ROUTLEDGE HANDBOOK OF AFRICAN POLITICAL PHILOSOPHY

The *Routledge Handbook of African Political Philosophy* showcases and develops the arguments propounded by African philosophers on political problems, bringing together experts from around the world to chart current and future research trends.

Africa's recent history has been shaped by the experiences of colonization, anti-colonial struggle, and postcolonial self-rule, so it is perhaps not surprising that political questions are also central to African philosophy. This exciting new handbook provides insights into the foundations, virtues, vices, controversies, and key topics to be found within African political philosophy, concluding by considering how it connects with other traditions of political philosophy. In doing so, this book provides important fresh perspectives that help us to gain a richer understanding of the challenges of coexistence in society and governance not just in Africa, but around the world.

This book will be an important resource for researchers and students across the fields of Political Philosophy, Political Science, International Relations, and African Studies.

Uchenna Okeja is a Research Professor at the Nelson Mandela University and Director of the Emengini Institute for Comparative Global Studies in Worcester, MA.

ROUTLEDGE HANDBOOK OF AFRICAN POLITICAL PHILOSOPHY

Edited by Uchenna Okeja

Routledge
Taylor & Francis Group

LONDON AND NEW YORK

Designed cover image: Ryan Green

First published 2023
by Routledge
4 Park Square, Milton Park, Abingdon, Oxon OX14 4RN

and by Routledge
605 Third Avenue, New York, NY 10158

Routledge is an imprint of the Taylor & Francis Group, an informa business

British Library Cataloguing-in-Publication Data
A catalogue record for this book is available from the British Library

ISBN: 978-0-367-56153-6 (hbk)
ISBN: 978-0-367-69842-3 (pbk)
ISBN: 978-1-003-14352-9 (ebk)

DOI: 10.4324/9781003143529

Typeset in Bembo
by codeMantra

CONTENTS

CONTRIBUTORS

Anthony C. Ajah (PhD) is a Senior Lecturer at the University of Nigeria, Nsukka. His background is in political philosophy, critical theory, philosophy of development, and narrative-identity studies. He is currently an AHP postdoctoral fellow, researching conceptual innovation and epistemic orientations in African Studies. His co-authored paper "Developmental Consequences of Identity-driven African Studies" was published recently in *South African Journal of Philosophy*.

Martin Odei Ajei (PhD) is an Associate Professor of Philosophy in the Department of Philosophy and Classics at the University of Ghana. His areas of research interest include African philosophy, applied ethics, political philosophy, and philosophies of liberation. He is the author of *The Paranormal: An Inquiry into Akan Metaphysics and Epistemology*, and *Africa's Development: The Imperatives on Indigenous Knowledge and Values* and editor of *Disentangling Consciencism: Essays on Kwame Nkrumah's Philosophy*.

Fatima Doumbia (PhD) is a Professor of Philosophy at Université Félix Houphöuet-Boigny in Abidjan, Ivory Coast. Her research fields are in Social and African philosophy. She is the author of "Des médiocres, des "rienneux" et autres zéros: sur le mépris social en Afrique" – "Mediocrties", Losers and other "Zeroes": On Social Contempt in Africa, published in *Diogène* vol. 263–264 (2018).

Edwin Etieyibo (PhD) is a Professor of Philosophy at the University of the Witwatersrand, South Africa. He is also an Adjunct Professor at the University of Alberta, Canada. He has expertise in ethics, social and political philosophy, applied ethics, African philosophy, critical thinking, philosophy for children, social contract theories/and history of. He is the author of *A Case for Environmental Justice* (Rowman and Littlefield, 2022).

Chielozona Eze (PhD) is a professor of Literature and Africana Studies at Carleton College. Prior to this, he was the Bernard J Brommel Distinguished Research Professor at Northeastern Illinois University. He is a philosopher and literary scholar, specializing in African and African-American literary and cultural studies. His areas of research interest include restorative justice, human rights, decolonial ethics, transitional justice, and cosmopolitanism.

Among his most recent publications are *Justice and Human Rights in the African Imagination: We, Too, Are Humans* (Routledge 2021) and *Race, Decolonization, and Global Citizenship in South Africa* (University of Rochester Press 2018).

Michael Onyebuchi Eze (Dr. Phil; PhD) teaches Africana studies at Fresno State University, California. He is a research associate at SA – UK Bilateral Research Chair in Political Theory, University of Witwatersrand, South Africa. His recent publications include "Decolonizing Humanitarianism: Beyond the Politics of Morality" (2022), "Ubuntu/Botho: A Theory of Humanism in African Philosophy" (2022), and "Religious Nationalism and Survival Politics in Contemporary Nigeria" (2022).

Katrin Flikschuh (PhD) is a Professor of Modern Political Theory at the London School of Economics. She works on the political philosophy of Immanuel Kant, the history of political thought, and modern African philosophy. She is the author of *Kant and Modern Political Philosophy* (CUP 2000); *What is Orientation in Global Thinking? A Kantian Inquiry* (CUP 2017); she has contributed numerous articles in the area of modern African philosophy.

Philip Adah Idachaba (PhD) is a Senior Lecturer in Philosophy at the Federal University of Lafia, Nasarawa State, Nigeria. His academic background is in Social and Political Philosophy, Transmodern Philosophy and History of Philosophy. He has authored articles in learned journals including the Frankfurt African Bulletin.

Polycarp Ikuenobe (PhD) is a Professor of Philosophy at Kent State University, Kent, Ohio, USA. His areas of research interest include African Philosophy, Philosophy of Law, Social and Political Philosophy, Moral Philosophy, Philosophy of Race, Informal Logic and Critical Thinking. He is an Associate Editor of the journal, *Philosophia*.

Elvis Imafidon (PhD) is a Lecturer in Philosophy and the Director of Centre for Global and Comparative Philosophies, SOAS University of London. He is also a Research Associate at the African Centre for Epistemology and Philosophy of Science, University of Johannesburg. His background is in the philosophy of difference, philosophy of corporeality, philosophy of healthcare, ethics, and ontology, primarily from African perspectives. He is the author and editor of several books including *African Philosophy and the Otherness of Albinism: White Skin, Black Race* (2019).

Albert Kasanda (PhD) is a Researcher at the Institute of Philosophy of the Czech Academy of Sciences and the University of Bayreuth. His research concentrates on African social and political philosophy, Afrophone philosophy, intercultural philosophy, and African social movements. He is the author of *Contemporary social and political Philosophy: Trends, Debates and challenges* (Routledge 2018) and co-editor of *Africa in a Multilateral world. Afropolitan dilemmas* (Routledge 2021).

Karabo Maiyane is a Lecturer in Philosophy at Nelson Mandela University and a PhD candidate at the University of Pretoria. His research focus is political philosophy, ethics, and epistemology.

Dennis Masaka (PhD) teaches Philosophy at Great Zimbabwe University, Zimbabwe, and is a Research Fellow at the University of the Free State, South Africa. His areas of research interest include the philosophy of liberation, epistemic (in)justice and global justice. He is the editor of Knowledge Production and the search for Epistemic liberation in Africa (Springer, 2022).

Bernard Matolino (PhD) is a Professor of philosophy at the University of Pretoria. His main research interests are in African political theory and race and racism. Among his most recent publications are *Consensus as Democracy in Africa* (NISC 2019) and *Afro-Communitarian Democracy* (Lexington Books, 2019).

Jacinta Maweu (PhD) is a Senior Lecturer at the Department of Philosophy, University of Nairobi, Kenya. Her main research interests include social and political philosophy, Media Ethics, Environmental Ethics and Philosophy of human rights. Her most recent publications include: "Equality, Difference and the Complementarity of African and Western Philosophy" in *Thinking Polyloguous: Considerations Concerning An Intercultural-Philosophical Minimal Rule* edited by Franz Gmainer-Pranzl and Britta Saal.

Thaddeus Metz (PhD) is a Professor of Philosophy at the University of Pretoria, South Africa. His background is in value theory, ethics, political/legal philosophy, and philosophy of religion. Among his more than 300 publications is *A Relational Moral Theory: African Ethics in and Beyond the Continent* (Oxford University Press, 2022).

Pius Mosima (PhD) teaches philosophy at the University of Bamenda, Cameroon and is currently affiliated with the Vrije Universiteit Amsterdam, The Netherlands and Wageningen University and Research, The Netherlands. His areas of research interest include African and Intercultural Philosophy, Globalization and Culture, and Political Philosophy. He has several peer-reviewed articles and book chapters on these topics. He is the author of Vital Force (Bloomsbury, 2023), and La philosophie au-delà des frontières: le cas de l'éthique africaine (Philosophy Beyond the Boundaries: The case of African Ethics (with Thaddeus Metz) (Harmattan 2023).

Nancy Oppongwaa Myles (PhD) is a Senior Lecturer of Philosophy at the Department of Philosophy and Classics, University of Ghana. Her areas of research interest straddle Ethics, Social-Political philosophy and African philosophy. Her current research works focus on personism, African democracy, multipartyism, and environmental sustainability.

Thierry Ngosso (PhD) is a Senior Research Fellow at the University of St. Gallen, Switzerland where he manages the Competence Center for African Research and Guest Lecturer of Philosophy at the University of Maroua and the Catholic University of Central Africa, Cameroon. He founded and manages the Ethics and Public Policy Laboratory (EthicsLab). His background is in political philosophy, ethics, and comparative philosophy.

Nanjala Nyabola is a writer and a researcher based in Nairobi, Kenya. Her research focuses on the intersection between technology and society. She is the author of Digital Democracy, Analogue Politics: How the Internet Era is Transforming Politics in Kenya (Zed, 2018); Travelling While Black: Essays Inspired by a Life on the Move (Hurst 2020); and Strange and Difficult Times: Notes on a Global Pandemic (Hurst, 2022). She is a PhD candidate at King's College London with a focus on African philosophies of personhood.

Isaïe Nzeyimana (PhD), a Rwandan national, is a Professor of Philosophy at the University of Rwanda. His several series of publications on "Philosophy and rationalities" constitute a Small Encyclopaedia of Philosophy for didactic use, written a posteriori following his experiences with students of different academic programs. His research and publication focus on metaphysics and philosophy and its application to the questions of education, development, philosophy of history and historiography, memory, politics and reconciliation

Omedi Ochieng (PhD) is an Associate Professor of Rhetoric, Race, and Decoloniality at the University of Colorado Boulder. He specializes in Africana philosophy & rhetoric, rhetorical theory & criticism, and comparative intellectual history. He is the author of two books: *Groundwork for the Practice of the Good Life: Politics and Ethics at the Intersection of North Atlantic and African Philosophy* (Routledge: 2017) and *The Intellectual Imagination: Knowledge and Aesthetics in North Atlantic and African Philosophy* (University of Notre Dame Press: 2018).

Uchenna Okeja (PhD) is research professor at Nelson Mandela University and Director of Emengini Institute for Comparative Global Studies. His background is in political philosophy, ethics, and critical theory. He is the author of *Deliberative Agency: A Study in Modern African Political Philosophy* (Indiana University Press, 2022).

Mitterand M. Okorie (PhD) is a Postdoctoral Research Fellow at the African Studies Centre, Rhodes University. His background is in conflict resolution, democratization and political philosophy. His publications have appeared on scholarly venues such as *Routledge Studies in Peace Conflict and Security in Africa*, *De Gruyter* and *Journal of Pan African Studies*.

Anthony I. Okpanachi (PhD) teaches philosophy at the Faculty of Arts and Humanities, Kogi State University, Nigeria. His research interests cut across epistemology, general history and philosophy of science, philosophy of social sciences, and African philosophy.

Jare Oladosu (PhD; JD) is an Associate Professor of Philosophy at Obafemi Awolowo University, Ile-Ife, Nigeria. He is a specialist in the philosophy of law. His other research interests are in social and political philosophy and applied ethics (environmental ethics and medical ethics). He is the co-editor of *Philosophy and Culture: Interrogating the Nexus* (Segundo Selo, 2020).

Oritsegbubemi Anthony Oyowe (PhD) is an Associate Professor of Philosophy at the University of the Western Cape. His areas of research interest include the point of interaction between metaphysics and ethics. He is the author of *Menkiti's Moral Man* (Lexington Books, 2022).

Ẹniọlá Ànúolúwapọ́ Ṣóyẹmí (PhD) is a Departmental Lecturer in Political Philosophy and Public Policy at Blavatnik School of Government, University of Oxford. She was previously a Max Weber Fellow at the European University Institute in Florence, Italy. Her book, Law's Moral Legitimacy is forthcoming with Hart/Bloomsbury Publishing.

Olúfẹ́mi O. Táíwò (PhD) is an Associate Professor of Philosophy at Georgetown University. He received his PhD in philosophy at the University of California Los Angeles. He has published in academic journals ranging from *Public Affairs Quarterly*, *One Earth*, *Philosophical Papers*, and the *American Philosophical Association Newsletter Philosophy and the Black Experience* and is the author of the books *Reconsidering Reparations* (Oxford University Press 2022) and *Elite Capture* (Haymarket Books 2022).

Mpho Tshivhase (PhD) is a Senior Lecturer at the Department of Philosophy at the University of Pretoria. Her research interests are existential uniqueness, personhood, and themes of love, autonomy, authenticity, death, aspects of race and feminism, as well as African ethics. Mpho was a 2021–2022 fellow at the Center for Advanced Studies in Behavioral Sciences (CASBS) at Stanford University. She was until recently the President of the Philosophical Society of Southern Africa.

Mfonobong David Udoudom teaches philosophy, and peace and conflict studies at the University of Nigeria, Nsukka. His background is in political philosophy and peace studies. He is a PhD research student at Rhodes University where his dissertation is focused on violent democracy.

Ajume H. Wingo (PhD) is an Associate Professor of Philosophy and the Director of the Law and Philosophy Program at the University of Colorado Boulder. His background is in Social, Ethical and Political Philosophy. He is the author of *Veil Politics in Liberal Democratic States*, published by Cambridge University Press (2003) in the series Studies in Philosophy and Public Policy.

PREFACE

The idea of editing a handbook on African political philosophy first occurred to me in 2014 when I taught a course on political philosophy. The questions posed by participants in the course made me realize that there was a need to produce a book that tracks the conceptual, methodological, normative discourses and new developments in traditions of political philosophy that enjoy little to no influence globally. The handbook model struck me as a natural fit for such a project.

Although I signed a contract with Routledge to develop the handbook on African political philosophy in May 2020, it took me more time than I had initially imagined to arrive at the publication stage in the development of the manuscript. While working on this project, I have received help from many people whose generosity I gratefully acknowledge. Many thanks are due to the authors of the chapters published in the handbook. Thanks are due especially to those who had to wait more than two years to see real progress with the publication process. I appreciate your understanding and encouragement.

Thanks to friends and colleagues that have supported me in many ways over the years. The final steps in the publication process commenced in late 2022. This coincided with my stay as a visiting professor at the Department of Philosophy at Utrecht University in the Netherlands. I thank the faculty and staff at the Ethics Institute where the Department of Philosophy is domiciled for the invitation. Thanks especially to Dorothea Gädeke, Joel Anderson and Karlijne van der Ende.

I have benefited a lot from my discussions with many colleagues at Rhodes University and other places. I appreciate their generosity and insights. It would have been impossible to complete this project without counting on the extra work my wife had to take on for the family. Many thanks to Oge, Aka, Beluchi and Nwando for your understanding and love.

Uchenna Okeja
Utrecht

1

AFRICAN POLITICAL PHILOSOPHY

Old Anxieties, New Imaginations

Uchenna Okeja

There are many anxieties afflicting the field of African political philosophy. Some of them arise from the contested history of African philosophy and others issue from the complicated intellectual history of African Studies. The first set of anxieties, that is, those that arise from the contested history of African philosophy, refers to the debate about whether and to what extent African philosophy is a 'different' kind of philosophy. It should be obvious why this debate is a source of anxiety for African political philosophy. For, if it is contested the sense in which African philosophy is indeed philosophy, a direct implication would be that a sub-field, such as African political philosophy, stands on a shaky foundation.

Although I recognize the importance of the first source of anxiety for African political philosophy, I prefer to preface my introduction to this handbook with a discussion of the second source of anxiety. The reason for this choice is that the second set of anxieties consists of different layers of inward-looking concerns that explain a lot of what is at stake in the field. Besides the fact that it is unhelpful to engage with a tradition of philosophy by questioning its legitimacy, I think we will better understand the nature, methods, and key questions of African political philosophy if we looked critically at the second set of anxieties that shapes the field, namely, the current constitution of African Studies.

Like other fields that study experiences in the African place, African political philosophy confronts challenges that arise from the reality that African Studies has remained largely a diaspora affair that is for the most part detached from the lived experience of the subject whose reality it is supposedly meant to improve. Not only are most of the celebrated exemplars of the field African diaspora scholars, but their work is also primarily sustained by the funding and recognition of foreign audiences. This situation raises a question about how thinking from a place shapes the imagination. As an intellectual practice, scholarship on Africa is constituted as a form of discourse undertaken by disparate individuals. Notwithstanding the diverse methodologies adopted and the different problems explored by African Studies experts, it would be plausible to say that the centring of their activities around a specific imagination of place plays an important role in shaping the sort of knowledge they construct about the object of their studies.

This is the case because the imagination of place that informs an intellectual practice in the humanities gives meaning to the propositions and concepts we employ in our analysis and construction of theories. The fact that African Studies has remained largely a detached

DOI: 10.4324/9781003143529-1

diaspora affair therefore implies that an attempt to delineate disciplinary boundaries, such as the one evoked by African political philosophy as a distinct field in African philosophy, must contend with complexities that attach to the constitution of the community engaged in the discourse we call African Studies.

To this end, an explanation of the impact of the current constitution of African Studies on the sort of knowledge created about African spaces and experiences must go beyond attempts to elucidate the factors responsible for the dispersion of African intellectuals in the present century. It is of course common knowledge that the crucial factors that contributed to the present circumstances of African Studies include the brain drain that occurred in the higher education sector due to the introduction of Structural Adjustment Programs in many African countries and practices like the career advancement requirement by universities that compel scholars in Africa to publish in so-called reputable international journals and presses. Due to the complex history of knowledge creation in African universities, the idea of international journals usually refers to journals that are published or indexed in databases outside Africa.

We can understand the impact of the current constitution of African Studies on fields like African political philosophy if we look beyond causal historical explanations. We must ask: how does the current constitution of African Studies impinge on theories created about African spaces and experiences? I will attempt to answer this question momentarily. But, before I do that, it is important to note that my aim in introducing the *Routledge Handbook on African Political Philosophy* with a preliminary note on the impact of the current constitution of African Studies on the knowledge we create about Africa is not intended as a shorthand for a value judgement. Said in another way, I do not intend by this preliminary comment to argue that it is morally good or bad that African Studies is a diaspora affair.

What I wish to emphasize instead is that the current situation of the scholarship on Africa has implications for the mapping of the history and analysis of core concepts and problems in African political philosophy. The point of concern here should become clearer when we consider the following issues: (1) the challenge of organicity in relation to the development of key ideas and theorists and (2) the lack of mentorship or skills transfer that is necessary for the development of an adequate orientation to scholarship on political reality as an action-guiding form of theorizing.

The first issue emphasizes that developing key political ideas and theories requires a specific form of organic relationship between scholars and the social and political reality they interrogate. Without such a relationship, political theories will be developed from a place of dislocation in which there is a lack of clarity about the linkages of audience, scholars, and the imagination of what defines valuable scholarship. An intellectual practice that is largely diasporic in form, even if not in content, implies a mismatch between the theories produced by participants in such intellectual practice and the interests or aspirations of those whose experience the theories are supposedly about.

This mismatch leads to an alienation that negatively affects the imagination of the dialectic between achievement and value. This is an important concern because the alignment of achievement and value in a knowledge tradition determines how we develop methods that are suitable for the context. Here, the alignment of achievement and value refers to the connection between a scholar's activities and an appreciation of the purpose of scholarship. In other words, what is implicated in this alignment is the intuition regarding what gives meaning to scholarly exertion and accomplishments. If achievement and value are aligned in a knowledge tradition, it will be clear in what sense and the sort of scholarly accomplishments that are valuable. The problem that arises when this alignment is disrupted is the blunting of the emancipatory power of ideas.

For keen observers of African Studies in the last three decades, it should be evident that it is not an exaggeration to say that there is a general blunting of the power of ideas proposed by theorists in the field. In fact, it would not be wrong to claim that the theorizing of social and political phenomena in African Studies in the last three decades is inversely related to emancipatory outcomes. In other words, the more experts working in the field of African Studies produce theories about social and political reality, the less the emancipation experienced by the people whose experiences and existential conditions supposedly constitute the main objects of such theorizing.

A situation in which theorizing becomes stagnated in this way could be described as a context in which social theory and political thought have transformed into a mere accumulation of theories. In such a context, progress in scholarship becomes a reference for the intensification and expansion of the accumulation of impotent concepts, methods, theories, and ideas. What I referred to earlier as the challenge of organicity in African political philosophy is the problem of self-definition in the field. This concern can be formulated in the form of a question: given the nature of the broader intellectual practice that shapes the study of African experiences, how should we define African political philosophy? In other words, how should African political philosophy be constituted so that it is not merely a shorthand for the accumulation of ideas and theories that lack emancipatory potential?

The search for an answer to this question is one of the key guiding motivations of the *Routledge Handbook on African Political Philosophy*. This is evident in the attempt made to ensure that sections of the handbook focus on innovative revision of concepts; exploration of new answers to old questions; formulation of new questions in light of critical emerging concepts and connecting African political theorizing to other forms of political thought. The chapters of the handbook provide an overview of key questions in African political philosophy while offering perspectives on how to develop political understanding without disregarding the imperative of emancipatory theorizing. I will return to the question of self-definition of African political philosophy towards the end of this introductory chapter. In the meantime, I want to discuss the second problem that arises from the current constitution of African Studies.

The issue I have in mind is the implication of the lack of mentorship and skills transfer on theory formation. Political philosophy is a contemplation, ideally, at the highest level of sophistication, of the ideal and challenges of co-existence in political communities. One of the prerequisites for engaging in such a reflection is having clarity about what it means to be a person. If one does not engage in this reflection with clarity about some fundamental categories, such as personhood, the result would be an inability to say with some level of conviction what is the most suitable form of political organization that is worth pursuing. This is the case because it is only by having clarity about the nature of the subject for whom a decent society is imagined that we can say with some degree of certainty the ideal of co-existence that a society should strive to achieve or preserve. But how does a functional consensus emerge about the fundamental categories that inform theorizing in a tradition of knowledge? My intuition is that a consensus emerges through robust discourses that guarantee that there is a strong linkage between theory and praxis.

The link between theorizing and praxis is always disturbed when extraversion becomes the dominant mode of discourse in a tradition of knowledge. In such a situation, the link between theory and praxis is distorted mainly due to the erosion of important safeguards that ensure that the requisite correctives accompany the process of inter-generational transfer of knowledge within a knowledge tradition. To be sure, having access to the publications and other medium in which an intellectual practice unfolds can give one insight into the ideas and theories espoused by the scholars working in that tradition. However, this is insufficient to make one an exemplar of a tradition of knowledge. In addition to having access to publications and related means of interlocution, there is the important requirement that an exemplar of a tradition of knowledge must develop certain sensibilities that shape the community of inquiry. Without a seamless and sustained inter-generational exchange in a shared space, which includes, but is not limited to a robust culture of exchange of ideas, the development of such sensibilities will either become severely constrained or totally impossible.

To this end, the impact of extraverted African Studies on African political philosophy is the distortion of the link between theory and praxis. As a field of study, political philosophy is an intellectual practice that has a clear teleology. Although political philosophers do not agree about many things, such as the adequate methodologies or conceptual tools to employ in their analysis, hardly any political philosopher would disagree with the suggestion that political philosophy is a meaningful endeavour dedicated to understanding the nature and dynamics of co-existence in society. If this is true, then the question to ask is what makes this form of scholarship meaningful. My intuition is that the meaning-giving factor for the field derives from its focus on improving human understanding to advance collective well-being.

If we accept this intuition as plausible, then it will be reasonable to argue that it is problematic for an intellectual practice that shapes a tradition of political philosophy to be largely of the form that African Studies currently embodies. What is problematic here is that the context in which African political philosophy unfolds distorts the sources of meaning for the field. This happens because the current constitution of African Studies negatively inflects the development of the sensibilities that exemplars of African political philosophy ought to embody. Surely, there is something wrong with a tradition of scholarship whose discourses unfold in contexts that are far removed from the location where the phenomena it studies manifest. To contextualize, imagine that there is such a thing as Siberian Winter Studies which, for various reasons, is now constituted as an intellectual practice that happens predominantly among the Siberian diaspora in West Africa. Such scholarship will surely have to contend with the challenge of understanding how its constitution distorts the link between theory and praxis.

Given these points, would it be correct to conclude that African political philosophy is impossible? What is implied in this question is whether it is plausible to argue that African political philosophy is doomed to remain an extraverted scholarship, and hence, a designation for research conceived to address a foreign audience. If one does not answer this question in the affirmative, what should one make of the impact of African Studies on the field of African political philosophy? It is important to consider these two questions because they enable us to formulate a viable conception of the nature and tasks of African political philosophy.

Regarding the first question, which raises a concern about the possibility of African political philosophy given the disciplinary practice that shapes it, an intuitive but insufficient answer would be to offer a *reductio ad absurdum* argument. This could be accomplished by arguing that what is at issue cannot be the impossibility of African political philosophy because if this was the case, it would be incomprehensible to talk about the idea of African political philosophy in any sensible way. But, since we are already engaged in a conversation about African political philosophy, albeit mainly in relation to its challenges, it will be false to raise a question about its possibility. Although this sounds like a clever argument, I think

4

there is more at stake than the argument captures. The question to which this reductio ad absurdum argument attempts to respond is to my mind a "so what" question. By this, I mean that it is a request for a clarification of why it is important to pay attention to the challenges that arise for African political philosophy due to the current constitution of African Studies. In other words, why does it matter that African political philosophy is confronted by several significant anxieties?

Understood in this way, the question about the possibility of African political philosophy can be best answered if we considered it alongside the second question about extraversion. Taken together, both questions point to a concern about how we should think about African political philosophy, given its foundational challenges. It seems to me that the way to proceed here is not to replicate the concerns that attach to the notion of African philosophy – that is, concerns related to whether African political philosophy exists and if so, what sets it apart from other ways of doing political philosophy. The history of contemporary African philosophy provides enough reason to show that this approach is unviable. Looked at carefully, the concern about how to define African political philosophy, considering its foundational anxieties, has little to do with the nature and pursuits of scholars working in this area of philosophy. Instead, the challenge of self-definition of African political philosophy derives from the politics of the canon in philosophy.

The question "how should we think about African political philosophy, given its foundational challenges" is in effect a demand for a justification of the field – or, as it is often expressed in academic philosophy, an explanation of why we should take the field seriously. Said in another way, why do we need African political philosophy to make meaning of African political experiences? Why is it not sufficient to simply mobilize the resources of subsisting ways of doing political philosophy to analyse and respond adequately to the political experiences in Africa – after all, African philosophers, as Kwasi Wiredu and Kwame Anthony Appiah rightly noted, are trained in both the Western and African traditions of philosophy (Appiah 1992, 85; Wiredu 1996, 137). Framed in this way, the problem becomes a matter of representation of voices and epistemic legitimation. This means that what is at stake is not the validity of theories advanced in African political philosophy, but a challenge to demonstrate why we need more than the available ways of speaking about political experiences. The cogency of this concern arises from the following argument: if the political experiences of people in Africa are at core human experiences, why does it not suffice to speak about them using the currently available metaphors, concepts, and theories of political philosophy?

It would not be convincing to argue, in response, that African political philosophy is necessary because contemporary political philosophy has shown that it is either uninterested or incapable of taking African experiences as a "normal" starting point of theory formation. This would amount to saying that African political philosophy is necessary because of the deficits of current ways of doing political philosophy globally. I think this is an unconvincing view because the importance of African political philosophy cannot be derived from the failures of other traditions of political philosophy, however grievous those failures might be. Besides, if the concern of African political philosophy is simply to correct the shortcomings of currently dominant ways of doing political philosophy globally, then it could go by any other name, such as global, postcolonial, intercultural or even decolonized political philosophy. Since this is not the case because the field retains the name *African political philosophy*, the concern conveyed by the question retains all cogency – or so it seems.

To answer the question, we need to make a distinction between how we *should* think about African political philosophy within the larger domain of the different traditions of philosophy and how to *describe* the nature and tasks of African political philosophy, given its

foundational challenges. This distinction enables us to separate anxieties about the legitimation of the field in comparison to other influential traditions from crucial questions about
the nature of the field. The first concern does not belong to the domain of African political
philosophy because the field is not primarily concerned with the study of the politics of
knowledge production or the implications of disciplinary boundaries. The second concern
relates to what it means to suggest that African political philosophy is an umbrella concept
that refers to diverse studies of political experiences that manifest in African spaces, especially with an eye on reshaping the conception of the ideal of co-existence in society.

Suggesting that African political philosophy is an umbrella concept that aims to achieve
the goals just stipulated is to assert that the field is a critical inquiry. It is a field where a diversity of methods or concepts are deployed in the study of the political experience of Africa
both in the continent and diaspora. The sort of meaning that results from the studies conducted in the field may be forward-looking, backward-looking or a combination of the two
approaches. The uniting thread of all three approaches, however, is the critical nature of the
inquiry they embody. This is to say that African political philosophers do not merely offer
a reconstruction of immutable beliefs said to be uniquely African. Instead, they question
assumptions and offer innovative, and sometimes counterintuitive, perspectives on political
experience and the ideal of co-existence in society that are grounded in arguments.

With this explanation of the idea of African political philosophy in mind, we can now
summarize the discussion of what I called earlier an internal discourse. The analysis so far
shows that the two major consequences of the current constitution of African Studies on
African political philosophy relate to the problem of self-definition and the distortion of the
link between theory and praxis. Scholars whose work could be categorized under African
political philosophy will have different views on these issues. Some of them might emphasize that the problem of self-definition is spurious because it echoes the sterile debate about
whether there is an African philosophy. Others might argue that any respectable political
philosophy must aim to conceive the best theory possible, the reason being that philosophy
does not, and should not, pretend to have any direct practical use. Still, some might argue that
since the concerns that derive from the so-called internal discourse are theoretical, African
political philosophy ought to look beyond the debate and focus mainly on finding solutions
to the concrete political problems in Africa, given the dire situation of the continent.

Regardless of what an African political philosopher makes of the so-called internal discourse in the field, the question that must be considered is how to do African political philosophy in a manner that is neither ahistorical, ignorant of the field's unique challenges but
nonetheless confident in the field's capacity to generate universally relevant ideas, methods,
theories or concepts. What I want to highlight with this observation is that the complicated
history and contemporary negligible influence of African political philosophy should not
occlude its imagination as a context for profound reflection on the human condition.

It is against this background that we should understand the goal and importance of the
Routledge handbook on African political philosophy. To be sure, modern African philosophy consists of a reflection on specific political questions. This is not an accident, given the political
condition of the continent. It is hardly a surprise to find that philosophers in every part of
the world focus their energies on articulating meanings of the most paradigmatic experiences
that shape the historical epochs in which they live. This point was clear to renowned British
philosopher, Bertrand Russell, who was perhaps the first to contextualize his account of the
history of Western philosophy by paying close attention to the historical and cultural milieu
of the philosophers. That African philosophy consists of a reflection on fundamental and
sometimes elusive questions about political life is a signal that major experiences that shape

the historical epoch of philosophers in this tradition have been largely political in nature. This should become clear if we recall that the modern history of Africa is shaped by the experience of colonization, anti-colonial struggle and the largely faltering experiment in self-rule.

This handbook has a two-fold rationale. On one hand, it is an attempt to systematize discourses in the African tradition of philosophy, by isolating theories that belong squarely to the sub-field of political philosophy, from those that fall under other distinct sub-fields. The importance of striving for this separation is to make clear that, although reflection on political experience is a central concern in African philosophy, it is not the only thing that is interesting in this tradition of philosophy. On the other hand, the handbook aims to develop further arguments propounded by African philosophers on political problems. Making such an effort has become imperative because of the need to expand the scope of the voices articulating views on global political concerns. In sum, the rationale for the handbook is to systematize and develop major theories in African political philosophy and to inflect, on this basis, global philosophical discourse on political concerns with ideas and theories firmly rooted in African political thought.

At a time when global politics is in a flux due to migration, terrorism, trade wars and different forms of intolerance, it is important to diversify the sources we can draw on to conceive answers to these challenges. Given its independent provenance, African political philosophy offers vital insights that can enable us to understand political challenges as universal human concerns that manifest concretely in different forms. By considering the history, sources, virtues, vices, controversies, concepts and connections between African political philosophy and other traditions of philosophy, the chapters contained in this handbook demonstrate that philosophy constitutes the creative self-expression of human beings. The handbook contributes refreshing and interesting new insights into the challenges of co-existence in society and governance. These insights should enable political philosophers everywhere to sharpen the validity of their propositions because they provide a chance for a comparative assessment of one's familiar concepts and theories.

The chapters of the handbook are categorized under five thematic sections – foundations and methods, political virtues and vices, controversies: normative debates and political praxis, emerging concepts and topics and parallels and global connections. Each thematic section provides a general definition of scope in the sense that it captures a broad range of issues that are loosely united by interconnections of the questions addressed. Although the sections are not conceived to suggest how African political philosophers should approach their work, they highlight through consideration of paradigmatic questions how theorists have approached inquiry in the field and the tendencies that have defined the literature produced over several decades.

In the first section, Foundations and Methods, there are six chapters dedicated to the discussion of the challenge of method and the foundational questions and concepts in the field. The foundational concepts of the state, freedom and nationalism are discussed in this section alongside consideration of the sources that scholars draw on to formulate their theories and two major sources of anxiety in modern African politics – namely, colonial modernity and genocide. How can literature enable us to understand the central categories of political philosophy, such as freedom, justice and recognition? What should we look out for in literature to understand its philosophical depth?

Chielozona Eze answers these questions in his chapter *Literature as a Source of Political Philosophy*. Some of the key concepts that have shaped contemporary political life in Africa include freedom, nationalism, citizenship and the state. In addition, the unique experiences of colonial modernity and genocide have changed the political imagination in the continent in ways that are difficult to comprehend. To help us understand these concepts and experiences, Katrin Flikschuh discussed the idea of the state in her chapter *The State in Africa and the African State*. Ajume Wingo tackles the idea of freedom in his chapter *A Free Person as a Maker of Surprises* and Michael Onyebuchi Eze takes up the analysis of citizenship and nationalism in his chapter *Citizenship Under Siege: Contemporary African Nationalism and the Trauma of Modernity*. Polycarp Ikuenobe provides us with an analysis of modernity in his chapter *Tradition and Modernity* and Isaie Nzeyimana tackles another tragedy of modern African political life, genocide, in his chapter *Pragmatic History in a Post Genocide Society*.

Moving forward, the chapters that make up section two of the handbook turn our attention to perennial concerns in postcolonial political experience in Africa, namely, the challenge of political vices and virtues. There is hardly any discussion of political life in modern Africa that does not in some way invoke paradigmatic problems, such as corruption, communal life, and ethnic and other forms of differences. How should we think about these concepts as political vices? Are there political virtues we can point to that manifest in the African context? The seven chapters in this section help us to answer these questions. The authors offer not just rigorous conceptual analysis but also perspectives on how to understand and mitigate the sufferings, crises and confusions generated by the long careers of these vices in the political firmament of different countries in Africa. Included in this section are the chapters Anthony Oyowe – *Community*, Dennis Masaka – *Deliberation, Manipulation and Consensual Polity*, Edwin Etieyibo – *Disharmony as a Political Vice*, Elvis Imafidon – *Difference and Exclusionism*, Mitterand Okorie – *Corruption*, Albert Kasanda – *African Civil Society and Jacinta* Mwende – *Election, Violence and Political Legitimation*.

Section three contains six chapters that deal with controversies in the field. Like every other sub-field of philosophy, African political philosophy is shaped by several debates. Most of these debates have yielded significant insights, such as the reason we ought to discard or rethink certain categories of political thought, the limits of freedom and the ways to creatively enrich imported concepts. In her chapter, *Deliberation, Dependence and Freedom*, Eniola Soyemi articulates a conception of democratic freedom by drawing on the work of two prominent philosophers, Kwasi Wiredu and Emmanuel Chukwudi Eze. Drawing on Wiredu and Charles Mills in his chapter *Uncommon features: Defending Ideal Theory with Model-to-World Inference*, Olufemi Taiwo demonstrates how an ideal theory could be conceived as a useful tool for doing the sort of philosophy that is opposed to social injustice.

Focusing on the intractable problem of democracy in Africa in his chapter *Development as an Alternative to Democracy*, Bernard Matolino articulated a view on why Africa should seek to democratize through development. In her chapter, *Pluralism and Social Cohesion*, Nancy Myles tackled one of the perennial controversy in African political experience, namely, how to imagine politics in contexts characterized by multiple languages, ethnicities and cultures. In their chapter *Democracy and Development*, Philip Idachaba and Anthony I. Okpanachi draw on the works of Ali Mazrui and Joseph Agbakoba to propose that the way forward for Africa is to construct a hybrid conception of democracy. Martin Ajei rounds off the section with his chapter *Development and Human Rights in Africa: A Theoretical Proposal* in which, among other things, he argued for the need to understand the implications of the history of social formation in conceiving a viable ideal of development.

It cannot be denied that religion plays a crucial role in the political life of African countries. The influence is so exaggerated in some cases that one could speak of apocalyptic politics.[1] Thus, section four begins with a chapter on religion and politics in Africa. In his chapter *Religion and Politics: Learning to Navigate a Slippery Slope*, Jare Oladosu discussed how religion and its influence on politics constitute a man-made factor that detracts from the project of democratization in Africa. Emerging topics, such as the use of autonomous weapons in wars and violent democracy are discussed alongside emerging concepts such as Africa's burgeoning digital public sphere and the modes of speaking about the marginalization of women. These issues are discussed in the chapters by Karabo Maiyane – *Autonomous Weapons and the Future of War in Africa*, Nanjala Nyabola – *Africa's Digital Public Sphere*, Fatima Doumbia – *Talking about the Marginalisation of Women in Africa*, and Anthony Ajah and Udoudom Nfonobong – *Violent Democracy and the Promise of Peace*.

Section five, which is the concluding section, contains five chapters that discuss the connection of African political philosophy to theories developed in other traditions. Also contained in this section are considerations of how to resolve global problems using insights from paradigmatic concepts in African political philosophy. In this regard, concepts like Pan-Africanism, harmony, and Ubuntu provide the foundations for critique and conceptualisation of new imagination. These tasks are undertaken in the chapters by Pius Mosima – *Pan-Africanism as Cosmopolitanism*, Thaddeus Metz – *Political Philosophy in the Global South: Harmony in Africa, East Asia and South America*, Thierry Ngosso – *Non-State Actors, Freedom and Justice: Should Multinational Firms be Primary Agents of Justice in African Societies*, Omedi Ochieng – *Africa in the Political Imagination of the African Diaspora* and Mpho Tshivhase – *Ubuntu: A Critique of Superiorization*.

One thing that is noticeable in contemporary African political philosophy is the omnipresence of democracy. Most of the current debates refer in some way to the challenges, promises, failures or even the incapacity of this way of organizing co-existence to address modern challenges arising from the so-called postcolonial condition. This is understandable, given that politics in postcolonial Africa is largely a faltering experiment in democracy. Even the military dictatorships that have caused so much anguish and disorientation in the continent are reactions to the failures of democracy. The current challenges arising from democracy should not be disregarded because one wants to focus on excavating so-called traditional ideas to show that African political philosophy has its own, albeit nameless, equivalents of the Western greats or theorizing a utopian future form of governance, say post-democracy.

Postcolonial political experiences matter because they have a lot to teach us about what constitutes a profound political philosophy of the present. We cannot presume that only theorists whose experiences are informed by the enjoyment of the positive fruits of contemporary political systems have something to teach the world. with regard to democracy, for instance, more could be learned from those whose experiences consist largely of injuries inflicted on the body and mind by the theories and practice of modern political systems.

To conclude, it is important to underscore two points. Firstly, I want to emphasize that the currently negligible influence of African political philosophy should not discourage anyone interested in pursuing in-depth personal or structured postgraduate study of the field. This handbook is an attempt to map and present in a critical but accessible manner the questions, concepts and theories that have informed the work of African political philosophers. The worry about the field's marginality is indeed real due to career concerns and the prestige factor in academic philosophy. This concern reflects in the sense of disquiet that some philosophers with an African heritage feel about the reception of their work if it is labelled African thought. I think the push towards more global awareness in curriculum design holds a lot of promise for real positive change. Besides, like the prominent political philosopher, Olufemi Taiwo, rightly argued, "the primary motivation for pursuing knowledge is simply to push back knowledge's frontiers" (Taiwo 2014, 81). Regarding the anxieties about losing one's *universal voice* because of being regarded as an 'African philosopher', it is important to always bear in mind Handel Wright's caution that an attempt at ontological reinvention by fiat is an illusion (Wright 2002, 4).

Secondly, it is important to move beyond thinking about African political philosophy as either a derivative discipline from Western philosophy or a practical plan for solving the myriad political problems in the continent. It is true that many African philosophers are trained in Western philosophy. But, it is also true that their engagement with African political philosophy is a conscious choice. Besides, education in Western philosophy does not in any way impose on anyone an incapacitation to be able to do only Western philosophy. Although most, if not all, African political philosophers will be delighted to see that their theory helps to resolve political challenges in the continent, the field of African political philosophy does not have the single goal of solving practical problems. The field is a domain of critical inquiry about political experiences that manifest in the African space.

Notwithstanding the old anxieties that arise from African Studies, I agree with Oyeka Owomoyela that "even if Europeans had not invented African Studies, Africans would have had to invent it", the reason being that African Studies contribute critical insights to the project of self-discovery of Africans amidst the "cultural amnesia" Africans must learn to live with and overcome (Owomoyela 1991, 177). We must be alert to the old anxieties that accompany theorizing in African political philosophy, just as we must also affirm and build on the new imaginations that emerge from efforts to overcome these challenges.

Note

1 Thanks to Asonzeh Ukah for discussions about apocalyptic politics in Africa – a situation where religion does not only replace secular sources of knowledge for practical action and political decision making but also colonizes the entire horizon of imagination of the future of states and political systems.

References

Handel Wright, Editorial: Notes on the (Im)Possibility of Articulating Continental African Identity, *Critical Arts* 16:2 (2002), 1–18.

Kwame Anthony Appiah, *In My Father's House: Africa in the Philosophy of Culture*, New York: Oxford University Press, 1992.

Kwasi Wiredu, *Cultural Universals and Particulars*, Bloomington and Indianapolis: Indiana University Press, 1996.

Olufemi Taiwo, *Africa Must Be Modern: A Manifesto*, Bloomington and Indianapolis: Indiana University Press, 2014.

Oyekan Owomoyela, Africa and the Imperative of Philosophy: A Skeptical Consideration, in: Tsenay Serequeberhan (ed.), *African Philosophy: The Essential Readings*, New York: Paragon House, 1991, pp. 156–186.

PART I

Foundations and Methods

2

LITERATURE AS A SOURCE OF POLITICAL PHILOSOPHY

Chielozona Eze

Introduction

It is, no doubt, ironic to suggest literature as a source of political philosophy in Africa, especially given that Plato, the father of political philosophy, banished it from the republic (Plato 2000). To be clear, Plato was speaking specifically of poetry. It is, however, important to bear in mind that at his time, poetry was the umbrella term encompassing nearly everything we now understand as literature. Poetry for him was an imitation of the real and therefore fails to say anything meaningful to the Republic; poetry is not pragmatic and does not lead to moral life. But even if we were to remain within the relatively limited understanding of literature (poetry) at the time, Plato's student Aristotle disagreed with his master, arguing in his *Poetics*, that through the very act of imitation, poetry can lead to an ethical life and a better life in the community, hence also political. I follow Aristotle's example and argue that literature is not only a potential source of political philosophy but is indeed essential in conceiving a functioning political unit. However, for that to be possible certain elements of the image of society and the human person must be present. It helps therefore to pose guiding questions in that regard: What image of the human person is portrayed in the African narrative? What are the structures of the society depicted? What virtues guide the relationships between individuals on the one hand, and between the individual and the state on the other?

I understand politics primarily in the form explained by Hannah Arendt as the exercise of speech in the polis (Arendt 1958). The act of speech presupposes freedom and the awareness of right. Political philosophy is understood as the articulation of the ideas guiding how individuals relate to one another within a given state and to that state as a body. These include the notions of freedom, justice, fairness, and rights. When I read works of literature in view of understanding the underlining political philosophy, I shall be looking for situations that excite thoughts about the ideal state. I shall be asking, explicitly or implicitly, whether individuals have rights and are able to exercise them. I shall be asking questions that probe the quality of the individual speech, that is, his or her ability to exercise freedom and responsibility in the polis. Like in *The Republic*, I follow Plato's footpath to inquire about the place and condition of justice in the society portrayed in *Things Fall Apart*. To that effect, it is important to note that a literary work such as *Things Fall Apart* does not need to formulate a specific

DOI: 10.4324/9781003143529-3

political philosophy or even a particular vision. It suffices to arrive at a picture of what ought to be from that of what is not.

To engage the above gesture toward political philosophy, I first provide a sketch of the importance of literature for our political imagination. I then discuss an example of the image of the human person in Africa. I conclude with a meditation on *Things Fall Apart*, one of the foundational literary texts in African literature.

The Importance of Literature for Our Imagination

Literature deals with reality indirectly via literary elements, and more specifically through figures of speech such as metaphor, metonymy, characterization, etc. I thus conceive literature in my discussions here as an expanded conception of poetry, or as Aristotle has defined tragedy, as

> an imitation of an action that is admirable, complete and possesses magnitude; in language made pleasurable, each of its species separated in different parts, performed by actors, not through narration; effecting through pity and fear the purification of such emotions.
>
> *(Poetics, 10)*

The definition suggests that literature is no more than recreating aspects of our world in ways that can help us comprehend them. It is the act of insinuating a new world by creating associations between two or three elements in the already-known world.

Literature is about narratives; it is about the stories we tell ourselves. In telling stories, we present not just characters but also worldviews; in reading or listening to stories, we confront others and sets of judgment. In texts, readers are asked to imagine the lives of people (characters) they will never meet. This meeting becomes truly ethical and political when the relation is initiated in form of questions, or identification with characters, worldviews or events, or rejection of the same. Either way, judgment is involved. According to Arthur W. Frank, "Stories teach people what to look for and what can be ignored; they teach what to value and what to hold in contempt" (*Letting Stories Breathe* 46). Every choice of material in a story reveals the value system of the person who makes that choice. Also, the way a story is arranged—what is highlighted and what is suppressed—says much about what is important and what is less so. Through a subtle and often complex system of figures, signs, and symbols, stories thus shape our values and display our political philosophical dispositions, that is, our conception of freedom, justice, rights, and obligations. The portrait of a particular world at the expense of others necessarily directs our imagination toward that world and all it embodies.

Judged from the above ideas, Plato could be said to have had a literary mind. He was a great storyteller. Consider for instance his allegory of the cave, which forms the basis of his theory of knowledge. Consider also his political philosophy, presented in form of a well-told story in his famous book, *The Republic*. Character "A" otherwise known as Socrates, sets out to inquire about the nature of justice. He enters into dialogue with several characters in his quest. Plato, thus presents us: a situation, an action involving characters, and a dialogue. This is as much as we can say about literature conceived as a recreation of an aspect of our world in story formats. Plato deploys the riches of dialogue—an important literary element—to portray his vision of a just city. I think it helps to provide a more detailed discussion of Plato's display of the named literary element and the vision of society he seeks to explore. Discussing it is also important in view of my stated goal of explaining the nature of justice in *Things Fall Apart*.

In book one of *The Republic*, Plato recounts an important dialogue between his master, Socrates, and Thrasymachus on the question of justice. Thrasymachus answers "that justice is simply what is good for the stronger" (15). Through his dialectic, enhanced by analogies, Socrates brings his interlocutor to the understanding that it is not always the case that one does what is good for the stronger or what is in one's own self-interest; a sailor does not pilot the ship well for his self-interest, neither does a good doctor attend to a patient because of self-interest. Socrates concludes that justice is to act in the interest of the weak, not the strong, just as a doctor acts in the interest of the sick. Ultimately, justice is in the interest of the common good because it seeks to maintain balance in the polity.

Plato's positive theory of justice is presented in the form of analogy, which he treats on the microcosmic level (the individual) and macrocosmic (the State).[1] Justice is a virtue, a quality of the individual mind; to understand it, one has to comprehend how the soul, which is composed of three elements: appetite, emotion, and reason, work. Each of these elements must not perform tasks other than its own. Plato states that the individual has to establish a balance or harmony between these three; he has "quite literally, to put his own house in order, being himself his own ruler, mentor, and friend, and tune the three elements just like three fixed points in a music scale" (141). Harmony in the self or "self-discipline is the agreement about which of them should rule - a natural harmony of worse and better, both in the city and in each individual" (126). The soul is to the individual what the city is to the rulers. The art of bringing to harmony the different often contradicting impulses or faculties in the soul is, therefore, a model of justice in the city. Justice in the polis is therefore a harmonious relationship between the opposing parts; the unlimited assertion of one part is as loathsome as is an unlimited assertion of self or one group over others. On that basis therefore, an individual cannot be denied what has been granted to others without unhinging the harmony that ought to exist among different parts of society.

Deriving from Plato's conception of justice as a balance between the various interest groups within society, we have an idea of how a city is to be organized. It must be one in which balance is maintained in the real world of individuals with diverse inclinations, orientations, lifestyles, or general pursuit of happiness. For example, social injustice, which often manifests itself in forms of institutional racism, caste system, sexism, homophobia, and so on, can be understood as when a particular party or group in a given society is systematically excluded from participation in active citizenry or when they are denied rights and freedom that others enjoy.

Of course, I do not seek to turn Plato into a fiction writer. He remains first and foremost a philosopher. But just as he made ample use of literary elements, so do fiction writers also produce works that contain philosophical truth that must be teased out. *The Republic* and literary works such as *Things Fall Apart* are fundamentally different given their declared genres. What they have in common, however, is the excitement of our imagination toward a certain vision of society.

The Human Person in the African Imagination

Recognition is the immediate implication of our attention to the structure of relationship with one another. We discover one another as conditioned by our common humanity. As the Nigerian-American philosopher Ifeanyi Menkiti (2004) states, individuals acquire personhood only in the community. In action and speech, we recognize one another as beings without whom our existence as humans would not be possible. Personhood is attained not in the abstract, but in being with others, in the daily exercise of encounter and, I would add, in the practice of the ordinary virtues with others. We are, as it were, exposed to one another, for without the other, speech would not be possible.

Menkiti articulates what I refer to as the symbiotic relationship between community and the individual, captured in popular Africa saying: "I am because we are." The notion of "I am because we are" speaks to the fact of "an individual, who recognizes the sources of his or her own humanity, and so realizes, with internal assurance, that in the absence of others, no grounds exist for a claim regarding the individual's own standing as a person" ("On the Normative Conception of a Person," 324). The conception of the individual human, Menkiti argues, is best approached as a journey, an ontological progression, from the past to the present. It is this journey, conducted within a given community, that grants the individual the status of personhood. This journey is not to be understood as a person just getting old, but rather as "the emergence of moral, or quasi-moral, qualities considered useful to the enrichment of the human community, or at least useful to the internalized rejection of attitudes directly inimical to community, that accounts for the shift in classification" (325). The emergence of moral qualities in the individual as a result of the journey suggests that to be a person is to attain a certain degree of moral maturity. For him, "personhood is the sort of thing which has to be achieved, the sort of thing at which individuals could fail" (326).

I characterized the relationship between the individual and community in the African imagination as symbiotic precisely because it is not a one-dimensional affair; the individual benefits from the community as much as the community does from the individual. Two things stand out in Menkiti's thought about the relationship between the individual and community in regard to personhood: First, given that the journey to personhood takes place in the community, the community must provide the individual with the much-needed ambiance to achieve moral maturity. It cannot demand from the individual duties and responsibilities it is not ready to provide to the individual. Second, the community must extend the same condition to every individual. Whereas it is the community that confers personhood, the condition for conferring it cannot be fickle and selective. This suggests that justice is the condition without which the individual cannot be expected to achieve personhood. Citing John Rawls, Menkiti (330) underscores this particular aspect of the role of the community in the emergence of a moral agent, arguing that those who are capable of a sense of justice are owed justice in the first place.

Against the backdrop of Menkiti's profound observations about the human person in the African community, it is only logical that the first question to engage any effort to articulate a working political philosophy for any society must be whether the state (community) has provided a just condition for the flourishing of every individual. Only when this is established can we demand duties and responsibilities from such individuals.

Things Fall Apart and the African Literature

My choice of *Thing Fall Apart* as the basis for my discussion of how to extract political philosophy from a literature lies largely in the fact that it is the most recognizable novel to come out of Africa. A lot has been written about the enormous impact of the novel on African postcolonial culture and discourse. Most importantly, it gave postcolonial African culture a definite shape and direction. In his essay, "Chinua Achebe and the Invention of African Culture," Simon Gikandi highlights Achebe's roles in Africa's intellectual history, crediting him with the invention of modern African culture. By African culture, Gikandi (4–8) means above all, culture as it is discoursed and "circulated within the institutions of interpretation." In this, there is the preeminent role of literature in the making of African subjects. *Things Fall Apart* did not exclusively institute, or even shape modern African culture that is characterized by nationalist consciousness. That honor belongs to African anti-colonial heroes such as Kwame Nkrumah, Jomo Kenyetta, Nnamdi Azikiwe, Obafemi Awolowo, etc. We cannot forget Leopold Sedar Senghor's *negritude* that gave Africa a putative right to the exclusive possession of full, untainted humanism. However, it is correct, as is implied in Gikandi's arguments, that *Things Fall Apart* gave these ideas and impulses a narrative format, a human face.

In tune with the above assessment of the narrative, Achebe himself writes that he would be quite satisfied if his novels, especially the ones set in the past, taught his African readers that "their past - with all its imperfections - was not one long night of savagery from which the first Europeans acting on God's behalf delivered them" ("The Novelist as a Teacher," 45). In his extensive commentaries on his works and in his interviews, Achebe might have indeed enormously influenced the interpretation of his work decidedly in the direction of the culture-clash paradigm. He mentions Joseph Conrad and Joyce Cary, whose stereotypical images of Africa in their respective novels forced him to "fight back." It is the need to take back the discourse about one's culture and existence that constitutes, in Achebe's words, the "overpowering urge to tell a story" ("*Home and Exile*, 38)

Most responses to the novel express glowing admiration of its role in redeeming and shaping African culture (Innes, *Critical perspectives on Chinua Achebe*). In "The Plight of a Hero in Achebe's Things Fall Apart" Patrick Nnoromele states that Okonkwo is a hero who embodies Igbo traits. Romanus Muoneke esteems Okonkwo as one "held up to the present as a model of courage, hard work, strength determination, and commitment to social values" (*Art, Rebellion and Redemption,* 100). It bears to note that the novel belongs to what Eileen Julien has described as an extroverted narrative, that is, a narrative that is turned outward, as opposed to being introverted, turned inward (695). Extroverted narratives are largely guided by the mindset of resistance rooted in opposition. It is, of course, one thing to highlight other people's negative image of oneself in their narratives, it is another to articulate one's own image of self and one's world. What exactly is the image of African persons and their communities in *Things Fall Apart*? Can we truly work with the African images portrayed in the narrative given that the story was crafted as a counter-narrative? We must highlight the most obvious thing about the work, which is that it is a work of fiction, and therefore the futility of expecting a realistic, or even factual depiction of African lives. Ato Quayson highlights the many problems associated with reading *Things Fall Apart* and African literature as representations of reality; he suggests a multi-tiered reading that highlights the many cultural subtexts (118).

The story of *Things Fall Apart* is woven around the fate of a central figure, Okonkwo. As Charles Larson argues in *The Emergence of African Fiction*, Achebe's design is to paint a complete picture of a community that has been impacted by external factors. This becomes evident, according to Larson, as we read a detailed presentation of the traditional marriage arrangement, the marriage itself with emphasis on bride price, childbirth, divorce, and finally "the funeral rites surrounding death. The emphasis is almost always on the group instead of the individual" (43). Larson argues further, that even though the second part of the novel is about Okonkwo's exile, he is "increasingly kept in the background, for Achebe's intention in the central section of his novel is to record the coming of the white man into Eastern Nigeria, and the communal rather than individual conflict" (52). He concludes his observation by arguing that the story "is not the story of the pacification of individuals but of entire tribes of people and even beyond that" (60).

Regardless of whether *Things Fall Apart* is about an individual or a tribe, one thing stands out rather prominently: the demise of that person or the tribe, which the novel set out to record, was caused by an external force. At least this is the conclusion the village people arrive at. It does seem that there is no way one can go around this conclusion, following the narrative structure. Thus, what is primary is the moral consideration, wrapped in the simple question of who is responsible for things going wrong in that community. For the leaders of Umuofia community, one thing is certain: they did not cause it; they are innocent. Left on their own, the status quo could go on unchallenged; expressed in political philosophical terms, the relationship between the individual and state was perfect. But was it? Was there harmony between the different parts of the polity?

Solomon Iyasere, among other commentators, points out some of the subtle and indeed more profound issues the novel engages with such as the inflexibility of tribal codes and their application in the formal decrees of the Oracles. It is in Okonkwo, he argues, that the inflexibility of that society is most manifest. The "obsession with proving and preserving his manliness dominates Okonkwo's entire life," and predisposes him to a "monochromatic view of what people should be, with men and women performing sexually-defined tasks" (96–104). Thus it could well be argued that the society's inflexibility brought about its falling apart. Could that inflexibility be a signifier of the absence of justice? Could it be indicative of the failure of that society to provide enabling conditions for the flourishing of the individual? Isidore Okpewho concurs that things fell apart because the Igbo did not allow for diversity, femininity, and pliancy in their world (Okpewho, *Chinua Achebe's Things Fall Apart*). Judged from their observations, the Umuofia society did not have the conditions that could have enabled individuals and groups to raise their voices and be heard.

Iyasere and Okpewho's interpretive trajectory did not gain as much traction as it deserved for various reasons which might have to do with the time period in which African societies still lived. The generations that experienced the brutality of colonialism are still alive. Indeed, the last two countries to gain independence or be formally free from the clutches of colonialism, Zimbabwe and South Africa, still grapple with the dire consequences of centuries of oppression. Affectively speaking, therefore, it appears just right that the African will be engaged with the question of how he was perceived and treated by the others more than how flawed his world was. Besides this reason, there is also the already mentioned interpretive trajectory that Achebe has vigorously pushed in his essays and interviews, and which failed to explore the political contexts of the community outside the gaze of the West. It is of course, not the goal of this essay to examine the merits or demerits of the above ideas about the novel. For my stated purpose, I concentrate on the world of the narrative; that is, I focus on the characters' self-perception in relation to rights and justice, their relation to one another, and to their polis. What was the standard of people's judgment in the world of *Things Fall Apart*? What was their conception of justice?

Quest for Justice in *Things Fall Apart*

It is generally agreed that John Rawls's conception of justice as fairness represents a more complete account of justice for our modern world. Space would not allow me to get into it now. The Golden rule has been suggested as helpful in appreciating this particular approach to justice. The notion of treating others as you would like them to treat you underscores the fundamental inviolability of the dignity of every individual and how justice helps us maintain that. In "Justice Through Deliberation and the Problem of Otherness," Uchenna Okeja argues that the primary condition for justice in society is the unconditional acceptance of the humanity of the other.[2] Justice is based on deliberation, he states, and this, in turn, is "contingent upon the intersubjective affirmation of a basic principle, namely, the principle of humanity" (10). Without acknowledging the basic fact of the dignity of every individual, no society can function in a somewhat acceptable civil manner. Recognition from our fellow humans is essential—primarily for our self-perception as humans, and secondarily for our exercise of citizenship. Even when we are aware that we possess dignity as humans, we still need others to affirm it in their relation to us. Their affirmation of our rights and dignity provides an enabling condition for our achieving personhood.

Postcolonial politics in Africa and racial politics in America have been largely about the right to recognition. The colonizers denied the colonized humanity and thus related to them in a typical Hegelian master/slave dialectic; the master does not recognize the slave because the slave is thought to not possess self-consciousness. But the master/slave dialectic is not restricted to the Western exercise of power on the colonized or racialized peoples of the world. In precolonial Africa (and indeed, in all feudal societies), the same dynamics took place in the relationship between the privileged and the less privileged, between the powerful and the powerless. *Things Fall Apart* is full of such cases, instances in which individuals and groups are denied basic recognition and are therefore not considered worthy enough to experience justice. I discuss only two of the instances: the fate of the members of the Osu caste system and the killing of Ikemefuna. On the basis of these instances, we recall the questions that will bring us back to the possibility of formulating political philosophical questions from literature. What exactly is the notion of freedom and human dignity in Umuofia society? Can we legitimately speak of individual rights in that society? If personhood is achieved, as Menkiti has argued, does that society provide an equal playing field for every individual to do so?

The *osu* caste system is a socio-political order rooted in ancient religious practices in which certain people are dedicated to deities as *pharmakós* (scapegoats). In *Things Fall Apart* an *osu* is defined as

> a person dedicated to a god, a thing set apart – a taboo forever, and his children after him. He could neither marry nor be married by the free-born. He was in fact an outcast, living in a special area of the village, close to the Great Shrine. Wherever he went he carried with him the mark of his forbidden caste … An osu could not attend an assembly of the free-born, and they, in turn, could not shelter under his roof.
>
> *(113)*

The descendants of those dedicated to the deities inherit their ancestors' fate in the same way that black people in America inherit the scourge of racism and are denied recognition by the system. From the onset therefore, the *osus* are placed outside the ambiance of empathy and consideration of justice precisely because they are not recognized as citizens with dignity. As the carriers of the communities' evils, the *osus* are regarded as *efulefu*—worthless—and are ignored by the clan not only in matters of social and political relevance but also in daily encounter. There is, strictly speaking, no encounter between them and the so-called freeborn.

The *osus* are featured mainly in relation to the advent of the new religion. When they saw that "the new religion welcomed twins and such abominations, [they] thought that it was possible that they would also be received" (113). They were thus among the first Igbo to convert to Christianity, together with some of the women whose twin children were taken from them and thrown away into the jungle because the Igbo considered twins anomalous.

The *osus* could, of course, not launch a revolution for recognition or a civil rights movement, given their negligible numerical strength. The new religion gave them what the old order denied them: a sense of worth, recognition as humans, albeit supported by the colonial power. From the perspective of Menkiti's conditions for personhood, we wonder, at least for the purpose of enhancing our deliberations, whether these people were expected to achieve personhood in that society given that doing so entails an unqualified recognition.

The *osus* were not only the first people to welcome the white man and convert to Christianity. Visiting Okonkwo in his place of exile, Obierika tells him how Umuofia has changed during the seven years of his absence; the white man has established missions, and the people of Umuofia have abandoned their old ways of life. The saddest news is that Nwoye, Okonkwo's first son, has joined the missionaries. Later in their discussion, Obierika observes that the white man has "put a knife on the things that held us together, and we have fallen apart." (124). It is not accidental that Obierika pronounces the judgment on the white man as the cause of their community disintegrating. He represents the elite of the old order that is being threatened by the colonial forces. By implication the concerns of the disfranchized members of his community (polity) is irrelevant. The most consequential questions we ought to ask in regard to his judgment include: why was it rather too easy for the members of the *osu* caste to join the new religion? Why was it easy for the society to collapse even without the white man firing a shot? Ironically, Christianity or even the colonial intervention could be seen as the advent of modernity in that space. Of course, we do not ignore Christianity's flaws or even the more obvious ones of the colonial forces. Despite these, however, the new forces provided an opportunity to think about the dignity of individuals and group such as the *osus* and the twins, and their relation to the community. I have addressed similar questions in "Nelson Mandela and the Topology of African Encounter," in which I argued that Nelson Mandela provided us with a new vocabulary with which we can best understand the contemporary African condition: encounter. Attempts to answer these questions objectively must first issue from the perspective of the outcasts, the grieving women, and Okonkwo's son. Could they have easily defected if they had experienced recognition as humans with dignity?

We consider one more incident that urges a rethinking of the freedom and dignity of the individual and his or her relation to the state (community): the killing of Ikemefuna, the boy from neighboring Mbaino, who had been taken as a ransom to Umuofia. He was raised in Okonkwo's household and had begun to call Okonkwo father. The Oracle had decreed that the boy be killed and Okonkwo made sure to carry out the dictates (40–43). Could Ikemefuna have been saved by a deft application of imagination and thoughts about the dignity of every individual? Why would he bear the consequence of the crime committed by another person? One might argue that the people were merely obeying the dictates of the Oracle. Obeying one's tradition, however, does not answer the question of justice and recognition. Obeying tradition does not make any killing justifiable; at least it does not exonerate the people from thinking about justice in its most basic form and exhibiting a certain degree of co-feeling toward the boy. Perhaps that co-feeling could have helped them to arrive at a more complex attitude to the world than blind obedience to tradition.

Conclusion

I have argued in "African Literature as a Handmaid of African Philosophy," that African philosophy can benefit from a close reading of African literature which has attained a more obvious status in global academia. I stated in the introductory part of this essay that in examining the image of the human person portrayed in the narrative as well as the structures of the society depicted, we are able to articulate the type of political philosophy that guides a particular society, or whether that society has one. Our considerations thus raise the question as to why the Umuofia society fell apart. Did the society fall apart because of the colonial intervention or because of a lack of coherent working political philosophy? It is safe to suggest that we have in the named society a blind allegiance to a tradition rooted in taboos and religious thinking rather than adherence to a rigorous political philosophy rooted in a thick conception of freedom and justice. Would consideration of justice in relation to the humanity of individuals such as Ikemefuna, who was sacrificed on the orders of the Oracle, have initiated far-reaching thought about an enduring political framework? Would a sense of justice, as conceived above, have given the people's political system a more profound over-arching philosophy?

In many ways, we might take *Things Fall Apart* as a cautionary tale for every society in which individuals or groups are denied recognition because of their phenotypical, physical, religious, or cultural difference from the normative group. This, I think, is a plausible interpretation and a line of serious intellectual inquiry. Justice as fairness and recognition of the dignity of every individual forms the basis of any political community. Based alone on Ifeanyi Menkiti's grounds for the emergence of a moral agent or personhood, we discover that the Umuofia community failed to fulfill the most fundamental condition for its citizens; it failed to provide conditions for justice. We can therefore not expect compliance within the polis from people who have been denied the basis for personhood. By compliance, we mean the exercise of basic duties of citizenship. We identify with a culture or a particular society precisely because it is what or where we feel affirmed. The outcasts had nothing in common with the rest of society because there was no basis for justice: they were not recognized. For them, therefore, things did not fall apart—they never stood together in the first place. To ignore these groups' concerns is to make the mistake of relating to society in the abstract.

To conclude, I return to my assertion to the effect that reading works of fiction can provide us with ideas with which to formulate society's political philosophy. This is definitely true about *Things Fall Apart* which, true to its genre as a work of fiction, does not deal directly with formal philosophy. What is said about the novel goes for many other novels set in realistic situations we can recognize as African.

Notes

1 Cosmos in the classical Greek tradition is not only "the world" or "the universe" but has connotations of just order—it is in this sense an antonym of "Chaos." A good state in Plato's philosophy would serve to represent the principle of order.
2 I have discussed the notion of justice in the African imagination elsewhere (Eze 2021).

References

Achebe, Chinua, *Things Fall Apart*. London: Heinemann, 1958.
Achebe, Chinua, *Hopes and Impediments: Selected Essays, 1965–1987*. Oxford: Heinemann, 1988.
Achebe, Chinua. *Home and Exile*. Oxford: Oxford University Press, 1978.
Arendt, Hannah. *The Human Condition*. Chicago, IL: The University of Chicago Press, 1958.
Aristotle. *Poetics*. Translated by Malcolm Heath. London: Penguin Books, 1996.
Eze, Chielozona. "African Literature as a Handmaid of African Philosophy." In *African Philosophical and Literary Possibilities: Re-reading the Canon*, edited by Aretha Phiri, 17–32. New York: Lexington Books, 2020.
Eze, Chielozona. *Justice and Human Rights in the African Imagination: We, Too, Are Humans*. London: Routledge, 2021.

Eze, Chielozona, "Nelson Mandela and the Topology of African Encounter." In *African Philosophy for the Twenty-First Century: Acts of Transition*, edited by Jean Godefroy Bidima and Laura Hengehold, 183–200. Rowman & Littlefield Publishers, 2021.

Frank, Arthur. W. *Letting Stories Breathe*. Chicago, IL: The University of Chicago Press, 2010.

Gikandi, Simon. "Chinua Achebe and the Invention of African Culture." *Research in African Literature*, 32.3 (2001). 4–8.

Innes, C.L. et al. ed., *Critical perspectives on Chinua Achebe*. Washington, DC: Three Continents Press, 1978.

Iyasere, Solomon. "Narrative Techniques in *Things Fall Apart*." In *Critical Perspectives on Chinua Achebe*, edited by in C.L. Innes and Bernth Lindfors, 96–104. Washington, DC: Three Continents Press, 1978.

Julien, Eileen. "The Extroverted African Novel." In *The Novel*, Volume 1: History, Geography, and Culture, edited by Franco Moretti, 667–700. Princeton, NJ: Princeton University Press, 2006.

Larson, Charles. 1972. *The Emergence of African Fiction*. Bloomington: Indiana University Press.

Menkiti, Ifeanyi A. "On the Normative Conception of a Person." In A Companion to African Philosophy, edited by Wiredu Kwasi, 324–331. Malden, MA: Blackwell Publishing Ltd., 2004.

Muoneke, Romanus. *Art, Rebellion and Redemption: A Reading of the Novels of Chinua Achebe*. New York: Peter Lang, 1994.

Nnoromele, Patrick. "The Plight of a Hero in Achebe's Things Fall Apart." In *Chinua Achebe's Things Fall Apart*, edited by Harold Bloom, 39–49. New York: Bloom's Literary Criticism, 2010.

Okeja, Uchenna. "Justice through Deliberation and the Problem of Otherness." *Angelaki: Journal of the Theoretical Humanities*, 24.2 (2019): 10–21.

Okpewho, Isidore editor. *Chinua Achebe's Things Fall Apart: A Casebook*. Oxford: Oxford University Press, 2003.

Plato, *The Republic*, edited by G.R.F. Ferrari and Translated by Tom Griffith. Cambridge: Cambridge University Press, 2000.

Quayson, Ato. "Realism, Criticism, and the Disguises of Both: A Reading of Chinua Achebe's *Things Fall Apart*." *Research in African Literature*, 25.4 (1994): 117–136.

3

THE STATE IN AFRICA AND THE AFRICAN STATE

Katrin Flikschuh

The State in Africa

State Failure and Statist Ideals

Numerous explanations have been offered by way of accounting for continental state failure or fragility. Perhaps the most common one explains state failure in Africa as the outcome of the conjunction of weak institutional structures and corrupt elites and leaders. Were institutions less weak or leaders less corrupt, so the suggestion, post-independent statehood would succeed better than it has done.[1] However, weak institutions are surely defining of weak statehood, and weak institutions all but *require* leaders to operate outside the realm of institutional accountability – in which case one might as well say that the state has failed because the state has failed. A different type of explanation blames political culture: incessant ethnic loyalties and attendant divisions work against the emergence of a civil society capable of acting as a fulcrum of shared civic interests that would in turn consolidate relations between citizens and state, rendering the latter more accountable to the former. Here the background assumption is the purported Weberian clash between 'tradition' and 'modernity': in the fulness of teleological time, the post-colonial state will transform tribalists into citizens and, with them, failing into functioning states. Yet this explanation begs the question as to why, short of buying into Weberian teleology, anyone *should* have an interest in statehood and attendant civic culture. *Pace* Weber, statehood is not the natural destiny of mankind – other forms of political association are in principle available. A third explanation points to the contrast between declaratory and constitutional sovereignty: unlike the state-building processes in Europe, African states are weak internally because African leaders inherited colonially established state boundaries and were never required to demonstrate sovereign territorial control internally.[2] This may be true – but why does it not simply show that states in Africa differ from – hence are not comparable to – states in Europe?

The above types of explanation tend to evaluate the failures and prospects of African statehood through the implicitly assumed lens of the European history of state-building. An alternative explanatory framework emphasizes the distinctiveness of the colonial state as a relevant precursor to the post-colonial state. More specifically, the colonial state is said to have been *structurally* distinct in that it lacked sovereign authority – the colonial state was

DOI: 10.4324/9781003143529-4

an extension of and subservient to the colonizing power to which it owed its existence.[3] The colonial state was also *institutionally* distinct in that it was based on the system of indirect rule, with the bifurcated functions between so-called 'traditional' sources of political organization and so-called 'modern' state bureaucracies.[4] This set relevant pathways to the post-independence emergence of the 'dual publics' famously identified and analysed by Peter Ekeh in 'Colonialism and the Two Publics'.[5] Finally, the colonial state was *normatively* distinctive in that the colonial powers saw no need to legitimize its existence to those subject to its coercive control. As Crawford Young has shown, the colonial state was experienced by colonial subjects as a 'crusher of stones' – an all-destroying machinery. This differs from Hobbes' *Leviathan* as that great mortal God which, whilst it keeps all in awe, nonetheless also crucially appeals to subjects' rational consent in this regard.[6]

Those who emphasize the distinctiveness of the post-colonial state when compared to the European state model might be hard-pressed to say whether or not the state in Africa has failed. As indicated, state failure is usually measured with reference to features and capacities that pertain to an implicitly assumed European ideal. If one takes the post-colonial state to be an altogether different kind of animal, assessing its failures and successes by standards relevant to European statehood makes little sense. Again, insofar as European statehood is assumed to set the standards for successful statehood in general, the post-colonial African state as successor to *colonial* statehood effectively emerged into independence stillborn: measured by European standards, the African post-colonial state was never a proper state in the first place. In short, anyone who accepts the structural and normative distinctiveness of the post-colonial state compared to the European model should measure the success or failure of the post-colonial state with reference to criteria relevant to the post-colonial norm. The trouble is, there is no such norm: the colonial state was at best a degenerative version of the European ideal. As the successor to the colonial state, the modern post-colonial state is a successor not to an ideal type but to the ideal type's degenerative version.[7] There is currently no theorized post-colonial ideal that supplies criteria of success or failure with reference to which actual post-colonial states could measure their performance.

In sum, the situation appears to be as follows: the very idea of state failure or success implies a relevant ideal against which actual states' performance is assessed. Current assessments of state failure and success implicitly assume a European ideal of statehood. If one accepts the distinctiveness of the post-colonial state, it is inappropriate to assess the African post-colonial state by criteria gleaned from the European ideal. One should instead assess actual post-colonial states with reference to a relevantly theorized post-colonial ideal. However, there is no ideal for degenerative state forms. We thus seem to lack relevant criteria by which to assess the success or failure of actual African post-colonial states. This in turn implies that we cannot in fact say whether African states have either failed or succeeded. Perhaps, by the standards of the colonial state as 'crusher of stones' the DRC as post-colonial successor to the Belgian Congo must count as a success story!

States' Interests and Citizens' Interests

Should we worry about African states' failure or success? When the relevant agencies measure state failure, what are the concerns and objectives that drive their measurements? Ostensibly, the concern is not with states as artificial agents in their own right but rather with the state as an institution designed to promote the well-being of its citizens. On this view, we should be concerned with state failure because we are concerned with the well-being of those who live within states. But what does well-being amount to here? The US-based think tank, The

Fund for Peace, measures state failure and citizen well-being by criteria that include security measures, economic development, governmental legitimacy, abidance by international human rights laws.[8] States that perform well on these dimensions are deemed to provide well for their citizens and are therefore said to be stable or non-fragile. These criteria are gleaned, as noted, from the European normative ideal of statehood. In respect of post-colonial states, they arguably measure nothing at all either way.

Given the lack of interest in the structural specificity of post-colonial statehood, there is reason to suspect that the stated concern with citizens' well-being is no more than part of the story. It is very comforting to think of the state as the first servant of the people – and it is of course a large part of states' legitimation narratives. But do states solely or even only primarily exist for the good of their citizenry? If that were so, the case for abolishing the state in Africa would surely be overwhelming, given its persistent failure in delivering the political goods enumerated by the Peace Fund. Yet there are no calls for abolishing states that persistently fail their citizens by the standards of the Fragile States Index. On the contrary, the point of the Index is to alert the international community to the necessity of averting state collapse. Too many Somalias would undermine the system of states. The stability of the international community of states would appear to be at least as large a factor, in concerns about state fragility, as citizens' well-being. Nor is a concern with international stability *prima facie* unwarranted. *Prima facie* it seems like a reasonable concern. Still, the interests of citizen well-being on the one hand and that of international stability on the other hand may end up conflicting. When they do, questions about the prioritization of legitimate interests should arise. Where states persistently fail their citizens, should they continue to be propped up for the sake of international security?

One may deny the possibility of conflicting interests – one may claim that citizen well-being and international stability go hand in hand. It is better for citizens of disparate countries to live in an internationally stable environment: one in which there are fewer wars, more international co-operation, better economic prospects, co-ordinated security, work, and social policies. There is, on this picture, no possible conflict between citizens' well-being and international stability – at least not in the long term; at least not all things considered; at least not if all states behaved as they should.

I am not so sure. Consider: a fairly sizable number of states are considered to be persistently failing or fragile, very many of them in Africa, though by no means exclusively so. According to the failed/fragile State Index, state fragility translates into reduced citizen well-being. As noted, however, the recommendation is not to disband fragile states but rather to strengthen them. The presumption appears to be that state strengthening is more like to increase citizen well-being than state dissolution. This presumption would possess more plausibility if alternatives to statehood had ever been given serious consideration or, more minimally, if suggested remedies to state fragility were adequate to the post-colonial state form in questions. As noted, however, the fragile state index recognizes only one state form, the classic European model, and proposes the administration to fragile post-colonial states of treatments tailored to the needs of a European-type state. This is akin to treating a cancer patient by way of sending her to the dentist. It raises the suspicion that citizen well-being may not be the only issue at stake – perhaps not even the most important one: a greater concern may be to preserve the overall state system by not allowing fragile states to fail. Conflicts of interest thus *are* possible between the citizenry of a fragile state and the international community. Current international practice suggests that the international community generally prioritizes international stability over citizen well-being.

Theorizing the Post-Colonial State

There is a strong Hobbesian presumption in Western political theory (and I suspect also in political science), that living in a state is better than not living in one. This is of course a theoretical construction and, again, part of the European normative ideal. According to Hobbes, life outside the state is 'poor, nasty, brutish, and short'. On Hobbes' account, state entrance is evidently better than the (only other proffered) alternative. And yet, according to Crawford Young, living inside the post-colonial state can often be a bit like living in the Hobbesian state of nature: here, the inherited state form is the problem, not the solution. One should guard against characterizing the failed or fragile post-colonial state as a *de facto* state of nature. After all, there are *no* state institutions in the state of nature; yet there are plenty of them in the post-colonial state, albeit dysfunctional ones (it would be a mistake to assume that dysfunctional institutions have no impact on citizens' lives). Nonetheless, if life in the fragile post-colonial state is as bad as or worse than life in the Hobbesian state of nature, would it not be rational to exit the post-colonial state? Many citizens of such states have in fact exited it: short of emigration (which many do in fact pursue) they have ceased to expect or hope for public services and provisions and are instead relying on non-statist forms of mutual protection and support.[9] Empirically, speaking such internal exit or exile from the state is difficult to register given that, short of emigration, the withdrawal does not manifest itself as physical removal from official state territory. Many citizens of the fragile post-colonial state thus withdraw from engagement with the state even whilst continuing to live within its territorial borders.[10]

I suggested that the hope of reforming the fragile post-colonial state by way of remedies that apply to the European state model is a futile enterprise. I also suggested that the international community has a strong interest in preserving the system of states. Given the non-applicability of European-style reform on the one hand and the non-availability of state disbanding on the other hand, the most plausible alternative would seem to lie in an explicit acknowledgement of the existence of the post-colonial state as a distinctive state form. Once its *de facto* existence was explicitly and generally acknowledged, one might begin the task of theorizing a possible post-colonial ideal. One might then be able to begin to specify relevant criteria of evaluation by which to measure actual post-colonial state performance as well as propose adequate institutional remedies to state fragility or failure. All of this may seem like a modest and even sensible proposal: however, it has some radical implications which, once considered, may help account for the general reluctance among state theorists and practitioners alike to acknowledge anything but a universal state norm (i.e., the European norm universalized). If it were explicitly acknowledged that the European state is but one possible form of statehood, the international community of states would have to begin to think of itself along the lines of a multi-cultural society characterized by non-negligible compositional differences among individual member states. This would have a considerable impact on international law and global policy-making.[11] These implications are highly inconvenient from the perspective of the international community. Even though not excusable, it is understandable that the question of compositional differences in modern statehood is rarely explicitly broached. Once again, the question is whether the inconveniences to the international community of states are sufficiently weighty to allow for the continuation of the current status quo in which many citizens of fragile states find themselves in an existential limbo – unsure as to whether they live in- or outside the state or somewhere in-between. From here on I shall assume, if only for the sake of argument, that the interests of those citizens should take priority over those of the international community. Given my argument so far, this implies that we ought to try to theorize a post-colonial norm against which actual post-colonial performance can be realistically assessed.

The African State

Post-Colonial Statehood and the Limits of Western Political Thought

I have suggested that despite international concern over state fragility in Africa and elsewhere, there is generally little appetite for acknowledging the structural distinctiveness of the colonially inherited state form on the continent. The tendency is instead to treat the European form as a universal norm and to measure post-colonial state performance by criteria gleaned from the European ideal. There are at least two reasons for the reluctance to depart from the assumption of a universal norm. One is political, and I have mentioned it already: acknowledging structural and normative diversity within the community of states would render international law- and policy-making an ever more complicated undertaking; no doubt it would also affect the power advantage enjoyed by those states that approximate the European norm most closely. The second reason is theoretical and, indeed, philosophical. It is fair to say that the impact of Hobbes' *Leviathan* on the philosophical imagination of political theorists in Europe (and the United States) has been overwhelming. European thinkers find it extremely hard to think politically *absent* the idea of the state. Our entire political vocabulary – from the idea of a state of nature to that of rights, liberties, and distributive justice – is state-based, i.e., it assumes the state as a relevant background institution. The relative failure of European or 'Western' political theorists to think beyond the state is reflected in the ill-fated global justice debate which blossomed during the 1980 and 1990s and into the 2000s before withering away on grounds of its failure plausibly to advance terms of debate beyond inherited Western, state-centric concepts and conceptions. Significantly, the global justice debate also demonstrates that the failure to rethink basic forms of political organization and institutionalization was not for want of trying: for a long time the aspiration was, after all, to think beyond and in that sense without the state.[12] At the same time, Western global theorists expended remarkably little effort on informing themselves about different historical conditions – let alone different theoretical frameworks – beyond the narrow remit offered by Western – indeed, Anglo-American political theory and practice. It seems relatively clear, moreover, that this failure in philosophical imagination feeds back into political practice. To return once more to the failed/fragile State Index: its conceptualization of relevant ideal criteria of assessment is informed by a state-centric philosophical tradition. The criteria – security, development, human rights – are taken on trust largely because they are treated as beyond theoretical reconsideration. The thought that states *should* secure citizens' well-being translates almost seamlessly into the expectation that, in principle, all states *could* do so: in that sense, the failure among theorists explicitly to acknowledge and theorize the heterogeneity of post-colonial state forms might be seen as a failure in political responsibility. Still, and even if one acknowledges the need to do so: given the hold on our philosophical imagination of the Hobbesian territorial all-powerful state, how can one begin to rethink or move beyond the European political ideal?

The Idea of the State in African Philosophical Thinking

Western political theorists have found it hard to think without or beyond the state; but what about African theorists? There is remarkably little sustained discussion of the statist idea in contemporary African philosophy. Indeed, once one begins to think about it, the contrast between Western theorists who cannot but think in statist terms, and African theorists, who seem reluctant to think in those terms, is striking. What one finds in the African philosophical literature are deeply engaged discourses on personhood and community.[13] A community is decidedly not a European state: a community lacks most of the features commonly deemed constitutive of the European state, including territoriality, a settled subject population, a monopoly of coercive authority and control internally, and the acknowledgement of sovereign status externally. The European state is conceived as an artificial agent which as such exists independently of its subject population, and which interacts with other states on the basis of state-specific interests that are in principle separable from the interests of its subject populations (hence, of course, possible conflicts between citizens and state interests). A community, by contrast, is typically conceived as an organically evolved political-cum-cultural association whose members collectively constitute it such that there is no division, in principle, between community and its constitutive membership. Nor is a community typically defined by its territorial extension, though it will of course typically have a habitat it calls its own. And whilst there will be institutionalized forms of accountability and control, the idea is anathema of a community as pursuing interests that are in principle separable from the collective interests of its constituent members (which is not to say that individual and collective interests cannot diverge).

Similarly, and as Ifeanyi Menkiti has recently reminded us, personhood and citizenship are not synonymous.[14] Although all citizens are persons, one can be a person without being a citizen. For Menkiti, personhood is ontologically and normatively prior to citizenship. At the same time, Menkiti believes that citizenship has come to occlude personhood; it has become normatively more important that one be a citizen than that one be a person (witness the treatment of non-citizens, such as immigrants or refugees). Insofar as citizenship in general is an attribute of modern statehood, Menkiti's position may reduce to the claim that modern statehood occludes personhood: citizenship is a state-based modification of personhood, and since for Menkiti personhood is ontologically and normatively prior to personhood, the modification amounts to a reduction in the richness of what it is to be a person. Menkiti does not go on to say similarly comparable things about state and community; I think, however, that Menkiti is likely to favour community over statehood precisely because he associates reductive citizenship with statehood and normatively rich personhood with community.

Arguably, Menkiti's preference for community/personhood over state/ citizenship generalizes: the preferred strategy among post-independent African philosophers has been to ask whether aspects of political organizations and governance historically found at the community level might not be scaled up to the post-colonial state level. Among the most influential of these latter attempts has been Kwasi Wiredu's idea of 'consensual democracy'.[15] According to Wiredu, the governmental style among the traditional Akan of present-day Ghana was consensus-based. Given the prevalence of the traditional African notion of 'palaver', Wiredu conjectures that consensus-based governance may have been the basic model of many other African communities and nations. Applied to the post-colonial state context, Wiredu takes consensual democracy to envisage a participatory but non-adversarial and therefore non-partisan mode of political consultation and decision-making. In fact, in calling it a 'no-party' model of democracy, Wiredu delimits consensual democracy from Soviet-style one-party systems and Western-style multi-party systems alike. Consensual democracy is thus not to be confused with the one-party systems established by early post-independence socialist leaders, such as Nkrumah or Nyeyere. Under Wiredu's consensual scheme, 'governments are not formed by parties but by the consensus of elected representatives. Government becomes a kind of coalition of citizens.'[16]

The immediate impetus to Wiredu's plea for consensual democracy were the ethnic conflicts that often erupted under systems of multi-party rule, in which members of different ethnic groups aligned themselves with ethnically defined parties. However, Wiredu's wider philosophical and political ambition may have been to 'indigenize' the post-colonial state by way of re-introducing elements from traditional forms of rule and governance. A similar strategy is pursued by Ajume Wingo who in a series of innovative articles seeks to reintroduce elements of traditional rule into modern state structures, ranging from non-party-based systems of public participation and accountability to a reminder of the significance of ancestral participation in the political life of communities.[17]

Wiredu's and others' attempts to integrate elements of traditional rule into post-colonial state structures have been criticized – especially by younger generations of philosophers. Emmanuel Chukwudi Eze, for example, doubts whether Wiredu's vision of consensual democracy 'is workable in the now largely secular states and, certainly, religiously pluralistic African Countries'.[18] Similarly, in his recent book-length analysis of Wiredu's proposal Bernard Matolino queries the superiority of consensual over majoritarian forms of democratic government.[19] Both Eze and Matolino in effect throw doubt on the adequacy of community-based forms of political organization and participation in relation to state-based governance: again, however, neither thematizes the post-colonial state directly.

Is this general failure among African philosophers to bring the post-colonial state into direct philosophical purview a reflection of their reluctance to accept the political reality of statehood in Africa? Or, alternatively, is it simply not clear, as Uchenna Okeja has suggested, whether African philosophers possess the conceptual resources necessary to think about the post-colonial state at a sufficiently abstract level? Taking the generational shift into consideration, it certainly seems as if philosophers of the period immediately following independence might have harboured the hope that the post-colonial state could be reformed from within by drawing on traditional forms of rule. By contrast, second-generation African philosophers appear more sceptical about the feasibility of this strategy. At the same time, they seem undecided as to available theoretical alternatives. Thus, in his book on the state of politics in post-independence Africa, Okeja emphasizes the philosophical importance of acknowledging political failure.[20] Post-independence generations, Okeja argues, have had to live with systematic and enduring political failure. Okeja's diagnosis goes a significant step beyond the writings of thinkers like Eze and Matolino, who express scepticism over the adequacy of a 'return' to traditional values in the face of modern statehood yet who retain some degree of confidence in the salvageability of the post-colonial state. By contrast, Okeja's comes as close as possible to a *philosophical* statement of state failure. This is not insignificant. Diagnosing state failure at the philosophical level is different from diagnosing state failure or fragility empirically. The latter failures will always remain contingent – always explicable in terms of these or those causal factors; as such, empirical failures always remain reversible. If the Nigerian state has failed empirically speaking, then it has failed to live up to its own possibility – but there is as yet every chance that it can do better in the future. To diagnose political failure at the philosophical level, by contrast, is not to make a conditional claim; it is to make an unconditional claim. Okeja might be proposing that the very idea of the state has failed in Africa. In that case, the Nigerian state has not failed to live up to its own possibility; rather, and at least as it stands now, the Nigerian state is itself an impossibility.

Okeja does not in fact go quite so far as to say that the state in Africa is an impossibility – at least he does not say so outright. He speaks of *political* failure, and he does intend this as a philosophical claim: the failure is non-contingent, which is to say that it was, in a sense, predictable. Nonetheless, to speak philosophically of *political* failure falls short of speaking of *state* failure. Okeja may be continuing the above-noted philosophical practice of *avoiding* direct engagement with the very idea of the state. This leaves his position somewhat ambiguous. On the one hand, when Okeja says that post independence generations have had to live with political failure, he is issuing a remarkable if depressing claim. He is saying, "let us stop pretending that the current political situation in Africa is salvageable via appeal to traditional values and concepts". On the other hand, when he develops his positive proposal in favour of thinking about politics in terms of deliberative agency, he is focused on the moral and political responsibilities of individual human agents whom he urges to take a conscientiously acknowledged attitude towards political failure. For Okeja, it is crucial that citizens in Africa acknowledge the fact that they are living with political failure – only once this is explicitly thematized, and only once it becomes a central feature in agents' political deliberations can possible remedies to political failure emerge. This is certainly an important dimension of overcoming political failure: but where, in all this, is the role of the state?

Conceiving the Post-Colonial State

Western theorists struggle to think politically without the state; African philosophers seem to find it equally difficult to think politically in statist terms. The reluctance may be both normative as well as conceptual: community may be preferred intrinsically, and even if it isn't, the available stock of concepts is communal more than statist. And yet, it seems unlikely that the wider international community would countenance a departure from some statist norm. (Here it is perhaps worth noting, even if only in parenthesis, that state fragility/failure is far more widespread than is generally acknowledged. Even if Africa is generally deemed to top the list of fragile states, the list is long and includes states in Southern America, in Eastern Europe, In Asia, in the Middle East. In many ways, the European state is the exception, not the norm – and yet we firmly continue to think of the latter as the normative ideal). But how does one even begin to get a grip on the post-colonial state? There is a large literature on post-coloniality: on otherness, othering, and hybridity. Much of it casts itself in terms that are self-consciously confrontational vis-à-vis 'mainstream' political analysis and theory. Indeed, often it is not clear what the target is: critique of Western thinking or concern to identify the distinctiveness of the post-colonial state. Within African philosophical and political thinking, post-modern and deconstructivist approaches appear to be less widespread than they are in recent European (and possibly Asian) writings on the post-colony.[21] I shall therefore not engage that literature here.

To my mind, within African theorizing, Peter Ekeh's by now classic contribution to post-colonial statehood continues to stand out.[22] Ekeh, recall, diagnosed the emergence of 'two publics' in the post-independence African state. In so doing Ekeh, was insistent upon conceptualizing this as a modern phenomenon: he explicitly distanced his analysis from the standard Weberian approach that expects the gradual displacement of 'traditional' structures by 'modern' ones. Ekeh's claim was not that a traditional public continued to co-exist alongside a 'modern' one. On the contrary, the point of the article was to show that the two publics are a creation of the colonial state with its system of 'indirect rule', so are a modern phenomenon, rather than signifying a clash between tradition and modernity. Ekeh further argued that the existence of the two publics gave state institutions a function fundamentally different from that of European state institutions: in the African post-colonial state, the latter is a resource base for *modern* communal politics.

My aim here is not to set out or to evaluate Ekeh's substantive position in any great detail; my sense is, however, that part of what makes Ekeh's contribution so enduring is precisely his ability to rise above the merely descriptive level to making a *conceptual* point. Ekeh saw something about the emergent structure of the African post-colonial state in general that seems to me not to have been captured with such analytic clarity since: he saw that there are *two* publics in the post-colonial state, and he saw that this is fundamentally at odds with European thinking about the state, in which there can only ever be *one* public. Of course, Ekeh did not give a complete account of the post-colonial state – he only gave a slither of it; and given that the article in question is nearly 50 years old, much has obviously happened since then. Nonetheless, it seems to me that Ekeh's analysis contained acute conceptual insight – and one question is whether current African philosophical thinking might be able to build on Ekeh's analysis.

There is another text that sticks in my mind, notwithstanding its somewhat unfortunate title. This is Patrick Chabal's micro-economic analysis of the modern African state in *The Politics of Suffering and Smiling*.[23] Much of Chabal's analysis is based on close observation of the daily actions and interactions of African citizens with their states and state officials. Chabal's analysis thus differs from that of Ekeh in that he focuses not on the 'political elites' who succeed in attaining to political office but on ordinary citizens who have learned to live with what Okeja calls 'political failure'. In often graphic detail, Chabal describes how citizens have developed strategies for coping with, responding to, or circumventing state structures and authorities. Take African states' colonially fixed territorial borders, for example, which not only bifurcated long-established communities but also cut across established trade routes, effectively curtailing intra-African, non-colonial economic activity and development. Cross-border communal trade and contact nonetheless continue, albeit with the additional obstacle of state borders that have to be negotiated as an inconvenience. In consequence, new opportunities for economic and revenue have developed. According to Chabal,

> The cost of negotiating borders, which is wholly a product of their presence, leads to the establishment of both formal and informal markets. The former is in the hand of the authorities, who can choose to tax the movement of people and goods as they see fit (...). The informal market arises either as a result of the subversion of the law – where, for instance, import/export restrictions are violated – or simply because it is cheaper to bribe the gatekeepers than to pay the official tax on trade.[24]

Chabal's point here is to demonstrate *agency* on the part of African traders who negotiate pointless state borders in ingenious ways in order to pursue sensible even if non-state-based economic activities. Chabal does not take the view that, if only the state were able to quash such informal markets, formal markets would perform more efficiently. On the contrary: it is the informal markets that perform efficiently despite the obstructions imposed by arbitrarily established political borders. Chabal thus inverts the formal/informal dichotomy, diagnosing the former, not the latter, as regressive and inefficient.

Chabal's analysis of the 'subject-client-citizen' triad offers another striking insight into ordinary African's daily negotiation of the post-colonial state. Whilst, in Europe, there was a historical development from subject to citizen, indirect colonial rule in Africa established subject – citizen dichotomy as a dual system. Natives were subjects, colonial official and settlers were citizens. Although independence resulted in the formal accession of natives to citizenship, path-dependent post-colonial institutions often continue to treat citizens as subjects. Frequently, official business can be successfully concluded only by way of citizens' appealing to clientilistic networks in order to avoid subjugating treatment by relevant state officials. According to Chabal,

> Africans (as others elsewhere in the world) are at one and the same time subject, client, and citizen. Not only do they inhabit all three political spheres but the very specificity of their contemporary condition is that the three interact in ways that it is important to conceptualise if one is to understand post-colonial politics on the continent.[25]

Again, as with Ekeh, it is not my intention here to consider Chabal's analysis in any great detail: my point is that the distinctiveness of Chabal's methodological approach – his micro-economic focus on persons' agency within and around post-colonial state structures – yields conceptual insights into the structure of modern African statehood that more mainstream, macro-level analysis fail to capture. The overall picture that emerges from Chabal's analysis is of the possibility of everyday agential transformation of institutional structures. These go largely unnoticed because the attention of mainstream theory and analysis stubbornly remains at the macro-economic level. It is possible, then, that African agents are transforming the structures of the post-colonial state under the eyes of political scientists and political theorists who are, as it were, asleep at their posts.

Conclusion

Where do these somewhat meandering reflections leave us with respect to thinking about the African state, or indeed, about the state in general? I am not too sure – at any rate, my conclusions are negative more than positive. By this, I mean that I have a better sense of what we should *not* continue to do than I have an idea of what we should do instead. I think what we should not continue to do is to perpetuate the pretence that the European norm can serve as ideal for all of today's states. Indeed, the more one thinks about it, it seems unlikely that the European norm can serve as an ideal to more than a handful of states. In a sense, the African post-colonial state may be less of an outlier, when it comes to the reality of statehood, than the European norm is. I noted in parenthesis, above, that although African states are usually assumed to top the list of failed state indices, there are many more regions in which statehood is fragile at best. Indeed, one needn't even look far beyond Northern Europe: the new states of the former Soviet Union spring to mind though, interestingly, these regions appear to be less frequently thematized under the failed state paradigm. Be this as it may, it seems to me clear that the European ideal of statehood has failed the African context both theoretically and practically speaking. Rather than asking why actual African states fail to live up to the European ideal, we should ask why the European idea continues to be preferred as the only available – or only acceptable – model of statehood. As indicated above, the reasons for this are likely to be political as well as conceptual. Politically, a community of structurally different states may be difficult to negotiate; conceptually, it simply requires an act of extraordinary philosophical imagination to overcome as dominant a paradigm as the Hobbesian state. But this then may be a reason for leaving the European model to one side, as it were, and for looking more directly at African statehood itself, avoiding, so far as is possible, any particular preconceptions about what it should look like. In one sense, I think that Okeja is right to thematize the fact of political failure in post-independent Africa: it is time to draw a line under hopes for eventual European statehood in Africa. In another sense, I wonder whether what appears to us like a failure in one guise could also be seen as a condition for the possible emergence of something very different under another guise. That is one reason why Chabal's analysis of ordinary people's active responses to state failure strikes me as a promising line of future inquiry.[26]

It is often assumed, especially among Western political scientists and theorists that bad though the colonial days no doubt were independence wiped the slate clean. The post–World War II (WWII) constitutional transfer of powers is frequently depicted as marking the moment at which former African colonies were welcomed as political equals into the newly founded international community of nations. Normative theorists sometimes cast the general post-war dismantling of empires as the moral triumph of state-based self-determination: post-war decolonization is seen as the third and final phase of a progressive historical movement that stretched from the American Declaration of Independence, through the French Revolution to the Universal Declaration of Human Rights. From this perspective, post-independence state failure in Africa looks like a golden opportunity recklessly squandered. And yet the thought of a slate wiped clean and of a new beginning is politically and normatively naïve in the extreme.

Here is another thought. When we say that state failure is widespread on the African continent, we are continuing with the well-established myth of African exceptionalism. We assume that statehood works tolerably well everywhere but in Africa. Indeed, the small Asian Tiger states of Hong Kong, Singapore, Taiwan, and South Korea – have at times been upheld as independence success stories compared to which the failures of Nigeria, say, or of the Democratic Republic of Congo stand out all the more markedly. Asia managed to modernize – why not Africa?! And yet: is Afghanistan a well-functioning state? Well, we might say, that situation is different. In fact, the entire Middle East is different insofar as there is the complicating factor of Islam. But are Moldova, North Macedonia, and Uzbekistan? Well, we might say, those societies are still in the throes of emergence and consolidation after Soviet rule: not really comparable? Is China a state? Well, China is China – another special case. But what about Greece, then, or Italy – could either function well as sovereign agents outside the EU framework? Which truly are the well-functioning states – and, assuming there are any, is it not they that are in the minority rather than the not-so-well-functioning, ailing states?

Notes

1 Robert Bates, *How Things Fell Apart. State Failure in Late Century Africa* (Cambridge: Cambridge University Press 2008).

2 Jeffrey Herbst, *States and Power in Africa. Comparative Lessons in Authority and Control* (Princeton, NJ: Princeton University Press 2000).

3 Crawford Young, *The African Colonial State in Comparative Perspective* (New Haven, CT: Yale University Press 1994).

4 Mamood Mamdani, *Citizen and Subject. Contemporary Africa and the Legacy of Late Colonialism* (Princeton, NJ: Princeton University Press 1996).

5 Peter Ekeh, 'Colonialism and the Two Publics in Africa: A Theoretical Statement', *Comparative Studies in Society and History* 17 (1975), pp. 91–112.

6 Thomas Hobbes, *Leviathan*, chps 13–16 (Oxford: Oxford University Press 1996; 1651 original publication).

7 For the classic statement of ideal constitutional models and their degenerate versions, see Aristotle, *The Politics* Bk VI (Harmondsworth: Penguin Classics 1985). Aristotle did not of course distinguish between the European state and the colonial state as its degenerate version.

8 Cf. https://fragilestatesindex.org/

9 James Scott, *Seeing Like a State. How Certain Schemes to Improve the Human Condition Have Failed* (New Haven and London: Yale University Press, 1998).

10 Patrick Chabal, Africa. The Politics of Suffering and Smiling. The phenomenon of state withdrawal is not confined to non-European states. For a highly instructive analysis of the phenomenon within contemporary Britain, see Insa Koch, Personalizing the State.

11 A modest beginning in this direction can in fact be found in John Rawls, *The Law of Peoples* (Cambridge, MA: Harvard University Press).

12 Two classic references in this debate include Charles Beitz, *Political Theory and International Relations* (Princeton, NJ: Princeton University Press 1979) and Thomas Pogge, *Realizing Rawls* (Ithaca, NY: Cornell University Press 1989).

13 One example among many is Dismas Masolo, *Self and Community in a Changing World* (Bloomington: Indian University Press 2010).

14 Ifeanyi Menkiti, 'The Concept of a Person and the Concept of a Citizen', unpublished keynote paper, University of Chicago, 17 April 2017.

15 Kwasi Wiredu, 'Democracy and Consensus: A Plea for a Non-Party Polity' in E. C. Eze (ed.), *Postcolonial African Philosophy: A Critical Reader* (Oxford: Basil Blackwell 1997), 303–312.

16 Kwasi Wiredu, *Cultural Universals and Particulars. An African Perspective* (Bloomington: Indiana University Press 1996), 189.

17 Ajume Wingo, 'Good Government is Accountability' in T. Kiros (ed.), *Explorations in African Political Thought* (Routledge and Kegan Paul, 2001), pp. 151–170; Ajume Wingo, 'Living Legitimacy: A New Approach to Good Government in Africa', *New England Journal of Public Policy* 16 (2001), pp. 49–71; Ajume Wingo, 'The Immortals in Our Midst: Why Democracies in Africa Need Them', *Journal of Ethics* 19.3 (Dec. 2015), pp. 237–255.

18 Emmanuel Chukwudi Eze, 'Democracy or Consensus? A Response to Wiredu' in Eze (ed.) *Postcolonial African Philosophy: A Critical Reader* (Oxford: Basil Blackwell 1997), 313–324, at 317.

19 Bernard Matolino, *Consensus as Democracy in Africa* (Grahamstown: AHP Publications 2014).

20 Uchenna Okeja, *Deliberative Agency: A Study in Modern African Political Philosophy,* Indianapolis and Bloomington. Indiana University Press, 2022.

21 But see Achille Mbembe, *On the Postcolony* (Berkely and Los Angeles: University of California Press 2001) and to some extent V.Y. Mudimbe, *The Invention of Africa. Gnosis, Philosophy, and the Order of Knowledge* (Bloomington: Indiana University Press 1988).

22 Ekeh, 'The two Publics', op. cit.

23 Patrick Chabal, *Africa. The Politics of Suffering and Smiling* (London and New York: ZED Books 2009).

24 Ibid., pp.135/136.

25 Ibid., pp. 96/97.

26 I would like to thank Martin Ajei, Caesar Atuire, Rowan Cruft, Uchenna Okeja, Eghosa Osaghae, Anthony O. Owoye, Paula Romero, Stephanie Wanga, Ajume Wingo, and all the MSc students on my course, 'Modern African Political Philosophy' for many fruitful hours of discussion on the topic of the Africa state.

4

A FREE PERSON AS A MAKER OF SURPRISES[1]

Ajume H. Wingo

Introduction

From the great urban centers to the hidden corners of the world, one can hear the resounding cry: "freedom!" Such yearning for freedom has given life to revolution and reform, mass movements, and countless individual acts of courage, defiance, and conscience. The voice that cries for freedom calls out for more than the mere necessities of life, but for a particular kind of life—one in which the individual is entitled to a say in how her community treats her and others, and ultimately one in which the individual does not live by the grace of some other person but by right. The very act of crying "freedom," in other words, is a declaration that there is more to life than *just* life. And it is a recognition—the same made by Aristotle 2,500 years ago—that even if the collective action we call "politics" began for the sake of survival, it has taken on a further purpose as a source of human flourishing.[2]

But what exactly is the relationship between freedom and politics? Attending to the works of modern political philosophers, one may conclude "not much." That is, freedom is an intrinsic quality of persons, regardless of their circumstances or conditions, and to the extent politics matters, it is only to constrain or accommodate that intrinsic quality. There may be states and situations in which this innate quality may be quashed for a time by particularly harsh or comprehensive means, but the underlying characteristics and dispositions are fixed. Freedom is the natural order of things, a quality that needs no special explanation. In such a view, it is not the existence of freedom that needs explaining, but the repression of freedom.

Alternatively, the possibility of freedom may be understood to be principally a consequence of a state's economic development. On this view, political freedom and the institutions that sustain it are thought to blossom more or less naturally when—and only when—a state becomes sufficiently wealthy. If true, this has the happy implication that perhaps the philosophical and sociological problems relating to liberalization and democratization can be circumvented through economic growth. The more troubling implication is that freedom will be next to impossible for those, like many of those living in Africa and other parts of the developing world, living outside of wealthy or rapidly growing states. And as if the material obstacles to freedom were not daunting enough, still others argue that freedom requires persons to sort through their emotions, desires, and false consciousness to reveal their true selves

DOI: 10.4324/9781003143529-5

in order to be free. But to fixate on the conditions for freedom, as so many contemporary political philosophers do, is to miss the object of interest—freedom itself.

This focus on how one *becomes* free strikes me as an odd way of getting at what freedom is. Even if political freedom can be referred to unambiguously as the output of some particular process—an already dubious claim—such an approach may be no more informative than if you were to describe Paris as "where you are if you float downstream on the Marne for four miles after it joins the Seine." At most, the characterization of the object of inquiry is indirect. So, for instance, a conception of "negative freedom" makes it hard to say what exactly this state of being free from external forces could be like. Similarly, "positive freedom" refers to being in the right position—having sufficient resources, being sufficiently authentic or independent—to do something more—presumably, to "be free" in some unspecified sense. It is, of course, important to ask *how* one becomes free. But it is no less important to ask what it is to be free—to be at the end stage of the process that is intended to produce freedom. This chapter is about that question—about freedom in its own right.

Defining Freedom

Our answer to the question of what freedom informs much of our other judgments about political power, rights, and legitimacy. Who should wield political authority, how should that authority be exercised, and in the service of what? Our views on each of those questions and more rely heavily on our understanding of freedom. So let us start with a very general view of political freedom as being a type of activity of a person in a community. On this view, freedom is a property of an individual—not a group or organization—and one that exists only by virtue of how that person acts within a group of other individuals, i.e., a community. The activity that deserves the name of political freedom, in this view, does not include quintessentially private activities relating to pure thought and conscience. Neither does it encompass those states of the human person such as intending, desiring, willing, capability, ability, and yearning that manifest themselves only "inside" a person. To be free demands instead that one act socially. In that sense, freedom is worldly, and is not simply evidenced by, but constituted by words and deeds.

But freedom is not, of course, just any kind of activity within a community: it is a particular kind of activity, caused and ordered by the free individual's will. An ant, notwithstanding the wonderful social organization of the anthill, is not free in any relevant sense. And neither is any citizen of a rigorously structured totalitarian state such as North Korea or of any crippled state like so many in Africa in which all one can do is to simply hang on and survive. The activities of such people are often intentional, purposeful, and informed—but their freedom is as illusory as that of a marionette or robot that, once programmed, carries out its functions in an orderly fashion.

So, what is it that distinguishes the activities of a free person? One clue is that the salient property of individuals we regard as unfree is that their actions are so predictable, either because they are constitutionally incapable of doing otherwise, or because the imperative of self-preservation compels them to act in a completely predictable manner. They behave like parts of nature. What that suggests is that the actions of a free individual must be unpredictable or surprising.

It may appear strange to tie political freedom to an individual's ability to surprise others. After all, the quality of being free purports to be a real property of persons, like one's height or character. "Being surprising," in contrast, is quite obviously relative to what is known about the individual: a stranger to me might surprise me in ways that would not surprise that person's close friends or family. To think of freedom in terms of the surprising nature of a person's behavior suggests that the behavior of an organism or even a complex mechanical object that I find very surprising would be free to me, but not to a scientist who understands the processes resulting in that organism's behavior or to the inventor who perhaps built the object in order to behave in that way.

And yet there is, I believe, a deep connection between a person's freedom and his capacity to surprise. To see that connection, consider what it means when we say a person has done something that is surprising. Surprising behavior is behavior that defies our expectations, that disturbs our assumption that we know the underlying order or patterns that should dictate individuals' actions. Surprising activities arise as if out of nowhere. Such behavior, no matter how surprising, is of course *potentially* predictable, just as we presume that other, perhaps equally surprising, complex behavior—the social lives of ants and bees, a plant's roots "search" for water and nutrients—is. And yet, as I explain below, the effect of a person's surprising behavior has a special effect on our view of freedom that the surprises the rest of the natural world produces do not.

The conception of freedom I propose here is a matter of how individuals behave in a community, and so depends on both the character of the individuals and that of the community in which they act. A community that can accommodate the surprising behavior of its members is one that flexes, bends, and restructures itself as novel beliefs and desires shape the behavior of the individuals in it in unforeseen ways. This ability to accommodate surprising activity requires not just a certain suppleness for institutions and regulations, but also demands that those in charge of those institutions and regulations—the government—pay attention to the beliefs and desires of the members of the community. In short, it is this attention and responsiveness to citizens that makes political freedom possible.

Free individuals interact with their communities. The possibility of surprising activity depends on the community's ability to accommodate such activities, and the pressure put on the community to develop institutions and norms capable of accommodating such activities comes from individuals making those kinds of demands. Thus, when internal disagreements arise, a responsive community will accommodate and channel those disagreements, rather than quashing them or expelling dissenters.[3]

The nexus between free individuals and their communities provides one important link between freedom and citizens' capacity to surprise. Another link can be seen through the privacy implied by the possibility of surprise. The capacity of citizens to surprise depends on there being some part of their lives that is walled off from the scrutiny of others—a private sphere in which they can develop plans for action on their own. That persons are capable of surprising others thus suggests that they have some degree of privacy, such that they can make decisions that are their own.

This view of freedom is consistent with the common association of predictability with merely mechanical or biological entities, rather than full moral persons. That is, a human being is, in the biological sense, just a particular kind of animal, no different in kind from a baboon, a bonobo, or any other animal in the wild. The survival instinct is common to human beings and animals alike and is anything but original. Instincts necessitate and conclude both human beings' and animals' activities and behavior in the service of survival and self-preservation. Contrast this understanding of human beings and animals to a common conception of a person. The idea of a person connotes a being of choice and a maker of surprises. Animals may manipulate the world in various predictable ways, but persons *make* their world.[4]

The activities of a free a person does not occur in a vacuum. In the first instance, we are born into the world and into particular circumstances: a family, a tribe, a nation, and more. It is in this world of fortuna—a world we never choose in the first place—that persons must make their way. The lucky ones are born into a well-ordered world, heir to decades or centuries of others' efforts. Others—like many African citizens—are unlucky enough to find themselves in a world of corrupt officials, bullies, and dictators. The world is, in fact, a congeries of constraints on action, and of all the various constraints on human activity, those most relevant to the conception of freedom are those imposed by other persons since an individual's freedom depends on how that individual act in her community.

A citizen with the capacity to make surprises also has the capacity to improvise as circumstances change. Such a citizen is not simply blown about by circumstances but can—like a skillful sailor harnessing the winds, currents, and tides—use the knowledge of her circumstances to reach her objectives. Indeed, a maker of surprises is free not in spite of the obstacles her circumstances present, but because of the way she deals with those obstacles. Perhaps the surprised action of an individual is best illustrated by Machiavelli's concept of *virtu* or the ability to take advantage of the opportunities that circumstances (he refers to as fortuna) thrust before each person. A free world is a world of fortuna inhabited by virtuosos.

A virtuoso of freedom is a person with self-control. She applies her virtuosity to act in and shape—indeed, to *make*—her world. The people of Nso (in the North West Region of Cameroon) refer to a maker of surprises as a *nyuy* (god), capable of deeds beyond human comprehension. Nso parents would name a child "god is a person" (*Nyuy Dze Wir*) or "One's god is another person" (*Nyuy Wir*) with hopes that their child has such command over her life. This kind of citizen-god is, for the Nso, the ideal of a person whose ability to act within her circumstances gives her the capacity to act deliberately, purposefully, and positively in her community.

Freedom is just that—freedom with no particular preordained goal apart from what individuals as makers of surprises set for themselves. That is to say, the activities do not have to make the world a better or worse place to be free, nor must they be directed to some particular end. But a free person *does* have to be capable of reflecting on and deliberately acting in light of her circumstances. Thus, while free actions may be in the service of a person's survival, they cannot be the product of a mere survival instinct or reflex as if a person was a slave. Instead, the life of a free person is one of deliberate choices, informed gambles on uncertain outcomes, and constant course adjustments in light of changing circumstances. A community of such free persons is likely to be vibrant and dynamic; mutating as each member adjusts his or her actions to the state of the whole and the actions of his or her neighbors. Its unity, at least as far as it makes sense to talk of a collection of such persons as unified, is not through some rigid structure imposed on them—it is the nature of free persons to work their way around such walls and barricades—but a structure that arises out of their interactions. Such a structure and organization cannot simply be willed into place from above.

Thus, we see that when persons get a taste of freedom, it is easy enough for them to topple governments, but rather more difficult to establish a replacement. For instance, in the so-called "Arab Spring," the rotten structures of several states in Egypt, Tunisia, and Libya fell quite quickly. It has, however, proved far more difficult to replace those rotten states in the short term with anything more resilient. A community of free persons requires not just effort on the part of individual citizens, but also time to reach an equilibrium state. As the aftermath of the Arab Spring suggests, the transition period from an authoritarian or totalitarian state to a free state is fraught with the risk of falling back into tyranny—or, perhaps more likely, into the chaos of a failed state.

At the Threshold of Freedom

Political philosophers have long thought of there being various thresholds of wealth, education, leisure, and trust needed before persons can be freed. According to John Stuart Mill, for instance,

> [l]iberty, as a principle, has no application to any state of things anterior to the time when mankind have become capable of being improved by free and equal discussion. Until then, there is nothing for them but implicit obedience to an Akbar or a Charlemagne, if they are so fortunate as to find one. But as soon as mankind have attained the capacity of being guided to their own improvement by conviction or persuasion (a period long since reached in all nations with whom we need here concern ourselves), compulsion, either in the direct form or in that of pains and penalties for non-compliance, is no longer admissible as a means to their own good, and justifiable only for the security of others.[5]

Rawls echoes Mill, insisting that "moderate scarcity" is a precondition for a free society. But while Mill and Rawls are surely correct to note the association between such thresholds of material goods and the possibility of freedom, it would be a mistake to conclude that freedom actually requires such thresholds to be achieved. The kernel of truth to the view that there are thresholds of material welfare that are required for freedom is that free individuals cannot be so preoccupied with their survival that they act purely from instinct as slaves or as the colonized do. But to imagine that "moderate scarcity" as measured on the scale of contemporary Western societies is neither realistic nor justified. It is not realistic, for that "moderate scarcity" threshold excludes many in the developing world from even the possibility of freedom. Nor is it justified, for the scarcity of material goods to any degree—moderate or severe—is simply another constraint on human action. The potential for a stable and free society is perhaps greater when, other things being equal, there are more scarce goods to divide. (It may be that the threshold requirement is most attractive to those who already enjoy freedom and wealth and are loathe to contemplate the sacrifices and difficult choices they would have to make to keep the former without the latter.) But other things are, of course, almost always not equal, and the traditions and norms of some very poor communities may be more amendable to freedom than those of more wealthy ones. And in any event, there appears to be no clear boundary between those communities wealthy enough to enjoy freedom and those that are not.

The most important condition for human freedom, then, is not that there be some sufficiently high level of material welfare, but life itself—and by life itself, I mean *vitality* or *courage*, the wellspring of any kind of human freedom. Many have taken credit for freeing slaves when they ought to have given the credit to slaves for finally taking on courage, responsibility, and control of their own lives. One can provide the condition for freedom by creating opportunities for individuals or by leaving them alone. But conditions by themselves make no one free, for freedom is an activity that the free person must undertake for herself.

There is, then, no forcing or making another to be free. Negative, positive, and Republican freedom,[6] understood as referring to certain conditions of freedom, thus falls short of capturing what freedom itself is—a state of action. A more accurate sense of freedom is suggested by Bernard Williams in his criticism of the animal liberation movement. Williams argues that obtaining freedom requires speaking for oneself:

> Oppressed human groups come of age in the search for emancipation when they speak for themselves, and no longer through reforming members of the oppressive group, but the other animals will never come of age: human beings will always act as their trustee.[7]

Williams thus sees the essence of freedom as a matter of free persons speaking—and acting—for themselves, rather than relying on others to assert their rights.

It is just this courage to act in their own interest and on their own behalf that those who are not free lack. The most daunting restrictions on freedom are those created by the inability or unwillingness of those who lack the freedom to stand up and attempt to direct themselves. This is particularly true in the case of Africa, where African elites and their Western sympathizers are very quick to blame Western colonialism for usurping the freedom of Africans. The history of slavery and colonialism has, to be sure, done great harm to Africans. But while the colonialists left Africa in the 1950s and '60s, the Western-trained African elites who have continued to govern most African states have done little to put the colonial mindset behind. Coupled with the inability of ordinary Africans to rein in the endemic corruption of their leaders, this failure by African elites has had tragic consequences. How does one begin to make sense of Africans allowing—indeed, facilitating—the rape of Guinea Conakry's natural resources by foreigners in exchange for Rolex watches and other Western trinkets?[8] How are the activities of these bands of Africans different from the peacocks strutting about in colorful plumage to attract sexual partners? The utter predictability of their greed makes them easy marks for anyone who wants to take advantage of them.

The truth is that colonialism—seen in the broadest sense as the state of powerlessness and servitude that plagues much of "independent" Africa even today—was not so much the cause of Africans' lack of freedom, but the result of that lack of freedom. As such, no amount of reparations from the Western world, no amount of wealth beneath the feet of Africans, no monitored elections, no leaders, no foreign military intervention, no human rights watchers, no NGOs, no foreign aid, and no African flight to Europe will render ordinary Africans free, as long as Africans continue to look outside of themselves for their emancipation.

The people of Nso refer to the spirit of surprise activities as "*selm*."[9] They divide "selm" into "*selm vifon*" (or "princely" selm, the quality of freedom attributable to prophets, heroes, saints, and messiahs) and "*vireem*" (or the destructive spirit of freedom that Western and African anthropologists often attribute to witchcraft in Africa). A "reem" is a free person who acts without concern for the consequences of his action on others. While both *selms* reflect the spirit of freedom as the making of surprises, one has constructive ends, while the other is merely destructive. Both, however, may be free, and so held responsible for his or her actions. Thus, tyrannicide in traditional societies in Africa was normally seen as a way of resetting the *legal* equality of persons as free and responsible agents in society. The restorative justice in putting the tyrant to death restores the supple quality of the society and the equality of persons as makers of surprises in an organized political sphere of activities.

The difference between what we would regard as tyrants and the more virtuous political leaders lie not in their ability to work their will in the world, for they have that quality in common. Rather, they are distinguished by the fact that tyrants work their will without regard for the effect on others' ability to control their own lives. The greatest champions of political freedom carefully exercise their powers leaving opportunities for others to do the same. The worst tyrants do the opposite, acting to impose their will and desires without concern for their effect on other's capacity to act. Such tyrants are wont to use human persons as canvases for their "artistic" endeavors in foisting their private vision onto the world. Isaiah Berlin saw the irony involved in praising the achievements that, notwithstanding their greatness, were bought with the sacrifices of countless unnamed individuals, remarking on "the sinister artist whose materials are men—the destroyer of old societies and the creator of new ones—no matter at what human cost: the superhuman leader who tortures and destroys in order to build on new foundations."[10] It is their arbitrary commands and their refusal to share the otherwise communal sphere of activities with others that make for evil. While heroes wait as it were for *fortuna* to open up channels that allow them to navigate the world, tyrants give no heed to *fortuna* when they act and, as such, are wont to leave disaster in their wake.

As I have argued above, there is no obvious material threshold needed for humans to be free beyond life itself. But that's not to say, of course, that merely being alive is sufficient for persons to be free. The tragedy for many is that while they are fully alive in a physical sense, they are dead inside, and lack either the capacity or the desire to act on their own behalf. Such beings exhibit all the complex behaviors of human organisms, but none of the surprising activities of a person.[11]

This divide between the life of the human organism and the life of the person is deeply embedded in the traditions and folk wisdom of the Nso. There is a proverb among those people that "should god die I will too." The "I" in this case is a divine aspect of the citizen, the maker of surprises. It is also said in Nso that "it is by god's activities that we know god," a recognition that the divine exists in this world in the way that we and other parts of the natural world act. The Nso, for instance, point to an awe-inspiring dance performance and say "that is Wirba Biin" meaning that Wirba Biin (who may or may not be alive) is/was the author of the dance. Wirba Biin in this case is synonymous with the dance she authored. So, if god is god's activities, so are the meme-like activities of citizen-gods. The life and death of a free person as the maker of surprises in this sense is more than just changes in physical qualities. Death is not merely the cessation of biological functions as it is the dearth of making surprises. The surprises are what make a free life, and while biological existence may be necessary, but it is never sufficient for a free life.

To lose one's freedom is thus not merely to cease physical activities, but to cease creating surprising activity. The people of Nso will refer to an "adult-do-little" or "adult-do-nothing"—a morose and reclusive person who has withdrawn from the society, the sphere of associative activities, and cocoons into themselves—as a dead person (or dead-life person), or *nkweyuv* or *kingwu ke wir*, not in spite of, but because of, their continued biological or clinical existence and activities. Other opprobrious terms such as "an empty person" (*wir kisang* in Lamso) or "useless person" (*onipa hun* in Akan) are used in the same way. The activity of a living-dead person atrophies into mere motions of necessities no different in kind from those of other living creatures.

As to why a person would cease to be free or decide against freedom is a puzzle not without causal explanations. No one captures this better than Shakespeare in *Julius Caesar*, Act II, Scene 2:

> Cowards die many times before their deaths
> The valiant never taste death but once.
> Of all the wonders I yet have seen
> It seems to me most strange that men fear,
> Seeing that death, a necessary end
> Will come when it will come.

Freedom, as I have presented it, implies independence and action that is often out of step with what is expected or tolerated. To act in such a way can be frightening. And we see this kind of fright manifested in many ways. We see people petrified into apelike imitators before tyrants and their threats to any independent action. We see the fear-struck faces of victims of genocide who find it easier to be heeded like cattle, broken like horses, making quivering sounds like animals while marching docilely to what they know will be their deaths than to defy their persecutors. We see it in the frozen faces of refugees in their flight, gripped by the most basic survival instinct. In a sense, the most terrifying quality of an autocratic or totalitarian regime is not the regime's ability to stymie political participation or to impose arbitrary constraints on people's lives, but the ease with which persons are transformed into bare humans, fit objects to serve as the canvas of the tyrant's vision of the world. Under a tyrannical regime, one's life becomes nothing but a plaything of fortune. Even if the despot is enlightened and benevolent, the message expressed is ever concise and precise: "you live at my whim." This message is neatly woven into the tyrant's formal and informal self-serving laws and institutions that surround victims' lives at every turn. Fear and the fear of death is always the underlying driver.[12]

Faced with the petrifying state of tyrannical affairs, persons may seek refuge by attaching themselves uncritically to the tyrant in the hopes of escaping persecution. This of course was Hobbes's conception of the relation of the sovereign to the res publica: "For by art is created that great LEVIATHAN called a COMMONWEALTH, or STATE (in Latin CIVITAS), which is but an artificial man... in which the sovereignty is an artificial soul, as giving life and motion to the whole body..."[13] This many-in-one mass of a human being can then be moved by a tyrant, first this way then another, in the service of the tyrant's vision of the world. In this state of affair, individuality disappears into the massdom.

You know that you are dealing with a socially dead citizenry when, as in many African states, mass protests amount to nothing but protest for survival. Unlike protests for genuine freedom, the apelike protests of a "massdom" are necessitated by physical needs. The tyrant can react in at least two ways. He can simply impose a curfew and wait them out (as the military juntas who overthrew the democratically elected government of Egypt did), knowing that as they get hungrier over time, they will be pulled back to their little subsistence farms or small shops. Or, if he wants to stop the hoarse noises more quickly (so as to avoid criticism from pesky outside observers or international watchdogs), he can simply increase the subsidies for the importation of rice, farina, and cooking oil from China, set a few heads rolling on the street, and then watch as protests from streets evaporate into thin air like the morning mist under the sun. What the so-called Arab Spring lacks which the human life-changing English, French, and American revolutions had in abundance was an informed and true conception of freedom from tyranny as conceived as the transformation of grace to right.

Uncritical allegiance to the state is but one form of what the people of Nso refers to as "death in life." social death. Another is a form of escapism that I refer to as "witdom." There is a category of persons who see the state authority as an obstacle to their freedom. They see freedom as what Isaiah Berlin says it is: the absence of external interference. Berlin bolsters his conception of freedom in his seminal piece "Two Concepts of Freedom" by approvingly quoting Bentham: "Every law is an infraction of liberty." As such, the state and with it the laws are seen as an enemy of freedom, as standing in the way.

In many parts of the world, for instance, ancient Greek and Rome, an individual would react against tyranny by taking himself out of the society, not physically but by retreating out of the sphere of communal activities deep in his head, "skull Kingdom." The life of the mind is and in some ways always has been a kind of castle that shields one's spirit of freedom from the outside physical and social world. Significant political thinkers and leaders who have transformed our world have, of course, needed an inner mental space in which to imagine an alternative world and develop their plans. But if one truly retreats into his mind with no activities in (spoken or written) words or in deeds, one ceases to be of any political consequence and becomes a mere curiosity. Politics is about action, and inaction of this sort implies social death.[14]

In both cases of "massdom" and "witdom," the individual moves away from politics and retreats to the zone of comfort in her inner sanctum. The utmost place of comfort is the sanctum of the "womb." The womb is a metaphor for immaturity: Immanuel Kant in an essay entitled "An Answer to the Question: What is Enlightenment?" define immaturity as the

> inability to make use of one's own understanding without the guidance of another. *Self-incurred* is this inability if its cause lies not in the lack of understanding but rather in the lack of the resolution and the courage to use it without the guidance of another. *Sapere aude!* Have courage to use your own understanding! is thus the motto of enlightenment.[15]

According to Kant,

> it is easy to be immature. If I have a book that has understanding for me, a pastor who has a conscience for me, a doctor who judges my diet for me, and so forth, surely, I do not need to trouble myself.[16]

The womb is that pristine, cozy safe homely home where there are no worries, no dreams, no fetters, no history, no consciousness, and consequently, no fears and freedom. Scare a child and see her rush for home and onto her mother's lap as close to the womb as she can. The nine months or so spent in a womb and the time spent prior to weaning the child leave an indelible impression on individuals who seek to recreate the womb at any opportune moment of their lives.

Next to the womb is the family, which provides another model of a place in which individuals may be free from potentially destabilizing surprises. As the Arab saying goes: "one is at ease at home around the comfort of family." Next to the family is the tribe or ethnic group which links disparate individuals through long, powerful bonds of kinship and shared history. The comfort of common blood and history is one reason why a group of people would seek a comforting imagined narrative, a comforting theocratic polity, and even racial identity in the polity.

Further than that are all sorts of elective clubs that seek, in some way or another, to reproduce the comfort of the womb. This includes all sorts of self-ghettoization, such as when groups gather to talk among themselves and about themselves like an association of African philosophers or other specialists. The attractiveness of the womb comfort could be seen in small dealings of life among those who seek to marry people sharing the same race, culture, and historical backgrounds. At each step, there is pressure to avoid the dislocations, the discomforts, and the disturbing surprises of pluralism, which demands so much energy, courage, attention, and sacrifice in order to negotiate the unexpected behavior of those unfamiliar others.

The retreat to comfort can be represented in a concentric pattern with the womb comfort at the center offering the most comfort and the least freedom and the ragged and discomforting world of politics at the outer circles offering the most freedom and the least womb comfort. The womb is of course a metaphor for a life devoid of constraints and fears. Everything outside of the womb can be surprising, discomforting and petrifying to a newcomer, even to adults. Since the womb is literally untenable, the closest thing to the womb is oneself and in one's head where one does not have to confront the petrifying world. The mind is a cozy place for many. There the frightening irrationality of the rest of life disappears. The mind is that politically dark place sealed from the outside variegated world of others, the sphere of associative communal activities. One would not be shocked to find that the dream of a tyrant is to be surrounded by thinkers.[17]

Historically Africans have attempted to avoid the menacing world of pluralistic politics, typically by relocating or "voting with their feet." This old traditions of non-confrontation and seclusion shed light on why Africa today has a disproportionate share of the world's refugees. The irony of this tradition of flight, however, is that it is not the place being fled, but the person in flight that is the problem. The flight itself does no good because the self that is the problem goes along to whatever place. An alternative to literal geographical flight is the metaphorical flight of escapism, a flight into the self. In this flight, one stays in the same geographical location and simply retreats from the petrifying political society into the comforting womb-like sanctum of the mind.

A stoic's retreat into quietude is an example of this kind of inner flight. Retreating from conflict in this way can be an effective way to carve out a tiny space of privacy in even the most repressive of environments.[18] It is, however, also an effective way for citizens to give over control of their lives to others as they nestle themselves in a comfortable and conflict-free zone of private—and apolitical—life. Isaiah Berlin tells us that this may have been so in Greece, where the Stoic ideal may have emerged as a reaction to the fall of the independent democracies before the centralized Macedonian autocracy and Rome after the end of the Republic. The affluence that allows individuals to satisfy their desires without having to act politically has a similarly isolating effect. As the novelist David Foster Wallace says in his well-known commencement address:

> Our own present culture has harnessed [the forces of frustration and greed in capitalism] in ways that have yielded extraordinary wealth and comfort and personal freedom. The freedom of all to be lords of our tiny skull-sized kingdoms, alone at the center of all creation.[19]

Likewise, the meditative practices of Eastern sages like Buddha may have been a response to autocracies. The quietism of thinking and of searching within one's mind as in the Eastern religious practices for one's higher self may be wonderful spiritually, but it is the fodder of a tyrant, a self-chaining scenario that has little or nothing to do with political freedom that is only possible in confrontation within the communal sphere of activities with others who are not likely to be like you, and who may care little about you or even hate you.

In the tradition of flight into the inner self, a Stoic like Epictetus simply trained himself not to desire what he could not have; the proverbial "sour grapes" scene. This course of training may be fulfilling from an individual perspective and may even in a sense "free" oneself from the passions, but it cannot lead to any genuine sense of political freedom. Political freedom in its most genuine sense is gained by confronting circumstances and acting in the world, not by withdrawing into the privacy of one's own mind to avoid any disturbing resistance to one's will. One may be necessarily sovereign within one's "tiny skull-sized kingdom," but sovereignty in such a lonely and isolated outpost is not freedom, but social death or "death in life."

The Audacity of Freedom

The life of a free person among other free persons is a demanding one, for to live among persons capable of making surprises means there is no knowing what the future holds. Dostoyevsky remarked on those whose need is "to surrender as quickly as possible the gift of freedom … with which, the unfortunate creatures, were born."[20] Freedom, like the exercise of the body for health, is not an activity that one can deputize or outsource, nor is it something that can be bottled in the United States like Coca-Cola and exported to the rest of the world. I have seen Africans praying to the Almighty God for their freedom or hoping that through elections some messiah in the name of a leader would deliver them from the grip of their tyrants. Such prayers are pointless, for freedom is an essentially human activity requiring human confrontation and negotiation with obstacles—especially other human beings.

The life of a free person requires navigating and negotiating a world loaded with constraints, be they natural or man-made. Tyranny is the constraint of constraints that must simply be gotten rid of for a free day to dawn, and this must be done even if by tyrannicide, the manner in which the ancients in African polities dealt with tyrants. Those who undertook this sacred task of emancipation never tasted death (at least, death in life). They are ready to ensure against their social death to kiss the gallows if need be. Death by kissing the gallows is a mere chimera, for life and death are not defined by mere superficial features. If there is any meaningful meaning in life, it is this kind for what deceased says is I am dying so all can live free. When Patrick Henry cried out to "give me liberty or give me death" he meant more than clinical death.

The maker of surprises needs audacity or courage. Courage is the wellspring of freedom, and any other source of freedom is at best a delusion. Courage is the mother of all virtues, what Churchill referred to as "the first of human qualities, because it is the quality which guarantees all others." Moses, Jesus, Prophet Mohammed, Buddha, Cincinnatus, Amenhotep (Akhenaton), Ngonnso, Washington, and Mandela are men and a woman from very different times and places who faced very different problems and obstacles. But what they shared—and what allowed each to overcome the problems and obstacles confronting them and their various communities—was their audacity to act in the face of the most daunting challenges. Many may think, intend, will and even know what, when, and how to do, but they lack one thing that men and women who set themselves apart in their deeds and (spoken or written) words have: the courage to act. The worst thing in the life of a free person is not to have not acted rightly; it is to have not acted at all.

Free action is reflective and requires among many things, the courage to act, and so to make all other human virtues possible. Fearlessness is tested during circumstances. To be courageous is to move beyond the zone of one's comfort. We start life in the womb, a very safe place free of obligations, consciousness, and fear. Out of the womb, one is thrust into unexpected and uncomfortable world full of obligations and everything to be afraid which by all accounts is the direct opposite of the womb. The tendency in the face of challenges is for grownups to retreat to the metaphorical womb when the going gets tough. In the uncomfortable and indifferent world, one has to make herself the primary focus and center of attention against all odds and that requires, above all else, the *audacity* to be a maker of surprises against all odds. Courage is the cultivated force that allows persons to move away from our concerns of the necessities of life and its preservation. It is this transformative cardinal virtue that put us at the doorstep of freedom.

To speak of courage is to speak of a grave matter of life. Hannah Arendt distinguished "courage" from merely the daring of a person who risks his life in order to feel "as thoroughly and intensely alive as one can be only in the face of danger and death," since "[t]emerity is no less concerned with life than cowardice."²¹ Courage—real courage—requires the willingness to always be on guard against oneself. Daredevils—those who seek the "rush" of danger for the sake of the experience itself—are little different from anyone else who retreats from the world in other ways. If anything, that form of escapism provides the luxury of being able to choose one's own obstacles, instead of having to fight one's way past, around, or under those that world throws up. A glimpse into a newfound political self can be a scary self of emptiness with nothing more uplifting than the desire to attempt to lose oneself for a fuller meaningful life through temerity or foolhardiness. For many, temerity involves taking illicit drugs or jumping off the cliff (bungee jumping) or committing outright suicide as a means of achieving the repose and the comfort of the womb. Such daring has little or nothing in common with courage manifested in the face of an ordinary person determined to face and overcome the ordinary obstacles in her life.

Tyrants are makers of surprises too, but let a courageous citizen challenge a tyrant's life and one sees a coward. Think of Saddam Hussein who betrayed his invincibility once a bunch of daring young men pursued him. He was found hiding literally in a hole. He was captured alive and eventually faced the noose as he cried out to the people he tormented for decades for mercy. He was a Shakespearean coward who died many times before his clinical death. A determined free citizenry can do wonders, and what is more daring in the realm of freedom than an act of tyrannicide? Think of the so-called "King of Kings" of Africa, Kaddafi. Determined young boys chased him down and shot him in the head while he cried out for their mercy. Bin Ali of Tunisia escaped overnight at the first sign of determined unarmed citizens to bring him to trial. If the tyrant Assad of Syria is still hanging in there, it is thanks not to his courage (he has none) but to Hezbollah, the Iranian and Russian missiles that wantonly kill his own citizens. In 1996, the pro-Soviet former president of Afghanistan, Najibullah, was castrated, dragged through the streets, and hanged by a people that he terrorized for years. No memorable words capture the realities of the lives of dictators better than Churchill's who said: "dictators ride to and fro upon tigers from which they dare not to dismount."

Among the most audacious surprises possible is for a legitimately elected leader to follow the law of the land despite all the temptations to circumvent the laws for their own selfish intentions. The most courageous of these is a leader's decision to leave power at the highest point of their rule at the height of their popularity and recognition, the very moment the general public is demanding their tenures for life. The few makers of surprises that human history has recorded include Cincinnatus, the legendary Roman general who helped overthrow a tyrant, but left power of his own volition and went back to his farm. Another is Washington. Having led the United States in freeing itself from the world's greatest power, he could have been president for life—but stepped down voluntarily. Still another is Mandela, who surprised the world by stepping down of his own volition when the culture in the entire continent is for "president for life." Julius Nyerere of Tanzania should be mentioned here as well. He did step down, but unlike the trio mentioned, he did so because of the unpopularity of his policies, yet he deserves to be mentioned if only as an honorable exception to the rule in Africa that leaders hang onto the offices as long as they can cajole the people or are forced to leave office through coup d'états or pressure from the international community or the combination of these factors otherwise through what Africans whimsically refer to as a "coup from heaven" (i.e., death in office).

The trio (mentioned above) made their marks in the political world not just in spite of, but because of the constraints on them. Akhenaton, an Egyptian pharaoh, founded the Aton religion that gave birth to monotheism. Moses created the conditions for freedom for the enslaved, ushered them out of their bondage and created a new nation for them. Jesus, who gave life to outcasts, was crucified like a common criminal, but lives on for billions today. Romulus and Lycurgus created the foundation for freedom in Rome and Sparta against all odds. Mandela challenged an entire regime of apartheid and ushered his people—both black and white—into a free world. Each had the audacity to steadfastly act in the face of the gravest challenges and odds.

While audacity or courage itself is not freedom, it is a wellspring of freedom. Courage, in turn, is a virtue that can be inculcated into a citizenry. The pedagogy of freedom ought to be demonstrative and not merely theoretical. The ancient Romans, for instance, taught the future full members of their society lessons of freedom though rituals that brought them face to face with the spirit and the images of freedom in the deeds of Romulus. The cardinal lesson inculcated in the citizenry was that of the courage to act in the face of adversity and in spite of the myriad fetters imposed by the world.

Indigenous Africans (most notably the people of Nso in Cameroon) did not only teach courage; they taught that the spirit of freedom was vitality in life. The audacity to carry on in life was made clear by the understanding in various African cultures that the universe was neutral or indifferent to the lives of human beings. Theirs was the spirit of self-assertion. No one was watching, directing, and taking care of them as if they were sheep in a flock. What they were and would become was a matter of what they made themselves. They, and they alone, were the ones responsible for their own lives.

For many traditional African cultures, an individual's control over his or her life was necessarily mediated by the way he or she related to other community members. This perspective is exemplified in proverbs such as "a person is a person because of another person" from a Zulu proverb, "*Umunto ngumunto ngabantu*" (a person is a person through other people). The sense of freedom for Africans thus has a much stronger communal basis than the highly individualist sense of freedom that has dominated Western thought since the Enlightenment. For Africans, it is quite natural to think of freedom, not as a lone activity in seclusion, but something made possible only through interactions with other persons. This highlights the sense of freedom as a kind of activity that emerges out of tension and opposition, and that demands constant attention and adjustments to ones surrounding.

To live in a free society surrounded by others equally capable of making surprises, calls for courage. African spirituality, which is constituted by the vitality of life in phenomenal action, exemplified in communal dances, theaters, arts, marketplaces, voluntary social organizations, all aim at pulling individuals out of themselves and into the world. African spirituality is thus a form of pedagogy of freedom par excellence. Its currency is the audacity to act in settings shared by a plurality of people. One can see this in African communal music, arts, and open theaters.

The character of African spirituality makes it an especially effective means of instilling this sense of freedom. The great religions of the world have their provenance in particular individuals. The Abrahamic religions, for instance, each has an ultimate lawgiver, a supernatural being outside of this world. African spirituality does not. Instead, it provides a view of the world in which individuals are here each on her own, with only her own mind and her fellow humans to lend her support. African spirituality is at a piece with individual responsibility. Significantly, the people of Nso have no word for "accident"—a result of their presumption that whatever happens in the realm of human affairs has the hidden hand of a human being in it. An event that Western cultures would interpret as an accident or fate, the people of Nso would go from one geomancer or diviner to another looking for the hidden causality in human beings. This places the burden of freedom on the actions of persons, responsibilities so heavy that most Africans welcome Western and Arabian Abrahamic religions partly because those religions offer relief from such burdens. It is not unusual nowadays to see Africans gathering in churches or mosques to pray for rain or for the end of a conflict, something that would not have been conceived of before the advent of the Abrahamic religions. The idea that everything that happened is up to Allah is now incorporated into many African languages, a practice that would seem bizarre to my African ancestors who knew that they were on this earth on their own, that the universe was not watching and cheering on them (a la Bernard Williams) and was therefore ready to take responsibility for whatever happened or did not happen in their lives. Living in such a world involved courage. African ancestors knew that every human being, whatever their will power, knowledge, or intention, needed above all the audacity to freedom.

The audacity to be free in many African societies like Nso is taught through the practice of bloodletting animal sacrifices. The sacrificial animals are typically the domesticated ones with whom one has formed intimacy such as chickens, goats, sheep, dogs, cats, and so on. Individuals partake in these sacrifices as a way of enlivening the spirit of audacity to freedom. Often the sacrificial blood rituals are made in the name of ancestors, but the essence of the ritual is the audacity to freedom. The people of Nso would say that power (or freedom) is in the blood and as such the idea of shedding blood gives one an additional power in the face of obstacles. They are ready to face the mother of all constraints to freedom, a tyrant.

In the traditions of African spirituality, those who live exemplary lives as makers of surprises are marked by their communities in fables, narratives, monuments, and so on. Among these are those who are able to free a people or surprise them with the originality of their actions and the effects of those actions in the lives of others. Their physical deaths are marked by grand celebrations that could bankrupt an extended family or community. The death celebration is uploading of the life of a maker of surprises' clinical death into a deathless social one to which all in search of an image of freedom can look to. For cultures of these sorts, the meaning in life is not in finding but in losing oneself to responsibilities, and it is this standing up against all the odds and taking on responsibilities to the world that freedom is found.

Notes

1 As any keen reader of Hannah Arendt will notice, I benefitted a lot from reading her work especially "What Is Freedom," in Peter Baehr, ed., *The Portable Hannah Arendt* (New York: Penguin, 2000).

2 In his words: "γινομένη μν το ζν νεκεν, οσα δ το ε ζν."

3 This ability to adapt and accommodate new developments is not limited to free communities, since any robust and resilient community—even the most unfree of them—must be able to adapt to often unpredictable circumstances. What's unique about free communities, however, is their capacity to accommodate and even encourage unpredictable behavior of its own members, rather than having to eliminate such behavior.

4 For a detail distinction between a "person" and a "human being" see Ajume Wingo, "The Aesthetics of Freedom," _____

5 John Stuart Mill, *Utilitarianism, On Liberty, Considerations on Representative Government, Remarks on Bentham's Philosophy*, ed. Geraint William (London: J. M. Dent, 1993), 79.

6 For the Republican Conception of freedom, see Philip Pettit, "The Republican Ideal of Freedom," in David Miller, ed., *The Liberty Reader* (Boulder: Paradigm Publishers, 2006), 223–242.

7 Bernard Williams, *Philosophy as a Humanistic Discipline* (Princeton: Princeton University Press, 2006), 141.

8 For the wanton exploitation of Guinea, see for example, Patrick Radden Keefe, "Buried Secrets," *The New Yorker Magazine*, July 8, 2003.

9 *Selm* is the base of *vitavi* or power or vitality.
10 Quoted in H. G. Schenk, *The Mind of the European Romantics: An Essay in Cultural History* (Frederic Ungar Publishing corporation, 1967), xvii.
11 Just as physical death may survive an individual's social death, there is a sense in which an individual's capacity to surprise could be said to survive her physical death, at least in narratives, songs, poems, books, sacraments, symbols, and ceremonies. The Romans, for instance, looked back to the founding of Rome for their image of freedom; in an important sense the 'narrative life' of Rome's founding outlived the lives of the founders. Similarly, the people of Nso look back to a woman by the name of "Ngonnso," the founder of their monarchical order for the true meaning of freedom. Ngonnso was a true maker of surprises in the founding of the state of Nso. The founding fathers of the United States can be seen in this light as well. The Washington Mall, named after the most venerable of the founding father, is adorned by a towering obelisk of the Washington Monument along with monuments dedicated to other great makers of surprises such Lincoln, Jefferson, Lincoln, Roosevelt and more recently Martin Luther King, Jr.. There is a national holiday dedicated after MLK and streets all over the nation are named after these figures, making sure that they are breathing in every citizen of the United States wherever they may be.
12 The great Irish poet, W. B. Yeats, wrote, viz: "man has created death." When the poet said man has created death, he is not denying that humans die. He is saying that unlike other biological lives like Tiba the dog or Fluffy the cat, humans are obsessed with death. That obsession with death is artificially created as (I dare to say) the most potent implements or instruments of violence far more than those manufactured by modern states, like fighter jets, tanks and Kalashnikovs. In unfree states the reaper is always hovering over the heads of Africans. The parallel to Yeats' poem is this "man has created hope." This is also not to say that we do not hope but to indicate a specie of hope created by the state and also accentuated by the so-called Prophets, the later—days pastors, sheiks and other sundry merchants of hope and fear as an instrument of the highest form of violence. These are the two pegs on which violence of the highest form is hung.
13 Hobbes, *Leviathan*, Introduction.
14 Descartes' view of persons as essentially "thinking things" could be seen as positing an essentially anti-political metaphysics, a world in which persons are essentially isolated intellects.
15 Immanuel Kant, "An Answer to the Question: What Is Enlightenment?," James Schmidt, Translator, originally published as "*Beantwortung der Frage: Was ist Aufklarung*" Monatsschrift (1784), 481–494.
16 Ibid.
17 For the same reasons Locke gave in arguing for the freedom of conscience, there is no particular reason for tyrants to be threatened by so-called freedom of thought. Thinking alone is not relevant to politics, so long as it is limited to mere thought; and as such, the idea of the freedom of thought is, to say the least, superfluous, because thought is not something that can be controlled and thought alone does nothing to the world of politics.
18 See, for example, the end of Terry Gilliam's black comedy *Brazil* for a dramatic illustration of this kind of retreat in which the protagonist "escapes" his torturer only after he becomes completely catatonic.
19 David Foster Wallace, "This Is Water."
20 Quoted in Bernard Cricks, "Freedom as Politics," in Peter Laslett and WG Runciman, eds., *Philosophy, Politics and Society* (Oxford: Blackwell, 1969).
21 Hannah Arendt, "What Is Freedom," in Peter Baehr, ed., *The Portable Hannah Arendt* (New York: Penguin, 2000), 448.

References

John Stuart Mill, *Utilitarianism, On Liberty, Considerations on Representative Government, Remarks on Bentham's Philosophy,* Geraint William, ed. (London: J. M. Dent, 1993), 79.
Ajume Wingo, "The Aesthetics of Freedom," In Boudewijn de Bruin & Christopher F. Zurn, eds., *New Waves in Political Philosophy* (New York: Palgrave-Macmillan, 2009), 198–219.
Bernard Cricks, "Freedom as Politics," in Peter Laslett and WG Runciman, eds., *Philosophy, Politics and Society* (Oxford: Blackwell, 1969), 194–214.
Bernard Williams, *Philosophy as a Humanistic Discipline* (Princeton: Princeton University Press, 2006).
David Foster Wallace, *This Is Water* (New York: Little, Brown and Company, 2009).

H. G. Schenk, *The Mind of the European Romantics: An Essay in Cultural History* (Frederic Ungar Publishing corporation, 1967).

Hannah Arendt, "What Is Freedom," in Peter Baehr, ed., *The Portable Hannah Arendt* (New York: Penguin, 2000), 438–461.

Immanuel Kant, "An Answer to the Question: What Is Enlightenment?" James Schmidt, Translator, originally published as "*Beantwortung der Frage: Was ist Aufklarung*" Monatsschrift (1784), 481–494.

Patrick Radden Keefe, "Buried Secrets," *The New Yorker Magazine*, July 8, 2003.

Philip Pettit, "The Republican Ideal of Freedom," in David Miller, ed., *The Liberty Reader* (Boulder: Paradigm Publishers, 2006), 223–242.

Thomas Hobbes, *Leviathan* (New York: Penguin, 2017).

5

CITIZENSHIP UNDER SIEGE

Contemporary African Nationalism and the
Trauma of Modernity[1]

Michael Onyebuchi Eze

Introduction

The Westphalian state is often understood as a discursive project that guarantees rights, obligations, and mobile citizenship.[2] Although creative nationalist impulses gave rise to the emergence of the Westphalian state, it is the same impulse in an excessive measure that ruptured the euro-modernist state. Where nationalist ideologies have colonized the state, citizenship, and rights were often undermined, as evidenced by the Nazis in Germany or Putinizm in eastern Europe. Nazi Germany thrived through the nationalization of the state, while Putinizm flourished through the vilification of history. In both instances, the present is imprisoned by the past, and history is pilloried as a prisoner of the moment. In the same breadth, while the past holds the present hostage, this past is simultaneously criminalized and glorified as an evocative moment to justify present commitments to violence. Herein, nationalist ideologies close the subjective borders of who may be admitted or excluded from a territory or endowed with rights of legal membership. Nationalism in this view, colonizes the structure of the state, expelling citizens on the basis of ideological ruptures and meta-physical narratives. Yet, the absence of nationalism has equally led to the rupture of the state. In this case, abstract rationality or demagoguery takes over the collective will. In states like Côte d'Ivoire, The Congo, Yugoslavia, and the former USSR, the national memory was expressive through the symbolic fusion between cult leadership and state bureaucracy.[3] Yet, if history is any instructive, "these modular operatives have always proven to be a disaster in the sociopolitical imaginary," for when a sudden vacuum emerges because of the demise of the cult leader or breakdown of bureaucratic dictatorship, "the national cohesion collapses since the country's integration is dependent on the cult character as an adhesive narrative of national imaginary" (Eze 2010a:194).

The aim of this chapter is to interrogate the sociopolitical reality of contemporary African citizenship as a residual narrative of the "sovereignty discourse" of colonial social space and historicity (Ibid.:31). Coloniality offers a promise of modernity in which the African world is "civilized" according to the European episteme. It is in this process of "civilization" that colonial violence displaced and reformatted the sociopolitical, cultural, and economic space of indigenous societies *á la* Euromodernism. The implication is that the colonized social space and agents at the same time become an agent and location of coloniality; modern and

DOI: 10.4324/9781003143529-6

primitive, a victim and perpetrator of a system that silences his/her presence and suppresses his/her history to nothingness. Frantz Fanon (1963) elucidates:

> Colonialism has not simply depersonalized the individual it has colonized; this depersonalization is equally felt in the collective sphere, on the level of social structures. The colonized people find that they are reduced to a body of individuals who only find cohesion when in the presence of the colonizing nation.

Drawn to Africa's political signification as a geopolitical region, possibilities emerge in which we may, albeit historically, begin to speak of Africa as a political construct. Despite the divergent cultures and histories, the politicization of African social space shared one thing in common – colonialism. Thus, three dominant ways of writing or speaking about Africa can only become articulated in three generalized senses: their experience during colonialism, liberation, and struggles (against imperialism) and attempts to reconcile with globalized modernity. This is not to suggest an entrapment to the past, but precisely because history is not a chronology of events, to make sense of the present and articulate a robust future, we first need to reconcile with the past. Homi Bhabha (2004:12) eloquently articulated:

> As literary creatures and political animals, we ought to concern ourselves with the understanding of human action and the social world as a moment when something is beyond control, but is not beyond accommodation…. the critic must attempt to fully realize, and take responsibility for, the unspoken, unrepresented parts that haunt the historical present.
> *(also, Mcleod 2000:220)*

Nations and Nationalism: Classical Debates

Nationalism in a classical sense is primarily concerned with forging a shared consciousness by way of religion, shared language, or tradition. Nation here is what one inherits by virtue of an inherited geographical territory, language, religion, or, as Kenneth Kaunda (1975:168f) explains, "the growing awareness amongst people in a given geographical area that since they were a nation, it was time they behaved like one." As Anthony D. Smith (2000:3) puts it, "By the term nationalism, I understand an ideological movement for the attainment and maintenance of autonomy, unity, and identity on behalf of a population deemed by some of its members to constitute an actual or potential 'nation.'" Yet, it also involves conscious coercion, invention, or willing imagination into a political community. This distinction is what colors dominant debates on nationalism, often codified as the primordial versus modernist arguments.

According to the primordial thesis, a nation is an *organic* formation constituted by shared language, history, blood, religion, or culture. From this primordial perspective, nations do not emerge *ex nihilo* and are not, as Vincent Pecora (2001:27) notes, artificial creation courtesy of

> intellectual demagogues out of thin air … nations are produced from bits and pieces of history that remain lodged in collective life, fragments that are then woven together in new ways by modern nationalism in search of an independent state.

Language specifically is often implicated as a core credential for collective identity and translated into political domains of influence. As Pecora puts it, "language tends to define identity in ways that are as profound as any political allegiance, attachment to the land, or religious belief" (Ibid.:21).

Drawn to the political history of Africa, it becomes necessary to recognize the variation contingencies to avoid inflicting epistemic violence through essentialist rendered discourses. Africa is neither one country nor a nation in the Euromodernism sense. It is often a tortuous adventure to make an epistemic generalization of Africa as having one homogenous culture, history, or tradition. Where it concerns religion, for example, in many indigenous societies, every village or kindred has a god or goddess. These gods are not arbitrarily absolute nor interested in missionary conquest of other peoples. The nature of these gods, on the one hand, offers a metaphysical expression of a shared primordial identity and, on the other hand, points to the internal divergence of these cultural variations. Thus, if religion would be a source of identity, then such a vision of the self is both essentialist and discursive, fixed and transitional, an ambivalent status that underscores the cultural differentiations, diversities, and plurality of Africa's sociopolitical and economic histories. This ambivalence ruptures any predictability for a political imagination based on a primordial organic history.

For the modernist thesis, the leitmotif is that nations and nationalism are conscious artifacts or projects. Nationalism is an artificial invention of intellectuals and not an organic project evolving out of shared history, memories, or common descent. Nations and nationalism are thus then, a conscious solidarity erupting through the historical fissures of memories and past sacrifices to animate present needs, desires, and aspirations as Ernest Renan (1882:19) suggests:

> The nations are not something eternal. They had their beginnings and they will end … A nation is therefore a large-scale solidarity, constituted by the feeling of the sacrifices that one has made in the past and of those that one is prepared to make in the future. It presupposes a past; it is summarized, however, in the present by tangible fact, namely, consent, the clearly expressed desire to continue a common life. A nation's existence is, if you will pardon the metaphor, a daily plebiscite, just as an individual's existence is perpetual affirmation of life.

A *daily Plebiscite* is suggestive of colonial statehood, which was a conscious modeling of the modernist thesis. It was an invention of imperial ideology. It was a state without coherent memory, and that lacked shared history, language, or common descent. The ontological coherence of this state was primarily by way of cohesion through a monopoly of violence. This is what Ernest Gellner (1983) means in arguing that the primordialist idea of the nation as an organic phenomenon is a *myth*. Nationalism appropriates "pre-existing culture and turns them into nations, sometimes invents them, and often obliterates pre-existing cultures … [it] …is not the awakening of nations to self-consciousness: it invents nations where they do not exist" (Gellner 1983:48f, 168). While deriding the primoridialists, Gellner it seems, merely displaces an old myth with a new myth. As a philosophical truth (λóyOç), myth is not necessarily falsehood or untrue. Myths are often functional "as a narrative to move the mind of communities" to action or inaction (Eze 2010b:108). Paul Veyne (1988:xii, 62, 65) notes:

> Men do not find the truth; they create it, as they create their history. And the two in turn offer a good return … sometimes … myths … are approximations of the idea … Myth is truthful, but figuratively so. It is not historical truth mixed with lies; it is a high philosophical teaching that is entirely true, on that, instead of taking it literally, one sees in it an allegory.

Myth becomes expressive as a "historical address" to order life as an "invented tradition" or become the creative impulse that draws people into "an imagined political community" (Anderson 2001:6; Eze 2010b:108; Hobsbawm and Ranger 1983).[4] In this context, for example, colonial state falls into such a myth that was invented for legitimate domination and imperial imagination. Colonialism thus seems to be a natural response to the rise of nationalism in Europe. Nationalism just like colonialism is a modernist European project which evolved in the past two centuries with the concomitant rise of capitalism, modern communication, and free market economy (Anderson 2001:6). Pre-existing cultures and nations were obliterated in the name of modernist aspiration of a colonial state. Yet, this was the model of the state adopted by most post-colonial African states. The modernist idea of nationalism was invoked but only insofar as it mediates resistance against foreign occupation. Herein, the very nature of the nation becomes signified from outside the borders as *mimicry* (of European modernity) and caricature of any rational cohesion. As Clifford Geertz (1973:278) noted, the new post-colonial African states were: "Naïve or apprentice painters ... seeking their own proper style, their own distinctive mode of solution for the difficulties posed by their medium. Imitative, poorly organized, eclectic, opportunistic, subject to fads, ill-defined, uncertain."

My purpose in this chapter is not to recycle old ideas but to show, albeit new levels of interrogation, how we may ask new questions that could perhaps mobilize new ways of thinking. There is intellectual fatigue in the colonial blame game, but the existence of such fatigue neither solves the perennial crisis of the post-colonial state alienation nor offers a creative adaptation to transcend the haunting ghost of our colonial past. My position is that contemporary African states were arbitrary states as opposed to historical states such as those of Europe or their North American colonies. In Africa, this arbitrariness of the state creation, as Fanon (1965:9) would argue, "sowed half-treasons, prevarications, rancors" which "jeopardized for several years" the future of many African states.

Modernity and the Logic of Coloniality

As indicated, the modernist thesis is specifically relevant to the formation of the colonial African space. Socially, colonialism legitimated the displacement of the native's social space, violation of cultures, and epistemicide. Economically, colonialism mandated racialist capitalism that codified new humanity that restricted access to citizenship, conflating race with capital and, above all, "dissolving *groups* of people with distinctive identities into *aggregates* of persons" (Comaroff and Comaroff 2006:32). What has become known as the "logic of colonialism" (Mignolo 2007, 2013). not only imposes material asymmetries on the colonized subject but fundamentally alters the colonized socioeconomic, cultural, and physical space. To this, one might add the imposition of what may be termed *teleological immobility* or an implied *discursive violence* as Fanon (1965:108) would have argued:

> Colonialism obviously throws all the elements of native society into confusion. The dominant group arrives with its values and imposes them with such violence that the very life of the colonized can manifest itself only defensively, in a more or less clandestine way. Under these conditions, colonial domination distorts the very relations that the colonized maintains with his own culture.

The discourse of colonialism was not only operative at the moment of conquest, it was a doctrine that became assimilated and regularized as the very nature of colonial and "post-colonial" identity. In most African societies, the fractured nature of decolonization in post colony guaranteed a specific transfer of power to selected elites without concomitant transformation of the ideology of the state thus inherited. Hence, while the focus was on the transfer of power, the structure of the state thus inherited was left colonized. Hence, while the subject of the state felt decolonized, the system and structures of colonialism, that is, the state, were left intact along with its oppressive structures of bureaucratic dictatorship. As often, systems and structures possess their own rationality, determining or framing accessibility to the sociopolitical or economic space as Fanon (1963:30) equally observes, "in the colonies the economic substructure is also a superstructure. The cause is the consequence; *you are rich because you are white, you are white because you are rich."* [my emphasis].

The colonial state, however, neither possesses the authority of tradition nor shared cultural consciousness to simulate self-determination in the Euromodernist nationalist paradigm. The colonial state, as the name suggests, is *colonial* to facilitate domination or imposition of a foreign sovereign over indigenous societies. It was a bifurcation in which racialized subjectivity enabled or disabled one's access to the sociopolitical and economic world. Within this colonial status quo, the numerical minority possessed a moral and sociopolitical majority (citizens) while the numerical majority became the sociopolitical, cultural, and economic minority (subjects). This bifurcation between citizen and subject was introduced through the direct and indirect rule systems. Direct rule used race to justify both an economic privilege and political domination. Specifically, it created a political majority out of a numerical inferior minority. Indirect rule justified the relegation of the numerical majority into a political minority. The political majority are those who have access to the state and the associated privileges of the civil law, generating what Mahmood Mamdani (1996:23) terms "race-based political identities." In French and Portuguese colonies, for example, even as Portuguese and French were spoken by a numerical minority, they constituted the minority subjective. For the colonized, a subjective upgrade is possible, but only through subjective denunciation (of one's history and culture) to embrace European modernist humanity by speaking Portuguese, converting to Roman Catholicism, dressing in European clothes, etc. Race constituted the material base that forged and reinforced this bifurcated ontology (see Eze 2018 for a detailed argument). A racialized moral hierarchy emerged, which defined the ontological essence of the colonial state in terms of accessibility, obligation, and rights. The colonial moral hierarchy possesses legitimation without consent, legitimation for oppressors without the consent of the oppressed.

This intellectual attitude is at the root of colonial enterprise and the binary mode of collective identity in Africa. The difference between the colonial state and the post-colony is that in the former, only certain races had access to Africa's overall political economy. In the latter, everyone had access to the political world while class (or political connections) delimited one's accessibility to the socioeconomic world. What is critical here, too, is that colonial "whiteness" is displaced with elitist subjectivity that forges a racialized essence for a new political majority. At this point, however, it is critical to pause and examine the historical moments animating the contemporary political unconscious of contemporary African nationalism. In the section that follows, I shall show how contemporary African nationalism derives its legitimation not in the way that history reproduces memories but from force and discursive violence.

Political Nationalism: The African Experience

To understand contemporary African nationalism, it is important to confront the critical complexities leading to its emergence. First, how colonialism created arbitrary political geographies. Second, the nature of resistance erupted in the face of domination. Third, how racial domination inspired a reactionary unifying moment of resistance amongst diverse ethnicities. Finally, how the arbitrary creation of the colonial state is ontologically linked to the violence, instability, and political conflict that haunts the post-colonialist state.

As shown earlier, the ontological conditionalities for European-type nationalism were incongruent with the African experience. The precolonial identities were rarely rigid in terms of a cohesive or impenetrable shared consciousness. Nationalism in Africa does not possess the same credentials characterizing the Euromodernist aspiration. First, aside from Ethiopia, most African territories were spheres of European colonial domination or white settlement. Second, being post-colonial, nationalism, therefore, is a performative political practice consciously created. As Kaunda (1975:468) rightly noted, the post-colonial state does not have the "advantage of a common language and culture to act as a cohesive factor to bind the people together" therefore, nationalism then invokes a new intentionality which "describes the goal of all our activity, if not the natural origins of our sense of solidarity … to create genuine nations from the sprawling artifacts the colonialists carved out all over the continent."

To create genuine nations is reflective of the very nature of the colonial state as primarily a political space of domination, existing only through a monopoly of violence. The territories were neither *genuine* nor *natural* in terms of shared origins, language, culture, or religion. To this extent, African nationalism becomes construed as an immediate response to colonialism, to create or make an inclusive national memory out of the ashes of the colonial state. I argue that it is the very absence of nationalism that has led to the rupture of the post-colonial state precisely because these states were not historical but rather emerged through arbitrary violence. This is not to suggest that *nationalist impulse* is a *conditio-sine-qua* non for the making of a modernist state in the civic sense; it is, however, a precondition for the formation of civic citizenship where none existed before.

The state inherited at independence flourished only with the mandate of colonial consciousness that was imposed from above. The people who lived in those territories had no say in the sociopolitical, cultural, or even geographical mapping of their inherited world. The colonial state was not only abstract and alienated from their lifeworld, but it also violated and truncated possibilities for *teleological mobility* of citizenship and belonging. Citizens are members of the post-colonial state not by choice but by the violence of history. According to Kwame Appiah (1992:287), this received or inherited ideal which suggests that the African post-colonial state as a site of a coherent universal is a false narrative that imposes epistemic violence on the differentiated traditions and complexities of Africa, which "grows out of a history of changing responses to economic, political and cultural forces." I argue that the very attempt to rehabilitate the post-colonial state's fixation on abstract modernism is what motivated and mobilized the various attempt of African elites to forge a national memory. The extent to which they succeeded is the focus of the remaining chapter.

The indigenous people's attempt to forge collective consciousness from historical exigencies of impossible circumstances is what I have termed somewhere as the "historical moments" of African nationalism (Eze and van der Wal 2020:195). These moments of history are not necessarily exclusive but mutually interchangeable. They are not necessarily linear; in fact, they consistently overlap. In adopting this approach, one begins to understand the residual impact of contemporary African political identity but, more importantly, as a cause and consequence of European coloniality.

The first, which is sometimes referred to as a wave of "primary resistance," equally denotes moments of "fragmented resistance against physical domination and revolt against institutional oppression or 'imposition of new institutions, or new forms of coercion" (Ibid.). This moment according to Coleman is best understood as "nativistic, mahdistic, or messianic mass movement" (Coleman 1954:406). This was the first creative impulse against physical domination and cultural resistance against colonial modernity.

The second moment constitutes the era of intellectual movement. The focus was to uproot colonialism at its intellectual roots while inspiring racialized black nationalism. This period saw the emergence of pro-African movements like Negritude, Pan-Africanism, Cuban Negrismo, et cetera. A new epistemic consciousness is invoked to displace the ontological legitimation of colonialism as an act of civilization. Where colonial "civilization" suggests assimilation into the European cultural ways of life with a concomitant denunciation of indigenous cultures and traditions, the second moment of resistance focuses on the subjective reclamation of the truncated African subject from this colonial absurdity. Instead of denunciation, African culture and history are reclaimed and celebrated as a necessary condition for political and psychosocial independence. On this view, political independence is only possible when the mind has become decolonized.

The third moment is a renewed vigor of physical struggles against physical domination. Drawing on the creative impulse of the intellectual movements and the experiences of World War 2 that demystified the myth of European superiority, militant rebellion emerged in different parts of the African continent in challenge to colonial authorities. The fourth moment is the era of political independence in which the colonial sovereigns affected the administrative transfer of authority from European to African executives. This phase ushered in the post-colonial phase with a national sentiment that is alien and unintelligible to the people.

Among many reasons for the rupture of the postcolonial state were (i) the non-decolonization of core state power, (ii) the continued politicization of ethnic differences for tribal domination of the state, and (iii) militarization of state institutions. These factors not only exacerbated the primordial differences but entrenched the colonial policy of divide and rule as the very form of the post-colonial independent state. The crisis in the fourth moment is what then yielded to the 5th moment, which is the era of coups and violent change of government. Upon this moment is also the era of neo-nationalist and religious movements that emerged in response to the crises of the state and the failure of its modernist aspirations. My position is that the post-colonial state is a perfect imitation of the colonial architecture, with the only difference being the change in leadership. The principle of the state is not guaranteed by the primordial thesis of self-determination. Self-determination is a character of national spirit. Rather, the principle of the state is guaranteed through the politics of violent cohesion. The symbols introduced remain salutary gestures of inclusion but only insofar as they legitimated elitist domination.

States without a Nation

If the colonial state thrives by way of racialist capitalism in which race defines accessibility to sociopolitical and economic world, the postcolonial state subverts this condition not by eliminating the ambivalence between race and human realities but by imposing a new form of alienation. Where colonial citizenship is based on race, in the post-colony, access to the state is based on the politicization of ethnicity. What both the colonial and post-African states shared in common is that both thrived by mobilization of ethnic and cultural differences for internal coherence. This coherence, however, was not sustained by way of self-determination but through the state's monopoly of violence.

Most of the post-colonial African states did not possess the minimum credential of nationalism in the classical sense. Appiah (1992:261) observes, "if the history of Metropolitan Europe in the last century and a half has been a struggle to establish statehood for nationalities, Europe left Africa at independence with states looking for nations." However, no sooner was this "moment of cohesion" against colonialism abate did "the symbolic register of national unity" became truncated with "the reality of our differences" (Ibid.:162). Thus, demonstrating the fallacy of the "modernist epistemology of colonialism" and its ubiquitous claim to "create affective bonding of political integration" (Eze and van der Wal, 2020). The notion of citizenship that emerged remained abstract and was neither constitutive of any shared social utopia nor congruent with the will of citizens, which they express by way of contracts, covenants, or obligations. The stunted integration naturally prevented the development of an active civil society, a situation well articulated by Anthony Smith (1986:275):

> Such states lacked the 'ethnic tranquility' which comes from knowing that the bulk of one's (the state's) population, especially at the political center, share a single culture and history, which in turn furnishes the myths, values, symbols and memories which the emerging state may 'take-for-granted' and promote in the efforts by state elites to maximize their control over manpower and resources within their territorial domains.

It becomes important to recognize, as Immanuel Wallerstein (1999:25) explains, that the "[liberation] movements came to power almost nowhere on their full terms, and the real change everywhere has been less than they had wanted." This political short-change is best characterized by what Wallerstein terms the "two-stage strategy," in which a liberation movement anticipates that once it "achieved power and controlled the state, it could then transform the world, at least its world" (Ibid.) But this dream of total sovereignty and auto-transformation is, in fact, an illusion. The two-stage hypothesis was adopted by many African elites in their various struggles for political independence. They hinged the total transformation of the post-colonial state on the acquisition of political power. Post-colonial realism nevertheless sets in amidst the constraints of an international global order which undermines previously held anticolonial ideologies and stifles substantive transformative initiatives.

The very attempt to forge solutions and accommodate the practicality of the world system is what forced many of the anticolonial/liberation leaders to harmonize the two-stage process and respond to the "undeliverable" promises of political liberation. For the African liberation leaders, the promise hinges on political freedom, thus, Kwame Nkrumah's famous call, "*Seek ye the political kingdom and everything will be added unto ye.*" On this motive, a coherent and prosperous post-colonial state is linked with political freedom. With a political kingdom, the state will thrive and self-imagine, as Nkrumah noted in reference to Ghana: "This country must progress politically – indeed political self-determination is the means of further realisation of our social, economic and cultural potentialities. It is political freedom that dictates the pace of economic and social progress" (Grundy 1963:440). Nkrumah's promise, however, fails to recognize (i) the diverse historical experience of colonialism; (ii) the cultural and historical differentiations of ethnicities and people constitute the inherited colonial space and (iii) that elitist post-colonial politics is not necessarily a shared good congruent with the aspiration of the political community.

Various attempts were made to generate a new national identity. First was the creation of a national flag. Second is the simulation of an indigenous national Anthem. Third was the change of colonial names to African ones. Finally, was the attempt by many African elites to develop a new political discourse to displace colonial ideology. They fashioned theories of sociopolitical and economic transition. In Tanzania, it was Ujamaa, in Guinea, it was *communaucratie*, in Ghana, it was consciencism, in Zambia, African Humanism, and so forth. Yet, theory without context rarely transforms reality. Both the anti-colonial and post-colonial contexts share a constitutive historical interest but not a substantive political practice.

A substantive political practice is what Kaunda (1975:468)means in arguing that having a nationalist aspiration is not synonymous to love for the *fatherland!* The vexing problem for him is "how we can transform nationalism into patriotism" in terms reflective of "a zealous love for one's country." This is all the more necessary since the very idea of a country is itself a modernist invention that gave rise to colonialism without any emotive or (natural) connection to precolonial Africans. Kaunda (Ibid.) further notes:

> Until independence few Africans were aware in this sense that they had a country … their loyalties were more restricted and fragmentary. Independence does not usher into existence a mature nation … it is little more than the realization of a dream which must then be clothed with reality. The loyalties that nationalism calls into being are at once too general and too restricted to warrant being called patriotism.

Kaunda recognizes that nationalism is not an automatic given and neither is patriotism which, according to him, falls within the realm of a creative innovation or what Renan earlier would term *daily plebiscite*. According to Kaunda (1975:470), patriotism is to be secured by way of what may be termed *transitional coherence* or *nationalistic continuity* and *ontological predictability*:

> To transform nationalism into patriotism … it is the leader's task to ensure continuity of public function by tackling the problem of succession … constantly at work finding and encouraging suitable young men to accept ever-increasing responsibilities, assessing their capabilities, their honesty, and their capacity for handling power. It must be borne in mind, of course, that a nation is not an inert, static thing. It is an organism which changes as it grows … So the leader's problem is not solely to ensure a supply of men with correct qualities … but also to predict what qualities are likely to be needed in ten or twenty years.

Accordingly, the two-stage theory Wallerstein (1999:25) rightly observes is "extremely naïve"; by (i) assuming that attaining political power is a sufficient basis for socioeconomic consent and (ii) adapting the "theory of sovereignty at its face value and assumed that sovereign states are autonomous." Granted that the colonial flags were lowered and a new abstract national anthem instituted, but to what extent do these abstract gestures have meaning for contemporary African identity? Do we have a collective African political identity? To what extent did these attempts forge a cohesive integration within these African states? Were these gestures primarily a discourse of power by the elites that produced them?

To recapitulate, the post-colonial African political identity and citizenship were mostly top-down in which monopoly of violence determined and defined the political temperament of the post-colonial state. The creative impulse of post-colonial nationalism would be signified by way of collective suffering, terrors, and humiliation of the colonial experience. Hence, resistance to this experience came to mobilize the emerging metaphysical sense of unity within the postcolonial consciousness. Yet, this sense of unity remains arbitrary and not historical. It is this arbitrariness that continued to haunt the African post-colonial state for various reasons, viz.: (i) the idea of unity it offered was not self-determined but primarily reactionary. It did not transform the inherited territory into an inclusive space. (ii) It merely negotiated the transfer of powers from one dominant elite to new dominant sets of elites, with the qualitative difference being the former is foreign and the latter indigenous. (iii) Socioeconomically, the state remained a primitive location for labor and resources for European industries without a mandate for "independent industrialization."[5] (iv) The post-colonial state was undiffused and continued to mediate colonial structure of violence to enforce both submission and cohesion within the geopolitical unit.

Tribalism as Nationalism

If the colonial political identity was determined by the racialization of difference between the colonialist and the Africans or citizens and subjects, in the post-colony, membership is bifurcated between elitist and peripheral citizens. Elitist here refers to those with access to the state through the monopoly of violence, tribalization, or political inheritance. A central feature of colonialism was indirect rule system which was introduced "to mitigate the settler-native dialectic by fracturing the race consciousness of natives into multiple and separate ethnic consciousness" (Mamdani 2001:23). The system negotiated the breaking of ethnic groupings into politicized ethnicities under the mandate of the colonial appointed representative. What became known as the tribe refers to this politicization of ethnic groups (see ibid, also, Eze 2010b:70). The political project of indirect rule assumes that every African belongs to a tribe under a chief. And where no chief existed, a warrant chief was invented. Yet as Terrence Ranger (1983:248) argues,

> Africans moved in and out of multiple identities, defining themselves at one moment as subject to this chief, at another moment as a member of that cult, at another moment as part of this clan, and yet at another moment as an initiate in that professional guild.

A view shared by W.M.J. Binsbergen (1976:73–75) in his work on the Chewa Identity:

> Historians fail to qualify the alleged Chewa homogeneity against the historical evidence of incessant assimilation and dissociation of peripheral groups....they do not differentiate between a seniority system of rulers imposed by the colonial freezing of political dynamics and the pre-colonial competitive, shifting, fluid imbalance of power and influence.

The tribalization of the native through the indirect rule system fractured the preexisting shared identities while effectively relegating them to positions of political minorities. As minorities, they cease to be a threat to the political majority (Mamdani 2001:25). In indirect rule, the myth of African homogeneity is normalized with politicization and/or emasculation of fluid ethnicity into a politicized group – the tribe. Accordingly, "ethnic discrimination in the customary sphere translated ethnicity from a cultural to a political identity" (Ibid.:29). The new independent state uncritically adopted the imposed collective memory that was mobilized through colonial historicity. This colonial "nationalistic" sentiment thus inherited did not reconcile the cultural and ethnic diversities within the post-colonial state. In a famous essay, *Two Publics of Morality,* the Nigerian sociologist argues that contemporary

African society was inevitably shaped by colonialism: "our post-colonial present has been fashioned by our colonial past. It is that colonial past that has defined for us the spheres of morality that have come to dominate our politics" (Ekeh 1975). The tribalization of the native population maintained continuity and coherence in the post-colonial state through "tactical maneuvers by the state to divide the people or to elite strategies to 'use' popular allegiances to gain advantage for themselves" (Mamdani 1996:187). For Ekeh, the core legacy of colonialism was this institutionalization of what he terms the two publics of morality: the moral primordial and nonmoral civic public. The former refers to the "primordial groupings, sentiments and activities" which shape an individual's *weltanschauung* in the public sphere. The primordial public is, accordingly, a moral sphere that shapes behavior and "occupies vast tracts of the political spaces that are relevant for the welfare of the individual, sometimes limiting and breaching the state's efforts to extend its claims beyond the civic public sphere (Ekeh 1975:107)."

The civic public, on the other hand, is amoral without any ethical imperative to model behavior in terms of culture, religion, or tradition. The civic is "based on civil structures: the military, the civil service, the police …it *has no moral linkages with the private realm*" (Ibid.:92). The civic public echoes Archie Mafeje's (1971:258) critical analysis of the post-colony as a site of "popular politics" in which the post-colonial subject "appeals to the tribe as an authority of tradition in order to exploit power differentials" (see also, Eze 2010a:80). Thus, as Ekeh (1975:93) noted, "the same political actors simultaneously operate in the primordial and the civic publics." As Mafeje (1975:258) further enunciates, the real difference is between a person

> who, on behalf of his tribe, strives to maintain its traditional integrity and autonomy, and the man who invokes tribal ideology in order to maintain a power position, not in the tribal area, but in the modern capital city and whose ultimate aim is to undermine and exploit the supposed tribesmen.

When the modernizing évolués took over the job of "modernizing" the inherited territories, they were only doing so with the idea of European nationalism, which again contradicts the reality on the ground. The new nation-states would be grounded on an alien metaphysical foundation, a move that further alienated the people already depersonalized by colonialism. The post-colonial state thus offers an illusion of change in the political baton of leadership without fundamental structural transformation of the inherited territory into a viable self-determined nation. If in Europe, therefore, the state exists to motivate what I described earlier as vertical and horizontal mobility of citizens within that political space, in Africa, the purpose of the state is to restrict this kind of mobility. The state is signified from outside the borders, legitimate only at the behest of the globalized neoliberal order. A shared collective identity has only become reproduced as politics of cohesion for the purpose of domination. Herein, we refer to cohesion from above, i.e. to stay together by the force of the state's coercive apparatus. One belongs to a state not because he or she desires but because one is forced by state powers. As a Nigerian street trader puts it, "*Nigeria is like a prison Island where everybody is forced to live together waiting for an opportunity to escape.*" What we have is merely a transference of power. The only difference is that the new oppressor is an African! The foregoing post-colonial disquiet showcases how the modernist processes of African nationalism primarily exude abstract collectivity legitimated through a monopoly of violence. Unlike the simulated European states, these African states were neither coherent in terms of culture nor possessed any shared political aspiration.

The post-colonial state is thus a site of competing identities and conflicting memories. The implication herein, as in many post-colonial states, was this politicization of ethnic difference with disturbing polarization. The impact of tribalism continues to shape the national imagination. Minority groups seeking independence from this imposed political unconscious were violently suppressed, as evident in the Biafra Civil war in Nigeria, the Matabeleland war in Zimbabwe, Rwanda, The Congo, etc. In Cameroun, language and ethnicity were legally used as modicum to disenfranchise or enfranchise accessibility (or membership) to the colonial and post-colonial state. The politicization of English and French languages as the location of sociopolitical and even cultural differences in contemporary Cameroon effectively undermined the assumed coherence of the state as a site of national memory. In Uganda's Idi Amin, citizenship was racialized to expel descendants of Ugandan Asians who came to the country even before it was officially colonized. In Côte d'Ivoire, President Henri Konan Bédié in 1995 coined the term *Ivoirité* to politicize ethnic difference and exclude Ivorian descendants of Mandinka ethnic group who migrated from the upper volta regions before Ivorian independence. In Nigeria, the regional state of origin determines one access to the federal state. Thus understood, the "apotheosis of independence is transformed into the curse of independence" (1963:77).

Dulce et Decorum est Pro Patria Mori: Citizenship beyond Modernity

The fallacy of the imposed statehood in Africa is the assumption that colonial statehood will naturally forge a shared and inclusive national consciousness. Nationalism cannot occur in the absence of shared history, tradition, culture, etc. As shown earlier, contemporary African states remain legitimated through inherited ideals of colonial dictatorship. For these states, coherence is maintained only by the state's monopoly of violence. Accordingly, the membership in these post-colonial states was neither self-will nor free association. Imposed from above, the state inherited was merely an abstract collection of people "devoid of even the smallest spark of human sympathy or fellow feeling" (Kedourie 1993: xiv). In this section, I suggest a new orientation for nationalism that (i) democratizes citizenship through the fusion of political power with political freedom; (ii) prioritizes the sovereignty of the people over the sovereignty of the state, and (iii) finally, an imagination where citizens assume ownership of the state in contrast to the inherited bureaucratic state that thrives through elitist dictatorship and tribal domination.

Dominant conversation on contemporary African political identity often evolves around the necessity of epistemic transcendence of colonial historicity. Two competing schools emerge with regard to the constitutive character of this post-colonial identity. The first is the Ibadan school of history which argues that colonialism is to be understood as merely an episodic moment in African history and not the totality of it (see also, Ekeh 1975). According to this view, the political unconscious of contemporary African identity ought to transcend the colonial moment and forge a new political imagination that is free from the emotive entrapment of coloniality. To fall back on colonialism is to deny agency and equally suffocate the culturally differentiated experiences and traditions within Africa. The core position herein is that African identity in terms of sociocultural, political, or even religious ideations preexisted colonialism, and to argue that these only become manifest at the point of encounter with colonial encounter is to reduce the African experience as a perpetual footnote to European historicity.

The second school is often associated with African academics, and statemen like Abiola Irele and Kenneth Kaunda are less optimistic. While they do not deny the internal differentiations and rich cultural traditions within Africa, they nevertheless argue for a realistic check on contemporary African political imagination. While pre-colonial Africa offers a historical location for subjective reclamation, contemporary reality makes it impossible to ignore the continued impact of colonial historicity. According to Kaunda (1975:468–477), the very idea of nationalism, when applied to Africa, is a misnomer! For Abiola Irele (1992:202), the timeless impact of colonialism is a phenomenon we cannot wish away; a predicament he enunciated beautifully in his "In Praise of Alienation":

> We are conscious of the irreversible nature of the transformations the impact of Europe has effected in our midst and which are so extensive as to define the really significant frame of reference of our contemporary existence. The traditional pre-colonial culture and way of life continue to exist as a reality among us, but they constitute an order of existence that is engaged in a forced march, in a direction dictated by the requirements of a modern scientific and technological civilization. It also happens to be the case that Western civilization ... provides the paradigm of modernity to which we aspire. Hence our mixed feelings, the troubled sense of acceptance and rejection ... the ambivalence we demonstrate in our response to Europe and Western civilization is in fact a measure of our emotional tribute; it is expressive, in a profound way, of the cultural hold Europe has secured upon us--of the alienation it has imposed upon us as a historical fate.

The problem with historical analogy, as I have shown somewhere, is the problem of epistemic coloniality or what I termed colonization of subjectivity (Eze 2010b:189). It reduces African historiography as a footnote to history. It remains residual without ontological agency, that is, existing only as a mirror of Europe. Yet, sometimes, looking at this mirror does offer epistemic spaces for creative regeneration. The question then is, how do we create a new nationalism colored with liberty, freedom, and self-determination? How do we forge a new order and centers of legitimation that is constitutive of our society which is the collective will of the nation? (See also, Kohn 1961:237). At the pain of historical analogy, I endorse Irele that this *historical fate,* even as imposed, can be managed. As Kohn (Ibid.:329) observes, the character of nations [are not]:

> Determined prehistorically or biologically, nor are they fixed for all time; they are the product of social and intellectual development, of countless gradations of behavior and reaction, some of which are hardly discernible in the flux of the past, from which the historian selects what seems to him to be the essential and characteristic elements in a pattern of almost confusing complexity.

In this *Social Contract Theory, Rousseau* argues that "the sovereignty of the prince" be replaced with the sovereignty of the people as the center and justification of the society. This was the emergence of a new democratic nationalism of which Rousseau would inspire. Rousseau's thought is traced to Calvinism with its emphasis on civic virtues and stoicism. Rousseau was a moderate revolutionary. He was averse to violent reforms, and unlike Diderot and Voltaire, who were diehard advocates of moral and intellectual progress of mankind as an essential key to social progress, Rousseau, for his part, was skeptical of "the parallelism of progress in civilization and the growth of moral consciousness" (Ibid.:240). Rousseau was not a nationalist in the classical sense. His advocacy for a new foundation of the state was patriotism, rational liberty, and justice (similar to Hobbes before him), *"civitas est persona una, cuius voluntas, ex pactis plurium hominum, pro voluntate habenda est ipsorum omnium, ut singulorum viribus et facultatibus uti posit ad paem et defensionem communem"* (De Cive 9). Unlike Hobbes however, the Prince cannot be "repository of the general will" even for the benevolent prince who understand the interconnectedness of a "just rule and the welfare of the people" (Ibid.:246). Accordingly, the state as "a community of men" in order to avoid dictatorship or imposed despotism on one person as a repository of the general will needs a different foundation. The state "must be a true 'corps moral et collectif,' a 'moi commun,' a collective self of which the individual becomes part, spiritually and physically" (Ibid.).

In Rousseau's ideal community, there is an obliteration between private and public ethics such that even the "reason of state, the dynamic self-interest of the community as the motivation for activities beyond the strict realm of morality" as wholly unacceptable (Ibid.:250). Nationalism is an attempt to relocate the free, autonomous individual within the community. My preferential adaptation of the term "nationalism" is a proposal for a continuity between the primordialist and modernist versions of nationalism. Rousseau's civic nationalism expresses an epistemic confluence. It accommodates both the primordial and modernists' claims of nationalism and moves to establish a historical continuity between the individual as both a primordial and modern subject. Unlike the German romanticists who made a distinction between the state (as a mechanical product of history) and nation (as an organic and eternal), the state in Rousseau is not prior to the lives of its members. In contrast to a society that prioritizes the law over the individual's good, Rousseau would go for an "austere community," that is, a community "based on reason, liberty, and good will."

In our context, the sovereignty of the state is thereby substituted with the sovereignty of the people. The sovereign will come from all persons who are united in a compact and have expressed a common will in the "volonté genérale," which, even if an ensemble of different individuals, will epitomize the ultimate end of a resolution as possessing a character of liberty and equality. The will is neither accidental nor arbitrary. It emerges as the free will of every member "of the reasonable and the good, of that virtuous attitude which should animate each member" (Ibid.:249). What this means is that an individual's relationship with the state is co-substantive. First, as Frederick of Prussia noted, "A king is the first servant of the state." (Kedourie 1993:3). A view that has much in common with the African saying that "A king is a king by the will of his people," which, according to Mogobe Ramose (1999:55,99.116) suggests *Kgosi ke kgosi ka batho* ('the sovereignty of the King derives from and belongs to its subjects'):

> To be a king is to accede to that position because of the consent of the people and to remain so far as long as the people have not withdrawn their consent … The King was king by the grace of the people and not the grace of God.

The point here is that our relationship with the state is not accidental but a metaphysical symbiosis in which our life flourishes when that of our community flourishes. The well-being of the individual is directly linked to the fatherland is what we learn from the Ancient Greeks, where Philopatros cautions Anapistemon:

> The good of society is yours without realizing it, you are so strongly tied to your fatherland, that you can neither isolate, nor separate yourself from it without feeling the consequence of your mistake. If the government is happy, you prosper; if it suffers harm, its misfortune will react on you. Similarly if the citizens enjoy an honest opulence, the sovereign prospers, and if the citizens are overwhelmed with poverty, the condition of

the Sovereign will be worthy of pity. Love of the father land is not therefore a mere concept of reason, it exists really.

(Kedourie 1993:3)

Conclusion

If the crisis of citizenship in contemporary Africa is the rupture of the state and the nationalism it inherited, then we have to uproot this past and forge a new beginning. Since colonial discourses offered a coherent universalism for the denigration and colonization of Africa it seems too that a "cultural synthesis" symbolizing the overall "historical consciousness of black struggles and experiences" is key for a new collective imagination, as Césiare notes:

> For me it is the call to Africa. I said to myself, it is true that superficially we are French. We are marked by French customs. We are stamped by Cartesianism, by French rhetoric, but if all this is broken through, if you go down to the depths, what you will find is fundamentally Negro.

(Tomich 1979:370)

A view endorsed by Fanon (1965:25): "It is the white who creates the Negro. But it is the Negro who creates negritude."

Accordingly, the future of political philosophy in Africa is to renegotiate then what constitutes a nation in our own terms, context, history, and contemporary experiences. If the euro-modernist state thrives through the presence of strong institutions, history has shown, however, that strong institutions without democratized citizenship only breed bureaucratic dictatorship. The context of Africa, therefore, demands a new orientation; a possession of history that is ours, a creation of a culture that is sympathetic, and a shared sense of fellow feeling.

But we cannot go into a past that remains beyond our momentary breadth. When the past is entrapped in the present, and the present becomes hostage to the past, nationalism becomes possible by way of violent acts of infusion of memories or vilification of the past. Political imagination becomes essentially an act of revenge for subjective reclamation. And so, it seems that our history has extended its long arm over us, over our destiny. The only solution is to uproot this past. Yet, to uproot it, we must understand it, its mechanics, and its workings. And then a conscious effort at nation-building and cultural reclamation of everyone. Herein, citizenship is not only defined as inherited colonial bureaucracy but an evolving practice that will inspire what I term a subjective purchase where everyone becomes a metaphysical shareholder of the state.

That is all!

Notes

1 To the Memory of Kenneth Kaunda (1924–2021).
2 Mobile citizenship is suggestive of subjective mobility in which membership in a particular state enables free movement of persons across geopolitical boundaries. Members of the European Union for example possesses what may be termed vertical and horizontal mobility. What this means is that the treaty of the EU States' conventions has granted rights of free movement or passage within EU borders. Beyond this however, being a member of the EU offers a collective sociopolitical, economic, and cultural capital for vertical mobility. Vertical mobility means that members of the

EU for example, could *easily* travel to a country like Burkina Faso or Tanzania without visa (or formality visas) on arrival but without reciprocity and even when these non-EU humans apply for EU visas, it is often under stringent conditions with most applications being denied.

3 State is here understood as bureaucratic dictatorship such as the former USSR or colonial statehood.

4 Benedict Anderson (2001:6) argues that the nation is

> an imagined political community and imagined as both inherently limited and sovereign … because the members of even the smallest nation will never know most of their members, meet them, or even hear of them, yet in the minds of each lives the image of their communion.

5 The Dutch buys cocoa beans from Côte d'Ivoire on the condition that they do not sell manufactured or finished chocolates to the EU. Is one of such examples of economic imperialism that long survived physical occupation of African territories.

Bibliography

Anderson, B. (2001). *Imagined Communities*. London: Verso.

Appiah, K. (1992). *In My Father's House*: *Africa in the Philosophy of Culture*. New York: Oxford University Press.

Bhabha, H. (2004). *The Location of Culture*. London: Routledge Classics.

Coleman, J. S. (1954). "Nationalism in Tropical Africa," *The American Political Science Review* 48, no.2 (1954): 404–426.

Comaroff, J. and Comaroff, J. eds. (2006). "Law and Disorder in the Postcolony: An Introduction" in *Law and Disorder in the Postcolony*. Chicago, IL: University of Chicago Press, 1–56.

Ekeh, P. (1975). "Colonialism and the Two Publics in Africa: A Theoretical Statement," *Comparative Studies in Society and History* 17, no. 01: 91–112.

Eze, M. O. (2010a). *The Politics of History in Contemporary Africa*. New York: Palgrave Macmillan.

Eze, M. O. (2010b). *Intellectual History in Contemporary South Africa*. New York: Palgrave Macmillan.

Eze, M. O. (2018) "Cultural Appropriation and the Limits of Identity: A Case for Multiple Humanity(ies)," *Chiedza, Journal of Arrupe Jesuit University* 20, no. 1 (May): 8–31:21.

Eze, M. O. and Van der Wal, K. (2020). "Beyond Sovereign Reason: Issues and Contestations in Contemporary African Identity," *JCMS: Journal of Common Market Studies* 58, no. 1: 189–205.

Fanon, F. (1963). *The Wretched of The Earth*. trans. C. Farrington. New York: Grove Press.

Fanon, F. (1965). *A Dying Colonialism*, trans. H. Chevalier. New York: Monthly Review Press.

Geertz, C. (1973). *The Interpretation of Cultures: Selected Essays*. New York: Basic Books.

Gellner, E. (1983). *Nations and Nationalism*. Ithaca, NY: Cornell University Press.

Grundy, K. W. (1963). "Nkrumah's Theory of Underdevelopment: An Analysis of Recurrent Themes," *World Politics* 15, no.3 (April): 438–454.

Hobsbawm, E. and T. Rangers, eds. (1983). *The Invention of Tradition: Past and Present Publications*. Cambridge: Cambridge University Press, 211–262.

Irele, A. (1992). "In Praise of Alienation" in V. Y. Mudimbe ed., *The Surreptitious Speech: Presence Africaine and the Politics of Otherness 1947–1987*. Chicago, IL: University of Chicago Press, 201–224.

Kaunda, K. (1975) "The Future of Nationalism" in G.-C. Mutiso, and S.W Rohio eds, *Readings in African Political Thought*. Lusaka, Zambia: Heinmann Educational Books, Ltd, 468–477.

Kedourie, E (1993). *Nationalism*. Oxford: Blackwell.

Kohn, H. (1961). *An Idea of Nationalism*. New York: Macmillan Company.

Mafeje, A (1971). "The Ideology of Tribalism," *The Journal of Modern African Studies* 9, no. 2 (August): 253–261.

Mamdani, M. (1996). *Citizen and Subject: Contemporary Africa and the Legacy of Late Colonialism*. Princeton, NJ: Princeton University Press.

Mamdani, M. (2001). *When Victims Become Killers: Colonialism, Nativism and the Genocide in Rwanda*. Princeton, NJ: Princeton University Press.

McLeod, J. (2000). *Beginning Postcolonialism*. Manchester: Manchester University Press.

Mignolo, W. (2007). Personal *Conversation*.

Mignolo, W. (2013). "Delinking: The Rhetoric of Modernity, The Logic of Coloniality and the Grammar of De-Coloniality" in W. D. Mignolo and A. Escobar eds., *Globalization and the Decolonial Option*. London: Routledge, 202–368.

Pecora, V. (2001). "Introduction" in Vincent P. Pecora ed., *Nations and Identities: Classic Readings,* Oxford: Blackwell Publishers, 1–42.

Ramose, M. (1999) *African Philosophy through Ubuntu.* Harare: Mond Publishers.

Rangers, T. (1983). "The Invention of Tradition in Colonial Africa" in E. Hobsbawm and T. Rangers eds., *The Invention of Tradition: Past and Present Publications.* Cambridge: Cambridge University Press, 211–262.

Renan, E. ([1882]1990). "Qu'est-ce qu'une nation?", trans. by Martin Thom as "What is a Nation?", in Nation and Narration, Homi K. Bhabha (ed.), London: Routledge, 1990, 8–22.

Smith, A. D. (1986). State-Making and Nation-Building" in John A. Hall ed., *States in History,* Oxford: Oxford University Press.

Smith, A. D. (2000). *The Nation in History: Historical Debates about Ethnicity and Nationalism.* Hanover: University Press of New England.

Tomich, D. (1979). "The Dialectic of Colonialism and Culture: The Origins of Negritude of Aimé Césaire." *Research Foundation of SUNY and Fernand Braudel Center* 2/3: 351–385: 363.

Van Binsbergen, W. M. J. (1975). "History of the Chewa" in H. W Langworthy ed., *African Social Research,* June 1976: 73–75.

Veyne, P. (1988). *Did the Greeks Believe in Their Myths? An Essay on the Constitutive Imagination.* Chicago, IL: The University of Chicago Press.

Wallerstein, I. (1999). *The End of the World as We Know It.* Minneapolis: University of Minnesota Press.

6

AFRICAN TRADITION AND MODERNITY

Polycarp Ikuenobe

Introduction

I examine the distinction between 'tradition' and 'modernity' and, the characterization of 'modernity' as an imperative, a normative standard for evaluating the African way of life, and the goal to which Africa's social and political ordering should aspire. Olufemi Taiwo expresses this imperative in the title of his book: *Africa Must be Modern: A Manifesto* (2014). And Kwasi Wiredu (1980) expresses this as follows: "what you do is to *modernise*" (p. 1). It appears that the call for Africa to modernize involves the call to adopt Western values, modes of living and thinking, which include principles of liberal democracy, rule of law, individualism, capitalism, and technological and scientific rational methods of inquiry (Appiah, 1992; Bodunrin, 1984; Hountondji, 1996; Taiwo, 2010; Wiredu, 1980). This call has engendered the debate regarding whether African traditional ideas and practices can provide the foundation for principles of good governance and modern living. This raises the following questions: (1) Is modernity necessarily good? (2) Is African tradition necessarily bad? (3) Should modernization in Africa involve the uncritical wholesale adoption of Western modernity? (4) Is it possible for modernization to draw from or blend with the good elements of African tradition?

I argue that 'tradition' is not necessarily bad, given the merits of the social-moral features of communalism, and that 'modernity' is not necessarily good, given the excesses of rugged individualism, liberal democracy, capitalism, science, and technology. As such, the process of modernization in Africa should involve the circumspective adoption of the positive elements of 'modernity' and 'tradition', and, jettisoning of their negative elements. In the first section, I critically examine the characterizations or purported features of 'tradition' and 'modernity.' I argue in the second section that, based on these characterizations or features, 'modernity' and 'tradition' are not distinct, but coextensive and blended. In the third section, I indicate how the blended nature of 'tradition' and 'modernity' can be exemplified in the modernizing efforts to ground liberal democratic governance on African communal tradition.

Characterization of Modernity and Tradition

African philosophers have been asked to provide the philosophical basis for Africa's modernization, in terms of articulating the principles by which Africans should deal with their

DOI: 10.4324/9781003143529-7

post-colonial realities. As such, they have been trying to articulate theories of social-political arrangements that will allow African states to modernize. The normative characterization of 'modernity, which assumes its inherent goodness, and the denigration of tradition, which implies the inherent badness of African traditions, begs the question of the nature and value of 'modernity'. It appears that 'modernity' may not necessarily be good, and 'tradition' may not necessarily be bad. Thus, modernization should not necessarily involve getting rid of African traditions; rather, it should involve a transformation of these traditions to meet the practical needs of Africans. Many of those who assume the honorific view of modernity usually engage in a kind of reductionism: they reduce modernity to only the positive elements of its scientific and analytic method and its liberal democratic and legal principles, but ignore its negative elements.

Although colonialism has had destructive effects on traditional values and ways of life, the relics of African traditions are still pervasive in people's lives. These surviving and persistent cultural traditions have, in part, made it difficult for many states to contend with their current situations. This raises questions regarding what modernity involves, the approach that Africans should take toward modernizing, and the value of modernization. Olufemi Taiwo (2010) sees the destructive effects of colonialism on African traditions as planting the seeds that could engender modernization. He argues that Africa can modernize only if it makes a clean break with tradition. This suggests a logical distinction between 'modernity' (as relics of European colonialism) and 'tradition' (ideas or ways of life that preexist colonialism), such that their distinct features and conditions make them mutually exclusive.

However, P. P. Ekeh (1983, pp. 11–13) has identified three social structures of 'modernity' that colonialism brought to Africa. The *migrated* social structures were brought wholesale in their original forms from imperial Europe to the colonized countries of Africa and juxtaposed with the new colonial situation. The *emergent* social structures were neither indigenous to Africa nor brought from Europe. They were generated by the colonial situation itself and are analogous to some structures in Europe. The *transformed* social structures are those indigenous pre-colonial institutions, traditions, and practices that were transformed to operate within the context of the newly created system of colonialism.

Many of these social structures indicate features of modernity, such as, a liberal legal system, which Taiwo (2010, pp. 45–56) argues, is a fundament of, and should provide the basis for, modernization in Africa. But is it possible for Africa to modernize in a way that addresses its unique problems without relying on some positive elements of its traditions? Answering this question requires a critical examination of 'modernity' and the mode that modernization must take in Africa. In my view, modernization must involve a blend of *the positive elements* of both modernity and tradition, or a transformation and an adaptation of certain cultural traditions to the new African situation. Thus, modernization cannot involve a complete rejection of tradition or a wholesale acceptance of all the elements of modernity.

'Modernity' indicates a period that was ushered in by the Enlightenment in Europe. It is characterized by or as a set of ideas and modes of thought that employs scientific, logical, rational, critical, and analytic methods of inquiry and thinking. These ideas and thoughts engendered ways of life that exemplify modernization, which involves adopting principles of social, economic, and political development. Modernity is now generally considered the paradigm way of living, thinking, and doing things, and a mark of civilization. The call for modernization is thus a call for Africa to transform or abandon its tradition, in order to develop its social, political, and economic systems.

We may appreciate this point by indicating the different elements of modernity: (1) The epistemological scientific elements, which involve empiricism, positivism, foundationalism, reliance on reason, analysis, objectivity, and critical reflection. (2) The metaphysical elements include physical ontology, atomism, realism, materialism, and a denial of idealism or spiritualism. (3) The logical elements include the universality of the formal standards of reasoning, and the idea that linguistic concepts can capture the essence of things and reality. (4) The social and political elements involve liberalism, democracy, rule of law, secularism, and the protection of individual rights and freedoms. (5) The moral elements include the moral sanctity of autonomy, voluntarism, individualism, human dignity, and individual choice or conception of the good. (6) The economic dimension involves capitalism and *laissez faire*.

These different features and elements of modernity are coextensive and mutually supportive, as exemplified in the connections among 4, 5, 6: the social-political, moral, and economic elements. We can also see connections among 1, 2, 3: the epistemological, metaphysical, and logical elements regarding the nature of singular reality and universal truth that reason in scientific inquiry must discover. The epistemological, metaphysical, and logical principles of modernity shaped the moral, political, and economic principles. The overriding issue of modernization that connects all these elements is, how Africa can acquire requisite intellectual virtues, epistemic methods, and devise a system of political governance, social arrangements that can address the current post-colonial situation. This would require creating the social, moral, political, and economic conditions that are conducive to the epistemological and logical aspects of modernity, in order to allow for adequate scientific inquiry and technological advancement.

An examination of the different elements of modernity will indicate that they all have positive and negative features. Such examination will help to determine which of these positive features of modernity Africans should draw from as a basis for modernization and technological advancement. For Wiredu (1980), this process of modernizing African traditions involves the infusion of the scientific method (undergirded by reason) into the dogmatic, irrational, authoritarian, communitarian, and anachronistic features of African traditions. As Wiredu (1980) argues,

> The habits of exactness and rigour in thinking, the pursuit of systematic coherence and the experimental approach so characteristic of science are attributes of mind which we in Africa urgently need to cultivate not just because they are in themselves intellectual virtues but also because they are necessary conditions for modernization.
>
> (p. 32)

This suggests that the intellectual virtues and epistemic features of modernity are inherently good. He underscores this by arguing that "logical, mathematical, analytical, experimental procedures are essential in the quest for the knowledge of, and control over, nature..." (p. 12). For him, this is important because what Africans need is how to live and manage their lives in ways that allow them to have some control over nature and their social conditions, which must involve science, technology, and economic development. Bodunrin (1984) makes a similar point by arguing that Africa needs the technological, scientific, and epistemological elements of modernity in order to develop socially and politically. He says: "Whether we like it or not we will have science and technology. We have to acquire the thought habits needed to cope with life in a technological age" (p. 20).

This idea is also implicated in Gyekye's (1997) view that the notion of modernity has gained a normative status, "in that all societies in the world without exception aspire to become modern, to exhibit in their social, cultural, and political lives features said to characterize modernity" (p. 263). This honorific nature of modern science, technology, epistemic methods, and habits is assumed without critical examination by advocates of modernization and critics of tradition. The vexing issue is whether the adoption of these modern epistemic principles, intellectual virtues, political system, ways of life, and social ordering must be founded on African cultural traditions or depart entirely from them.

The normative view of modernization and its implied imperative and inevitability, in contrast with tradition suggest that (1) we should not subject modernity to critical examination and (2) tradition has nothing to offer the efforts to modernize. The central argument is that African traditions have irrational and dogmatic features that will not allow Africans to develop and adopt social, political, and economic modes of life that engender scientific and technological advancement. For Gyekye (1997), the implication is that the irrationality and dogmatism associated with African traditions are significant drawbacks or pitfalls that make various elements of modernization impossible (pp. 242–58). Thus, critics have argued that Africa does not have legitimate traditional thought systems, including a philosophy of social and political arrangement and good governance.

The underlying idea is that such legitimate philosophical political ideas, beliefs, or thoughts must involve the modern processes and methods of coherent conceptual, critical and rigorous analyses of principles, ideas, and concepts; such are lacking in African traditions which are dogmatic, irrational, and spiritualistic. The criticism of African traditional beliefs, ideas, and thoughts is that they lack rational basis and practical applicability that will allow Africans to cope with life and their current reality. Odera Oruka (1987) underscores this criticism by arguing that, "Reason is a universal human trait. And the greatest disservice to African philosophy is to deny it reason and dress it in magic and extra-rational traditionalism" (p. 66). And Oruka among others argues that African traditions are characterized by supernatural beliefs, spiritual explanations, and religious dogmatism.

Modernization involves a rejection of such religious dogmatism. As Bertrand Russell (1945) indicates, modernity in Europe is characterized by "the diminishing authority of the Church and the increasing authority of science" (p. 491). This involved a rejection of the tradition of the Medieval period, which was characterized by the sole reliance on religious authority, dogmas, and spiritual or metaphysical explanations. Such rejection ushered in modernity, the acceptance of the authority of science and technology, and the adoption of the scientific method, which involves individuality and reason, experimentation, empirical test, critical and rigorous analysis. The result of the virtue of the scientific and rational method has been manifested in the industrial revolution and the advent of technology. Modernism was characterized by the view that there are universal and absolute truth-claims that are embedded exclusively in reason. Scientific inquiries and theories seek to bring universal rationality, unity, and simplicity to ways of seeing and doing things, organizing life, thinking about, explaining, and understanding phenomena in the world.

An important element of European modernity and its mode of inquiry is that it "has retained, for the most part, an individualistic and subjective character" (Russell, 1945, p. 493). This element is related to the first, in that the rejection of religious dogmas and the authority of the Church has opened up numerous chosen areas of inquiries by individuals, the growth of knowledge, and the ability of people to think for themselves by using subjective rational criteria for the universal validity of knowledge or justified beliefs. This required that one accepts beliefs based on one's own individual rational and critical consideration of the evidence, as opposed to what is dictated by any community, tradition, the Church, or their dogma. This highlights the necessity of individual rationality, rights, freedom, conception, and choice of the good, which are underpinned by metaphysical autonomy and voluntarism. These epistemological ideas are implicated in the focus on the political and legal elements of modernity regarding, the advocacy for liberal democracy as the mode of governance that will create the conditions and environment for individual rights, enterprise, freedom, rational thinking, inquiry, and choices.

Blending Modernity and Tradition

The criticism of the spiritual and dogmatic features of African tradition suggests that African philosophers who want to develop philosophical principles of modern governance in Africa cannot rely on its traditions. Wiredu (1980) argues that this effort to make African philosophy applicable, practical, and relevant to Africa's social development and modernization involves "the broad sense of the word in which philosophy is, so to speak, a guide to the living of life..." (p. 32). In his view, African philosophy that can provide a guide to living life must rely on critical analyses and rigorous inquiry, which will lead to applicable and adaptable principles to the African situation. Thus, some argue that the proper role of African philosophers is to critically examine African tradition in order to identify why Africans must get rid of it, instead of romanticizing or trying to rehabilitate it. Sogolo (1993) captures this view thus: "the major dilemmas of modern Africa today cannot be accounted for by romanticizing the past" (p. 192).

The characterization of African tradition and modernity, and the criticisms of African tradition, suggest that African tradition cannot inform the principles of modernity that Africans must adopt and how they adopt them. Taiwo suggests that accepting the features of African traditions cannot be helpful to the efforts to modernize. This suggests (1) that Africa is currently not modernizing, and (2) that 'modernity' is an *absolute holistic condition* that comes abruptly into existence, wholesale, in a single fell swoop, and then it stops, as opposed to a gradual process of change and modification of traditional and accepted ways of life. It suggests that modernity comes into being at a specific time frame, and during this time frame, all the principles or features of modernity are adopted and remain in place in absolute terms. In my view, traditions must inform the gradual process of African modernization!

Even in Europe, modernity did not come into existence abruptly; it was a gradual process of modifying 'traditional' and Medieval ways of life. Europe did not adopt modernity or get rid of its other traditions in a single fell swoop. This modification process has allowed for some form of coexistence in the continued blending of various traditions with elements of modernity. For instance, the irrationality and dogmatism of Christian religion of the Medieval tradition have coexisted with modern science, technology, and medicine. Harding (1998) argues that the universality, rationality, and objectivity assumptions of science have borrowed from the metaphysical assumptions and beliefs of Christian religion, involving a unity and predetermined nature as God's creation (pp. 56–58, 167, 181). Thus, modernity cannot be characterized in absolute terms. The process of 'modernization' is gradual in its move toward or a verisimilitude to the ideal of modernity, which is the superlative exemplification of *all* its principles and features. Modernization is a matter of degree. No cultural tradition or way of life is static. It is usually influenced by other cultures and is thus always evolving.

African traditions have been influenced by European modernity through colonialism and have been evolving in adopting some principles and features of modernity. In this sense, Africa is currently in the continuous and gradual process of modernization. No reasonable person would deny that Africa is modernizing or has some degree of modernity, especially in its adoption of elements of formal education, science, medicine, technology, and liberal democracy—no matter how limited. The imperative for Africa to modernize is meaningful only if it is understood as a call to expedite the modernizing process, or to draw attention to the slow pace of modernization and the efforts to achieve the ideal of modernity. Such a call is nonsensical if it is understood as saying that Africa is not modernizing at all or adopting to some degree some features of modernity. Such a view is simply absurd. This modernizing process has involved in part, as Ekeh indicates in his account of the colonial social structures, the modification of some cultural traditions to infuse into them some principles of modernity, in order to make them adaptable to African conditions and problems.

When certain aspects of cultural traditions are no longer useful or effective, people use basic practical (means-end) rationality to critically examine them, to find alternative ways of doing things and living. It appears that critics of African tradition conceive of science, rationality, reason, and critical reflections as features of modernity that came solely from the Enlightenment and exist exclusively in Europe. Sandra Harding (1998) has argued against this characterization of modernity and science as a normative standard because it is a way for Europe to elevate its thoughts as universally true and rational, in order to suppress or denigrate other cultural traditional forms of knowledge, rationality inquiry, science, and technology. According to Harding, "the suppression of other cultures' knowledge traditions also contributed to producing the illusion that only European sciences were and could be universal ones" (p. 181). In her view, other cultures and traditions have or had science and technology.

We must understand the ideas of 'rationality', 'science' and 'technology broadly to involve the empirical testing of hypotheses, knowledge production, and their application to ways of life, which are features of any culture. According to Boxill (1998),

> People do not normally think of their own culture as an experiment in living. They do not suppose that their culture's mores and practices are hypotheses about how life should be lived and that in following these mores and practices they are behaving somewhat like scientists subjecting hypotheses to empirical tests. Normally they act as their culture dictates because they don't think about it, or because they believe that alternatives are wrong, or sometimes because they cannot conceive of alternatives. Still a culture is an experiment in living in the sense that things happen as a result of people following its mores and practices, and people do learn from how and why these things happen. This is why cultures change.
>
> *(p. 117)*

Most cultural changes, which are rational and require critical reflection involve the epistemic elements 'modernity'. This view of culture underscores Harding's (1998) view that cultural traditions are, usually, the rational contextual toolboxes and basis for science, technology, and knowledge production (pp. 55–72). Thus, she argues for a multicultural view of science and technology by exploring the role of and contributions of different traditions to the global corpus of scientific knowledge and technology.

The process of 'modernization' in Africa must involve a critical examination and gradual blending of the reasonable elements of modernity and tradition that are relevant and applicable to the African situation. Many have suggested that besides adopting the intellectual virtues and methods of science, the most significant aspect modernization in Africa should involve the adoption of liberal democratic and legal principles that define the relationship between the individual and the community. According to Taiwo,

> Various components make up the modern way of life. They include … 'the principle of subjectivity'; a social ontology that represents the relation between the individual and the community and is manifested in the peculiar bifurcation between the state and civil society; …; a social epistemology in which reason plays a central role and knowledge is founded not on revelation, tradition, or authority but on conformity with reason; and … the near-religious attachment to the idea of progress. These conjointly make up the subject matter of the philosophical discourse of modernity.
>
> *(2010, pp. 15–16)*

The call for Africa to modernize is a call to articulate and adopt rational, political, legal, and social structures of modernity as the fundaments of their ways of life.

For Taiwo (2010, 2014), the intellectual virtues and epistemic principles associated with modernity cannot be acquired and used effectively for practical needs if Africa lacks legal, social, economic, and political conditions. In his view, modernization involves the acceptance of the supremacy of reason, rule of law, individualism, and liberal democratic principles as the social and political bases for organizing people's lives in Africa. The argument is that these liberal democratic principles are better in creating the proper environment for individuals to think freely, innovatively, engage in the rational and critical inquiry that conduces the adoption of science and technology. These liberal democratic principles emphasize individual autonomy, rights, and consent of the governed, and they prioritize the individual over the community. These principles justify the modern political, economic, and social conditions of individual liberty to freely make one's own rational choices and to pursue a conception of the good and life plans.

The liberal democratic principles of moral autonomy and individualism provide the basis for the capitalist and *laissez faire* economic elements of modernity, in terms of individuals' ability to freely create and accumulate wealth for individuals' own economic prosperity. It is with respect to this modern liberal idea of the sanctity of the individual, free choice, and property that advocates of modernity are opposed to the African communal tradition. The issue is whether this idea of individualism can (co-)exist within communalism, by maintaining a balance between them. Some argue that modernization in Africa must embrace individualism and abandon communalism. However, the adoption of individualism cannot be abrupt; it must be a gradual process that involves a rational effort to balance the positive features of individualism and communalism, and, getting rid of the negative features of each. But some have argued that the adoption of the principles of liberalism as a form of governance should be founded on African communal social, moral, and political traditions, so that the requisite modern principles of governance in Africa can be fully engrafted into them.

Thus, Taiwo (2014) among others have criticized African communal tradition because it fails to give priority to individual rights, dignity, freedoms, values, and ability to make their own choices regarding their own life. Taiwo's idea of modernity implies that Africa should not emphasize communalism, relationality, and solidarity, as the basis or form of social ordering, whereby

> the group or community is prior and superior to the individual and that the individual should always or in most cases be subordinate to and, from time to time, have her will bent to the interest and welfare of the community.
>
> *(Taiwo, p. 55)*

According to Taiwo (2014), the

> modern individual is a free being whose nature is typified by freedom. He is free to be whatever he wishes to be as long as he does not in the process impair the ability of others to similarly display or exercise their freedom.
>
> *(p. 45)*

The emphasis of modernity in Taiwo's (2014) view is on one's own individuality—the sovereignty of individual autonomy—and the respect for the individuality of others, "for their sheer membership of the human species [which] is what marks the modern age" (p. 46). He argues that the respect for individuality which is negotiated within the social ordering of the state or community is usually exemplified in the idea and practice of the rule of law and the primacy of human rights.

Taiwo's (2010) criticism of African communal tradition and the veneration of the individuality of modernity suggest that one's sense of individuality is inconsistent with the idea of community. However, Gyekye (1997, pp. 36–70) argues that African communal tradition is not inconsistent with modern individualism. He argues in favor of a moderate view of communitarianism that seeks to synthesize or balance the modern principles of individualism and African traditional principles of communalism. It recognizes the interests of individuals and the community, but requires a negotiation between the individual and community, by seeking to balance their interests. The communal tradition does not necessarily assume that the community has priority over the individual or vice versa. It indicates that an individual's dignity derives from, and individual's choices are made meaningful and circumscribed by, the community.

What Gyekye (1997) has characterized as radical communitarianism is criticized as specifying a communal conception of the good that is imposed on individuals, who are not at liberty to decide whether to choose such a conception. Thus, communalism is criticized as overemphasizing common interests, common ownership, the values of caring and mutuality, and the responsibilities to the community as a group, to the detriment of individual autonomy and freedom. This criticism of communalism, which assumes the liberal attitude of individualism, argues that the community vitiates one's individuality, rights, and autonomy; thus, it is authoritarian. The question about the inherent goodness of individual autonomy, which is raised by the plausibility and merits of communal relationality in the idea of 'relational autonomy', is ignored when it is used to criticize African communal tradition (Ikuenobe, 2015).

This criticism begs the question about the inherent value of the rugged individualism of modernity and absolute autonomy. It assumes without question that individualism, autonomy, and freedom are intrinsically good, such that individuals' autonomy and freedom must have moral priority over, and may not be circumscribed by, the community. Although Wiredu (1980) uses this modern liberal perspective to criticize the authoritarian nature of communalism in African tradition, he also observes that the criticism, "That our traditional culture was authoritarian is a distinctly modern comment" (p. 4). The suggestion is that this modern criticism assumes illicitly the intrinsic goodness of the modern liberal principles of individualism and autonomy. This suggests that Taiwo's view of the goodness of individualism as a feature of modernity that Africa must adopt is problematic because as many have suggested, Africa can adopt a form of communalism that gives credence to the individual.

The uncritical adoption of modernity has been criticized because modern individualism and liberalism have engendered extreme license, permissiveness, selfishness, and extreme capitalism. These have engendered a number of negative moral and social effects, such as greed, exploitation, moral indifference, and a lack of caring, consideration, and sympathy for others, as well as some of the social pathologies that correlate with the pervasive incidences of extreme deviant, criminal, and violent behaviors. These facts remind me of a profound statement made by a friend many years ago when she came newly to the United States. Based on the pervasiveness of moral decadence, violence, selfishness, indifference, lack of caring, and social pathologies she observed in old people's homes, the various places she worked, and her various interactions and experiences in many aspects of life, she said, "If what I see here is modernity or modernization, then I don't want Africa to be modernized". The implication is that Africa should maintain many of the moral and social communal aspects of its cultural traditions.

African Communal Tradition and Modernity

One may criticize her statement by saying that the problem is not modernization *per se*, but the manner of modernization and the peculiar exemplification of modernity in the United States. One might also argue that the peculiar moral and social pathologies we find in the United States do not exist in some modernized European and Scandinavian countries, because they have social welfare services and adopt principles that reflect traditional African communal and humanistic values of general welfare and caring. This is precisely the point of the statement or criticism! The implication is that the issue is not whether Africans should modernize, but how precisely they modernize. This will depend on the values and principles of modernization they adopt and internalize, and how they apply them in their behaviors and their social and political structures. Africa must modernize by blending those features of modern individualism and traditional communalism that focus on social welfare and emphasize human caring and solidarity.

We also cannot ignore the calamitous consequences of science and technology on the environment, air pollution, contamination of food, and the chronic and debilitating illnesses they have caused. Scientific methods and processes are extremely individualistic, competitive, uncaring, adversarial, and alienating; and they usually engender unproductive conflicts. Sometimes, scientific methods and processes encourage knowledge or discovery for its sake without consideration for its humanistic and moral effects or implications. The negative aspects of modernity, specifically, individualism and science, indicate that Africans must be circumspect in their approach to modernization, in terms of how and what to modernize. This kind of circumspection is not the approach advocated by many who criticize traditions and insist that Africa must modernize wholesale. They emphasize only the negative features of tradition but fail to highlight and balance them with the positive features.

Similarly, these critics highlight only the positive features of modernity and rarely highlight its negative features. Usually, they would rave about the virtues of individualism, rule of law, liberal democracy, capitalism, science, and technology, but ignore their negatives. When they do this, no one tells them that they are romanticizing European modernity. But whenever one talks about the positive features of African tradition in terms of its communal values, critics are quick to say that one is romanticizing Africa's past or tradition. Why is there asymmetry in the characterizations of, and differential attitudes toward, Western modernity and African tradition? This asymmetry involves seeing only the good in modernity but not the bad and, seeing only the bad in tradition but not the good. The failure to see the negatives in modernity and the positives in tradition is an error that Africans must be aware of in order to avoid it in their concerted rational efforts to modernize.

The project of political and economic modernization in Africa must be a balancing act. It involves creating social, economic, and political principles and structures that balance the need to rely on others, with the need for individual independence and interests. Such structures must rely on and be informed by traditional communal values and principles. This must require a critical evaluation of modernity and traditions in order to harness their good and avoid their bad. Many of the elements of modernity we find in Africa today are their negative features or the bastardization of the positives, such as some pervasive moral and social pathologies that did not exist in African communal traditions. As Bodunrin (1984) argued, "No doubt many things are worth preserving in our traditional culture—especially in the moral sphere—but we stand in danger of losing these if we do not take pains to separate these from those aspects that are undesirable" (p. 20). These valuable moral aspects of tradition must be retained in order for political and economic modernization to be meaningful for Africans.

As Wiredu (1996) observes, the necessary moral foundation for the success of democracy such as "those finely designed parliamentary palliatives, which in the United States or the United Kingdom, for instance, do mollify the opposition to some extent are in Africa often nonexistent, or equivalently, existent only on paper" (p. 177). This is because "the European organizational pieces that came to us were virtually disembodied of their moral contents, of their substratum of implicating ethics. And yet the imported models were never engrafted onto any existing indigenous morality" (Ekeh, 1983, p. 17). This underscores why the democratizing process of modernization must rely on the communal moral traditions and values of caring, humility, fraternity, solidarity, mutuality, and social structures, which could provide social welfare services and palliatives that would engender harmony in society. These traditional communal values can limit and ameliorate the vices of rugged self-centered individualism, the exploitative capitalism of modernity, and allow for individual freedom of rational critical thinking, choices, creative enterprises, and the entrepreneurial spirit. We can appreciate these communal values because, as Sogolo (2014) argues, one important element and consequence of modernization in Africa must be social harmony and a form of individual and social discipline.

Sogolo (2014) indicates that the value communalism, which includes solidarity, caring, and general welfare, had stabilizing effects in traditional African society, by engendering social harmony and discipline, and that those values have something to offer in today's society (pp. 85–94). In communal societies, an individual is seen as a social and corporate being whose life is inseparable from his community and ways of life that have positive social welfare values that are conducive to peace and harmony. Some have criticized such communal values as implying uncritical attitude and compliance with African traditional ideas, practices, and beliefs. In response to this criticism, Sogolo (2014) indicates,

> It could be that man's uncritical attitude to traditional institutions, his willingness to accept them and the ease with which he internalises conventional norms, are society's techniques for survival. It is for this reason that some philosophers attribute rationality to social institutions.
>
> *(p. 88)*

African communalism has a rational foundation that indicates that social institutions and traditions do have 'wisdom' that is better than, could rationally override, or balanced against individualistic experiences, thinking, and rational judgments.

One might understand the above comment regarding the *accepting attitude* as a willingness to rationally compromise or achieve consensus per Wiredu (1996). This attitude cannot be understood as uncritical group compliance that negates individual rational thinking. Such attitude is usually viewed by critics of African tradition as a dogmatic, irrational, and uncritical attitude that is identified as a negative feature of communalism. This *acceptance attitude* is not uncritical! It involves a form of rational acceptance of "wisdom embodied in traditions" (Partridge, Benn and Mortimore, p. 365). Such wisdom that underlies the "willing attitude of acceptance" is, in Wiredu's (1996) view, usually what engenders consensus, solidarity, and social harmony. The pertinent issue then is, how can Africa modernize by relying on the wisdom of traditions, transforming and adapting them to contemporary situations? Sogolo (1993, p. 41) argues for what might be called a 'transformational blending' of some traditional elements and 'wisdom' of African cultures into the modern. Similar to Ekeh's (1983) view of transformed social structures, he indicates that in some parts of Africa, "traditional, social and political institutions have given birth to new forms" (Sogolo, 1993, p. 42).

It is reasonable to argue that these new forms of social and political structures arose from critical examination and the rational process of modernization and modification of traditional structures. However, critics have argued that it is a waste of time and effort to try to recapture or reconstruct African communal tradition as a basis for modernization. In their view, not only is that tradition dogmatic, retrogressive, irrational, and significantly lacking in value, but there is also a practical problem in trying to reconstruct it because it is a *past* that is far too removed in time. Such tradition has been lost historically and it no longer exists in a meaningful form that can be reconstructed, because it has either been completely destroyed or irretrievably corrupted by colonialism. The alternative view by those who argue for modernization in terms of a transformational blending of tradition indicates that such reconstruction can be done because the traditional values and social and political structures, such as communalism and traditional rulership, still exist and are pervasive in people's lives.

As Sogolo (1993) argues,

> some of the social and political ideals, freedom, democracy, equality, justice, etc., which we seek to attain [in Africa today in the name of modernization] are intrinsically part of our traditional African social structures and that what we need are suitable institutions for realizing these virtues.
>
> *(p. 192)*

As such, some political theorists have sought to articulate modern viable social and political ideas and structures that rely on African traditions. Usually, these theories "start from the base that traditional African societies are structurally communalistic", with "the hope of formulating a new social and political formula that reflects the uniqueness of African society" (Sogolo, 1993, p. 193). Such efforts led Kwame Nkrumah (1970), Julius Nyerere (1968), and Leopold Senghor (1964) to argue for, and then, sought to adopt socialism in post-colonial states. They argued that socialism was a way to borrow from and transform African communal traditions, which have the egalitarian, redistributive, and social welfare values, principles, and practices that mirror socialism.

Although these leaders tried to use the idea of socialism to capture African social, political, and economic traditions based on the communal values of solidarity, general welfare, caring, and mutuality, they did not craft the proper political structures and institutions to effectuate these values. As such, their efforts were unsuccessful, and the adapted system of socialism did not take hold. In some African states, such efforts exploited and misappropriated the idea of communal solidarity to create one-party systems that manifested features of dictatorship where leaders held on to power and abused their authority to infringe on individual rights, liberties, and perpetuate corruption. However, it is unclear whether the failure of these efforts was because of the shortcomings of communalism or socialism, or the manner in which they were adopted, in that they were not sufficiently engrafted into the communal traditions.

Sogolo (1993, pp. 193–198) suggests that the problem with these efforts was the manner in which African communal traditional ideas, values, and structures were adapted to modern post-colonial situation. To underscore the idea that the democratization efforts of modernization in Africa should not abandon tradition, Wiredu (1996), Ramose (1999), and Ake (1996), suggest that African traditions had elements of democratic structures, values, norms, and practices that may be adequately harnessed and properly modified. However, critics who argue that modernization requires a clean break with tradition indicate that African social and political traditions were based on kinship, theocracy, and authoritarianism; and they deny that such traditions were democratic (Eze, 1997; Otubanjo, 1989). They argue that the kind of democratic governance required for modernization in Africa cannot be built on these traditional theocratic, tyrannical, authoritarian and kinship systems.

Sogolo (1991) described as 'fruitless' the debate regarding whether the traditional African social and political systems were authoritarian or democratic. He insists that there are positive features of tradition that Africa can draw from in its efforts to modernize and democratize. He added that, "My impression, however, is that the past of African politics was far more decent than what exists today" (1991, pp. 55–59). This raises the question of whether African traditions that are said to be in the 'past' are really in the 'past'. Are they so irretrievably removed from the present, or is the 'past' (tradition) coexisting and blending with the 'present' (modern)? As Sogolo (1993) argues, the reality of the post-colonial situation is such that "the African blends the traditional with the modern" (p. 41). In his view, all cultures are eclectic, in that "every thought system contains [elements of] both the traditional and the modern" (p. 41). Every culture has elements of 'tradition' because they have a long history, have been preserved over time, and passed down over generations, as well as elements of 'modern', in that some of these traditional beliefs have been critically examined, tested, modified, and adapted to current situations.

Wiredu (1996) has argued that 'tradition' and 'modernity' do coexist in Africa because many people still hold and exhibit traditional African values, ethos, and sensitivities, including the communal values of consensus, solidarity, and common good, and other-regarding attitude of caring. Ekeh (1983) also argued that there is something good about African traditional 'past', which, he suggests, currently coexists with the 'present'. For instance, in his distinction between the 'civic public' and 'primordial public', the former represents elements of 'modernity', while the latter represents elements of tradition. Communal moral norms and values have significance and applicability in the primordial public of tradition, but they are absent or insignificant in the civic public of modernity. These communal norms contributed to social harmony in African communities. For instance, relevant interactions in the 'civic public' of government institutions usually manifest the modern features of individualism, liberal democracy, the rule of law, and the values of individual rights, autonomy, and liberty, while the 'primordial public' manifests the traditional features or norms of communalism and the values of duty, caring, familial, ethnic, cultural ties, common good, general welfare, and consensus.

Wiredu (1996), Gyekye (1997), Bujo (1997), Wingo, (2006), and Romose (1999) have argued that the traditional African values and ways of allocating political power and authority, which one might argue, still exist in the primordial public, may lend themselves to non-party and consensual systems of democracy. These systems could avoid the usual conflict between or among political parties; instead, it could engender consensus among people after due deliberation. As Sogolo (2014, p. 88) suggests, traditional communal ethos and attitudes had stabilizing effects, and in Wiredu's (1996) view, they provided a way of resolving conflicts and pruning down divergent interests for the sake of common good and harmony (pp. 173, 177). This is because people will be motivated by the goal of achieving and promoting the values of common good, general welfare, togetherness, solidarity, and harmonious communal relationships, which make individual life, freedom, and wellbeing possible. The values of freedom and wellbeing are exemplified at the communal level where individuals have harmonious communal and caring relationships with others, which provide the basis for political decisions and governance at the state level. Some African philosophers such as Ani (2014); Eze (2008), and Matolino (2012) are skeptical. They have raised questions about the nature that such consensus would take in Africa's practice of liberal democracy and how realistic such consensus would be in multi-ethnic states with conflicting interests.

Conclusion

The non-integration of modern and traditional structures and values have created serious social and political problems in Africa. A plausible explanation is an assumption that modernity is inherently good, and tradition is inherently bad. Therefore, modernization must involve a complete break with tradition because tradition lacks any value that modernity can draw from. Some have argued that some communal moral and social elements and attitudes of African tradition are demonstrably valuable; they still exist and hold strong sway among people today. And these positive features can be relied on as the moral anchor for modernization in Africa.

References

Ake, Claude, *Development and Democracy in Africa*. Washington, DC: Brookings Institution, 1996.

Ani, Emmanuel, 'On Traditional Consensus Rationality'. *Journal of Political Philosophy*, vol. 22, 2014, pp. 342–365.

Appiah, Kwame Anthony, *In My Father's House: Africa in the Philosophy of Culture*. New York: Oxford University Press, 1992.

Bodunrin, P. O., 'The Question of African Philosophy'. In Richard A. Wright, Ed. 1984. *African Philosophy: An Introduction*. New York: University Press of America, 1980, pp. 1–23.

Bujo, Benezet, *The Ethical Dimension of Community: The African Model and the Dialogue between North and South*. Cecilia Namulando Nganda (trans.) Nairobi: Paulines Publications Africa, 1997.

Boxill, Bernard, 'Majoritarian Democracy and Cultural Minorities'. In Arthur M. Melzer, Jerry Weinberger, and M. Richard Zinman, Eds. *Multiculturalism and American Democracy*. Lawrence: Kansas University Press, 1998, pp. 107–119.

Ekeh, Peter P., *Colonialism and Social Structure. An Inaugural Lecture*. Ibadan: University of Ibadan Press, 1983.

Eze, Emmanuel, 'Democracy or Consensus? Response to Wiredu'. In *Postcolonial African Philosophy: A Critical Reader*, Emmanuel Eze, Ed. Oxford: Blackwell, 1997, pp. 313–323.

Gyekye, Kwame, *Tradition and Modernity: Philosophical Reflections on the African Experience*. New York: Oxford University Press, 1997.

Harding, Sandra, *Is Science Multi-Cultural?* Bloomington: Indiana University Press, 1998.

Hountondji, Paulin, *African Philosophy: Myth and Reality*. Bloomington: Indiana University Press, 1983.

Ikuenobe, Polycarp, 'Relational Autonomy, Personhood, and African Traditions'. *Philosophy East & West*, vol. 65, no. 4, 2015, pp. 1005–1029.

Matolino, Bernard, 'Democracy, Consensus, and Africa'. *Philosophia Africana*, vol. 14, 2012, pp. 105–124.

Nkrumah, Kwame, *Consciencism: Philosophy and Ideology for De-Colonization*, Rev. Ed. New York: Monthly Review, 1970.

Nyerere, Julius, *Ujamaa: Essays on Socialism*. New York: Oxford University Press, 1968.

Oruka, Odera, 'African Philosophy'. In Guttorm Floisted, Ed. *Contemporary Philosophy: A New Survey, Vol. 5: African Philosophy*. Dordrecht: Martinus Nijhorff, 1987, pp. 47–65.

Otubanjo, Femi, 'Themes in African Traditional Political Thought'. In J. A. A. Ayoade and A. B. Agbaje, Eds. *African Traditional Political Thought and Institutions*. Lagos: Center for Black and African Arts and Civilization, 1989, pp. 1–14.

Partridge, P. H., S. I. Benn, and G. W. Mortimore, 'The Rationality of Societies'. In Benn and Mortimore Eds., *Rationality and the Social Sciences*. London: Routledge and Kegan Paul, 1976, pp. 353–375.

Ramose, Mogobe, *African Philosophy through Ubuntu*. Harare: Mond Books, 1999.

Russell, Bertrand, *A History of Western Philosophy*. New York: Simon and Schuster, 1945.

Senghor, Leopold Sedar, *On African Socialism*. Trans. Mercer Cook. London: Pall Mall, 1964.

Sogolo, Godwin, 'The Futures of Democracy & Participation in Everyday Life: The African Experience'. In B. Van Steenber77/gen, R. Nakarada, F. Marti, and J. Dator, Eds. *Advancing Democracy and Participation Challenges For the Future*. Barcelona: Centre UNESCO De Catalunya, 1991, pp. 55–59.

Sogolo, Godwin, *Foundations of African Philosophy*. Ibadan: University of Ibadan Press, 1993.

Sogolo, Godwin, 'Ethical and Socio-Cultural Foundations of National Security'. *African Journal for Security and Development*, vol. 1, no. 1, 2014, pp. 85–94.

Taiwo, Olufemi, *How Colonialism Preempted Modernity in Africa*. Bloomington: Indiana University Press, 2010.

Taiwo, Olufemi, *Africa Must be Modern: A Manifesto*. Bloomington: Indiana University Press, 2014.

Wingo, Ajume, 'Joy in Living Together'. *Journal of Political Philosophy*, vol. 14, 2006, pp. 186–202.

Wiredu, Kwasi, *Philosophy and an African Culture*. London: Cambridge University Press, 1980.

Wiredu, Kwasi, *Cultural Universals and Particulars: An African Perspective*. Bloomington: Indiana University Press, 1996.

7

PRAGMATIC HISTORY IN A POST-GENOCIDE SOCIETY

Isaïe Nzeyimana

Introduction

If one was to ask the question, "what is the function or purpose of history?" The most likely response would be: to gain knowledge of the past. How to know the past in the disconcerting diversity of its object? To its temporal extent, since the mind of the historian must go to coincide with the origins, is added the thematic complexity, methods of causal explanation and interpretation or donation of a meaning, or projections as to the use of the results. Théophile Obenga overburdens historians and thinks they should also use the results of other sciences; they should proceed by the overall integration of methods, the crossing of cross-sources, the ordering of these elements, and the search for the overall movement of all these elements.[1]

Since in terms of knowledge what is required is objectivity, understood as the correspondence of historical thought with the object, total object, by instinct, we realise that such objectivity is discouraging. Practitioners, on their part, see two great defects in history: that of disinterested truths and the lack of useful formulas. We will then want to rewrite history to bring it into line with political choices. If each political regime wrote its own history, there is a risk that it might condemn its people for the lack of awareness of history because too many versions of history create a lack of consistency and clarity about the past. Also, since all politics is a reasoned choice, how do we deal with historical truths that hinder or are incompatible with political choices? How to hold together contradictory individual or collective memories that are nevertheless true for those who hold on to them? Rwanda sought to overcome these contradictions by erecting, outside the usual academic spaces, new schools of history teaching. In this case, Rwanda is not the only model. According to Dominique Maingueneau,

> History is an essential component of the collective memory of a people or a nation. It serves as a point of reference, a common base on which the identity of a social group is built. It is therefore obvious that it is an important political issue. Political mastery of the past is a way of giving the people a constructed corpus of reference that can be used as a point of reference or an object of rejection. Numerous studies bearing, in particular, on the vision of history transmitted by school textbooks, show this misuse of the past for political purposes.[2]

DOI: 10.4324/9781003143529-8

We take as provisional the history of immediate consumption, taught to resolve questions of extreme urgency, leaving openings to the definitive academic history touching on questions deemed immediately disinterested but which carry the memory of humanity.

History and Pragmatism

A conscientious reader of history does not take long to realise that history is a political and ideological enterprise and that it is designed for a specific purpose or to attain specific objectives. It is along these lines of pragmatism that the history of Rwanda is written in distinct moments, each moment emphasising one purpose over another. Thus, (1) the oral history of the people of the Royal Court is produced for the purpose of the dynasties, the spirit of the people and the national memory; (2) the colonial history is written with the aim of occupation and introduction of external models of government; (3) the history of the two 1st Republics is written with the purpose of revolution and independence; (4) the post-genocide history is written out of the purpose of remembering the genocide and the liberation of July 1994. To read each of these moments, in a sincere way, it will be necessary to place oneself on the side of each of these objectives. On that question, Spinoza writes the following:

> To engage in a reasoned reading of the existing works on a given subject would be supposed to particularise the life and mores of the author of each book, the goal he proposed, who he was, on what occasion, in what time, for whom, in what language finally it was written, but also "into what hands it fell, why men decided to admit it into the canon, how the books recognised as canonical were brought together in a body.[3]

Basically, the antecedent historiography commits a serious error and nothing is more humiliating than to be reduced to its exterior, like the question or even the suspicion of wanting to consider mankind according to race, ethnicity, colour of their skin, the length of their limbs. Yet it is our troubled story, like that of Oedipus, the accursed king driven from his kingdom and who wandered blind. On such occasions, like cursed Oedipus, I remain speechless, also disturbed by the presence of the one who thinks of me thus, more forbidden than a child.[4]

For new generations, this model is changing. The method does not consist of a decree that will erase the categories of colonial historiography, but of changing the historical project. It is by changing the project that we also manage to change the direction of historical research. Make no mistake about it, the elementary laws of criticism allow us to abandon a model of thinking and to imagine new directions of research, according to the practices of organised scepticism, methodical doubt and falsifiability.

Thus, the abandonment is total. As Fourez would say, when you abandon a hypothesis, you never abandon an isolated proposition, but a whole direction of research or interpretation. The abandonment of one model and the acceptance of another is not done according to the logic of pure rationality; it can follow our daily existence, often not reducible to a clear rationality. Again, Fourez Gérard specifies that we do not abandon a scientific model for purely scientific reasons.[5]

The paradigm shift in the history of Rwanda appears as a requirement for the destiny of the Rwandan people, but also as an intellectual requirement because intelligence only finds its true role if it is also pragmatic, because to think is to resolve problems. If Buakasa Tulukia Mpansu[6] emphasises that the model of thinking must be able to explain, suggest useful interventions, and allow them to be anticipated, from this point of view of pragmatics, the history of Rwanda is true insofar as it allows programmes to be carried out of effective reconciliation. In this sense, history is elevated to the status of a political instrument and because all politics is also a pedagogy, the new spaces for teaching history make reasoned choices, such as: (1) the choice of educationalists, (2) the bracketing of certain questions; (3) the overcoming of a historiography of controversies and insistence on the fundamentals of a national history, one and indivisible, (4) the pedagogy of contradictory memories; (5) the choice and worship to be rendered to historical figures.

Bracketing Certain Questions

Schools and universities are famous for their ability to promote intellectual curiosity and to stir up disinterested truths. In addition to these "flaws", the leaders of the paradigm shift do not know if they have all completely made the necessary breaks with the habits and historical corpora designed for colonial and republican projects. In these doubts, which we must above all not risk, we must supplement the usual official frameworks for the teaching of history with ancient spaces such as "Ingando", "Itorero" and other occasions of a meeting or gathering of more than one person.

To guarantee the effectiveness of the history tool, the new educational spaces favour educationalists trained in the history of an inclusive nation, and who are equipped with simple formulas that allow the choice of facts undoubtedly in accordance with the new Revolution.

To voluntarily forget a certain category of questions, especially those which are unresolved, or point to an undesirable resolution, can be the only way to protect the person who, in a rotating way, is a victim of the use of wrong judgements. Failing to consider everything, the selection of historical facts and their interpretation is motivated by the Renaissance of ancient Rwanda, source of ideas, values and practices that can inspire the management of contemporary Rwanda.

The new model has this disposition of extreme sensitivity: to abandon the facts likely to have interpretations of separation, to insist instead on the traces of a common history, eliminating a series of questions that are no longer considered relevant or those perceived as capable of causing disharmony.

Going Beyond a Historiography of Controversies

It is often said that the history of Rwanda is divided. Disagreements revolve around the meanings of sites, dates, events and historical figures, some of which are honoured and acknowledged and others which are forgotten and excluded. It is true that, as individuals, the historical figures of the Monarchy and the Republics have passed, some gently, others in disaster. However, in their passage, they left behind a substantial, incorruptible and indivisible reality; beyond all reproaches, they built a *Nation, a national conscience, a State, a People and a Sovereignty.* It is now these universals that make it possible to collect all historical "ethnic" and "regional" affiliations. These affiliations, by constantly referring to each other, extend into the perpetual continuum of a Rwandan Nation.

Pedagogy of Contradictory Memories

Rwandan society is still fragile, with individual memories, sometimes in contradiction, yet all true. The question that arises then is whether contradictory memories can all be true. Wouldn't that be an oxymoron? It is however, a possibility. It imposes a very singular pedagogical attitude of going to meet the other in their individual memory. Apart from the great occasions of commemoration or celebration of the National and official Memory where the discourse must go in the same direction, where the whole Nation is looking in the same direction, in other circumstances, it is important for an educationalist to have good choices of examples, always dialectical, which take into account opposing memories, *a priori*, because it will be malicious to ask if there are those in the classroom who carry them. For example: the memory of an orphan or a widow of the genocide and that of an orphan and a widow of the atrocities of the war, although the times and the circumstances are different, they both experience the same feelings. The memory of an exile from the First Republic and that of another from the October 1990–1994 war, although the times and circumstances are different, they both experience the same feelings of emptiness or loss. It is in this way that Rwandans are and must come together around a problem, each one finding the account of his/her memory and feeling listened to by the others.

Between the two contradictory memories, it is impossible for the teacher to remain neutral or indifferent: he also has his own memory or recollection of history which may fall into the version of the past held by one or more groups among his audience. It is important for this teacher to understand history as something dynamic in which different people hold different accounts of, and to cover different sides of this history by considering each one according to their time, their age, their environment, and their sensitivities. In this sense, the space of history teaching can be considered a site of empathy. As such, the individual who occupies this space must muster the courage of not only showing empathy, but should also commit themselves to listening, understanding and feeling – with individual memories, collective memories, national memory and official memory.

The challenge is daunting, that is, the need to listen to all individuals and acknowledge collective memories, and find ways to link them.

Like most things that concern the human condition, the history of Rwanda is opposed to binary logic, and rather receptive to dialectical logic, as this holds the contradictions together. The pedagogical victory will always be on the side of the one who borrows Pascalian reason according to this formula: "the heart has its reasons that the reason does not know". The reasons of the heart are what make it possible to read, through the silence, the faces of a people, sometimes innocent, sometimes guilty or cluttered by memory. In the absence of such attention, is there any pedagogue who has not yet read, through silence, the signs of approval or disagreement?

Pedagogy According to Ages

On the one hand, can adults conversant with the history of the dynasties, colonial or republican, quickly learn the new paradigms, which necessitates breaking with their memories? For them, suddenly adopting a new way of reading history requires what Gaston Bachelard calls "an epistemological break" which is a labour of patience.

On the other hand, should the new generations, still innocent, be informed of the shame of their history? For them, pedagogy is confronted between two options of equal force: (a) informing young people of their history at the risk of importing into their imaginations the problems they do not yet have; (b) silence the horrible, terrifying, and shameful questions in their story, with the risk that they will learn them from other sources. To these confidant sources, they will however not fail to pay attention and take this information as discoveries.

Survivors, widows and widowers, genocide sites, prisoners of genocide crimes, refugees of genocide crimes on the run or taken hostage by the genocidaires on the run, etc., all these situations will require explanations. It is impossible to be silent or to run away from the question, because young people, especially children, ask their questions directly, such as "why this or that?" In logic, there is a fallacy called "*ignorance of the question*". It occurs when what is demonstrated is not what was requested. In effect, we pretend to prove something but we voluntarily or involuntarily go off-topic. It is often used to answer or rather escape awkward questions, which, honestly, required silence and discretion. However, sometimes the silence in front of an attentive and an overly curious interlocutor is not always possible.

Historical Figures

In addition to the spaces of *Ingando* and *Itorero*, Works of Public Interest, Genocide Commemoration, Heroes' Day, and Liberation Day serve the same purpose of teaching history. Each of these celebrations takes up a whole week, day and night, in preparation for the great day of the celebration; it highlights the heroism of Rwandan historical figures.

It is the essence of philosophy to admire great figures and great cultures. One of the most prominent in this genre was Auguste Comte who would devote a religion, a worship and a high mass to them at the Cathedral of Paris; and the other is Hegel, who admires great men even in their troubled times of history. His admiration is mainly for Alexander the Great and Napoleon:

> I saw the Emperor, this soul of the world, leaving the city to go on a reconnaissance. It is indeed a marvellous impression, he exclaims, to see such an individual who, concerned here on one point, mounted on a horse, extends over the world and dominates it, etc. Such progress has never been possible only thanks to this extraordinary man, whom it is impossible not to admire.[7]

On which ground are they great? In his book, *Reason in History*, Hegel recognises historical figures under the following traits: (a) they are heroes because they were able to break with static societies and common morality; (b) they draw their actions from the will of the universal genius; (c) they are idealists; (d) they have an intuition of duration and continuity, never of discontinuity; (e) they are the ones who perceive the next race very early; (f) they are the best possible; (g) they are soul conductors; (h) they are passionate and have great interests; (j) they need a particular morality; (k) they create peoples.

They are idealistic and communicate immediately with "creative intuition", according to Bergson's words. Their greatness is measured by their degree of idealism. As idealists, they place the ideal at such a high level that the man concerned with immediacy finds them visionary. They are simple and ordinary like the idea or the universal, modest, humble, frank and sincere because the universal they seek to accomplish, they have drawn it from themselves, without having invented it; they only awakened what was hidden deep within their people; they understood the fundamental aspiration of their people and made it their ideal.

Great men are creators of their peoples, but paradoxically, historical men are also created by their peoples and arise or emerge from them.

We recognise great men by their speeches and actions, always elevated to what is universal, constantly distinguishing the cyclical from the essential, devoting their energies to this essential, leaving the cyclical to their technical administrators.

An intellectual trait dominates among historical figures: whereas the common man is preoccupied with the triviality of worldly life – petty possessions, honours, vainglory – the historical man is driven only by the ideal. Momentary uprooting of man from his immediacy, which also pulls him from the finitude that every man carries within himself and immerses him in the infinite, according to Pascal's expression of the "infinitely small and infinitely large".

Great historical men or figures have great passions and great interests. In *Reason in History*, Hegel makes the following statement:

> The first image that history offers us is that of human actions as they derive from needs, passions, interests, from the idea men have of them, from the goals they set for themselves, from their character and qualities. So much so that, in this spectacle of activity, it is these needs, these passions, these interests, etc. which appear as the only motives.[8]

Hegel makes the point that nothing great has been accomplished in the world without passion. We therefore say that nothing was done without being supported by the interest of those who collaborated in it. We call this interest passion when, repressing all other interests or goals, the individual projects itself onto an objective with all the inner fibres of its will and concentrates its forces and all its needs in this goal. In this sense, we must say that nothing great has been accomplished in the world without passion.[9]

Yet, by pursuing selfish interests and acting through the passions, reason tricks the particular and selfishness: by striving for itself, the individual satisfies common needs at the same time. This is the case of a leader who struggles to become a president, a scientist who spends his life in laboratories, a merchant who makes import–export transactions, a bourgeois who builds large buildings, an artist who creates large works, etc. Essentially, all those people we meet in life act directly for their interests, but they serve the universal.

Is it not paradoxical that a history as troubled as that of Rwanda can have heroes? This is because optimism does not make it possible to reduce historical figures to the contingency of negative moments alone. Optimism is also realism because no one doubts that beyond the powers of family and birth (*Akazu* of *Ubuhake*), institutionalised clientism, regionalism and ethnic balance, historical figures have left a substance: Rwanda as a Nation, a State, a Sovereignty and a People.

From what intuition these historical figures decided to carry out conquests of enlargement and unification of Rwanda and to devote their energies and their sacrifices to it, alternating peace and wars? From what intuition did these historical men create the spirit of the universalisable Rwandan people without having travelled and learned from contacts with other civilisations? Such men are great because they have drawn their actions from the will of the universal genius. No need to find models for them: they have no models; if they had role models, they would only be second-class great. They are their models and creator of the models that the others, the most talented, will follow.

If all the politics know how to honour the great figures with celebrations it is because history is a real component of the politics, and tribute paid to the heroes could be a school of history, especially of the history of the dominant ideology, as a kind of materialisation of a political message. Thus, a passage from *History and Politics* by Gisèle Séginger is even more eloquent:

> History is an essential component of the collective memory of a people or a nation. It serves as a point of reference, a common base on which the identity of a social group is built. It is therefore obvious that it is an important political issue. Political mastery of the past is a way of giving to the people a constructed corpus of reference that can be used as a point of reference or an object of rejection. Numerous studies, bearing in particular on the vision of history transmitted by school textbooks, show this misuse of the past for political purposes.[10]

However, the idea that history should be dedicated to the honouring of military and political heroes deserves to be interrogated. Difficulties arise when only political and military heroes occupy the space as if life outside of politics has no right to flourish.

For example, when one consults the *Atlas Historique Illustré* [Historical Atlas], in its pages devoted to the Glossary of 600 characters, or Great names in history, one regrets the same narrowness of horizon limited to the political, military and religious profile. The reason is such that politicians do brilliant actions and it is themselves who come back to organise their own celebrations, forgetting the contributions of others, often ordinary people whose patience, vigilance and ideas contributed to their greatness. In this kind of voluntary forgetfulness, politicians are like athletes. An athlete trains, takes a pole, holds it tightly and jumps. By jumping, at the top, he/she leaves the pole behind, having exhausted its utility.

On the other hand, at the end of the twentieth century, around 31 December 1999, journalists made a review of the great moments which marked the century, with a broadening of the horizons to artists, musicians, painters, poets, writers, sportsmen, philosophers, scientists, etc.

Worship is not a question of means, but of symbol. The Rwandan State, by broadening the horizons, will not lack symbolic honours in favour of men and women who are not on the list of soldiers and politicians, who are on the silent and discreet list of other actors: artists, writers, scientists, industrialists, technicians, bureaucrats, amongst others.

Blaise Pascal distinguishes between two kinds of size: establishment size and natural size. The greatness of establishment depends on the will of men, who have rightly believed in having to honour certain states and attach certain respects to them. Dignities and nobility are of this kind. Natural magnitudes are those which are independent of the imagination of men because they consist in the real and effective qualities of the soul and the body, which render one or the other more estimable, such as science, light of the spirit, virtue, health and strength. Does Rwanda lack these men, still alive, to whom the community recognises the lights of the spirit?

Rwanda Needs Heroes Who are Still Alive

The law, the right and the bureaucracy were created among men to remind them, and to constrain them to act in the direction of what is good and just. But the force of the law alone is not enough to guarantee order. A society is also held together by humans, great in their wisdom, who, in the event of disagreements, say yes or no, true or false, good or bad, permitted or forbidden, with the certainty of being listened to. This is the case of customary chiefs in certain African societies, religious leaders, senior executives in the judiciary in ultra-modern societies who, without the filing of law, command, recommend or prohibit by their ancestry and charisma.

They are great, not only by their position, but also by their greatness of soul, because it is possible for a person to occupy a high political, religious, military, administrative or magisterial position, while not remaining great by this only common status. Only their presence summons obedience because they act according to the virtues of wisdom, intelligence, science, justice, friendship and prudence, considered cardinal.

Rwanda celebrates heroes. The heroes have the function of indicating what is permitted or even encouraged. They have a symbolic, practical and ethical function through their mere presence. However, Rwandan heroes are recognised and celebrated for having been. Dead heroes did not fight alone. It is a mistake to believe in the witnesses of vivid events whenever, for the sake of insistence, they report the heroism of a single man/woman in isolation from the contexts that produced it and from other positive people who fought with him or her, making believe that the hero in honour was exceptional, that he fought alone.

We can, of course, start from the heroes already established, find in their immediate entourage the men/women who fought with the dead heroes and grant them symbols, a kind of "Nobel Prize". Such men/women, fortunately still alive, will serve as a moral authority that tempers recourse to law or brute force, because they are the ethics, the right way, the mores and the living law.

Is it not paradoxical that a history as troubled as that of Rwanda can have heroes? This is because optimism does not make it possible to reduce historical men to the contingency of negative moments alone. Optimism is also realism because no one doubts that beyond the powers of family lineage (Monarchy, *Akazu* of *ubuhake*), institutionalised clientelism, regionalism and ethnic balance, historical men left a substance: Rwanda as a Nation, a State, a People and a Sovereignty.

From what intuition, these men decided to carry out conquests of enlargement and uni-fication of Rwanda and to devote their energies and their sacrifices to it, alternating peace and wars? From what intuition did these historical men create the spirit of the universalisable Rwandan people without having travelled and learned from contacts with other civilisa-tions? Such men are great because they have drawn their actions from the will of the univer-sal genius. No need to find models for them: they have no models; if they had role models, they would only be second class great. They are their models and creator of the models that the others, the most talented, will follow.

The new educational and public spaces of the school of history: *Ingando, Itorero*, and other civic education meetings are used to manage the questions that the same history has imposed on us. But its insistence reminds us that there are two levels of history: the "original" his-tory of witnesses, often indirect to history, surely close to political actors, and the academic history of historians. Speculative academic history enjoys a superiority that it draws from its **reflexive distance** and from the eternal questions of human heritage because it belongs to the whole of theoretical knowledge which presupposes no other ends than itself.

Understanding the Past from the Present

In the past, men lived and acted from day to day without worrying too much about future. It will only be in the present that the understanding of the development that brought about the present will take shape, in retrospect. Is it then true to say that the present state gives meaning, and the meaning to the past? This is because the successes, like the worries of the present, send us back to back to what had happened and which can explain what is happening now, by virtue of the fact that the cause is always prior to the effect.

The past is therefore the night light of the present, awaiting the conditions that will make it hatch and expose it to the light of day. Thus, history is a science of the pilot causes and the conditions of hatching which will cause an event to occur in the now and here and not elsewhere. The example can be drawn from the explosive social events that take place in the world, in a specific place and time. Reflecting on them, all the minds from here and else-where, taken worry, they sigh: Ah, this catastrophe could have fallen on us too!

> Just as neither the sun nor the planets are aware of the laws which regulate the move-ments of one in relation to the other, so the individuals who pursue their particular ends, and even those who play a historical role, are not aware of the end where the story leads them, etc.[11]

Historical science then has this advantage: where other sciences of extreme rationalism dissociate the faculties of knowledge, in historical imagination, memory and reason are reconciled. It is in the enchantment or the anxieties of the present that the imagination reconstitutes, even approximately, what had happened, supplying the reason with the materials for correspondences, connections and causal explanations.

Conclusion

Depending on the moment, certain historical sites and monuments are adorned and erected to the rank of honourable national museums. Sometime later, the same sites are minimised into oblivion, in the guise of rewriting history. Historical figures alternate between heroism and posthumous condemnations. A date celebrated does not know if it will still be celebrated on the following anniversary. Is it essential that historical figures follow one another as antagonists, each totally refusing to find the positive in the other?

The effort of the mind is then to preserve, without struggle, individual memories that are contradictory yet all true. The challenge for historiography will then be to reconcile individual memories, collective memories, and national memory with official memory. The need to build a reading grid is imposed, which is not the refusal of partiality in history, but a donation of meaning to this partiality.

Controversies in history then mean disagreement about projects that have indicated what facts to retain and how to interpret them. The same projects explain, by recurrence, the forgetting of other facts, yet as obvious as those chosen by the user of the story. In this sense, pragmatism is a reading of history through final causality, asking whether the project or the intended end is fair or unfair. Thus, from the question of historical truth, or of epistemology, we move on to that of the ethics of the political objectives that history has come to support and justify.

The new pedagogical spaces for teaching history, such as I*ngando, Itorero,* the Works of General Interest Camps, Heroes' Day, and the Celebration of the memory of the genocide, have the merit of weakening the legitimate use of the terms "ethnic groups" and to remove them from objective content.

Notes

1 Théophile Obenga, "Sources et techniques spécifiques de l'histoire africaine, aperçu général" in Histoire générale de l'Afrique. pp. 98–111.
2 See Les livres d'école de la République (1870–1914): discours et idéologie, Paris, Le Sycomore, 1979, 343 pages, quoted by Gisèle Séginger, http://fr wikipedia/wiki/histoire, note 40.
3 Spinoza Baruch, Œuvres, 1984, pp. 716–717 and 725–726.
4 Henry Bauchau, Œdipe sur la route, Paris, J'ai lu, 2000.
5 Gérard Fourez, La construction des sciences, p.68.
6 Buakasa Tulu Kia Mpansu, « Trois questions sur les modèles en sciences humaines », in problèmes des méthodes en philosophie et sciences humaines, pp. 147–156.
7 Jacques D'Hondt, Hegel, le philosophe du débat et du combat, Paris, Librairie générale française, 1984, p. 57.
8 Hegel, La raison dans l'histoire, p. 102.
9 Hegel, La raison dans l'histoire, pp. 108–109.
10 Dominique Maingueneau, Les livres d'école de la République (1870–1914): discours et idéologie, Paris, Le Sycomore, 1979, 343 pages, quoted by Gisèle Séginger, http://fr wikipedia/wiki/histoire, note 40.
11 Les philosophes par les textes, Classe de Terminal, Paris, Ferdinand Nathan, 1974, p. 207.

References

Baruch, Spinoza, *Œuvres*, Paris, Gallimard, 1984.

Fourez, Gérard, *La construction des sciences*, Bruxelles, De Boeck Université, 1996.

Gadamer, Hans–Georg, *Vérité et méthode : les grandes lignes d'une herméneutique philosophique*, Paris, Seuil, 1976.

Hegel, *La Raison dans l'histoire*, translated by Kostas Papaioannou, Angleterre, Librairie Plon, 1965.

Hegel, *Leçon sur la philosophie de l'histoire*, translated by J. Gibelin, Paris, J.Vrin, 1963.

Hegel, *Précis de l'encyclopédie des sciences philosophiques,* Trad par J. Gibelin, Paris, Librairie philosophique, 1978.

Ricœur, Paul, *Temps et récit, III*, Paris, Éditions du Seuil (Coll. « Points Essais »), [1988], 1991.

PART II

Political Virtues and Vices

8

COMMUNITY

Oritsegbubemi Anthony Oyowe

Introduction

One of the distinguishing marks of contemporary philosophical and political thought in Africa is that it aims to foreground community. African thinkers typically ask how might our theories about self and the world look if we began with the assumption that the community rather than the individual is basic. The dominant theories of nature, mind and personhood in metaphysics, truth and knowledge in epistemology, ethics and value in moral philosophy, as well as democracy and justice in political philosophy, frequently make explicit reference to community. Not only are these ideas characterised in such a way that they evince one or more communal features, the rationales for and justification of them invoke the principle of community. This is probably why Dismas Masolo noted quite aptly that community is both an axiomatic principle around which experience as well as reflection on experience revolves and a distinctive mark of African philosophical thought (Masolo 46, 51). To adapt Senghor's famous remark that ours is a community society, ours is a community philosophy (Senghor 94).

Yet, the community remains undertheorised as an idea in its own right, quite apart from cognate terms such as relationality. Moreover, it is common to examine community in relation to some other more prominent ideas, like personhood and value, or as part of larger theories like *Ubuntu*, communitarianism, communalism and collectivism under which it is routinely subsumed.

In this essay, I aim to track the ways in which the notion of community has been understood in some of the contemporary debates and to articulate several senses of it. The essay is divided into four parts. For each part, I articulate a notion of community, illustrating it by referencing selected philosophers, and then briefly problematising the relevant conception. This does not mean that the relevant philosophers do not appeal to other senses of community. On the contrary, what one often finds is that different conceptions of community might feature in the writings of one and the same philosopher. Although the aim is not to be exhaustive, what emerges are four broad senses of community: reified, constitutive, functionalist and end-state notions of community. I conclude with general comments on the politics of community.

DOI: 10.4324/9781003143529-10

Reified Notions of Community

In recent work, Masolo has broached albeit without necessarily endorsing what is arguably the most controversial sense of community: the idea that it is a *thing*—an entity with its own essential structure or set of distinctive intrinsic properties (see especially his 2004, 2009 and 2010). He offers us two paths to understanding this view. One path leads us through the early controversies regarding meaning and method of African philosophy. On one side, proponents of ethnophilosophy held that philosophy—or thought in general—can be the property of a group. Talk of Bantu philosophy, for example, is not only not incoherent, they held, but also aptly describes African philosophy. However, in endowing a collective with a philosophy, they did not only presuppose a collective mind as Bodunrin has noted, but also took for granted the idea that community is something to whom thought or a philosophy can be attributed. That is, they treated it as a *thing* existing independently of the individual minds of its members. Put differently, unless it is intended as a *façon de parler*, to posit a Bantu philosophy was in effect to entertain the view that community is a thinking thing in its own right. On the other side, opponents of ethnophilosophy denied that a philosophy could properly be attributed to a collective consciousness—a thinking community, so to speak. Hountondji, in particular, viewed philosophy as a property of an individual's consciousness, which his critics saw both as an opposition to the idea of a collective philosophy and as a rejection of the idea of community as a "thinking collectivity" (Hountondji 91; for an analysis of the debates, see Masolo 1994 and 2010).

The other path takes us along the discourses on personhood. Indeed, debates on the nature of the self have been the most productive site for engaging with the idea of community. Here, too, Masolo tells us that community has been construed either in terms of "self as a metaphysical collectivity" or "as a natural formation" (489). I take this to mean two related points. First, community is not an artificial kind, the outcome of a social contract among rational and self-interested individuals for mutual advantage. It is *partly* what Gyekye means when he says communal belonging is not optional—generated by individual choices and preferences (38–39, 42; partly, because, as far as I can tell, he does not endorse a reified notion of community). Second, since community is not artificial, the implication is that it is an aspect of the essential structure of the natural world, independent of us (i.e., human minds). Understood as a metaphysical collectivity or natural formation, community, as in the Dogon case, becomes the prototype self by virtue of which individual selves are constituted (Masolo 489).

However, it was Menkiti who gave this notion of community its clearest formulation. He held that community is an extended self and that each individual person is a part of that extended self (325; see also, Menkiti 179). Ikuenobe also interprets Menkiti's use of an organically fused "we" as referring to the community *as* a self (Ikuenobe, *Philosophical Perspectives on Communalism* 56). Here, I simply identify it as what Menkiti describes as an extended self, where extension can be thought of spatially and temporally. In other words, personhood is grounded in community construed as something temporally and spatially extended.

Menkiti's reference to an extended self must be understood against the backdrop of his other point that in the idea of community, there is "an *organic* dimension to the relationship between the component individuals" (Menkiti 180, emphasis as in original). In other words, Menkiti is asking us to think of the relationship between component parts of community in the same way parts of a living organism are linked to each other. In short, as a living organism capable of replicating itself across time. Two points are worth highlighting in this regard.

First, by way of compelling biological imageries, he impresses on his readers the organic nature of community. In one place, community is likened to a shared gene pool, by which each and every individual is capable of self-identification. Put simply, one way to ground the identity of individuals as persons in community is to genetically (re)identify them within a specific lineage. The result is that each person is immediately situated as part of a larger whole: a *community* that extends across space and time. Consider, for example, how something as mundane as a DNA or paternity test immediately situates one within a complex network of relationships with other persons––forbears and contemporaries alike. In fact, Menkiti's other imagery drives home the point about the temporal extension of community. Past and future generations of persons, he tells us, are linked together in a "thoroughly fused collective 'we'" by the umbilical cord (Menkiti 172). Here, too, the picture that emerges is that each person is a *part* of a temporally extended *thing*––i.e., community––with some parts in the distant past, others in the present and still others in the future. Because the imageries appeal to parts of an organism, it is not unreasonable it seems to me to hold that Menkiti's organic sense of community is an invitation to view it as a living organism temporally (and spatially) extended.

The second point concerns the way Menkiti characterises the persistence of community. According to him, community is a "stubborn *perduring* fact of the psychophysical world" (Menkiti 172, my emphasis). Notice first his appeal to perdurance theory. In mainstream discourse on persistence, something is said to perdure (as opposed to endure) if and only if it has temporal parts. Put differently, a perduring thing exists over time in virtue of its parts existing at different times. In the same way, parts of an object occupy different regions of space (my head is here, my hands are there, etc.), so too temporal parts of community (past, present and future generations of persons) exist at different points in time. What I wish to stress is that by construing the persistence of community in this way, Menkiti unequivocally locates it in the same category as other metaphysical entities capable of persisting over time. Now, notice in addition that community is described as a "*fact of the psychophysical world*" (172, my emphasis). Here, I believe Menkiti is stressing the point that community is a metaphysical entity––something with independent reality and a natural kind––something that belongs to a class of objects discoverable in the natural world. Community in this sense reflects something about the structure of the world, independently of us. It is not surprising then that he writes: "the reality of the communal world takes precedence over the reality of individual life histories…" (Menkiti 171).

The sense in which community is an entity should now be clear. In Menkiti, it consists of four more basic ideas. First, that community is a natural kind––with a distinct essence. Second, it is a particular natural kind namely, a biological kind, insofar as its existence takes the form of a living organism with individual persons as its parts organically fused. Third, community in this organic sense perdures by having temporal parts across time. This explains why and how one and the same community can have different properties at different times––its temporal part differ. Lastly, like other persisting metaphysical entities, community exhibits mind-independent reality.

Reified notions of community have either been tempered or roundly criticised. Below, I draw attention to three different engagements with it. Developing the Akan idea of person, Wiredu notes that although remarks like, *it is the community that defines the person*, are common, the community does not do any defining strictly-speaking; it is individuals who do the defining using shared rules (338). He says this most probably because he is being careful not to be read as underwriting the view that community is an *entity* capable of undertaking certain kinds of actions in the world. Before then, he had warned: "we must not hypostatize the notion of the community" (Wiredu 334). What I take from Wiredu is that we can reasonably describe the community as metaphorically doing things, like defining persons, without treating it as a metaphysical entity or natural kind.

Whereas Wiredu tempers the view, Masolo and Matolino have been more critical. The former interrogates the idea in the context of migration in the global world. Conceived as an entity with an essence, community takes the form of a single, bounded, fixed, unchanging *thing*, entirely closed in on itself. On the one hand, Masolo worries that this prevents an adequate grasp of human subjects as beings who are, like the *ombasa* (i.e., travelling) plant, capable of inhabiting multiple communities at once (52). More clearly, essentialising community entails natural borders between human groups, thus shutting individuals within their supposedly "natural" community. On the other, by reifying community, we essentialise differences between groups of people, not merely in terms of

> their supposedly fixed metaphysical constitutions, such as race or ethnicity, but also that these assumed differences lead to other differences … which we proceed to argue, however wrongly, to be warranting of differential treatment of people who are dissimilar in those terms.
>
> *(Masolo 53; see also, Masolo 668)*

For Masolo, episodes in our recent history, like the Rwandan genocide and the Holocaust, are painful reminders of the consequences of essentialising community.

Finally, Matolino opposes the idea that community is a *thing* because it involves a category mistake. As I understand him, we rightly classify mind-independent kinds as entities. However, he argues, if we take mind-independence as a criterion for deciding what counts as an entity, community fails the test. In the context of his analysis of personhood, Matolino contends that community cannot plausibly be a constituent of person because it is an exemplification of the practices and activities of persons (144–157). To think otherwise, that is, to reify it, is to commit a category mistake.

In conclusion, while we must heed Wiredu, Masolo and Matolino, and resist the impulse to reify community, we need not abandon the intuition that in some important sense community is more than the sum of its parts. Elsewhere, I have suggested that community is a social (as opposed to a natural) kind (see Oyowe, *Menkiti's Moral Man*, especially Ch. 5; for a similar idea, see Ikuenobe's *Menkiti's Account of the Social Ontology of African Community and Persons*). Adopting this perspective would allow us to still talk about community as an entity, as Wiredu desires, albeit a social entity. Moreover, it circumvents the negative consequences of essentialising community to which Masolo draws attention; social entities lack an essential nature. We would not be involved in a category mistake; community belongs in a social (not a natural) ontology. Even the Ethnophilosopher's intuition that community exhibits a collective mind can be rescued, as Bodunrin seemed to have envisage (171).

Functionalist Notions of Community

Functionalist notions of community are far more common relative to reified notions. One reason for this might be that they do not involve any ontological commitments about the nature of community. On this approach, what makes some human association community rather than something else or similar is not the metaphysical kind it is, its constitution or internal structure, including the way its different parts are organised. Instead, community is defined in terms of one or more of its functions or by specifying its causal role(s) within a complex system or set of processes, including especially in the formation of personal identity as well as in the evolution and sustaining of shared values. In short, community is defined not by what it is made of but by what it does.

Consider, for example, how Ikuenobe deploys the notion of community in his work on personhood. He makes explicit its role within a range of activities and practices, including especially the complex processes by which individuals come to internalise values and ultimately acquire personhood. "Community is at the center of every activity, practice, belief, and value," he writes. "One's community helps to shape one's ways of life, values, attitudes, ways of seeing things and methods of doing things. A community also shapes the moral and social identity of an individual that indicates his or her moral personhood" (*Philosophical Perspectives on Community* 53–54; see also, *The Idea of Personhood*, 118, 120). The community is also able to place demands on individuals––demands which constitute themselves to individual persons as reasons for acting (120, 123; see also his *Social Ontology, Practical Reasonableness and Collective Reasons for Action*). Further to its role in practical reasoning, Ikuenobe assigns a prominent role to community in the fostering and exercise of what he calls relational autonomy. "The community," he writes, "expands the scope of substantive choices and makes them meaningful or valuable by providing the options of goods from among which one can choose freely ..." This is significant because the "the moral autonomy to choose any substantive option would depend on what a community provides." Thus, rather than limit, community plays a fundamental role in expanding and enhancing individual autonomy (Ikuenobe 14,15,17,121).

Before him, Menkiti held that community defines the person by functioning as a catalyst and prescriber of norms in virtue of which it confers person-status on its members. In taking up these roles, the community, he says, "steps in" to assist the individual in the transformation from human being to person (Menkiti, *Person and Community* 171, 172, 174; *On the Normative Conception of a Person* 326). In a recent paper, Metz suggests some other way community may be causally involved in personal identity. Although he is focused on relationality, rather than community, he may still be read, given the origination and historical versions of relationality he samples, as allowing that a community one has been in in the past or over the course of a life plays a role in forging selfhood in one (216). One final example of appeal to a functionalist conception of community is due to Motsamai Molefe, who not only interprets Menkiti as appealing to a functionalist notion of community, but also seems to embrace it as one possible way of understanding community. Citing Amato and Eze approvingly, he implies that community functions as a social incubator and enables individuals to attain levels of moral perfection (Molefe 19–20, 61–62).

What is common to all these examples is the following idea: community is *that* which performs certain kinds of functions or occupies particular roles in relation to the development and overall functioning of the individual person. What its nature is or its constituent parts are remains unspecified. While this makes functionalist accounts compatible with the next broad notion of community, we shall consider namely, constitutive conceptions of community––different lists of constituents or the basic building block of community might result in the same range of functions attributed to community, by itself it appears to leave out something central: an account of *what* it is that has the relevant function or in virtue of *what* these functions obtain. An account of *what* in virtue of which community performs these functions and occupies certain causal roles is the primary virtue of constitutive conceptions of community to which we shall shortly turn.

There may be other reasons why one might find functionalist conceptions less appealing. For one, functionalists tend to stress the positive functions of community, including its role in forging personal identity and nurturing moral values, and not the role of community in bringing about other undesirable outcomes. Community may enable individuals to develop personhood and values, but it might also become the means for social conditioning and indoctrination, as well as the exclusion and oppression of some (see Oyowe 2022, Ch. 4 and Menkiti 2017). As with constitutive conceptions, some believe that what is needed is the inclusion in our conception of community the idea that the relevant functions are directly constrained by moral norms. This is what proponents of end-state conceptions of community set out to do. However, before looking closely at end-state conceptions, it is important to see how constitutive conceptions of community fill an important gap in the understanding of community in African discourses.

Constitutive (and Structural) Notions of Community

Constitutive notions of community specify the conditions under which some association or group counts as community. Alternatively, they explain what it is about the current situation that makes it the case that there is a community, and not something else or similar. This way of understanding community differs from reified notions in that those who propose it do not typically make inflationary claims such as that community is part of the basic structure of the universe, a natural formation or an entity with an independent reality. It also differs from functionalist conceptions of community in that it tells us what community is made up of, rather than merely what it does. It is important to note that many of those who focus on constitution often pair it with some view of the form or structure community typically takes. In other words, in addition to specifying its building blocks, they also offer a sense of how these building blocks might be organised. Seen from this perspective, constitutive (and structural) conceptions (henceforth, I use the less cumbersome "constitutive") are more appealing than their functionalist counterparts. By clarifying what community *is*, we are better able to understand why it has the functions or is able to occupy the causal roles the functionalist ascribes to it.

We have already seen that Wiredu warns against hypostatising community—i.e., attributing an independent and real identity to it. Instead, he recommends a way of thinking of community that focuses on the way its constitutive parts are organised. On the one hand, Wiredu characterises community as a series of concentric circles of kinship relations involving many individuals. This is exemplified first and foremost within the household, extended family, lineage and then spirals outward to the clan and society at large (Wiredu 15; see also Wiredu 333, 335). On the other, he clearly broadens the scope of relations that constitute community by characterising it as a configuration of interests within a particular context. In his words: "the community is simply a certain contextualisation of individuals with respect to their locations and to their perceptions of their interests and of those of others" (334). As I understand him, where interests are configured in view of the group as opposed to particular individuals, a community is in place. This does not mean that we simply aggregate individual interests, far from it. "Community is not just an aggregation of individuals existing as windowless monads …," he writes (Wiredu 13). It is instead a complex configuration of relations between individuals, their interests, as well as how these interact with and are mediated through various institutions and practices in a given cultural context. Such a configuration, which is capable of orienting individuals in the world, is not fully explained by merely aggregating their interests.

Wiredu is not alone in affirming a constitutive view of community. Gyekye, for example, implies that at the very minimum a shared way of life, which consists of social relationships, values, interests, goals and a common good, is constitutive of community. "What distinguishes a community from a mere association of individuals," he writes, "is the sharing of an overall way of life." This means that "... each member acknowledges the existence of common values, obligations, and understandings and feels a commitment to the community that is expressed through the desire and willingness to advance its interests" (Gyekye 42). Like Wiredu, Gyekye believes that these building blocks of community may be arranged in several different ways: a shared way of life may be exemplified in a family, clan, village, city, neighbourhood, nation-state and as well as the international community.

Similarly, Metz has proposed albeit without endorsing by itself what seems to me a constitutive view of community. For him, relationships involving shared identity among individuals constitute (at least one sense of) community, where shared identity consists of a common sense of self, common ends, common reasons for acting, coordinated actions toward common ends and projects etc. (335). Where these more basic facts and relations are in place, one finds some instance of community. Like Wiredu and Gyekye, he thinks that the constituents of community might be arranged in different ways with the result that community can be instantiated by several human associations: family, clubs, churches, schools, firms and nations.

For Ikuenobe, the emphasis is on "enduring traditions, structures, interests, values, beliefs, and transcendental selves, which cannot be pinned down or reduce to the set of individuals and institutions that make up the community" (56). What is interesting in Ikuenobe's approach is that it appeals to facts beyond individuals, stressing traditions and a social structure, as constituents of community. To have a community in place is not just to have individuals with various interests standing in appropriate relations to each other, sharing identity or a way of life, it also requires an enduring tradition: customs, institutions, beliefs, values, rationales and modes of justification and many other background conditions. Of course, the point is implied in the views put forward by Wiredu, Gyekye and Metz, but Ikuenobe makes it explicit. What he also makes explicit is that community consists of a rather expansive set of relations. Specifically, in terms of its structure, it encompasses the living and the living-dead, i.e., ancestral persons (Ikuenobe 54–56, 63–64).

In general, constitutive notions specify both the basic building blocks and make-up of community. And, as earlier noted, fare better than their functionalist counterparts. Even so, they face difficulties of their own. Some of these come from my reading of Masolo's interrogation of the idea of community. As I understand him, the stress on facts like shared identity, interests, way of life and enduring traditions, runs the risk of reflecting "characteristics of natural homogeneity among inhabitants" (Masolo 656). As noted earlier, Masolo believes that in an increasingly globalised world characterised by human migration, the idea of "community as a homogenous social unit" is difficult to sustain.

Moreover, it is unclear to what extent shared identity, interests, way of life and enduring traditions must hold for there to be community. Consider that something like a shared way of life comes in degrees. Some members of a community may share the relevant way of life to a larger extent than others. Others might share only certain aspects. Does one have to share in *all* aspects of a way of life or an enduring tradition, for there to be community between oneself and others? Relatedly, can one share identity and a way of life with two groups whose ends are radically different? More clearly, can one simultaneously share identity and a way of life with Catholics and with pro-choice movement? I understand Masolo to be making the point that if these constitutive elements are stated strongly, deemed to be all-or-nothing, there is a risk on the one hand that individuals may not be able to belong simultaneously to multiple communities with diverse interests and on the other that some in a given community might place a "conditional demand" that for one to be part of the "we," i.e., to share identity or a way of life with us—in short, to be part of *this* community, one must first abandon another (Masolo 665). Either way, the threats of undue restriction and exclusion loom large.

Reflecting on the "topology of community," Masolo further suggests that we think of community as constituted by the "participative choices" of individual persons as well as their "responses to and within given political, economic, and other forms of cultural contexts" (653). This is a central feature of the conception of community the *older* Menkiti also stresses, as he reflects on the reality that communities are also sites of oppressive and repressive practices. For him, the basis of community weakens to the extent that the "willingness of the individual to participate" is undermined (Menkiti 466–467). This idea of elective community has been powerfully captured by Okeja, who has given philosophical expression to one of Menkiti's poems reflecting on the notion of elective community.

For those who might worry that shifting attention to participative choice and willingness leaves community hostage to the individual, it is perhaps more meaningful to read the point by Masolo, Menkiti and Okeja as an invitation to specify which constitutive features of community are *morally important*. Shared identity, interests, way of life and traditions may constitute community but they are not morally important in themselves. Terrorist, racist and sexist groups meet these conditions of community. However, these, as well as communities that unduly restrict and exclude, are not the sort of communities we should advocate. On this way of thinking, perhaps rather than stress participative choice and willingness, we should insist that the appropriate notion of community is one that reflects some moral ideal. The next broad notion of community involves precisely this sort of move.

End-State Notions of Community

End-state conceptions take for granted many of the building blocks of community constitutive conceptions specify. However, they differ in that end-state conceptions include the proviso that for some human association to count as community, it must reflect some moral ideal. In other words, the relevant constituents of community must be subject to direct normative constraints. In some cases, end-state conceptions require that the constituents of community conform to some normative standard, e.g., mutual respect—this means that shared identity or a shared way of life characterised by frequent abuses of human dignity does not constitute community. In other cases, they specify an ideal state of affairs that must be realised for some human association to count as community, e.g., equality—relationships involving shared identity constitute community only to the extent that they exhibit equality among persons. Or, enduring traditions constitute community only to the extent that they do not discriminate along gender lines, for example. However they are framed, what end-state approaches have in common is that they specify some normative standards or ideal state of affairs that tell us what community ought to look or be like. Because they provide some yardstick for morally evaluating what should count as community, they extend our understanding of community beyond constitution.

End-state conceptions of community have significant support. In what follows, I focus on two examples. The first is due to Wiredu. Earlier, we noted that Wiredu puts forward a constitutive conception of community. What was not stressed is that in addition to kinship ties and the interests of individuals, which are constituents of community, he also specifies that certain kinds of ethical relationships that must hold for there to be community proper. The ethical component of community involves relations of solidarity. In his words, "people are brought up to develop a sense of bonding within large kinship circles. This solidarity starts from the household and radiates outward to the lineage and, with some diminution of intensity, to the clan at large" (Wiredu 15; see also, Wiredu 337). In other words, from this strongly substantive and ethical perspective, concentric circles involving a network of kinship and broader social ties, including the wide range of interests that frequently erupt in them, may be necessary but not sufficient for community. To count as community, these relationships must be characterised by solidarity, which, according to Wiredu, entails a range of rights and obligations.

Elsewhere, Wiredu implies that community should reflect the ideal of consensus—a state of affairs in which there is a suspension of disagreement in the face of conflicting interests so as to facilitate collective action (Wiredu 374, 380). Recall that earlier we characterised Wiredu's constitutive view of community as a configuration of among other things individuals' perception of their interests. Here, Wiredu may be read as adding a normative criterion: that differing interests must be aligned with what he calls a "rock-bottom identity of interests." The reason is that "ultimately, the interests of all members of society are the same, although their immediate perception of those interests may be different" (Wiredu 306). For another example of the view that community properly understood reflects the communal ethos of solidarity and consensus, see (Ramose 139–140). Similarly, Ikuenobe stresses a non-conflictual relationship between individual and collective interests (Ikuenobe 77, 82–83).

The second is due to Metz, who stresses a different sort of value. Like Wiredu, he supplements the constitutive conception of community we earlier attributed to him with the requirement that relationships involving shared identity among individuals must be grounded on goodwill (Metz 338, 335–338). The reason is that shared identity by itself is not morally important. Elsewhere, he implies that community is grounded in relationships involving identity and *solidarity* or harmony among people. In his words, "a promising conception of community includes both kinds of relationship." (Metz 26). It is end-state precisely because it requires that community reflects some ideal state of affairs, thus excluding from the category of community human associations, e.g., terrorist associations, which exhibit shared identity but lack goodwill or solidarity.

While end-state conceptions may look attractive, they present unique difficulties. I read interventions by Emmanuel Eze and Michael Eze as efforts to interrogate the utopian idea of community in Wiredu's consensual democracy. For the former, consensus is not characteristic of community, but only one moment of it. For the latter, it precludes differences among other things. Elsewhere, in *Personhood and the Strongly Normative Constraint*, I expressed concern that such idealisations might render what is being accounted for rare to find indeed. The same may be said of end-state communities. But here is a further worry. They are implicitly perfectionist. This points to two specific problems. One is that they frequently assume that a particular end-state conception of community is objectively good, thus problematically ruling out the possibility of plural goods, including especially individualism as a distinct good. For one such defence of individualism, see Molefe. Another is that many of the implicit perfectionist ends—e.g., consensus, solidarity, harmony etc.—could be realised by questionable means, including those that undermine human dignity. End-state conceptions rarely confront this fact, with many preferring instead to simply idealise community.

The Politics of Community

The foregoing reflection on the idea of community is born out of a sense that the task of taking stock of the ways philosophers in the African tradition have deployed the idea has often been taken for granted. It must be acknowledged, however, that the critical literature on community that emerged in contemporary African philosophical and political thought has not been primarily about conceptualising it. The idea of community has dominated politics, policy, legislation, political discourse, the development of the African Charter on Human and Peoples' Rights, academic philosophical writing, etc. by way of compelling philosophers and jurists to reflect on what precisely its role should be in relation to the individual. More clearly, the idea of community is at the centre of a larger inquiry into the question of whether and to what extent ostensibly liberal values, including especially individual rights, autonomy, democratic equality, could be accommodated within an African brand of communitarianism grounded on communalism (as opposed to cultural individualism, broadly but perhaps inaccurately ascribed to Western societies, see Masolo 2004 and Wiredu 2008) and expressed through various incarnations of socialism.

The origins of the politics of community are well known. As prominent African revolutionaries and later statesmen took up the mantle of leadership, they were confronted with the challenge of imagining and defining the political futures of their respective states. In response, they searched for African pathways to socialism founded on ideas of communalism and humanism rooted in traditional African thought patterns. The subsequent failure of Africa's twentieth-century experiments with socialism was followed by the prevalence of one-party dictatorships, the president-for-life syndrome, the suppression of civil liberties and political opposition, and gross human rights abuses, under ideologically-inflected notions of community. This was at the political level. At the cultural level, various self-serving and dubious idealisations of community were still being marshalled by a patriarchal elite to normalise and justify beliefs and practices that violated the human rights of women and children in particular. However, by the late 1980s, there were deliberate calls for democratic reforms and a greater need to account for individual rights and freedoms within, yes, the parameters of African cultures and traditions, specifically the revaluation of the ideal of community, but nonetheless in a manner that would transcend the distortion and abuses of same that prevailed in the previous era.

African political philosophy flourished on the heels of these developments. Two related critical discourses are illustrative. The first concerns the discourse on human rights within the framework of communitarian thinking. The second had to do with the (re)conceptualisation or appropriation of democracy in a way that is continuous with African thought, traditions and values.

With regards to the proper relation between individual and community, and the related issue of human and individual rights, Gyekye offered a neat taxonomy of perspectives that would structure the debates. On the one hand, extreme communitarians affirmed the primacy of community, and defined the self wholly in terms of it, thereby retaining the old intuition that community is the first principle around which all other values, including individual and human rights, revolve. Still, when compared to what held sway in the previous era, what strikes me as radically different in the intellectual articulations and justifications of variants of extreme communitarianism was the acknowledgement *at the very least* that rights were important even if *secondary* to the duties the individual had to the group. On the other hand, proponents of moderate communitarianism vehemently protested against the conservatism of extreme communitarianism, and in contrast sought to provide a greater recognition of rights and even a higher normative status for rights within a communitarian scheme. To a large extent, these and other disagreements that played out in the discourse were already crystalised in the *African Charter of Human and People Rights*, which sought to negotiate some balance between the claims of the community and the individual.

On the issue of democracy, Wiredu's appropriation of traditional Akan democratic principles and practices for a modern African context stands out. The outcome was consensual democracy which opposes itself to majoritarian democracy, which Wiredu faults for many of the political ills and failures in Africa. Unlike majoritarianism, consensual democracy is founded on a more robust sense of representation––that is, the combination of formal and substantive representation, thereby making it *strongly* representative. Emmanuel Eze's reply to Wiredu remains a classic. His concerns centred around the way Wiredu represents traditional Akan principles and practices, understands political interests, and elevates a moment in democratic practice and process to a necessary requirement. Much of the discourse since that early exchange between Wiredu and Eze has focused on other philosophically fascinating issues related more to *consensus* in consensual democracy. And while there is no doubt at all that a robust interrogation of consensus as an ideal has ensued, it appears to me that the idea and role of community in shaping their respective positions have not been sufficiently brought to the foreground. As I see it, although he is clearly rooting for many of the democratic ideals we most cherish, Wiredu's frequent use of phrases, such as "rock bottom identity of interests", seem to me his way of channelling in new ways old ideas about the primacy of community in theorising the nature of political interests and political reasoning. Likewise, Eze's reference to "an individuated structure of desire" seems to me to locate him squarely in the opposite camp.

References

Amato, Peter. "The Menkiti-Gyekye Conversation: Framing Persons." *Filosofia Theoretica*, vol. 7, no. 2, 2018, pp. 33–47 *AJOL*, https://www.ajol.info/index.php/ft/article/view/179033. Accessed 30 Aug. 2021.

Bodunrin, Peter O. "The Question of African Philosophy." *Philosophy*, vol. 56, no. 216, 1981, pp. 161–179. *JSTOR*, http://www.jstor.org/stable/3750739. Accessed 30 June 2021.

Eze, Emmanuel Chukwudi. "Democracy or Consensus? A Response to Wiredu." In *Postcolonial African Philosophy: A Critical Reader*, edited by Chukwudi Eze, 313–323. Cambridge: Blackwell Publishers Ltd, 1997.

Eze, Michael. "What Is African Communitarianism? Against Consensus as a Regulative Ideal." *South African Journal of Philosophy*, vol. 27, pp. 386–399. *Taylor & Francis*, https://www.tandfonline.com/doi/abs/10.4314/sajpem.v27i4.31526. Accessed 15 June 2021.

Gyekye, Kwame. *Tradition and Modernity: Philosophical Reflections on the African Experience*. New York: Oxford University Press, 1997.

Hountondji, Paulin. *The Struggle for Meaning: Reflections on Philosophy, Culture, and Democracy in Africa*. Ohio: Ohio University Press, 2002.

Ikuenobe, Polycarp. "African Communal Basis for Autonomy and Life Choices." *Developing World Bioethics*, vol. 18, no. 3, 2018, pp. 212–221. *Wiley*, https://doi.org/10.1111/dewb.12161. Accessed 15 June 2021.

Ikuenobe, Polycarp. "Menkiti's Account of the Social Ontology of African Community and Persons." In *Menkiti on Community and Becoming a Person*, edited by Edwin Etieyibo and Polycarp Ikuenobe, 95–114. Lanham, MD: Lexington Books, 2020.

Ikuenobe, Polycarp. *Philosophical Perspectives on Communalism and Morality in African Traditions*. Lanham, MD: Lexington books, 2006a.

Ikuenobe, Polycarp. "Social Ontology, Practical Reasonableness and Collective Reasons for Action." *Journal for the Theory of Social Behaviour*, vol. 49, no. 3, 2019, pp. 264–281. *Wiley*, https://doi.org/10.1111/jtsb.12202. Accessed 15 June 2021.

Ikuenobe, Polycarp. "The Idea of Personhood in Chinua Achebe's Things Fall Apart." *Philosophia Africana*, vol. 9, no. 2, 2006b, pp. 117–132. *PDCNET*, https://doi.org/10.5840/philafricana2006924. Accessed 15 June 2021.

Masolo, Dimas. *African Philosophy in Search of Identity*. Bloomington: Indiana University Press, 1994.

Masolo, Dismas. "Narrative and Experience of Community as Philosophy of Culture." *Thought and Practice*, vol. 1, no. 1, 2009, pp. 43–68. *AJOL*, https://www.ajol.info/index.php/tp/article/view/46306. Accessed 15 June 2021.

Masolo, Dismas. Rethinking Communities in a Global Context." In *The African Philosophy Reader*, edited by Pieter H. Coetzee and Abraham Pieter Jacob Roux, 653–670. New York: Routledge, 2003.

Masolo, Dismas. *Self and Community in a Changing World*. Indianapolis: Indiana University Press, 2010.

Masolo, Dismas. "Western and African Communitarianism: A Comparison." In *A Companion to African Philosophy*, edited by Kwasi Wiredu, 483–498. Oxford: Blackwell Publishing Ltd, 2004.

Matolino, Bernard. *Personhood in African Philosophy*. Durban: Cluster Publications, 2014.

Menkiti, Ifeanyi. "Community, Communism, Communitarianism: An African Intervention." In *The Palgrave Handbook of African Philosophy*, edited by Afolayan Adeshina and Falola Toyin, 461–473. New York: Palgrave Macmillan, 2017.

Menkiti, Ifeanyi. "On the Normative Conception of a Person." In *A Companion to African Philosophy*, edited by Wiredu Kwasi, 324–331. Malden: Blackwell Publishing Ltd., 2004.

Menkiti, Ifeanyi. "Person and Community in African Traditional Thought." In *African Philosophy: An Introduction*, edited by Richard Wright, 171–182. Lanham, MD: University Press of America, 1984.

Metz, Thaddeus. "African Conceptions of Human Dignity: Vitality and Community as the Ground of Human Rights." *Human Rights Review*, vol. 13, no. 1, 2012, pp. 19–37. *Springer*, https://doi.org/10.1007/s12142-011-0200-4. Accessed 30 June 2021.

Metz Thaddeus. "Toward an African Moral Theory." *Journal of Political Philosophy*, vol. 15, no. 3, 1997, pp. 321–341. *Wiley*, https://doi.org/10.1111/j.1467-9760.2007.00280.x. Accessed 30 June 2021.

Metz, Thaddeus. "What Is the Essence of an Essence? Comparing Afro-Relational and Western-Individualist Ontologies." *Synthesis Philosophica*, vol. 65, no. 1, 2018, pp. 209–224. https://hrcak.srce.hr/clanak/320926. Accessed 30 June 2021.

Molefe, Motsamai. *An African Philosophy of Personhood, Morality and Politics*. New York: Palgrave Macmillan, 2019.

Molefe, Motsamai. "Individualism in African Moral Culture." *Cultura, International Journal of Philosophy of Culture and Axiology,* vol. 14, no. 2, 2017b, pp. 49–68. *PDCNET*, https://doi.org/10.3726/CUL.2017.02.03. Accessed 28 July 2021.

Okeja, Uchenna. "Before a Common Soil: Personhood, Community and the Duty to Bear Witness." In *Menkiti on Community and Becoming a Person*, edited by Edwin Etieyibo and Polycarp Ikuenobe, 219–236. Lanham, MD: Lexington Books, 2020.

Oyowe, Oritsegbubemi Anthony. "A Social Ontology of 'Maximal' Persons." *Journal for the Theory of Social Behaviour*, vol. 52, no. 1, 2022, pp. 147–163. *WILEY*, https://doi.org/10.1111/jtsb.12312. Accessed 30 Aug. 2022.

Oyowe, Oritsegbubemi Anthony. *Menkiti's Moral Man*. Lanham, MD: Lexington Books, 2022.

Oyowe, Oritsegbubemi Anthony. "Personhood and the Strongly Normative Constraint." *Philosophy East and West*, vol. 68, no. 3, 2018, pp. 783–801. *JSTOR*, https://www.jstor.org/stable/26529854. Accessed 28 July 2021.

Ramose, Mogobe. *African Philosophy Through Ubuntu*. Harare: Mond Book Publishers, 1999.

Senghor, Leopold Sedar. *On African Socialism*, trans. and intro., Mercer Cook. London: Pall Mall Press, 1964.

Wiredu, Kwasi. "An Oral Philosophy of Personhood: Comments on Philosophy and Orality." *Research in African Literatures*, vol. 40, no. 1, 2009, pp. 8–18. *JSTOR*, http://www.jstor.org/stable/30131182. Accessed 20 Aug. 2021.

Wiredu, Kwasi. Democracy and Consensus in African Traditional Politics: A Plea for a Non-Party Polity. In *Postcolonial African Philosophy: A Critical Reader*, edited by Chukwudi Eze, 303–312. Cambridge: Blackwell Publishers Ltd, 1997.

Wiredu, Kwasi. *Cultural Universals and Particulars*. Indianapolis: Indiana University Press, 1996.

Wiredu, Kwasi. "Social Philosophy in Postcolonial Africa: Some Preliminaries Concerning Communalism and Communitarianism." *South African Journal of Philosophy,* vol. 27, no. 4, 2008, pp. 332–339. *TAYLOR & FRANCIS*, https://doi.org/10.4314/sajpem.v27i4.31522. Accessed 28 July 2021.

9

DELIBERATION, MANIPULATION, AND A CONSENSUAL POLITY

Dennis Masaka

Introduction

Rational deliberation is considered an important ingredient of a successful democratic culture. The reason is that it creates platforms for the voices of the governed not only to be heard but to influence governance decisions and policies. The aim is to curtail tendencies towards the tyranny of a few under the pretence of exclusive right to govern or lead. Conceived as such, deliberation would appear to be an attractive way of conducting the affairs of the state. However, for such deliberations to lead to authentic agreed outcomes, they need not to be anchored on manipulative behaviour. This is a behaviour that inclines parties to deliberations to sway decision-making processes in a certain preferred direction of the manipulators under the guise of a genuine deliberative process or dialogue. This results in a bogus deliberative process meant to cheat stakeholders into endorsing decisions to which they have no or marginal decisional influence.

Hidden in this sham of a deliberative process is the vice of manipulation which is a form of political vice. Political vices are dispositions that are entrenched in people and they have the potential to jeopardise the expected functions of political institutions to ensure the attainment of political virtues such as equality, human dignity and honest participation in governance of various segments within a particular space. As Mark E. Button aptly puts,

> political vice, as a general category, is the habitual disposition to act in ways that would install a part over the whole without justification, or, contrawise, it describes the attitude and settled disposition that motivates the "whole" (or those who claim to speak on its behalf) to ignore and/or dominate over a part without sound reason.
>
> *(Button, 2016: 15–16)*

It is important to note that the vice of manipulation has partly swayed opinions on a suitable democracy model for countries in Africa between majoritarian democracy emerging from Euro-North American world and a typical African consensual polity, such as one espoused by Kwasi Wiredu (1995; 1997; 2007; 2011). The understanding has been that the former, because of its structural nature, is saddled with the loathed manipulative tendencies while

DOI: 10.4324/9781003143529-11

the latter is considered not to have these deficiencies mainly because everyone is *party* to the decisional processes whose purpose is never to produce winners and losers but legitimately agreed outcomes by all or representatives of interest groups. As a result, the deciding factor becomes partly a normative issue that is a consequent of structural differences between the two democracy models. Wiredu (1995; 1997; 2007; 2011) has consistently shown his dislike for multi-party majoritarian democracy on account of its structural nature that ignites manipulation as a way through which the consent of people is contentiously attained. At one point he states that 'the Hobbesian competition for votes among seekers after political power involves such intensive efforts in the manipulation of the voters that the representative status of the eventually triumphant candidates must be deeply uncertain' (Wiredu, 2007: 156). While Wiredu (2007: 156–157) points to the structural aspect of multi-party majoritarian democracy as a reason for the occurrence of manipulation, he claims that this vice is absent in a consensual polity. My contribution to this debate is to question the assumed absence of manipulation in a consensual polity. I seek to show that it might not be totally immune from some nominal traces of this vice. The contention is that while it is not an expressed strategy of rational deliberation from the reading of Wiredu (1995: 54) choosing rather 'persuasiveness' or 'persuasion' (also termed 'rational[1] persuasion' in Wiredu's later works) as indicative of consensus-seeking deliberative processes, I argue that it is unpersuasive to totally deny manipulation's sublime and subtle role in consensual deliberation if rational 'persuasion' is to be critically understood. However, in arguing thus, I am not defending its necessity but rather highlighting its marginal influence in the arduous process leading to the attainment of consensus. But then, what is at stake is to posit a compelling position that persuasion is not totally devoid of some marginal traces of manipulation which I consider to be a tall order, yet a necessary one. On the same note, I do not posit that manipulation and persuasion are synonymous terms (Bakir, Herring, Miller and Robinson, 2019: 316) because doing so will be to trash substantive differences that exist between them. While I argue that deliberations in a consensual polity are not completely immune to some marginal traces of manipulation, I consider it as a more attractive democracy model because of its essential structural attributes which might make occurrences of traces of manipulation largely tenuous and less of influence in the greater scheme of consensus-seeking rational deliberation.

I have set out three sections to pursue the thesis of this chapter. In the first section, I briefly present Wiredu's (1995; 1997; 2007; 2011) account of consensual polity highlighting his efforts to show that it is not troubled with the vice of manipulation that afflicts deliberations in a multi-party majoritarian democracy. In the second section, I give a critical appraisal of Wiredu's (2007: 156–157; 2011: 1058) implicit distinction between manipulation and persuasion. The aim is to establish whether manipulation can legitimately be said to be absent in a consensual polity. In the final section, I put to test a fact implicit in Wiredu's (1995; 1997; 2007; 2011) idea of a consensual polity that dialogue or deliberation is non-manipulative. As I posit, to claim that a consensual polity is non-manipulative is not compelling enough especially when one realises that persuasion as a legitimate strategy for reaching consensual outcomes may not be immune to some traces of manipulation (*see* Bakir, Herring, Miller and Robinson, 2019: 316). The structural composition of a consensual polity on its own may not, on the face of it, cure it of possible manipulative tactics of some parties to consensus-building even if they could be of nominal influence to the overall decisional process. Despite this, I defend consensual democracy as a promising option for countries in Africa reeling from problems associated with multi-party majoritarian democracy.

Wiredu on the Merits of Consensual Democracy

Proponents of a consensual polity credit it with a number of virtues that present it as essentially different and more attractive than liberal tradition's multi-party majoritarian democracy (Wiredu, 1995; 1997; 2007; 2011; Masaka, 2019). For that reason, those who are opposed to the performance of multi-party majoritarian democracy in countries in Africa often cite a consensual polity as a refreshing and credible corrective to a number of serious problems that the former has been associated with over the years. Of particular interest in this chapter, is the vice of manipulation associated with a multi-party majoritarian polity and, in turn, thought to be absent in a consensual polity. In this light, it is necessary to present briefly Wiredu's (1995; 1997; 2007; 2011) idea of consensual democracy and show how it, as he claims, is better than a multi-party majoritarian polity. I use some examples from Africa to show that deliberations in a multi-party majoritarian dispensation are replete with the vice of manipulation that substantially put to question the input of some stakeholders in running the affairs of the state.

While noting that conflicts were common in African societies, Wiredu (1995: 53) argues that the good thing is that when resolutions were negotiated, the reason was the attainment of consensus. Consensus was considered to be attractive as it is an outcome of deliberations where the positions of parties are strictly taken into account. By this reasoning, the idea defended by Wiredu (2011: 1066) is that consensual democracy could as well work well in present-day countries in Africa if sufficient thought is put into it. Part of its attractive features is that dialogue or deliberation is a preferred mode of settling issues without necessarily implying that parties to it will cease to hold their divergent positions which they held prior to reaching compromise positions. Wiredu (1997: 304) aptly puts across this idea when he states that 'where there is the will to consensus, dialogue can lead to a willing suspension of disagreement, making possible agreed actions without necessarily agreed notions'. This is in part an admission that people or their representatives may not be swayed by the need for consensus to drop positions they uphold even though they agree that it is a noble thing to reach compromise positions. Dialogue will work towards reaching consensual outcomes, that is, 'what needs to be done' and not the attainment of unanimity of perspectives both intellectual and ethical (Wiredu, 2011: 1057). This means that consensus requires compromises to be made by parties to deliberations. While this appears to be an insurmountable challenge for attaining consensus, Wiredu (1995: 54) thinks that the 'residual minority' can willingly 'suspend disbelief' in a prevailing option in order to attain consensus. There is a proviso to this in the absence of which compromise positions may not be attained. As Wiredu (1997: 304) argues,

> the feasibility of this depends not only on the patience and *persuasiveness* of the *right people* but also on the fact that African traditional systems of the consensual type were not such as to place any one group of persons consistently in the position of the minority.[2]

Because of the thoroughness of rational deliberations leading to consensual outcomes, it is a more taxing way of attaining consensus compared to alternatives such as one based on the majority principle which Wiredu (2007: 169) strongly opposes. This reason is that the majority principle deprives the minority of having their will influencing decision-making. Consensual democracy provides an embracing system of governance because decisions are reached through rational dialogue by people or their representatives in governing councils (Wiredu, 1997: 308; 2011: 1057). The defining character of these rational engagements by parties is that of participation and corporation and not competition or confrontation with an eye on sectional appropriation of power. Parties in a consensual polity are considered to be an embodiment of independent thought which is necessary for rational deliberations or dialogue that lead to consensual outcomes. In pleading for the building of a consensual governance model for use in present times through tapping from indigenous African model, Wiredu (1997: 309) is aware that times have changed and political life is now more complex than it was in the past. Multi-party majoritarian democracy peddlers have taken advantage of a consensual polity's supposed unsuitability in present circumstances to defend the indispensability of liberal majoritarian polity for countries in Africa especially in light of the existence of various ethnic groups within states. But then, Wiredu (1997: 310) sees merit in a consensual polity to smother tensions, competitions and confrontations resident in a multi-party majoritarian polity by ensuring that groups are conceived as special-type parties to deliberations whose outcome is consensus. The idea is that the complexities of presently constituted states desperately need the mechanism of consensus governance to accommodate group interests. As a result, no interest group or party is left out of decisional processes and 'this is nothing short of a matter of fundamental human rights' (Wiredu, 1997: 311). The reason is that democracy by consensus is rule by the consent of the people and not by the consent of the majority of the people. With this in mind, it can be noted that the structural nature of a majoritarian polity is apt to be burdened by the vice of manipulation while that of a consensual polity gives way to rational persuasion as a way of seeking the consent of parties. And the consent that is consistent with a consensual polity is one attained through legitimate means (Wiredu, 2011: 1058), that is, through rational persuasion.

Persuasion and Manipulation

In the previous section, I noted Wiredu's (1995; 1997; 2007; 2011) efforts to show that his idea of a consensual polity is distinct from a multi-party majoritarian polity both in terms of its structural dynamics and moral attributes. As a result, Wiredu (2011: 1063) prefers a democracy model that uses rational persuasion in deliberations as a method of seeking the consent of the people than one that uses manipulation to give a façade of the same. My main worry in this section is not with the structural differences between these two models of democracy in terms of how decisional processes are conducted, but with insinuations that rational persuasion could be said to be immune from traces of manipulation. My take is that it might not be compelling to claim that the two strategies of seeking the consent of the people may not influence each other in some small measure. In this section, I first seek to bring to the fore Wiredu's (2007; 2011) implicit distinction between persuasion and manipulation as opposing methods of getting the consent of people. In the last part, I demonstrate that consensual democracy is not totally devoid of some elements of manipulation. The purpose here is not to pose a false equivalence between manipulation and rational persuasion but simply to show that they might influence each other in some nominal way. Nevertheless, because of the substantive role that rational persuasion plays in a consensual polity, it remains an attractive option for countries in Africa.

Wiredu (2007: 156–157) is open about how manipulation plays an influential role in multi-party majoritarian politics. He cites use of financial resources to sway the views of voters in the preferred direction of vote manipulators. This means that the electioneering process becomes riddled with this vice. Support of the electorate is then garnered through chicanery and deception often under the veneer of empowering the electorate. This is despite the fact that the efforts towards empowerment are intricately linked to voter mobilisation efforts of political gladiators. The electorate is often promised, as it were, heaven on earth.

This simply means that what political competitors promise the electorate is rarely fulfilled in letter and spirit despite claims that they are well-meaning promises. What appears more disturbing is negative campaigning that is meant to draw votes to a certain political brand or individual while presenting political opponents in a bad light (Wiredu, 2007: 156). This is an art that has become refined in some countries in Africa leading to rising political tensions. Command of huge financial resources and state machinery such as media are essential accessories for voter manipulation. Some sitting African governments have well exploited this advantage to manipulate voters to vote for them while they lambast opposition parties for, among many vices, being unpatriotic, sell-outs and agents of subversive foreign powers. The fact that opposition political parties are denied an opportunity to articulate and defend their own positions and programmes using the same state machinery, especially in cases where there is no vibrant private media, is a cause for serious concern. This places command and control of money and the state machinery at the centre of vote manipulation. This is especially worse in countries in Africa where opposition political parties have generally weak financial base to fight it out with ruling political parties and possibly influence voters to support them.

If it is accepted that there is a 'causal link between the command of financial resources and the command of voter allegiance' (Wiredu, 2007: 156), then it becomes easier to understand why multi-party majoritarian democracy is a source of a number of conflicts in Africa. The reason is that political parties in power will use their command of financial and state resources to remain in power, while opposition political parties will, for a considerable time, remain mired in opposition. However, this does not altogether cleanse opposition political parties of the vice of manipulation especially when one realises that much of what they promise the electorate is largely not put into practice or fulfilled in relatively small and insignificant political offices they may occupy in the state. But then the usual excuse, that at times is merited, is that the majority party is always working towards making opposition members of parliament and councils fail to deliver their promises to the electorate. Seen from this angle, the vice of manipulation seems to afflict participants in multi-party majoritarian politics both the ruling and opposition parties though the former get the mantle by virtue of command and abuse of state resources for party purposes. The impression that this creates then is that manipulation is a result of the structural composition of a multi-party majoritarian polity. It becomes an instrument for the attainment of political power for individuals and political party elites. The manipulated voters are left counting loses. This serves to show one critical moral deficiency that proceeds from the structural composition of a multi-party majoritarian polity. Wiredu (2007: 161) laments the stampede for power acquisition and retention for the reason that 'the quest for power easily excites passions, and this is why rational dialogue does not come easily in the relationship among political parties'. It is for this reason that he takes a consensual polity to be structurally disposed to use rational persuasion as a means of seeking the consent of people in cases where matters require its service. Since parties in a consensual polity are *party* to decisional processes, consensus-seeking deliberation is considered to be ethical and rational as no party is geared towards self-appropriation of power but in fact seeks to attain consensual positions.

While Wiredu's (2007: 169) position concerning the structural differences between a consensual polity and a multi-party majoritarian democracy appears compelling, the same might not be said of 'rational persuasion' and 'manipulation' that respectively somehow constitute the normative aspects of these two models of democracy. Wiredu (2007: 155–156) has not gone to the extent of trying to articulate their differences especially considering that they partly help to sway decisions on which democracy model could be more attractive.

Questions pertaining to the meanings and import of the terms 'persuasion' and 'manipulation' are important in the process of getting the consent of the governed. While an implicit distinction between the two is noticeable in Wiredu's (1995; 1997; 2007; 2011) case for a consensual polity and aversion to a multi-party democracy, it is important to go beyond this and try to establish whether the two terms do not share some essential attributes in common thereby rendering the implicit distinction rather superfluous.

I take Norbert Paulo and Christoph Bublitz's (2019: 58) understanding of manipulation

> as influence that (at least) one person exhibits over another and that alters choices, opinions or beliefs of the targeted person in a way that she does not approve of, and that does not correspond to the demands of rational thought

as its operational definition in this chapter. By its very nature, manipulation embodies deception and sublime coercion of a person by another so that he or she takes the preferred position of the latter. The intention is to dupe the targets. Manipulation is expressly immoral. Its messengers present it to their targets as *the truth*. It deliberately misleads and makes false assertions that are presented as truths. The targets may fall for it believing the messenger's message to be true and well-intentioned yet it is manipulative. This is a strategy that political parties in a multi-party majoritarian democracy have perfected and employed more often without visible signs of moral regard. At the same time, the electorate in countries where multi-party majoritarian democracy is at play may resign to this immoral strategy of garnering their votes and political support given the regularity with which it is employed by some politicians and political parties to attain the same effect. Paulo and Bublitz (2019: 56) make an important observation that 'the legitimacy of a government is cast in shadows if it is elected after it manipulatively altered citizens' opinions and if the alteration caused the electoral outcome, i.e. if voters would have voted differently without the alteration'. This makes manipulation a contentious part of political deliberation. The fact that it has been employed with regularity by political parties to negotiate votes does not at all make it right and beyond reproach. It simply makes its outcomes subject to contested legitimacy. It is partly because of the manipulative nature of multi-party majoritarian democracy emanating from its structural composition that its critics have no faith in it as model that ought to underpin more humane and germane governance in Africa. In different degrees, both consensual and multi-party majoritarian polities require the consent of the people even though this consent is sought differently. Wiredu (2007: 163) also notes that decisional consensus requires 'a shared commitment to basic morality' and that majoritarian democracy is no exception. Nevertheless, democracy by consensus is said to be more appealing because it more substantively reflects the consent of the people. And this consent is key, especially in instances where people hold different opinions on what is to be done.

Rational persuasion or dialogue that Wiredu (2011: 1062) considers to be a germane way of attaining decisional consensus has not been clearly articulated in his submissions specifying how it operates to make those who were initially hesitant to agree to what needs to be done *to do so* after being persuaded. Such explicit articulation is necessary if persuasion is to legitimately assume a higher moral status in deliberations compared to manipulation. In the absence of an explicit definition of the term 'persuasion' in Wiredu's (2011: 1062) submissions on democracy by consensus, one is tempted to tap from other writers on what it could mean especially when conceived in relation to the term 'manipulation'. But in doing so, one has to be mindful of the hazards of steeping into a straw man in invoking meanings of these terms that Wiredu (2011: 1062) himself seems not to have committed to explicitly articulate. To mitigate this possibility, it is necessary to estimate as close as possible what Wiredu (2007; 2011) conceives these terms to mean from his works. However, as I will show, such efforts do not help an inquisitive reader to view manipulation and persuasion as completely incompatible terms. What can be discerned from Wiredu (2011: 163) is that rational persuasion makes possible decisional consensus because of the shared perspectives of *parties* to dialogue. Because the motivation for persuasion is never for one party or its segments to win over others but for rational and morally respectful engagement of parties to reach consensual outcomes, manipulation appears not to have any place in consensus-seeking deliberations. As such, persuasion in deliberative sessions is done in the spirit of robust, inclusive participation of parties to produce germane consensual outcomes. Manipulation becomes its complete opposite as outcomes of deliberative processes mediated by it not only lack in moral import but produce deceptive notions of agreed outcomes. While manipulation in political deliberations is underpinned on the need to control its targets' minds and behaviours for self-serving purposes of manipulators (*see* Nichols, 1987: 27), rational persuasion is underpinned by a desire to cooperatively arrive at what needs to be done by parties to deliberations.

Ralph G. Nichols (1987: 15) is one thinker who has tried to be more explicit about the distinction between manipulation and persuasion. In this connection, he states that,

> there are vast differences between manipulation and persuasion. One is short-lived, fluctuating, and divisive; the other is long-lasting, trust-building, and unifying. Manipulation is the attainment of compliance based upon illusion, intimidation, or fear. By contrast, persuasion is the attainment of commitment based upon reality of need, discernment and conviction.
>
> *(Nichols, 1987: 15)*

At stake, here are the virtues of persuasion and correspondingly the vices of manipulation that, on balance of scale, makes the former compellingly better grounded to produce outcomes that genuinely tap from robust and respectable engagements of participants than the latter. It would appear beyond contest that if one were to choose between manipulation and persuasion to underpin deliberations that respect the rights of parties to it to be heard and for their submissions to substantively influence decisional consensus, then it could be none other than rational persuasion. This is on account of its attractive attributes that makes it rather unmatched by manipulation as basis of deliberation. When issues are debated objectively, the outcomes are bound to be well received by parties because they emerge from and reflect their input in deliberative sessions. But then, in the cited work, Nicholas (1987: 15) has not intimated on possible shared attributes between manipulation and persuasion, that is if according to his understanding, they do have any. Non-focus on possible points of convergence, might not necessarily mean that there aren't any which could be of some importance in this chapter's thesis that persuasion may not on face of it be immune from nominal traces of manipulation. Similarly, Wiredu (2007) has not, as I see it, come clear on possible traces of manipulation in the operations of rational persuasion which is considered to be part of rational dialogue in political deliberations.

Use of the qualification 'rational' that prefixes the term 'persuasion' in Wiredu's (2011) later works on democracy by consensus could be conceived as a way of trying to fortify it from what one might be conceived as a blurred distinction between it and manipulation. On face of it, this appears to separate 'rational persuasion' from 'persuasion' in general on account of its conception as a legitimate and objective means of attaining decisional consensus. But this might not successfully prove that some traces of manipulation may not creep into processes of decisional consensus even when it employs rational persuasion as a means of attaining it. Earlier on in this chapter, I noted that in one of his earlier works on a consensual polity, Wiredu (1997: 304) implores that a compromise position can be attained through the 'persuasiveness of the right people'. One might not be blamed for thinking that such moments of persuasion by the 'right people' on the 'residual minority' might involve the smuggling *in* of some manipulative tactics to make the latter agree to what needs to be done. This might have traction especially when one realises that certain positions polarises opinion to the extent that reaching agreed positions is a colossal task. With this in mind, the leap from a situation of entrenched positions of disagreements of opinion through rational persuasion of the 'residual minority' to one of compromise on what needs to be done may involve the use of some coercive influence especially given their transitory moment of residual minority position. This could be an instance of a moment that I consider to be a window for some traces of manipulation to creep into deliberations leading to consensual outcomes. Rational persuasion as a concept may not be immune from instances of manipulative tactics directed at the residual minority in seeking to attain what needs to be done. More importantly, the adjustment of interests of individuals and parties in the process of seeking decisional consensus may give way to manipulative tendencies. While manipulation is conceived in extremely negative terms in efforts to present rational persuasion as a legitimate means of reaching compromise consensual positions, it would appear to be too simplistic an assessment. The position I take is that for all claims of negative attributes, manipulation also employs persuasive tactics especially in negotiating for votes in a multi-party majoritarian polity. Yes, the dominant means of attaining the consent of voters in a multi-party majoritarian polity is manipulation but persuasion might play an ancillary role to aid its successful consummation. It is not uncommon for political contestants to use persuasive tactics in the greater scheme of manipulating voters for their self-serving reasons. I take this to be a plausible notion of the operations of manipulation in political deliberations typical of multi-party majoritarian democracy. But then the persuasion might be of a degree insignificant to be the overarching means to substantively influence deliberations. The same could be equally said concerning the workings of rational persuasion as the principle by which decisions are reached under a consensual polity. In its operations, rational persuasion may involve less significant encroachment of manipulation to decisional processes. This appears rather difficult to deny especially when one comes to accept that polarisation of opinions on what needs to be done cannot be easily broken even by the most robust rational dialogue that parties might engage in. In such a case, rational persuasion could be supplemented by manipulative tactics to have the residual minority to be *party* to compromise positions in decisional consensus.

The idea defended so far is that manipulation and rational persuasion might not be plausibly conceived as polar opposites but as concepts that in some way influence each other such that the operations of one is to some extent influenced by the other. If this is acceptable, an interlocutor might proceed, it would be largely unpersuasive to lambast manipulation while praising rational persuasion as legitimate means by which consent is attained in light of the stated connections. But such an assertion by an interlocutor loses sight of the fact that rational persuasion in consensus-seeking deliberations is the overarching principle of deliberation. The suggested nominal influence of manipulation in the overall principle of rational persuasion may not demean the attractive aspects of a consensual polity. It might not overall compromise the structural attributes of a consensual polity which makes it more appealing to a multi-party majoritarian polity. In the following section, I proceed to show that despite the possible nominal influence of manipulation in the operations of rational persuasion, a consensual polity remains an attractive option for countries in Africa.

Wither a Consensual Polity?

Having posited that rational persuasion may be aided by nominal manipulative tactics, I now proceed to argue that such nominal levels of manipulation are essentially not harmful to the creation of a consensual polity underpinned by robust and legitimate deliberations. This is the standout position that I defend in this section. Drawing from this, I argue that democracy by consensus remains an attractive option that allows legitimate deliberations by parties leading to consensual outcomes. Its structural nature and underlying principle of participation by including *all* either physically or by representation to rational dialogue platforms makes it the best option for countries in Africa reeling from intemperances of multi-party majoritarian democracy and the corresponding problem of representations of interest groups in governmental power and structures.

A case has been made on the problems of manipulation as a means of seeking the consent of the governed. While it finds conditions for significant manifestations in a multi-party majoritarian polity on account of its structural nature, it has been intimated that its tentacles may to some measure impinge on a consensual polity whose mode of operation is the participation of parties in rational deliberations as opposed to sectional competition to ascend to power. Drawing from this understanding, the structural compositions of multi-party majoritarian democracy and democracy by consensus emerge to be key in deciding a model that promises more sustainable and objective rational deliberation anchored on authentic participation in decisional processes of governance. I take a consensual polity to be a promising option for countries in Africa precisely because of its structural composition and modes of operation that puts at its centre legitimate and exhaustive deliberations as the foremost mode of decision-making. The reason for this is that the means by which consent of parties is sought proceeds by way of rational persuasion though manipulative tactics may in moments play some nominal role in the overall decisional processes so I argue. Nevertheless, such moments of nominal manipulation may not be harmful to the substantive use of rational persuasion as the preferred means of conducting deliberations. One who is accustomed to problems that multi-party majoritarian democracy has inflicted in Africa might be compelled to go for an alternative that has better credentials especially in ensuring that there is authentic participation of parties or interest groups in governance either through direct participation or by way of representation. Authentic participation of parties in deliberations where *no one* is left out will go some significant way in making interest groups feel and be assured that their input will have decisional influence. Since such deliberations are anchored on rational persuasion and all-embracing participation as operational principles, *no one* will be left out. A system of this nature that is not anchored on seeking consensus by deceptive and manipulative means will possibly not create the kind of rancour and acrimony known to be associated with multi-party majoritarian democracy. Just like any other model of governance, a consensual polity may have its own downside. On balance of scale, it is more disposed to produce decisional outcomes that are not only sustainable and appealing to parties because they *own* them, but also because issues are effectively deliberated and the outcomes are more reasoned out.

Honest and committed rational deliberations leading to consensual outcomes are a standout quality of a consensual polity. It is a common cause that one of the key issues plaguing countries in Africa is that governance is essentially an elitist enterprise with marginal or no involvement of governed in decisional processes that impact their lives. Significant segments of populations might feel that they are left out of decisional processes such that they conceive government and governance to be far removed and disconnected from their daily issues and concerns. Essentially governance does not speak to their concerns but reflects whims of the ruling elite. This is despite claims usually emanating from governments that their policies are people-centred when in fact they largely reflect what they deliberate in elite platforms reflecting what they think the governed possibly want and think. Such a model of democracy has serious flaws. With this in mind, honest and committed rational deliberation that is promised by a consensual polity offers a compelling alternative. What is important to note is that any decision that affects interest groups or parties within a state must legitimately be an outcome of their deliberative processes. This calls for the processes leading to consensus to be authentically inclusive. As I see it, this is the point at which deliberation is a key attribute. Rational deliberation is the process and consensus is the outcome (Ani, 2014: 347). The outcome cannot be praised when the process is flawed and deceptive. For this reason, the process of deliberation ought to be inclusive and genuine in order for it to give us legitimate consensual outcomes. And a consensual polity seems to give just that refreshing dimension to governance, especially in countries in Africa where the predominant use of multi-party majoritarian democracy has largely produced more chaos than envisaged thriving democratic culture.

But then despite its impressive credentials centering on genuine inclusive and robust deliberations foregrounding consensual outcomes, its operational possibilities for countries in Africa and elsewhere have not been sufficiently tested. By this, I mean that it essentially remains an idea to be implemented following its dislodgement as a model of choice in some African societies at the inception of colonial conquest. A consensual polity's chief proponent, Wiredu (2007: 170) has acknowledged the need to revisit it with the aim of using it as the model for deliberative democracy in Africa when he states that 'by all the visible signs in Africa now, we need to re-learn the ways of consensus, both conceptually and existentially. Political consensus might then be added unto us'. Both 'conceptually' and 'existentially' the mettle of democracy by consensus has been put to doubt by its prominent critics. Bernard Matolino (2012; 2013; 2016) and Emmanuel Ifeanyi Ani (2014) come to mind. More generally, they doubt the conceptual articulation and operational promise of a consensual polity in present-day countries in Africa. These are profound concerns that require serious attention. Wiredu (2007: 170) himself has highlighted the need to continue thinking about this idea until it is consummated in concrete implementation for the betterment of countries in Africa. Though critics raise important points about its possibilities of concrete implementation given the complex nature of the modern state, it can hardly be denied that consensual democracy is an attractive option that could help countries in Africa overcome internecine conflicts and rancour that have troubled them since 'independence'. I use the term 'independence' with caution because its veritable attainment for countries in Africa is seriously in doubt. In this light, the focus might need to be on what a consensual polity would promise and then see to it how it could be consummated to provide a compelling option to multi-party majoritarian democracy. And from an analysis of how rational deliberation operates as a process leading to consensual outcomes, it appears convincing that a consensual polity has better and more inclusive democratic credentials. However, its conception of *parties* has often been viewed as essentially pointing to one-polity inclinations. Wiredu's (2007: 1066) idea of parties that participate in rational deliberations as opposed to political parties driven by the desire for the sectional appropriation of power has not been well appreciated. Indeed, a consensual polity has multi-parties but their mode of operation is robust and inclusive participation in deliberation in order to arrive at consensual outcomes. As a result, they are different from the rancorous political parties of multi-party majoritarian polity that have brought serious problems to some countries in Africa. A mode of deliberation in which views and concerns of *all* are represented and reflected in consensual outcomes is really one to praise than lambast.

Concluding Remarks

In efforts to show the structural attractiveness of a polity that prides rational deliberation to produce consensual outcomes, David Bohm's (1996) idea of dialogue is instructive. The spirit of dialogue, for Bohm (1996: 7), is that 'nobody is trying to win. Everybody wins if anybody wins'. The cravings to win against opponents is an overarching character of multi-party majoritarian democracy. But in doing so, it exhibits its fatal structural and ethical flaws as manipulation underpins deliberation and negotiations for the consent of the governed in such a polity. Critics of a consensual polity may not see what they perceive as attributes of parties in the special kind of parties that participate in rational deliberation. However, these parties that participate in rational deliberations make a profound difference to the rancorous and divisive political parties of multi-party majoritarian democracy that have placed some countries in Africa perpetually in election modes and accompanying problems that are an anathema to political peace and stability that are so essential to economic development. Possible operational challenges of a consensual polity in the present modern state aside, it offers a refreshing dimension of rational deliberation where *everyone* feels his or her influence in the decisional processes and their consensual outcomes is treasured.

Notes

1 This qualification to the term 'persuasion' could be indicative of Wiredu's (2011: 1062) realisation that conceived on its own without this appellation, persuasion might not be easily separated from, say, manipulation.
2 The italics in this quotation are my own.

Works Cited

Ani, Emmanuel Ifeanyi. "On Traditional African Consensual Rationality." *The Journal of Political Philosophy* 22.3 (2014): 342–365.
Bakir, Vian, Herring, Eric, Miller, David, & Robinson, Piers. "Organized Persuasive Communication: A New Conceptual Framework for Research on Public Relations, Propaganda and Promotional Culture: A New Conceptual Framework for Public Relations and Propaganda Research." *Critical Sociology* 45.3 (2019): 311–328.
Bohm, David. *On Dialogue.* New York: Routledge, 1996.
Button, Mark. E. *Political Vices.* Oxford: Oxford University Press, 2016.
Masaka, D. "Kwasi Wiredu's Consensual Democracy and One-Party Polities in Africa." *South African Journal of Philosophy* 38.1 (2019): 68–78.
Matolino, Bernard. "Democracy, Consensus, and Africa: An Investigation into Consensual Democracy's Contribution to African Political Philosophy." *Philosophia Africana* 14.2 (2012): 105–124.
Matolino, Bernard. "The Nature of Opposition in Kwasi Wiredu's Democracy by Consensus." *African Studies* 72.1 (2013): 138–152.
Matolino, Benard. "Ending Party Cleavage for a Better Polity: Is Kwasi Wiredu's Non-party Polity a Viable Alternative to a Party Polity?" *Acta Academica* 48.2 (2016): 91–107.
Nichols, Ralph. G. "Manipulation versus Persuasion." *Journal of International Listening Association* 1.1 (1987): 15–28.
Paulo, Norbert & Bublitz, Christoph. "Pow(d)er to the People? Voter Manipulation, Legitimacy, and the Relevance of Moral Psychology for Democratic Theory." *Neuroethics* 12 (2019): 55–71.

Wiredu, Kwasi. "Democracy and Consensus in African Traditional Politics: A Plea for a Non-party Polity." *The Centennial Review* 39.1 (1995): 53–64.

Wiredu, Kwasi. "Democracy and Consensus in African Traditional Politics: A Plea for a Non-Party Polity." *Postcolonial African Philosophy: A Critical Reader.* Ed. In Emmanuel Chukwudi Eze. Cambridge, MA: Blackwell Publishers Ltd., 1997. 303–311.

Wiredu, Kwasi. "Democracy by Consensus: Some Conceptual Considerations." *Socialism and Democracy* 21.3 (2007): 155–170.

Wiredu, Kwasi. State, Civil society and Democracy in Africa. Reclaiming the Human Sciences and Humanities through African Perspectives Volume I1. Ed. In Helen Lauer and Kofi Anyidoho. Legon, Accra: Sub-Saharan Publishers, 2011, 1055–1066.

10

DISHARMONY AS A POLITICAL VICE

Edwin Etieyibo

Introduction

Harmony is a beautiful thing in several contexts, and this is perhaps best illustrated in music. So, imagine that you're dancing or singing along to your favourite music or song. You may not know the full lyrics or perhaps, you only know parts of it, but that does not deter you from engaging with the music, as you sing some words and hum others. Given how you're feeling as the song is playing you can tell that there is something special or good going on. The song does something to and for you; it resonates with you, and it moves you, your sensation, limbs and the rest of your body to react positively and joyfully; in fact, it does move you to dance (which you don't often do).

What are we to make of you and the song? One direction that we can take this to is to say that your appreciation of the music is caused or mediated by a number of things or factors. But whatever these are; there is certainly a pleasing or stimulating feeling that it produces in you. One may speak of what is going on—the song, all the sensation and your bodily reaction—in terms of harmony. More of this in a moment. I used this imagery or idea of music to accomplish two things. The first is to flag the notion that the claim that harmony is a beautiful thing doesn't seem misplaced. Second, to signpost the idea that harmony often features in the background and may be unrecognizable to one confronting it. By doing this I might be said to be introducing the sense in which one might think of harmony as something valuable—at least it seems so in music given its role and value in creating some experiences for you or the listener of the music.

Given what I have said about harmony and much of what goes on in music, I want to suggest that harmony is an important concept and if it is then disharmony is also important, inasmuch as it is, one might think, antithetical to harmony. Although I am suggesting here that harmony and disharmony are important concepts it seems curious why they have not got that much consideration (or very elaborate and explicit attention and discussion) in the philosophical literature, and certainly in the African philosophical literature. Even when the concepts are mentioned or examined, they haven't really been discussed in ways that point us to the sense in which harmony can be construed as a virtue and disharmony as a vice. This is a very significant insight but, for now, I set this consideration or worry aside. Owing to this lack thereof, a discourse on harmony and disharmony as a virtue or vice or harmony as

DOI: 10.4324/9781003143529-12

desirable and disharmony as undesirable is bound to run into some issues, not the least that of source material and an inability to present what some of the major discussions and positions on harmony and disharmony are. This is not to say that there are no ideas in the literature that one can draw on to talk about harmony and disharmony. That is certainly what I will be doing in this chapter. This, therefore, makes my endeavours here a largely exegetical and interpretative one, rather than an excavatory or analytically discursive one.

In a nutshell, what I will be doing in this chapter is to draw on ideas here and there on harmony and disharmony to make sense of the idea of harmony as desirable ethically and politically and disharmony as undesirable ethically and politically. In particular, I will be drawing on harmonious existence and being or a *we-mode of being* in African ontology or metaphysical worldview, the notion of "consensus" in consensual democracy, and on "harmonious or communal relationships" in personhood and Ubuntu to highlight the notion of harmony as a virtue (or valuable) in contrast to disharmony as a vice (or dis-valuable). Ultimately, the thesis that I defend is that there is a plausible case to be made for the view that disharmony is a vice (and insofar as it is, it is a political vice) that undermines the proper practice of politics in Africa.

I will be arguing for this thesis in a less somewhat explicit way. What I mean by this is that my argument for the thesis will be presented in some roundabout way. Constituting the argument that I will be advancing for the thesis will be my discussion of a number of things in connection with harmony and disharmony and the African Union as an exemplification of political practice in Africa. This discussion I hope will show why and how harmony is valuable, and the sense it is and why and how disharmony is not valuable and, the sense it is not, and the importance of embracing harmony as part of the proper practice of politics in Africa. My discussion of harmony in this chapter is divided into three parts. In the first part, I examine harmony as a virtue and disharmony as a vice. In the second part, I analyse some aspects of African philosophical ideas and understanding to highlight and show the way that harmony and disharmony may be drawn from these. Finally, in part three, I discuss an aspect of African political realities (the African Union) and how some of its failures constitute marked examples of disharmony in the political sphere or practice.

Harmony and Disharmony, Virtue or Vice?

Should we desire harmony? Is harmony valuable, and, if it is, what makes it valuable? And why should we prize and pursue harmony? These are important questions that have some bearing on the question of whether disharmony is a vice, or in particular, whether disharmony is a political vice. In this section, I will briefly examine what is meant by harmony and disharmony and the sense in which one may think of these two concepts as valuable or dis-valuable and/or virtuous or vicious.

Understanding Harmony and Disharmony

To enable us understand disharmony, it may be helpful to first of all understand harmony. When one thinks of harmony one may quickly think of music, where the concept has gained as much fame. Here, I come back to the image of singing or humming a favourite song that I began with. Recall the point I made about the music doing something to or for you in the sense that it resonates with you and it moves you to react or to dance and the point about the pleasing or stimulating feeling that it produces in you. I remarked that all of this implicate us in some talk of harmony, even when the listener is unaware of harmony (lurking in the background) in the song that he or she sings or hums to. One's positive engagement with the song may be explained by the meditation of the melodious tune, not the least, the lyrics or musical notes, etc. given that in music, harmony is used in reference to the amalgamation of concurrently sounded notes in music to produce harmonies and chord progressions that produce in the listener some pleasing effect. Having said this, I should remark that harmony can also mean the sound of two or more musical notes that are heard simultaneously.

But harmony is used also in other contexts besides music; in fact, in almost every other context. In photography for example, harmony refers to the combination of similar elements throughout the frame that creates certain visually stimulating images. In design, harmony is said to exist when all components of some particular design fit together. And in art, harmony refers to the creation of cohesiveness by emphasizing the similarities of separate but related parts. What comes out from the sense of harmony here is that harmony refers to some sort of balance or unity of entities or parts or simply some togetherness of elements or parts of some *thing* or object, which may result in some pleasant effect.

As I have indicated, harmony can be used to designate almost everything; certainly things besides music, photography, design and art. Harmony also does play a role in human-to-human relationship, which is my interest in this chapter. In particular, I am interested in harmony in reference to human affairs or activities and the sort of implications that one can draw in terms of politics broadly construed. So, if one keeps in mind the idea of harmony as referring to the balance or unity of entities or parts, then harmony as understood in the context of humans or human relationships and human activities will refer to the balance or unity that exists in those relationships or activities or community. Accordingly, when one says, "There's harmony among members of so and so community," one seems to be saying that there is an absence of conflict and divisions in that community. Harmony then as describing human affairs as free from conflicts and divisions is a description of the relationship of humans and their activities as members of a group (or community) and a description that points to some accord or agreement in action or opinion or feeling etc., or more generally, about some sort of peaceful co-existence among humans—the existence of balance or unity in some particular domain of activities.

This way of thinking of harmony provides us with one way of understanding disharmony, particularly if we think of it as the opposite of harmony. Like harmony, disharmony can also define relationships between and among entities. Broadly, it refers to a number of disparate parts or entities that are out of sync or some imbalance or disunity of entities or parts. If disharmony suggests the idea of imbalance or disunity with reference to certain entities or parts, then used in reference to humans and their affairs it will mean the presence of conflict and divisions among humans and their activities and in the community. That is, when disharmony is used to designate humans and human activities one means the absence of unity or accord or agreement in action or opinion or feeling, etc. That is to say, human activities and relationships are disharmonious when there is the manifestation of disunity or disagreement or the presence of conflict or some hostilities among humans. To take disharmony to characteristically designate humans, their relationships and interactions with one another in this way is to emphasize that those activities or relationships are discordant. A feature of discordance is its conflicting nature or *confliction-ness*. Thus, one can speak of disharmonious relationship or activities when one speaks of something being out of tune or *off*-balance, in this case, the relationship or activities.

There are a couple of important questions that need to be asked here and which are of interest to me. The first is, "Why is harmony valuable or desirable and why is disharmony not valuable and desirable?" And the second question, which is related to the first is this: "What makes harmony valuable or a virtue and disharmony not valuable or a vice?"

Underlining these questions is the thought about the importance of harmony and the need to embrace it and abjure disharmony.

My general view is that harmony is a virtue and disharmony a vice and this, I think, carries some normative or prescriptive injunction, which is that one ought to act in ways that are harmonious or avoid behaviour that engenders disharmony. Although I will not be providing a robust or full argument for the claim that harmony is a virtue and disharmony a vice, I will be suggesting some ways of thinking of them as desirable and not desirable, and consequently as virtuous or vicious.

Even though one may think that harmony does not feature as a virtue in the Hellenic tradition or among some of the cardinal virtues that we find in Socrates, Plato, and Aristotle such as wisdom, moderation/temperance, courage/bravery, justice, piety, or in the discussion of the four cardinal virtues of prudence, justice, fortitude, and temperance in classical European philosophy and Roman Catholicism I think it is important to consider it as a virtue—whether as a personal virtue or as a virtue of social institutions. To take harmony as a virtue of social institutions is to take it as a political virtue and, correspondingly, disharmony as a pollical vice (the way I am suggesting that we do in this chapter). Harmony as a virtue of social institutions and disharmony as a vice of social institutions should not come as a surprise. The thought of harmony and disharmony as a virtue and vice of social institutions respectively is consistent with the notion that some virtues can both be of personal character and of society or social institutions. We see this with justice as a virtue that extend beyond personal virtue into the social, as we see in Plato's idea of justice in the city in the *Republic*,[1] Aristotle's discussion of justice as a virtue of character in Nicomachean Ethics[2] and as a virtue of constitutions and political arrangements in Politics,[3] and finally, in John Rawls' understanding of justice as "the first virtue of social institutions" in *A Theory of Justice*.[4]

The line of thought that I will be advancing in making a case for harmony as a virtue (and desirable or valuable) and disharmony as vice (and undesirable) is that as long as the notion of harmony enables humans to flourish (i.e., coexist less violently or more peacefully and to live in more beneficial ways that advance our various conceptions of the good) it is a virtue or desirable and to the extent that disharmony does the opposite or does not enable human flourishing it is a vice or not desirable. This thought suggests that the justification of the virtue of harmony and the vice of disharmony is a consequentialist one. That is true. Of course, it is possible for one to also argue for the desirability or virtue of harmony and undesirability or vice of disharmony on deontological or virtue ethics grounds. Harmony as virtue and disharmony as vice on deontological ground will point to valuing harmony because of its rule-enabling nature or for its own sake and not for its consequences and harmony as virtue and disharmony as vice on virtue ethics grounds will be concerned with showing that what ought to underlie our ethical lives is the development of various virtues and character traits including those associated with harmony. These remarks now put me in a position to be able to make a case, in the next section, as to why one might think of the virtue of harmony as valuable which, normatively, one ought to desire and embrace, and the vice of disharmony as dis-valuable and which, normatively, one ought to eschew and not desire.

The Virtue of Harmony as Valuable and the Vice of Disharmony as Dis-valuable

With regard to human affairs, one prominent area where harmony and disharmony are discussed is environmental ethics, or more broadly in connection with the relationship between humans and nature or the environment. In environmental ethics discussions, harmony is treated as a value or desirable and humans are encouraged to pursue it. In choosing to act, humans are encouraged to value an interconnected relationship with nature, and they do so by displaying appropriate moral sensibilities toward nature. They display such sensibilities when they live in harmony with nature. The sort of harmonious relationship emphasized here is what environmentalists such as ecocentrists generally call for when they argue that a sustainable relationship of humans with nature is one whereby living harmoniously with nature is to live in balance and agreement with the natural environment.[5]

The idea of harmony with nature is an idea of the interconnectedness and interrelatedness of human relationship with nature. It is simply the idea of balance. We certainly see this environmental idea in the broad outlines of eco-philosophy and the work of J. Baird Callicott[6] and Aldo Leopold's *Land Ethics*,[7] as well as discussions of the metaphysical underpinning of environmental consciousness in African philosophy.[8]

There are other contexts or cultures as well where harmony as balance is discussed. In Japanese culture and worldview, harmony is taken to be one of the most fundamental values.[9] As well, in Confucianism, harmony is prized as a value that incorporates some peaceful state of the mind or an action or some outcomes of an action.[10] In healthcare setting, Emiko Konishi, Michiko Yahiro and Naoko Nakajima have indicated the connection between harmony and the display of politeness and respect by nurses for other persons and how the outcome of harmonious practices of nurses proved beneficial to their patients in virtue of creating peaceful, harmonious relationships for all. As I indicated above in connection with justice in Plato's *Republic*, harmony is touted as important for the proper flourishing of the soul (with regard to Plato's' psychology) and the city (in respect of his politics or political view).[11] Indeed, Plato's discussion of harmony *ala* justice as the balance between the three parts of the soul and the three parts of society should be understood within the context of his view of justice as a master virtue (justice in the city is the same thing as justice in the individual).[12] In line with Plato's psychology, Neal O. Weiner has discussed the importance of harmony for health in general and mental health in particular, especially in the balance between the body and soul, and as understood in psychiatry.[13] I have argued elsewhere that within the African worldview of illnesses and health, the notion of metaphysical or psychophysical harmony plays a crucial role.[14]

The above discussion of harmony as balance in nature, psychology and health suggests to us that harmony is a virtue or at least a value that ought to be prized; and accordingly, that disharmony is a vice that should be shunned because it is not valuable. We can see why harmony is treated as valuable or a virtue and disharmony as a vice or a dis-value. The idea is that harmony brings together and leads human towards some beneficial state of affairs in virtue of some balance that is vital to either the individual (as in balance of the soul and body) or the larger whole (as in the flourishing of the communal or society). By contrast to the alluring nature of harmony, disharmony ought to be avoided because it tends to pull down and create an imbalance state of affairs; such imbalance detracts from unity among individuals or social flourishing.

African Philosophical Ideas and Understanding

In this section, I will be looking at three areas in African philosophy or African philosophical ideas and understanding in relation to harmony. These are: harmony and disharmony in African ontology or metaphysical worldview; harmony and disharmony in consensual democracy; and harmony and disharmony in personhood and Ubuntu.

Harmony and Disharmony in African Ontology or Metaphysical Worldview

One might say that the ideas of harmony and disharmony that have been discussed so far and the suggestion that harmony is a good thing or a value or virtue that ought to be embraced, on the one hand, and that disharmony is a bad thing or a dis-value or vice that one should have nothing to do with, on the other hand, introduce us to some definite ontology or metaphysics. That is, it is one thing to discuss harmony, or its nature and it is another thing to talk about whether it should be desired, pursued and embraced or not. When one focuses on the latter (harmony should be pursued and disharmony abjured) one is engaged in normative thinking which prescribes some course of action but in being prescriptive one needs to justify such posture. One justification for such is to point to the metaphysics or ontology that grounds the normative thinking and that is what I want to highlight here.

The idea of a "desirable harmony" (that is harmony which is valuable and ought to be desired) is grounded on the notion of harmonious existence and being of some ontology—one such ontology is the ontology of an African metaphysical worldview, according to which entities coexist in harmony. The notion of harmony and disharmony in African ontology or African metaphysical worldview is brought out in the idea of interconnectedness and interrelatedness of entities or beings. Lesiba J. Teffo and A.P.J. Roux have introduced us to this idea:

> African metaphysics is holistic in nature. Reality is seen as a closed system so that everything hangs together and is affected by any change in the system ... African metaphysics is organised around a number of principles and laws which control the so called vital forces. There is a principle concerning the interaction of forces, that is between God and humankind, and material things. These forces are hierarchically placed, they form *a chain of beings.* In this hierarchy, God, the creator and source of all vital forces, is at the apex. Then follow the ancestors, then humankind, and the lower forces, animals, plants, and matter.[15]

In suggesting the notion of a harmonious existence and being, Teffo and Roux point to a closed system, everything hanging together, a holistic metaphysics, etc. Polycarp Ikuenobe and Edwin Etieyibo have previously argued that this metaphysics is an ontology of a *we-mode of being* sort—an ontology that speaks of a way of existence or *beingness* that prizes togetherness, interconnectedness and interrelatedness.[16] Cleary, from this, one can say that in an African metaphysical worldview, harmony is something that has an ontological underpinning and one aligns oneself with a "prescriptivist ontology" when one values harmony and avoid disharmony. On this understanding, harmony is valuable because existence is understood as *a we-mode of being,* and disharmony is not valuable because it diverges from *a we-mode of being* or aligns with the perspective of an *I-mode of being.*

This notion of an ontology of a *we-mode of being* will further be reinforced in the next two sections, when I discuss consensus and consensual democracy, personhood and Ubuntu. The connection between an African ontology of *a we-mode of being* and topics such as consensus, consensual democracy, personhood and Ubuntu should not be surprising given the relationship between metaphysics or ontology and other areas of social and political life or philosophy such as ethics and socio-political philosophy.[17]

Harmony and Disharmony in Consensual Democracy

The idea of harmony and disharmony comes out in the notion of "consensus," a notion that is employed in consensual democracy. Consensual democracy is one of the most important topics in African political philosophy. Kwasi Wiredu resurrected the idea in contemporary African political philosophy by pointing to how it was practiced in traditional African communities, in particular among the Akan and then moves from there to attempting to make a case for why it should be looked at in contemporary politics in Africa especially given that, as he argues, it is a better iteration of democracy for Africa compared to majoritarian or multi-party democracy.[18] For consensual democracy, consensus plays a role because it is the mechanism by which issues and matters are decided. That is to say, it is a decision procedure that allows parties or participants in a political matter or an issue that affects a group or the society to arrive at a conclusion that is beneficial for all. For Wiredu, such conclusion brought about in consensual democracy by consensus may simply be one where parties agree on actions even if they don't agree in notions or beliefs.[19] How then does harmony come up in consensus and why is it a virtue and disharmony a vice?

First, harmony comes up in the sense that the entire purpose of consensus is to get agreement in action (unquestionably, it would be great if there is also an accord in notion or belief). That is, there has to be an agreement on what has to be done and this agreement is one that entails a balance of thought in the direction of some unity. Every participant or all parties are normatively required to put aside differences in beliefs in order to come to some agreement in action. Of course, agreement does not come about on a platter of gold. There have to be discussions, debates and disputations and from this rational persuasion is advanced or provided which allows all parties to come to some agreement, some unity or harmony in what has to be done going forward. From this then and the fact that harmony comes up in consensus we are able to see how and why it is that it can be said that harmony is valuable, or a virtue and that disharmony is not valuable or a vice.

The simple thought here is that if the normative injunction in consensual democracy is for participants or all parties to strive towards consensus if and only if they so desire to go forward with certain actions, then consensus and or striving for harmony can only be but a *good* thing. Consensus *qua* harmony is good politically. It is good politically because it facilitates the possibility for any political action or behaviour and leads to the achievement of some desired outcome, which is *agreed action*. Accordingly, one can say that harmony is desirable and a virtue inasmuch as it is a *good* thing or valuable and correspondingly disharmony is a bad thing or a vice just in case it leads or takes parties or participants away from some beneficial political action. The vice of disharmony is underscored by the fact that it does not lead to what consensus requires, a unity of action even if not in belief or notion. To embrace disharmony when matters of public or communal importance are being debated is to poke communal life where it hurts most, namely, to undermine the very foundation of consensual democracy, which is to achieve some outcome that is understood and perceived to be beneficial for the community, and which is possible only when parties align their behaviour or direct their thoughts to some particular unified action.

Harmony and Disharmony in Personhood and Ubuntu

Personhood and Ubuntu constitute two of some of the hottest topics or hotly debated subjects in African philosophy. Both personhood and Ubuntu exhibit features that speak to the concepts of harmony and disharmony. This is so because at their core is the notion of "community" or harmonious relationship, or simply a uniting or coalescing in a "we." Desmond Tutu speaks of the "we" of Ubuntu in the following passage:

> When we want to give high praise to someone we say, "*Yu, u nobuntu*"; "Hey, so-and-so has *ubuntu*." Then you are generous, you are hospitable, you are friendly and caring and compassionate. You share what you have. It is to say, "My humanity is caught up, is inextricably bound up in yours.[20]

The point about unity, as advanced by Ubuntu, goes beyond the idea of individuals or persons having solidarity with others. Rather, it relates exclusively to the idea of one being inextricably bound together with others in some common communal fate and life. Tutu shows how to think of this when he says:

> A person with Ubuntu is available and open to others, affirming of others, does not feel threatened that others are able or good, for he or she has a proper self-assurance that comes from knowing that he or she belongs in a greater whole and is diminished when others are humiliated or diminished, when others are tortured or oppressed.[21]

When one talks about Ubuntu one is largely implicated in discussions of personhood insofar as the notion of personhood has a moral dimension that speaks of the "I" or individuals as members of a community that are required to fulfil certain moral obligations that are beneficial for the "we" or important for relationships. The point is that the "we" or "communal" in the Ubuntu aphorism as expressed by John Mbiti "I am because we are, and since we are, therefore, I am" is meaningful in the context of communal moral life and such a life is one where persons work harmoniously and in good faith with others or as Mogobe Ramose puts it, where they form humane relations:

> [For Ubuntu, to] be a human be-ing is to affirm one's humanity by recognising the humanity of others and, on that basis, establish *humane relations* with them.... One is enjoined, yes, commanded as it were, to actually become a human being.[22]

Thus, to speak of Ubuntu and personhood is to speak aphoristically of humans *qua* persons being persons through other humans *qua* persons. This introduces us to the idea of that which is constitutive of persons or personhood, where the thought is that for Ubuntu, the "I am" is an "I only in the "we," and each and everyone is normatively enjoined to reorient or reorder their behaviours so that their actions advance or establish *humane relations,* namely, are other regarding rather than self-regarding.

On a normative account of person or personhood, relationships or the capacity to commune or being in community (i.e., exercising the capacity), where being in community means exhibiting a *we-mode of being* is integral to what makes one a person and accordingly one who follows through on what Ramose calls the injunction to form a humane relationship is said to be a moral person, morally speaking. To live then morally means that one is a person, and one lives morally when one behaves in ways that enhance relationships or beneficial for the "we" or community. Stated differently, living morally or moral persons seek to promote activities that are not disharmonious.

From the discussion above, we can see how harmony and disharmony feature in personhood and Ubuntu and what makes one a vice or not of value and the other a virtue and of value. Just to reiterate, for personhood and Ubuntu, one is commanded to form *humane relations* or commune with others. One does this when one lives harmoniously with others, and it is only then that it can be truly said that one is a person that has acted morally. Ifeanyi Menkiti has reminded us that personhood is not automatic but something a person can fail or succeed at. He says:

> For personhood is something which has to be achieved, and is not given simply because one is born of human seed.... As far as African societies are concerned, personhood is something at which individuals could fail, at which they could be competent or ineffective, better or worse.[23]

There are several things that one can take from all of these. One of which is that if one proves to be incompetent at becoming a person or fails at personhood one has failed to live morally in at least one sense and this is in the sense of harmonious existence, that is, a failure in living harmoniously with others in the community, or a failure to properly commune with others, or a failure to effectively exercise the capacity to commune. The point *simpliciter* is that an individual or an 'I' that is unable to see or carry themselves as part of a "we" and carries on in life as an "I" is a moral failure or a *non-person*. Moral failings or non-personhood is not desirable, therefore one who desires to be a person is better off to prize harmony over disharmony and given how beneficial harmony is to the notion of persons or living a moral life and to the promotion of communal activities and fostering relationships, harmony turns out to be a virtue and disharmony a vice.

Speaking of harmony, Tutu says it is not only one of the great goods in African moral thinking (along with friendliness and community) but the greatest good. Indeed, as the summum bonum, it is a good that he thinks ought to be embraced.

> Harmony, friendliness, community are great goods. Social harmony is for us the *summum bonum*—the greatest good. Anything that subverts or undermines this sought-after good is to be avoided like the plague. Anger, resentment, lust for revenge, even success through aggressive competitiveness, are corrosive of this good.[24]

Along the thought of harmony as communing properly with others, Thaddeus Metz has expressed harmony in the context of right actions as follows: *"An action is right just insofar as it produces harmony and reduces discord; an act is wrong to the extent that it fails to develop community."*[25]

If we are to embrace the virtue of harmony because of its value, then disharmony, as a vice has to be shunned. It has to be avoided because disharmonious behaviour flies in the face of or undermines the logic of the communal organization of African societies. Menkiti has presented to us how the requirement of obligations (the ethics of duty) is important for the organization of traditional African societies and how this is different from the organization of traditional Western societies.

> [I]t becomes quite clear why African societies tend to be organized around the requirements of duty while Western societies tend to be organized around the postulation of individual rights. In the African understanding, priority is given to the duties which individuals owe to the collectivity, and their rights, whatever these may be, are seen as secondary to their exercise of their duties. In the West, on the other hand, we find a construal of things in which certain specified rights of individuals are seen as antecedent to the organization of society; with the function of government viewed, consequently, as being the protection and defense of these individual rights.[26]

What this tells us is that if the communal organization or nature of society is to be maintained, then behaviour and actions that promote peace, togetherness and unity are to be embraced and those are certainly not the sorts of actions and behaviour that are associated with disharmony but rather with harmony.

African Union and African Political Realities in the Context of Harmony and Disharmony

What I want to do in this section is to draw on the above discussion of harmony as valuable and disharmony as not valuable to discuss the specific context of political experiences or realities in Africa. In order for me to be able to generalize about political experiences and life in Africa I will be using the African Union (AU) as a foil for this discussion and engagement. I think this method is apropos, not because I think that the AU exhaust politics in Africa but because it gives us a glimpse of the sort of thinking in terms of harmony and disharmony that may generally be at play at the macro-political level (the level of continental bodies) in contradiction to micro-political level (the level of individual societies or countries in Africa).

Uniting Africa in the AU

Anyone familiar with events on the continent or goings on in Africa will probably have their views or ideas about why the continent is where it is in terms of development or why by and large many of the countries in the continent are not doing that well politically and economically. Undeniably, the point that many countries in Africa are not doing well politically and economically can be said of many countries in other continents or parts of the world. But I am not concerned with other countries in other parts of the world. I am concerned with countries in Africa. And surely, one is allowed to discuss issues in Africa (which may also be present or implicated elsewhere) without having to discuss issues in every or other parts of the world. Additionally, and perhaps the most important point, this chapter is for a volume that is about Africa, i.e., African political philosophy.

One may point to all sorts of ills plaguing the continent but here I am less concerned with these ills. Rather, my focus is on what these ills may be symptomatic of. One may take these ills to be representative or indicative of things like poor leadership, brazen and crass corruption, political disengagement or absence of communal engagement and active citizen participation, and lack of political vision etc., which may be symptomatic of something more fundamental. In any case, in the midst of these ills, there is unquestionably the lurking around or in the background of the big monster of disharmony, which is visible to anyone that is capable of cutting through the chase, i.e., through all the political shenanigans and madness in the continent. It is this monster that I am interested in, or simply the sense in which harmony and disharmony are implicated in African political realities as exemplified in some of the activities of the AU. So even if one disagrees with me and claims that the ills plaguing many of the countries in Africa are not symptomatic of disharmony the fact that there's something to be said about the importance of engaging with harmony and disharmony in African political realities insofar as harmony is desirable and disharmony is undesirable makes it worthwhile engaging with harmony and disharmony in the way I am doing in this chapter or suggesting one should do. And since I am focusing on the continent and not on one individual or particular countries in the continent, I think that, a place to begin with in our engagement with harmony and disharmony in the context of African political realities is the AU given that one of its mandates or vision is "unity."

The AU is an intergovernmental organization that on July 9, 2002 replaced the Organisation of African Unity (OAU), which was established on May 25, 1963 in Addis Ababa, Ethiopia.[27] What is interesting here is that the AU replaced the OAU, and in doing some dropped the word "unity," even though unity is still fundamental to the AU. One of the main objectives or aims of the OAU (and indeed among the first set of listed objectives) is *"To promote the unity and solidarity of the African States."*[28] This objective of the OAU is carried over by the AU. In its Constitutive Act and Protocol on Amendments to the Constitutive Act, one of the listed aims of the AU is stated as follows: "[Achieving] greater *unity and solidarity*[29] between African countries and their the people" (sic).[30] It is this talk of or reference to unity and solidarity (which I emphasized) that implicates the AU in discussions of harmony and disharmony, and which I am interested in.

Challenges, Problems and Failures of the AU

Since its inception, the AU has faced many challenges and problems— challenges and problems that have beset the continent for many decades. These include chronic poverty, high unemployment rate, corruption, political instability and not the least, armed conflicts, civil wars, terrorism and violent extremism. Anyone interested in the achievements of the AU can point to all the good things that they have done. I have no problem with these achievements, but I won't be focusing on them in this chapter.[31] My interest and focus rather are to point out the things that they have failed to do, which I want to claim is indicative of disunity or activities that are disharmonious. I will begin by making a comparative move, a move that will see me highlight these failures by pointing to another continental body, the European Union, in particular, highlighting its successes or achievements in contradiction to the AU.

The European Union (EU) is a political and economic union of 27 member countries in Europe. Officially, the EU was founded on November 1, 1993 in Maastricht, Netherlands.[32] The EU was not always as big as it is today. When European countries started to cooperate economically in 1951, only Belgium, Germany, France, Italy, Luxembourg and the Netherlands participated. The EU inherited many of its present obligations and aims from the European Communities (EC), which was founded in the 1950s. And its metamorphosis has been propelled by a number of treaties such as the *Treaty of Paris* (or the *Treaty establishing the European Coal and Steel Community*), which was signed on April 18, 1951 and the *Treaty of Rome* (or the *Treaty establishing the European Economic Community*), which brought about the creation of the European Economic Community (EEC) or the European Communities (EC).[33]

If one goes with the official incarnation of the EU, the OAU/AU is older. Yet, the EU, which does not have "unity" as one of its values or objectives (or at least explicitly so), seems to have done more for its members in Europe and unified them more than the OAU/AU has unified the continent or achieved for its members in Africa for decades. For a start, the EU has a single currency but the AU does not. About three decades ago the OAU and its replacement the AU through the Abuja Treaty, which was signed on June 3, 1991 in Abuja, Nigeria committed to the aim of a common currency under the African Monetary Union[34] by around 2020.[35] We are now in 2023 and we can hardly see any movement in this area.[36] And as Osterholt (2021) has noted, "most countries have not signed this proposal as some decided to form their own currency unions, some want to delay the starting date and some are already using currencies from other countries." To say here that the AU is swimming in an ocean of disunity is to understate the fact.

Secondly, the EU won, in 2012, the Nobel Peace Prize "for advancing the causes of peace, reconciliation, democracy and human rights in Europe"[37] Or as the 2012 Nobel Prize

Committee said that the 2012 Nobel Peace Prize was awarded to the EU because "for over six decades [it has] contributed to the advancement of peace and reconciliation, democracy and human rights in Europe."[38] That the EU won a peace prize for the job it did to advance peace and reconciliation is a testament to its work, vision and dedication. With all the problems on the African continent: internal and external ethnic tension, armed conflicts, wars, etc. one will think that the AU has a veritable ground and environment for them to push towards peace and unity in Africa. Or stated differently, the number of conflicts and wars in Africa are many and more than enough to win a continental body many Nobel Peace Prizes. For example, the wars or armed conflicts that have been waged in Africa by both state and non-state actors in Africa between 1990 and 2015 are in the region of about 630, which account for over 75% of conflicts in the world.[39] The sarcastic point here is that if the AU has done even a tiny little bit to push towards peace and help stabilize the continent, as a body, and as part of fulfilling its objective and mandate of "unity" it would have at some point won at least one Nobel Peace Prize.

The above point and its connection to one of the mandates of the AU in terms of unity and solidarity are that peace and security have continued to elude the continent. The AU has remained essentially an observer during the last several years while the continent is being bedevilled, devastated and ravaged by civil wars, armed conflicts and terrorist attacks.[40] Some conflicts have been raging for decades. The armed conflicts and terrorists' attacks cover the following regions: The Sahel area (Mali, Burkina Faso, Northern Nigeria, Chad, Sudan and Eritrea); around the Lake Chad (Cameroon, Chad, Niger and Nigeria); the region of the Horn of Africa (Somalia, Sudan, South Sudan and Kenya); and in the Great Lakes area (Burundi, the Democratic Republic of Congo, Rwanda and Uganda). While some of the most prominent civil wars are those in Libya, South Sudan and Cameroon, the most notable armed confits include the ones in Western Sahara, the Maghreb region "involving Al Qaeda in the Islamic Maghreb, the Somali civil war, and the Allied Democratic Forces and Lord's Resistance Army insurgencies in Uganda and the DRC."[41] And in terms of conflicts by non-state actors, we have those of the "Tuareg separatist and jihadist insurgencies in Mali, Boko Haram in Northern Nigeria, jihadist and militia insurgencies in Burkina Faso, al-Shabaab in Somalia, and the ethnic war in the Central African Republic."[42]

In 1999 when the AU metamorphosed from the OAU it changed its Constitutive Act. This change allowed it to intervene in the internal affairs of member states. To shows its commitment to this change, the AU adopted in 2016 the Lusaka Road Map to end conflict by 2020. Unfortunately, the AU has not lived up to this change and challenge as it has failed and unwilling to mediate in some cases such as the bloody conflicts in Cameroon and Libya.[43] So, although one may point to some peace efforts that the AU is making in Sudan's Darfur region and Somalia; there are a number of conflicts by non-state actors like the Jihadi insurgencies in Lake Chad Basin and Northern Mali, the war in Libya and the Anglophone Ambazonia separatists conflict in Cameroon that "have turned Africa into a greater theatre of conflict than ever before."[44]

AU, Harmony and Disharmony

Given the above discussion, the following question becomes germane: in view of the mantra of the AU as a body for unity and solidarity why has it failed in these important areas? Some have attributed the failure and ineffectiveness of the AU to a number of factors. One of those is internal divisions. Let me use the example of the conflict in Libya that I highlighted above as one of the most prominent civil wars or conflicts in Africa to underscore the point about internal divisions in the AU.

Citing the example of Libya and the failure of the AU to intervene in the conflict in the country but rather elected to play an observer role, the AFP says that the AU passivity dates

> back to 2011, when African members of the UN Security Council endorsed military intervention, even as the AU's Peace and Security Council opposed it…A Nigerien source recently explained that the AU remains divided on Libya, claiming that Egypt, for example, doesn't want the AU to get involved.[45]

This view seems to be echoed by Linnéa Gelot who has highlighted that the impression of the AU by the international community is that it is much too weak, divided and disorganized to deal considerably with the civil war in Libya.[46]

Gelot's point about the weak, divided, and disorganized nature of the AU in Libya may be said to also apply to what is happening at the moment in Sudan. As I write this, heaving fighting has broken out in Sudan between the military leader of Sudan Abdel Fattah Abdelrahman al-Burhan and the Mohamed Hamdan Dagalo (generally referred to as Hemedti) who is commander of the paramilitary of the Rapid Support Forces of Sudan. Both army generals were allies and worked together not only in toppling and overthrowing in 2019 Sudanese President Omar al-Bashir in 2019 but also played a key role in the military coup in 2021.[47] In midst of the ongoing armed clashes there has hardly been any meaningful movement from the AU even though the fighting has been going on for almost a week. While countries like Egypt and South Sudan have offered to mediate in the conflict, the AU has only seen it fit to express deep concern about the situation and to call on the forces of al-Burhan and Hemedti to protect civilians and swiftly embrace a peaceful solution and inclusive dialogue, as well as warning against external interference in the crisis in Sudan.[48] If that is all that the AU thinks and hopes that it can do for now, then Gelot is right, for countries like Türkiye, the US, UN, as well as some other international actors have done the same thing that the AU has done. They have expressed concern over the fighting in Sudan and called on the warring parties to commit themselves to the transition process and dialogue.[49] In fact, the US has done more than the AU. There was a brief period of ceasefire (a 24-hour ceasefire) that was brokered on Tuesday April 18, 2023, by the US Secretary of State, Antony Blinken after he separately telephoned al-Burhan and Hemedti "to express 'grave concern' about civilian deaths and to urge them to agree to a ceasefire."[50] More worrying is that the armed conflict has been preceded by months of rising tensions between both rival factions of the armed forces, which has now spiraled into an all-out battle for control of Sudan.[51] During this period, the AU seems to have remained passive or not done anything to try and get the parties to deescalate the situation.

The issue of internal divisions also appears to be evident in another area, that of an African candidacy for the World Trade Organization and United Nations Security Council. Isaac Mugabi describes the AU's failure and ineffectiveness as that of a child that has refused to grow up:

> [T]he AU seems to be more a case of a child, who despite turning 18, seems stuck in puberty — a child unable to get up in the morning and clean up its messy room, a child who is permanently squabbling with its siblings. This is evidenced by the AU's failure to back a single candidate for the next head of the World Trade Organization, or even more embarrassingly, for the recently vacant UN Security Council seat.[52]

A number of things come up from the above. There is a reference to divisions in the AU regarding the conflict in Libya. Mugabi speaks of permanent squabbling of siblings (or members states or parties in the AU) concerning candidacy for the World Trade Organization and United Nations Security Council. And with regard to a single currency for the continent, there is division in AU on how to move forward. All of these are quite clearly issues that speak to a lack of unity or harmony. Simply put, they do speak to the absence of harmony and thriving of disharmony. A conclusion that one can draw then is that the failures of the AU in the areas that I have discussed are failures that point to disharmony, where these failures and the internal divisions that they are consequences of exemplify the presence of political vice. As a follow up to this, I would claim that if the AU is to follow a little more of its own mantra of unity and solidarity and to appreciate the importance of harmony as valuable or a virtue and to pursue harmony committedly and religiously the continental body would have made much more progress and achieve a little more peace in Africa.

Conclusion

What I have done in this chapter is to provide an exegetical and interpretative notion of the concept of harmony as a contrast to disharmony, and as constitutive of activities that are by definition in sync or describable as being in balance or unity. This exercise is meant to place me in a position to argue that harmony and disharmony are valuable (or desirable) and dis-valuable (not desirable), respectively. The upshot of this is that if harmony is valuable then it ought to circumscribe our activities, ethically and politically. One acts consistently with harmony and eschews disharmony when they seek out peaceful relationships, when they refuse to divide and align themselves with others such that in effectively communing there is an agreement in actions. As I have indicated, this seems to be lacking in some of the activities of the AU, which have prevented it from accomplishing as much as it ought to have accomplished given its broad aims and vision of "unity." This conclusion should be a worry for anyone interested in political progress in Africa, economic development and some semblance of stability and unity. This is particularly so given the claim that I have advanced that harmony is desirable and disharmony undesirable and that the failures of the AU in the areas that I have discussed highlight the problem of the absence of proper practice of politics in Africa.

I now want to end by raising one issue for my endorsement of harmony. By arguing that disharmony is a political vice, I have, at the same time, suggested that harmony is desirable and a good thing. One may wonder whether harmony particularly in the pollical space, as I have done in consensual democracy, does not endorse an authoritarianism regime or fascist tendencies where the views of others or the minority are brushed aside. This is certainly a legitimate point to make and one that was made by participants when I presented parts of the paper to the Centre for Ethics, Philosophy and Public Affairs (CEPPA).[53] As I flagged in my response during the Q&A after the talk, I noted that I did, in some way, anticipate this issue in my 2020c essay on "African Consensual Democracy, Dissensus and Resistance," where I argued that there may be some difficulty with consensual democracy in accommodating resistance and opposition. This is partly what I said in the essay:

> I now come to the question of the possibility of resistance. The kernel of this problematic is encapsulated in the question: If resistance is opposition, how then does one resist? The idea here is that even if we agree that the impact on the disposition to resistance by the cultivation of the disposition to compromise is not negative, the kind of resistance that is available to decision-makers will be a lame one, what might be called "lame duck opposition." In the regime of the disposition to compromise, one may be forbidden

from protesting since that will undermine the fact that we have agreed with the decision. As well, one cannot remind others that one is unhappy with the decision or express the wish or desire to reverse one's view, as this suggests that one is distancing oneself from the decision. And protest (whether overt or covert, verbal or through actions) is essential for resistance. So, what we are left with is the possibility of resistance without any *real* or *actual* resistance, almost akin to the distinction between formal freedom and effective freedom.

My response at the CEPPA talk was to say that what makes the point legitimate is that it goes to the heart of how to think of decision making in social and political spaces and that if one understands that consensus is continuously iterated and an unremitting give and take process, then authoritarian or fascist tendencies may be eschewed insofar as it is the case that in following through on consensus in pollical decision making participants are constantly reminded of the need to be respectful of everyone and the process. I now want to add that whether one thinks of the issue of authoritarianism as problematic and pervasive for consensus and consensual democracy will depend partly on how one parses out the interests of parties in relation to both the communal and individuals. If one parses the interests atomistically such that they align with or are sensitive to strictly the individual, then one might worry about some form of authoritarianism lurking behind consensus. However, if one parses the interests non-atomistically, i.e., communally, such that they align with or are sensitive to strictly the community, then one would not worry about the problem of authoritarianism in consensus. In the latter view, one takes communal flourishing to be of paramount importance such that harmony is all the more important and consensus, as both a practice and decision procedure for achieving harmony, becomes imperative and a *sine qua non*.

Notes

1 Plato (380 BC/1950)).
2 Aristotle (2000).
3 Aristotle (1995).
4 Rawls (1971/1999).
5 See Jordan and Kristjánsson (2017).
6 Callicott (1989, 1994, 1999), Callicott and Ames (1989).
7 Leopold (1949).
8 See Ekwealor (2012) and Etieyibo (2017a).
9 Konishi, Yahiro and Nakajima (2009).
10 Konishi, Yahiro and Nakajima (2009).
11 Robinson (1995).
12 Plato (380 BC/1950).
13 Weiner (1993).
14 Etieyibo (2014).
15 Teffo and Roux (1998: 138).
16 Ikuenobe (2020); See also Etieyibo (2020a, 2020b).
17 For the view that metaphysics does inform African ethics or axiology or how ontology or metaphysical view grounds other areas of philosophy see Obiajulu (2015); Ogbonnaya (2018) and Etieyibo (2017b).
18 Wiredu (1996, 2001).
19 For some discussion of Wiredu's consensual democracy see Emmanuel Eze (1997); Edward Wamala (2004); Matolino, (2013); Ani (2014a, 2014b); Ani and Etieyibo (2020); Etieyibo (2000c).
20 Tutu (1999: 31).
21 Tutu (1988: 4–5).
22 Ramose (2002: 52).

23 Menkiti (1984: 172, 173).
24 Tutu (1999: 35).
25 Metz (2011: 334).
26 Menkiti (1984: 180). See also Gyekye (2003 and 2010) for some further discussion of the ethics of duty in African societies, moral system or worldview.
27 The OAU existed from 1963 to 1999. The AU was founded in Durban, South Africa.
28 Emphasis is mine.
29 Emphasis is mine.
30 African Union (n.d).
31 My not focusing on the achievements or successes of the AU should not be interpreted to mean that I am only interested in finding fault with the AU. One reason that I am focusing on the failures of the AU and not its successes is that the former and not the latter help me advance the idea of harmony and disharmony in the political landscape in the AU viz-a-viz Africa or African nations. For a highlight and review of some of the successes or achievements of the AU as well as some of its failures see Tieku (2019).
32 The 1992 *Maastricht Treaty* is the foundation treaty of the EU, and it was an agreement between the 12 member States of the European Communities.
33 See European Union (n.d1, n.d2).
34 The expectation is that African Monetary Union will create an African Central Bank and an African Economic Community.
35 See Milkiewicz and Masson (2003) and Osterholt (2021).
36 Miriri (2009).
37 European Union (n.d2).
38 Noble Prize Organization (n.d).
39 *The Conversation* (2020).
40 See Mbaku (2016).
41 *The Conversation* (2020).
42 *The Conversation* (2020).
43 See Mugabi (2020).
44 Mugabi (2020).
45 AFP (2020).
46 Gelot (2016).
47 The fighting is reported to have started on Saturday April 15 in Sudan's capital, Khartoum and in a handful of other cities. And as of Tuesday April 18, 2023, 270 people have been reported killed in the armed clashes (Yeung, Rebane, and Picheta (2023b).
48 See Elbagir, Qiblawi and Orie (2023); Africanews with AFP (2023); TRTWorld (2023b).
49 TRTWorld, 2023a.
50 Burke, 2023; See also Yeung, Rebane, and Picheta (2023b).
51 Declan (2023).
52 Mugabi (2020).
53 Etieyibo (2023). This talk was presented virtually on Zoom.

References

AFP (2020), "African Crises: The Ineffectiveness of the African Union," *The North Africa Journal*, February 7, 2020. Available at: https://north-africa.com/2020/02/african-crises-the-ineffectiveness-of-the-african-union/, accessed October 3, 2021.

African Union (n.d.), "About the African Union," https://au.int/en/overview.Africanews with AFP (2023), "African Union Chief to Travel to Sudan as Fighting Spreads," *Africannews.com*, Sunday April 16. Available at: https://www.africanews.com/2023/04/16/african-union-chief-to-travel-to-sudan-as-fighting-spreads/, accessed April 19, 2023.

Aristotle (1995), *Politics*, translated by Ernest Barker and revised by Richard Stalley, Oxford: Oxford University Press.

Aristotle (2000), *Nicomachean Ethics*, Roger Crisp (ed./trans.), Cambridge: Cambridge University Press. doi:10.1017/CBO9780511802058.

Ani, Emmanuel Ifeanyi (2014a), "On Agreed Actions Without Agreed Notions," *South African Journal of Philosophy* 33 (3): 311–320.

Ani, Emmanuel Ifeanyi (2014b), "On Traditional African Consensual Rationality," *Journal of Political Philosophy* 22 (3): 342–365.

Ani, Emmanuel Ifeanyi and Etieyibo, Edwin (2020), "The Consensus Project: The Debate So Far," in *Deciding in Unison: Themes in Consensual Democracy in Africa*, Emmanuel Ifeanyi Ani and Edwin Etieyibo (eds.), 1–17, Wilmington, Delaware and Malaga: Vernon Press.

Burke, Jason (2023), "Sudan Ceasefire Fails to Contain Fighting Amid Reports of Gunfire," *The Guardian*, Wednesday April 19. Available at: https://www.theguardian.com/world/2023/apr/18/humanitarian-aid-impossible-as-fighting-in-sudan-traps-millions, accessed April 19, 2023.

Callicott, J. Baird (1989), *In Defense of the Land Ethic: Essays in Environmental Philosophy*, Albany: State University of New York Press.

Callicott, J. Baird and Ames Roger T., eds. (1989), *Nature in Asian Traditions of Thought: Essays in Environmental Philosophy*, Albany: State University of New York Press.

Callicott, J. Baird (1994), *Earth's Insights: A Survey of Ecological Ethics from the Mediterranean Basin to the Australian Outback*, Berkeley: University of California Press.

Callicott, J. Baird (1999), *Beyond the Land Ethic: More Essays in Environmental Philosophy*, Albany: State University of New York Press.

Elbagir, Nima, Qiblawi, Tamara, and Orie, Amarachi (2023), "Rival Generals are Battling for Control in Sudan: Here's a Simple Guide to the Fighting," *CNN* Monday April 17. Available at: https://edition.cnn.com/2023/04/16/africa/sudan-military-clashes-explained-intl/index.html, accessed April 19, 2023.

Ekwealo, Chigbo (2012), "Metaphysical Background to Igbo Environmental Ethics," *Environmental Ethics* 34 (3): 265–274.

Etieyibo, Edwin (2014), "Psychophysical Harmony in an African Context," in *Symposium on the Metabolism of the Social Brain*, October 25–26, Berlin: Akademie der Künste.

Etieyibo, Edwin (2017a), "Anthropocentricism, African Metaphysical Worldview, and Animal Practices: A Reply to Kai Horsthemke," *Journal of Animal Ethics* 7 (2): 145–162.

Etieyibo, Edwin (2017b), "Ubuntu and the Environment," in *The Palgrave Handbook of African Philosophy*, Adeshina Afolayan and Toyin Falola (eds.), 633–657, New York: Palgrave Macmillan.

Etieyibo, Edwin (2020a), "Menkiti as a Man of Community," in *Menkiti on Community and Becoming a Person*, Edwin Etieyibo and Polycarp Ikuenobe (eds.), 251–264, Lanham, MD: Lexington Books.

Etieyibo, Edwin (2020b), "An African Ethics of Duty and Cultural Justice and Injustice," *Inaugural Lecture, University of the Witwatersrand*, Wednesday September 23, 2020.

Etieyibo, Edwin (2020c), "African Consensual Democracy, Dissensus and Resistance," in *Deciding in Unison: Themes in Consensual Democracy in Africa*, Emmanuel Ifeanyi Ani and Edwin Etieyibo (eds.), 135–148, Wilmington, Delaware and Malaga: Vernon Press.

Etieyibo, Edwin (2023), "Disharmony as a Political Vice," talk presented to the Centre for Ethics, Philosophy and Public Affairs (CEPPA), St Andrews University, Scotland, Thursday March 23, 2023.

European Union (n.d.1), "About the EU," https://europa.eu/european-union/about-eu_en, accessed September 20, 2021.

European Union (n.d.2), "The EU in Brief," https://europa.eu/european-union/about-eu/eu-in-brief_en., accessed September 20, 2021.

Eze, Emmanuel Chukwudi (1997), "Democracy or Consensus: A Response to Wiredu," in *Postcolonial African Philosophy: A Critical Reader*, Emmanuel Chukwudi Eze (ed.), 313–323, Oxford: Blackwell.

Gelot, Linnéa (2016), "The Role and Impact on the African Union," in *Political Rationale and International Consequences of the War in Libya*, Dag Henriksen and Ann Karin Larssen (eds.), Oxford Scholarship Online: Oxford University Press, DOI: 10.1093/acprof:oso/9780198767480.001.0001

Gyekye, Kwame (2003), "Person and Community in African Thought," in *The African Philosophy Reader*, 2nd edition, P. H. Coetzee and A. P. J. Roux (eds.), 348–366, New York: Routledge. Previously appeared in Gyekye, Kwame (1992), "Person and Community in African Thought" in *Person and Community: Ghanaian Philosophical Studies*, 1, Kwame Gyekye and Kwasi Wiredu (eds.), 101–122, Washington, DC: Council for Research in Values and Philosophy.

Gyekye, Kwame (2010), "African Ethics," *Stanford Encyclopedia of Philosophy*, http://plato.stanford.edu/archives/fall2011/entries/african-ethics/.

Ikuenobe, Polycarp (2020), "Menkiti's Account of the Social Ontology of African Community and Persons," in *Menkiti on Community and Becoming a Person*, Edwin Etieyibo and Polycarp Ikuenobe (eds.), 95–114, Lanham, MD: Lexington Books.

Jordan, Karen and Kristjánsson, Kristján (2017), "Sustainability, Virtue Ethics, and the Virtue of Harmony with Nature," *Environmental Education Research* 23 (9):1205–1229.

Konishi, Emiko, Yahiro, Michiko and Nakajima, Naoko (2009), *The Japanese Value of Harmony and Nursing Ethics, Nursing Ethics* 16 (5): 625–636.

Leopold, Aldo (1949), *A Sand County Almanac*, New York: Oxford University Press.

Menkiti, A. Ifeanyi (1984), "Person and Community in African Traditional Thought," in *African Philosophy: An Introduction*, Richard A. Wright (ed.), 171–181, Lanham MD: University Press of America.

Metz, Thaddeus (2011), "Ubuntu as a Moral Theory and Human Rights in South Africa," *African Human Rights Law Journal* 11 (2): 532–559.

Milkiewicz, Heather and Masson, Paul R. (2003), "Africa's Economic Morass—Will a Common Currency Help?" *Brookings Policy Brief Series*, July 1, 2003, Available at: https://www.brookings.edu/research/africas-economic-morass-will-a-common-currency-help/, accessed October 3, 2021.

Miriri, Duncan (2009), African Union Sees Single Currency by 2021," *Reuters*, March 4, 2009, https://www.reuters.com/article/ozatp-africa-currency-20090304-idAFJOE5230HR20090304, accessed October 10, 2021.

Mugabi, Isaac (2020), "Opinion: African Union Turns 18 But Still Hasn't Grown Up," *DW Made for Minds*, July 8, 2020. Available at: https://www.dw.com/en/opinion-african-union-turns-18-but-still-hasnt-grown-up/a-54094274 accessed October 6, 2021.

Noble Prize Organization (n.d.), "The Noble Peace Prize 2012," Available at: https://www.nobelprize.org/prizes/peace/2012/summary/, accessed October 1, 2021.

Osterholt, Katharina (2021), "Is It Beneficial for the African Union to Introduce a Common Currency?" Munich, GRIN Verlag, Available at: https://www.grin.com/document/193726, accessed October 7, 2021.

Plato [380 BC] (1950), *The Republic of Plato, Translated into English with an Analysis and Notes* Golden Treasury Series). John Llewelyn Davies and David James Vaughan (eds., trans.), London: Macmillan and Co.

Ramose, Mogobe (2002), *African Philosophy Through Ubuntu*, rev. ed., Harare: Mond.

Rawls, John (1971) (revised 1999). *A Theory of Justice*, Cambridge, MA: Harvard University Press.

Robinson, T. M. (1995), *Plato's Psychology* (2nd Edition), Toronto: University of Toronto Press.

Teffo, Lesiba J. and Roux, A.P.J. (1998), "Metaphysical Thinking in Africa," in *Philosophy from Africa: A Text with Readings*, P.H. Coetzee and A.P.J. Roux (eds.), 134–148, Johannesburg: International Thomson Publishing Southern Africa.

The Conversation (2020), "Why the African Union has Failed to 'Silence the Guns': And Some Solutions," June 30, 2020, Available at: https://theconversation.com/why-the-african-union-has-failed-to-silence-the-guns-and-some-solutions-139567, accessed October 3, 2021.

Tieku, Thomas Kwasi (2019), "The African Union: Successes and Failures," Available at: https://doi.org/10.1093/acrefore/9780190228637.013.703, accessed October 6, 2021.

TRTWorld (2023a), "Türkiye, UN, US Urge Ceasefire, De-escalation as Fighting Erupts in Sudan," Sunday April 16. Available at: https://www.trtworld.com/africa/t%C3%BCrkiye-un-us-urge-ceasefire-de-escalation-as-fighting-erupts-in-sudan-67111, accessed April 19, 2023.

TRTWorld (2023b), "African Union Warns Against External Interference in Sudan Crisis," Tuesday April 18. Available at: https://www.trtworld.com/africa/african-union-warns-against-external-interference-in-sudan-crisis-67154, accessed April 19, 2023.

Tutu, Desmond (1988), Sermon in Birmingham Cathedral, April 21, Transcript Published by the Committee for Black Affairs, Diocese of Birmingham.

Tutu, Desmond (1999), *No Future Without Forgiveness*, New York: Random House.

Walsh, Declan (2023), "Rival Generals Unleash Fighting in Sudan, Dashing Dreams of Democracy," *The New York Times*, Monday April 17. Available at: https://www.nytimes.com/2023/04/15/world/africa/khartoum-sudan-fighting.html, accessed April 19, 2023.

Wamala, Edward (2004), "Government by Consensus: An Analysis of a Traditional Form of Democracy," in *A Companion to African Philosophy*, Kwasi Wiredu (ed.), 435–441, Maiden, MA: Blackwell Publishing Ltd.

Weiner, Neal O. (1993), *The Harmony of the Soul: Mental Health and Moral Virtue Reconsidered*, Albany: State University of New York Press.

Wiredu, Kwasi (1996), *Cultural Universals and Particulars*, Bloomington: Indiana University Press.

Wiredu, Kwasi (2001), "Democracy by Consensus: Some Conceptual Considerations. *Philosophical Papers* 30 (3): 227–244.

Yeung, Jessie, Rebane, Teele and Picheta, Rob (2023b), "Ceasefire Crumbles Amid Chaos in Sudan as Death Toll Reaches 270," *CNN*, Tuesday April. Available at: https://edition.cnn.com/2023/04/18/africa/sudan-fighting-intensifies-students-intl-hnk/index.html, accessed April 19, 2023.

11

DIFFERENCE AND EXCLUSIONISM

Elvis Imafidon

Introduction: From Identity Politics to Differentia-Politics

The question of identity is at once an ontological, epistemological, ethical, and political question. It is a question about the idea of my very *being* as an individual, or of our *being* as a collective; a question of *knowing* who I am as an individual or who we are as a collective. The identity question is also a question about rights, justice, freedom, duties and obligation of others to the self and of the self to the other. But answering these ontological, epistemological and ethical questions about identity seems to depend largely and very crucially on the agency and power to take charge of, to answer, and to define, the idea, knowledge and value of identity, or at the very least, the agency and power to question and critique existing narrative and construction of these identities. More so, essentially political questions of identity or identity politics are more obviously manifest in lived experiences. Agius and Keep (1–2) rightly say that,

> The power of identity to manifest as a unifying and divisive force pervades social, cultural, economic and political relations. Economic crises, war and conflict, struggles over resources and equality, and questions of exclusion and belonging are premised both overtly and subtly in claims about identity. This finds expression at and between the individual and collective level… Questions of 'who we are' shape our subjectivities and the world we inhabit, but… questions of identity have been fixated on 'identity politics'

This is perhaps why identity politics seem to foreground and dominate identity discourse and scholarship than say, identity ontology, identity epistemology and identity ethics even though these different strands of it are more interconnected and interdependent than may be obvious and even though other strands of it such as identity ontology, although less obvious and more latent in the scholarship on identity today, ought to take a more primordial place. Thus, identity politics although an essentially contested and slippery concept itself, has become a very useful concept in the last few decades in the social sciences and humanities for scholars to explain exclusion, belonging, conflicts, class struggles, queerness, activism, civil rights movements and the like. As Mary Bernstein (47) puts it,

> The term identity politics is widely used throughout the social sciences and the humanities to describe phenomena as diverse as multiculturalism, the women's movement,

DOI: 10.4324/9781003143529-13

civil rights, lesbian and gay movements, separatist movements in Canada and Spain, and violent ethnic and nationalist conflict in postcolonial Africa and Asia, as well as in the formerly communist countries of Eastern Europe.

Scholarship about postcolonial conflict, struggles and exclusion in sub-Saharan Africa in general and Nigeria in particular has therefore seen identity politics as a useful and important concept and theoretical framework to analyse these lived experiences (e.g., Konrad-Adenauer-Stiftung 1–154; Tarimo 297–308; Alumona and Azom 291–306; Etieyibo, Musemwa and Katsaura 361–366; and Green 1197–1226). For example, in an Introduction to the conference proceedings for the conference entitled Politics of Identity and Exclusion in Africa: From Violent Confrontation to Peaceful Cooperation held at the University of Pretoria in July 2001, published and co-funded by the Konrad-Adenauer-Stiftung Foundation, Hussein Solomon (5) says that,

> From Angola in the south-west through the Congos to Sudan in the north-west, a conflict zone exists which passes through the heart of Africa. Over the past four decades this has accounted for the death of millions, while contributing to the displacement of millions more. More depressing is the fact that contagion has occurred and now affects areas in Southern Africa, North and East Africa and West Africa. Many of these conflicts are intrastate and their roots often lie in contested perceptions of ethno-religious identity... The aim of the conference was to understand the root causes of the politics of identity and exclusion, which has so scarred this beloved continent of Africa.

Alumona and Azom (292) further explain some of the consequences of identity politics in Africa:

> ... in different parts of Africa the fallout of identity politics has led to ugly developments such as genocide in Rwanda, civil war in Nigeria, Liberia, and Somalia, apartheid in South Africa, and frequent ethnic violence in Kenya. In another vein, the fallout of identity politics in Africa has also been responsible for several secessionist attempts as found in the following cases: Belgian Congo 1960, Uganda 1966, Nigeria 1967, Djibouti 1991, and Senegal 1991. Presently, the resurgence of separatist movements in Nigeria has to do with identity politics.

Therefore, identity politics is no doubt a very useful concept for theorising and analysing identity-based lived experiences in African societies and exploring the power play between different groups, but it is a limited theoretical framework and conceptual tool. This is because identity politics takes as its focal objective the politics of constructing, and the power and agency to construct and define, an essentialist conception of the self, of what is or ought to be the self in which anything not fitting within become residues of identity. Identity politics in this sense, unlike identity ontology, which would acknowledge the factuality of the plurality of identities, implies an amplification of a notion of the self as superior to other notions. We can easily see how this has played out in human history for instance, white identity politics and male identity politics and how they resulted in racism and patriarchy. As the tables turn in our post-world, we see similar situations in which masculinity and heterosexuality take derogated places as residues of feminist and gay politics of identity. A crucial aspect of identity politics is thus to construct a narrative of the different, the other, or the alleged residues of the self, a construction geared towards presenting the self as real and ideal and excluding the other as far from ideal. It has the tendency to play down on the factuality and necessity of difference, portrays difference as a threat to identity and undermines the role difference plays in the formation and understanding of the multiplicity and diversity of identities.

My intention in this chapter is to show that much of our troubling lived experiences do not emerge primarily from who we say we are – identity politics – but from how we say the other is different from us and how we downplay differences in favour of the self – differentia-politics. While there is no thick line between identity politics and differentia-politics as both could as well be conceived as two sides of the same coin, it does a disservice to identity and alterity studies to focus solely on one side of the coin as this does not allow for a robust perspective. I am particularly interested in analysing how identity politics and differentia-politics dominate sub-Saharan African political experiences with particular reference to how these manifest in the Nigerian polity. The goal is to explore how an understanding and analysis of identity politics and the politics of difference in African political experiences can lay a solid foundation for the theorisation of African political philosophy. I am particularly interested in exploring the theory of relationality embedded in African philosophical thought such as Ubuntu in navigating the pitfalls of identity politics and differentia-politics and constructing endogenous African political philosophy. In pursuance of this, I begin in the section that follows by examining two approaches to the analysis of difference, differentia-ontology and differentia-politics. I then examine in the next section how differentia-politics forms the key foundation for forms of exclusion, violence and crises in the Nigerian polity, exploring two key aspects of the manifestation of differentia-politics. In the final section, I analyse how a shift to differentia-ontology through the hermeneutic ethic of Ubuntu is crucial in deconstructing differentia-politics and promoting inclusivity amidst diversity.

Exploring and Exploiting Difference: From Differentia-Ontology to Differentia-Politics

Ontology, the study, discourse and theory of being, of what is, what it means to be, to exist and to be real, occupies a central place in philosophical inquiry and many perspectives have emerged from different philosophical traditions. For example, Heideggerian and Sartrean discourse of being and existence in the twentieth century saw a shift from the dominant focus in traditional Western ontology on substance ontology or a metaphysics of presence to fundamental, existential ontology (Heidegger 33; Sartre 570), both representing two major approaches to the discourse of being in Western philosophy. Relational ontology has dominated the discourse of being in African philosophy literature (Teffo and Roux 192–208; Lajul 19–49) as the African understanding of being is theorised around shared energies and forces, co-dependency and relationality of beings and reality, and meaningful existence is understood as the equilibrium and togetherness that is sustained in the community of beings. However, a rarely explored perspective of being in the existing literature on ontology in various philosophical traditions is the existential factuality of difference, what I will simply call here, differentia-ontology, as a distinct approach to the discourse of being from say, substance ontology, fundamental ontology and relational ontology.

Differentia-ontology is the discourse of being that explores difference, uniqueness, dissimilarity and distinctness as a fundamental and defining quality of being: to-be is to-be-different. Being, as one of its fundamental qualities, consists of beings exhibiting qualities of dissimilarity and distinctness from other beings such that being different as an entity, an event or process is not an accident of being, but the very substance of it. Differentia-ontology therefore consists of explicitly reformulating the question of being in a way that takes seriously the factuality of difference. But this will largely depart from the human-centric, for example, Dasein study of being in Heidegger's *Being and Time* (Section 1 of the Introduction), as the only being who asks the question of being. This is essentially because although, Dasein remains the being who would formulate and theorise the question of difference, Dasein remains only one of the manifold of beings that exhibit and manifest difference and the sole focus on the ontological analysis and interpretation of the being of Dasein would be a very limited approach to a robust differentia-ontology. Differentia-ontology would therefore also involve exploring the structure of difference, its temporal, transcendental and finite natures, questions of factuality, existentiality, authenticity and relationality of difference, and questions of the dread for, denial of, misunderstanding of, veiling of, and disclosure of difference. Differentia-ontology is therefore not focussed on the empirical study of differences in beings – ontic differences – or the question of the difference of beings as observable, but rather on a more primordial question of the being of difference, how differences come into being and how being is in reality a manifestation and unfolding of difference. The all-important task of differentia-ontology – the study of the being of difference – is not of immediate concern or the primary focus in this paper. It is of course, the ideal project of the study of difference to be explored more fully elsewhere. The primary focus at this point is the deliberate and non-deliberate exploitation of ontic differences that permeates human society primarily for the control of power and resources.

Difference as ontic factuality is palpable and permeates existence and reality, but while differentia-ontology explores the fundamental nature of the ontic factuality of difference and the existential manifolds of differences with the objective of unravelling being as diverse and inclusive, the politics of difference or differentia-politics as manifested in human societies exploits these manifolds of ontic and concrete differences to entrench exclusion by formulating, constructing categories, contradictories and negations such as being and non-being, entity and non-entity, superaltern and subaltern, self and other-than-self, real and unreal. Differentia-politics is the politicisation of difference that has taken root and reigned in human society for as long as human history, often in a manner that supresses and shadows factual, authentic, and ontic differences. It continuously ensues from an interplay of recognition, misrecognition, non-recognition, refusal to recognise and a radical ethnocentric gaze on ontic differences. In the case of recognition of difference, it often happens by recognising a form of difference, elevating it to the status of identity for a particular form of being and by implication, elevating it over and above other manifestations of differences of that form of being for the main purpose of power and resource control.

Politics of difference does not happen, therefore, without the normative construction and narrative of difference by the elevated form of difference and such a narrative and construction always has the utilitarian goal of putting the constructor's form of difference on top of the ladder to enjoy certain rights and privileges and subjugating other forms of differences under its control. The subjugated forms of difference would have to sacrifice and suspend their forms of difference and attempt to become the elevated difference to enjoy those same rights and privileges. The politicised and problematic categories of inferior and superior, developed and underdeveloped, civilised and uncivilised, religious and non-religious, black and white, literary/cultured and vernacular languages are a few examples of the politicisation of differences that elevate a form of difference over others.

The politics of difference is manifested in every aspect of the African experiences including its polity. Imafidon (2–3) write that,

> … difference stands under a manifold of experiences in African traditional and modern societies. The othering in African traditional and modern societies of disabled and queer beings from human beings and of the male folk from the female folk and the xenophobic and xenophilic feelings for the foreign other in traditional and modern Africa spaces; the othering of the self from the other based on ethnic, political, and religious differences; the othering of the other based on economic status and class; and the notorious history of the racial othering of Africans by non-Africans and vice versa are clear manifestations of the experience of, and importance of, difference in African societies.

In what follows, I examine how the politics of difference manifests in two aspects of the Nigerian experience leading to sustained and increasing exclusion, violence and crises: (i) ethnic politics; and (ii) the politics of naming and labelling.

Differentia-Politics and Exclusion in Nigerian Polity

Nigeria is a place booming with differences, uniqueness and dissimilarities. The politicisation of such differences is key to understanding the plethora of exclusion, marginalisation and developmental crises that manifest in the Nigerian polity. One of the most influential forms of differences that impact the lived experiences of Nigerians is ethnic differences. As a country with over 250 ethnic groups, there exist a huge diversity of ethnic differences and these differences are exploited in ways that breed crises, violence, exclusion, marginalisation and underdevelopment. This differentia-politics in the exploitation of ethnic differences manifests in several ways including but not limited to the categorisation of ethnic groups as major (superior) and minor (inferior) and the clamour for the suspension of ethnic differences for the sake of the one, the Nigerian identity. Concerning the first, the differentia-politics of ethnicity or ethnic politics manifests itself in the categorisation of some ethnic groups as major ethnic groups and others as minor ethnic groups. This categorisation is not merely descriptive as often painted in terms of ethnic groups that have larger populations, but also normative and political as such ethnic groups are portrayed as superior and more important than the minor ethnic groups. Thus major ethnic groups such as the Yorubas, Igbos and the Hausa-Fulanis enjoy superior, privileged positions than minor ethnic groups such as the Edo, Tivs, Ijaws, Ibibios and the Kanuris. This has significant implications in terms of marginalisation and exclusion for the minor ethnic groups and in terms of power and resource control for the major ethnic groups. For example, the allegedly more important, superior and major ethnic groups subsumes under it many unique and different ethnicities from itself, failing to recognise, and by implication, suspending and supressing, their difference. The Biafra agitation, for example, which is an agitation by the Igbo ethnic group subsumed under it other unique and different ethnicities in places like Benue Uyo, Calabar, Edo and Delta, leading to marginalisation and agitations. Recently, the Anioma people and the Benin people of Nigeria have dissociated themselves from the Biafra agitation on the basis that it fails to recognise their uniqueness and differences and simply subsume them under the Igbo ethnic group and identity. (See Vanguard News 3 Mar 2016; and Vanguard News 5 Nov 2018; Chiluwa 357–381.) The question of which ethnic groups are at the centre of the Nigerian polity as different from those at the margins also influence significantly politics and resource distribution in the country, resulting in uneven distribution of resources, injustice and marginalisation of many ethnic groups. For even within the agitation for justice and fairness in the distribution of political power and resources, the agitation is often essential for fair and equal distribution among the major ethnic groups in the country. Thus a superior–inferior, major–minor, superaltern–subaltern categorisation of ethnic groups in Nigeria and in several other African countries persists and becomes the foundation of exclusion, marginalisation and oppression.

Concerning the second – the clamour for the suspension of ethnic differences, a common trend in the Nigerian polity is to demonise the recognition and discourse about difference in ethnicities as inimical to the Nigerian identity and progress. It is a quest to sacrifice ethnic differences for the one Nigeria in a manner that assumes that the recognition of different ethnicities and the recognition of the one Nigeria cannot happen at the same time; one must be foregone for the other. The same agitation for the suspension of ethnic identities for the survival of one Nigeria saturates scholarship on Nigerian governance and development in form of reports, articles, books and discourses in general. Ethnicity is often described in these literature as the cause of underdevelopment and the major challenge to governance in Nigeria. In the words of Ukoha Ukiwo (7),

> The vilification of ethnicity as the scapegoat of all vices associated with the Nigerian body polity has made the subject a dominant theme in the study of Nigerian political economy.... Thus, analysts interested in such diverse issues as nationalism, decolonization, national integration, political parties, military intervention, corruption, economic development, structural adjustment, democratization and violent conflict have all considered the variable of ethnicity. This was the case even in the 1960s and 1970s when the major intellectual traditions felt ethnicity was of secondary importance as an explanatory variable; at best an epiphenomenon and at worst a mask for class privilege...

But ethnicity is an ontic factuality. In being together – being-with-others, we form bonds and we develop shared linguistic, cultural, religious and even political values, and build ethnic identities with which we become affiliated in terms of ethnicity. Denying our affiliation to ethnic identities or denying ethnicity is no different from denying our collective being and existence. But this is exactly what the clamour for the suppression and rejection of ethnic identities in Nigeria in favour of the one identity, Nigeria, calls for. For example, although the Niger Delta in Nigeria produces the highest quantity of oil and clamours for a fair share of the gains from its production for the development of its region in Nigeria, the government of the day is quick to request that the Niger-Deltan's gives up its identity and produce for one Nigeria and allow for equal distribution of its resources to all Nigerians. The mistaken assumption here is that ethnicity is a harmful creation in the Nigerian polity when in fact, the creation of Nigeria is even more recent to the longstanding and primordial existing ethnic groups within Nigeria. Claude Ake (1) once aptly puts it that,

> Ethnic groups are, to be sure, inventions and constructions in some measure, but they are also decidedly real, even in the sense that states [or nations] are said to be. Before the colonial era, some parts of Africa had what may be described as ethnic polities - political societies with governmental institutions in a local space where territoriality and ethnic identity roughly coincided. Colonial rule, which amalgamated disparate ethnicities into the chaos called the colonial state, largely created the fluid abstract ethnicity which is so evident today by dissociating ethnicity from autonomous polity and territoriality... The concreteness of ethnic groups is invariably affirmed by ethnic markings which society

categorically pins on them, markings which underscore the social existence of ethnicity even when they are arbitrary or shifting.

More so, the clamour for the suspension and rejection of ethnicity in Nigeria often emerges from the space of a major ethnic group – often the ruling group – when it seeks to reap benefits from the resources and labour of the minority group by using the claim of one Nigerian identity, a purely political move. The North for example is quick to invoke the one Nigeria claim when pushing to enjoy the same benefits from crude oil as the minority groups in the Niger Delta that produce it and by implication, are more impacted negatively and environmentally by the effects of such production. The result is the non-recognition, marginalisation, exclusion and suppression of ethnic differences, which in turn leads to agitations, violence, clamour for recognition, identity crises and the rejection of the all-unifying one Nigeria. Once perceived as a threat to ethnic identities, the created Nigeria is bound to be rejected as we see continually playing out in the quest for Biafra state and Oduduwa republic, both emerging from ethnic consciousness.

Besides ethnic differences and the embedded politics is the politics of naming and labelling. The linguistic turn in ontology draws our attention to the indispensable role language, naming and labelling play in the unveiling, unfolding and unconcealing of being. Heidegger's famous lines in the Letter on Humanism (217) aptly capture the ontic factuality of language as the house of being when he says:

> Language is the house of being. In its home man dwells. *Those who think and those who create with words are the guardians of this home.* Their guardianship accomplishes the manifestation of being insofar as they bring the manifestation to language and maintain it in language through their speech.[1]

But there seems to be the taken-for-granted assumption in this very important capturing of the indispensable role language plays in the unfolding of being that 'those who think and those who create with words', the guardians of our very existence as it were, do so apolitically and purely ontologically.

The creation of words that have defined and troubled human history for ages such as race, whiteness, blackness, able-bodied, disabled, queer, civilised, barbaric, rational, emotional and so on, often were done for essentially political reasons of domination seizure and control of power and resources. The very idea that there are 'the ontological existential guardians' who seem to be the ones qualified to define and represent our realities in words already points to the distinction between a certain class of persons and the rest of us.[2] Such a distinction seems to exist in all human places particularly because since language is inseparable from place, the linguistic turn in ontology is by implication, a topological turn (Malpas), for in place, there are the guardians and masters of the language of the place that defines reality, unfold existence and create meanings for the rest. And this creation of words to represent realities does not happen as a realist, objectivist representation through words of our lived experiences and realities, it happens very politically.

In Nigeria and many African states and globally of course, language in general, and labelling and naming in particular, become political tools wielded to create, interpret, becloud, veil, sustain and defend manifold differences and realities. One obvious example is that of Boko Haram. Boko Haram, a group that has repeatedly referred to itself as the Nigerian Taliban and has obvious links and connections with other terrorist groups all over the world, is a notorious terrorist group in Nigeria. The United States Council on Foreign Relations shows that due to the activities of Boko Haram, as of January 14, 2022, nearly 350,000 have been killed in North East Nigeria since 2009, and about 3,100,000 people have been displaced in Nigeria. This of course does not take into account many other factors such as the widespread Boko Haram-led killings and kidnappings all over the country. But the Buhari-led Nigerian government has been very reluctant to label Boko Haram as a terrorist group although this is a factual reality. But for political reasons, the government has taken it to open itself to *differentiate* Boko Haram from other terrorist groups by giving it more subtle names and labels such as banditry, insurgency and militancy. In a recent response to The Economist (October 24, 2021), despite calls by Nigerians for the government to treat Boko Haram strictly as a terrorist group, President Buhari through his spokesperson, Garba Shehu, still describes the group as not different from bandits. But interestingly, the same government is quick to describe the Indigenous People of Biafra (IPOB) group as a terrorist group when ironically it is the Boko Haram that is seen as a terrorist group globally and not the IPOB group. As Mayowa Tijani explains it,

> IPOB and Boko Haram took two different routes to the terrorism tag. For Boko Haram, the government was reluctant, they wanted to negotiate, northern elders were against attacks on Boko Haram. In IPOB's case, the government was enthusiastic, and did it before many Nigerians ever saw the group as a long-term threat… [But] Internationally, the world generally recognises just Boko Haram as the major terrorist organisation in Nigeria. If you travelled to the United Kingdom, for example, and mentioned that you are a member of Boko Haram, you are likely to be arrested on the basis of that name only. For IPOB, the story is different. They have not been designated as a terrorist organisation globally.
>
> *(The Cable October 26, 2021)*

What is more intriguing is that prior to the Buhari-led government, Boko Haram and other affiliated 'bandit' groups in the Northern part of the country have been labelled as terrorist groups. For example,

> On May 24, 2013, a federal high court in Abuja ruled in favour of the Nigerian government that Boko Haram was a terrorist organisation. In effect, Boko Haram did not become a terrorist organisation in Nigeria until four years after it started carrying out major attacks in the country.
>
> *(The Cable October 26, 2021)*

But the present government is reluctant and hesitant to align itself with this terrorist label in ways that clearly indicate ethnic politics, favouritism and a differentia-politics meant to sustain resource and power control in the Northern part of the country. As Sallek Yaks Musa writes in The Conversation (October 18, 2021),

> The atrocities and motivation of the bandits have assumed an insurgent-type criminality. But the government is reluctant to label the groups as terrorists or insurgents. President Muhammadu Buhari has been accused of sympathising with the perpetrators, who appear to be of his ethnic affiliation. He has been accused of emboldening the groups over his quest to reclaim and reestablish grazing routes despite the open rejection of open grazing by half of Nigeria's 36 state governors. Critics argue that his lopsided appointments of mostly northerners like himself, against the constitutional

federal character principle, explain his failure to take a tough stance against the attacks on Nigerians by the Fulani.

There is therefore no doubt that the way the current Nigerian government treats IPOB is very different from the way it treats Boko Haram, an internationally known terrorist group. The Buhari-led government is known to handle Boko Haram terrorism with kids' gloves offering amnesty, funds, rehabilitation and resettlement in communities to any member who 'repents' while hundreds of thousands of those displaced by Boko Haram remain stranded refugees in their own country (Premium Times, August 30, 2021). The emphasis on the uniqueness and difference of Boko Haram as not terrorist enough to be labelled terrorist remains a politically fruitful route to exploit by the Nigerian government for the sake of control of power and resources for the North.

Thus, differences are ontic, real and factual and can be explored for the beauty and richness of the diversity and plurality of being and such exploration can if properly done, result in authentic inclusivity amidst diversity that can emerge from a genuine understanding of difference. But the focus on the self rather than on being in general as an inclusive whole leads to the self's exploitation of differences for its own sake as clearly seen in the Nigerian ethno-politics and politics of labelling. In the section that follows, I examine an aspect of African philosophical tradition that can allow for a fruitful encounter with difference resulting in a shift from differentia-politics to differentia-ontology through the hermeneutic ethic of Ubuntu

Deconstructing Differentia-Politics: Ubuntu as a Relational Hermeneutic Ethic

The factuality of difference results in a hermeneutic burden, the burden to interpret and understand the ontic difference that stands in-between the self and the other. But from the foregoing, what is obvious is that our lived experiences, as exemplified in ethnic politics in Nigeria, are permeated not with attempts to understand our differences and see how they can contribute to an aesthetically and robustly inclusive and diverse society but with attempts to create and construct differences as narrated by the self for the purpose of power and resource control. If a return from differentia-politics to the factuality of difference is desired, the hermeneutic burden must be taken seriously and this immediately imposes on us interpretive ethical duties which include the duty of recognition, the duty to be empathic, and the duty of openness. The duty of recognition is the duty to recognise the other and the differences that lie between the self and the other. It is an affirmation and acknowledgement that the self is only an aspect of the unfolding of being and thus not a yardstick for the affirmation of the being of others. It is the recognition of the factuality and potentiality of difference and that the self exists as a form of difference. But this is only preliminary for actual interpretation and understanding to take place, for to recognise is not the same as to understand what one recognises. The duty of empathy and care on the other hand emphasises awareness of, sensitivity towards, and vicariousness for, the other,

> The emotional capacity for first-personal empathetic experience, in which I feel like another and therefore can come to care for the other, becomes the phenomenological warrant of a shared ontology of empathic ability which assures us of our common humanity.
>
> *(Kogler 311)*

But the duty to empathise and care in the pursuit of the hermeneutics of difference is also limited since being empathic does not bring about understanding of the other's difference and may have the tendency of imposing our ethnocentric perspectives on others, for if we have shared empathy, we should also have shared experiences. This completely makes the other's difference a-contextual and a-cultural. As Kogler (312) puts it.

> The problem consists in the conflation of empathy with pre-communal feeling-states that are experienced by the individual. This suggests that moral understanding is grounded in the empathetic-emotional identification of the self with the experiential states of the other. Yet the fact that the other experiences these states in a particular cultural and social setting, which defines the full experience of the other as a human being, is thereby ignored. The emotional bridge is taken to cross, as it were, the different contexts to establish a direct emotional community with the other. Emotional empathy not only invites the aforementioned problem of assimilative understanding, but also reduces the other's experience to its pure a-contextual and a-cultural core

The duty of openness is at the heart of hermeneutics of the other and of difference because such a quest for interpretation and understanding is essentially a quest to be open to something beyond the self. It is the ethical disposition towards openness that enables hermeneutic to take place, allowing the exercise of interpretation and understanding not only to prepare to recognise and acknowledge difference and the other, but to allow the other to be the other (Botts 498–518). But again, being open is not necessarily understanding. Thus, recognising, empathising and care for, and being open towards the other and towards difference are essential first-step ingredients for truly encountering, putting oneself in the position to, and setting the stage to, understand and interpret the factuality of difference. But this is not enough. The actual understanding must take place for authentic diversity that results in building community, reciprocity and inclusivity to take place. African philosophy of Ubuntu provides an important hermeneutic ethic for this to happen.

Ubuntu as African communitarian philosophy is a political, moral, ontological, and existential philosophy that has been defended by African scholars as a unique and authentic African philosophy that defines the African way of life and forms the basis for an African identity, as well as distinguishes African cultures from other (mostly) liberal, non-African cultures (Imafidon 115–126). I do not wish to go into the key debates about Ubuntu here. But the most salient point about Ubuntu is that it carries with it the most significant philosophy of the sub-Saharan African peoples – a person is a person through other persons. In the words of Bolden (799), Ubuntu,

> ... is a Zulu/Xhosa word, with parallels in many other African languages, which is most directly translated into English as 'humanness'. Its sense, however, is perhaps best conveyed by the Nguni expression 'umuntu ngumuntu ngabantu', which means 'a person is a person through other people'.

But this is a restrictive and narrow interpretation of Ubuntu. A broader interpretation from the lived experience of African peoples is that a being is a being through other beings. One of the core principles implicated by this understanding of Ubuntu is what I would call the relational hermeneutic principle. A person is a person through other persons, or a being is a being through other beings is essentially hermeneutical or interpretive, breeding an important theory or principle of interpretation and understanding of one another and our differences. My understanding of myself, the notion or idea of who I really am, my personality, cannot be completely disentangled from what the other, others around me, others I relate to, think of me. This is the key point made by Ubuntu hermeneutics: interpretation is relational, intersubjective and not merely subjective. This is crucial for the relationship that exists between the self and the other and the difference between them. In alterity interpretive discourse, the assumption is that the other is simply interpreted by the self while in reality, the self is also undergoing constant and continuous interpretation by the other. A genuine account of ourselves is never complete without the other's perspective. To instantiate, the interpretation of Boko Haram by specific players in Northern Nigeria as banditry is incomplete without taking seriously the other's interpretation as terrorism. The other's interpretation is vital for a critique of the self's understanding of itself and its difference. A relational hermeneutic understanding provides a fruitful space for intermingling and checkmating self's difference and the other's difference. It prevents the self from, and consequently deconstructs, a constructed narrative of difference that is political for the sake of power and resource control. It allows authentic self, other and difference to emerge in an existential space that emphasise a co-dependency ethos that inhibits marginalisation and exclusion, where the self is intrinsically dependent on the other and the other on the self in understanding and creating their identities and differences. A relational hermeneutic ethic would thus regard as impermissible any action or inaction that threatens the diverse community of being since all beings rely and depend on one another not only for survival but for understanding.

Conclusion

We have examined the factuality of difference as fundamental to the very essence of being and how such factuality is veiled, overshadowed and obscured by a politicised narrative of difference for the sake of self, evident from the ethnic politics and the politics of labelling in the Nigerian polity. The politics of difference is thus an identity politics in disguise forged and constructed to sustain power and resource control for the self while ensuring the marginalisation and exclusion of the other on the one hand and a complete disregard for ontic differences on the other. The shift from differentia-politics back to the factuality of difference therefore requires a hermeneutic ethic that emerges from a hermeneutic burden to understand and interpret the other and the difference in between. This hermeneutic ethic must transcend duties of recognition, care, openness and empathy, which though essential and necessary duties that put one in the place of hermeneutic encounter with difference, are not sufficient. An African relational hermeneutic ethic grounded on the philosophy of Ubuntu has been sketched out here as an option to explore for a robust hermeneutic of ontic differences, one that allows for the recognition of the interdependence of diversity which invariably necessitates inclusion and inhibits exclusion and marginalisation.

But the politics of difference is not always intended to breed exclusion. In many cases, the goal is justice, reparation, recognition, decolonisation and liberation. In fact, it is the way through which supressed, marginalised and misrepresented forms of differences in human history retake power to redefine and voice their differences, which is key for any form of liberation, decoloniality, reparation, justice and the building of communities to emerge. However, while the goal of the politics of difference is not always to exclude, even within the most noble goals, exclusion often becomes the consequence once the politics of difference is not coated or accompanied with the ethics of relationality, which Ubuntu as a theory provides, Therefore, a robust theorisation of African political philosophy of identity and difference highlighted here with reference to the Nigerian polity, must necessarily weave together the political, ontological, ethical and epistemological dimensions of identity and difference for a meaningful theory to emerge as none of these dimensions can independently form a reliable basis to develop an adequate understanding of identity and difference. While not within the scope of the present chapter, a political philosophy of difference needs to be thoroughly theorised with all its dimensions as a robust theoretical approach to the understanding of identity and difference.

Notes

1 Emphasis is mine.
2 Heidegger mentions members of the guardians of our being in several of his essay speaking particularly of poets and philosophers, obviously of Greek and German origins, and the role they play in creating and unfolding being for the rest of us. For example, being very fond of poetry and its role in the unconcealment of being, Heidegger writes that "Poetry, however, is not an aimless imagining of whimsicalities and not a flight of mere notions and fancies into the realm of the unreal. What poetry, as clearing projection, unfolds of unconcealment and projects ahead into the rift-design of the figure, is the open region which poetry lets happen, and indeed in such a way that only now, in the midst of beings, the open region brings beings to shine and ring out." (Heidegger 197)

References

Agius, Christine. and Keep, Dean. "The Politics of Identity: Making and Disrupting Identity". *The Politics of Identity: Place, Space and Discourse*. Christine Agius and Dean Keep (eds.), Manchester University Press, 2018, pp. 1–11.

Ake, Claude. "What Is the Problem of Ethnicity in Africa?" *Transformation*, Vol. 22, 1993, pp. 1–14.

Alumona, Ikenna. M. and Azom, Stephen. N. "Politics of Identity and the Crisis of Nation-Building in Africa". *The Palgrave Handbook of African Politics, Governance and Development*. Samuel Ojo Oloruntoba and Toyin Falola (eds.), Palgrave Macmillan, 2018, pp. 291–306.

Bernstein, Mary. "Identity Politics" *Annual Review of Sociology*, Vol. 31, No. 1, 2005, pp. 47–74.

Bolden, Richard. "Ubuntu." *Encyclopaedia of Action Research*. David Coghlan and Mary Brydon-Miller (eds.), Sage, 2014, pp. 799–801.

Botts, Tina F. "Hermeneutics, Race and Gender". *The Routledge Companion to Hermeneutics*. Jeff Malpas and Hans-Helmuth Gander (eds.), Routledge, 2015, pp. 498–518.

Chiluwa, Innocent. "A Nation Divided Against Itself: Biafra and the Conflicting Online Protest Discourses". *Discourse and Communication*, Vol. 12, No. 4, 2018, pp. 357–381.

Etieyibo, Edwin, et al. "Identities, Exclusionism and Politics in Africa". *African Studies*, Vol. 79, No.4, 2020, pp. 361–366.

Green, Elliott. "The Politics of Ethnic Identity in Sub-Saharan Africa". *Comparative Political Studies*, Vol. 54, No.7, 2020, pp. 1197–1226.

Heidegger, Martin. *Being and Time*, trans. John Macquarrie and Edward Robinson. Basil Blackwell, 1985.

Heidegger, Martin. "Letter on Humanism". *Basic Writings*. David Farrell Krell (ed.), Harper Collins Pub, 1993a, pp. 213–266.

Heidegger, Martin. "The Origin of the Work of Art". *Basic Writings*. David Farrell Krell (ed.), Harper Collins Pub, 1993b, pp. 139–212.

Imafidon Elvis. "Africa and the Unfolding of Difference: An Introduction". *Handbook of African Philosophy of Difference*. Elvis Imafidon (ed.), Springer, 2020, pp. 1–12.

Imafidon, Elvis. "African Communitarian Philosophy of Personhood and Disability: The Asymmetry of Value and Power". *International Journal of Critical Diversity Studies*, Vol. 4, No.1, 2021, pp. 115–126.

Kogler, Hans-Herbert. "Ethics and Community". *The Routledge Companion to Hermeneutics*. Jeff Malpas and Hans-Helmuth Gander (eds.), Routledge, 2015, pp. 310–323.

Konrad-Adenauer-Stiftung. *Politics of Identity and Exclusion in Africa: From Violent Confrontation to Peaceful Cooperation*. Konrad-Adenauer-Stiftung, 2001.

Lajul, Wilfred. "African Metaphysics: Traditional and Modern Discussions". *Themes, Issues and Problems in African Philosophy*. Isaac E. Ukpokolo (ed.), Palgrave Macmillan, 2017, pp. 19–49.

Malpas, Jeff. "'The House of Being': Poetry, Language, and Place". *Paths in Heidegger's Later Thought*. Gunter Figal, et al. (eds.), Indiana University Press, 2012, pp. 15–44.

Sartre, John-Paul. *Being and Nothingness: An Essay on Phenomenological Ontology*, trans. Hazel E. Barnes. Routledge, 1958.

Tarimo, Aquiline. "Politicization of Ethnic Identities: The Case of Contemporary Africa". *Journal of Asian and African Studies*, Vol. 45, No.3, 2010, pp. 297–308.

Teffo, Lesiba. J. and Roux, Abraham. P. J. "Metaphysical Thinking in Africa". *The African Philosophy Reader*. P. H. Coetzee and A. P. J. Roux (eds.), Routledge, pp. 192–208.

Ukiwo, Ukoha. The Study of Ethnicity in Nigeria. *Oxford Development Studies*, Vol. 33, No.1, 2005, pp. 7–23.

12

CORRUPTION

Definitional Ambiguities and Current Imaginations

Mitterand M. Okorie[1]

Introduction

> For it cannot be denied that the most outstanding and resilient problem that has beset and blighted the politics of the new nations (or nation-states) of post-colonial Africa is political corruption
>
> *(Gyekye, 2015, p.353)*

The extract above, in exploratory terms, is at the centre of my discussion in this chapter: the claim that political corruption is the most prominent problem of post-colonial Africa. The ideation of corruption as Africa's most concerning political problem is a widely held view among scholars and policymakers in Africa. African citizens and leaders equally allude to the damaging effects of corruption and how vastly more developed the continent would be if corruption did not exist. For example, the Chairperson of the African Union (AU) Commission, Moussa Mahamat opined that "corruption is undoubtedly the most pressing governance and development challenge that Africa is confronted with today…" (Fagbadebo, 2019, p.9). At the AU Summit in 2018 themed *Winning the Fight Against Corruption: A Sustainable Path to Africa's Transformation*, President Muhammadu Buhari of Nigeria identified corruption as "one of the greatest evils of our time" (Fagbadebo and Dorasamy, 2021). Ironically, the UK Prime Minister, David Cameron had in 2016 called Buhari's Nigeria, a "fantastically corrupt" country (BBC News, 2016, Paragraph 1).

From crumbling healthcare and educational infrastructure to poor economic growth and intensifying poverty levels, corruption is directly and indirectly linked to the crisis of governance in Africa (Olanipekun, 2021; Van den Bersselaar and Decker, 2011). If Africa fails to stop corruption, it is said, corruption is most likely going to stop Africa (Udombana, 2003). In short, so compelling is this notion of corruption as an existential threat to African nations that the AU declared July 11 every year as 'African Anti-Corruption Day' in commemoration of continental dedication towards fighting corruption (Fagbadebo, 2019). Yet, what really is corruption? Is it a compendium of all governance-related infractions? Is it a buzzer for all illicit acts undertaken by public officials to advance self-serving objectives? Igboin (2016) reckoned that corruption is a problematic and elusive concept, which causes many scholars to deliberately avoid defining it. There is merit to the veracity of this claim, but the elusiveness of a concept should compel us to wrestle with it, not avoid it. The problem has been that, as various African thinkers repeatedly summon corruption to account for Africa's political and development challenges, it has come to assume a commonsensical status.

The word corruption (or political corruption, both are used interchangeably in this work) is used to refer to several illicit acts ranging from bribery, misuse of public money, laundering of state funds, state capture, nepotism and related acts and practices considered to be legally transgressive for public officials. Each of these actions which are constitutive of corruption is too broad in itself to be lumped together, and deserves to stand on its own merit. In lumping them together, it is impossible to know which of the corrupt practices are being referred to in relation to how they impact politics. The question I seek to deal with in the chapter is whether this near-obsessive focus on corruption as the most outstanding political pathology in contemporary Africa impedes what should be other imaginative interrogations of the African political condition.

The chapter is sectioned into four parts. The first section deals with the definitional ambiguities and the sweeping nature of the term 'corruption', contending that the broadness of the term has made it a term of convenience for thinkers who dissect political failure in contemporary Africa. The second section undertakes an exploratory appraisal of how corruption as the most concerning political problem in Africa is currently framed. It highlights how the extant literature identifies corruption as arising from a failure of the moral character of African leaders and a failure of state institutions in Africa, and then interrogates the utility and deficiencies of both perspectives. In the final section, I discuss the need to move beyond 'corruption' as the most outstanding problem in contemporary Africa into broader imaginative territories.

Definitional Ambiguities: What Is Corruption?

The term 'corruption' is an etymological adaptation of the Latin verb 'corruptus' (to break) and literally means broken object (Udombana, 2003). The Cambridge Dictionary defines corruption as "illegal, bad, dishonest behaviour, especially by people in positions of power." In academic scholarship, corrupt acts have often referred to issues such as bribery, embezzlement of public funds, fraud, nepotism, insider trading, money laundering and state capture by vested interests (Fagbadebo, 2019; Fagbadebo and Dorosamy, 2021; Gyekye, 1997; Udombana, 2003). In the African context, when corruption is mentioned, names and images of several kleptocratic regimes come to mind. African leaders who illegally amassed wealth running into several billions of dollars include General Sani Abacha of Nigeria, Houphouet Boigny of Ivory Coast, Mobutu Seseko of Zaire, Mouza Traore of Mali (Olanipekun, 2021). Even in contemporary times, one reason why elections in Africa and the tussle for political power generally remained violent is for its ability to introduce individuals into formal channels of wealth accumulation (Okorie, 2018; 2021; 2022).

When it comes to discussing corruption empirically, scholars have often referred to the definition of corruption by Transparency International (TI) and the use of its Corruption Performance Index (CPI) to make inferences on how corrupt a country is. TI (2021) defines acts of corruption as bribery, diversion of public funds, officials using public office for private gain without facing consequences, excessive red tape in the public sector which incubates opportunities for corruption, nepotistic appointments in the civil service, state capture by narrow vested interest, lack of legal protection for people who report cases of corruption and lack of access to information on public affairs or government agencies. Each year, TI measures how over 180 countries perform against the above-mentioned infractions. A country's rank on the CPI is its position relative to the countries in the index. A country's score is the perceived level of corruption in the public sector on a scale of 0–100, where 0 means highly corrupt and 100 means very clean. Each country's score is drawn from a combination of 13 or more corruption surveys and assessments.

Given this perception of empiricism, TI's assessment of corruption is often cited with a degree of confidence. Yet, if one is to assume that TI's index is empirically robust, it is important to pay closer attention to the proclamations or conclusions scholars come to on the basis of the organization's reports. The fact that African countries tend to rank the lowest on the CPI typically accounts for the suggestion that corruption is the most resilient problem that blights the politics of post-colonial Africa (Gyekye, 2015), or that political corruption has done the greatest harm to Africa's economic and developmental aspirations (Udombana, 2003). The understanding of corruption as implicated in African politics mostly draws from how it has been conceptualized by TI. In doing so, understanding the failure of politics in Africa simply comes down to ticking a list of bullet points on each country's flag. For example, the investigator would only need to look out for a number of elements such as: (1) do politicians of country X embezzle state funds, (2) are contracts and tenders acquired through patronage networks and other inappropriate channels, (3) are licenses for mining or extractive activities acquired through bribery, (4) are positions in government dominated by the president's friends and members of his ethnic group? If all or majority of these boxes are ticked, the investigator then concludes that corruption is at the centre of the country's problems and that such a country is in decline as a result. This linear logic underlines the current imagination of corruption in contemporary Africa and its place in accounting for the failure of politics. There are two reasons why this is an unhelpful way of analysing political failure in Africa.

First, when a scholar or an expert implies that corruption is an outstanding problem for a given African country, what do they really mean? Which of the corrupt acts do they refer to or are they implying that all corrupt acts recognized in the TI's CPI are operational in such a country? If we mean bribery, wouldn't it be important to focus on how bribery poses a political problem for the country? And then study in what capacity bribery threatens the stability of the state and the material well-being of citizens. If by corruption, we mean embezzlement, financial misappropriation, money laundering, state capture, fraudulent tender processes, etc., then each of these governance-related infractions ought to be independently studied in order to identify how they impact governance. With such intricate details glossed over, clarity on the nexus between corruption and political failure is bound to be ambiguous.

Second, it is necessary to note that the governance-related infractions which are identified as corrupt acts are not restricted to Africa. Perhaps, not with the same degree of brazenness but they occur in countries across continents. China is a veritable example that challenges the concomitant effects of corruption on a country's development aspirations. For example, between 2014 and 2022, China consistently hovered between 26% and 45% in the CPI report of TI but in the same period pulled 800 million of its people from the International Poverty Line (World Bank, 2022). Former U.S. President, Donald Trump's administration consistently appointed his close friends and family members into his cabinet, but such a degree of nepotism would never be considered a blight to U.S. democracy nor referred to as something more than a questionable leadership style. That these issues are not found to be hindrances to the development aspirations of China and America but are expected to do so for African states deserves to be questioned. Clearly, concepts and theories that confirm our most basic assumptions travel with little difficulty (Ferragina, 2009), and the term 'corruption' is one such. Yet, the inadequate conceptualization of the term means that it is unhelpful in getting us to the heart of Africa's political challenges.

Current Ideations of Corruption in Africa

The existing ideation of corruption as the most outstanding problem in Africa has been argued to arise from two factors. The failure of the moral character of African leaders and the failure of state institutions in post-colonial Africa. While both factors are seemingly interconnected, they possess different constitutive elements. I therefore unpack them separately to ensure clarity in how they have been studied in relation to how they account for the failure of politics in Africa.

Corruption as a Failure of the Moral Character of African Leaders

Corruption as a political pathology in African states, has been argued, stems from the moral depravity of politicians or officeholders in Africa. In his acclaimed work, Gyekye (1997, p.194) mentions that political corruption in Africa flourishes due to weak political leadership whereby leaders who are themselves corrupt cannot exert discipline in the polity. As such, bribery, fraud and other related schemes are allowed to thrive and compromise the quality of governance. However, this moral failing, Gyekye (1997) goes on to argue, is not exclusively limited to the political leader who is only part of an ecosystem of amoral actors within an amoral society. In effect, individual members of the society cannot be divorced from the politicians who are from among them and whom they vote into elective offices. In cementing his claim that political corruption is fundamentally "a moral problem" (Gyekye, 1997, p.209), he suggests that a *commitmental* moral revolution is necessary to inculcate and dispose society towards moral beliefs, values and principles. Olanipekun (2021) objects to Gyekye's (1997) argument of tarring all of society with the brush of corruption, arguing instead that even if the wider society is corrupt, leaders are expected to be of upright moral character. Whatever the case, it is unlikely that a society that is fundamentally virtuous can repeatedly produce and defend amoral leaders. One can take for example that barely one year after a politician wins an elective position in Africa, they would arrive in their place of worship and pledge to reconstruct a new and often grandiose worship centre. When the pledge is made, the entire congregation breaks into a frenzy of applause, including the religious leader who then invites the politician to the altar for special blessings. Sometimes, the officeholder may have a backlog of unpaid salaries to government employees under his care. He might be issuing government contracts and tenders to his relatives and without due process. Schools in his domain might be closed because the teachers are on strike due to poor wages. Yet, his donation to the worship centre is greeted without question as to how an individual who owned nothing of worth a year before could finance the building of a grand edifice on his own. In the next electioneering period, such an officeholder may then return to the worship centre to mobilize for votes, using his donation as a mobilizational tool. In such a scenario, the failure of moral character cannot be restricted to the politician alone (even though an officeholder is expected to be of a higher moral rectitude), but that of the generality of individuals within the society. Gyekye's (1997; 2015) claim is therefore not without its merit. Moreover, conceptual frameworks like prebendalism, which is the utilization of public office to dispense public resources, support groups (Joseph, 1983) and Neopatrimonialism, the vertical distribution of state resources from political patrons to secure the loyalty of clients in the general population (Bratton and Van de Walle, 1994), allude to the widespread nature of the amorality that incubates corruption in African states.

De Sardan (1999) argues however that corruption does not arise as a result of any intrinsic moral failure of the individual; rather, it is an acquired habit occasioned by the survivalist interactions of everyday life in Africa. In almost all African countries, Sardan suggests, a driving license can be bought from the inspector, without due process. Public officials may attempt to curb this infraction by including additional personnel to check the inspector, he mentions. Yet, far from curbing the illegal act, the individual seeking the license would suddenly have one more person to bribe. In time, this practice becomes normalized and attains an almost irreversible status. Ganahl (2014) posits that since the private economy in Africa is often in a stagnant state and public sector employment is often poorly remunerated, the individual in contemporary Africa may not have the luxury of being a moral purist. He is faced with a burning need to depend on bribes and other underhanded methods to compensate for his poor wages.

Osaghae (1995) maintains that corruption in Africa arises from the moral failings of a reprobate political class. In articulating this, however, he mentions that this moral failing is not peculiar to Africans or Africa because the material gain motivation for engaging in politics has universal applicability. The problem has been that in African countries, the state is the major means of socio-economic reproduction, which has been seized by a highly opportunistic class whose involvement in politics is restricted to achieving self-serving objectives. One has to concede here that in societies of the Global North, political leaders have risen to chart a prosperous course for society by demanding higher moral standards from themselves. Europe's move from feudalism to liberal democracy underscores this evolution. More recently, one can see that even in China, a one-party state, the Chinese Communist Party in 2011 instituted the death penalty in the Chinese Criminal Code for officeholders found guilty of substantial financial mismanagement (Lui and Faerber, 2011). Such action is often likened to class suicide since the political class is essentially eliminating the ability to profit from their positions. The fact that a similar degree of selflessness has hardly been replicated by the political class in Africa somewhat aligns with Gyegke's (1997) stance on corruption being attributable to a personal moral failing.

That said, Gyekye's (1997, p. 215) point is that the commitment to moral principles will drive effective law enforcement in a democracy; but not the reverse. Although not completely without merit, this proposal underplays the role of law in guiding the behavior of citizens or enforcing morality. Such prescriptions are what Okeja (2022, p.27) argues to be the problem-solution approach to comprehending African political experiences because they isolate layers of causes to link with effects. Take for example, since Africans have been made to believe that amoral leaders promote and advance corruption in the polity, thereby sabotaging progress in society, they spent the entire 1960s and even now in 2022 (as with Mali and Burkina Faso), jubilantly welcoming military coups that topple 'corrupt' civilian regimes. Repeatedly, one also sees opposition parties in African democracies riding to power on the coattails of anti-corruption sermons, only to end up worse than the administrations they replace. One could take for example the 'Mai Gaskia' (Hausa word for *The Honest One*) sloganeering for Muhammadu Buhari during the 2015 election that eventually propelled him to power (Akhaine, 2022) could not hold for longer, as the corruption, he was elected to eliminate festered and worsened under him. The same could be said of George Weah of Liberia, also popularly elected by a people who wished to take a break from establishment politicians. However, Weah sought to quickly amend the country's constitution to enable him to run for an additional term in office (Nyei, 2020). In South Africa, Cyril Ramaphosa had presented himself as a clean break from his predecessor, Jacob Zuma, who was implicated in multiple financial infractions (Madonsela, 2019). Yet, a few years after, he too was implicated in a financial scandal known as the Phala-Phala farmgate (Maseko, 2022). In other words, citizens gravitate uncritically to supposed moral leaders to ensure good governance by eradicating corruption in the belief that finding a moral leader is enough to transform the system. Ending corruption, they assume, would automatically ensure a good life, as though good governance and corruption are not mutually exclusive. Little is also said about the meagre per capita income and tax base of most African states, and that absent of corruption, government revenues are nowhere near enough to guarantee the good life for all. Surely, one may argue that the smaller a country's tax revenue is, the less it can bear being looted or embezzled. But this means that the discussion must isolate embezzlement of state funds and not 'corruption' as the political pathology in focus. And then proceed to examine the relationship between embezzlement of state funds and political failure while also answering the question of why such governance-related misdeeds do not lead to political failure in non-African climes.

Another deficiency with the claim that corruption stems from the moral failing of Africans ignores the strict accountability standards by which Africans hold leaders of their community organizations, village groups, diaspora community gatherings or even religious groups. In these associations, financial improprieties are hardly recorded, due to the emotional investment and sense of identification they feel towards the organization. And because the price of embezzling the collective fund of the organization is exceedingly high. Hurting the interest of those with whom one shares such close bonds of association or kinship portends serious reputational damage. Such a lack of integrity may lead to alienation from the community. People may refuse to marry into such a person's family in a bid to avoid being yoked with a thief. Such a person's spouse or children also faces an improbable chance of being endowed with any sort of fiscal responsibility in such an organization. Further, given contemporary migratory trend in Africa, one can observe the teaming number of Nigerian medical, technological and academic professionals moving to countries in the Global North. Many of these individuals rise to the zenith of the professional ladder in these countries and occupy positions where financial responsibilities are part of their duties. Yet these Africans exercise the highest form of financial prudence and exude integrity. One way to explain this moral probity is that these individuals are encouraged to live up to the ideals that have been cultivated and are held sacred in their adopted countries. Also, institutions in the West tend to have structures and layers of oversight that make it hard, even pointless to engage in primitive accumulation.

There is also an implicit recognition that their actions form part of a social contract of playing by the rules as a means of co-creating a progressive and healthy society. If such professionals are thrown back into their countries of provenance where millions of people strive to game the system, they would come to grief as a result of playing by the rules. Thus, there may be something wrong with the system in which Africans are forced to navigate their lives, and this dovetails to the second strand of the discourse on society and corruption in contemporary Africa as discussed in the next section.

Corruption as a Failure of Public Institutions in Post-Colonial Africa

An equally prominent ideation of corruption in Africa and its existential implications for the state is on how the failure of public institutions accounts for it. A plethora of studies and theories have been developed to point out how corruption threatens the stability and existence of the state, because state institutions not only enable it but are also undermined by it. Indeed, large-scale theft or embezzlement of public resources is both a historical and contemporary reality of politics in Africa. Whether it is the massive fraud in state-run companies in Zimbabwe that cost the country up to $800m between 1999 and 2001 (Udombana, 2003), or the diversion and laundering of $193m by Nigeria's accountant general—Mr. Ahmed Idris in 2022 (Eboh, 2022), public institutions in Africa are known to be too effete to prevent such privatization of state resources. In both academic and policy discussions, these instances of official malfeasance are discussed as events that threaten the survival of the state.

This weakness of public institution and the large-scale corruption it fosters, it is argued, are direct vestiges of Africa's colonial experience. In the assessment of political corruption in Africa, Ekeh's (1975) theory of *two publics* remains one of the most cited works and provides anatomical insight into the rot that plagues state institutions in post-colonial Africa. Ekeh (1975) argues that colonialism created two publics in Africa; the primordial public (the realm of kinship, tribe, ethnic association) and civic public (the realm of public administration). And that for many Africans, their primary loyalty lies with the primordial public where their affairs are guided by moral probity even though they interact with the civic public in the most amoral ways. According to Ekeh (1975), the oppression inherent in the colonial experience (punitive taxation, high-handedness, corruption), drew a wedge between Africans and the colonial authorities. The sphere occupied by the colonising power became the civic public and was considered amoral. In contrast, the primordial public was one in which the social exchanges between people of similar ethnic origin and was based on mutual reciprocity and a commitment to fairness. When colonialism eventually ended, the educated African class (Ekeh termed them 'African bourgeoisie') who took over from the British simply perpetuated the dysfunctionality of settler-native social exchanges where structures of public accountability could not effectively evolve.

Mamdani (1996), Nkrumah (1970) and Afigbo (1972) have also extensively explored the prevalence of abuses of power by native authorities which characterized British colonial rule in Africa. Since it was necessary for the colonial authorities to wield power illegitimately than having no power at all, indirect rule which leveraged on alliances with abusive and loathed local authorities became a feature of politics. Colonial chiefs, as Mulinge and Lesetedi (1998) mention, were encouraged to use their positions to retain part of the taxes unjustly levied and forcefully collected from their people. The colonial state was never designed to respond to the democratic demands of the people or develop a sense of citizenship in them, but rather to exploit the people and the land through the imposition of an alien bureaucracy. This alienated the people from the state, which they viewed as a transactional reality that reproduces and perpetuates transaction politics (Adebanwi, 2017). On account of this, corruption in contemporary Africa can be traced to the historical process of colonialism (Osoba, 1996). Besides, the crop of Africans who were part of the administrative chain of command in the colonial period inherited the very institutions which showed little regard for accountability to the people. Political independence therefore did not create a break from the past. Instead, a combination of neo-colonial objectives of the departing colonial authorities and the character of the independence constitutions created powerful central executives who subjected state institutions to their whims. Power came to belong, not to the people, but to the 'Big Man' (Szeftel, 2000) who could better the lives of his coteries and support groups similar to the colonial era.

In what was his fourth novel, *A Man of the People*, Achebe (1966) painted a portrait of Nigeria and the political corruption that characterized the immediate aftermath of self-rule (Ekaney, 1977). The story's protagonist, Chief Nanga was emblematic of the 'Big Man' who often dominated space and towered above state institutions. Not only did he embezzle state funds without repercussions, but he also routinely introduced acolytes into formal channels of primitive accumulation. Gaining power in Achebe's mythical country thus becomes a desperate affair for the ruling elites who perceive public offices as an opportunity to share in the spoils of independence. As the political parties amass support groups and engage in violent clashes, law and order became threatened. Finally, the lack of capacity for state institutions to prevent this thievery and abuse of power became untenable as the military moves in to topple the government. Achebe's imagination of corruption and the state here also leans into the belief that corruption arises from the weakness of public institutions in Africa, which is an apparent fallout of the colonial experience. Returning to Ekeh (1975), political corruption has seemed irreversible in Africa because unlike in Europe where citizens moved from feudalism to democracy (with a genuine social contract), the post-colony has not evolved in that regard. There is no generalized morality in the private and public realm, as officeholders who would not exploit their clan have no qualms about defrauding the state.

The logic of colonialism being responsible for current weaknesses in public institutions in Africa has its merit, though such perverse state–society relations may have occurred without colonial contact. Banfield's (1958) observations in the small Italian town of Chairomente (mentioned in the book as Montegrano) indicate that Europeans who acted in this way did not do so from colonial contact. That said, it is undeniable that the weakness of public institutions contributes to the plunder of state resources by avaricious elites in Africa. These weak institutions are also unable to protect the population from multinational companies who collude with state elites when necessary to serve their own interests. Those in the extractive sectors engage in extractive activities that bring about ecological disasters to the host communities without being held to account. However, these accounts of corruption being a function of weak public institutions fail to identify how the global financial system—essentially western institutions—provides the channels to effectively secure monies or assets looted by African political elites. Wealth of African nations is only able to depart Africa through clandestinely efficient services offered by Euro-American corporations, which then undercut local measures to fight corruption. Moreover, some of the most egregiously corrupt African leaders have and continue to enjoy a cosy relationship with western leaders on account of being thought economically or geopolitically useful. In other words, the focus on the lack of strong public institutions to halt corruption tends to ignore the exogenous factors that undercut political consciousness in African states.

From Concept of Convenience to Imaginative Interrogations

As I have argued in earlier sections of this work, interrogations about the political experience in Africa have to transcend 'corruption' as currently defined because they only offer a list of infractions signifying nothing in particular. Yet, given its triggering quality, the term typically activates, for scholars or policymakers the pressure to outline 'recommendations' and 'solutions' to 'kill corruption before corruption kills Africa'. Not that seeking solutions to germane political problems isn't a necessary undertaking, but it is equally important to consider why the failure of politics in post-colonial Africa has remained resistant to these anti-corruption recommendations. There is a need to consider whether these recommendations are not being squandered on the wrong problems. Of course, scholars like Mamdani (1996) have long suggested that corruption does not particularly possess the 'catastrophic' effect bequeathed on it. Countries thrive in spite of corruption, and countries can fail in the absence of it. The rapid industrialization of South Korea occurred against the backdrop of high levels of clientelism (Szeftel, 2000). China has and continues to dominate global trade for nearly two decades, without being hamstrung by its corruption challenges.

Again, one can look at Nigeria and the various times it faced an existential threat shows that corruption had nothing to do with it. Its periods of political instability such as the Civil War (1967–1970), its Niger Delta problem (2005–2009) and currently its Boko Haram problem (2009–till present), arose over issues pertaining to (in)justice and identity, and not corruption. These periods were the most pivotal in the country's history and threatened the very foundation of its existence as they gave rise to multiple zones of ungovernability. Sections of the country did not feel wanted and attempted to refuse identification with it until certain terms were met. The ongoing civil wars in Ethiopia (Tigray conflict) and Cameroon (Anglophone crisis) which are strong existential concerns for both countries have little to do with 'corruption'. Perhaps, African thinkers underplay the acrimonious nature of the colonial borders in Africa and the elusive quest for unity within these geographical accidents.

What is also being ignored is that a number of African countries would cease to exist and in fact dissolve into new, homogeneous nations if referenda for independence were conducted across the continent. In effect, a variety of post-colonial states in Africa are held together by the force of arms and the guarantees of the international community. This sense of alienation from the state by its citizens (since the political experience is one of the catastrophic disadvantages) effectively robs the state of a galvanizing force that should typically propel it for greatness. These problems should equally count as some of the most outstanding problems in contemporary Africa. History reminds us that whenever the material well-being of citizens is threatened, they often seek comfort in their ethnic or primordial enclaves. There, they may begin to romanticize self-determination or any new political arrangement that tears away from the failing one.

There is also the challenge of Africa's inability to move from a net importer to a net exporter of goods and services. As a continent experiencing a youth bulge, there is too little by way of employment to keep the majority of its people productive and to grow the tax base commensurate to the needs of the population. It is true that monies continue to be siphoned and moved to clandestine accounts overseas by African politicians. Still, the combined annual budgets of all the countries in West Africa are less than the gross annual profit of Apple Inc. This level of (un)productivity in economic terms hurts Africa perhaps even more than officeholders embezzling state funds.

Thinkers of the African political experience must wrestle with the challenge of inertia in the politics of contemporary Africa, which is occasioned by a sense of powerlessness (Okeja 2022, p.155). This is the feeling among the general population that politics is a meaningless cycle of the impossible where periodic elections produce new sets of politicians without new sets of outcomes. Electioneering periods throw up supposedly popular candidates, from old guards leveraging on ethnic support to charismatic, unorthodox politicians with messianic slogans. Yet, the mood of the general population quickly transits from boisterous hope to the same sullenness and inertia which reigned in the periods before electoral campaigns. Hence, the presence of corruption in African states does not quite capture this lack of meaning in politics nor can it be said to threaten the existence of the state as currently imagined. Perhaps, it is also time for scholars to ask: Why do we vote? Why do elections matter in Africa if political outcomes do not change? Why are countries on the continent which are glaringly loathed by their citizens (or substantial sections of its population) still in existence, and are such countries capable of progress under these conditions?

Again, one needs to refer to Ekeh (1975; 1994) and his argument on the lack of evolution of the African person from an oppressed subject under colonial rule to a citizen with genuine privileges. An individual or a people who are not afforded the privileges of citizenship would typically have no incentive to commit themselves to the moral ethos that eschews corruption as Gyekye (1997) imagines. Consider for example how the government of the United States of America would conduct a daring operation in the riskiest geography in the world to extract an abducted American citizen. Or how the government of Britain, or Japan, would plunge into the depths of the world in search of a countryman on a holiday trip who is suddenly reported missing. Citizens of such nations are acutely aware of the duties they owe the state on account of the privileges they derive therefrom.

In contrast, what does it mean to be Nigerian, Cameroonian, Gambian, etc., in Africa today? If citizens of these countries would rather embark on the dangerous voyage to Europe on a dinghy than endure the powerlessness that characterizes everyday life in the continent, then it is impossible to get such a citizen to choose the well-being of the country over theirs if such a choice is to be made. Let us also consider, for the sake of argument: what does the African who forgoes the opportunity of embezzlement while in office and chooses to remain an upright public servant get? Hardly the assurance that others would aspire to hold the reins of office in good faith as he has done. Rather, such refusal to enrich himself while in office would come to haunt him, because his successor would embezzle everything in sight, including his pension fund. This crisis of ownership of the state by its own citizens is at the heart of many problems that plague post-colonial Africa, including the problem of its opportunistic and self-serving elites. This crisis of ownership of the state is at the heart of the miseries that plague Africa today; 'corruption' is only one of the many consequences of it.

Conclusion

This chapter explored how the concept of 'corruption' has been examined by scholars of the African condition. It wrestles with the definitional ambiguities of the term, and points out how the lack of clarity over what scholars mean when they say a country is 'corrupt' impedes understanding of the failure of politics in contemporary Africa. The chapter also examines the extant literature on corruption as Africa's most resilient or outstanding problem. The exploration indicates that the scholarly perspective on why corruption manifests so acutely in African politics is divided between those who believe corruption to be a failure of the moral character of African leaders and those who essentialize corruption as a failure of public institutions in Africa. While both perspectives are important in making sense of the failure of politics, they also overstate the role of corruption as a pathology of the post-colonial state. And this crowds out the space for other germane interrogations of the African condition.

Note

1 Postdoctoral Research Fellow, Centre for African Studies, Rhodes University, South Africa.

References

Achebe, C., 1966. *A Man of the People*. London: Heinemann Educational Books
Adebanwi, W., 2017. Africa's 'two publics': Colonialism and governmentality. *Theory, Culture & Society*, 34(4), 65–87.
Afigbo, A.E., 1972. *The Warrant Chiefs: Indirect Rule in Southeastern Nigeria, 1891–1929*. Longmans.
Akhaine, S.O., 2022. Populism in Africa and the anti-corruption trope in Nigeria's politics. In *The Palgrave Handbook of Populism* (pp.485–496). Palgrave Macmillan, Cham.

Banfield, E.C., 1958. *The Moral Basis of a Backward Society.* New York: Free Press.

BBC News, 2016. David Cameron calls Nigeria and Afghanistan 'fantastically corrupt'. 10 May. Available at https://www.bbc.co.uk/news/uk-politics-36260193 [Accessed on 12 October 2022]

Bratton, M. and Van de Walle, N., 1994. Neopatrimonial regimes and political transitions in Africa. *World Politics, 46*(4), pp.453–489.

De Sardan, J.O., 1999. A moral economy of corruption in Africa? *The Journal of Modern African Studies, 37*(1), pp.25–52.

Eboh, C., 2022. Nigeria's accountant general faces corruption charges after arrest. *Reuters*, May 17. Available at: https://www.reuters.com/world/africa/nigerias-accountant-general-faces-corruption-charges-after-arrest-2022-05-16/ [Accessed on 12 July 2022]

Ekaney, N., 1977. Corruption and politics in Chinua Achebe's" a man of the people": An assessment. Présence Africaine, 104, pp.114–126. https://www.jstor.org/stable/24349492

Ekeh, P.P., 1975. Colonialism and the two publics in Africa: A theoretical statement. *Comparative Studies in Society and History, 17*(1), 91–112.

Ekeh, P.P., 1994. The public realm and public finance in Africa. In Kinyanjui, K., Himmelstrand, U. and Mburugu, E. (Eds), *African Perspectives on Development: Controversies, Dilemmas and Openings* (pp.234–258). London: James Currey.

Fagbadebo, O., 2019. Corruption and the challenge of accountability in the post-colonial African states: A discourse. *Journal of African Union Studies, 8*(1), pp.9–32.

Fagbadebo, O. and Dorasamy, N., 2021. Political leadership, corruption, and the crisis of governance in Africa: A discourse. *African Renaissance (1744–2532), 18*(1), pp.27–52.

Ferragina, E., 2009. The never-ending debate about the moral basis of a backward society: Banfield and 'amoral familism'. *Journal of Anthropological Society of Oxford, 1*(2), pp.141–160.

Ganahl, J.P., 2014. *Corruption, Good Governance, and the African State: A Critical Analysis of the Political-Economic Foundations of Corruption in Sub-Saharan Africa* (Vol. 2). Universitätsverlag Potsdam.

Gyekye, K., 1997. *Tradition and Modernity: Philosophical Reflections on the African Experience.* Oxford: Oxford University Press.

Gyekye, K., 2015. Political corruption: A philosophical inquiry into a moral problem. *Philosophy and Politics: Discourse on Values, Politics, and Power in Africa, 10*(2), p.353.

Igboin, B.O., 2016. Traditional leadership and corruption in pre-colonial Africa: How the past affects the present. *Studia Historiae Ecclesiasticae, 42*(3), pp.142–160.

Joseph, R.A., 1983. Class, state, and prebendal politics in Nigeria. *Journal of Commonwealth & Comparative Politics, 21*(3), pp.21–38.

Lui, Y. and Faerber, G., 2021. CSR Blog: Corruption and the death penalty in China: Political Win v. Criminal law development. *The SAIS China Studies Review.* July 1. https://saiscsr.org/2021/07/01/csr-blog-corruption-and-the-death-penalty-in-china-political-win-v-criminal-law-development/ [Accessed on 12 July 2022]

Madonsela, S., 2019. Critical reflections on state capture in South Africa. *Insight on Africa, 11*(1), pp.113–130.

Mamdani, M., 1996. *Citizen and Subject: Contemporary Africa and the Legacy of Late Colonialism.* James Currey.

Maseko, N., 2022. South Africa's clean President Ramaphosa faces his own scandal. *BBC News*, August 1. Available at: https://www.bbc.com/news/world-africa-62289552 [Accesed on 11 August 2022]

Mulinge, M.M. and Lesetedi, G.N., 1998. Interrogating our past: Colonialism and corruption in Sub-Saharan Africa. *African Journal of Political Science, 3*(2), pp.15–28.

Nkrumah, K., 1970. *Class Struggle in Africa.* London. Panaf Books Ltd.

Nyei, I.A.B., 2020. Liberia. In Awedoba, A.K, Kamski, B., Mehler, A., and Sebudubudu, B. (Eds), *Africa Yearbook Volume 16: Politics, Economy and Society South of the Sahara in 2019.* (pp.121–129). Leiden: Brill Publishers.

Okeja, U., 2022. *Deliberative Agency: A Study in Modern African Political Philosophy*, Bloomington: Indiana University Press.

Okorie, M.M., 2018. Presidential amnesty and resource militancy in a petro-state. In Obi, C. and Oriola, T. (Eds), *The Unfinished Revolution in the Niger Delta.* (pp.60–76). Routledge.

Okorie, M.M., 2022. Populism in the ANC and the 2019 xenophobic violence in South Africa. In Schapkow, C. and Jacob, F. (Eds), *Nationalism and Populism: Expressions of Fear or Political Strategies?* (pp.71–96). De Guytner. DOI: 10.1515/9783110729740-005

Okorie, M.M., 2021. Like Kwazulu-Natal, like rivers state: The implications of prebendalism on elec-toral contest. *Journal of Alternative Perspectives in the Social Sciences*, *11*(1), pp.41–72.

Olanipekun, O.V., 2021. Political corruption in Africa: Revisiting Kwame Gyekye's moral solution. *The African Review*, *48*(1), pp.122–139.

Osaghae, E.E., 1995. Amoral politics and democratic instability in Africa: A theoretical explora-tion. *Nordic Journal of African Studies*, *4*(1), pp.17–17.

Osoba, S.O., 1996. Corruption in Nigeria: Historical perspectives. *Review of African Political Economy*, *23*(69), pp.371–386.

Szeftel, M., 2000. Clientelism, corruption & catastrophe. *Review of African Political Economy*, *27*(85), pp.427–441.

The World Bank (2022). Lifting 800 Million people out of poverty – New report looks at lessons from China's experience. Press Release, April 1. Available at: https://www.worldbank.org/en/news/press-release/2022/04/01/lifting-800-million-people-out-of-poverty-new-report-looks-at-lessons-from-china-s-experience [Accessed on 30 April 2022]

Transparency International - T1, (2021). The ABCs of the CPI: How the corruption perception index is calculated. December 20. Available at: https://www.transparency.org/en/news/how-cpi-scores-are-calculated [Accessed on 12 July 2022]

Udombana, N.J., 2003. Fighting corruption seriously-Africa's Anti-corruption convention. *Singapore Journal of International & Comparative Law*, 7, p.447.

Van den Bersselaar, D. and Decker, S., 2011. "No longer at ease": Corruption as an institution in West Africa. *International Journal of Public Administration*, *34*(11), pp.741–752.

13

AFRICAN CIVIL SOCIETY

Albert Kasanda

Introduction

A range of scholars and political thinkers consider that the awareness about civil society emerged, in Africa, in the last two decades of the last century. For them, this society concentrated on the struggle against postcolonial regime that was viewed as authoritarian and undemocratic rule. To put things positively, this dynamic aimed at both the rehabilitation and instauration of liberal democracy in Africa. This statement can be considered partly true because, as it will be explained further, civil society emerged in Africa a long time before the end of the last century, and it aimed at several purposes.

This analysis divides into three sections. The first section explores the theoretical debate about the concept of civil society and its application to African social and political reality. The second section focuses on theoretical typologies or representations of civil society in African contexts. The third section examines challenges regarding the future of African civil society, particularly regarding its relationship with the state.

Debating African Civil Society

The idea of civil society became popular in Africa in the context of criticism concerning African postcolonial state and the subsequent democratic turn that took place in the last quarter of the twentieth century. Despite its popularity, this idea does not refer to a definition that can be accepted unanimously, because of its long history as well as because scholars and political thinkers provide various interpretations about. Bratton (1994, 52) observes that

> Not only did the concept evolve in distinctively European historical and cultural milieux, but its usage by political philosophers has changed dramatically over time [...] As a result, its contents for purposes of comparative political analysis in the late twentieth century is highly contestable. Analysts who have tried to apply the concept to non-Western politics have found it "unwieldy" and "complex".

DOI: 10.4324/9781003143529-15

Two tendencies characterize the debate on the concept of civil society regarding Africa. On the one hand, critiques of the application of the concept of civil society to African social and political realities, and on the other hand protagonists of such an application.

Criticizing African Civil Society

Critics of African civil society consider the application of the concept of civil society to African reality as inappropriate. They rely on the Western roots of this concept to denounce potential ambiguities in the use of this concept, regarding for example the relationship between both the African state and African societies, as well as the weakness of African market as a mode of economic regulation. Scholars such as Patrick Chabal and Jean-Pascal Daloz (1999), Maxime Haubert and Pierre Philippe Rey (2000), to mention but a few, count within protagonists of this approach. Chabal and Daloz (1999), for example, consider that the idea of civil society anchors in Western social and political philosophy. As such, it expresses the Western worldview including, for example, the notion of individual rights, and the relationship between the state and the society. Therefore, for them, it is inappropriate to make use of such a concept to speak of African reality. In this respect, they observe that

> [...] the emergence of a properly institutionalized civil society, led by politically independent citizens, separate from governmental structures, is only possible where there is strong and strongly differentiate state. Only then is it meaningful to speak of a "counter-hegemonic" civil society. Historically, however, the only instances of the development of civil societies of this type have occurred in Europe- where their formation was fortuitous, or rather unplanned and unpredictable. The situation in contemporary Africa is, at this stage, historically so different that it is hard to see how it could evolve in the same direction- at least in the foreseeable future.
>
> *(Chabal and Daloz 1999, 21)*

It can be observed that, for these critiques, the want of sharp distinction between state and society represents a stumbling-block for the emergence of a properly institutionalized civil society in Africa. The African political system can't be viewed as like the Western counterpart. The want of a clear distinction between both the African state and the society implies, for Chabal and Daloz (1999, 17), a "constant interpenetration, or straddling, of the one by the other". Subsequently, for both the scholars, the use of the concept of civil society about African social and political reality is inappropriate. This criticism stands on a narrow interpretation of the African postcolonial state which is viewed as static and authoritarian. Indeed, the postcolonial African rule relied on African precolonial culture to impose its own approach to the world as well as to the power. It stifled all stray impulse of civil society through its hegemonic structures.

Jean-Francois Bayart (1993) proposes a different perception of the state in Africa. For him, it is understandable that African state gets involved with family kinship, social ties, and all kinds of strategic alliances. It is on this kind of network that the African state's balance and legitimacy rely. Bayart perceives the African state as *"Etat rhizome"*, since this state is involved in a complex network of social and political relationships by virtue of its own survival and expansion. He describes this process in the following terms:

> [...] the postcolonial State operates as a rhizome rather than a root system. Although it is endowed with its own historicity, it is not one-dimensional, formed around a single

genetic trunk, like a majestic oak tree whose roots are spread deep into the soil of history. It is rather an infinitely variable multiplicity of networks whose underground branches join together the scattered points of society.

(Bayart 1993, 220)

This model of state was predominant in postcolonial Africa, as most of the African leaders relied on this paradigm to rule. One of the multiple effects of this consisted of the strangulation of civil society's dynamic and all political alternative to the benefit of authoritarian rule. In this context, every social and kinship interstice was considered an opportunity for both the state and the elite to emerge. The former aimed at expanding its dominance while the latter intend to keep its financial and political privileges.

Antagonists of the idea of African civil society also evoke the weak influence of the market in Africa to sustain the inexistence of civil society. For them, the proliferation of informal mechanisms excludes African economy from the ruling standards of the market, and subsequently, this process contributes to marginalizing this continent. This singularity impedes the establishment of a balanced relationship between the state, the market, and the society. It also turns complex the use of the concept of civil society as economic standards are not clearly identified and matched.

It can be noted that Antagonists of the concept of African civil society stand on an ethnocentric premise considering Europe as an immovable centre of gravity of humankind's thought and development. For them, nothing like salvation can be achieved without Europe. Both the democracy and the development of non-Western people should stand on Western paradigm to be successful. This way of thinking not only includes ethnocentric approach to foreign people and cultures, but it also implies a linear view of humankind's evolution by pointing out Europe as exclusive and mandatory paradigm of social and political development of humankind. Scholars such as Levi-Strauss (2007), Mudimbe (1998), and Mbembe (2013), to quote but a few, have brilliantly denounced the limits of such an ethnocentric view.

It is worth observing that the idea of civil society is not the only concept concerned regarding the encounter between Western and non-Western people. Ideas such as democracy, human rights, constitutionalism, equality, liberty, and good governance, which also are rooted in Western culture and philosophy, are equally used to speak of African struggles. Despite of their Western origin, these concepts have been adopted – and subsequently adapted – by a variety of people and cultures all over the world. The idea of democracy, for example, is even viewed as one of the world's leading political and normative principle, regardless of its foreign origin and regardless of ups and downs of people willing to rely on it as their normative and political reference. Kervegan (1996, 127) reminds that

> [La] démocratie ne désigne plus un régime parmi d'autres, mais semble être l'horizon de tout ordre politique légitime. L'accession de la démocratie au statut de l'idéalité normative se traduit par le fait que cette notion recouvre désormais plus que les institutions définies, un ensemble des valeurs : les droits de l'homme.
>
> (Democracy no longer refers to a political regime among others, but it seems to be the horizon of any legitimate political order. The fact that democracy got normative status can be explained by the fact this notion now includes more than defined institutions, that means a set of values: human rights).

As already evoked, the critiques of the application of the concept of civil society to Africa stand on a narrow interpretation of this concept. They reduce its perception to only one view consisting of opposing civil society to the state. For them, the civil society is exclusively viewed as a « counter-hegemonic society » (Chabal and Daloz 1999, 21). Contrary to such a reductionism, it is worth reminding other possible views of this society. It can be noted that the concept of civil society had received multiple interpretations though Western philosophy. Aristotle, for example, perceived the civil society (*polis*) as the equivalent of a political community (*Koinonia politiké*). Thinkers such as Ferguson considered it as the expression of progress and good manners, while Hegel opposed it to the state, and Marx approached it through economic category and the antagonism of social classes (Kasanda 2005, 10–14).

Protagonists of African Civil Society

For the defenders of the idea of African civil society, this concept includes a compound of social and political experiences of African people and their daily struggle for a living. According to them, making use of this concept will not transform African people's experience into a mere and pale copy of the Western process. Nothing like a nonsensical mimicry. They postulate the universality of civil society since it is intrinsically linked with democracy. They think that the notion of civil society embodies universal beliefs that are to be shared by every humankind society regardless of its cultural, social, and political singularity. These beliefs include, for example, principles and practices concerning human rights, democracy, legitimacy, and control of power. In sum, the defenders of the idea of African civil society including for example Harbeson (1994) and Young (1994) think that this concept represents a common and universal legacy transcending both cultural and political cleavages.

The resort to the idea of universalism as an argument in support of the application of the concept of civil society to African experience requires a bit of prudence and criticism. It is important to keep in mind what the concept of universalism itself does refer to. Does this word imply a totalitarian expansion of a model of civilization (Mudimbe 1998; Fornet-Betancourt 2011, 194) or does it refer to something different? In other words, does this word refer to an endless expansion of Western cultural and political imperialism? Protagonists of the application of this concept to African social and political reality seem far from such an interpretation. Their approach to universality implies pluralism, recognition of the other and dialogue.

For the protagonists of the idea of African civil society, the link between civil society and democracy is also invoked in support of their postulate. According to them, democracy and civil society are intimately tied so that they can be considered as revealing each other. Democracy presupposes the existence of civil society, and inversely civil society constitutes a sign of the achievement of democracy. As various scholars observed, the mobilization of civil society for democracy has been most striking in Africa in recent years. Thus, it can be considered as unmistakable to think of African civil society as an essential structure for the entrenchment of democracy in the continent (Sithole 1998, 27–28). For thinkers such as Gautier Pirotte (2007, 87), for example, there is no democracy without civil society. For him, civil society constitutes itself a kind of epiphany for democracy, as he wrote that

> Il n'y a pas de démocratie sans société civile où que ce soit. […] la société civile [est] à la fois un élément actif du processus de démocratisation et un indicateur du degré d'avancement de ce processus.

(There is no democracy without civil society wherever it can be [...] civil society [is] at a time an active factor in the process of democratization as well as a sign of progress achieved in this process).

Paradigms of African Civil Society

Relying on the premise that the concept of civil society has multiple meanings and various articulations, it can be pointed to a few paradigms that show the dynamism of this society in both the African history and political thought. This presentation divides into three sections following the conventional approach dividing African history in terms of the precolonial period, colonial rule, and postcolonial era as well as the globalization period.

Precolonial African Civil Society

A range of African scholars and political leaders sustain the existence of the precolonial African social and political organizations including civil society (Gyekye 1997; Wiredu 1998). For them, the concept of civil society refers to structures aiming at balancing traditional authority and promoting social peace. Unfortunately, these structures were victims of the colonial system which made them disappear. Wiredu (1998), for example, considers that regardless of the want of performing theoretical background, precolonial African societies assumed civil society's duties through integrative mode. The advent of colonial rule broke down this mode of regulation. In this respect, he notes that

> One way in which colonialism injured Africa was through the rupture it caused in the integration of the civil with political aspect of her social life. That integration was one of the strong points of traditional society. Indeed, in traditional life the distinction between the state and civil society was largely inoperative.
>
> *(Wiredu 1998, 241)*

Wiredu thinks that precolonial African communities were organized based on the principle of continuity between African state and the civil sphere. According to him,

> in traditional milieu the state itself can be seen as a special organization for the pursuit of mutual aid; and its underlying principle bears the same analogy to moral principles as those of the civil institutions and practices of traditional communalism.
>
> *(Wiredu 1998, 243)*

In this perspective, Wiredu considers that every extended kinship linkage plays an important paper in social relationship. He observed himself that

> the smallest kinship set-up to which any young adult belongs with a lively sense of belonging is already a significant society.
>
> *(Wiredu 1998, 241)*

For Wiredu, in precolonial societies, the "sense of obligations and rights and of reciprocity is developed on the basis of natural feelings of sympathy and solidarity" (Wiredu 1998, 242). The idea of continuity between state and civil society relies on an up-streaming principle of adjustment of the interest of both the individual and the community. This principle aims at promoting solidarity between community members avoiding irrationality and conflicts. To illustrate his postulate, Wiredu makes use of a metaphor of a crocodile having two heads and only one stomach. According to him,

> [the] adherence to the principle of consensus was (…) based on the belief that ultimately the interests of all members of society are the same, although their immediate perceptions of those interests may be different. This thought is given expression in an art motif depicting a crocodile with one stomach and two heads in struggle for food. If they could but see that the food was, in any case destined for the same stomach, the irrationality of the conflict would be manifest to them.
>
> *(Wiredu 1997, 306)*

The Wiredu's approach to precolonial societies seems a bit romanticized, since he passes over silence antagonism, rivalry, and conflicts structuring power relationship in the evoked precolonial societies. He seems to be worried by one thing principally, to making of African precolonial values the cornerstone of an alternative mode of governance which he thinks should be based on consensus and no-party rule (Wiredu 1998, 252).

Various African scholars including Gyekye (1997), Wamala (2004), and Teffo (2004) excavated African precolonial values and traditions to assert the existence of the precolonial civil society. Now the question is how can these excavated precolonial values be made relevant to current African social and political context and challenges. To be coherent, such a project must benefit from permanent and critical vigilance, that means an endless hermeneutical process. Such a process entails constant interpretation of African heritage in light of the burgeoning social and political configurations.

African Civil Society as a Mode of Resistance against the Colonial Rule

The colonial rule placed African communities under its tutelage and subsequently established with them a relationship based on the principles of domination and dispossession. Young (1994, 38) observes that during colonial rule

> […] much of the social space within which a society might become civil was blocked. By *legal concept*, the colonized was a "subject" with highly circumscribed civil and political rights. *Economically*, the colonial subject was a unit of labor, (…). In *religious terms*, the African was a *fetishist* awaiting redemption by Christian conversion (unless a secondary zone of salvation through Islam blocked the path). *Culturally*, the African domain required sorting and labeling through an often- alien classificatory schema. *The radical reordering of political space* imposed by the colonial partition deconstructed potential civil societies.

It seems obvious that during the colonial era, African civil society developed through interstices and multiple shades. It sometimes appears as the mirror of the pattern of dominance of African people, sometimes it reveals itself as a tool for African resistance and rebellion against colonial rule, and undemocratic regimes (Breytenbach 1998).

Mamdani (1996) explores the evolution of African civil society in his seminal book *Citizen and Subject. Contemporary Africa and the Legacy of Colonialism*. In the book, he deals with the issue of the postcolonial African state's failing including its chronic crisis, conflicts and groping of democratization process. For Mamdani, the failing of African postcolonial state has its roots in African colonial past rather than in any substantial lack of ability of African people to rule themselves. The source of the crisis of African postcolonial state is the mode of governance inherited from colonization. For him, the logic that governed South African apartheid regime, for example, was the same one that was deployed through colonial rule all over the African continent, since it was based on Lugard (1858–1945)'s considerations according to which black people were like children. They should be ruled and not treated as if they were equal to white people.

Colonial rule implies dualism and disconnection between urban area and rural area, modern and traditional rules, civilized and uncivilized. The former group was treated as citizens and ruled according to modern law. They were part of civil society. The latter one was governed through indirect rule with emphasis on traditional authority and customs. They were not viewed as part of civil society. In other words, Lugard's distinction was used in support of racist and oppressive system, as well as to deny African people's aptitude for both democracy and civil society's organization.

It can be noted that for different reasons and making use of different arguments, Mamdani reaches a similar conclusion as the one advanced by already evoked critiques of the application of the concept of civil society to African realities. For him, civil society didn't exist in Africa and the current use of this concept is, as concerning the idea of African state for example, based on mistaken and illusory premises. Contrary to this opinion, Breytenbach states that "the roots of civil society go back far in history, and is not alien to Africa" (1998, 40). Standing on this premise, he denounces the silence of African historiography on this issue, particularly regarding African pre-independence era. For him, this silence constitutes a "curious omission" whose effect consists of ignoring all kinds of African resistance against colonial policies and emergent forms of civil society (Breytenbach 1998, 39). Breytenbach argues that there have been multiple forms of resistance in African history including for example:

> the Sierra Leone hut tax revolt, Samori Touri's uprising against French, the Herero-Nama and Maji-Maji resistance against the Germans, and the Bambatha rebellion, Chilembwe and Harry Thuku protests the British.
>
> *(Breytenbach 1998, 39)*

These forms of resistance may not be properly considered as expressing African civil society. But considering that they have been displayed as instances of collective action aiming at redressing colonial grievances, and interacting with colonial state, they could be viewed at least as "proto-civil society" (Breytenbach 1998, 40). Breytenbach's claim relies on an up-stream postulate according to which there are two distinct historical epochs that deal with the role of civil society in Africa: African protest colonial policies, and anti-authoritarian resistance against undemocratic regimes in independent Africa.

African Civil Society as the Expression of Culture and Civilization

The idea of African civil society as expressing the rejection of the colonial rule expanded from the beginning of colonization up to nationalist struggles for emancipation that started soon after the Second World War. This epoch also witnessed the rise of voluntary associations that were mainly grievance-driven and aimed at reforms rather that the destruction of colonialism. These associations relied on collective action, and they were organized on account of a relatively permanent associational base, and in interaction with the colonial state (Breytenbach 1998, 39). Here, civil society seems to rime with civilization. It can be equated with the mainstream thinking for which Europe was the unique and exclusive reference of humankind civilization. It was in such a context that Belgian colonizer, for example, created in Congo (DRC) the famous social category of *Evolués*. This category includes people who could justify through their education, social, civic behaviour, and life standard their aptitude to benefit from civil rights and better consideration from colonizers. These people were viewed as "civilized", – thus members of civil society – in opposition to their fellow countrymen who did not match the required standard. This category of people represented a kind of mirror of the prevailing ruling system in opposition to local communities which were considered as the realm of conservatism, obscurantism, and subsequently the want of civil society.

The local elite who joined the category of *évolués* got quickly disenchanted since the ruling authority hardly paid attention to their expectations for reform, particularly for them to enjoy similar consideration as white people were. Because of this disillusion, they changed their mind. They became aware of their own dignity as indigenous as well as concerning the relevance of their struggle for emancipation. This period can be considered as the rise of African nationalist self-assertion. It developed by the end of the Second World War, and it was clearly independence driven. As Young (1994, 38) observed:

> In the final years of the colonial state – after World War II in most of Africa– a swiftly intensifying voice of protest emerged. At the time the rise of nationalist self-assertion appeared to herald the birth of civil society, even if that term was not employed. A proliferating web of associational life knit society together in ways that supplied the structuration indispensable for the impending nationalist challenge. (…) If one defines civil society by its organizational life, one might suggest that the decolonization era was its golden age.

In sum, it can be noted that nationalist self-assertion relied on a philosophy of resistance against colonial rule. This resistance followed two main trends including the claim for human being dignity, and the criticism of failures of colonialism. Aimé Césaire (1976) and Frantz Fanon (1975; 1979) count within theoretical spearheads of this resistance.

Civil Society in Postcolonial Africa

African civil society also expanded as criticism of African postcolonial state which stood, for decades, as an integral state. The concept of the integral state is due to Gramsci who used it to refer to the whole machinery of rule and hegemony of the ruling class. Young (1994, 39) thinks that this concept refers to

> A design of perfect hegemony, whereby the state seeks to achieve unrestricted domination over civil society. (…) The integral state requires not only the autonomy from civil society achieved through comprehensive instruments of political control but also suzerainty, if not monopoly, extending over social and economic vectors of accumulation.

This paradigm of state-dominated Africa since the early 1960s up to the last two decades of the twentieth century. African leaders who assumed political power upon the demise of colonial rule evoked varied pretexts in support of this mode of governance. Focusing on the preoccupation with national unity and development, for example, they promoted hegemonic mechanisms leading to stultifying the emergence of political pluralism and associational life. In doing so, they quelled the growth of a strong and self-supportive civil society. In this regard, Appiah (1992, 158), for example, denounces the violence with which African leaders such as Nkrumah annihilated the emerging Ghanaian democracy, suppressed political pluralism, and persecuted or sent into jail political rivals and opposition's leaders. Remembering his father's prosecution by Nkrumah, he notes the following:

> I grew up also believing in constitutional democracy, or to speak more precisely, believing that what those words stood for was important. When my father and his friends were locked up by Kwame Nkrumah in the early sixties, I was too young to think of it as anything more than a family tragedy. But the time they came out, I knew that the abolition of the legal opposition in 1960 had been a blow against democracy, that it had led naturally to imprisoning those who disagreed with our president and what my father called the « graping sycophants » who surrounded him, that all this evil began when multiparty electoral democracy ended.

Nkrumah was not an exception in putting an end to electoral and representative democracy in Africa. Many other African countries including Cameroon, Togo, Chad, Zaïre (DRC), Malawi, and Zambia underwent the same process under the supervision of their respective leaders, particularly during the three decades following the emancipation period. Because of the already evoked pretexts of unity and development, African leaders launched authoritarian regimes aimed at annihilating diversity and political pluralism. Contrary to Young's statement according to which the decolonization period was the golden age of African civil society (Young 1994, 38), it can be considered that postcolonial era was a time of coercion, muzzling and the extinction of attempt of this society. Sithole (1998, 27) observes in this respect that

> [the] subordination to nationalist movement intensified after independence when one-party rule was introduced. The hegemony and imposition of the one-party state in most African countries stultified the growth and independence of associational life, thus preventing the growth of a strong self-supportive civil society.

Facing African state's authoritarianism, a range of people relied on passive resistance, while active resistant social forces developed within spheres such as churches, university campuses, and to some extent through trade unions (Sithole 1998, 27). They became spearhead of anti-authoritarian resistance and awakening of African civil society. Their agenda can be approached according to two perspectives: the struggle against undemocratic regimes and the consolidation of democracy in African countries.

The resistance to authoritarian regime took place by the late 19980s and early 1990s. It expanded through claims concerning the disclosure of corruption, accountability policy, and the abomination of the one-party rule. Its manifestations were similar in most African countries, as the African people's desire and determination were clearly the same: to put an end to undemocratic regimes once forever. It is worth reminding that it was in this context that national sovereign conferences took place in various African countries (Young 1994, 43). These conferences represented an important political experience ever done by African people, as it consisted of a national debate between people representatives (from all social and political groups) to lay foundations for a new political contract. As an effect of this process, new political prospects emerged in Africa. In this respect, Breytenbach (1998, 41–42) observes that

> The rise of constitutionalism, the flourish of civil society, and the comeback of parliaments (...) new political parties were formed; former social movements were rejuvenated; apolitical groups also adopted political agendas; new leaderships arose in many parts of Africa; the public agendas were broadened to include socio-economic issues.

The consolidation of democracy in Africa prolongs the challenge to put an end to authoritarian regimes, particularly concerning ways and means to prevent denounced regimes to be back again. In this respect, a range of NGOs integrating African civil society concentrates on issues that are essential to the improvement of democracy in Africa, such as human rights, public accountability, capacity building, gender equity, and people's participation in decision-making spheres, to quote some few (Tripp et al. 2009; Kabarhuza et al. 2003). The exploration of these specific duties leads to a main debate concerning the interpretation that involved NGOs give to the concept of democracy and how far do they manage to sustain its achievement. Does this word exclusively refer to a procedural requirement (regular elections, for example) or does it imply the balance of social forces? How far can African civil society resist African leaders' permanent temptation to rule endlessly their respective countries? As already observed, the paradigm of liberal democracy dominated African democratic turn that took place in the last decades of the twentieth century. It is my feeling that such a paradigm is hardly sustainable because elections don't constitute sufficient evidence of democracy particularly in Africa where such a procedure is often marked by great distortions and massive irregularities.

In addition to that, democracy relates to social sphere, that means the development of social network aiming at the balance of social forces that, translated into strong people organizations, can successfully oppose the temptation of many African leaders for endless presidential mandate, for example. In this respect, it is worth reminding the struggle of African youth movements such as « Y en-a-marre », « Balai citoyen », « Filimbi » and « Lucha ». Those groups are principally constituted of young people who regardless of their religious belief, educational level, ethnic origins, and sex, stand for democracy and political alternation in Africa. They claim the strict respect of the nation's fundamental law and the full achievement of human rights. They are persuaded that Africa is the place where they have to be, their real homeland. So, they feel committed to fighting and making it a better place to live. They essentially rely on non-violence, and they make use of strategies such as theatre, arts, music, citizenship's capacity building, to mention a few means at their disposal, to promote social and political change. In other words, the emergence of those youth movements attests to the renewal of African civil society through a new and civic consciousness. It is my belief that those movements reflect a renewed African nationalism in accordance with the current challenges facing the African continent. As an illustration, let's roughly sketch the philosophy and some subsequent deeds of those youth movements.

The "Y en a marre" was launched as a citizen movement in 2011, in Senegal, by a group of Senegalese rappers and journalists. This movement can be viewed as the Senegalese sentinel of democracy. It aims at promoting a society shaped by civic values such as citizen participation, respect for laws and the constitution of the republic, the fight against corruption and impunity. Relying on a range of citizen initiatives, this dynamic overcame the carelessness and nepotism of President Wade's regime. Thus, it contributed to the emergence of the "Senegalese spring". This movement participates actively in the consolidation of achievements of the evoked spring as well as in the citizen control of the public action.

The concept of "Broom Citizen" (*balai citoyen*) is a metaphor standing for the idea of cleaning of Burkinabe society from the political corruption. It also calls the citizens to take control of their political and social destiny. In other words, this expression refers to the emergence of a new civic consciousness centred on justice, democracy, and the commitment of everyone to a better society. The social dynamics known under this name echoed in Burkina Faso in 2013 and it stands on the political legacy of Thomas Sankara (1949–1987). This movement played a central role in the fall of President Blaise Compaoré in 2014, notably through the political sensitization of young people and several protest's actions and civic resistance. The leaders of this movement do not envisage transforming it into a political party or a kind of springboard for the conquest of the political power. On the contrary, they think of remaining a critical conscience regarding the evolution of democracy and the respect of human rights. Through music, empowerment sessions and various events, they work to awaken the consciousness of the younger generations.

The word Filimbi comes from Swahili, and it means whistle. It is used as a metaphor inspired by the sport sphere to express the will of the defenders of this movement to whistle the end of the game concerning corruption, authoritarianism, and lack of respect for fundamental laws, particularly concerning the duration of the presidential term and political alternation. Filimbi is a platform of citizen movements that see themselves as "deliverers of democracy" (*accoucheur*). They prefer non-violence against the disproportionate violence of the state. They are aware that this commitment requires determination, patience, and perseverance. The activists of Filimbi took a model from the emblematic figure of Nelson Mandela.

The Movement "Struggle for Change" – Lutte pour le Changement LUCHA)- emerged in 2012 as one of the platforms of Congolese civil society. It mostly brings together young people dreaming of a new and prosperous DRC, where democracy and peace reign. The protagonists of LUCHA believe very little in the capacity of international institutions and foreign NGOs to reverse the course of things in the DRC. For them, change must come from inside. Despite the repression that they suffer from Congolese authorities, the activists of LUCHA rely on their own sense of sacrifice to bring about the long-awaited change. They take a paradigm for their struggle the figure Patrice Emery Lumumba, the Congolese national hero. The LUCHA's protagonists mainly develop non-violent actions such as the sits-in, theatre, protest march, campaigns of sensitization, and civic initiatives such as street sweeping.

In sum, it can be noted that African civil society is more active than ever. The emergence of the evoked platforms testifies to this dynamism. New social and political actors, especially young people, are struggling for the emergence of a new Africa where democracy, human rights, and human excellence are a priority for all. Those platforms bring to light the change in both political philosophy and paradigms occurring in the continent. Contrary to conventional perception, young people are taking the lead for social and political change regardless of their educational level, ethnic origin, or religious belief. Through their action, they challenge modes of governance that have been common in Africa such as authoritarianism and gerontocracy.

African Civil Society and the Challenge of Globalization

Current prevalence of neoliberal thought, particularly through globalization process, constitutes an important vector regarding the agenda and the development of civil society in Africa. It is worth outlining phenomena such as terrorist attempts, massive migration of

African people (internal and external migrations), ecologic disasters, armed conflicts and poverty, tutelage of international funding agencies, and the incidence of world-ruling powers, which also have a great incidence on the development of the civil society in Africa. In other words, this society faces multiple challenges. This section does not aim at exploring all of them. It shortly focuses on one that seems to be central: the relationship between African civil society and the state.

The relationship between state and civil society, as developed in Africa, raises the question to know whether African state and civil society can evolve as antagonist or supplementary to each other. What can be the role of civil society in a context where, due to globalization process, the idea of nation-state has been transformed and adapted to the market requirements? Protagonists of the neoliberal worldview denounced African postcolonial state as flawed, weak, and ineffective regarding growth, democracy, and liberalization. Regardless of the varied vectors that originated this situation, defenders of neoliberalism postulate to ditch such a state, and subsequently to search for its replacement. They highlight civil society as the alternative to African state and spearhead of African development. In arguing so, they relegate African state to a marginalized position for the benefit of global market principles (Willame 1996). Now the question is to know how far civil society can validly substitute the state in Africa.

First, it is worth recognizing that African state underwent (and still undergoing) multiple changes due to various configurations at work in the world. Despite these transformations, this state remains the established reference for African people's citizenship in the current world-ruling system, since it is the only institution habilitated to act with the required authority to ensure security and peace, order, stability, and equity within a given territory. In this respect, the idea to substituting African state with civil society seems more destabilizing and emasculating of African countries than ever. This kind of ambition should be revised downwards or considered with a bit of prudence and moderation, since it has been noted that despite its failures, current African state is still the only one institution to represent the people as well as to ensure unity and stability.

Secondly, it is important to unmask neoliberal sophism opposing civil society to African state and turning them into rivals each other. This perception dominated African transition era, as it relied on a subtle mirage mixing ruling political regime and state as administrative and political structures organizing people's social and political life in a definite territory. The sliding achieved on account of this mirage had as an effect the evoked opposition between civil society and state; consequently, it aimed at supporting – or to some extent improving- economic and political liberalization of African countries (Bratton 1994, 63). As the euphoria for political change slew down in Africa, it seems relevant to rediscover the very role of civil society and its fundamental relationship with the state. Various social and political thinkers including Hegel, Hobbes, Locke, Rousseau, to mention but a few, sustain the existence of an intrinsic link between state and civil society. According to them, both institutions are intertwined, and they mutually influence each other. In this respect, Osaghae (1998, 270) observes that

> [The] state is transformed by a changing civil society; civil society is transformed by a changing state. Thus, state, and civil society form a fabric of tightly interwoven threads, even if they have their own independent patterns.

This existence of common threads doesn't imply a fundamentally antagonistic development, but it refers to a critical and supportive relationship leading to promoting, for the state, the capacity to identify and express common good; while it makes possible, for civil society's members, the sense of state ownership, decision-making participation and accountability. In this respect, African civil society is called to turn aside from beaten tracks and deal with its specific challenges including, for example, the consolidation of democracy through limitation of presidential mandate, respect for African countries 's fundamental chart, the achievement of human rights, accountability, and equity. In other words, this society is called to tackle all deviations of the state about common good and people's well-being. Instead of opposing the state, it has the duty to rescuing and rehabilitating values constitutive of *vivre ensemble*.

Conclusion

Relying on the European origin of the concept of civil society and a Euro-centric reading of history, some scholars, and political theorists including for instance Chabal and Daloz (1999) as well as Haubert and Rey (2000), dispute the use of this concept to designate the current social and political dynamism of African societies. Some others, standing on the requirement of democracy and the existence of an intrinsic link between democracy and civil society, support the use of this concept for non-Western societies including the African ones.

Civil society developed in Africa along its own path, marked by milestones such as precolonial era, colonization, and the struggle for emancipation, postcolonial time, and the impact of globalization. These moments left a deep mark on the deployment of African civil society which, subjected to globalization and the onslaught of neoliberalism, is proving to be more dynamic than ever.

Finally, it should be observed that, despite the difficult and winding road ahead, African civil society is today a key player, since African states and international institutions can hardly do without it when it comes to analysing issues relating to the fight against climate change and the environment, gender, the promotion of youth, sustainable development or even conflict management. It can be noted that African civil society is a main social and political actor in its own right. It is the bearer of the utopia of another possible world, governed by the values of justice and democracy.

References

Appiah, Kwame Anthony. *In My Father's House. Africa in the Philosophy of Culture.* Oxford: Oxford University Press, 1992.

Bayart, Jean-Francois. *The State in Africa: The Politics of the Belly.* New York: Longman, 1993. (Translated from the French by Mary Harper, Christopher and Elizabeth Harrison. The French version: Bayart, Jean-Francois. *L'Etat en Afrique. La politique du ventre.* Paris: Fayard, 1989).

Bratton, Michael. Civil Society and Political Transitions in Africa. In Haberson John W., Rothchild, Donald and Chazan, Naomi (eds). *Civil Society and the State in Africa.* Boulder and Convent Garden: Lynne Rienner Publishers, Inc., 1994, pp. 51–81.

Breytenbach, Willie. The Erosion of Civil Society and the Corporatization of Democracy in Africa. In Yacouba Konaté (ed.). *Etat et société civile en Afrique. Actes du Colloque international interdisciplinaire. Abidjan (13–18 juillet). Quest Special* issue, Vol. 12, n°1, 1998, pp. 39–46.

Césaire, Aimé. *Discours sur le colonialisme.* Paris: Présence Africaine, 1976.

Chabal, Patrick and Daloz, Jean-Pascal. *L'Afrique est partie! Du désordre comme instrument politique.* Paris: Economica, 1999.

Fanon, Frantz. *Peau noire, masques blancs.* Paris: Le Seuil, 1975.

Fanon, Frantz. *Les damnés de la terre.* Paris: Maspero, 1979.

Fornet-Betancourt. *La philosophie interculturelle. Penser autrement le monde.* Paris: L'Atelier, 2011.

Gyekye, Kwame. *Tradition and Modernity: Philosophical Reflections on the African Experience.* New York and Oxford: Oxford University Press, 1997.

Harbeson, John W. Civil Society and the Study of African Politics. A preliminary Assessment. In Haberson John W., Rothchild, Donald and Chazan, Naomi (eds). *Civil Society and the State in Africa.* Boulder and Convent Garden: Lynne Rienner Publishers, Inc., 1994, pp. 285–300.

Haubert, Maxime and Rey, Pierre Philippe. *La société civile face au marché. Le changement social dans le monde postcolonial.* Paris: Karthala, 2000.

Kabarhuza, et al. *La société civile congolaise. Etat des lieux et perspectives.* Bruxelles: Colophon, 2003.

Kasanda, Albert. Considérations sur la société civile congolaise: un apport conceptuel. In Houtart, Francois (ed). *La société civile socialement engagée en République démocratique du Congo.* Paris: L'Harmattan, 2005, pp. 9–22.

Kervegan, Jean-Francois. Démocratie. In Raynaud, Philippe and Rials, Stéphane (eds). *Dictionnaire de philosophie politique.* Paris: PUF, 1996, pp. 127–133.

Levi-Strauss, Claude. *Race et histoire.* Paris: Gallimard, 2007.

Mamdani, Mahmoud. *Citizen and Subject. Contemporary Africa and the Legacy of Late Colonialism.* Princeton: Princeton University Press, 1996.

Mbembe, Achille. *Critique de la raison negre.* Paris: La Découverte, 2013.

Mudimbe, V.Y. *The Invention of Africa. Gnosis, Philosophy, and the Order of Knowledge.* Bloomington and Indianapolis: Indiana University Press, 1998.

Osaghae, Eghosa E. Rescuing the Postcolonial State in Africa. A Reconceptualization of the Role of Civil Society. In Jacouba Konate (ed). *Etat et société en Afrique. Actes du Colloque international Interdisciplinaire.* Abidjan (13–18 juillet). *Quest, special issue:* Vol. 12, n°1, 1998. pp. 269–282.

Pirotte, Gautier. *La notion de société civile.* Paris: La Découverte, 2007.

Sithole, Masipula. Civile Society and the Struggle for Democracy in Zimbabwe. In Jacouba Konate (ed). *Quest, special issue: Etat et société en Afrique. Actes du Colloque international Interdisciplinaire.* Abidjan (13–18 juillet). Vol. 12, n°1, 1998, pp. 27–38.

Teffo, Joe. Democracy, Kingship, and Consensus. A South African Perspective. In Wiredu, Kwasi (ed.). *A Companion to African Philosophy.* Malden and Oxford: Blackwell Publishing, 2004, pp. 443–449.

Tripp, A.M. et al. *African Women's Movements. Transforming Political Landscapes.* Cambridge: Cambridge University press, 2009.

Wamala, Edouard. Government by Consensus. An Analysis of a Traditional Form of Democracy. In Wiredu, Kwasi (ed.). *A Companion to African Philosophy.* Malden and Oxford: Blackwell Publishing, 2004, pp. 435–442.

Wiredu, Kwasi. The State, Civil Society, and Democracy in Africa. In Jacoub Konate (ed.). *Etat et société civile en Afrique. Actes du Colloque international interdisciplinaire, Abidjan (13–18 juillet). Quest Special Issue,* Vol. 12, n°1, 1998, pp. 241–252.

Willame, Jean-Claude. Trajectoire de la démocratie, gouvernance, concepts de base pour l'analyse. *Cahiers Africains,* n°23–24, 1996, pp. 9–25.

Young, Crawford. In search of civil society. In Haberson John W., Rothchild, Donald and Chazan, Naomi (eds). *Civil Society and the State in Africa.* Boulder and Convent Garden: Lynne Rienner Publishers, Inc., 1994, pp. 33–50.

PART III

Controversies

Normative Debates and Political Praxis

14

DELIBERATION, DEPENDENCE, AND FREEDOM

Ẹniọlá Ànúolúwapọ̀ Ṣóyẹmí

Introduction

This chapter focuses on two prominent scholars—Kwasi Wiredu and Emmanuel Chukwudi Eze—the interlocution between whose work has sparked renewed and refocused enquiries into questions of democracy and deliberation within contemporary African political thought and philosophy. The chapter proposes that, despite their disagreements, a normative understanding of communal rationality, and of dependency, lies at the heart of both Wiredu's and Eze's arguments concerning the consensual possibilities for democracy's practice. The nature of the democratic freedom that both Wiredu and Eze envisage for African countries, and for the no-less post-colonial societies beyond the continent's borders, depends on taking seriously the major challenge both these scholars pose—what if there are more morally agreeable ways of thinking about the things that order our politically determinant interactions with each other?

Kwasi Wiredu's central problem is simple: the majoritarian form of democracy that structures the political practices of most modern industrialised societies is unsustainable and morally hazardous. For Wiredu, the majoritarian archetype of democracy—found in countries like the United States and the United Kingdom—undermines the very notions of fairness and participation, by which such systems are supposedly defined. It is not merely the practical problem of representation in large, complex modern societies that concerns Wiredu. While the modern operation of representation seems to confuse the arm-wringing of groups and individuals through manipulative finance and manic electioneering for the voluntary consent of politically persuaded populations,[1] the fundamental problem should not be conceived as only a modern phenomenon.

Indeed, for Wiredu, the Athenian format to which this widespread model of representation traces should be thought no less problematic for having been direct—since no less was Athenian democracy based on decision-making by majority vote. Never mind the pre-exclusion of women and slaves, Athenian democracy kept intact the problem that 'a substantial part of the citizenry suffered veritable disenfranchisement *in the matter of decision-making*.'[2] One of the consequences of this sort of democracy is that it 'does not necessarily ensure that the decisions of the governing body reflect the consent of ... even a large proportion of the citizens.'[3] Against majoritarianism, Wiredu therefore questions: 'is it not possible ... for human wit to devise a kinder, gentler, and more rational system of governance?'[4]

DOI: 10.4324/9781003143529-17

Wiredu proposes a reconstruction of the traditional governance practices of various precolonial African societies, including his own Ashanti—part of the Akan. The distinctive socio-political feature of such societies was decision-making by consensual deliberation.[5] African deliberative practice was, according to Wiredu, further distinguished by certain moral structures that made possible its consensual outcomes. The kind of democratic deliberation that made genuine reconciliation possible on political matters depended on an underlying rationality of communality and discourse, and not on voting numbers. This also made feasible the possibility of inclusive agreement on action regarding even those matters where moral accord was unattainable.[6]

A similar estimation of numerous precolonial African histories seems to have inspired the political ideologies of several of Africa's post-independence leaders—for instance, Leopold Senghor,[7] Kwame Nkrumah,[8] Ahmed Sekou Touré,[9] Kenneth Kaunda,[10] and Julius Nyerere. Indeed, the latter's socialist programme was not, to his mind, grounded in any specifically Marxist philosophy. But rather, in Nyerere's own understanding that 'the organisation of traditional African society … was such that there was hardly any room for [the] parasitism [capable of producing] 'a leisured class…In traditional African society everybody was a worker.'[11] Despite his repeated admirations[12] for such post-independence figures, however, the analytical motivations for Wiredu's own political theorising are not ideological.[13]

Wiredu is, further, distinguished from other scholars like Kwame Gyekye,[14] Mogobe Ramose,[15] Edward Wamala,[16] and Joe Teffo[17]—whose work also explores the nature of consensus—because Wiredu's analysis is not motivated by the notion that the ideal of consensus, of radical democratic representation, is unique to Africa's historical experiences. He recognises it could not be.[18] He recognises also, however, that the normative value contained in such ideals is most certainly contextualisable by, at least, a deep set of historical experiences rooted in a not-insignificant African geography. Should our imaginations permit the ideational influence from Africa's examples to other parts of the world, then we would do well to pay closer, more positive, analytical attention to Africa's historical geographies.[19] The somewhat derogatory classification of Wiredu's democratic theorising as part of a romantically rear-faced 'return to the source'[20] mode is, I think, therefore, unjustified, and simplistic.[21]

Emmanuel Chukwudi Eze's intellectual agenda is equally morally urgent. For Eze, as for Wiredu, the practical difficulties of political life in many modern African countries requires solutions rooted in a specific kind of normative enquiry—one shorn of the inadequacies and assumptions of the kind of political theorising that has failed to make itself familiar with other worlds beyond narrow European histories and geographies. Eze adds another requirement— that of engaging the histories of African countries as continuously evolving parts, themselves rooted in modernities of their own making.[22] For Eze, the anthropological reification of past African "traditions" should have no part in envisioning Africa's political futures—futures as connected to everything that has gone before as they will be to all that comes after.

For Eze, then, the promise of Wiredu's ideas is let down by two things. First, they appear rooted in too uncritical a view of Africa's precolonial past.[23] Second, they take too little from that past what is known to have been degraded by those parts of the "enlightenment" philosophies responsible for giving colonial imposition its moral justification. It is, for instance, unlikely to Eze that precolonial African political systems were able to sustain such thorough-going deliberative practices simply, as Wiredu seems to say, due to the 'persuasiveness' of their 'rational' discourse.[24] What could be supposed responsible for making the "rationality" of Akan public discourse so intrinsic to that community as apart from the perhaps not-at-all "rational" features that tied together communal life in most precolonial African spaces?

Further, while the ancestral mythologies that united communities in traditional African societies might have their modern equivalents in many countries—'the flag, …the

Motherland… God,'[25] and so on, most African countries suffered from a double-sided issue. Their post-colonial condition made them no longer intimately connected to the ancestral mythologies that sustained their forefathers at the same time as being forced into state structures the flags of which continue to mean even less. If we agree that consensual democracy is, for its own sake, a better form of democratic governance than its majoritarian alternative, then Africa, and indeed everyone else, will need something different from what obtained in traditional African societies to sustain, in modernity, the forms of political governance and association those societies appear to offer us as examples.[26]

Over the intervening 20 years, the interlocution between Eze and Wiredu has inspired fresh scholarship on numerous topics—the nature of the public sphere,[27] the role of disagreement in democratic practice,[28] and of rationality in deliberation. In the latter area, Eze's arguments have generated debate about the influence of so-called "non-rational" factors in deliberative settings, and the extent to which these should be prevailed upon by "reason" and "rationality."

In this chapter, I wonder, however, the extent to which the latter discourse has been sustained largely by Eze's interpretations, and others', of rationality as contextualisable primarily, or only in an individualised sense.[29] And whether such an interpretation has served to stifle developments towards an understanding of the communal rationality on which Wiredu's thesis most surely relies, and to which some of Eze's own ideas point. I hope some of the developments made here will be as useful for intervening in some of those debates as they are for reassessing our understandings of the points at which Wiredu's and Eze's ideas meet.

This chapter will be divided into three further sections. In the next section, I propose that Wiredu's ideas about consensual democracy challenge us to think about deliberation in ways that ought to reframe some of our understandings about rationality. I argue that the normative understanding of communal rationality Wiredu offers is capable not only of sustaining the type of deliberative practice he envisages but, also, of providing the wider moral foundations that recommend such practice. But perhaps Wiredu does not, himself, go far enough in his arguments to secure the moral foundations of the communal rationality by which his thesis is, most assuredly, structured. Eze's critique is instrumental to increasing understanding about the communal rationality that not only grounds Wiredu's thesis but, also, leads us to a better reckoning of Eze's own ideas about the requirements of a "true" democracy. In section three, I outline a notion of communal and consensual dependency that I suggest is at the normative root of the kind of democratic practice capable of offering the solution that both Wiredu and Eze fundamentally seek. Finally, I conclude by outlining a view regarding the universal value of the type of political theorising that is serious in its critical and normative examinations of specifically African geographies and histories. I want to suggest that any disconcertment elicited by some of the ideas currently occupying African political theory and philosophy may simply be the correct result of an intellectual agenda deeply invested in coming to less narrow understandings of those political phenomena of concern to us all.

Rationality and a Radically Consensual Politics

In the specified African context of both Wiredu's and Eze's concern, the majoritarian model of democracy—first exported, now adopted by many African countries—has been especially calamitous. As Eze describes, in numerous African countries, the appeal to and demand for 'democratic ideals … whose historical examples are rooted in the modern European traditions,'[30] have enabled the maintenance of a democratic façade. These are fabrications in which the political class and organs of state are more substantiated by foreign governments than they are by the will of those they claim to serve.

Such is the global draw of multiparty electoral politics that simply the pretence to it in countries like 'Nigeria, ...Liberia, Rwanda' has allowed dictators and popular politicians alike, regardless of the substance or sanctity of their local support, to maintain 'untransformed the mechanisms of autocratic, dictatorial, and terroristic ...state power'—and with the stable, if not always unwavering, political, and military support of external governments.[31] It was against the destructive effects on Africa's societies of reducing real participation to the outsized and illegitimate influence of 'World Bank officials, Western NGOs [and]... the African elite' that those such as Claude Ake had, long ago, pleaded.[32]

What has made the effect of majoritarian electoral politics appear uniquely problematic in Africa's political contexts is the fact that throughout most of the continent, there has been a bifurcation between indigenous ethnic communities and the post-colonial structures of modern states and governments.[33] 'The ethnic stratification of nearly all contemporary African states has ensured that [, under multi-party electoral democracy,] many ethnic groups will be politically marginalized.'[34] The effect of which has been, as Richard Joseph had already theorised within the first three decades of independence, that many 'are compelled to pursue [electoral] democracy for the very reason they are unable to rely on' its ability to directly and effectively represent 'their particular subgroup of the population.' Multiparty electoral politics, in many African states was now a means to subvert state resources, through "democratic" contestation, for the political and economic interests of ethno-linguistic groups, each of whose adequate representation that same democracy was incapable of guaranteeing.[35]

It is unsurprising that the addition of a governance model uniquely reliant on electoral contestation by majority vote should be negatively explosive to externally constructed political entities housing newly stratified ethnic communities most of which are minimally, if at all, connected to the governing structures claiming to represent them.[36] It might be more noteworthy that the efforts of the present period which ought, as Wiredu states, to be dedicated to rectifying the problem of modern African states not yet the creations of their inhabitants,[37] have instead, in many cases, been put to devising ever greater pretences to majoritarian democracy—the beneficiaries of which are not the local population.[38]

The problems of majoritarianism seem to have most acutely lent themselves to Africa's political contexts, and this has made finding its replacement, across much of Africa, a matter of 'life-and-death.'[39] However, the problem of majoritarian democracy is not, so far as Wiredu is concerned, solely traceable to the modern particularities of African countries. For political societies with different stories of state formation, perhaps the problems of adversarial politics will manifest themselves decades after they have in African countries, and perhaps for different reasons, but majoritarianism presents fundamentally deleterious moral consequences regardless of the society in question. As such, the 'valid' possibilities for its solution 'ought to be a concern for our whole species,'[40] and envisaging the historical possibilities of a radically consensual politics has become morally necessary.[41]

But what exactly does Wiredu mean by a consensual politics? And precisely what could be radical about it? If securing and maintaining the power of distinct (or distinguishable enough) political parties using electoral mechanisms determines the political ordering of majoritarian systems, what Wiredu calls a system of decisional consensus would be a means of ensuring, through deliberative procedure, that *all* parties (that is, the rightful associations of groups and individuals expressing concern or interest on any given issue) agree to the decisions made under that system. By such a procedure, the notion of political majorities and minorities would become temporary states, manifest only during the deliberative process and disappearing once a decision is made.[42] By consensual democracy then, Wiredu means a form of political organisation in which the persistent notion of "winners" and "losers" is eradicated along with the organisation of political parties for the sole purpose of 'appropriating' governmental power.[43]

By consensus, Wiredu does not simply mean cooperation. Though consensual politics relies on political cooperation, the latter is a feature of many sites of political organisation, including of the very majoritarian forms of Wiredu's normative opposition.[44] The difference between consensus and cooperation is not simply that one takes in the other while the latter does not, necessarily, contain the former in its definition. There is also a temporal difference. Where cooperation under many forms of political organisation will be specific to a certain time and matter, cooperation under a consensual democracy will be sustained not only by concrete political mechanisms but, also, by a permanent—or potentially permanent—mode of *being* with one another.[45] It is why, as Martin Odei Ajei's explains, 'a liberal majoritarian system that employs deliberation and arrives at consensus in decision-making will not be characterised as a consensual democratic system, for the phenomenon of consensus will not be … *intrinsic* to it [emphasis added]'.[46]

Wiredu's organisational references for a system of consensual democracy are the varied precolonial political systems of numerous African societies—in particular, that of the Ashanti.[47] In the Ashanti political system, Wiredu says, there 'is never an act of formal voting.'[48] The election to the head of the political unit (lineage) was by extensive 'consultations and discussions' such that once a person had been elected, it was not so much that they had been voted for than that they had been agreed to. The 'pursuit of consensus [as] a deliberate effort to go beyond decision by majority opinion,'[49] Wiredu states, was applied throughout all areas of the Ashanti political process where a decision had to be made. In council or municipal matters, for example, after the selection of representatives by consensual agreement, it was the responsibility of those representatives to engage the adult members of the town in extensive consultations over all matters requiring a decision that would be agreeable to every member.[50]

If the problem of majoritarianism is that it takes the voting consent of the majority for the right to represent all adult persons in all political matters (including even on those matters where the opinion of the voting majority does not accord with that of the party they have, nevertheless, voted to power) for so long as the winning party is in office,[51] then the nature of representation under the Ashanti political system would seem to be radical in its ability to secure substantive representation in all matters of political decision-making for every adult member. This, Wiredu explains, was achieved by the fact that, as a rule, consensus was the mode of electing all members of the political councils, including the council heads, and 'the king of the Ashantis, at the highest level of traditional government.'[52] Moreover, the content of decisions carried out by council was not only achieved by consensus in council but, further, by the consensus and approval of the population through consultations with 'the young people's association' that was constituted in every Ashanti town.[53]

Perhaps more radical was the absence of a party structure. If Wiredu's descriptions are accurate, the institutional feasibility of the Ashanti system relied on the fact that such parties as did exist were not organised solely to secure political power, and to keep it to the exclusion of all others. Under the Ashanti system, all existing parties were 'partners in power' and, as such, there could be no party "out" of power.[54]

I do not believe Wiredu aims to paint a falsely utopian picture of Africa's precolonial histories, since those histories are not set apart from the rest of the world's by a paucity of wars and conflicts.[55] Wiredu's point, however, is that there are other ways—besides multi-party majoritarianism—of organising political life that better meet society's representative needs and democracy's own moral ambitions. At least two difficulties arise from Wiredu's attempts to secure the consensual possibilities for our democratic futures in the example of Africa's deliberative past, and Emmanuel Eze articulates them well.

First, Wiredu acknowledges that 'the conditions of traditional political life were surely less complicated than those of the present. The kinship networks that provided the mainstay of the consensual politics of traditional times are simply incapable of serving the same purposes in modern Africa,' and in most other places.[56] Yet, as Eze correctly assesses, in his own analysis Wiredu undervalues the role of such ancestral and kinship ties in supporting the picture he paints of consensual practice among the Ashanti, and perhaps elsewhere in precolonial Africa.[57] Eze suggests that this, also, causes Wiredu to overestimate the role of "rationality", that it was—as Wiredu states—by 'logical persuasiveness [and]…simply rational discussion'[58] that consensus was had in the Ashanti political system.[59] Both analytical issues present Eze with a normative dilemma: if we determine that consensual politics holds radical possibilities for our democratic futures, but the ties that secured the foundations of its practiced past no longer exist or are too different to be relied upon, then by what should the future of a radical consensual democracy be organised?[60]

For Eze, Wiredu's ideas that individuals can achieve decision-making consensus (that is, consensus about what is to be done),[61] even when they have no moral or normative substance tying them together, that there can be 'agreed actions without necessarily agreed notions'[62] simply by 'rational dialogue,' is not only an inadequate representation of Ashanti 'social conditions,'[63] it is further a misunderstanding of what is to be considered "rational" where 'the possibility of absolute justice' cannot be guaranteed.[64] Competition and conflict must be perceived as "rational" in a world where people first experience themselves as individuals—and where, as a result, even 'agreed notions do not necessarily produce agreed actions.'[65] Those things, therefore, that we may perceive as "irrational" or as without 'reason'—nondialogic mythologies of communal belonging, for example—may be of the utmost significance.[66]

If, for the present purpose, we understand rationality to mean, simply, the grounds on which we structure, and the reasons by which we explain the orders of our societies[67] then, perhaps inadvertently, Eze's critique identifies what we may call a communal rationality, capable of grounding his and Wiredu's arguments about the nature of human interaction and the character of reason in a consensual conception of deliberative democratic practice. I want to suggest that what those such as Emmanuel Ifeanyi Ani have called 'extraneous factors,'[68] and what Eze himself describes as criteria beyond the realm of "reason" do, indeed, come under a morally defensible rationality of their own. It may seem 'extreme'[69] for Eze to understand that the legitimation and 'exercise of public power relies heavily on mythologies and symbols' of communal belonging, whose authority over us is often more profound than the legitimacy we imagine accords to dialogue made reasonable by other criteria.[70] Such a position seems absurd, however, only if we imagine it irrational for people to consider more seriously, with greater faith, the ideas and arguments of those they are capable of proving equipped, if only to themselves, with a communal affection—and, in particular, on those decisions capable of affecting some of the most personal, intimate, and paramount areas of our individual and communal lives.

Eze might be mistaken to suggest that the bonds of community achieve legitimating effects for 'little or no "reason".'[71] In truth, what he really seems to mean is that the character or nature of reason by which those things we achieve only through communal engagement—such as deliberation and the kind of democracy that could be its outcome—cannot be grounded in purely 'ordinary,' or individualised bases of rationality.[72] Eze's mistake then, is to unduly uphold "reason" and "rationality" to special status, when they belong as concretely to his and Wiredu's normative tasks, as they have been wielded by the differing philosophical agendas of others.[73]

There is a communally based understanding of society's organising principle capable of securing the challenge that Emmanuel Eze sets out for Wiredu—that many modern, secular, culturally pluralistic societies, no longer held together by precolonial traditions (I believe this applies as much to non-African countries as it does to societies on the continent) must find new ties of social and communal attachment untethered to the dominance of state power.[74] This communally based rationality is outlined by Wiredu himself though he does not, I think, sufficiently defend it in his arguments regarding consensual democracy.

A communal rationality informs a certain kind of behavioural ethics that guides how we interact with one another in any given society. It is an ethics that 'if all the members of any community were to run completely short of due regard for the interests of other people in their behaviour, that community would regress into brutish chaos. Conduct cognizant of that constraint is what morality is.'[75] A communal rationality, therefore, positively accepts our moral dependencies on each other. Its major normative prescription is that we ought to consider 'the interests of others' in our outward actions.[76] That those to whom we have been considerate in our actions will, in their own actions, be more likely to consider us with greater care in turn.

For a thorough understanding of the operations of a consensual democracy, this notion of communal rationality is not to be brought under a purely individualised explanation of deliberative reasoning.[77] Rather, a communal rationality is what makes Wiredu's use of individual reason and rationality sensible. Take, for instance, what Wiredu describes about the importance of compromise and reciprocity to decisional consensus—this is where deliberative participants come to unified acceptance of a decision even where what Wiredu calls 'normative consensus'—that is, agreement as to moral beliefs—cannot be reached.[78] Decisional consensus, Wiredu states, depends on 'the willingness on the part of all concerned ... to contemplate with equanimity the prospect of not getting ones way all the time. Interpersonally, such a frame of mind... translates into a reciprocity that can have far reaching consequences.' Wiredu goes on,

> [t]he point, now, is that the right compromises are made not by virtue of any additional inquiries into facts and values but out of a certain kind of commitment to the general good. Such compromises are not irrational on this account, but their rationality is a rationality of attitude.[79]

Wiredu also states, 'rational dialogue is a necessary condition of consensus. But it does not of itself yield consensus.'[80]

Underlying Wiredu's ability to speak of decisional consensus as the 'prize' to 'rational discussion'[81] and 'dialogue'[82] is the logic that structures of consensual deliberative practice sustain, and are sustained by, a different kind of rationality to the purely individualised one that is at least partially necessary at the point of deliberating. A behavioural communal ethics that enables any given society to approach not only the politically determinant interactions of its inhabitants, but all sub-political social interactions, with an aim to consensus is of the utmost importance to Wiredu's understanding of consensual democracy.[83] It is only this communal rationality, which must underrun the human interactive function within society,[84] that is capable of making possible the procedural operation of governing structures by which political decisions are reached and agreed to by all through individually reasoned discussion.[85]

Emmanuel Ifeanyi Ani has noted the problem in Wiredu's attempt to dislocate decisional consensus about what *is* to be done—which Wiredu states relates most directly to consensual democracy—from a 'cognitive' or 'normative consensus' about what *ought* to be done.[86] As with Ani, I do not think most stable-minded people agree to *do* a thing they also believe is *not* the right thing to do—not without those reservations that permanently threaten an agreement's undoing.[87] Note that this is not equivalent to a person agreeing to an action with others though they do not necessarily align with all the normative points leading to that agreement, and as such being capable of reaching a compromise on a political decision though they are not especially wedded to some of the normative ideals behind them. The mistake that I think surrounds some of Wiredu's conceptions is the idea that the latter situation is the one that defines the majority of politically determinant interactions in which we find ourselves.[88] Rather, in a not-small number of instances, most of us do not simply hold an opinion on a matter, we hold a *belief* that as much influences our decisions about what to do on a matter as it may relate to a normative ideal.[89] Our ability to come to decisional consensus will, therefore, in many cases depend on being persuaded into normative consensus with others. As Wiredu himself notes,

> there is no such thing as compromise as to beliefs regarding what ought to be done. One cannot say with any degree of propriety something like "I believe that we ought to do A, but, in the interests of the community, I am going to believe that we ought to do B".[90]

Wiredu's argument that the two kinds of consensus he identifies can be agreeably separated leads him to the further point that it is by "rational" dialogue and discussion that people are persuaded to decisional consensus even where such a mechanism may be insufficient to normative consensus.[91] I suggest that Wiredu is able to make this separation between decisional and normative consensus, and further to foreground the importance of individually reasoned dialogue in attaining the former because the society Wiredu imagines capable of supporting his ideas is operated by a communal rationality that makes possible high degrees of communal trust,[92] 'reciprocity', and 'compromise,' among participants who though they may not have the same normative beliefs in all relevant things, are yet able to, as Wiredu says, willingly suspend any 'disbelief'[93] that on matters of political concern, each fellow inhabitant will deliberate with reciprocity and with the interests of the others in mind, just as she will have proved herself to behave in all other areas of social engagement. Individualised reason, and the explicability it is capable of giving the deliberative dialogue of Wiredu's understanding, is mediated through a communally based rationality.

The reason of communal interdependency, of what Wiredu calls 'communalism'[94]—what Gyekye has called 'moderate communitarianism'[95]—and which lies at the unifying heart of Wiredu's deliberative thought is, further, what explains the latter's ability to speak of human beings as having a 'rock bottom identity of interests.'[96] The understanding is not, as some seem to have taken it, that even within morally tight-knit communities the specified material interests of its individuals will be identical.[97] It is, rather, a normative prescription—that the nature of our communal dependencies on one another, in any given society, makes it desirable, morally advisable, that we find ways of making compatible those among our material interests that accord with an ethics of communal reciprocity. For even within such an ethical remit, there will be wide room for divergencies of particularistic concern.[98]

Eze's challenge is that

> the interests of some members... of a society may be to dominate the rest, for the sheer morbid enjoyment of power... how is such ... "interest" of the dictator reconcilable with that of the dominated? [For example] ... How do the commercial interests of a Texan oil company, or the Anglo-Dutch Shell... to get oil out of the soil as quickly... as possible, coincide with the ... survival interests of ... the Ogonis?[99]

But this is, I think, Wiredu's precise point. Where, as in Eze's Ogoni example, the presented material interests of one group seek to threaten the very existence of another, we do not, on at least one side, have the presentation of a true or ethical interest, nor indeed a set of persons mutually engaged in a communal rationality they could be equipped, by deliberative consensus, to sustaining.

Wiredu is not engaging us simply to think about how we may better practice deliberation as a means of securing practicably tolerable negotiations to morally intolerable concerns,[100] or for the benefit of deliberative decisions whose major epistemic value is not the moral sustenance of a communal rationality.[101] He is asking that we envisage the kinds of communities even capable of supporting a thorough-going consensual deliberative practice and requiring, in turn, of being morally maintained by the formalised political structuring of such engagements.

In this case, our conceptualisations of deliberation cannot be about the supposedly "objective" quality of decisions arrived at in settings under which participants are forced to accept each other's assumed equalities, moral or otherwise.[102] Nor can our ideas about deliberation be merely about the procedural justification conferred through its mechanics.[103] Rather, where (consensual) deliberation is made sense of as an operational support for, and outcome of, a communally oriented rationality, then deliberative settings become capable, as Wiredu notes, of presupposing and coping with 'original position[s] of diversity.'[104] They become sites in which our equalities, freedoms, and interests are not assumed but, persistently—communally—interrogated and, if needs be, reciprocally recalibrated.[105] By a communal rationality does deliberation become a means of assessing, regenerating, and sustaining the ties by which modern communities, through their own agencies, come to reimagine and remake themselves.

Freedom and the Reason of Consensual Dependency

Perhaps the most intriguing part of Eze's challenge to Wiredu is Eze's understanding that the impetus to append consensus to an ideal of democracy may not save us from the fact that democracy, 'truly' speaking, is not really defined by the mode of its operation. It is, rather, 'a political culture' capable—depending on the time and the place—of being continuously moulded by the society that operates it, and to the needs of that society.[106] It is difficult to disagree. But the question Wiredu is forcing us to answer is whether there are mechanisms for operating democracy that would seem more seamlessly compatible with that very spirit or "culture" that Eze suggests belongs to a "true" democracy. Indeed, he is forcing us to question the very moral grounds that seem to uphold the now most popular operation of democracy, and to query whether there are no preferable others.

Possibly in answer, Emmanuel Eze writes,

> It seems to me that a society opts for [a democratic] form for political life for the reasons Wiredu tells us the Ashantis had: "Two heads are better than one," or, as the Igbos say *Onwe gi onye bu Ọmada Ọmachara*: No one individual is Mother Wisdom. Political Wisdom comes in many forms and democracy becomes, in deed, a market place of *competing* — not just consenting or consensing — ideas. The only "consensus" primary to democracy ... if any — is the initial, formal agreement to play by a set of rules... Thus we cannot reduce democracy to one moment of its [possible] outcomes, decisional representation or consensus.[107]

Eze notes that this transformation of democracy into 'a market place' of competition results from the fact that human beings are, by the nature of our existences within society, incapable of achieving an 'absolute' form of justice.[108] We live in a 'condition of relativized desires' and democracy 'is one of the several sorts of social framework that a people adopt in order to mediate the struggles and the conflicts that *necessarily* arise from the necessarily competitive nature of individuated identities and desires.'[109]

There is another way of interpreting the underlying truth behind Eze's arguments. Certainly, the relative condition of our existences would seem to provide the justifiable basis of our conflictual relations in society and the justification, therefore, of an adversarial operation to democratic politics. More fundamentally, however, our inability to attain absolute justice—that is, a form of justice that seeks no reflection against any interests or desires outside those that can be determined to belong, singularly, to any single one of us—is, positively, the product of the fact that we live, for better or worse, under a condition of human dependency. The 'guarantee ... of absolute justice' is,[110] *rightly*, unavailable to beings who are, also, not free absolutely. We depend on one another precisely for the reason of Eze's concern—our 'individuated identities and desires' do not occupy spaces of absolute freedom.

Such a relativised understanding of freedom denotes not simply that each person is free up to the limit that others are not.[111] It is, further, that each of us depends on the active aid of others if we are to attain many of the ends in pursuit of which each of us seeks to exercise the sphere of freedom in which we are, at minimum, free from the constraint of others. The operational condition here is dependency. This is not a dependency to be secured simply as a matter of logical necessity and exclusively upon the power of the political state for the false promise of moral independence from every other.[112] It is, rather, nearly the opposite.

The dependency, here, is on one another, in voluntary acknowledgement of the fact that freedom, justice, in an absolute sense, unqualified and without reference to any others, is infeasible, meaningless, and with little to morally recommend it. The moral substance of our dependencies comes from choosing to beneficially regard their nature and choosing also, by deliberation, to structurally sustain these dependencies. It is this recognition of communal dependency, which is—perhaps ironically—illuminated through Eze's reservations about the import of consensus to a fundamental view of democracy, that also sustains Wiredu's thesis about the significance of reciprocity and compromise to decisional consensus.[113]

Additionally, it is the protection of the very individual of Eze's considerations that is sought by a consensual form of democracy and the logic of communal dependency that underpins it. 'All persons,' Wiredu says, 'have the moral right not to have their interests and concerns affected by actions or forbearances that do not enjoy their consent.'[114] The right, Wiredu says, amounts to 'a fundamental human right.'[115] Such a view supremely recognises the intolerableness of a political arrangement that could claim to formally structure our communal dependencies to the discount of any one among our number. In such a case, by which others will that person's share of free action be unjustly absorbed? And upon the just share of which others will the wrongful gain eventually encroach? If it is possible that a consensual form of democracy is that under which the interests of every individual, if not every individual interest, is most credibly protected, precisely because of the notion of communal dependency that upholds it,[116] then perhaps we should consider consensus—despite Eze's suspicions, and upon his own suppositions—constitutive of a fundamental conception of democracy.

We may interpret Wiredu's arguments in favour of consensual democracy as, also, an appeal that we make a particular kind of moral choice regarding deliberation—that it become, not a means of assuming shared equalities, but of structuring the possibilities for their persistent regulation. And that we choose to accept the promise of deliberation's mechanics so long as we are, also, convinced by the reasons capable of sustaining and rationalising its operation.

In defence of what he calls an 'ordinary' philosophical—what I have been calling an "individualised" —notion of reason, Eze writes: if 'I could not know that *this* is a tree if there were no tree in existence, neither could I cognitively recognise the existing object for what it is without my capacity to form its concept, such as *tree*.'[117] "Reason," and all the features of humanity that arise from its function must, therefore, be understood to take its most fundamental meaning from the autonomous mental activity of each individual human being.[118] It seems true that because we are all individually capable of conceptualising the object of a tree, for example, that the seat of reason must also be located in the individual mind. I do not aim to deny this. Simply to add, that the subjective interest each person may have in observing a tree and calling it one does not seem unrelated to the fact that numerous others are similarly subjectively interested in the nature of trees, their elements, uses, the reasons for their unqualified being. This, in no way, amounts to the conclusion that a tree is not a tree (or whatever name we might give it) unless we all agree that it is. It is, however, to say that in a great number of cases, our interests are given both practical and intellectual outline by the fact that we are, gratefully, rarely ever the only ones productively interested in a subject, nor engaged by any object capable of being brought under conceptual subjectivity.

My concern here is not simply one of language, nor of the socialising agencies that make communicative action possible.[119] I, also, do not wish to be misinterpreted as suggesting that communal interests are what *determine* individual ones. I am suggesting, however, that regardless of the multi-various factors that may determine the active interests and goals of any given individual, those interests would seem to also be given substantive meaning (not least to the individual holder of that interest), by the fact that they can usually be identified with by a rarely insignificant number of others (who may, again, have come to those interests for their own equally incalculable reasons). This applies even to those interests in which we might imagine ourselves solitarily engaged, for there are few ideas held in a single mind alone or sustained entirely by the efforts of any one individual's reason, no matter how great that individual seat may seem.

If the moral and intellectual substance given by the community to the individual is not, at least, unequal to that the individual may give to the community, then the reason of communal dependency would seem to provide the necessary and sufficient grounds for the proposal that in those matters of social and political life that seek the regulation of our actions, and which threaten always the balance of our freedoms in relation to those of all others, that we order our communal interdependencies by the consensus and agreement of all. By doing so, we give our dependencies a moral substance. The resulting *consensual* dependency will be in no way a subordination of the 'interests of the individual to those of the community,' or vice versa. It will be simply a moral understanding that recognises and accepts the 'symmetrical' and mutually substantiating relationship between the two.[120]

In the recent literature that has proceeded from the communication between Emmanuel Eze's and Kwasi Wiredu's intellectual ideas, there has been a tendency to follow a line of thinking that sees an individualised rationality as rationality's "pure" form and as, therefore, logically exclusionary to any communally based structure of reason capable of ordering political society. In fact, this line of examination has rendered unintelligible, and beyond "rationality's" bounds, what it calls those 'scaffolding elements' which may, in any given society, be the structural source of a communalised mode of behaviour.[121] Even according to those arguments where the latter is deemed of some significance—in particular, to the structure of "epistemically sound" deliberations—the apparent disparity of 'factors' capable of being subsumed by the notion of communality has seemed enough to defeat the latter's consideration as a form of rationality and, therefore, as a sustainable, dependable, means by which we may validly structure our political societies.[122]

But there is no necessary concession in the understanding that if, 'for the individual, community life is not optional'—with the latter understood as more than merely political association—then this is justly the result of the primacy of each individual capacity, which the community both supports and utilises in its definitions of itself.[123] Nor do developments in such normative understandings warrant the claim that our individual capacities are "supplied" by the community. It suffices simply to acknowledge that most of us, in significant areas of our lives, benefit from the moral and intellectual assistance of others, regardless of the "ultimate" source of these.[124] The morality of a radically consensual politics is, therefore, furnished by the understanding that we are all, *individually*, capable of considering—as much as we are of ignoring—the fact that there are few of our outward actions not consequential to the needs and interests of numerous others whose deeds affect, also, the manner of each of our own lives.

On the strength of Wiredu's plea, the especial concern of this chapter has been to not take for granted what Eze says he 'assumes'— that 'society and history are constructed, made by individuals or groups of individuals acting... within and out of relationships to nature, to self, and to others.'[125] If an understanding of communal rationality makes consensual democracy practicable, that of a communal dependency—and the possibilities for a *consensual* dependency—morally validate it.

Uchenna Okeja has argued that the kind of consensual deliberative practice envisaged by Wiredu should not be interpreted as itself 'a form of [traditional] African democracy.' But as, instead, the 'practices of deliberation that made genuine democracy possible.'[126] At the core of Wiredu's arguments, however, is not simply a theoretical reflection on an African traditional past.[127] His arguments are, more importantly, a normative examination of precisely how *true* a democracy is made possible by societies for who consensual deliberation is the reflexive practice of individuals who think of their outward actions always in relation to others' interests.

It can, surely, not be any kind of democracy, and what is "genuine" about it may be precisely what Eze describes: that the ultimate end of a true democracy's procedural engagements must be its own internal sustenance, by which all the moral possibilities imagined by the community that defines itself by it are mutually supported.[128] Is it not such a democracy that characterises a form of political representation the fundamental procedure for which is not morally distinguishable from the inner social function that operates the community that operates it?

Conclusion: African Political Philosophy and Deliberative Democratic Theory

'What difference,' Emmanuel Eze asks, 'does history make to thoughts of method?'[129] I would like to pose the question another way: what difference does history (and our perceptions of it) make to the method of our thoughts? If the difference is substantive then there are, I think, few other areas of political theory and political philosophy more capable of meeting a present challenge than the one critically specified by the historical (not particularistic)[130] experiences of an African geography.

That "challenge" is a post-colonial world, which is the result of an imperial project whose aim—'with an air of normality,' and 'with arguments drawn from science, morality, ethics, and a *general* philosophy [emphasis added]'—has been to 'change the uselessly unoccupied territories of the world into useful new versions of the European metropolitan society.'[131] The 'past degradations of our humanity, degradations of humanity tout court are [therefore as] fresh... in subjective memories... [as they are deeply embedded in all our] critical public institutions.'[132] There are few other branches of political theory and philosophy that ought to be more unafraid, more critically equipped, and with not so much left to lose in providing some modest, but invaluable contribution to what an honest, genuinely 'humanist,' world might look like.[133]

But perhaps the difference made by historical perspective to an intellectual agenda is not so great. Perhaps Wiredu is inaccurate in his assessments that the 'tendency to identify government by the consent of the people, that is, democracy, with government by the consent of the majority is … born of *excessive* [emphasis added] fixation on Anglo-American models of democracy.'[134] In other words, that there appears an unjustifiable, and 'politicised' determination to outline the universalisable structures by which we are all fated to determining our lives on the basis, mostly, of the historical view and experiences of not more than a few—refusing to the majority, the right of intellectual contribution.[135]

Perhaps it is, also, a mistaken assessment that many of the normative presuppositions that foreground the bulk of mainstream theorising on deliberation and deliberative democracy—for instance, the often problematically unproblematised assumption of participants' free equality in the practice of "ideal" deliberations[136]—receive their logical justifications from arguments the historical contexts for which have recently been examined to call into question the intellectual credibility of some among their authors.[137] Even were we to accept, as normative prescriptions, an ideal of human freedom and equality as elemental to our notions of deliberation and democracy, we are, at the very least, forced by a post-colonial reality not to assume the elements of their nature, and further to acknowledge the necessity of critically assessing the intellectual methodologies by which we might justify their eventual attainment.

Ani has noted that 'political paradigms should be examined primarily on their normative potential, much more than on their alleged antecedents in an ancient society that is difficult to access and examine today.'[138] With this, we should have little disagreement. But it is, I think, also misguided to believe that our honest assessments about the normative preferability of a thing can, or should, be divorced from the historical contexts that often situate them, deepen their meaning, and guide their logical extension, critique, and improvement.

The idea that a political theory and philosophy that takes at least some of its analytical inspirations from an African historical source should be assumed automatically contrary to, or exclusive of, the ambitions of a universalisable political theory and philosophy is, i believe, only the result of a current disciplinary predicament in which many of the historically contextualisable assumptions that guide our work have, until far too recently, remained either hidden, inexplicitly stated, or uncritically examined. I do not believe that such a trend has been to the betterment either of our theories or to the societies we intend to be advanced by them.

If African political theory and political philosophy should only succeed in preventing the negation of the 'historical shapes of our freedoms'[139] and that of every other moral idea we seem to hold dear, then the field will, I think, have proved its universal value, not least to our theories of deliberation and democratic practice.

Notes

1 Kwasi Wiredu, "Democracy by Consensus, Some Conceptual Clarifications," *Philosophical Papers* 30, no. 3, (2001): 228–229.
2 Ibid, 230.
3 Ibid, 230.
4 Ibid, 232–233.
5 Kwasi Wiredu, "Democracy and Consensus in African Traditional Politics: A Plea for a Non-party Polity," in *Postcolonial African Philosophy: A Critical Reader,* ed. Emmanuel Chukwudi Eze (Cambridge, MA: Blackwell Publishers, 1997), 303–304.
6 Ibid, 304–305.
7 Leopold Sedar Senghor, *On African Socialism,* trans. Mercer Cook (New York: Praeger, 1964).

8 Kwame Nkrumah, *Consciencism: Philosophy and Ideology for Decolonization* (London: Panaf, 1970).

9 Ahmed Sekou Touré, *Strategy and Tactics of the Revolution* (Conakry, Guinea: National Printing Press, 1977).

10 Kenneth Kaunda, *A Humanist in Africa* (London: Longman, 1966).

11 Julius K. Nyerere, *Ujamaa: Essays on Socialism* (New York: Oxford University Press, 1968).

12 Kwasi Wiredu, "Social Philosophy in Postcolonial Africa: Some Preliminaries Concerning Communalism and Communitarianism," *South African Journal of Philosophy* 27, no. 4 (2008), 332–333; Wiredu, "A Plea for a Non-Party Polity," 303; Kwasi Wiredu, *Cultural Universals and Particulars: An African Perspective* (Indianapolis: Indiana University Press, 1996), 145–146.

13 Indeed, Wiredu is despondent with what he deems to be the lack of progress of politics and philosophy in African societies that has resulted from having left the 'propagation' of political philosophies in the hands of, however well-intentioned, ideologically based party machines. *Cultural Universals,* 146.

14 Kwame Gyekye, *Tradition and Modernity: Philosophical Reflections on the African Experience* (Oxford: Oxford University Press, 1997), Ch. 4.

15 Mogobe B. Ramose, "African Democratic Tradition: Oneness, Consensus and Openness: A Reply to Wamba dia Wamba," *Quest* 6, no. 2 (1992): 62–81.

16 Edward Wamala, "Government by Consensus: An Analysis of a Traditional Form of Democracy," in *A Companion to African Philosophy,* ed. Kwasi Wiredu (Oxford: Blackwell Publishing, 2006).

17 Joe Teffo, "Democracy, Kingship, and Consensus: A South African Perspective," in *A Companion to African Philosophy,* ed. Kwasi Wiredu (Oxford: Blackwell Publishing, 2006).

18 Kwasi Wiredu, *Cultural Universals,* 190.

19 Ibid, 149.

20 Amilcar Cabral, *Return to the Source* (New York: Monthly Review Press, 1973).

21 Emmanuel Ifeanyi Ani, "On Traditional African Consensual Rationality," *The Journal of Political Philosophy* 22, no. 3 (2014): 346–347; Emmanuel Chukwudi Eze, "Democracy or Consensus? A Response to Wiredu," in *Postcolonial African Philosophy: A Critical Reader,* ed. Emmanuel Chukwudi Eze (Cambridge, MA: Blackwell Publishers, 1997), 313.

22 Eze, "A Response," 313–314.

23 Ibid, 316.

24 Ibid, 317.

25 Ibid, 317.

26 Ibid, 317–318.

27 See Uchenna Okeja, "Palaver and Consensus as Metaphors for the Public Sphere," in *The Oxford Handbook of Comparative Political Theory,* ed. Leigh K. Jenco, et al. (New York: Oxford University Press, 2019).

28 Uchenna Okeja, "Justice through Deliberation and the Problem of Otherness," *Angelaki: Journal of the Theoretical Humanities* 24, no. 2 (2019); Bernard Matolino, "The Nature of Opposition in Kwasi Wiredu's Democracy by Consensus," *African Studies* 72, no. 1 (2013); Emmanual Ifeanyi Ani, "On Agreed Actions without Agreed Notions," *South African Journal of Philosophy* 33, no. 3 (2014).

29 Emmanuel Chukwudi Eze, *On Reason: Rationality in a World of Cultural Conflict and Racism* (Durham, NC: Duke University Press, 2008), 82–89.

30 Eze, "A Response," 313.

31 Ibid, 313–315; Wiredu, "A Plea for a Non-party Polity," 309; Said Adejumobi, "Elections in Africa: A Fading Show of Democracy?" in *Government and Politics in Africa*, ed. Okwudiba Nnoli (Harare: AAPS Books, 2000).

32 Claude Ake, "The Unique Case of African Democracy," *International Affairs* 69, no. 2 (April 1993): 239–240.

33 Peter Ekeh, "Colonialism and the two Publics in Africa: A Theoretical Statement," *Comparative Studies in Society and History* 17, no. 1 (Jan. 1975), 92.

34 Wiredu, "Democracy by Consensus," 233.

35 Richard Joseph, *Democracy and Prebendal Politics in Nigeria: The Rise and Fall of the Second Republic* (Cambridge: Cambridge University Press, 1987), 4.

36 Wiredu, "Democracy by Consensus," 233–234.

37 Ibid, 233–234.

38 Eze, "A Response," 315; Ake, "The Unique Case."
39 Wiredu, "Democracy by Consensus," 233.
40 Wiredu, *Cultural Universals*, 190.
41 Wiredu, "Democracy by Consensus," 233.
42 Ibid, 237.
43 Ibid, 238–239.
44 Ibid, 234.
45 Ibid, 238.
46 Martin Odei Ajei, "Kwasi Wiredu's Consensual Democracy: Prospects for Practice in Africa," *European Journal of Political Theory* 15, no. 4 (2016): 448.
47 Wiredu, "A Plea for a Non-party Polity," 303–305.
48 Ibid, 305.
49 Ibid, 307.
50 Ibid, 305.
51 Ibid, 307–308.
52 Ibid, 306–308.
53 Ibid, 306, 308.
54 Ibid, 308.
55 Ibid, 303–305, 309.
56 Ibid, 309.
57 Eze, "A Response," 316–318.
58 Wiredu, "A Plea for a Non-party Polity," 305–306.
59 Eze, "A Response," 317–319.
60 Ibid, 318.
61 Wiredu, "Democracy by Consensus."
62 Wiredu, "A Plea for a Non-party Polity," 304.
63 Eze, "A Response," 318.
64 Ibid, 319–320.
65 Ibid, Note 12, 323.
66 Ibid, 317–318.
67 The fundamental question, and meaning, of rationality is nearly endless in the various cannons of philosophy across the globe and will not be dealt with here. My modest aim is to mark out the ways in which the term has been used in, and which most appropriately relates to, the theory of consensual democracy.
68 Emmanuel Ifeanyi Ani, "On Traditional African Consensual Rationality," *Journal of Political Philosophy* 22, no. 3 (2014): 351–352.
69 Ibid, 347–348.
70 Eze, "A Response," 317.
71 Ibid.
72 Eze, *On Reason*, 82–89.
73 Ibid. Chapter 5, 250.
74 Eze, "A Response", 318.
75 Kwasi Wiredu, "On the Idea of a Global Ethic," *Journal of Global Ethics* 1, no.1 (2005): 45.
76 Kwasi Wiredu, "Society and Democracy in Africa," *New Political Science* 21, no. 1 (1999): 34–35; Wiredu, "Preliminaries Concerning Communalism," 33.
77 As Ani attempts, "African Consensual Rationality."
78 Wiredu, "Democracy by Consensus," 235–237.
79 Ibid, 237–238.
80 Ibid, 237.
81 Wiredu, "A Plea for a Non-party Polity," 306–307.
82 Wiredu, "Democracy by Consensus," 236–237.
83 Wiredu, "A Plea for a Non-party Polity," 303; Wiredu, "Society and Democracy," 36.
84 Ajei, "Prospects for Practice," 445–451, 457.
85 Wiredu, "Democracy by Consensus," 237.
86 Ibid, 235–238.
87 Ani, "On Agreed Actions," 316.
88 Wiredu, "Democracy by Consensus," 236.

89 Ani, "On Agreed Actions," 313–316.

90 Wiredu, "Democracy by Consensus," 236–237.

91 Ibid, 236–237.

92 It is perhaps not too dissimilar a notion underlying Robert D. Putnam's notion of social capital. See *Making Democracy Work: Civic Traditions in Modern Italy* (Princeton, NJ: Princeton University Press, 1994).

93 Wiredu, "Democracy by Consensus," 236–237.

94 Wiredu, "Society and Democracy," 33–44; Wiredu, "Preliminaries Concerning Communalism," 333–334.

95 Gyekye, *Tradition and Modernity*, Ch. 2. For further discussion: Ifeanyi Menkiti, "Person and Community in African Traditional Thought," in *African Philosophy: An Introduction*, ed. Richard A. Wright (Lanham, MD: University Press of America, 1984); Segun Gbadegesin, *African Philosophy: Traditional Yoruba Philosophy and Contemporary African Realities* (New York: Peter Lang, 1991).

96 Wiredu, "A Plea for a Non-party Polity," 306; Ajei, "Prospects for Practice," 451.

97 See Eze, "A Response," 318–320; Bernard Matolino, "A Response to Eze's Critique of Wiredu's Consensual Democracy," *South African Journal of Philosophy* 28, no. 1 (2009): 39–40.

98 Wiredu, "Society and Democracy," 34.

99 Eze, "A Response," 318.

100 As might be part of Matolino's concern "A Response to Eze's Critique," 40.

101 This seems to me the task taken on, for example, by Ani, "African Consensual Rationality." See Wiredu, "Society and Democracy," 33–36.

102 For such arguments, see Joshua Cohen, "Deliberation and Democratic Legitimacy," in *The Good Polity: Normative Analysis of the State,* eds. Alan Hamlin and Philip Petit (Oxford: Basil Blackwell, 1989), 17–34; Joshua Cohen, "Procedure and Substance in Deliberative Democracy," in *Democracy and Difference: Contesting the Boundaries of the Political,* ed. Seyla Benhabib, (Princeton, NJ: Princeton University Press, 1996), 95–119; Joshua Cohen, "Reflections on Rousseau: Autonomy and Democracy," *Philosophy and Public Affairs* 15 (1986): 275–295.

103 For such arguments, see Amy Gutmann and Dennis Thompson, *Democracy and Disagreement* (Cambridge, MA: Belknap Press, 1996); Amy Gutmann and Dennis Thompson *Why Deliberative Democracy* (Princeton, NJ: Princeton University Press, 2004); Jurgen Habermas, *Between Facts and Norms: Contributions to a Discourse Theory of Law and Democracy,* trans. William Rehg (Cambridge, MA: MIT Press, 1996); Jurgen Habermas, *Legitimation Crisis* (Boston, MA: Beacon Press, 1975); Jurgen Habermas, *Communication and the Evolution of Society,* trans. Thomas McCarthy (Boston, MA: Beacon Press, 1979); Simone Chambers, "Democratic Deliberative Theory," *American Review of Political Science* 6 (2003): 307–327; David Estlund, "Beyond Fairness and Deliberation: The Epistemic Dimension of Democratic Authority," in *Deliberative Democracy: Essays on Reason and Politics,* ed. James Bohman and William Rehg (Cambridge, MA: MIT Press, 1997), 173–204; Ani, "African Consensual Rationality."

104 Wiredu, "A Plea for a Non-party Polity," 304; Wiredu, "Democracy by Consensus," 235–236.

105 For such examinations, see Okeja, "Justice through Deliberation."

106 Eze, "A Response," 321.

107 Ibid, 321.

108 Ibid, 320.

109 Ibid, 320.

110 Ibid, 320.

111 Isaiah Berlin, *Four Essays on Liberty* (Oxford: Oxford University Press, 1969).

112 See Jean Jacques Rousseau, *Social Contract,* trans. Judith R. Masters (New York: St Martin's Press, 1978), 77; Jean Jacques Rousseau, *Emile,* trans. Allan Bloom (Basic Books, 1979). See also, Arthur Melzer, *The Natural Goodness of Man.* (Chicago, IL: University of Chicago Press, 1990), 98–99.

113 Wiredu, "Democracy by Consensus."

114 Ibid, 231.

115 Wiredu, "A Plea for a Non-party Polity," 307.

116 Wiredu, "Society and Democracy," 34–35; Ajei, "Prospects for Practice," 448, 451.

117 Eze, *On Reason,* 86.

118 Ibid, 84–85

119 For such examinations, see Wiredu, *Cultural Universals,* Chapters 7 and 8; Jurgen Habermas, *The Theory of Communicative Action, Volume 1: Reason and the Rationalization of Society,* trans. Thomas

McCarthy (Cambridge: Polity Press, 1984); Jurgen Habermas, *The Theory of Communicative Action: Volume 2*, trans. Thomas McCarthy (Cambridge: Polity Press, 1987).

120 Wiredu, "Preliminaries Concerning Communalism," 334; Gyekye, *Tradition and Modernity,* 36–41.

121 Bernard Matolino, "Rationality and Consensus in Kwasi Wiredu's Traditional African Politics," *Theoria: A Journal of Social and Political Theory* 63, no. 146 (March 2016): 36–55.

122 Emmanuel Ifeanyi Ani, "Some Implications of Arguing that Deliberation is Purely Rational," *Journal of Indian Council of Philosophical Research,* 37: 303–313.

123 Gyekye, *Tradition and Modernity,* 42–44; also, D.A. Masolo, "Western and African Communitarianism: A Comparison," in *A Companion to African Philosophy,* ed. Kwasi Wiredu (Oxford: Blackwell Publishing, 2006), 495–496.

124 I agree with Eze that it is not necessary, for our purposes, to be drawn into the argument between an "internalist" and "externalist" camp about whether man's capacity to reason has a source prior to her existence among other human beings or whether our reason is always mediated by all those socio-historical and material experiences that define what is, at least, perceptible to us about human existence. *On Reason,* 82–83.

125 Eze, *On Reason,* 84.

126 Uchenna Okeja, "Palavar and Consensus," 573.

127 Ajei, "Prospects for Practice," 446–447.

128 Eze, "A Response," 320–321

129 Eze, *On Reason*, 137.

130 Ajei, "Prospects for Practice," 458.

131 Edward W. Said, *The Question of Palestine* (New York: Vintage, 1980), 77–78.

132 Eze, *On Reason*, 144.

133 Ibid, 144.

134 Wiredu, "Democracy by Consensus," 233.

135 Uchenna Okeja, "Palavar and Consensus," 574.

136 For further discussion, see Iris Marion Young, "Communication and the Other: Beyond Deliberative Democracy," in *Democracy and Difference: Contesting the Boundaries of the Political,* ed. Seyla Benhabib, (Princeton, NJ: Princeton University Press, 1996), 120–127; Jane Mansbridge, "Using Power/Fighting Power: The Polity," in *Democracy and Difference: Contesting the Boundaries of the Political,* ed. Seyla Benhabib (Princeton, NJ: Princeton University Press, 1996), 53–60.

137 See Emmanuel Chukwudi Eze, *Race and the Enlightenment* (Oxford: Blackwell Publishing, 1997). On Kant, see Robert Bernasconi, "Kant's Third Thoughts on Race," in *Reading Kant's Geography,* eds. Stuart Elden and Eduardo Mendieta (New York: SUNY Press, 2011); Emmanuel Chukwudi Eze, "The Colour of Reason: The Idea of "Race" in Kant's Anthropology," in *Postcolonial African Philosophy,* ed. Emmanuel Chukwudi Eze (Cambridge, MA: Blackwell Publishers, 1997), 103–131. On Locke, see David Armitage, "John Locke, Carolina, and the "Two Treatises of Government","* Political Theory* 32 (2004): 602–627; Duncan Ivison, "Locke, Liberalism and Empire," in *The Philosophy of John Locke: New Perspectives*, ed. Peter R. Anstey (New York: Routledge, 2003), 86–105; Barbara Arneil, "Trade, Plantations, and Property: John Locke and the Economic Defense of Colonialism," *Journal of the History of Ideas* 55 (1994), 591–609.

138 Ani, "African Consensual Rationality," 347.

139 Eze, *On Reason*, 144.

References

Adejumobi, Said. 2000. "Elections in Africa: A Fading Show of Democracy?" In *Government and Politics in Africa*, edited by Okwudiba Nnoli, 242–261. Harare: AAPS Books.

Ajei, Martin O. 2016. "Kwasi Wiredu's Consensual Democracy: Prospects for Practice in Africa." *European Journal of Political Theory* 15 (4): 445–466.

Ake, Claude. 1993. "The Unique Case of African Democracy." *International Affairs* 69 (2): 239–244.

Ani, Emmanuel I. 2020. "Some Implications of Arguing that Deliberation Is Purely Rational." *Journal of Indian Council of Philosophical Research* 37: 303–313.

Ani, Emmanuel I. 2014. "On Agreed Actions without Agreed Notions." *South African Journal of Philosophy* 33 (3): 311–320.

Ani, Emmanuel I. 2014. "On Traditional African Consensual Rationality." *Journal of Political Philosophy* 22 (3): 342–365.

Armitage, David. 2004. "John Locke, Carolina, and the Two Treatises of Government." *Political Theory* 32: 602–627.

Arneil, Barbara. 1994. "Trade, Plantations, and Property: John Locke and the Economic Defense of Colonialism." *Journal of the History of Ideas* 55: 591–609.

Berlin, Isaiah. 1969. *Four Essays on Liberty.* Oxford: Oxford University Press.

Bernasconi, Robert. 2011. "Kant's Third Thoughts on Race." In *Reading Kant's Geography,* edited by Stuart Elden and Eduardo Mendieta, 291–318. New York: SUNY Press.

Cabral, Amilcar. 1973. *Return to the Source: Selected Speeches of Amilcar Cabral.* New York: Monthly Review Press.

Chambers, Simone. 2003. "Democratic Deliberative Theory." *Annual Review of Political Science* 6: 307–326.

Cohen, Joshua. 1996. "Procedure and Substance in Deliberative Democracy." In *Democracy and Difference: Contesting the Boundaries of the Political,* edited by Seyla Benhabib, 95–119. Princeton, NJ: Princeton University Press.

Cohen, Joshua. 1989. "Deliberation and Democratic Legitimacy." In *The Good Polity: Normative Analysis of the State,* edited by Alan Hamlin and Philip Petit, 17–34. Oxford: Basil Blackwell.

Cohen, Joshua. 1986. "Reflections on Rousseau: Autonomy and Democracy." *Philosophy and Public Affairs* 15: 275–295.

Ekeh, Peter. 1975. "Colonialism and the Two Publics in Africa: A Theoretical Statement." *Comparative Studies in Society and History* 17 (1): 91–112.

Estlund, David. 1997. "Beyond Fairness and Deliberation: The Epistemic Dimension of Democratic Authority." In *Deliberative Democracy: Essays on Reason and Politics,* edited by James Bohman and William Rehg, 173–204. Cambridge, MA: MIT Press.

Eze, Emmanuel C. 2008. *On Reason: Rationality in a World of Cultural Conflict and Racism.* Durham, NC: Duke University Press.

Eze, Emmanuel C. 1997. "Democracy or Consensus? A Response to Wiredu." In *Postcolonial African Philosophy: A Critical Reader,* edited by Emmanuel Chukwudi Eze, 313–323. Cambridge, MA: Blackwell Publishers.

Eze, Emmanuel Chukwudi. 1997. "The Colour of Reason: The Idea of "Race" in Kant's Anthropology." In *Postcolonial African Philosophy,* edited by Emmanuel Chukwudi Eze, 103–140. Cambridge, MA: Blackwell Publishers.

Eze, Emmanuel Chukwudi. 1997. *Race and the Enlightenment.* Oxford: Blackwell Publishing.

Gbadegesin, Segun. 1991. *African Philosophy: Traditional Yoruba Philosophy and Contemporary African Realities.* New York: Peter Lang.

Gutmann, Amy and Dennis Thompson. 2004. *Why Deliberative Democracy.* Princeton, NJ: Princeton University Press.

Gutmann, Amy and Dennis Thompson. 1996. *Democracy and Disagreement.* Cambridge, MA: Belknap Press.

Gyekye, Kwame. 1997. *Tradition and Modernity: Philosophical Reflections on the African Experience.* Oxford: Oxford University Press.

Habermas, Jurgen. 1996. *Between Facts and Norms: Contributions to a Discourse Theory of Law and Democracy.* Translated by William Rehg. Cambridge, MA: MIT Press.

Habermas. Jurgen. 1987. *The Theory of Communicative Action: Volume 2.* Translated by Thomas McCarthy. Cambridge: Polity Press.

Habermas, Jurgen. 1984. *The Theory of Communicative Action, Volume 1: Reason and the Rationalization of Society,* Translated by Thomas McCarthy. Cambridge: Polity Press.

Habermas, Jurgen. 1979. *Communication and the Evolution of Society.* Translated by Thomas McCarthy. Boston, MA: Beacon Press.

Habermas, Jurgen. 1975. *Legitimation Crisis.* Boston, MA: Beacon Press.

Ivison, Duncan. 2003. "Locke, Liberalism and Empire." In *The Philosophy of John Locke: New Perspectives,* edited by Peter R. Anstey, 86–105. New York: Routledge.

Joseph, Richard. 1987. *Democracy and Prebendal Politics in Nigeria: The Rise and Fall of the Second Republic.* Cambridge: Cambridge University Press.

Kaunda, Kenneth. 1966. *A Humanist in Africa.* London: Longman.

Mansbridge, Jane. 1996. "Using Power/Fighting Power: The Polity." In *Democracy and Difference: Contesting the Boundaries of the Political,* edited by Seyla Benhabib, 46–66. Princeton, NJ: Princeton University Press.

Masolo, D.A. 2006. "Western and African Communitarianism: A Comparison." In *A Companion to African Philosophy,* edited by Kwasi Wiredu, 483–498. Oxford: Blackwell Publishing.

Matolino, Bernard. 2016. "Rationality and Consensus in Kwasi Wiredu's Traditional African Politics." *Theoria: A Journal of Social and Political Theory* 63 (146): 36–55.

Matolino, Bernard. 2013 "The Nature of Opposition in Kwasi Wiredu's Democracy by Consensus." *African Studies* 72 (1): 138–152.

Matolino, Bernard. 2009. "A Response to Eze's Critique of Wiredu's Consensual Democracy." *South African Journal of Philosophy* 28 (1): 34–42.

Melzer, Arthur. 1990. *The Natural Goodness of Man.* Chicago, IL: University of Chicago Press.

Menkiti, Ifeanyi. 1984. "Person and Community in African Traditional Thought." In *African Philosophy: An Introduction,* edited by Richard A. Wright, 171–181. Lanham, MD: University Press of America.

Nkrumah, Kwame. 1970. *Consciencism: Philosophy and Ideology for Decolonization.* London: Panaf.

Nyerere, Julius K. 1968. *Ujamaa: Essays on Socialism.* New York: Oxford University Press.

Okeja, Uchenna. 2019. "Justice through Deliberation and the Problem of Otherness." *Angelaki: Journal of the Theoretical Humanities* 24 (2): 10–21.

Okeja, Uchenna. 2019. "Palavar and Consensus as Metaphors for the Public Sphere." In *The Oxford Handbook of Comparative Political Theory,* edited by Leigh K. Jenco, Murad Idris, and Megan C. Thomas, 565–579. New York: Oxford University Press.

Putnam, Robert D. 1994. *Making Democracy Work: Civic Traditions in Modern Italy.* Princeton, NJ: Princeton University Press.

Ramose, Mogobe B. 1992. "African Democratic Tradition: Oneness, Consensus and Openness: A Reply to Wamba dia Wamba." *Quest* 6 (2): 62–81.

Rousseau, Jean Jacques. 1979. *Emile.* Translated by Allan Bloom. United States of America: Basic Books.

Rousseau, Jean Jacques. 1978. *Social Contract.* Translated by Judith R. Masters. New York: St Martin's Press.

Said, Edward W. 1980. *The Question of Palestine.* New York: Vintage.

Senghor, Leopold S. 1964. *On African Socialism.* Translated by Mercer Cook. New York: Praeger.

Teffo, Joe. 2006. "Democracy, Kingship, and Consensus: A South African Perspective." In *A Companion to African Philosophy,* edited by Kwasi Wiredu, 443–449. Oxford: Blackwell Publishing.

Touré, Ahmed S. 1977. *Strategy and Tactics of the Revolution.* Conakry, Guinea: National Printing Press.

Wamala. Edward. 2006. "Government by Consensus: An Analysis of a Traditional Form of Democracy." In *A Companion to African Philosophy,* edited by Kwasi Wiredu, 435–442. Oxford: Blackwell Publishing.

Wiredu, Kwasi. 2008. "Social Philosophy in Postcolonial Africa: Some Preliminaries Concerning Communalism and Communitarianism." *South African Journal of Philosophy* 27 (4): 332–339.

Wiredu, Kwasi. 2005. "On the Idea of a Global Ethic." *Journal of Global Ethics* 1 (1): 45–51.

Wiredu, Kwasi. 2001. "Democracy by Consensus, Some Conceptual Clarifications." *Philosophical Papers* 30 (3): 227–244.

Wiredu, Kwasi. 1999. "Society and Democracy in Africa." *New Political Science* 21 (1): 33–44.

Wiredu, Kwasi. 1997. "Democracy and Consensus in African Traditional Politics: A Plea for a Non-Party Polity." In *Postcolonial African Philosophy,* edited by Emmanuel Chukwudi Eze, 303–312. Cambridge, MA: Blackwell Publishers.

Wiredu, Kwasi. 1996. *Cultural Universals and Particulars: An African Perspective.* Indianapolis: Indiana University Press.

Young, Iris Marion. 1996. "Communication and the Other: Beyond Deliberative Democracy." In *Democracy and Difference: Contesting the Boundaries of the Political,* edited by Seyla Benhabib, 120–136. Princeton, NJ: Princeton University Press.

15

UNCOMMON FEATURES

Defending Ideal Theory with Model-to-World Inference[1]

Olúfẹ́mi O. Táíwò

Introduction

Defenders of ideal theory in social and political philosophies insist that its abstractions and idealizations are justifiable or even indispensable; detractors maintain that these will irretrievably distort reality, pointing out important aspects of political life that are un- or misrepresented by theory.[2] They argue that ideal theory works on a picture of the world too removed from how the world actually works to guide efforts to fix its problems, thus failing to meet a core obligation they take political theory to have.[3]

One particular cohort of these detractors, most prominently Charles Mills, advance an even more pointed and worrying version of this criticism: they argue that ideal theories and theorists, by virtue of their failure to take into account specific features of various forms of actual historical domination, act as unwitting or negligent accomplices in oppressive structures, both within professional philosophy and society more broadly.[4] Mills bases his argument on Onora O'Neill's distinction between abstractions and idealizations, arguing both that the going ideal theories don't merely fail to represent as much as they could (abstraction) but that they introduce falsehoods (idealization).

This argument sits in implicit tension with some other available approaches in Africana philosophy. I argue that Ghanaian philosopher Kwasi Wiredu's writing on "consensual democracy" serves as a prominent example of ideal theorizing within African philosophy, and aim to defend it here from Mills' objection.

Key to the defense from Mills' argument against ideal theory is a point made by Leif Hancox-Li in "Idealization and Abstraction in Models of Injustice", where he argues that many researchers in the literature have gotten something fundamentally wrong.[5] Whether our theories are ideal or non-ideal, whether they involve "idealizations" or "abstractions", in the strictest sense, they just don't themselves do what the participants in the debate accuse them of doing: make claims about the actual world.[6] Then, these particular criticisms of ideal theory rest on something of a category mistake. Alongside Hancox-Li, I argue that many of the supposed problems with ideal theory (and benefits to non-ideal theory) are not problems based on the content of our theories at all, but how we take those features to relate to features of the world that the model is built to investigate – that is, what I call *model-to-world inference*.[7]

DOI: 10.4324/9781003143529-18

On the view argued for here, the better target for Mills' criticisms are bad practices and norms of model-to-world inference, and that the proffered distinction between ideal and non-ideal theory is at best orthogonal to the concerns that Mills and other scholars invoke to motivate abandoning ideal theory. In part I, I will clarify the difference between Mills and Wiredu's metaphilosophy with respect to ideal theory, arguing that defenders of non-ideal theory have an overly narrow conception of how models can inform. In part II I will explain why the criticisms of ideal theory fail and suggest a different diagnosis of the problems in political philosophy attributed to ideal theory by Mills. In part III, I conclude with some preliminary suggestions for different ways forward in Africana social and political philosophy, again taking cues from Wiredu's example.

Theories, Models, and Common Features Contrasting Mills and Wiredu

Many concerns about ideal theory rest on the relationship critics that ideal theory has with the real world. Mills worries that these abstractions either tacitly represent the problems of oppression as simple deviations from the ideal that don't require serious consideration or theorization, or that theorizing about changing the world must start with ideal theory.[8] Others are concerned that will lead to misdiagnoses of social problems, since the idealized version of the world may as such exclude the features of the world that we need to understand flaws – including the history and basic nature of historically specific forms of oppression.[9] Thus, ideal political theories like Rawls' as such involve either a claim about what aspects of the real world are of core importance to understanding how it operates or a claim about what aspects of the world one must keep track of to improve it.

While Rawls' theory of justice can be interpreted as a verbal model aiming to succeed on this sort of criterion, the general aim pursued by ideal theory should not be construed as solely the province of white bourgeois analytic philosophers in the Global North. As political theorist Adom Getachew chronicles in her work *Worldmaking After Empire*, the African anti-colonial activists of the 60s and 70s were also thinking about the abstract rules of a new world order organized around non-domination as an ethical principle and a New International Economic Order as a concrete set of political principles.[10] They had an immediate struggle to fight and win – the fight for national independence from colonial powers. But they didn't want to stop there – they also wanted to use the power they hoped to win to reshape their political structures and lives.

How best to do this restructuring? Getachew refers to their practices of answering this question as a "worldmaking" view, and it's a natural fit with the normative understanding criterion. Moreover, worldmaking was part and parcel of the overall political struggle in which the anti-colonial activists were engaged. As such, the non-ideal theorists have no special claim to the stance of social justice (other than the rhetorical advantages caused by the erosion of cultural memory that followed the global defeat of left projects for justice over the tumultuous years that followed).

Ghanaian philosopher Kwasi Wiredu provides an important example of one worldmaking sort of enterprise that philosophers responding to the anti-colonial political situation have used ideal theory to deliberate about. Throughout a series of books and papers, Wiredu articulates and defends a view of the ideal democratic structure for African societies.[11] He takes "consensual democracy", to be a governance form that is rooted in African traditions and that was prevalent before European colonialism, but also takes it to respond to the continent's new challenges for governance left in the wake of the European colonial era. This theory, and the debates it proliferated, have been a fruitful site for African theorists and theorizing.[12]

A number of reasons count in favor of interpreting Wiredu's argument as an instance of ideal theory. First, Wiredu's account is that of the ideal African democratic form – it does not analyze any particular African society, though it is informed by historical analysis of African traditions. Both he and his dissentors discuss idealizations and/or abstract relations between abstract classes or groupings of people, considering how organizing around "lineages" might contrast fruitfully with party systems, and how the outcome of consensual deliberation might better position "minority" groups for social cooperation than under a party system.[13] While Wiredu makes reference to some actual history, the scope of the specific historical structures it considers does not come close to matching the scope of societies the argument aims to prescribe actions for – Wiredu's historical investigations largely revolve around Ashanti social structure, a society that occupied much of what is now Ghana. For the people of Benin or Guinea-Bissau to adopt governance principles mined from this history is not obviously a non-ideal theoretic response to their particular political situation. From their perspective, the kind of theorizing Wiredu is doing is fact-insensitive, which counts in favor of viewing it as an ideal theory on Volacu's conception thereof, which treats fact sensitivity as a consideration relevant to the classification of a theory as ideal or non-ideal.[14]

Then, non-ideal theorists' insistence that ideal theory must make reference to specific categories and histories of oppression gains artificial plausibility because it takes place in the domain of Anglophone political philosophy, in which the defenders of ideal theory are associated with old white men like Rawls. But the substance of his criticism seems to throw those of us interested in doing the kind of theory Wiredu was doing under the same dialectical bus. Wiredu's highly idealized approach is not a failure to understand the complexities of the particular political histories that structure political life on the continent. Far to the contrary: it is motivated by those very complications. Wiredu does not theorize about the particular history of, say, the social categories of Hutu and Tutsi relations in Rwanda because he is trying to guide political action on the scope of the entire continent, which calls in favor of the kinds of abstractions that will guide decision-making in Togo as well. The kind of generality and abstractions that ideal theory trucks in, in this context, don't constitute an attempt to ignore political context but, one might imagine, a constructive response to the intractability of the alternative: attempting to navigate what is by some measures the world's most diverse continent by a political approach that avoids generalizing across different groups and histories.[15]

Models and Theories

If the preceding is right, then there's something to be said for abstraction and generalization in general. But what role should these play in theorizing, and to what extent should we rely on them? I turn here to a more pointed discussion of theories and theorizing, to help bring out the stakes of the disagreement between Mills and Wiredu.

Theories, whether about racial justice or about the migratory patterns of buffalo, involve or are constituted by abstract relationships between abstract concepts.[16] We build theories because there's something in the world we want to understand or navigate practically, and we think the network of concepts we build through theory will help. Theories generate principles that we can use to guide our investigation and observation of phenomena in the world.

But it takes some work to apply the principles to the world and things within it. One reason for this is that theory is not connected to the world in the same sense that our empirical observations are. One important sense in which theory is disconnected from the world gives rise to some of the anxieties that inform Mills' attack on ideal theory. Theory involves abstractions and idealizations from the messy details of the real world: some features of the target phenomena and its worldly context are left in and some are left out. Theorists' decisions about which to leave in and which to leave out are quite meaningful, as both defenders and detractors of ideal theory have rightly maintained. Our choices at the levels of abstraction at which political philosophers tend to operate (whether ideal or non-ideal theorists) will especially constrain and load the deck for various downstream effects of the theory, whether its effects on our concrete political projects or even just the attention hierarchies of philosophy as an academic discipline.

To establish a connection to the world that we build theories to help us understand and navigate, theory makes use of models and functionally similar tools. A model is an "interpreted structure": a device that purports to inform us about "target systems": phenomena in the world or the aspects of them we're interested in learning about.[17] There's a tight relationship between theories and models: on one candidate's positive view of theories applying to (at least) the domain of the natural sciences, the "semantic" view of theories, theories simply are sets of models.[18] Less ambitiously, we might content ourselves with observing that theories make use of models as tools that mediate between theory and world.[19]

When we see models discussed as models, they are often formal mathematical models (e.g. systems of equations) or computations models. These are important and scientifically useful classes of models, but they are not the only sort. We can build replicas of natural phenomena with physical materials (concrete models) or verbally articulate chains of ideas that stand in for models that could be fleshed out with any of our other modeling approaches (narrative models). This last sense of "model" is the sense that most obviously applies to political philosophy.

Rawls' theory of justice, for instance, is particularly amenable to re-description as a series of verbal models. Rawls begins with an initial, guiding model of the "well-formed society". The well-formed society resembles the world on some dimensions, in that it is populated by people with moral powers that we take each other to generally have, and is governed by familiar-sounding structures like a political constitution. It is also helped along by some important and load-bearing abstractions (e.g. from the contingencies of a particular political history or demographic composition) and idealizations (e.g. that the society is "closed" to outside forces) from things that are true about the actual world.

From there, other models are introduced that extend some of the initial assumptions and suspend others: perhaps most notably, the original position and the second, international tier of Rawlsian theory, which eliminates the assumption of a closed society that was used to develop the conception of domestic justice). The end goal of these was to investigate the principles of justice that would govern Rawls' well-formed society and the supposedly separate principles that would govern a global consortium of such societies, which may inform our orientations toward the less-than-perfectly formed societies we find in the world.

Desiderata for Models and Theories

One way of characterizing ideal theory in political philosophy is to point out its regulative function: ideal theory there produces a characterization of the just society, which we can use as an evaluative standard for the various versions of non-ideal reality that history puts on the table.[20] Valentini insists that there are three separate debates misleadingly grouped under this heading: (1) whether full or partial compliance is assumed by a theory; (2) the extent to which a theory is "utopian" rather than "realistic"; and (3) whether the theory is conceived as a conception of the "end-state" at which justice is achieved or is a "transitional" account of how we might make our society more just.[21] Hamlin and Stemploska treat the distinction between idealization and abstraction as a fourth.[22] Whichever characterizations of the debate we accept, the crux of the issue is the extent to which theories match up to the target phenomena in the world, and what justifications succeed or fail to vindicate the use of these theories when they do not.[23]

The question of what justifications we can give for theories and models turns on the prior question of what it is that we can accomplish with them. There are a multiplicity of desiderata for theories and models, each implying different standards of evaluation. Since not all of them require or even involve relationships between features of the world and corresponding features of the model, the different desiderata imply differences in which model-to-world inferences are licensed – that is, what descriptions of the world we can take a theory or theorist to be committed to because of what their theory or model looks like.

The desiderata considered here adapt the distinctions offered in Michael Levins' seminal paper "The Strategy of Model Building in Population Ecology" which explains these as a response to the complications of "overlapping but not identical goals of understanding, predicting, and modifying nature" to reflect the kinds of considerations relevant to political philosophy and normative theorizing.[24]

One possible desideratum is descriptive accuracy. This desideratum licenses the sort of models that we build to get a deeper understanding of how target systems in the world function. Levins uses the example of a tendency in fishery biology to build models tightly around the variables relevant to the short-term behavior of the organism of interest. When we improve a model with respect to this criterion, we make the model itself resemble the target system in the world more strongly. This sounds like what non-ideal theorists have in mind when they complain that ideal theory distorts reality, and that non-ideal theory is better suited to studying the real-world effects of oppression. In the extreme case, we can adopt an ideal on which we try to make the model match the target system as perfectly as possible, which philosopher of science Michael Weisberg calls "completeness".[25]

Since features of a model built according to this criterion are attempts to match features of the world, such a model may license model-to-world inferences from features of the model to descriptive commitments about what the target system is actually like. This seems to fit Mills' implicit picture of how political theories ought to relate to political realities, and would provide a stable ground for interpreting a theory's silence about race and gender as an affirmative statement that these are unimportant axes of oppression in the actual world.

But there are other desiderata that we might use to evaluate models and refine them, which wouldn't license such model-to-world inferences. Another is predictive accuracy, a desideratum geared and predicting the behavior of a target system or elements within it. Fulfilling this criterion is often in tension with the previous one. Levins gives the example of "clearly unrealistic" models: in biology, he describes mathematical models that investigate biological phenomena with equations that neglect critical aspects of the descriptive story like the effect of a species' population density on its own rate of increase, which he likens to models in physics that assume frictionless surfaces or "perfect" gases.[26] These models nevertheless achieve other goals: for instance, they allow us to predict population dynamics across many species.

We refine models with respect to this criterion when their *output* – predictions – more strongly matches the behavior of the target system or its constituent parts. But that may not involve making the model *itself* more representative of the real world at all – it might require introducing more or different idealizations, or changing the relative contribution of unrepresentative parts of the model to its output. Accordingly, there's no stable relationship between the elements of models built to excel at this desideratum and any particular description of the world – then, model-to-world inferences that treat a model's content or omissions as statements about what the target real-world phenomenon is like are unlicensed.

Action guidance is a third potential desideratum. To meet this criterion, a model should provide useful and actionable predictions about the world, or otherwise inform practical projects in which we are engaged. This is tightly related to the previous criterion, since the most obvious ways of using models practically hinge on how well they do at predicting behavior of or in a target system. But this criterion focuses on a subset of predictions: the ones relevant to our potential practical intervention. A model that succeeds in this way gives us actionable intelligence, which could be increased even by a refinement of a model that degrades overall predictive accuracy.

For example, a political communication model may recommend a series of ads that genuinely increase a candidate's vote share in an election, despite (or even because!) it makes incorrect predictions about how the total viewership will respond. This might correspond, for example, to a situation where the model predicts that an ad will help out a candidate by convincing "independent" voters not to vote for the other party's candidate, when it in fact simply convinces a higher share of them (whose minds were already made up) not to skip election day. This would be a case where the model succeeds despite resting on a blatantly false "description" of the world – yet another case where we are not licensed to infer directly from the features of the model to descriptive claims about the corresponding feature of the world.

A fourth criterion for models: normative understanding.[27] This criterion is also related to the previous criterion, but perhaps the most peculiar to political philosophy and ethics.[28] The action guidance criterion uses the practical aims we already have to evaluate the models: but those practical aims, themselves, ought to be evaluable. What interventions ought we be trying to make, and what would their consequences be? What should our long-term goals be, supposing we succeed in the short term at eliminating the obstacles that prevent us from long-term control of our social environment? Several of these are among the reasons Rawls gives for his method of inquiry in Justice as Fairness: A Restatement.[29]

Models can also be used to investigate these questions, since they represent ways both of clearly stating and investigating the causal connections of the world we hope to intervene in. We may be interested in setting targets, evaluating long-term objectives that may be a ways off from an immediate practical perspective, or simply directly evaluating current aspects of our current world without commitment to any particular practical response.[30] The models or theories we construct for such purposes may diverge even further from a description of the actual world than with the previous criterion, as we wheel in heavily idealizing assumptions like "full compliance", the assumption that everyone will do as our moral standard or rule requires.[31] The models or theories involved with reaching this criterion are perhaps least likely to license any particular inferences from the content of the models to any particular descriptive claims about the real world.

Beyond Common Features

Directly Answering the Non-Ideal Theorists

I now focus on the negative arguments that switching to non-ideal theory is unlikely to help us diagnose or solve the problems Mills and other theorists have attributed to ideal theory.

The main problem with the arguments against ideal theory as such is that the problems attributed to ideal theory as such are better described as problems with model-to-world inference.

First, a brief refresher of Mills' case against ideal theory. In "Ideal Theory as Ideology", Mills asks, echoing much of the non-ideal theory literature that followed:

> Can it possibly serve the interests of *women*, white and nonwhite, to ignore female subordination, represent the family as ideal, and pretend that women have been treated as equal persons? Obviously not. Can it possibly serve the interests of *people of color* to ignore the centuries of white supremacy and to pretend that a discourse originally structured around white normativity now substantively, as against just terminologically, includes them? Obviously not. Can it possibly serve the interests of the *poor and the working class* to ignore the ways in which an increasingly inequitable class society imposes economic constraints that limit their nominal freedoms and undermine their formal equality before the law? Obviously not.[32]

But, as this paper suggests, I don't think this is quite as obvious as advertised. It *is* obvious that there is a non-accidental connection between the tendencies of ideal theories and ideal theorists to the forms of oppression and domination Mills points out. What is not obvious is that the connection is causal in the particular way needed for the argument to go through: that the privileging of ideal theory over non-ideal theory *itself* exacerbates these structures of domination, whether in the domain of philosophy or more generally.

Of course, we could give an alternative etiology of the problem, which would in turn suggest a different functional relationship between philosophers' reluctance to engage real-world forms of oppression and domination and the social structures they are thereby ignoring. Perhaps the tendency of the literature to ignore actual injustice reflects the preferences selected for by an unfair world, but exerts no causal influence on that world's unfairness. For example: perhaps it is true that classical music aficionados are overrepresented among philosophers. But if it were also true that both classical music and academic philosophy select for a certain class background we could explain the covariance here without suspecting that we had uncovered evidence that classical music appreciation among academic philosophers is a significant aspect of the class-based disadvantage inherent to capitalism.

Without the veneer of analogy: perhaps it is simply the case that philosophers' reluctance to engage real-world forms of oppression and domination and their penchant for ideal theory are simply both symptoms of the same disease – that philosophy selects for the people least likely to take it upon themselves to research oppression – rather than the latter causing or enabling the former. Then, the reluctance of philosophers to engage real-world forms of oppression and domination is explained by the sociological forces that produce *philosophers* in general, not the theoretical decisions that produce ideal theory, and ideal theory plays no role in the explanation.

A more serious challenge to Mills' framing of the issue here involves returning to the two key assumptions referred to in the introduction: the common features account of models' role in knowledge production, and the related assumption that models should be taken to make descriptive claims about real-world systems. Recall that a *common features account* of what makes theories or models informative requires that they share common features with the aspects of the real world they investigate.[33] This would ground the model-to-world inference that Mills makes here, when he takes it that the targeted aspects of the ideal theory "model" are committed to describing real-world political systems.

For all he says here, Mills could even be read as presupposing a much stronger claim: Weisberg's *completeness* ideal for models, the representational ideal on which every aspect of the target system must be represented in the model).[34] However, my arguments against his position work equally well against the weaker "common features" reading of his argument's implicit commitments, which seems the more charitable interpretation of his position. For the remainder of the chapter, I will assume the common features reading in my response.

Mills' discussion here involves not only this narrow view of models, but the second mistake as well, which is helped along by the first. Reading a common features account working in the background would make sense of why Mills identifies the assumption of equality among persons as a distortion of the actual world rather than simply a potentially innocuous or even informatively distortive feature of the relevant models as such. Such an account of how political theories work, after all, would take them to be making implicit claims about the real-world counterparts of their component features. That is why the kind of idealizations Rawls makes about the well-formed society amounts to pretending that "women have been treated as equal persons" in the real world rather than simply a description of the model world under construction.[35]

In "Idealization and Abstraction in models of Justice" Hancox-Li introduces an effective response to this point by discussing an abstract "collaboration game" model developed by Justin Bruner and Cailin O'Connor.[36] Agents play the game multiple times and maximize their payoffs by using strategies that have proved effective for them or other players in the past. Bruner and O'Connor show that, when the population is divided into a majority and a minority group, this division effects what strategies the players employ and learn from: majority players make larger demands of minority players, and minority players prefer to collaborate with other minorities or not at all. Hancox-Li points out that the model predictions are consistent with a real-world phenomenon: women preferring to collaborate with women in multiple fields of inquiry.[37]

But Bruner and O'Connor's model of abstract "minorities" maximizing numerical payoffs does not reflect a number of complications that actual women face. One idealization Hancox-Li focuses on is that players in Bruner and O'Connor's model only learn from previous versions of this same collaboration game. Women researchers, on the other hand, have presumably learned about gender in a variety of contexts before they ever became researchers (in home, in early education, etc.). Is the model distorting reality in an objectionable way? Hancox-Li's answer:

> It might seem that I have made a dodgy move in claiming that the model can *remain silent* on other sources of learning instead of *introducing the falsehood* that they do not exist [emphasis his]. I confess that I find it hard to distinguish clearly between these two alternatives, since "remaining silent" and "introducing a falsehood" *may only be metaphorically applied to models, as opposed to speakers or texts* [emphasis mine]. Some readers may have the intuition that omitting other sources of learning in the collaboration game counts as introducing a falsehood even if we are interested only in the question of how people learn from collaboration alone. But if we follow these readers' intuitions and take the exclusion of real-world causal factors from a model to always be introducing falsehoods, we are led to the conclusion that all social-science models introduce falsehoods, and are thus idealized in the way that Mills deplores.[38]

Hancox-Li's point involves distinguishing between the content of a model and a description of a target system. Empowered with the previous section, we can also flesh this point out further. First, Mills seems to assume that we should treat models as descriptions of the target system and hold them to the criterion of descriptive accuracy. However, three out of the four possible model desiderata considered here would license viewing the model as potentially informative or useful without saddling it with the expectation that it should be built on common features shared with the part of the real world we aim to use it to learn about.

I don't mean here to advocate for this particular construal of "normative understanding" models as a reading of Rawls or anyone else in particular. Instead, I mean to point out two things. First, if Rawls failed to adequately theorize about race, his use of ideal theory is not the reason why. The claim that racial justice (or any other sort) is not an important category from the standpoint of justice is in no sense implied or licensed by its omission from a proffered model of justice.[39] Models, unlike researchers, do not speak. As such, we should be slower to decide what it means that x or y is not represented in a model.

Secondly, if those of us invested in racial justice (or any other sort) mean to accomplish it, we shouldn't decide what the possibilities for an entire approach to knowledge production are by way of these sorts of arguments, which I argue misunderstand the possibilities for models and modeling in our moral and political life. If we, for example, took the relevant criterion for models serving an "ideal" political theory to be something like "normative understanding", then the models produced to provide normative understanding could play the role of adjudicating between the appropriateness of different racial justice-pursuing strategies, which could be planned out using still other models.

Theory in the Natural Sciences Goes Far Beyond Common Features

Reflection on the use of models in the natural sciences helps explain a broader point about them that explains why they might fit *worldmaking* projects: that they can be informative even when they do not resemble the aspect of the world that they are meant to inform us about. Sometimes they are informative about the world precisely because of their dissimilarities or distortions. Discussions about models among our colleagues, especially on the subject of explanation in the philosophy of science, are potentially informative for political philosophers on this issue.

Morrison and Morgan describe models as "partially independent" of both the world and the theories they help precisify. Models themselves and their constituent parts represent aspects of the theory that informs their construction, things or relationships in the world that motivated the inquiry in the first place, or both at once.[40] They are inspired by, guided by and are sometimes even logically deducible (or otherwise directly derivable) from the theory or theories they derive from.[41] But the extent of their independence is important: they often respond to or contain elements meant to represent empirical features of the world that have been observed but have no counterpart in a guiding theory of a target system, and even in some cases include elements that contradict the principles of the guiding theories.[42] Independence, then, can be thought of as a constraint on the inferences that are licensed by features or behavior of the model: a model is independent of the world or a theory to the extent that it features relationships with no real-world or theoretical analog.

This is no mere cop-out caveat designed to save time and ward off objections about this or that hastily designed feature of some model. The independence of models and theories from the real world can be a functional aspect of their role in knowledge production. For instance, Nancy Cartwright gives the example of "Galilean experiments" in which "unrealistic assumptions are not a hindrance but a necessity", when a researcher's model ignores all other factors to maximize potential understanding of the factor of interest.[43] Speaking more generally in "Models as Mediators", Morrison and Morgan explain that it is the partial independence from both theory and world that allows models to perform the function that they do – that is, it's *because* the model isn't fully determined by either the theory or that data that either expected or unexpected predictions or other output of the model or other behavior of its components is informative.[44] We compare the behavior or predictions of the model with the relevant, non-identical features of the real to adjust our model, our background theory, our understanding of the real world, or some combination of these.

Batterman and Rice even identify an entire class of models that are overall neither similar to nor representative of the real world, which they call "minimal models".[45] Even such "thoroughgoing caricatures of real systems" can be informative, if the features the model does have nevertheless inform us about the phenomenon of interest.[46] They use the Lattice Gas Automaton computational model of fluid flow to illustrate their point. In this model, a set of point particles are arranged on a hexagonal lattice. A set of rules dictates how these particles move, when and if they collide, and how collisions alter the trajectory of the colliding particles. This is not how molecules move in actual fluids – the model-to-world inference that real particles move in a hexagonal lattice-like fashion would involve a misunderstanding of the model. Yet, the large-scale behavior of the model predicts large-scale behaviors of actual fluids.[47]

Minimal models are just one way to put pressure on a common feature account as a total explanation of what makes models informative. Lauren Ross and Mazviita Chirimuuta identify still other examples of models in neuroscience whose explanatory utility doesn't depend on similarity to the target system, some of which may be "minimal models" in Batterman and Rice's sense and some of which may be yet another method to learn about the world other than rebuilding it in miniature.[48]

All the kinds of models these authors consider share *some* common features with their target systems, but this observation by itself is trivial – we could always engineer "common features" by simply relaxing our standards of what counts as common. What defenders of the common features account would need to invalidate the point being made here is to establish that the common features between the model and target system explain why the model is informative. That does not seem to be the case in either of Batterman and Rice or Chirimuuta's cases.

I don't rely on any of these authors' specific descriptions of how their specific models of interest explain and inform. What's important about their examples is what they reveal about the role of models in explanation quite generally: that similarity to the world is not a limitation on how, why, or whether models inform. If this is so, then this takes some of the wind out of the sails of Mills' objection against ideal theory, that ideal theories are too dissimilar from the messy unjust world to inform us about them.

Reconsidering the Role of Common Features in Ideal Theory

The discussion in philosophy of science is not a perfect parallel to the discussion in political philosophy on ideal theory – but that is in part because the discussion in philosophy of science on models and explanation is live to a fuller spectrum of ways we can learn about the world than the ideal theory debate is. David Kaplan's "3M constraint" requires both that the components of a model correspond to components of the target system and that relations between these also correspond to causal relations between the parts of the target system – a particularly strict version of a common features account of models and a clear competitor to the "minimal models" approach to understanding why models explain.[49] But Kaplan and Carver) are clear that this is a constraint on *explanation*, in particular, at most demarcating those models that explain from those that do not.[50] They treat as open the well-established possibility that even models that do not properly explain (in the particular mechanistic sense they defend) might nevertheless meet some other standard of informativeness (e.g. "empirical adequacy").

The lesson for political philosophy, then, is that the approach assumed by non-ideal theorists is not actually required. Having a background theory that pre-judges which aspects of the real world are causally relevant, and then populates the model with just those features that matter is only one way to proceed – the only way that Mills, Knight, and others seem to hold that political ideal theory could work. Political philosophy ought to take a page from this book and avoid tying its own hands with demands for representation – which involves casting a critical eye on the criticisms of ideal theory that presuppose similarity between theory and models.

Pair Rawls' and Wiredu's theory with Batterman and Rice's discussion of large-scale fluid flow, for example. Rawls does not suppose that his toy society in *A Theory of Justice* is much like any society in the real modern world, much less all of them: for instance, Rawls explicitly concedes that we may live in a "corrupt society" rather than the "well-ordered" one he prefers to theorize about, but sees value in this very fact. Ideal theory can tell us ways in which our social world might have been different and might well become different in the future.[51] Similarly, while Wiredu does seem to claim that many African societies that have had consensual democratic bases, he can neither charitably be read as making this claim about literally all of them nor as equating Zulu political history of consensual structures with that of Ashanti's political history with the same. Then, to recommend consensual structures for all African societies is not to treat Asanteman as a universally and trans-historical description of all African societies but is better understood as an act of idealization past relevant sociohistorical differences.

Also similarly, Batterman and Rice claim we needn't (and in fact shouldn't, given what subsequently became proven about sub-atomic particles - like the fact that they exist) think that the model of fluid flow provided by the Lattice Gas Automaton (LGA) model resembles how particles in flowing fluid actually move. Nevertheless, a wide variety of engineering contexts make use of the model.[52] To criticize the LGA model because it represents particles as moving along a hexagonal lattice (and particles are not in fact constricted in this way) would involve a fundamental misunderstanding of how the model is attempting to inform us about the world. Using the LGA needn't involve licensing the model-to-world inference that real-world particles move in a lattice-like fashion – just that representing the movement of particles this way can help the model make useful predictions about the flow of actual fluids.

Similarly, defenders of Wiredu's theory of consensual democracy need not argue that the entire African continent (comprised of well over a billion people) will return to exactly those structures of conversation and social organization that structured the much smaller Ashanti society. Nevertheless, ethical principles developed with reference to that society and a set of abstract values might well be informative for the continent. Likewise, defenders of Rawlsian theory can concede that neither the members of the Rawlsian original position nor the interactions among them are much like real-world interactions between people who find themselves enmeshed in histories of domination, yet Rawls' model could still be informative.[53]

Answering an Objection: Is Normative Theory Special?

One distinction that might seem particularly useful to the anti-ideal theorist is the distinction between theories with descriptive and normative ends. So far, I have mostly confined my discussion to a treatment of models as such, leaving many possible distinctions by the wayside. I've cut wildly across different environments and domains of inquiry that feature models, and different kinds of models and model-like reasoning. But perhaps there are moral norms governing normative theorizing that do not apply to other kinds, and these norms either independently require something of a "common features" approach to theory and model building in political philosophy or otherwise account for the success of arguments in favor of common features-based theories that might otherwise fail.

The objection gets going something like this: some theories and acts of theorizing are primarily about understanding the world. Maybe Galileo was just curious about whether or not Jupiter had any moons, and that by itself was a good enough reason to find out. This sort of theorizing is perhaps more common in the natural and social sciences, which licenses their ways of building and evaluating theories and models, or at least differentiates their practices from those that are appropriate in more normatively oriented disciplines.

But other theories are – or at least should be – in the business of making the world better. It would be callous and objectionable to spend a good deal of social resources developing a theory of a disease that we did not intend to cure or treat. This last analogy is especially on the nose, since this seems something like the charge laid at the feet of ideal theory.

What exactly is different about theorizing that is normatively laden? One possibility is that our acts of theorizing are in and of themselves morally laden. The objection that stems from this position is that ideal theory is objectionable because of what it *does* – abstracts from real-world conditions of oppression and injustice – rather than what comes of its so doing.

But it's hard to read those who attack ideal theory as having meant this version of the objection. Mills, for example, asks whether the idealizations of ideal theory can possibly "serve the interests" of women and of racially oppressed people, which implies a consequential argument. But the plausibility of this argument hinges far too much on the particular examples. It's a good deal easier to say how the idealizations of Wiredu's ideal theory might serve the interests of, say, ethnic minorities on the African continent who might be ignored altogether in contexts like Nigeria's, where explicit reference to ethnicity (particularly by the larger groups) has historically driven domination and conflict.[54] It is less likely that Mills has pointed out a crucial problem with ideal theory *as such* here and more likely that Mills has identified particularly important aspects of social domination that any theory or model, ideal or not, could benefit from including.

It's also worth taking a second look at how the burden of proof has been assigned here. It is less than obvious what the practical payoff of an opposition to ideal theory in favor of explicit theorizing about oppressed groups will be. Adolph Reed and Merlin Chowkwanyun argue that a spate of social science inspired by motivations like Mills' has uncovered a great deal of evidence about a great many specific racial disparities in specific contexts, but this very specificity comes with a considerable cost: obscuring the very causal factors that we would need to intervene on to prevent them.[55] In the aptly titled article "Fuck Nuance", sociologist Kieran Healy argues persuasively that nuance is only superficially attractive as a criterion of social theory, and may serve as an impediment to learning when valued inappropriately.[56] Pointing out racial disparities may be good argumentative fodder against those who deny the existence, reach, or importance of racism. But suppose we already were persuaded that racism exists and pervades society. Does it materially and significantly help the racial justice struggle to spend social resources proving that discrimination pervades kindergarten education slightly more in Tulsa than it does in Kansas City? Would such granularity "serve the interests" of Black and brown students in either case, who are confronting a system of racial injustice that cuts across the differences in their contexts? It is precisely the kind of unity across differences that motivates the use of idealizations and abstractions. Non-ideal theorists seem to take it for granted that more empirical and historical analysis of the racial origins of such disparities is of practical use in responding to them, but it is far from clear how such a focus helps, which undermines the advantage of practical relevance they take themselves to have over ideal theorists. This challenge is particularly pressing if the attentional/resource cost or research design that allows us to uncover the disparity precludes investigation of the sort of factors that might explain what is different about Tulsa rather than simply reveal that Tulsa is different.[57]

The possibility that replacing ideal theory with empirically laden non-ideal theory could be counterproductive pushes back effectively against even the more deontological framing of the problem: that it's somehow intrinsically immoral or unjust to theorize without explicit reference to axes of oppression like race, gender, and disability. It seems plausible that whatever principle would recommend making explicit reference to these would be a subsidiary principle in a larger set of principles oriented around the broader themes of racial, gender, and disability justice. How could it be more morally weighty to follow the subsidiary principle that recommends that we socially signal via our models that we care about, say, racial justice, than to actually advance the political project of dismantling structural racism? Shouldn't a higher-level principle override in this sort of instance? If not, what could count in favor of constructing our set of racial justice principles in so self-defeating a fashion? Opponents of ideal theory should tell us.

Even if we take Mills to have correctly assigned the burden of proof, the same kind of arguments that undermined the principle-based advocacy of abandoning ideal theory also undermine an approach that focuses on the consequences of different kinds of theorizing. We can group the consequences under consideration by domain.

First, consequences internal to academia. Perhaps "ideal theory" of the Rawlsian or Wiredian sort will lead to bad consequences in the discipline itself because ideal theory will act as an ideology or will otherwise signal strong commitments to researchers about what aspects of the world are important to a description of how it works. That is, maybe not explicitly theorizing about gender, disability, or race communicates that a political philosopher need not learn about these phenomena to effectively do their job.

But we could even concede to Mills that the particular ideal theories, as received by the discipline, function ideologically in this sense without being further committed to preferring non-ideal theory or avoiding ideal theory. We could, for instance, adopt a race, ability, and gender-blind (for example) ideal theory and pair it with a non-ideal theory or set of these that were conscious about the aforementioned aspects of identity, thus fulfilling both the desiderata of theorizing about oppression explicitly and whatever ideal theories might be good for. Or we could campaign to change how philosophers are educated on axes of oppression directly: by changing the content of graduate requirements, holding symposia on these issues for mid-career philosophers, and other interventions of this sort.

If any of these are potentially effective responses, then the criticisms of ideal theory are perhaps better directed at the lacunae of appropriate, matching non-ideal theories rather than at the content of the ideal theory. If it is inadequate, we are owed an answer why – and, again, an appeal to what the ideal theory has or lacks seems orthogonal to the problem, unless it is established that an ideal theory *precludes* examination of systems of oppression. That strong claim is not established by observing that the ideal theory simply doesn't itself examine oppression in the desired ways. It is hard to attribute whatever negative consequences stem from oppression-silent ideal theory to the content of the ideal theory itself, rather than the broader epistemic environment in which it intervenes.

Second, the consequences external to academia. Perhaps anti-ideal theorists are concerned about the effects of ideal theory in the world – either downstream of the previous set of concerns, because of the influence philosophers' reception of theory has outside of the discipline, or perhaps in some direct sense that bypasses how other philosophers respond to ideal theory. The latter seems implausible, given how seldom academic papers are read at all.[58]

Also, the earlier response helped along by Reed and Chowkwanyan puts pressure on the most plausible explanation of the problem here: that theorists' inattention should be understood as a negative consequence of social justice. But say we had gotten rid of ideal theory and that resulted in theorists taking axes of oppression more seriously, as the non-ideal theorists advocate for. Would that have been a positive development for the struggles for social justice? Perhaps, but perhaps not – if what researchers do when they study social justice is distracting or otherwise counterproductive. There seems to be at least some evidence that at the very least, despite laudable intentions, researchers' effects on the injustices they study are not uniformly positive. Yet more reason that we ought to focus on the actual effects our theories have, rather than the abstract categories we sort them into.

Conclusion

Ideal theory is a tool – nothing more, nothing less. The most skillfully designed guitar won't play beautifully while used as a door stop; the car with the finest engine will not outrace a lemon while it's in park. We would know straightaway what had gone wrong with the reasoning of any person who looked to find flaws in the guitar or the car themselves in these cases for the explanation of why they failed to be a part of bigger and better things. Similarly, those who are concerned about ideal theory have learned the wrong lesson from its misuses and non-uses. If we want ideal theory, or philosophy in general, to serve the cause of ending oppression then it is our task to appropriate it and set to that purpose, or to find a tool that is better based on *its* potential use and not the present machinations of its owners.

There are other ways to navigate the world besides rebuilding it in miniature. The debate about the relative virtues of ideal theory vs. non-ideal theory is, at best, simply orthogonal to both the question of how to avoid the risks that have thus far been attributed to problematic idealizations and the more important question of how theory could be emancipatory or progressive. At worst it is a costly and self-undermining distraction from more pressing concerns: if the problems pinned on ideal theory are actually problems with model-to-world inference, then switching to non-ideal theory would at best solve the problems indirectly and accidentally, and risks obscuring them or worsening them.

Perhaps ideal theory isn't hegemonic and ideological because of what it *does* contain (problematic idealizations or abstractions) but because of what the broader field *doesn't*: a sustained, systematic or otherwise intentional way of working from our models to practical projects. That would provide guidance each step of the way about which model-to-world inferences were licensed by our various theories. As things stand now, the problems identified with ideal theory and its accoutrement apply more strongly and directly to our interpretation of models than to our construction of them.

To make this point about model-to-world inference is not to defend ideal theory as currently practiced, but to contend that ideal theory itself as an approach is a confused choice of target and it is unclear what a move to non-ideal theory would do to remedy the problem as understood in this way. I criticize the debate as it stands precisely because I share the motivation to avoid the field's current pitfalls, and thus see the presentation of non-ideal theories as a solution to or even necessarily an improvement with respect to these problems as misleading about what theory that takes those problems seriously would look like. Unlike our colleagues in other fields and even other corners of philosophy, model-to-world inference is vastly undertheorized in political philosophy and endangers the relevance and helpfulness of our work as a field.

Even if it is so that race, gender, disability, and other such categories ought to be represented such specifically in "theory" (done by theorists in their professional capacity), this is no argument for them needing to appear in *theory* in the strong sense (as direct components of relevant theories). That is, *that* they should be on the agenda of political philosophers ought to be separated from the question of *how*. If it turns out that we don't need to explicitly think about gender or race to do a specific kind of political theorizing, it does not follow either that these phenomena are unimportant or that we do not need to think about race to do political philosophy more generally speaking. We could challenge the wholly unmerited association of abstraction with importance directly by appropriately valuing applied, translational, and other forms of philosophy other than ideal theory rather than the overcorrection of demonizing a perfectly legitimate theoretical enterprise.[59]

As mentioned in the introduction, the argument in this paper is not in the least designed to defend political philosophers' *use* of models, be they Rawlsian or Wiredian or in some other camp. But ideal theory as such is neither an explanation of nor a defense of this tendency of some philosophers. It's hard to see why discussions about the adequacy of Wiredu's theory itself should stand or fall on the good or bad behavior of Rawlsians – or why our appraisal of the general theoretical approach should be sensitive to either camp's, as opposed to a sober analysis of what the approach could be if it were held in better hands.

Ideal theory may have a positive role to play. We may find ourselves with questions like Rawls about what to hope for out of a just social system. We may find ourselves in a context like Wiredu's – he wrote in the aftermath of the massive transformation of African politics that followed the successful anti-colonial movements of the 60s and 70s and the unsuccessful attempt to forge a just way forward from there. He had to abstract heavily from particular African histories to respond to the total range of contexts he was interested in: the full African continent. Ideal theory was useful for these enterprises and is likely useful for still others.

If theory really has the causal role in either supporting or potentially dismantling systems of oppression that non-ideal theorists speak as though it has, then that is all the more reason to evaluate our theories with a ruthless focus on their adequacy. If our theories really are genuine ammunition in the fight for justice, a little idealization is a small price to pay.

Notes

1 Thanks to: Serene Khader, David Estlund, Bryce Huebner, James Mattingly, Leif Hancox-Li, Simon Căbulea May.

2 For a compelling example of this sort of argument, see Farrelly 2007. Colin Farrelly, "Justice in Ideal Theory: A Refutation," *Political Studies* 55, no. 4 (2007): 844–864.

3 See, for example, the argument provided by Knight on disability, which argues that we should "move away from ideal theory and grapple with complex power relations that arise in the real world in order to produce theories capable of guiding action toward emancipatory change." Amber Knight, "Disabling Ideal Theory," *Politics, Groups, and Identities* (2018): 1–17.

4 Charles W. Mills, "'Ideal Theory' as Ideology," *Hypatia* 20, no. 3 (2005): 165–183.

5 Leif Hancox-Li, "Idealization and Abstraction in Models of Injustice," *Hypatia* 32, no. 2 (2017): 329–346.

6 The distinction is O'Neill's. Roughly, abstractions refer to things that are ignored by a theory (the danger being that they may be relevant to real-world instances of the target phenomena) and idealizations refer to falsehoods about phenomena introduced by a theory, perhaps for simplicity or

another sense of convenience. Onora O'Neill, "Abstraction, Idealization and Ideology in Ethics," *Royal Institute of Philosophy Lecture Series* 22 (1987): 55–69.

7 Cartwright is already wise to this – for example, her distinction between models as parables and as fables appeals to differences in what I would call model-to-world inference: "The advantage of thinking of what happens here in terms of Lessing's account of morals and fables is that it makes clear that there is nothing wrong with the initial experiment. What is wrong vis-à-vis applicability elsewhere is the level at which the conclusion is described. "Nancy Cartwright, "Models: Parables v Fables" (Beyond Mimesis and Convention, Springer, 2010), 28.

8 Mills, "'Ideal Theory' as Ideology," 168.

9 See, for example: Elizabeth Anderson, *The Imperative of Integration* (Princeton University Press, 2010), 4–5; Knight, "Disabling Ideal Theory."

10 Adom Getachew, *Worldmaking after Empire: The Rise and Fall of Self-Determination* (Princeton University Press, 2019).

11 Kwasi Wiredu, "Democracy by Consensus: Some Conceptual Considerations," *Philosophical Papers* 30, no. 3 (2001): 227–244; Kwasi Wiredu, "Democracy and Consensus in African Traditional Politics: A Plea for a Non-Party Polity," *The Centennial Review* 39, no. 1 (1995): 53–64; Kwasi Wiredu, *Cultural Universals and Particulars: An African Perspective* (Indiana University Press, 1996).

12 See, for example, this recent edited volume: Emmanuel Ifeanyi Ani and Edwin E. Etieyibo, eds., *Deciding in Unison: Themes in Consensual Democracy in Africa* (Vernon Press, 2020).

13 I agree with Hamlin and Stemplowska that the difference between abstraction and idealization is insufficiently clear to apply to complex cases. For a critical discussion of Wiredu's point on minority groups in particular, see Etieyibo. Alan Hamlin and Zofia Stemplowska, "Theory, Ideal Theory and the Theory of Ideals," *Political Studies Review* 10, no. 1 (2012): 50–51; Edwin Etieyibo, "African Consensual Democracy, Dissensus and Resistance," *Deciding in Unison: Themes in Consensual Democracy in Africa* (2020): 135.

14 Alexandru Volacu, "Bridging Ideal and Non-Ideal Theory," *Political Studies* 66, no. 4 (2018): 887–902.

15 "A Revealing Map of the World's Most and Least Ethnically Diverse Countries," *Washington Post*, accessed July 27, 2021, https://www.washingtonpost.com/news/worldviews/wp/2013/05/16/a-revealing-map-of-the-worlds-most-and-least-ethnically-diverse-countries/.

16 Nancy Cartwright, "Models and the Limits of Theory: Quantum Hamiltonians and the BCS Models of Superconductivity," *Ideas in Context* 52 (1999): 242.

17 Michael Weisberg, *Simulation and Similarity: Using Models to Understand the World* (Oxford University Press, 2012), 15, 172.

18 I do not take a stance here on the precise relationship of theories to models, as it is enough for my purposes that there is one. Cartwright, "Models and the Limits of Theory: Quantum Hamiltonians and the BCS Models of Superconductivity," 241; Robert W Batterman and Collin C Rice, "Minimal Model Explanations," *Philosophy of Science* 81, no. 3 (2014): 349–376.

19 Margaret Morrison and Mary S. Morgan, "Models as Mediating Instruments," *Ideas in Context* 52 (1999): 10–37; Nancy Cartwright and Robin Le Poidevin, "Fables and Models," *Proceedings of the Aristotelian Society, Supplementary Volumes* 65 (1991): 55–82.

20 Ingrid Robeyns, "Ideal Theory in Theory and Practice," *Social Theory and Practice* 34, no. 3 (2008): 346.

21 Laura Valentini, "Ideal vs. Non-ideal Theory: A Conceptual Map," *Philosophy Compass* 7, no. 9 (2012): 654–664.

22 Hamlin and Stemplowska, "Theory, Ideal Theory and the Theory of Ideals."

23 Volacu suggests a two-axis schema: fact sensitivity/insensitivity on one axis and prioritization of desirability/feasibility on the other. I more or less agree with Volacu's schema here and take it that my sentence here roughly approximates these axes. Volacu, "Bridging Ideal and Non-Ideal Theory," 893.

24 Richard Levins, "The Strategy of Model Building in Population Biology," *American Scientist* 54, no. 4 (1966): 422.

25 Michael Weisberg, "Forty Years of 'The Strategy': Levins on Model Building and Idealization," *Biology and Philosophy* 21, no. 5 (2006): 626.

26 Levins, "The Strategy of Model Building in Population Biology," 422.

27 This corresponds to something like what Sen labels the "transcendental" approach to justice. Amartya Sen, "What Do We Want from a Theory of Justice?," *The Journal of Philosophy* 103, no. 5 (2006): 215–238.

28 See, for example, Estlund's distinction between "concessive" and "aspirational" theory – the former makes concessions in theorizing about how we can expect people to respond, the latter does not. Both, Estlund thinks, are kinds of theory that are potentially worth doing. David Estlund, "Utopophobia," *Philosophy & Public Affairs* 42, no. 2 (2014): 113–134.

29 John Rawls, *Justice as Fairness: A Restatement* (Harvard University Press, 2001), 2–5.

30 Estlund makes the last point about the separability of evaluation and (any particular) practical intervention in: David Estlund, *Democratic Authority: A Philosophical Framework* (Princeton University Press, 2009), 265–267.

31 Hamlin and Stemplowska, "Theory, Ideal Theory and the Theory of Ideals."

32 Mills, "'Ideal Theory' as Ideology."

33 Batterman and Rice, "Minimal Model Explanations," 351–357.

34 Weisberg, "Forty Years of 'The Strategy': Levins on Model Building and Idealization."

35 Mills, "'Ideal Theory' as Ideology."

36 Justin Bruner and Cailin O'Connor, "Power, Bargaining, and Collaboration," 2016.

37 Hancox-Li, "Idealization and Abstraction in Models of Injustice," 337.

38 Hancox-Li, 339.

39 Tommie Shelby argues for something like this in: Tommie Shelby, "Racial Realities and Corrective Justice: A Reply to Charles Mills," *Critical Philosophy of Race* 1, no. 2 (2013): 145–162.

40 Recall that on the semantic view theories simply are sets of models, in which case this argument works just as well for "theories". But, as before, I decline to take a stance here on the precise relationship between theories and models. Morrison and Morgan, "Models as Mediating Instruments," 11.

41 Stephan Hartmann, "Models and Stones in Hadron Physics," *Models as Mediators: Perspectives on Natural and Social Science* 52 (1999): 2.

42 Michael Redhead, "Models in Physics," *The British Journal for the Philosophy of Science* 31, no. 2 (1980): 147.

43 Cartwright, "Models: Parables v Fables," 23.

44 Morrison and Morgan, "Models as Mediating Instruments," 17.

45 Batterman and Rice, "Minimal Model Explanations."

46 Batterman and Rice, 350.

47 Batterman and Rice, 360–361.

48 Lauren N Ross, "Dynamical Models and Explanation in Neuroscience," *Philosophy of Science* 82, no. 1 (2015): 32–54; Mazviita Chirimuuta, "Minimal Models and Canonical Neural Computations: The Distinctness of Computational Explanation in Neuroscience," *Synthese* 191, no. 2 (2014): 127–153.

49 David Michael Kaplan, "Explanation and Description in Computational Neuroscience," *Synthese* 183, no. 3 (2011): 347.

50 David Michael Kaplan and Carl F Craver, "The Explanatory Force of Dynamical and Mathematical Models in Neuroscience: A Mechanistic Perspective," *Philosophy of Science* 78, no. 4 (2011): 602–603.

51 Rawls, *Justice as Fairness: A Restatement*, 37–38.

52 Batterman and Rice, "Minimal Model Explanations," 357.

53 For a brief defense of Rawls whose basic strategy makes use of this possibility, see David Wiens, "Against Ideal Guidance.," *Journal of Politics* 77, no. 2 (April 2015): 433–446.

54 Usman Mohammed, "Corruption in Nigeria: A Challenge to Sustainable Development in the Fourth Republic," *European Scientific Journal* 9, no. 4 (2013).

55 Adolph L Reed and Merlin Chowkwanyun, "Race, Class, Crisis: The Discourse of Racial Disparity and Its Analytical Discontents," *Socialist Register* 48 (2012): 149–175.

56 Kieran Healy, "Fuck Nuance," *Sociological Theory* 35, no. 2 (2017): 118–127.

57 Reed and Chowkwanyun, "Race, Class, Crisis: The Discourse of Racial Disparity and Its Analytical Discontents," 152–153.

58 Biswas and Kirchherr claim that the average peer reviewed paper is fully read by "no more than ten people" but do not explain how they arrived at this number. Asit Biswas and Julian Kirchherr, "Prof, No One Is Reading You," *Text, The Straits Times*, April 11, 2015, https://www.straitstimes.com/opinion/prof-no-one-is-reading-you.

59 "Translational" philosophy is "about creating a practical intervention to address a real-world problem", relating theory to the real world in a practically oriented sense. The authors distinguish

this from applied philosophy, which relates theory to real world phenomena in an epistemically oriented sense. Margaret Little et al., "Ethics Lab," *A Guide to Field Philosophy: Case Studies and Practical Strategies*, 2020.

Works Cited

Anderson, Elizabeth. *The Imperative of Integration*. Princeton University Press, 2010.

Ani, Emmanuel Ifeanyi, and Edwin E. Etieyibo, eds. *Deciding in Unison: Themes in Consensual Democracy in Africa*. Vernon Press, 2020.

Batterman, Robert W, and Collin C Rice. "Minimal Model Explanations." *Philosophy of Science* 81, no. 3 (2014): 349–376.

Biswas, Asit, and Julian Kirchherr. "Prof, No One Is Reading You." *Text*. The Straits Times, April 11, 2015. https://www.straitstimes.com/opinion/prof-no-one-is-reading-you.

Bruner, Justin, and Cailin O'Connor. Power, Bargaining, and Collaboration. In T. Boyer, C. Mayo-Wilson & M. Weisberg (eds.), *Scientific Collaboration and Collective Knowledge*. Oxford: Oxford University Press, 2022.

Cartwright, Nancy. "Models and the Limits of Theory: Quantum Hamiltonians and the BCS Models of Superconductivity." *Ideas in Context* 52 (1999): 241–281.

Cartwright, Nancy. Models: Parables v Fables. In *Beyond mimesis and convention: Representation in art and science*, pp. 19–31. Springer, Netherlands, 2010.

Cartwright, Nancy, and Robin Le Poidevin. "Fables and Models." *Proceedings of the Aristotelian Society, Supplementary Volumes* 65 (1991): 55–82.

Chirimuuta, Mazviita. "Minimal Models and Canonical Neural Computations: The Distinctness of Computational Explanation in Neuroscience." *Synthese* 191, no. 2 (2014): 127–153.

Estlund, David. *Democratic Authority: A Philosophical Framework*. Princeton University Press, 2009.

———. "Utopophobia." *Philosophy & Public Affairs* 42, no. 2 (2014): 113–134.

Etieyibo, Edwin. "African Consensual Democracy, Dissensus and Resistance." *Deciding in Unison: Themes in Consensual Democracy in Africa*, Emmanuel Ifeanyi Ani and Edwin Etieyibo (eds.), Wilmington, Delaware and Malaga: Vernon Press., 2020: 135–148.

Farrelly, Colin. "Justice in Ideal Theory: A Refutation." *Political Studies* 55, no. 4 (2007): 844–864.

Getachew, Adom. *Worldmaking after Empire: The Rise and Fall of Self-Determination*. Princeton University Press, 2019.

Hamlin, Alan, and Zofia Stemplowska. "Theory, Ideal Theory and the Theory of Ideals." *Political Studies Review* 10, no. 1 (2012): 48–62.

Hancox-Li, Leif. "Idealization and Abstraction in Models of Injustice." *Hypatia* 32, no. 2 (2017): 329–346.

Hartmann, Stephan. "Models and Stones in Hadron Physics." *Models as Mediators: Perspectives on Natural and Social Science* 52 (1999): 326.

Healy, Kieran. "Fuck Nuance." *Sociological Theory* 35, no. 2 (2017): 118–127.

Kaplan, David Michael. "Explanation and Description in Computational Neuroscience." *Synthese* 183, no. 3 (2011): 339.

Kaplan, David Michael, and Carl F Craver. "The Explanatory Force of Dynamical and Mathematical Models in Neuroscience: A Mechanistic Perspective." *Philosophy of Science* 78, no. 4 (2011): 601–627.

Knight, Amber. "Disabling Ideal Theory." *Politics, Groups, and Identities* 8, no. 2 (2020): 373–389.

Levins, Richard. "The Strategy of Model Building in Population Biology." *American Scientist* 54, no. 4 (1966): 421–431.

Little, Margaret, Elizabeth Edenberg, Sydney Luken, and Jonathan Healey. "Ethics lab: harnessing design methodologies for translational ethics." In Evelyn Brister and Robert Frodeman (eds), *A Guide to Field Philosophy*: Case Studies and Practical Strategies, New York: Routledge, 2020: 66–79. Routledge, 2020.

Mills, Charles W. "'Ideal Theory' as Ideology." *Hypatia* 20, no. 3 (2005): 165–183.

Mohammed, Usman. "Corruption in Nigeria: A Challenge to Sustainable Development in the Fourth Republic." *European Scientific Journal* 9, no. 4 (2013): 122–123.

Morrison, Margaret, and Mary S Morgan. "Models as Mediating Instruments." *Ideas in Context* 52 (1999): 10–37.

O'Neill, Onora. "Abstraction, Idealization and Ideology in Ethics." *Royal Institute of Philosophy Lecture Series* 22 (1987): 55–69.

Rawls, John. *Justice as Fairness: A Restatement.* Harvard University Press, 2001.

Redhead, Michael. "Models in Physics." *The British Journal for the Philosophy of Science* 31, no. 2 (1980): 145–163.

Reed, Adolph L, and Merlin Chowkwanyun. "Race, Class, Crisis: The Discourse of Racial Disparity and Its Analytical Discontents." *Socialist Register* 48 (2012): 149–175.

Robeyns, Ingrid. "Ideal Theory in Theory and Practice." *Social Theory and Practice* 34, no. 3 (2008): 341–362.

Ross, Lauren N. "Dynamical Models and Explanation in Neuroscience." *Philosophy of Science* 82, no. 1 (2015): 32–54.

Sen, Amartya. "What Do We Want from a Theory of Justice?" *The Journal of Philosophy* 103, no. 5 (2006): 215–238.

Shelby, Tommie. "Racial Realities and Corrective Justice: A Reply to Charles Mills." *Critical Philosophy of Race* 1, no. 2 (2013): 145–162.

Valentini, Laura. "Ideal vs. Non-ideal Theory: A Conceptual Map." *Philosophy Compass* 7, no. 9 (2012): 654–664.

Volacu, Alexandru. "Bridging Ideal and Non-Ideal Theory." *Political Studies* 66, no. 4 (2018): 887–902.

Washington Post. "A Revealing Map of the World's Most and Least Ethnically Diverse Countries." Accessed July 27, 2021. https://www.washingtonpost.com/news/worldviews/wp/2013/05/16/a-revealing-map-of-the-worlds-most-and-least-ethnically-diverse-countries/.

Weisberg, Michael. "Forty Years of 'The Strategy': Levins on Model Building and Idealization." *Biology and Philosophy* 21, no. 5 (2006): 623–645.

———. *Simulation and Similarity: Using Models to Understand the World.* Oxford University Press, 2012.

Wiens, David. "Against Ideal Guidance." *Journal of Politics* 77, no. 2 (April 2015): 433–446.

Wiredu, Kwasi. *Cultural Universals and Particulars: An African Perspective.* Indiana University Press, 1996.

———. "Democracy and Consensus in African Traditional Politics: A Plea for a Non-Party Polity." *The Centennial Review* 39, no. 1 (1995): 53–64.

———. "Democracy by Consensus: Some Conceptual Considerations." *Philosophical Papers* 30, no. 3 (2001): 227–244.

16

DEVELOPMENT AS AN ALTERNATIVE TO DEMOCRACY

Bernard Matolino

Introduction

Post-colonial sub-Saharan Africa's struggle with democratizing, as understood and practiced in developed countries, has been long and is on the verge of confirmed failure. Statistically, the most generous of reports put democratic countries at less than 10, on the entire continent. Other reports claim that Africa's dictatorial regimes or unfree regimes are on the rise. The reasons for Africa's failure are many and have been canvassed at length. My aim is to argue that the difficulty associated with Africa's democratic standing might be largely influenced by socio-economic realities that are inconsistent with the expectations of Western democracy. In particular, I seek to argue that Africa's developmental needs, which remain stunted, actively work against the cementing of democracy. In addition, I will seek to demonstrate that the development of democracy in the West, was a very specific project that reflected a prevalent social and epistemological orientation. That social and epistemological orientation, I shall argue, is not prevalent in Africa. I will divide this chapter into four sections. In the first section, I spell out the major features of Western democracy and how those features, as a specific historical and social construction, do not appear on the African continent. In the second section, I will seek to argue why development should be taken as a necessary precursor to a stable political dispensation on the continent. In the third section, I will outline what Africa needs to do to realize its developmental potential. In the last section, I sketch what an African democracy inspired by developmental imperatives might eventually do for Africa.

Democracy as a Western Success and Africa's Failure

Democracy, particularly in developed Western European countries and Northern American countries such as the United States of America, has come to represent what is desirable about a free and fair polity, a just state, exemplary protection of civil liberties, economic progress leading to decent living standards of citizens, and human progress. The exemplary nature of democracy, in these regions of the world, is actively sought and promoted in other regions of the world including sub-Saharan Africa. However, what is quickly forgotten are the histories of the democratic examples, specifically, how they came to be democratic (Popper, 1994: 204–205; Rawls, 1993: xxi–xxix). Other aspects that are quickly forgotten are how the

DOI: 10.4324/9781003143529-19

histories of these regions' interactions with Africa have ultimately shaped these democratic regions' material and intellectual progress as well as how they have impacted Africa's material, intellectual, and democratic decline (see Adebajo, 2010: xiii–xvii; Kebede, 1999: 8).

While there has been a lot written about the genesis and entrenchment of democracy in the Western world, what is not always sufficiently emphasized is how Western democracy as a political system is a response to social, historical, economic, political, and intellectual forces that shaped very particular societies in very particular ways (see Strauss and Cropsey (1963) 1987: 907–934). What is of interest, for my purposes, is how Western democracy is a product of years of intellectual engagement in response to social conditions. If we look at all Western political philosophers be it from Hobbes to Rawls, Machiavelli to Habermas, we find two interesting facts about their work. The first is that their reflections are specific to their societies in their attempt at understanding human beings and their social environment. The second is that they have contributed to the establishment of a tradition that places emphasis on a particular interpretation of the world that is consistent with a certain ideal – an ideal of their place of origin. Whatever differences exist between them and whatever the significance of those differences, they are about the intellectual reflection of the peculiarities of a space that has forced an intellectual response from its thinkers. Two of these peculiarities have got to do with the ownership of property and the relationship between central authority (that has come to be known as the state) and the individual. To this, we could add issues such as fair distribution of material goods, the importance of public office (including its assumption and termination), separation of powers among organs of state, and how relationships between private individuals are to be governed. While these issues are truly human issues with the capability for universalization, what cannot be denied is that they rose with a specific force in the Northern hemisphere. A large part of the enlightenment thinkers, for example, dedicated themselves to defending private property and individual rights. Such a defense did not emerge from nowhere, neither were ideas of property and civil rights the most attractive among a bunch of competing ideas. On the contrary, these ideas were responses to the reality of living under authoritarian regimes that thought they had a God-given right to rule. These regimes saw ordinary people as not deserving of rights, freedoms, and other entitlements similar to those enjoyed by the ruling classes. This is how ideas on representation, popular government, and responsible and accountable exercise of power emerged. Ideas of the enlightenment about government were largely in rebellion with monarchical power. The birth of the United States of America as an independent country was in response to unfair decisions taken in a body that the people of the then colony were not represented. The US constitution, which is held as a model of democratic constitutions, was partly inspired by enlightenment ideas on freedom, representation, and property, and partly by the history of Britain's mode of ruling conquered lands.

The French revolution and the American quest for independence, for example, were to become historic occasions that represented the establishment of a new order. An order that prioritized certain principles of governance over older claims by the monarchy and the colonial power that was Britain. The political order that was being established was in tandem with the generation of new ideas about the nature of humans, and their intellectual powers which led them to explaining things without reliance on God. Trust or belief in human capacity extended into all areas of life. The political system had to reflect such new-found power. Ideas about human subjectivity in relation to government became centered on contractarianism. The ideas promoted by contractarianism represent the cultural shift that was taking place in Europe and Northern American colonies. That culture became the new norm. A norm that represented how life was understood and was going to be lived.

The core elements of this new outlook were cultural, religious (with the emergence of Protestantism), economic, and new methods of knowing represented by the advances in science with philosophical backing. All these elements combined to transform society. They set their societies on a path of epistemological, material, and political progress that had never been witnessed before. Political gains were not registered in isolation or opposition to other gains happening in society. Political gains happened because of shifts that had occurred elsewhere. In fact, the political disposition became a reflection of the general disposition that permeated the whole of society.

Over the years the Western world (particularly the mature democracies of the United States, Canada, England, and France) have perfected this way of life that was initiated in the enlightenment. All systems of thought, behavior, and production are a continuation of the core emphasis of the enlightenment. Notwithstanding criticism of the enlightenment's inadequacies, there is no doubt that its spirit is the author of the modern world (Keita, 2011: 116). That spirit is so evident in the countries that I have just mentioned. Any attack of that spirit is an attack on the values of these countries. And these values are taken as representative of what true humanity is, what the enlightened and progressive humanity is about. The defense of these values as well as their continued protection is a defense of the Western heritage of humanity.

The West then took it upon itself to oversee that its values, systems of life, and beliefs were spread around the world. However, they chose to go about this through an objectionable way – conquest. From ordinary curiosity about the nature of difference between whites and non-whites, colonial powers quickly became merchants of discrimination and plunder. Behind this discrimination and plunder was the firm belief that the white race, by virtue of its civilization, was a superior race to all other races, particularly Africans. This superiority was not conceived in nice and polite intellectual terms. At times its barbarity, probably indistinguishable from hatred, was on display in places such as the modern-day DRC with King Leopold's excesses being probably the worst. Other occurrences included various acts of murder and displacement all over the continent. With time, colonial powers ceremonially relinquished their hold on Africa by granting her nominal independence. That independence came with the requirement that Africa was now to join the fully civilized world by, among other things, democratizing. That road, as already stated above has been long and is now on the brink of collapse.

We could infer two things from the foregoing. The first is that modern Western-inspired democracy is not internally generated in Africa. I need to explain this a little bit. I do not mean that there was no sense of democracy or some version of representation or popular and accountable governance. Those types of democracies died together with the death of the dominance of traditional societies. Just as the cultural, social, religious, and economic dominance of traditional societies has been compromised or decimated, so has its political order and democratic usefulness. Africa's internal journey was disrupted by the colonial episode. Its own resources that would have been responsible for inspiring its people to generate a heritage worthy of defending were replaced by alien and oppressive systems. Successors to these systems were incapable of inspiring anything beyond the rhetoric of the equality of black people and their right to total emancipation. The journey, then, from traditional Africa to modern Africa was interposed by disruption. This disruption was so deep that Africa was left with two options, to reinvent itself or to re-engineer its traditional roots. Neither option has been successful. The traditional roots, some have argued, are too remote for verification and usefulness. The attempt to re-engineer ourselves have been sporadic and incoherent at best. It has been informed by reactions to external forces. There has never been an intellectual culture or deep-seated belief committed to democracy. The public space, in Africa, is not seized with the same spirit as the one that seized enlightenment in Europe. The second is that Africa certainly needs a thoroughgoing reform, an internally generated and internally driven reform. A reform that aims at overhauling the entirety of Africa's dominant systems so that they can be replaced by new ones. However, what we need to engage with is what these new systems are going to be and how they are going to be of benefit to Africa. If there is a relationship between all resources in society (both intellectual and material) and that society's political inclination and practice, then we have to look carefully at what Africa's resources are and how they have a bearing on our current state (not just the political one).

Today's measurements of democracy are greatly tipped in favor of mature Western democracies. However, what is not recognized is that the type of democracy under discussion is an extension of a heritage of a particular people. That heritage has two sides to it. The first is the internal dynamic of their ability or privilege to determine their own history. That privilege includes being allowed to encounter their own historical facts in ways that are self-determined. The second is how the same people have been at the forefront of denying other people not only their humanity but the same freedom to be self-determining while engaging with their own internally generated historically factors. From slavery to colonialism, to neo-colonialism, Westerners have shown adeptness at destructive interference with non-Westerners' ways of living and thinking. This has taken various forms from direct control to sponsored destabilization. This is followed by pressure for the destabilized regions to fully democratize, by the same instigators of that destabilization. What obtains is how some regions are seen as democratic examples yet others are consigned to the bin of democratic disaster.

What must be reckoned with is that Africa has not been responsible for authoring some of these failures. In particular, Africa has not been responsible for how its right to authoring its history was violently abrogated (see Oliver and Atmore, (1967) 2007). Africa was also not responsible for the destruction of systems that were in place and neither was it responsible for the forcible imposition of alien systems that have failed to resonate with the reality dominating Africa. Africa is not responsible for the systematic dismantling of its viability. It would not be stretching it, if one was to arrive at the conclusion that Africa's being interfered with was not only meant to exploit it while benefitting Europe, but it was also meant to ensure that Africa would fail. Its failure was supposed to be registered on several fronts including, democracy, modernization, and self-determination. It is hardly surprising that Africa occupies the station it is currently at. Hence in the next section, I will seek to argue why Africa needs to prioritize development as a precursor to a stable democratic dispensation.

The Relevance of Development for Stable Politics

The idea of development is multi-faceted (see Rodney, 1972: 3; van Haften et al., 1997). It covers numerous aspects of human existence which at times have different bearings and meanings (see Ake, 1996: 8–9). There is no single definition of what development is, or at the very least there is no single definition that covers all aspects of development. However, this does not mean that we can never have a conceptual understanding of what we are referring to when we invoke the term development. For example J.C.A Agbakoba writes:

> A development theory establishes the basis and model of human aspiration based on human nature. This is commensurate with the goals of development. The goals include the notion of justice, security, basic needs—food, clothing, shelter—employment,

psychological needs such as self-esteem and other elements of self-realization. The factor that one can see underlying these aspirations is the principle of consistency taken as both transcendental and immanent.

(2005: 78)

In addition, Agbakoba holds that there is a dialectical relationship between material and non-material development in society.

What I find appealing in Agbakoba's view on development is his connection of the idea of development to satisfying a model of human aspirations which are founded on human nature. What this means is that human aspirations are not going to emerge from nowhere. They are going to emerge from something that we know about humans – what they are. Hence Agbakoba's assertion that the only way that aspirations can be satisfied is through knowledge, which is subdivided into technological and organizational knowledge.

The reason why I find Agbakoba's notion of development appealing is that it is human and knowledge centered. It seeks to satisfy specific things about humans. How this will be done will be through knowledge. Knowledge of three sorts; knowledge as we understand it in philosophy, knowledge about how things are set to be achieved, and knowledge of what tools to use to attain the envisaged development. All these types of knowledge have not been too prominent on the African continent. Knowledge, for example, as knowledge for knowledge's sake or as knowledge pursued to access truths about us or our nature has always been marginalized. Africa's claim to fame is collectivism that finds defense in notions such as communitarianism, defense of tradition or culture, and deference for the old (both ideas and people). Rigorous examination of propositions, refutation of proofs, and a search for new knowledge are not something that is routinely insisted on. Africa's approach to knowledge has steadfastly swung between two unhelpful extremes of conservatism and respect for authority. To make my case I will use the example of politics and philosophy. Politics has remained somewhat unable to transcend the restrictions of appeals to traditional resources. This is so true of the dominant but contrasting schools of political theory; democracy by consensus and African socialism. Their desire to make their starting point a justification of the authenticity and efficacy of the past, trivializes present concerns. It also diverts thinking away from the present as more and more intellectual resources are invested in purifying the past. With respect to philosophy, the continent's practitioners of this revered trade have seen it fit to spend more than a quarter of a century debating on whether such a discipline exists and if it does, in what form it does so. Philosophy's own contribution to Africans both materially and immaterially, is not significant. When it comes to organizational knowledge, Africa's chaotic public institutions are testimony to the continent's lack of appetite to engage with what it means to be organized, to have that knowledge of how things are run and how to run things efficiently. In respect of technological knowledge, not only has Africa lagged behind it has almost contributed nothing to the modern world's overwhelming technological advancement. It could be that we don't have knowledge of how to develop our own technologies or it could be that we are overwhelmed with what others have produced. Yet it is important that we develop such knowledge for our own development. If all these types of knowledge were to be pursued with vigor, for the benefit of humankind, Africa could begin to get somewhere. That somewhere, a place that is unknown but has continuously proven to be elusive to Africa, will not come through insistence on the importance of democratizing in the same fashion as the West has done. It will come through Africa's development.

Development, as a reference to pursuing human aspirations based on human nature aided by knowledge, will lead to a change in how things are done in Africa in respect of the humans who occupy this space. Humans in this space have suffered, for a long time, under oppressive regimes that do not care about responding to their aspirations. From colonial times to the present day, there has been an assortment of assaults on the basic dignity and progress of humanity. The question must be, what will development do? The answer is to be found in how we conceive development as capable of addressing the fundamentals of the problems Africa is faced with. While development can be taken as relevant in addressing developmental problems, I suggest that it can go beyond that by addressing political and human issues.

Since development is multi-faceted, one clear aspect where it has been lacking on the continent has been on harnessing knowledge to benefit the residents of this continent. Africa is not an ignorant place. We have people on this continent who are trained in all forms of Western systems of knowledge. Many African-born individuals have excelled in the major Western universities as professors, while others have made it to the top of their chosen careers. Africa has pockets of excellence that have succeeded in mimicking Western ways of doing things. To varying degrees, one can come across service provision, houses, and lifestyles that can compete or outdo their Western counterparts. Yet Africa's overall material development levels remain low with poverty widespread. What this shows, at least in my reading, is Africa's failure to systematize or tame Western modes for Africa's benefit. Some aspects of those modes of knowledge are even responsible for the denigration of Africans. The question then becomes what has Africa to do to develop itself. The answer is that Africa must be responsible for generating knowledge and systems that are best suited for Africa.

In the present context, there are two things that are lacking in Africa. Both these lacks have to do with how knowledge is utilized. The first is what we can transform about our material standing. In this respect, I do not refer to personal or private access to monetary benefits that lead to individuals enjoying materially comfortable lives. On the contrary, I refer to what is commonly known as the wealth of a nation. While our own economists refer to fancy economic measurements in replicated forms as they are used in the West, we neglect to come to terms with what it would take for us to create nations that are by definition considered wealthy. Why is it that none of the African countries are interested in becoming as wealthy as Switzerland? Why is it that none of our African countries are interested in becoming technologically advanced as Japan or as clean as Denmark or Sweden? The issue of Africa's failing has to do with the neglect of the people who occupy this place. There has been no investment in the welfare of the people. There is nothing being done to collectively ensure that there is mass upliftment of the people. Such upliftment would involve the development of systems of knowledge that account for what the people are – as Africans and humans – and what that upliftment would require (technologically and organizationally). It might be the case that we may not need to end up as wealthy as Switzerland or as clean as Denmark, but what cannot be denied is that the human condition in Africa is very dissatisfactory. It needs to be improved so that as many Africans as possible have access to clean water, nutritious food, decent shelter, working public services, and all sorts of material things that make life secure and enjoyable. Slums and run-down villages, outdated township houses, and derelict colonial city center building can no longer be the definition of Africa. We also need to overturn the image of Africa as only efficiently captured by starving children dressed in dirty clothes. To do that takes special bureaucratic knowledge that is capable of implementing plans and actions that are transformative in nature.

The second lack, which has driven Africa's current malaise, is a citizenry that is knowledgeable, empowered, interested, and civic enough to take long-term interests in the creation of a viable partnership between itself and political authority. There are various factors that work against citizens' intellectual empowerment. Material poverty has ensured that chances of a decent education that is meant to advantage children from their first year in school, are reduced to almost nil for the majority of citizens. Access to information is limited by a lack of access to objective and neutral portals whose sole aim is to inform and empower citizens. Citizens do not know what their standing is in relation to the state. They remain ignorant of their role as contributors to the making of a state that would be of service to them. The average citizen is deprived of knowledge about their civic status and entitlements. I am not referring to the glib demand of protection for one's rights or freedom from violations. Rather, what I refer to is a thoroughgoing understanding between the state and its citizens on what their project is. Further to this shared understanding must also be a clear understanding of what the respective parties' duties and privileges are in that project. What has led to the citizenry failing to be responsible knowers and participants of public life can be owed to a variety of factors but I will cite the most fundamental. While quite a vast majority of Africans are schooled people, they lack the awareness of what political citizenship is about. Many have mistaken political citizenship to be an equivalent to party political loyalty and activism. There should be a difference between one's understanding of their duties toward the public space and the politics thereof and her loyalty to some political ideas or beliefs she may have. Political citizenship, as I conceive it, is beyond partisan politics as it is the fundamental commitment that each citizen has to the creation of a state that is viable for its inhabitants. While there may be differences about what makes that state viable, there must be agreement that each citizen is obligated to respecting such a fundamental feature of citizenship. The second aspect that has contributed to citizens' failure to be responsible knowers and participants in the public sphere is how that public sphere has always been shaped and influenced by toxic machinations that seek to undermine the interests of the majority. Modern African politics is built on post-independence toxicity which was inherited from colonial toxicity. This toxicity is premised on the need to contain citizenship in order to oppress, control, and place them in a submissive posture. The post-colonial government has retained the same level of suspicion as the colonial government. At times the tyranny of the post-colonial government has been quite bad as it has even reversed a few benefits that were afforded "the natives".

Full human development will free humans and the spaces they occupy, including the political. As long as humans remain stunted in their development, both material and intellectual, the political space will also be stunted. There cannot be a political space that is fully developed yet its citizens/participants are stunted (with no knowledge and besieged by hunger). A developed political system is only generated and sustained by developed individuals.

What Needs To Be Done for Africa's Development

In this section, I outline what needs to be done for Africa to initiate its developmental project. The development I have in mind is modeled on Agbakoba's insistence on knowledge as the foundational framework. For my present purposes I shall limit my discussion to Agbakoba's idea that a "development theory establishes the basis and model of human aspiration based on human nature" (2005: 85). What this phrase implies, in respect of knowledge, is that there must be a firm understanding of human nature which will then inform us what the range of human aspirations could be. Knowledge of human nature is generalizable to all humans. Yet we could have reason to think of Africans as entitled to be exempted from this generalization. We could say either because of their history or because of their social circumstances, they deserve a distinct account of human nature. In African philosophy, this sort of commitment is evident in notions such as personhood and theorization on the foundations of African politics.

However, I think there is a lingering problem with such an approach. At the very least, there is one issue that assails African forms of knowledge, which have a direct impact on development. The issue has to do with the notion of African difference. This idea started with the curiosities of colonial-era anthropologists who were out to understand what made the African tick. It was extended by ethnophilosophers, socialists, and other cultural zealots who sought to defend some pure version of what it is to be African. While I admit that there are distinctions between and among different people, the African difference has not always been used to advance Africans. In most cases, it has been used as a defense of the purity of African heritage. Knowledge, under this approach, has been understood as a retrieval of African traditional resources to either inspire the present or guide us to a desirable future. However, I suggest, caution is necessary when attempting to articulate the African distinction. Such caution must be on how Africans see themselves in relation to their past. As Kwasi Wiredu once remarked, many years ago, for better or worse that past is gone. Maybe the question we should ask is what has also gone with that past. Maybe we should also allow ourselves to let certain things go with that past. While I am not opposed to retrieving one's past I think there are dangers when we think of the past in terms of the development I have in mind. One of those dangers has to do with the past's impotence in aiding us to achieve the sort of development we need. The Africa of today is an Africa that is part of the modern world (see Vaughan, 2006). As already stated that entry into the modern world was through the violence of colonial domination. What Africa needs to do is to reckon with the fact of modernity. Old knowledge systems are not going to be of much use in the current era. While it is possible to have knowledge of both eras, there is a further need of knowing how to integrate both sets of knowledge to either create a hybrid that works or jettison what has outlived its relevance. The problem with both systems of knowledge is that they evoke different commitments to the world. It is not easy to simply propose that there are possibilities of hybrids being formed. Such hybrids must be followed by commitments. Unfortunately, we cannot have a hybrid commitment. I think the conflict between the African systems of knowledge that are steeped in modernity and ones that are steeped in tradition, will always be a source of conflict. That conflict will extend itself to serious aspects of life such as identity and human purpose. Once these areas are characterized by conflicted commitments knowledge to organize will be severely hindered, as the conceptual commitments are not coherent.

The above problem may lead to further problems, particularly those that will affect organizational and technological knowledge. In order to forestall such problems, there is a need for Africa to commit itself to its future. Such a commitment involves both imagination and knowledge creation that will take Africa to recognizable development levels. When I refer to the imagination, I have in mind first an acknowledgment that the disruption to our past was so severe that it represented an effective death of the link between us and that past. Another necessary acknowledgment would be that we have not done very well in the project of modernity. All our public institutions and practices have failed to exhibit a modern ethos. On the contrary, these institutions and practices have demonstrated contradiction and confusion. The contradiction is sponsored by the contrasting loyalties they must show to both traditional and modern demands. The confusion arises from a fundamental misunderstanding of what public institutions are supposed to do in the modern era. The paralysis in public service seen in a decayed public building, unreliable medical services, and patchy government service, shows confusion about what the role of these entities in modern life should be. Their failure at their mandate, though, is a reflection of failure at modernity.

Imagination refers to thinking in creative ways, in the light of the above acknowledgments, how we can restore humanity in Africans beyond the refrains of disruption and Africa's own failings. It is to re-think and re-direct our humanity toward new knowledge about ourselves in the current environment. Such knowledge has to point to new beginnings which are reflective of all things we know. Such beginnings must sufficiently reflect a movement from commitment to unsustainable epistemologies to ones that we are able to take full responsibility for as people who are existing here and now. This taking of responsibility is indispensable to the creation of new forms of knowledge. Those new forms of knowledge, in turn, are indispensable to development.

Democracy and a Developed Africa

In this last section I will attempt to outline what democracy will do for a developed Africa, at least in the sense of development I sketched above. I think one of the basic errors committed by those interested in advancing democracy in Africa, has been to think that democracy is a forerunner to development. The suggestion has been that if Africa gets its democratic practices right, then all else will fall in place. I have attempted a different understanding. What I have sought to argue is that polities must reflect the thinking and commitments that their people take seriously. If polities do that, then they will be in service of the people by enabling the realization of aspirations. My argument proceeds from the view that democracy is a political value that was orchestrated by people for the purposes of meeting governance needs. Such needs may have other values that are both capable of being incorporated into the value of democracy or could stand alone as worthwhile. These values may include justice, equality, representation, freedom, accountability, honesty, etc.

The current state of affairs regarding the relationship between democracy and Africa is that democracy has become an ideal that has proven elusive for Africa. It may even be that it is actually a system that has been imposed on Africa while having no prospect of living up to that system. As an expression of political value, Africans appear to be willing to accept that they must democratize. They might even go on to claim that the fact that Africa is not democratic is not the fault of ordinary Africans but is due to the shenanigans of the political elite who are opposed to democracy for their personal benefit. However, I would choose to believe differently. Let us imagine that the whole of sub-Saharan Africa could fully democratize and be absolutely free like South Africa. Let us imagine that all constitutions would be modeled on the South African one, that all judiciaries would be free and courageous as the South African one, and that all elections would be free and fair to the extent that there would be no need for foreign/international observers. If all this was to be attained, in the same magical way that South Africa's democratic transformation and standing was attained, what benefit would this be to Africa?

I suggest that the answer to this question is to be found in South Africa's current reality. While the political transformation of 1994 from a racist pariah overseeing the criminal apartheid system to a full democratic system with the freest constitution in the world, was lauded as a political achievement that was just about it. While there was true democratic transformation a number of social and economic problems have locked South Africa into a less-than-desirable standing in many respects. I will enumerate a few of these less-than-charming areas. South Africa's division between those who have and those who do not have is extreme, if not the worst in the world. Expensive and world-class real estate overshadows shanty towns with little or no amenities. Rural communities remain largely impoverished and excluded from mainstream economic activity. Violent crime has become a permanent part of South African topography. This is coupled with unabated violence against children, women, and those who identify as lesbians. Unemployment has remained high and both uneducated and educated youths are generally gloomy about their prospects of finding meaningful work. Civil litigation and access to justice are prohibitively expensive effectively ruling out the indigent from accessing justice. While South Africa's infrastructure is the most developed on the continent, the country itself is far from being considered as developed or middle income. It is a country of divisions along all conceivable lines ranging from race to class to gender. It is also a first-world country to some citizens while it remains a third-world country to others. Even South African universities are divided along lines of formerly white and black universities, with the former regularly and proudly featuring in global university ranking lists while the latter is never mentioned on such lists.

I could go on describing the social and economic problems of South Africa as well as the reasons for them. However, I think the point I am attempting to make can be appreciated. The imposition of democracy on South Africa did not benefit South Africa in other areas. As a society, it has remained divided largely on the same lines as it was during apartheid. This mismatch between democratic gains and social and economic realities demonstrates how democracy is not the answer to Africa's problems. What if we were to invert the South African reality and imagine things differently? Let us imagine that an average African country did not choose to pursue democracy exclusively. It chose to pursue development. It started development in its capital by doing basic things such as cleaning streets, repairing buildings, getting government services back on track, and eliminating corruption. The result could be different from the South African case. It could be that such a country after a while will have a democratic system that is well appreciated by all its citizens, one they are intellectually responsible for and connected to. It could also be the case that the democratic system itself will find resonance with social and economic conditions which would push the country into a developmental standing that is meaningful for all citizens. Some have argued that this is what will eventually unfold with Rwanda, yet others have reservations about such a possibility.

Whatever the final outcome of Rwanda and South Africa in respect of the problems and opportunities they are presented with, respectively, I am certain of one thing. Democracy will not thrive in places that are economically and socially broken. If it thrives in such places it will be an artificial existence and practice of democracy for its own sake. Such existence and practice would not benefit anyone except minimalist satisfaction of democratic demands and accompanying bragging rights. However, we have to ask what good is it for people to live in a flourishing democracy when some of the citizens have no work, no decent accommodation, and access to amenities, and they experience living in their country in vastly different ways.

If Africa's development was to be in tandem with its democratic growth we would see an increased appreciation of democracy's true meaning and operations. There would be respect for the defense of democracy by all social players. Rules of engagement and disengagement would be slowly formulated and agreed on over long periods or over generations. This is how I envisage this to work out. In the beginning, there would be not much of shared values or aspirations on social, economic, and political fronts. However, as people pursue common goals of development, they also begin to desire to protect the gains they have made. They soon realize that the only way to protect their developmental gains is by invoking the political to protect and oversee their aspirations. Aspirations will never be generated by political systems, they will only be protected by those systems after humans have decided that those aspirations are worthy of protection. Once that decision is made, then the same humans will seek to implement systems that protect their aspirations in ways that make sense to them.

Democracy, then becomes a crucial supporter of the social and economic conditions that are either beginning to emerge or that have already been established by the people. In order for the people to move from a loose association of individuals, probably with shared aspirations, to full citizens, they need to have common desires about the protection of their individuated desires. The existence of a desire to protect their desires will ultimately lead to the creation of an order that is capable of fulfilling any range of desires that people have committed themselves to. Democracy is an engineered guardian that people create and volunteer themselves into and are willing to protect, in the hope it protects them. Expecting democracy to work in places where avaricious attitudes and shameless search for opportunities to fulfill such attitudes have become dominant, which is Africa's reality with its political elite and its long line of hangers-on and enablers, is hopeless. Democracy, on its own, will never cure the ills, divisions, and poor attitudes of any given society. A society's own internal convictions and commitments will drive democracy.

If Africa were to develop and when Africa was to develop, democracy might have a natural fit with such a developed Africa. This will not be because a developed Africa will be in line with democratic demands. Rather, it would be due to people being responsible for developing desires that they think are worth the invocation of democracy. It is then that democracy's usefulness would be patent. It could also be the case that Africans will eventually develop a system that is not quite democratic albeit functional. Such a system may just as well, following Agbakoba, be in line with human nature and the desires they so express.

Conclusion

My aim has been to argue that democracy will not take root in Africa since it is an imposition that does not rhyme with stated aspirations. I have sought to present a view that takes development to be a necessary precondition for democracy. Unlike the old insistence on the necessity of democracy as a precondition for Africa to develop, I have sought to show that a developed Africa is likely to be receptive to democratic values. Its desire for democracy will not be based on the attraction of democracy for developed places but it will be based on the necessity of democracy as an effective regulatory political principle for places where development's interests demand to be protected. Without development, the citizens and their concomitant public institutions are caught up in a vicious cycle of dysfunction and confusion about their purpose. Democracy, by its nature, is not well-suited to manage such a space and its citizenry. My conviction is that as much as development is incremental so will be the democratic appeal on the African continent.

References

Adebajo, A. 2010. *The Curse of Berlin: Africa after the Cold War.* Scottsville: UKZN Press.

Agbakoba, J.C.A. 2005. Theoretical Considerations on the Impact of Worldviews on Development. *Journal of Philosophy and Culture*, 2(2): 76–86.

Ake, C. 1996. *Democracy and Development in Africa.* Washington: The Brookings Institute.

Kebede, M. 1999. Africa's Quest for a Philosophy of Decolonization. *Philosophy Faculty Publications*, 32. https://ecommons.udayton.edu/phl_fac_pub/32

Keita, L. 2011. Philosophy and Development: On the Problematic African Development – A Diachronic Analysis. https://codesria.org/IMG/pdf/7-3.pdf

Oliver, R. and Atmore, A. (1967) 2007. *Africa since 1800*. Cambridge: Cambridge University Press.

Popper, K.R. 1994. *The Myth of the Framework: In defence of science and rationality*. New York: Routledge.

Rawls, J. 1993. *Political Liberalism*. New York: Columbia University Press.

Rodney, W. 1972. *How Europe Underdeveloped Africa*. Nairobi: East Africa Educational Publishers Ltd.

Strauss, L. and Cropsey, J. (eds). (1963) 1987. *History of Political Philosophy*. Chicago: The University of Chicago Press.

Van Haften, W. et al. (eds). 1997. *Philosophy of Development: Reconstructing the Foundations of Human Development and Education*, vol 8. Springer, Dordtrecht. doi: 10.1007/978–94-015–8782-2

Vaughan, M. 2006. Africa and the Birth of the Modern World. *Transactions of the Royal Historical Society*, 16: 143–162.

17

PLURALISM AND SOCIAL COHESION

Nancy Oppongwaa Myles

Introduction

The topic of pluralism and social cohesion is an important one in Africa's political experience given the incontestable fact of her multi-ethnic, multinational, multi-lingual and multi-cultural constitution on the one hand (Hino et al), and her claimed largely communitarian orientation on the other (Senghor 49, 93–94; Mbiti 141). Though the attempt has been made by some thinkers to defend a moderate kind of communitarianism (Gyekye; Ikuenobe; Majeed), African communitarianism overall is hardly contested (Famakinwa; Matolino).

Notwithstanding the claimed African communitarian posture and a consequent higher degree of cohesiveness at the ethnic-group level, there is a need for emphasis on the value of state-level social cohesion even in the face of a pronounced ethnic diversity and the intricacies of African socio-political systems for accelerated growth and development outcomes (Easterly et al). Colonialism and the post-colonial political experiences of the African peoples further fuel the argument for a return to a socially cohesive tradition that, it is argued, has been undermined considerably by the advent of the forcibly forged states of Africa today (Wiredu and Oladipo).

But how should one understand pluralism, especially from an African perspective? Is pluralism antithetical to the pursuit of state-level cohesion? Should the search for social cohesion imply homogeneity? Should the presence of many diverse persuasions undermine a sense of a common bond? This chapter engages these questions as it pertains to the African context and offers a perspective on the extent to which we can shape political imagination today, given global political realities and the specific context of experiences in the African continent and diaspora.

Ethnicity and Pluralism in the African State

It is an indisputable fact that many states around the globe today are ethnically and culturally heterogeneous. The African state is no exception. Not only is the idea of a racially pure and culturally homogeneous society counterfactual to Africa and its states now, the pursuit of the same in the name of ethnic cleansing or genocide is now generally rejected (Serageldin).

DOI: 10.4324/9781003143529-20

Yet, accepting and promoting pluralism, in the normative sense of the term not merely descriptive, has become difficult to implement because of the nagging and resilient problems it unleashes for the African state given its striking diversity. Nigeria, for instance, is a notoriously plural society whose mix includes "Yoruba, Hausa/Fulani, Ibo, Ijaw, Tiv, Idoma, Nupe, Urobo, Birom, Ibibio, Efik, Anang, Ebira, Ekiti and a lot more, that space will not allow to mention" (Ajayi et al). The constituent ethnic groupings are at best classified as a "medley" because they may "mix" but they do not "mingle" in significant respects for, "it is not hard to notice that each ethnic group holds its own culture, language and religion, its own values, ideas and patterns of human relations" (Ibid). According to David et al (1), "today less than a third of South Africans often or always talk or socialize with someone from a different racial group". The perception of people who live in a society in terms of perceived or actual inequalities, the degree of societal trust and the extent of persons' attachment to their national identity, undeniably affect the level of social cohesion of that society (Langer et al).

The foregoing points up a phenomenon for Africa generally that cannot be ignored or overstated which is that the peoples' sense of identity, even if logically deficient (Appiah) or historically questionable (Myles, "Multiculturalism"), is firmly tied to the sub-national groups which they believe they *naturally* hail from and therefore share kinship ties primarily with. The observation of Herder should be germane here:

> A nation is as *natural* a plant as a family only with more branches. Nothing therefore is more manifestly contrary to the purpose of political government than the unnatural enlargement of states, the wild mixing of various races and nationalities under one scepter; ... such states are but patched up contraptions, fragile machines, for they are wholly devoid of inner life (Herder 324, emphasis mine).

For some tribes such as the Nuer of East Africa, kin was so important in all authority, rights and obligations such that fictive inventions of blood relation were made where people would treat even their guest-friends as family, to the extent that women counted as men where necessary (Evans-Pritchard 180–9). By this thinking, many contemporary African states already would not hold the claimed natural ties that make for a genuine nation-state. The *sense* of natural belonging is what is nurtured into a system of shared foundational beliefs and values based on which members understand themselves and interpret their experiences. The psychological and emotional connection that the member feels toward her ethnic, cultural or language group, the sensitivity and extreme interest in the integrity of the group, the commitment to protect, sustain and seek to preserve the same emanates from this thinking. Mbiti perhaps captures this well in his famous summation: "I am because we are and since we are therefore, I am" (Mbiti 141).

Thinking of themselves as sharing a common ancestry, language, history and culture gives rise to a more pronounced ethos of cohesion, solidarity, fellow-feeling, mutual recognition, loyalty and most importantly a sense of belonging together in a way that non-members do not, even in the face of intra-ethnic disputes which would not be infrequent anyway. Allusions to such intra-ethnic tensions can be seen in Wiredu's view of "agreed actions without agreed notions", both in principle and in practice, in his discussion of the culture of consensus pursuit as a key element in decision-making in traditional Akan social and political dealings (Wiredu, "Democracy"; Ani). Busia's observation reinforces this allusion when he writes,

> When a council, each member of which was the representative of a lineage, met to discuss matters affecting the whole community, it had *always* to grapple with the problem

of reconciling sectional and common interests. In order to do this, the members had to talk things over: they had to listen to all the different points of view. So strong was the value of solidarity that the chief aim of the councilors was to reach unanimity, and they talked till this was achieved (Busia 28, emphasis added).

The sense of belonging together is not easily watered down by distance, forced integration through power-play such as colonial rule, war and conquest, or economic or political migration. The common aims, aspirations and goals engendered by the sense of belonging together further drives members' concern for the well-being of the group and the interest in the flourishing of its members, institutions and norms. Thus, it is commonplace for the African to express their nationality in terms of the ethnic group Fante or Ibo rather than Ghanaian or Nigerian, respectively.

It should also be stressed that Africa is a continent with a very high linguistic diversity estimated at 1250–2100 official and spoken native languages, not to mention the dialects which are not always mutually understandable (Heine and Nurse). If it is correct that "... wherever a separate language is found there a separate nation exists..." (Fichte 215) and "the essence of nationality lies in language" (Mises 12), then African communitarianism and the consequent sub-national social cohesion referred to would be prominent and near-impossible to extirpate. Sharing a common language then would constitute, to a large extent, the context of social identity and induce interdependence and ethnic consciousness which draws members further closer together and serves as a basis for unity.

It is worth mentioning here and now that persons may live together geographically and even share the goods that may emanate from their mutual engagements but that would not in itself guarantee an attachment to, and a responsibility toward the flourishing of that shared life. That is, sharing a common geographical location would not necessarily guarantee the *sense of belonging* together underscored by the African's notion of ethnic membership discussed so far. It would be far from correct to think that Ghanaians, for instance, can be created from the colonialist-imposed boundaries of demarcation that created a territory called Ghana. The recent Western Togoland Secessionist uproar in Ghana should give credence to the case being made so far (Ker-Lindsay). Rather, it would have to be the *sense* of belonging together which derives chiefly from attachment to common aims, aspirations and goals, and the claimed common biological ties that members believe they share regardless of their physical location. In the words of Etzioni (127):

first, a web of affect-laden relationships among a group of individuals, relationships that often crisscross and reinforce one another, and second, a measure of commitment to a set of shared values, norms and meanings, and a shared history and identity – in short, to a particular culture.

Thus, one would find copious expressions of ethnic allegiance and loyalty from Ghanaian maxims such as these: *"okyeman, yen nhwe mma nennsei"* (we will not sit aloof and watch the Akyem *nation* be destroyed) and *"obi pe adee ako Kotoko a, yenni no aboro"* (you do not frustrate the one seeking to bring something good to Kotoko (Asante nation)). The Ndebele of Zimbabwe also maintain, "The king is the people. To respect the king is to respect oneself. He who despises our king despises us. He who praises our king praises us. The king is us" (Sithole 96–97). Such expressions of ethnic allegiance and attachment can only be disregarded at the peril of the larger multi-ethnic state. For, ensuring social justice, participation and inclusion, curbing corrupt leadership, mitigating the corrosive force of extreme inequality and circumventing the path of ethnic-driven warfare as the only means of redress at the state level would all be better addressed by an informed admission of the African people's ethnic ties and the implications thereof. Where members relate to the larger state as an insensitive and distant other who wields unjustified coercive force of control and exploitation, the outcome is a subversion of all that is perceived to be connected to the state (Ihonvbere). It is instructive to note how the label *aban adwuma* (government work), reminiscent of the colonial times, still informs the perception and approach to work in state institutions (Gyekye 128, 256).

The pertinent and most basic question for such a context, therefore, is how to weld, forge or solder the various constituent parts of Africa's states into a collective whole, though not one (Allen), to create what has been called a metanationality from the several constituent sub-nationalities (Gyekye). In other words, the concern is how to de-emphasize ethnic and racial identities and transfer those attachments and allegiances to the larger metanational state, Ghana for instance, to engender a sense of metanational identity, culture, belonging and consequently increased social cohesion also at the metanational level. In responding to this daunting question, one suggestion is

> since most of the less developed states contain a number of nations, and since the transfer of primary allegiance from these nations to the state is generally considered the *sine qua non* of successful integration, the true goal for such contexts is not 'nation-building' but rather 'nation-destroying' (Connor, "Nation-building" 336; *Ethnonationalism* 42). Others would, however, focus on how Africa can use her striking ethnic diversity rather as a strength to drive growth and development of the continent instead of as roots of discord and instability.
>
> *(Hino et al; Ajayi et al 938)*

However, in the urge to forcibly create a unity from diversity, the tendency has been to generate disaffection and a charade of seeming unity at the cost of denied identities and unhealed wounds (Momoh). The Ewe and Nzema of Ghana, for instance, have been forcibly separated from their ethnic groups of Togo and Cote D'Ivoire respectively by the crack of the overlord's whip during the false partitioning of Africa. The same is the case with the Hausa of Nigeria who has been coercively separated by a thin line of the colonialist from other members of their ethnic group. The dire consequences of such imposition are still felt today. There is a need for a reconceptualization of the post-colonial African state even if the option to forge a metanational *whole* seems the most viable way to go.

The African State as an Encorporated "Self" and Its Interests

A general view of the state which has gained currency in contemporary political thought is one that presents it as a form of political association (Kukathas, "A definition"), to which the constituent people(s) belong, owe allegiance and obedience and regard as embodying their collective will, or acting for their common good through institutional agents empowered to do so by its citizens. The underlying assumption for this thinking is that states so empowered are capable and well-advised to serve, and actually do serve, the interests of their populations even when they are found beyond the state's boundaries in certain contexts.

Understanding the state in such terms cannot mean a mere collectivity of persons or groups of persons but something more. In the view of Creveld (52–58), the state emerged because of the supposed shortcomings of the many forms of political organization that existed before it such as clans, tribes and dynasties and their chiefs, lords and kings respectively. The literature of contemporary political theory thus recognizes the state as a *corporate* entity: a unified "self" different in significant respects from those forms of political association that preceded it in Africa, for instance.

The state today is conceived as a corporate entity, a legal person, with its own interests and a capacity not only to act "as *if* it were a real, flesh-and-blood, living" being, but can also be held responsible for its actions and inactions (Creveld 1). As a legal person, unlike a people or a public, self-preservation and survival is fundamental to its being. It is seen as an entity able to hold property, have rights and duties, powers and liabilities that belong to itself and not to any of the actual persons who comprise it, nor are these rights and duties reducible to these constituent persons. This is so even though as a corporation; it cannot exist without the concrete persons who constitute it. Creveld argues that the modern state's property, raised by levying of taxes, imposition of tariffs and the like, cannot be said to belong to any of the actual persons who exercise authority in the name of the corporate entity. So, even though the state as an *abstract* corporate entity can neither be seen, heard nor touched, it owns accrued property that it cannot use on itself but only has a sole responsibility of redistributing among its agents through whom it exercises power and among others whom it chooses to favor out of obligation.

The state as a single abstract sovereign entity, for contractarians like Hobbes, is necessary to preserve order, peace and stability in the face of challenges to peace posed by, among other things, other political associations he describes as in the "state of war". But a single abstract sovereign entity need not be *necessary* to serving peace and order. Besides the fact that the state, such conceived, sometimes acts in ways that rather destructs the peace and order of its indigenous populations, there is ample evidence to the effect that peace and order prevailed in societies that had no unified state apparatus (Creveld 1; Obioma) prior to the state.

Not only has order existed without the state such conceived, but Hobbes' postulation of a voluntary agreement to transfer power to a sovereign corporate agent in a Hobbesian "state of war" social context could not be possible if the "state of war" per his own argument could not allow the making or keeping of agreements (Kukathas, "A definition" 363). But since Hobbes' own argument suggests that it is possible to make and keep agreements even in what he calls the "state of war" prior to the social contract with the state, then a non-unitary government system should be conceivable, viable and effective to the maintenance of peace and order especially in the context of a plurality of nation-communities such as prevails in post-colonial Africa.

On the contractarian's assumption that the state as a corporate unitary entity is formed to enhance humans' natural freedom, women's for example, by making it possible for us to be subject not to others but to ourselves through the laws we legislate for ourselves as embodied in what has been labeled the general will, there is a fundamental objection. An identifiable challenge is that if subjects have different competing and conflicting interests and some can prevail only at the expense of others, then the claimed freedom served by the state would only be an illusion for some because at least some subjects' interests would be subordinated to that of others. The deciding factor(s) in most instances would favor the one(s) who holds the reins of power. Lamenting the Nigerian situation, Ajayi et al writes:

> The state of bondage in which we find ourselves in Nigeria is not imposed by nature but by man. It is however, the natural impulse of men to seek for freedom, an impulse unacceptable to the beneficiaries of the unjust status quo. It is a fact that the benefactors who make peaceful change impossible will also make violent changes inevitable, thus

the alienation, subjugation and obvious marginalization suffered by the other ethnic nationalities in the hands of the ruling ethnic group and their military allies, led to agitation and the fight for self-determination.

(Ajayi et al. 936)

The corporate state then might only serve interests of persons who have managed to capture it for their own purposes. If this concern has any merits, then the claim that the corporate state is *necessary* for serving freedom to its subjects and curtailing imbalance in status, class, ethnic groups, among others, in a better way than the political associations preceding it, may also not be wholly plausible after all. It may rather be a tool used by some agents to deprive at least some subjects under its corporation of the very freedom it claims to enhance. This seems largely so for post-colonial Africa where most of its states are not self-evolved by their subjects but have been *forcibly created*, and their systems and institutions imposed on the peoples only to meet the set ends of the inventors of those states.

Yet, arguing from the unquestioned assumption that the imposed state offers cultural, economic, political and ethical advantage over the forms of political associations that preceded it, the *in*corporation of persons or nation-groups into the larger single *corporate* state has become the dominant concern and preoccupation of contemporary political thought generally. As such, arguments aimed at correcting the injustices of colonialism and the consequent empires created rather inadvertently end up actually offering a justification for them (Kymlicka). This complaint is legitimate if advocates rather argue for a suppression of local and particular nationalities and identities to ensure the integrity of the created states or colonies by appealing to the same considerations that motivated colony and empire builders. The undesirable consequences of a blind defense of a unitary state are not far to see in multinational and multicultural Africa where most of the created post-colonial states to a large degree can be, in the words of Herder, said to be patched up contraptions or fragile machines which are wholly devoid of inner life (324.).

The point of concern for these contexts is that little to no attention is given to the palpable incongruence that arises between the interests of the imposed single sovereign abstract entity and its varied and disparate populations. The consequences of such disregard have been detrimental, especially in the various instances where the project has been *en*corporation and not simply *in*corporation of persons or groups into the corporate state. The difference between the two challenges, as I see it, is that whereas *in*corporation entails one thing including or *becoming* a part of the other, *en*corporation depicts the forceful *bringing into existence* of a wholly new condition or thing. The quest to incorporate constituent sub*nations* in Africa as a whole is itself a herculean one given the extent of diversity. That process should be gradual and non-coerced not imposed and abrupt. But to seek to *create* states by a crack of the whip is one main source of distrust in the relationship between the people(s) and the ruling agents of post-colonial African states. This undermines the people's sense of ownership of governance and that needs to be confronted more directly. For, the argument for the being of the *en*corporated states bears significant resemblance with that of empire and therefore, to the extent that the case for empire creation is questionable, so and even more is the case in defense of state as an *en*corporation.

The point of critical importance for this chapter is that the creation of both state and empire in these contexts involved the forcible suppression, absorption or destruction of already functioning societies and their *self*-evolved systems of law, institutions of learning and forms of civil life. These forms of life, for most of post-colonial Africa, have been disrupted and replaced by new structures of the colonialist state that in most cases sit uneasily with the indigenous traditions which hardly comprehend them (Abudu). This state of affairs already undermines trust and the people-centeredness expected to undergird democracy in principle and practice. The thought that the state and its imperial rule foster economic growth in its colonies is, at best, overstated. The entire colonial apparatus in Africa, it has been argued, was rather engineered to grow imperialist economies after three centuries of plundering that continent (Lauer and Anyidoho). To claim that imperial states civilized hitherto savage, barbaric or unsophisticated societies is only "a substantial alibi which accompanied the equally squalid lie that" (Lauer and Anyidoho 1037) there was the need to carry the art of government to the "inferior" races of distant lands. If one considers the bloodiness of wars of resistance waged by indigenous populations and the history of subjugation of local elites and populations, one is likely to be unconvinced that an imposed unitary state established peace and freedom.

Toward Genuine Self-Rule in the Encorporated State of Africa

Subjects of many post-colonial states, in Africa especially, are still grappling with the challenge of addressing the colonial legacy of *encorporated* states and how to treat constituent nation-groups in such already pluralist societies. Advocates of multiculturalism acknowledge the need to recognize the claims of minorities for recognition by, or protection from, society in such states (Kymlicka; Kukathas, "Multiculturalism"). Most of the debates about multiculturalism in political philosophy are thus focused on the extent to which such claims should be accepted, and how far recognition should be extended. Kymlicka, in an important distinction he draws between groups' claims for *external protections* and their claims for *internal restrictions*, helps draw out the central issue in the multiculturalism debate. The advocacy is that in dealing with the claims of minority cultural groups of the encorporated colonial states, the state should protect groups from undesirable interferences from outside society by ensuring that they have the means for cultural survival, but not by tolerating any group's efforts to control or restrict the freedom and equality of its members.

A fundamental problem identifiable with such a conception however is that, for all the concern for the well-being of the sub-groups it champions, the theory is grounded in a commitment to the interests of the corporate *abstract* unitary entity called state. Such a commitment, I seek to suggest, makes it difficult to pursue or sustain any *genuinely* pluralistic social organization, purportedly advocated for, since the test of every measure is whether it harms – or fails to enhance – the interests of the supposed neutral entity called the state.

As earlier argued, the contemporary state, in sum, seems to be a created "unitary space that enacts a single system of social interaction, or society", and which requires that every type of social transaction pass through its organs (Cavanaugh 30). The African state today has evolved to the point of subsuming and absorbing every aspect of society under its single authority since contemporary political thought takes it for granted that it has the right

> to a monopoly of all the force within the community, to make war, to make peace, to conscript life, to tax, to establish and dis-establish property, to define crime, to punish disobedience, to control education, to supervise the family, to regulate personal habits, and to censor opinions.

(Cavanaugh 28)

The problem with the creation of such a unitary structure, however, is that it makes diversity or deep pluralism near-impossible. For, the limits of diversity – ethnic, cultural, religious or ethical – is set by the need to preserve the integrity of the state as a single ethical and political unit and, therefore, the diversity of constituent nation-groups, especially the minority, may be recognized and regarded as worthy of consideration yet cannot be given any independent weight because there is no space for such perspectives.

To further defend the point I make, a unitary state cannot be limited since there would be no forces to compete with it. As the people develop a direct relationship with the state their reliance on other forms of association diminishes and those associations, and all it means to their *being,* wither away. On the other hand, to the extent that those associations resist the centralizing and absorptive tendencies of state life, they incur the hostility of the state, which cannot by its nature tolerate the threat that pluralism poses to its existence. This seems to be the point of the pluralists who maintained that a limited state could only exist "where social space was complexly refracted into a network of associations, that is, where associations were not 'intermediate associations,' squeezed between state and individual, at all" (Cavanaugh 32). If diversity or pluralism then is seen as a threat to the survival of the unitary state as argued, then the only options available to the state, as conceived, are either eliminating non-conforming/dissenting groups or absorbing them by regulating and *transforming* them into components of the whole. It is important to understand that the negative effects of such transformative oppression do not affect only social institutions but also impact negatively on individual psychologies.

This tendency was noticed early by Rousseau who understood that the survival of the state depended on its *creation* of *citizens* – persons whose first loyalty was to it – not *men*. For, as actual men rather than citizens, Rousseau understood that persons could not be ruled even by themselves since there would be so many different people, with their own inclinations and tendencies, shared with clusters of others. To be subjects of the abstract entity then, citizens had to be *forged* from actual concrete human persons who are already constituted by both individual *and* communal relations.

The point of the foregoing then is that democracy fails at its core if it *uncritically* admits of a rule by an entity called the state which *the* governed people, do not consider to be constitutive of their "self" and thus, unable to meet the fundamental requirement of "self-rule". In other words, democracy as "self-rule" is greatly undermined if it is rather focused on the preservation of the state as a sovereign force even where its rule and interests do not coincide with that of the people supposed to be living under its sovereignty. The notion of we-the-people embedded in the concept of democracy would be lost. The argument for this chapter therefore is to defend a conception of statehood in post-colonial Africa that takes seriously and reconciles, as much as possible, the various ramifications of self-rule in practice for, it is only in this that democracy in Africa would be democratic and consequently effective and viable.

Reconceptualizing Statehood in Africa for a Meaningful Social Cohesion

The problems outlined in the preceding sections call for a rethinking of the current political order which is chiefly focused on how to maintain the integrity of the state as it is now. African democracies would have to be constructed in the light of persons who are at once members of ethnic groups *and* also citizens of the metanational state both of which are in constant dialogue and perpetuating flux and whose members would consider themselves as a collective "we" even in the face of the various shades of diversity. This is contrary to the rule by an imposed entity whose subjects do not consider themselves to be part of its collective "self". Oshagae's conviction clarifies the point:

> ... a federal union is a *voluntary* union and that the Nigerian federation as it presently exists is an anomaly because the various groups have not been allowed to decide whether they want to continue to belong to it or not since the British "forced" them into union in 1914.
>
> *(343, my emphasis)*

The viability of African democracies lies in taking the concept seriously as what it is: a self-rule evolved by the constituent *persons* themselves, who are a complex blend of individuality *and* communality (Myles, "The Individual"), out of their interactions, experiences and shared meanings, for their own flourishing *simpliciter*.

Accordingly, any rule that aims at social cohesion would have to put on the democracy tag understood as self-rule. A democratic society must center on "the people" as the ruled but also as the ruler. But who "the people" refers to is the fundamental notion that is often distorted, misplaced or misunderstood. Conceiving of democracy as "the-people-centered" does imply that not only would the people own, possess or wield the power of self-determination or self-sovereignty but more importantly, that they would, and should, administer, regulate, control and execute the actual exercise of this power. The people would have to make decisions concerning the affairs of the state, nation, polity or group toward their own well-being. Such decision-making would have to be based on principles, guidelines, codes, systems and formulations that should be born, not imposed, of the hopes and aspirations of the people, and/or borrowed, adapted and adopted, fashioned, nurtured, refined and shaped by their goals, values and ideals, to reflect their wishes, desires and expectations (Gyekye). Without such involvement of the people in the making of the governing rules and governance itself, their intellectual and psychological sense of proprietorship would be immensely undermined and that would in turn affect their interest in, and commitment to, the course of the collective in pursuit of its own ends. Thus, a state, nation or any collective qualifies to be named a democracy not merely by attributions or claims of ownership of political power, but more importantly, by the degree of actual expression of the constituent people's will, involvement, participation and inclusion in self-governance; in how much of a say or control members actually have and are able to contribute to decisions concerning their rule of themselves toward their own set aims and aspirations even if through representation.

Yet, paradoxically, not attaining a full grasp of the notion of people-centeredness and its concrete realization is one main underlying reason for most of the discontents undermining social cohesion at the metanational level in Africa. First, in the context where a well-defined, unambiguous collective "we" has been established the almost insurmountable hurdle of achieving true representation and its concomitant challenge of ensuring all-inclusiveness and participation pertains. But second, more crucial, and often overlooked, is the context where the discontent stems from members' non-attachment to, or non-identification with, the state, nation or polity in question because that collective is forcibly composed or amalgamated into a "we". When membership is compelled, democracy as "*we* the people" is greatly undermined and rendered unfruitful. Dahl (Ch. 12) notes cultural diversity, among others, as a potential threat to modern democracies and advocates for some level of homogeneity as necessary for effective democratic decision-making.

There is therefore the need to confront this concern seriously; to take another look at the current artificially created multinational states and re-think of governance in two ways: the choice, on the one hand, of seeking to protect the integrity of such an artificial metanational state, even if that would be tantamount to a perpetuation of an already unjust situation, by consciously eliminating members' allegiance from constituent nations to favor dominant constituent nations where possible. This might mean creating *citizens*, not human persons with natural social attachments, who are molded along a single model individual, according to Rousseau (cited in Canovan); citizens whose loyalty would compulsorily have to be directed by the state to itself, being an artificial entity, through the creation of a "unitary space that enacts a single system of social interaction, or society" (Cavanaugh 30) just to ensure its own continuous survival.

On the other hand, it is still open for choice a rejection of the perpetuation of what is no less an injustice entailed in contemporary political discourse which solely aims at how to build a more stable and just state, only by subordinating and unifying the disparate nations within its territory and absorbing the rights and responsibilities of the plurality of these social groups (Cavanaugh 26). The latter option advocates for granting true liberation to persons who have collectively suffered an abrupt suppression or destruction of their already functioning societies. Any attempt at reparation would, therefore, call for a de-statization outlook of governance at all levels to correct their damaged, transformed or obliterated forms of life and sense of identity which underscores the natural sociality of all human persons, and which fosters respect for the freedoms and rights of the person. The argument in the foregoing need not mean a total breakdown of state structures. The point being made is that emphasizing membership in constituent nations is rather a better means to creating and strengthening a "self-evolved" multinational state that the members of constituent nations can identify with and most importantly *own*.

It should be stated that these options may hold in varied forms for many post-colonized compelled states of Africa. While some states like Ghana and Botswana have continually worked at responding to the colonial heritage differently, Ghana continues to have its fair share of the inherent challenge of that regime. Botswana may be hailed as Africa's best democracy in recent times since it has successfully held multi-party elections since independence in 1966. However, Botswana's relatively smaller population size is largely ethnically homogeneous compared to the several multinational and tribal constituents of a large part of colonized Africa. This means it will not be a good example of the *compelled* states inherited from colonialism which is under scrutiny. The peculiar circumstances of Botswana perhaps make its democracy yet to be tested by a strong opposition since a single party, evolved by *the people* from their traditions of chieftaincy, has ruled since the colonial regime ended. Botswana's first post-colonial president Seretse Khama, grandson of Khama III the Good, only succeeded his father to the chiefship of his people at a tender age. His own son Ian Khama also became president of Botswana in 2008 after Seretse Khama's successive terms (Encyclopedia Britannica). One may therefore exercise reservation in attributing the positive story of Botswana since independence to a successful development of the Western colonial model by its "decent leaders". It would rather seem more defensible to argue that the people's homogeneity, coupled with their sense of belonging with the rulers, and their *adaptation* of the imposed system of rule may be better reasons for the hailed successes of Botswana.

However, the demand these challenges make on its adherents is a re-think of democracy as a work in progress, conducted by *the people* –a defined collective at any point in time whose constituents identify themselves as such–to whom this work affects and thus requires constant attention toward restructure and re-form by *the people* as and when the social and political demands of the said peoples emerge. To be concise, it is the central role that any collective peoples must play in self-determination that is to be fully appreciated, defended, instituted and pursued for that system to be properly labeled as a democracy and thus to attract the allegiance and loyalty of the owners of that rule to foster social cohesion even amid disparate plurality.

Conclusion

The paper introduced the topic of pluralism and social cohesion as an important one in Africa's political experience given the incontestable fact of multiplicity of language, ethnic groups, cultures, and nations and the largely communitarian posture of Africa against the background of a conceptually devastating history of extensive colonialism.

It has been maintained that there is a need for emphasis on social cohesion at the state level just as pertains to a higher degree at the ethnic-group and other sub-group levels to promote accelerated development and progress for such a context especially. It goes without saying that a cohesive society would be instrumental in bridging the perceived or actual gaps arising from social and economic inequalities, whether vertical or horizontal, which would in turn aid the building of quality, inclusive and effective public and private institutions (Easterly et al; Anda et al). A sufficient social cohesion fosters cooperation, solidarity and trust across the various group boundaries that are not uncommon to the African context given its composition and history. Pursing the "glue" that binds society together is thus crucial to the very human well-being of the persons that constitute the society and reason to consider social cohesion as an important political virtue in itself besides its valuable contribution to accelerated development and progress.

However, it has been stressed that a socially cohesive society would not be achieved by a strike of an overlord's whip to forcibly align human persons, who are constituted by natural sociality and a consequent sense of belonging, fictive or actual, to an abstract authority called the state which they may not feel a sense of attachment, allegiance or loyalty to because of past and present injustice.

In response to the diagnosed African situation, the chapter calls for a rethinking of the current political order which is chiefly focused on maintaining the integrity of such imposed states indiscriminately. The proposed view is that the state's rule, like that of any social or political organization, would be a genuine "self-rule" and therefore a legitimate democracy only if the effort is exerted into attracting allegiance and loyalty of constituent members to voluntarily *own* its rule. Such a posture is better able to foster genuine social cohesion at the state level even amid avid plurality.

Works Cited

Abudu, Assibi. "Salvaging Ghana's Surreal Democratic Process." *Reclaiming the Human Sciences and Humanities through African Perspectives Vol. II*, edited by Helen Lauer and Kofi Anyidoho, Sub-Saharan Publishers, 2012, pp. 1044–1054.

Allen, Danielle. *Talking to Strangers: Anxieties of Citizenship since Brown v. Board of Education.* The University of Chicago Press, 2004.

Ajayi, Johnson Olusegun, and Bernard Owumi. "Ethnic Pluralism and Internal Cohesion in Nigeria." *International Journal of Development and Sustainability*, vol. 2, no. 2, 2013, pp. 926–940.

Ani, Emmanuel. "On Agreed Actions without Agreed Notions." *South African Journal of Philosophy*, vol. 33, no. 3, 2014, pp. 311–320. doi:10.1080/02580136.2014.931750.

Appiah, Kwame. *In my Father's House: Africa in the Philosophy of Culture.* Oxford University Press, 1992.

Busia, Kofi. *Africa in Search of Democracy.* Praeger, 1967.

Canovan, Margaret. "Arendt, Rousseau, and Human Plurality in Politics." *The Journal of Politics*, vol. 45, no. 2, 1983, pp. 286–302. www.jstor.org/stable/2130127.

Cavanaugh, William. *Migrations of the Holy: God, State, and the Political Meaning of the Church.* Wm. B. Eerdmans Publishing Co, 2011.

Connor, Walker. "Nation-Building or Nation-Destroying?" *World Politics,* vol. 24, no. 3, 1972, pp. 319–355. doi:10.2307/2009753.

Connor, Walker. *Ethnonationalism: The Quest for Understanding.* Princeton University Press, 1994.

Creveld, Martin van. *The Rise and Decline of the State.* Cambridge University Press, 1999, doi:10.1017/CBO9780511497599.002.

Dahl, Robert. *On Democracy.* Yale University Press, 1998.

David, Anda, et al. "Social Cohesion and Inequality in South Africa." *SALDRU Working Paper Number219,* 2018. www.opensaldru.uct.ac.za/bitstream/handle/11090/900/201821 9_Saldruwp.pdf?sequence=1.

Easterly William, Joseph Ritzan, and Micheal Woolcock. "Social Cohesion, Institutions, and Growth." *Economics and Politics,* vol. 18, no. 2, 2006, pp. 103–120. doi:10.1111/j.1468-0343.2006.0016.x.

Encyclopedia Britannica. www.britannica.com/biography/Seretse-Khama (Accessed August 16, 2022).

Etzioni, Amitai. *The New Golden Rule: Community and Morality in a Democratic Society.* Basic Books, 1996.

Evans-Pritchard, Edward Evans. *Kinship and Marriage among the Nuer.* Oxford Clarendon Press, 1951.

Famakinwa, Olanipekun. "Moderate Is Kwame Gyekye's Moderate Communitarianism?" *Thought and Practice,* vol. 2, no. 2, 2010, pp. 65–77. ajol.info/index.php/tp/index.

Fichte, Johann. *Addresses to the German Nation.* Translated by Reginald Foy Jones and George Henry Turnbull. Greenwood Press, 1979.

Gyekye, Kwame. *Tradition and Modernity: Philosophical Reflections on the African Experience.* Oxford University Press, 1997.

Heine Bernd, and Derek Nurse, editors. *African Languages: An Introduction.* Cambridge University Press, 2000.

Herder, Gottfried. "Ideas for a Philosophy of History." *Herder's Social and Political Thought: From Enlightenment to Nationalism,* edited by Frederick Barnard, Oxford University Press, 1965, p. 324.

Hiroyuki Hino et al., editors. *From Divided Pasts to Cohesive Futures: Reflections on Africa.* Cambridge University Press, 2019.

Ihonvbere, Julius. "The Nigerian State as Obstacle to Federalism: Towards a New Constitutional Compact for Democratic Politics." *Federalism in Africa: The Imperative of Democratic Development,* edited (Vol 2.) by Aaron Tsado Gana and Samuel Egwu, African Centre for Democratic Governance. AWP, 2003, pp. 187–211.

Ikuenobe, Polycarp. "Matolino's Misunderstanding of Menkiti's African Moral View of the Person and Community." *South African Journal of Philosophy,* vol. 36, no. 4, 2017, pp. 553–567. doi:10.1080/02580136.2017.1387994.

Ker-Lindsay, James. *Western Togoland: Ghana's Ewe Independent Movement.* 23rd October, 2020. youtu.be/HGrHFjN2y1M.

Kukathas, Chandran. "Multiculturalism." *The Routledge Companion to Social and Political Philosophy,* edited by Gerald Gaus and Fred D'Agostino, Routledge, 2013, pp. 505–516.

Kukathas, Chandran. "A Definition of the State." *University of Queensland Law Journal,* vol. 332, no. 2, 2014, pp. 357–366. ink.library.smu.edu.sg/sossresearch/2917.

Kymlicka, Will. *Multicultural Citizenship: A Liberal Theory of Minority Rights.* Oxford University Press, 1995.

Langer, Arnim, et al. "Conceptualizing and Measuring Social Cohesion in Africa: Towards a Perceptions-Based Index." *Social Indicators Research,* vol. 131, 2017, pp. 321–343. doi:10.1007/s11205-016-1250-4.

Lauer, Helen and Kofi Anyidoho, editors. *Reclaiming the Human Sciences and Humanities through African Perspectives Vol II.* Sub-Saharan Publishers, 2012.

Majeed, Hasskei M. "Moderate Communitarianism Is Different: A Response to J. Famakinwa and B. Matolino." *Journal of Philosophy and Culture,* vol. 6, no.1, 2018, pp. 3–15. doi:10.5897/JPC2018.0019.

Matolino, Bernard. "Radicals versus Moderates: A Critique of Gyekye's Moderate \Communitarianism." *South African Journal of Philosophy,* vol. 28, no. 2, 2009, pp. 160–170. doi:10.4314/sajpem.v28i2.46674.

Mbiti, John. *African Religions and Philosophy.* Anchor Books, 1970.

Mises, Ludwig Von. *Nation, State, and Economy: Contributions to the Politics and History of our Time.* Translated by Leland Bennett Yeager, New York University, 1983.

Molefe, Motsamai. "A Defence of Moderate Communitarianism: A Place of Rights in African Oral-Political Thought." *Phronimon,* vol. 18, no.1, 2017, pp. 181–203. doi:10.25159/2413-3086/2668.

Momoh, Abubakar. "Civil Society and the Politics of Federalism in Nigeria." *Federalism in Africa: The Imperative of Democratic Development,* edited (Vol 2.) by Aaron Tsado Gana and Samuel Egwu. African Centre for Democratic Governance. AWP, 2003, pp. 163–186.

Myles, Nancy O. "Multiculturalism and the Notion of Cultural Identity." *University of Ghana Readers: A Celebration of Philosophy & Classics,* edited by Kofi Ackah et al., 1st ed., Ayebia Clarke Publishing Limited, 2013, pp. 147–164.

Myles, Nancy O. "'The Individual' in the Individualism-Communitarianism Debate: In Defence of Personism." *Legon Journal of the Humanities,* vol. 29, no. 2, 2018, pp. 242–264. doi:10.4314/ljh.v29i2.9.

Obioma, Chigozie. "Africa Has been Failed by Westernization. It Must Cast off Its Subservience." *The Guardian,* 12th November 2017, www.theguardian.com/commentisfree/2017/nov/12/africa-failed-by-westernisation-must-cast-off-its-subservience.

Osaghae, Eghosa. "Structural Adjustment and Ethnicity in Nigeria", *Research Report No 98*, Nordiska Afrikainstitutet, 1995. www.files.ethz.ch/isn/97898/98.pdf.

Serageldin, Ismail. Lecture. "The Making of Social Justice: Pluralism, Cohesion and Social Participation." *Ninth Annual Nelson Mandela Lecture,* Johannesburg, 23rd July, 2011.

Senghor, Leopold. *On African Socialism.* Translated by Mercer Cook, Praeger, 1964.

Sithole, Ndabaninigi. *African Nationalism.* Oxford University Press, 1959.

Wiredu, Kwasi. "Democracy and Consensus in African Traditional Politics: A Plea for a Non-party Polity. " *The Centennial Review,* vol. 39, no. 1, 1995, pp. 53–64. www.jstor.org/stable/23739547.

Wiredu, Kwasi and Olusegun Oladipo. *Conceptual Decolonization in African Philosophy: Four Essays.* Hope Publications, 1995.

18

DEMOCRACY AND DEVELOPMENT

Philip Adah Idachaba and Anthony I. Okpanachi

Introduction

Is the move towards democracy in African countries an indication that political outcome will be aligned with the desired economic outcome? Does the embrace of democracy guarantee development? These are the questions that are of concern in this chapter. The need to examine these questions again has become quite pressing and important due to some of the recent events in Africa. From August 2020 to January 2022, no less than seven (7) military coup d'états have been executed in six African countries. There is even a palpable fear of coup contagion in the continent. More worrying in these coups is that it is democratically constituted governments were ousted from power. A common motivating factor for the military interventions, as alluded to by the coup plotters, is the inability of these democratically constituted governments to demonstrate competence in good governance in order to guarantee security and economic prosperity for the people. Thus, we have the case of democratically constituted governments unable to guarantee development. In a place like Guinea, there were news reports of widespread jubilations among the people, and they praised the soldiers as saviours. This sudden surge of 'democratic recession' or 'coup epidemic,' which results from the failure of democratic regimes to guarantee development, demands that we take a critical look at the question of democracy and development in Africa.

More impetus for critically taking this look draws from the fact that the events mentioned above seem to be a contrast to the initial impression that gave motivation to the drive for democracy in Africa. Some of the policy documents about the development situation in Africa following the end of the Cold War give these impressions. In February 1990, a meeting of various groups representing non-governmental grass-root associations, United Nations Agencies and governments converged on Arusha, Tanzania. The meeting was convened under the auspices of the United Nations Economic Commission for Africa (UNECA) and it resulted in the *African Charter for Popular Participation in Development and Transformation*. The charter observed that the absence of democracy is the primary cause of deep crises in Africa (UNECA, 1990, 17ff). At the 26th summit of the Organisation for African Unity (OAU) in Addis Ababa, a declaration titled *The Political and Socio-Economic Situation of Africa and the Fundamental Changes Taking Place in the World* was adopted by the OAU. The declaration acknowledged that a political environment that guarantees human rights and the rule of law

DOI: 10.4324/9781003143529-21

would be more conducive to accountability and probity than the present environment and that "popular based political processes would ensure the involvement of all...in development efforts" (OAU, 1990, para 10). These impressions have not proven to be quite correct given the widespread underdevelopment in Africa, despite the spike in democracy.

The exploration of this question of democracy and development in available literatures have followed two basic trends. The one challenges the operationalisation of democracy in Africa, insisting that there are elements of democracy in traditional Africa. Thus, Africa's development consists in looking back and retrieving these traditional democratic elements for implementation in contemporary practice. The other insists that democracy has never been allowed to take roots in Africa. For this group, what is required is that democracy should be allowed to take proper roots. Only then can there be development in Africa. Both positions have their limitations, and the goal of this chapter is to find a middle ground between these positions, which balances out the shortfalls of the perspectives. To accomplish this mission, we explore, in some detail, the arguments from both sides as evident in the literature. In doing this, attention will also be given to highlighting the weakness of each. The final proposal for this chapter is that rather than returning to tradition or completely aligning with modernity, with regard to democracy and development, what is required is a hybrid. To construct the hybrid system we propose, arguments are drawn from the proposals by Ali Mazrui and Joseph Agbakoba.

Understanding and Contextualising Democracy and Development

There are two perspectives regarding the understanding and contextualising of democracy and development. The first perspective focuses on the historical trajectory of democracy. The second view revolves around the tangible outcome of democratic practice in terms of public good, human flourishing and well-being. Although we will examine both perspectives, our major focus will be on discussing how African political theorists understand the role of democratic practice in relation to public good, human flourishing and well-being on the African continent in the postcolonial era. Our discussion of the perspective that focuses on how democracy developed on the continent will unfold as an effort to contextualise the practice of democracy in Africa. This will serve as a groundwork for considering the various perspective regarding the capacity of democracy to guarantee public good and human flourishing on the continent. Before we proceed with these substantive tasks, it is important to indicate how we use the main concepts implicated in our discussion, namely, democracy and development.

In terms of its conceptual origin, democracy is a combination of the Greek words, *demos* meaning 'common people' and *kratos* meaning 'rule.' Thus, democracy means the rule of commoners. While this definition of democracy is clear enough, problem arises at the level of the operationalisation of the rule of the people (Osabu-kle, 2008, 2). How is the rule of the people to be understood in concrete terms? Given the size of societies and states today, even though direct rule was possible at some time, such a rule is no longer feasible today. The large size of societies today makes it necessary that a few be selected to oversee decision-making for all. This is the perspective of J. S. Mill (2009). Commenting on this perspective from Mill, W. A. Lewis avers that democracy has two meanings: its primary meaning is that all those who are affected by a decision should have the chance to participate in making that decision. Its secondary meaning is that the will of the majority shall prevail (Lewis, 1965, 64). By this understanding, democracy as the rule of the people is the arrangement of government such that everyone affected by a decision participates in it and the position of the majority prevails. As a result, party politics, elections and voting have crystallised as the most popular way of realising majority rule or operationalising it.

The current fascination for democracy has not always been the case. As far back as the time of Plato, democracy was considered as the rule of the 'mob' (Plato, 1997, 1156). In the case of Aristotle, it was a perverted form of constitutional government. That is, a constitutional government which is an ideal form of government is what deteriorates into a democracy (Aristotle, 1991, 130ff). Through the Middle Ages, given the influence of religion on the affairs of men, the political disposition was largely that of the divine right of kings (Figgis, 1914). The current fascination for democracy is therefore the outcome of historical factors. One of such factors is the rise of liberalism. Due to the emphasis, it places on individual autonomy, it is considered the forerunner of recent western democracy (Njoku, 2002, 169). Scholars like C. B. Macpherson argue the politics of competition brought in the bourgeois sense of freedom in which the society not only forced people to be free but also compelled them to adopt self-chosen market behaviour (Macpherson, 1965, 6–8). The commercial society let in by the bourgeoisie needed a responsive politics which was pursued at the exclusion of the electorate. As the electorate demanded a voice and wanted to be included, democracy came to be added to the competitive market economy (Macpherson, 1965, 6–8; Moore, 1966). This explains why democracy subsists today.

Development is another concept that is of concern to this essay. Although there are many definitions of the concept, in simple terms, development can be understood as a type of change. This type of change is positive and it is not haphazard or accidental. It is rather a purposeful, goal-oriented change that presupposes a knowledge of the ends to which the change aspires. Beyond this knowledge of ends, the change demands choices about value. This means that some values need to be upheld in the process of accomplishing the kind of change development represents. About human beings, the end of this kind of change is self-realisation. Thus, development can be understood as the "process by which human beings seek the maximum realisation of themselves" (Agbakoba, 2019, 56). It is a positive and progressive transformation of capacities and capabilities and the freedoms thereof. This is a sense of development as positive freedom which is central to Armatya Sen's idea of development as freedom. This idea of development as self-realisation through positive freedom has universal and particular dimensions. The values, orientations, attitudes, ideas, practices and objects necessary for the self-realisation of individuals across the globe are its universal dimension. The modification and adaptation of these universal dimensions to suit particular geographical and/or sociocultural contexts refers to the particular dimensions of development.

From all the foregoing, development can be understood as the positive freedom we need for self-determination and self-realisation. The centrality of positive freedom in this regard has to do with the fact that freedom is both an end and a means for accomplishing development. By this definition, there are two levels to the understanding of development. The first is the imagination that development is about the satisfaction of basic needs like a dignified existence free of hunger, unemployment, and disease. Secondly, and more importantly, development is framed in terms of deliberate efforts at fulfilling political imperatives such as freedom of the individual, equal and fair treatment before the law and freedom from being victimised by the state (Matolino, 2018, xii). At the first level of the understanding of development, authoritarian states can also accomplish development. But at the second level of development, only democratic social arrangements can be said to have the requisite disposition to accomplish the task of development. It is reasonable to conjecture that it will be almost impossible for a state which allows for the liberties at the second level of the understanding of development to be unable to guarantee the first level of development. This is what makes democracy a worthwhile arrangement for society to pursue. It has the double advantage of meeting development at both the first and second levels. Authoritarian arrangements are most likely only to meet development at the first level. This level of interconnection between democracy and development is what will be the core of our discussion in this chapter.

From the Rhetoric of Self-Governance to the Grammar of Development in Africa

Post-development scholars have emphasise that the problematisation of poverty, most especially in colonial spaces, was a result of the contact between such places and ethno-European modernity. It is within a modernity-inspired understanding of life that poverty becomes a problem. They claim that addressing the problem refers to efforts at development (Rahnema, 1991; Escobar, 1995; Willis, 2005). Thus, the discourse of development becomes the focus of scholarly and governance attention only at a certain point in time. Against this background, colonialism in Africa can be seen as an attempt at developing Africa in line with a modernity-inspired conception of the world. Throughout the experience of the domination of colonialism, Africa's reaction was couched in the rhetoric of self-governance. In this rhetoric, emphasis was on expelling the colonisers so that Africans can govern themselves. It was in the aftermath of colonialism that the grammar of development was born.

The emergence of postcolonial Africa is primarily a result of effort of independence movements across the continent. These movements ensured the end of colonial rule and accomplishment of self-governance for many African states. Despite the success of nationalist movements, it was obvious from the beginning of independence that power and not development was the driving force for the nationalist movements. The quest for power engenders a number of negative sentiments among the African people. Putting this point rather succinctly, Claude Ake notes that "besieged by a multitude of hostile forces that their authoritarianism and exploitative practices had engendered, those in power were so involved in the struggle for survival that they could not address the problem of development. Nor could they abandon it" (Ake, 2001, 7). Even though the idea of development was already vaguely implicit in the ideology of nationalist movements, the full adoption of the grammar of development (ideology of development) was based on the fact that the rhetoric of self-governance had run its course. Something was needed to replace it.

The argument is that to eradicate the humiliation of colonisation, Africa needed to catch up. Catching up meant developing. As it eventually turned out, the popularity of the grammar of development amongst African leaders shortly after independence "was not so much an ideology of development as a strategy of power that merely capitalised on the objective need for development" (Ake, 2001, 9). The implication of this is that African leaders, in their quest to sustain themselves in power, made every effort to show that they were offering development, since colonial rule was no longer an issue. Some theorists have argued that post-independence leaders continued with the same strategies with which they ended colonialism in the quest for development. But the strategies required to accomplish the task of ending colonisation were completely different from that required for accomplishing development (Ayetti, 2005). Consequently, Ake argues that "the ideology of development itself became a problem for development because of the conflict between its manifest and latent functions" (Ake, 2001, 9). It was while Africa was embroiled in the crisis of development that the wave of democracy hit the continent.

Between Democracy and Development in Africa

The discourse on the causal relationship between democracy and development has been very broad in comparative politics and political philosophy. One of the main perspectives advanced is that economic development is what determines the level of democracy and also sustains democratic institutions within a state (Lipset, 1959; Almond, 1991; Przeworski and Limongi, 1997). This view is challenged by the fact that there are nations that enjoy economic property without having in place established democratic institutions. Samuel Huntington explains this in his description of an indirect evolution from economic development to democracy using the instance of Latin American states (Huntington, 1968). A second perspective stress that development does not lead to democracy, the argument being that authoritarian counties like China employ 'the breaking of strategic coordination' as a means of avoiding democratisation (Mesquita and Down, 2005). A third perspective is that democracy guarantees development. For this school of thought, democracy and democratic institutions are key prerequisites for development (Leblang, 1996; Brown and Hunter, 1999; Zweifel and Navia, 2000; Siegle, Weinstein, Halperin, 2004). The fourth view is that democracy does not matter in development. Although, politics influences the economy, regime type does not have any role in accomplishing development (Przeworski, Alvarez, Cheibub, Limongi, 2000). As a result of this diversity of opinions on the question of the causal relationship between democracy and development, Liang-Chih Evan Chen argues that this is an inconclusive controversy (Chen, 2007, 31).

From an African standpoint, the opinions articulated in these arguments lead to the consensus that there is a form of relationship between democracy and development. Although the nature of this relationship is unclear, one can emphasise that there is such a connection. To this end, Yakubu Ochefu argues that "… from our definition of democracy and development, it is clear that both are inexorably linked. Development is primarily an economic concept and is operationalised at the level of society by political systems such as democracy" (Ochefu, 2007, 26). Furthermore, Larry Diamond avers that, "Africa cannot develop without democracy, and democracy in Africa ultimately cannot be sustained without development" (Diamond, 2005). These positions suggest that the possibility of accomplishing development in Africa is linked to democracy and the survival of democracy in Africa has to do with the perpetuation of development in Africa.

Challenging the Operationalisation of Democracy in Africa

Despite the position above regarding democracy and development in Africa, there are still perspectives that challenge the operationalisation of majoritarian democracy in Africa. The operationalisation of democracy is mostly through party politics. In this system, political parties put forth candidates in an electoral contest for power. The candidate with the highest number of votes becomes the representative of both the party and people. In postcolonial Africa, there are positions that challenge this mode of operationalising democracy, insisting that this approach has impeded the project of development rather than contribute to its realisation. The propensity towards one-part rule in Africa is anchored on this sentiment.

Specifically, "one valid point which was made again and again by one-party persuaders is that there is no necessary connection between democracy and multiparty system" (Kasanda, 2015, 46). In fact, for Julius Nyerere, political parties in Africa have a different source of motivation when compared to political parties in Europe and America. Quigley quoting Nyerere submits that political parties in Europe and America

> came into being as the result of existing social and economic divisions - the second party being formed to challenge the monopoly of political power by some aristocratic or capitalist group. Our own parties had a very different origin. They were not formed to challenge any ruling group of our own people; they were formed to challenge the *foreigners* who ruled over us. They were not, therefore, political "parties" i.e., factions but nationalist movements. And from the outset they represented the interests and aspirations of the whole nation.
>
> *(Quigley, 1991, 616)*

Because of this difference in motivation, party politics in Africa need to be one-party system.

Kwasi Wiredu's advocacy for a non-party politics in Africa represents a new chapter in the challenge to the operationalisation of democracy in Africa. Wiredu insists that democratic elements exist in African cultures in the form of consensus where people gathered under trees to talk in villages until they agree. The aim of this negotiation is "reconciliation rather than the mere abstention from further recriminations or collisions" (Wiredu, 1995, 53). This reconciliation is possible because "ultimately the interests of all members of society are the same, although their immediate perceptions of those interests may be different" (Wiredu, 1995, 57). In this kind of consensus democracy where there are no political parties, representation is not just formal but substantive. It is substantive in the sense that representatives are directly loyal to their constituents because there are no political parties to mediate the loyalty of the representative to constituents.

For Wiredu, multiparty democracy is adversarial and breeds unhealthy struggles. Non-party democracy does not suffer from this deficiency. Taking this line of thought a step further, Joe Teffo makes the case that there is democracy in traditional Africa. In substantiating his view he highlights the fact that in traditional Africa a king is born not elected and his powers are regulated by a group of elders in council. Thus, the king cannot make pronouncements that are not in alignment with the decision of elders in council. The elders in council deliberate to agree and not so that the winner takes it all. The fact that the king is checked by the elders in council and these elders always deliberate to arrive at a consensus shows a deeper sense of democracy which is way above the merits of majority rule and could be a viable democratic option for Africa (Teffo, 2004, 443–448).

Extolling further the positive aspects of consensus politics in Africa, Edward Wamala introduces the demographic component to highlight the uniqueness of democracy in the African context. In his opinion, democracy emerged in Africa, just like in the Greek polis, because the size of the population allows for the full participation of the citizens. For the Ganda people of Uganda, before the development of monarchical socio-political structures, society was constituted by independent patrilineal totemic tribes headed by *Omutaka*. *Omutaka*, as the head of the clan, presided over a cultural hierarchy in which the different descending segments were headed by *Bataka* (clan leaders) of descending social ranks. The monarchical system emerged in Buganda when the more powerful *Bataka* outcompeted the weaker ones in the struggle for power with the more powerful ones becoming *Ssabataka* (leader of clan leaders). The weaker ones remained in their original *Bataka* position. This was the foundation for centralisation of power in the Ganda state.

The *Ssabataka* was also head of the religious activities of the clan. While the *Ssabatak* seeks to expand his power over the *Bataka*, it sometimes created friction which makes some *Bataka* to break away and form another settlement. To avoid strained relationships, the *Ssabataka* incorporates democratic principles in the exercise of power. This is to enable them to avoid any form of legitimation crisis. The key democratic element in this context is consensus. The *Bataka, Ssabataka* and the people rely on a constant quest for consensus in their political interactions. Once party politics is introduced into this kind of system, it usurps the direct interaction between the people and the clan leaders. Besides, political parties are usually desperate for power in a manner that was unimaginable in traditional societies. Wamala identifies the rule of personality in the traditional context and this means that the monarch knows his subjects individually and works with them as persons. The introduction of the party system of politics adversely affects this system of personal rule as well (Wamala, 2004, 435–441).

These perspectives on consensus have been criticised from many angles. Arguments have also been advanced to show why it is flawed to imagine one-party politics as the solution to current African predicament (Nyongo,' 1992, 90–96). The agitations against and eventual collapse of the one-party system of politics is considered as a proof that the system is unviable. The non-party system proposed by Kwasi Wierdu has been scrutinised from various angles. But what is of interest for this essay is T. Carlos-Jacques' classification of Wiredu's understanding of non-party politics as a type of one-party system. That there was really no difference between Wiredu's non-party proposal and the one-party politics that was already in practice in parts of Africa (Jacques, 2012, 1017ff). In response to Jacques, Helen Lauer argues that Wiredu was quite clear in his efforts at drawing the lines between his propositions about a non-party polity and the widely practiced one-party polity in Africa (Lauer, 2012, 41–59). The most prominent critic of Wiredu's proposal of non-party democracy was Emmanuel Chukwudi. The case Eze made against Wiredu's proposal is that the interest of all human beings cannot be the same. The only point when interest could be completely identical is when no one in a society is able to "develop an *individuated* structure of *desire* – the absolute guarantee against (inclination to, or suspicion of) greed and (infliction of, or fear of) domination" (Eze, 1997, 313–323). This situation is practically impossible in human societies. It underscores the difficulty in practically accomplishing the reconciliation which Wiredu thinks consensus can bring.

Although Bernard Matolino insists that T. Carlos-Jacques' reasons for claiming that Wiredu's non-party politics is same as one-party are not cogent, he still maintains that there is good reason to take Jacques' critique seriously. For Matolino, a close reading of Wiredu's idea of Party$_1$, Party$_2$, Party$_3$ and Party$_{1.3}$, shows that such an understanding of party is not tenable and that by those categories a non-party polity is not different from a one-party polity (Matolino, 2016, 101–106). Matolino argues about Walama's case for consensus that consensus could be a form of majoritarianism as against what its advocates will have us believe. Particularly, within the context of the relationship of friction, Matolino (2016, 103) proposes that:

> When the tension had reached a point of no return, the single *mutaka*, who, together with his people, were in disagreement with the *Ssabataka* were ultimately left with no option but to remove themselves from the *Ssabataka's* rule and land. What this shows is that there was a certain consensus which was acceptable to further the inherent communocratic nature of consensus societies and those who refused to abide by this consensus were only left with one option: leave. This may give credence to those who suspect that consensus is nothing more than a ruse of majoritarianism in another form.

Matolino is convinced that "what is needed is not so much a spelling out of the traditional scaffolding of consensus, as we see in Teffo and Wamala, but an attentive demonstration of how these scaffoldings will work as transformed modern scaffolding and what modern institutions it will subsequently develop and argue for" (Matolino, 2018, 188).

Besides the arguments articulated by Matolino and Carlos, the positions of Teffo and Wamala still require further scrutiny. Predominantly, kings are born not elected in the African context. Teffo was quite correct on this. However, he wrongly proceeds from this position to justify the democratic credentials of the African experience. His process of thought is wrong in this case because, although elements of democracy can be deciphered from traditional African governance, evidence from precolonial Africa suggests that governance was largely autocratic. Precisely, the fact that a king is born not elected implies that the people do not have any direct influence on the constitution of kingly powers. Consequently, they cannot make legitimate claims as to how the power of the king is exercised. Even the council of elders that is referred to as checks to the powers of the king in traditional society, at best, only plays advisory roles. A clearer picture of power constitution in the African context and checks on it is properly construed when attention is focused on the metaphysical basis of power. In traditional African society, political power and authority derive from possession and control of the vital force of a political unit. This is a spiritual force that can exhibit its influence on both physical and no-physical nature (Agbakoba, 2004, 143). Power is therefore guaranteed by metaphysical abilities. In many African societies, the process of the appointment, coronation and installation of a king eventually transforms such a king into a deity. This means that the person who exercises kingly power becomes of one nature with the power: a metaphysical being. Within such context and following the African flow of hierarchy of beings, which holds that the vital force of influence resides in the superior being and not the inferior, the king cannot offend his subjects, only his subjects can offend him. Given the enormous power bestowed on the king, his power can only be regulated by: (i) the taboos attached to the office and (ii) fear of incurring the wrath of the patron deity or spirits that protect and oversee the welfare of the group (Agbakoba, 2004, 144). It is only by this means that there could be checks on kingly powers. Thus, whether the political system is a hereditary or non-hereditary monarchy or even partially a democracy, the authoritarian principle is present, and the power of the king is only divinely limited. The implication is that kings cannot act arbitrarily because it is incumbent upon them to maintain a kind of cosmic and spiritual balance in their territories (Agbakoba, 2004, 147). About this point, Eze is quite correct to argue that Wiredu's idea of consensus democracy "might need further evidence to make a successful case that the king and chiefs actually ruled, and believed, along with their subjects, that authority could be legitimised on through the secular virtue of persuasiveness of ideas" (Eze, 1997, 313–323). Eze's suggestion amounts to a claim that efforts at demonstrating that Africa had a form of democracy miss the point about the nature of political power in this context.

The understanding of the rule of personality as presented by Wamala does not reflect a complete picture of the practice in the African context. We see this in the fact that vitalism is very important in the African ontological outlook. Vital force is what drives change in things and what a thing is depends on its vital force. A thing is essentially the forces and power it displays. This leads to the idea of voluntarism in African traditional thought. Voluntarism in human beings stresses the role of self-preservation in this world and the perfection of the self in the struggle for dominion as the highest good. This is the basis for the kind of personality that tends to personalise all social relations and enforces a rule of the personality as against the rule of law. In the rule of such personality, there is an aversion to the realisation of social relations based on formal structures and the rules that spell out rights and duties which are supposed to be operated as objectively and impersonally as possible (Agbakoba, 2010, 8). This understanding of the rule of personality aligns more with the reality in African political contexts than its overly simplistic presentation in Wamala's works. Understood in this way, the rule of personality explains the excesses of power in the precolonial setting, which have continued to hold sway even in postcolonial times.

Democracy as Conducive to Development in Africa

Despite the arguments about how democracy has adversely affected development in Africa, there is still some general disposition to accept that democracy is largely conducive to development in Africa. One of the most popular efforts to demonstrate this can be found in Claude Ake's *Democracy and Development in Africa*. Although a Political Scientist, Ake's intuitions have huge philosophical implications that warrant close attention. Ake argues that even with the forays the newly industrialised countries (NICs) from Asia are making despite being anti-democratic, there is a tendency to cast aside the democratic credentials of this anti-democratic regimes. For him, the NICs have incorporated qualities like accountability, transparency, predictability, rule of law and competition. These are 'redeeming features' that made the *Asian Miracle* possible. This goes to show that democratic ideals are part of a genuine effort at development. How have these two played out in Africa?

Ake's answer begins with the observation that "it is not so much that development has failed as that it was never really on the agenda in the first place" (Ake, 2001, 1). This means that the African experience is not that of a failure of development, but developing Africa has never been the focus right from colonisation even to the postcolonial experience. He argues that the nature of colonialism in Africa was antithetical to any form of development on the continent. In the postcolonial period, "gaining of independence was not a matter of nationalists marshalling forces to defeat colonial regimes. More often than not, it was a matter of the colonisers accepting the inevitable and orchestrating a handover of government to their chosen African successors, successors who could be trusted to share their values and be attentive to their interests" (Ake, 2001, 4).

Since postcolonial leaders were selected based on the level of alignment with the ideals of the erstwhile colonisers, the implication was that they did not have development on their agenda. They saw development as a rhetoric to retain power. Even when efforts were made to develop by African leaders, such efforts were often at variance with the agenda of the metropolitan sponsors of powerholders. This led to what Ake calls "a confusion of agendas" (Ake, 2001, 18–41). Despite this confusion, the effort of African leaders with regard to development could at best be termed "improbable strategies" (Ake, 2001, 42–97). Beyond the inefficiency of the effort of African leaders in the quest for development, there is the issue of "the development by underdevelopment by the agents of development" (Ake, 2001, 114). This points to the marginalisation of Africa in world economic affairs, which explains why Africa now occupies a marginal position with regard to the rest of the world. This is as a result of deliberate marginalisation of Africa.

To accelerate development in Africa, Ake outlines what he calls *a residual option* as an appropriate paradigm to accomplish development in Africa. This option is residual because it begins from what is left after separating out the confusions, irrelevancies, frills and distortions that stand in the way of strategising development in Africa. It is a paradigm and not a blueprint or action plan because it is about "the logic, values, principles and general path of movement for development in Africa." It is more of a "theoretical structure of experience whose practical operation will vary depending on historic circumstance of each country" (Ake, 2001, 124). Ake's residual option is a kind of political philosophy for African emancipation. After separating out the confusions, irrelevancies, frills and distortions that stand in the way of development in Africa, what is left, Ake thinks, is the energy of ordinary people.

The kind of democracy that will guarantee development for Africa is one which is powered by the energies of these ordinary people. It is a kind of democracy in which the people are not only just voting, but one in which ordinary people have real decision-making power. Such a democracy emphasises concrete political, social and economic rights, as opposed to abstract individual rights. It emphasises collective rights as it does with individual rights. It is a democracy of incorporation. He calls it 'participatory social democracy.' The sense of participation here is unique because it is linked to communality. He argues that "people participate not because they are individuals whose interest are different, and need to be asserted, but because that are part of an interconnected whole" (Ake, 1993, 243). The form of democracy that is motivated by this level of participation ensures the development that makes ordinary people its agents, means and end. Using the power of decision-making acquired from participatory social democracy, people will be able to determine how development can unfold.

One of the obvious pitfalls of Ake's discourse on democracy and development is that he is not very clear on how social participatory democracy can be achieved. At some point, Ake suggests that accomplishing this democracy

> could mean, for instance, a second legislative chamber, a chamber of nationalities, with considerable power in which all nationalities irrespective of their numerical strength are equal. It could mean consociation arrangements, not only at the national level but even at regional and community levels. It will also entail such arrangements as proportional representation and an electoral-spread formula like the one used in Nigeria, by which a party must secure a stipulated minimum percentage of votes over a large part of the country to win.
>
> *(Ake, 2001, 132)*

The three possibilities suggested by Ake have disadvantages that make his proposal untenable. The idea of a second legislative chamber of nationalities with equal powers irrespective of numeric strength is hardly imaginable in a nation with strong tribal leanings. Besides, democracy is a game of numbers. When numbers do not count, there is hardly any democracy. As for consociation arrangements, "specialist in constitutional engineering have been mounting a number of criticisms against it, the points in question include the fixation of group boundaries and identities, the lack of competitive oppositional politics and the tendency towards gridlock and disintegration, which can be the direct outcomes of adopting consociational... institutions" (Mine, Katayanagi and Mikami, 2013, 12). The third suggestion of proportional representation leaves much to be desired. The suggestion could have been a good one if the arrangement is working in such places as Nigeria where it is practiced. Proportional representation has simply not yielded democracy, let alone development for Nigeria.

Hybridity and the Prospects of Democracy and Development in Africa

The positions regarding the operationalisation of democracy in Africa and how democracy is conducive to development in Africa, point to a dilemma that African political philosophy is yet to resolve. Put in another way, these positions leave us with "two opposing systems that have different, but equally untenable, recommendations for Africa. On one hand, we have the view that consensus will be a promising starting point for realising the democratic goals and aspirations of the continent and its people. On the other hand, we have the recommendation that the success of majoritarian multiparty democracy must be allowed to take root if the continent is to be successful" (Matolino, 2018, 199–200). A tenable option is one which adopts elements from both sides and forms a workable democratic and development frame for Africa. Our suggestion is to seek a form of hybrid between the traditional and the modern. This is the case because a return to the past is no longer possible and a total adoption of the modernist ideas will not be fruitful either.

In constructing a hybrid of the traditional and the modern, we draw on the views of Ali Mazuri and Joseph Agbakoba. Mazuri suggested ways to attain hybridity in democratic practice in Africa, just like Agbakoba who suggests a hybrid perspective on development. We attempt to bring both hybrid perspectives together to outline a proposal about the nexus between democracy and development. For Mazuri, the primary economic problem has never been a structural adjustment. The problem has always been how to carryout cultural re-adjustment. This re-adjustment would not be a demotion of African culture (Mazuri, 2002, 17). This cultural re-adjustment requires creating a balance of African continuity with cultural borrowing from western modernity. In his words, "until now, Africa has borrowed Western taste without western skill, Western consumption pattern without western production techniques, urbanisation without industrialisation, secularisation without scientification" (Mazuri, 2002, 17).

This is the reason Africa needs a cultural rather than structural adjustment to create a new equilibrium in taste, values and skills. This proposal by Mazuri brings the critical cultural element into conversation with efforts to democratise development. This element has been lacking in previous perspectives on democracy. When cultural elements are mentioned in the discourses on democracy, they are only romanticised and not critically interrogated for the purpose of democracy. This appeal to culture also resonates well with the proposal of Samuel Huntington about why culture matters in democracy (Huntington, 1991, 20ff). The attention to culture moves the focus of accomplishing democracy from the level of institutions to agents.

Agbakoba's thinking on development as an organicist venture gives impetus to the intuitions of Mazuri about democracy in Africa. Organicist conception of development, according to Agbakoba, understands development to be more of internalist than an externalist affair. The internalist approach "holds the view that the internal state of a society initiate and direct the development of a society by responding constructively to internal and external stimuli and/or by adopting or rejecting such stimuli" (Agbakoba, 2019, 64). Based on this conviction, Agbakoba suggests that the continued insistence on colonialism as the reason for the development deficit in Africa is no longer tenable. His argument is that colonialism was as effective in Africa because of internal dispositions inculcated by African traditional worldview. Agbakoba advocates what he calls the cultural-development thesis which "emphasizes the role of culture in the development of a state or community" (Agbakoba, 2010, 1). The thesis is similar to the proposition that 'culture matters' (Harrison and Huntington, 2000). Agbakoba believes the agential integrity of traditional Africa led to a situation of poor cultural firewalling. This is why African agential receptivity is unable to deal with the effects of colonialism even long after it had ended. In his estimation, the reason some other societies were able to recover from the onslaught of colonisation is because their cultural firewalls were strong enough to sieve out all received threats to agential integrity. In Africa, this was not the case. Thus, there is a need for cultural re-adjustment to enable development.

From Mazrui's perspective, cultural re-adjustment is necessary to accomplish the democratisation of development. Agbakoba shows that cultural re-adjustment is vital to accomplish development. The cultural re-adjustment required must proceed from Africans themselves. Although the "coloniality of power" (Quijano, 2000) could still be a threat to an unhindered accomplishing of the project of democratising development, Africa is yet to demonstrate sufficient creativity and determination in fully exploiting the advantage of the freedom it already has. One way to accomplish this re-adjustment is to embark on a sustained and persistent "critique of elite norms within the African context" (Okeja, 2020). Predominantly, elite norms in Africa reflect the basic elements of the rule of personality as seen in flagrant disregard of the rule of law due to status in society. These norms have been so elevated in the African context to the extent that non-elites aspire to such norms. Consequently, democracy easily snowballs into government of friends and cronies, by friends and cronies, for friends and cronies. Development suffers, ultimately.

Conclusion

We began by asking whether the move towards democracy in African countries is an indication that political outcome will be aligned with the desired economic outcome? Does the embrace of democracy guarantee development? To address this question, we considered the arguments of those who challenge the operationalisation of democracy in Africa and those who think democracy is conducive to development. Going beyond both arguments, then we propose that a hybrid approach to democracy and development in Africa is a viable way forward. Our conclusion is that internal agential considerations are vital to make democracy work for development in Africa. Until aspects of internal agency are addressed through the instrument of critique of elite norms, democracy and development will remain elusive and misaligned in Africa.

Works Cited

Agbakoba, Joseph. "Traditional African Political Thought and the Crisis of Governance in Contemporary African Societies." *Journal for the Study of Religions and Ideologies*, vol. 7, 2004, pp. 137–154.

Agbakoba, Joseph. "Values and Developing Administrative Instruments for the African Cultural Environment." *Uche Journal of the Department of Philosophy University of Nigeria*, Nsukka, vol. 16, 2010, pp. 1–17.

Agbakoba, Joseph. *Development and Modernity in Africa: An Intercultural Philosophical Perspective*. Köln: Rudiger Köppe Verlag, 2019.

Ake, Claude, "The Unique Case of African Democracy." *International Affairs*, vol. 69, no.2, April, 1993, pp. 239–244.

Ake, Claude. *Democracy and Development in Africa*. Ibadan: Spectrum Books Limited, 2001.

Almond, Gabriel A. "Capitalism and Democracy." *Political Science and Politics,* vol. 24, no. 3, 1991, pp. 467–474.

Aristotle, *Nicomachean Ethics. The Complete Works of Aristotle*, vol. 1, edited by Jonathan Barnes. Princeton: Princeton University Press, 1991.

Ayetti, George. *Africa Unchained: The Blueprint for Africa's Future*. New York: Palgrave Macmillan, 2005.

Brown, David S. and Wendy Hunter. "Democracy and Social Spending in Latin America, 1980–1992." *The American Political Science Review,* vol. 93, no. 4, 1999, pp. 779–790.

Chen, Liang-chih Evans. "Development First, Democracy Later? Or Democracy First, Development Later? The Controversy over Development and Democracy." 2007, http://www.democracy.uci.edu/files/docs/conferences/grad/chen.pdf

de Mesquita, Bruce Bueno and George Downs. "Development and Democracy." *Foreign Affairs*, vol. 84, no. 5, 2005, pp. 77–86.

Diamond, Larry. "Democracy, Development and Good Governance: The Inseparable Link." Maiden Annual Democracy and Governance Lecture of the Ghana Centre for Democratic Development, Accra, 2005.

Escobar, Arturo. *Encountering Development: The Making and Unmaking of the Third World*. New Jersey: Princeton University Press, 1995.

Eze, Emmanuel. (ed.), *Postcolonial African Philosophy: A Critical Reader*. Oxford: Blackwell, 1997.

Figgis, John Neville. *The Divine Right of Kings*, 2nd Edition. Cambridge: The University Press, 1914.

Harrison, Lawrence and Samuel. P. Huntington (eds.), *Culture Matters: How Values Shape Human Progress*. New York: Basic Book, 2000.

Huntington, Samuel P. "Democracy's Third Wave." *Journal of Democracy*, vol. 2, no. 2, 1991, pp. 13–34.

Huntington, Samuel P. *Political Order in Changing Societies*. New Haven: Yale University Press, 1968.

Jacques, Carlos. "Alterity in the Discourse of African Philosophy: A Forgotten Absence." *Reclaiming the Human Sciences and Humanities through African Perspectives*, Vol. II, edited by Helen Lauer and Kofi Anyidoho. Ghana: Sub-Saharan Publishers, 2012, pp. 1017–1030.

Kasanda, Albert. "Analyzing African Social and Political Philosophy: Trends and Challenges," *Journal of East West Thought*, vol. 5, no. 1, 2015, pp. 29–50.

Lauer, Helen. "Wiredu and Eze on Good Governance." *Philosophia Africana: Analysis of Philosophy and Issues in Africa and Black Diaspora*, vol. 14, no. 1, 2012, pp. 41–59.

Leblang, David. "Property Rights, Democracy and Economic Growth." *Political Research Quarterly*, vol. 49, no. 1, 1996, pp. 5–26.

Lewis, Willian Arthur. *Politics in West Africa*. Toronto: Oxford University Press, 1965.

Lipset, Semour M. "Some Social Requisites of Democracy: Economic Development and Political Legitimacy." *American Political Science Review*, vol. 53, no. 1, 1959, pp. 69–105.

Macpherson, Crawford Brough. *The Real World of Democracy*. Toronto: Canadian Broadcasting Corporation, 1965.

Matolino, Bernard. "Ending Party Cleavages for a Better Polity: Is Kwasi Wiredu's Non-Party Polity a Viable Alternative to a Party Polity?" *Acta Academia*, vol. 48, no. 2, 2016, pp. 91–107.

Matolino, Bernard. *Consensus as Democracy in Africa*. Grahamstown, South Africa: African Humanities Program, 2018.

Mazuri, Ali. "Who Killed Democracy in Africa? Clues of the Past, Concerns of the Future." *Development Policy Management Network Bulletin*, vol. IX, no. 1, 2002, pp. 15–23.

Mill, John. *Considerations on Representative Government*. Waiheke Isaland: The Floating Press, 2009.

Mine, Yoichi, Mari Katayanagi and Satoru Mikami. "Comparing Political Institutions: Institutional Choice and Conflict Prevention in Africa." *Preventing Violent Conflict in Africa: Inequalities, Perspectives and Institutions*, edited by Yoichi Mine, Frances Stewart, Sakiko Fukuda-Parr and Thandika Mkandawire. Palgrave: Macmillan, 2013, pp. 10–39.

Moore, Barrington, Jr. *Social Origins of Dictatorship and Democracy: Land and Peasants in the making of the Modern World*. Boston: Beacon Press, 1966.

Njoku, Francis. *Philosophy in Politics, Law and Democracy*. Nekede: Claretian Institute of Philosophy, 2002.

Nyongo,' Peter. "Africa: The Failure of One-Party Rule." *Journal of Democracy*, vol. 3, no. 1, 1992, pp. 90–96.

Ochefu, Yakubu. "Democracy and development in West Africa: How Integral is the Relationship" *NESG Economic Indicators*, vol. 13, no. 1, January – March 2007, pp. 25–32.

Okeja, Uchenna. "A Letter to the Victims of Hope: A Lamentation and Reflection." A panel presentation at the One-Day Virtual Workshop of the Association of Philosophy Professionals of Nigeria (APPON) on the theme: Intercultural Philosophy and the Challenge of Development in A Post Covid-19 Africa on the 15th of December, 2020.

Organisation of African Unity. "Declaration on the Political and Socio-economic Situation in Africa and the Fundamental Changes Taking Place in the World." 1990, http://archives.au.int/bitstream/handle/123456789/715/AHG%20Decl%201%20XXVI_E.pdf?sequence=1&isAllowed=y

Osabu-Kle, Daniel Tetteh. "Western Democracy: Is it Applicable in Africa?" *The Bulletin of Fridays of the African Union Commission*, vol. 1, no. 3, April, 2008, pp. 2–14.

Plato. Republic. *Plato: Complete Works*, edited by John M. Cooper and D. S. Hutchinson. Indianapolis/Cambridge: Hackett Publishing Company, 1997.

Przeworski, Adam, and Fernando Limongi. "Modernization: Theories and Facts." *World Politics*, vol. 49, no. 2, 1997, pp. 155–183.

Przeworski, Adam, Michael E. Alvarez, Jose Antonio Cheibub, and Fernando Limongi. *Democracy and Development: Political Institutions and Well-being in the World 1950–1990*. New York: Cambridge University Press, 2000.

Quigley, John. "Perestroika African Style: One-Party Government and Human Rights in Tanzania." *Michigan Journal of International Law*, vol. 13, no. 3, 1992, pp. 611–652.

Quijano, Anibal. "Coloniality of Power, Eurocentrism, and Latin America." *Nepantla: Views from South*, vol. 1, no. 3, 2000, pp. 533–580.

Rahnema, Majid. "Global Poverty: A Pauperising Myth." *Interculture*, vol. XXIV, no. 2, 111 (Spring 1991), pp. 4–51.

Siegle, Joseph T., Michael M. Weinstein, and Morton H. Halperin. "Why Democracies Excel." *Foreign Affairs*, vol. 83, no. 5, 2004, pp. 57–71.

Teffo, Joe. "Democracy, Kingship and Consensus: South African Perspective." *Companion to African Philosophy*, edited by Kwasi Wiredu. Blackwell: Blackwell Publishing Ltd, 2004, pp. 443–448.

United Nations Economic Commission for Africa. *African Charter for Popular Participation in Development and Transformation*. Arusha, United Republic of Tanzania, 1990.

Wamala, Edward. "Government by Consensus: An Analysis of a Traditional Form of Democracy." *Companion to African Philosophy*, edited by Kwasi Wiredu. Blackwell: Blackwell Publishing Ltd, 2004, pp. 435–441.

Willis, Katie. *Theories and Practices of Development*. New York: Routledge, 2005.

Wiredu, Kwasi. "Democracy and Consensus in Traditional Politics: A Plea for a Non-Party Polity." *The Continental Review*, vol. 39, no. 1, 1995, pp. 53–64.

Zweifel, Thomas D. and Patricio Navia. "Democracy, Dictatorship, and Infant Mortality." *Journal of Democracy*, vol. 11, no. 2, 2000, pp. 99–114.

19

ELECTION, VIOLENCE AND POLITICAL LEGITIMATION

Jacinta Mwende Maweu

Introduction

This chapter examines the recurrent electoral violence that has become part and parcel of political competition in most countries in Africa since the re-introduction of multiparty politics in the early 1990s and how this in turn affects political legitimation. Elections are necessary instruments of representative democracies prevalent in most African societies. Although there has been a remarkable increase in periodic elections and advancements in the quality of democracy across the continent generating a sense of optimism for multiparty politics, this development has been closely accompanied by another, much more worrying trend, of election-related violence (Adolfo et al. 2012). Electoral violence continues to erode people's faith in democratic processes, undermine the sustenance of democracy, the integrity of elections, trust in governing institutions and pose a threat to peace and security in the continent. It is a widely held belief in contemporary political philosophy that democracy is necessary for political legitimacy (Burchard 2015).

The wave of political liberalization that swept through most African countries in the early 1990s brought with it lots of hope, optimism and enthusiasm for the flourishing of democracy. But this has since turned into pessimism with most countries in Africa sliding back to the usual 'big man,' neo-patrimonial and chaotic politics that had characterized sub-Saharan Africa in the pre-1990s. It appears that the liberal democratic notion of elections being one of the many ways of choosing leadership, enhancing political legitimacy and disposing of old governments in a political system (Kellner 2010), does not have a meaningful impact in most contemporary African contexts. In almost every African country, there have been allegations of 'stolen elections' causing post-election violence on a large or small scale. Therefore, although multiparty elections have clearly become a regular institution in Africa, there are still many doubts about the meaning, quality and significance of these elections in the consolidation of democracy (Gillies 2011).

Throughout Africa, there has been an over-emphasis on elections as though they are sufficient instruments of democracy. The trend has been that as long as a country holds periodic elections no matter how shambolic, it is an illustration of democracy. But as is evident, mere periodic elections are not a sufficient measure of democracy. For democracy to be actualized, the electoral processes through which political competition is channelled

DOI: 10.4324/9781003143529-22

must be fair, citizens must enjoy basic freedoms of association, expression and access to information, and the judiciary must be free to rule impartially on election petitions and any other issue pertaining to the conduct of the polls as well as rulings governing the constitution of political parties and eligibility of candidates (Bratton 2008). The legal and political conditions under which elections are organized must also be seen to be free and fair. All of this form part of the key ingredients of the democratization processes. The conduct of elections and the environment under which they are held is therefore crucial to the quality of democracy and subsequent political legitimacy hence the focus should not be entirely on the actual voting. Although democratic institutions and procedures, including elections, have been introduced and/or reinforced since the (re-)introduction of multiparty politics in sub-Saharan Africa in the early 1990s, the underlying structures of power in society and the norms governing the political system have often not yet been transformed. This has continued to undermine democracy and political legitimacy in Africa even with the new political strategy of forming coalitions to facilitate power sharing to resolve political conflicts after disputed elections.

This chapter is organized into four sections including this introductory section which gives a general overview of the main arguments presented in this chapter. Section two focuses on elections and political legitimation in Africa and analyses the rationale and credibility of periodic elections in Africa as a reflection of the will of the people on the ground. The question of whether fraudulent/'stolen' elections, which are the most common in Africa are valid sources of state legitimacy is discussed. Section three focuses on multiparty politics and electoral violence in Africa. The factors that have enabled electoral violence to continue to taint and derail free and fair electoral competition in sub-Saharan Africa, even as multiparty politics remains the most dominant mode of access and transfer of political power are discussed. Section four analyses and critiques the emerging trend of the formation of political coalitions commonly known as consociational democracy in most African countries as the solution to end electoral conflicts and/or violence. This chapter ends with a conclusion that summarizes the main arguments presented.

Elections and Political Legitimation in Africa

Ideally, elections should reflect the will of the people. They should be avenues for citizens to exercise their democratic right, to define their destiny by electing leaders who will make a difference in their lives for the better. But what has been happening in most countries in Africa calls for a redefinition and re-examination of the value of elections as a means of political cum state legitimation and the promotion of democracy. Elections seem to have become mere rituals to endorse the power of the minority political and economic elite hence there is declining trust in supposed democratic institutions. According to Willems (2012), the meaning of electoral democracy, the right of the citizens to vote and the legitimacy of political leadership is lost if even with periodic elections, millions of ordinary citizens do not see any substantial improvement in their living standards.

The major problem of electoral democracy in Africa has largely to do with how true the will of the people is reflected in the results of elections (Fayemi 2009). As Kasanda (2018) observes, African political philosophy is concerned with people's everyday life, everyday experience of alliances and collective actions and one cannot therefore analyse the practicality of democracy independent of the experiences of the ordinary citizens' experience. Kasanda (2018: 31) identifies three classical concerns of political philosophy that are central to African political philosophy: the well-being of African citizens, the power and the suited paradigm for social and political organization. These factors are relevant to our discussion in this chapter because they help us assess and critique the rationale for periodic elections as the hallmark of democracy and political legitimation in Africa at a time when the credibility and integrity of elections are under scrutiny globally. In most African countries, the democratic gains that ought to come with these periodic elections seem to be reduced to entrenching the power of a few political elites and what is acceptable to these elites frequently provides the boundaries of democratic politics (Ksanda 2019; Steyn 2008).

According to Gilley (2009: 5), political legitimacy is the right to rule granted by citizens to political authorities or political regimes 'grounded in common good or shared moral evaluations'. "Legitimacy involves the capacity of a political system to engender and maintain the belief that existing institutions are the most appropriate or proper ones for the society" (Lipset 1959: 86). Political legitimacy is often perceived as the *de facto* ability of a political regime to secure acceptance based on belief as opposed to securing compliance based on coercion alone (Weber 1984). Legitimacy is a classic topic of political philosophy and deals with questions such as: What are the right sources of legitimacy? Is a specific political order or regime worthy of recognition?

As a normative concept, political legitimacy refers to some benchmark of acceptability or justification of political power or authority and possibly obligation. Political authorities generally advance legitimacy claims in an attempt to convince citizens about their right to rule and citizens can in turn either accept these legitimation claims or reject them depending on the congruence of the claims with their expectations or legitimation demands (Grauvogel and Von Soest 2014). Political legitimacy implies the popular acceptance of a government, political regime, or system of governance. It is a virtue of political institutions; the justification of coercive political power (Gaus 2014; Ripstein 2004; Rawls 1993). For an institution or a political agent to be legitimate means both that its exercise of political power is generally permissible, and that subjects generally have a genuine or moral obligation, as opposed to a mere legal obligation, to accept their laws and decisions (Peter 2019).

Every regime must be perceived to have a basic minimum amount of legitimacy to avoid rebellion, protests or collapse. Therefore, whether a political body such as a state is legitimate and whether citizens have political obligations towards it depends on whether the coercive political power that the state exercises is justified (Rawls 1993). As Reyes (2010: 146) notes, 'all governments need to legitimize their rule, to justify their right to promote their authority as a means to gaining popular support, or at least, acquiescence, without which they are likely to collapse. Political legitimacy is considered as a basic condition to rule and therefore every regime tries to justify its reign to enhance its credibility and acceptability. Free, fair and regular elections are generally regarded as the basis of political legitimacy and the incorporation of people's development needs into public policies (Fayemi 2009: 106).

The question of whether elections are valid sources of state legitimacy is particularly critical in emerging democracies in Africa and elsewhere, where trust in institutions is increasingly becoming shallow and the authority of the state remains contested (Lajul 2020).

Empirical research (Sil and Chen 2004; Gibson and Caldeira 2003) suggests that states with high levels of legitimacy gain the voluntary compliance of their citizens, are more stable and possess greater developmental capacities (Hurrelmann et al. 2007; Englebert 2002). Therefore, state legitimacy determines government performance and vice versa (Redie 2020). When the public distrust the police and courts and feel that elected officials are not responsive, people are less likely to view the state as a legitimate wielder of political power and authority (Carter 2011: 24). In most African countries, the state uses the police to 'keep peace' during election-related violence, elected leaders especially the executive ignore court orders with impunity and the citizens feel neglected by their leaders at the grassroots. This paints a blurred picture of how legitimate political power wielders are in the African setting today.

Multiparty Politics and Electoral Violence in Africa

Competitive elections are by their very nature conflictual processes aimed at mobilizing divergent interests in society and stimulating political competition between political actors (Kovacs and Bjarnesen 2018: 13). Although elections are not inherently a source of violence, they can deepen or reawaken political, ethnic, regional and religious tensions which can spill over into violence, especially in cases where electoral management institutional frameworks are weak (International Peace Institute report 2011; Fjelde and Höglund 2014). Electoral violence is by definition 'any activity motivated by an attempt to affect the results of an election either by manipulating the electoral procedures and participation or by contesting the legitimacy of the results' (Laakso 2007: 227–228). Electoral violence continues to taint and derail free and fair electoral competition in most countries in sub-Saharan Africa, even as multiparty politics remains the most dominant mode of access and transfer of political power. The existence and destructive force of election-related violence challenges political transitions, aspects of nation-building and democratization itself (Stremlau and Price 2009: 5). Although violence has been a long-standing feature of the democratization process in Africa, its recent manifestations have assumed an unprecedented magnitude and a changing form and character. This has tended to put the democratization process on the line in many African states, threatening the prospects of democratic stability and consolidation (Omotola 2010: 52). As Voltmer and Kraetzschmar (2015) observe, elections in transitional democracies can often function as a 'Pandora's box' by showcasing weak institutions, legacies of authoritarian regimes and unresolved conflicts.

As Adolfo et al. (2012) observe, although the causes of electoral violence are multifaceted, they can be summarized into structural factors and factors related to the electoral process and electoral contests. Structural factors are those that relate to the underlying power structures prevalent in most transitional democracies in Africa characterized by informal patronage systems, poor governance, exclusionary politics and the socio-economic uncertainties of losing political power in states where almost all power is concentrated at the centre. Factors related to the electoral process and the electoral contest itself includes failed or flawed elections, election fraud and weak or manipulated institutions and institutional rules governing the electoral process. After the re-introduction of multiparty politics in most countries in sub-Saharan Africa in the early 1990s, it was fallaciously assumed that multipartyism equals democracy, despite the lack of a strong clear relationship between the two (Kanyinga et al. 2010). As Mueller (2020: 349) observes, political parties remained deeply personal non-programmatic vehicles for ethnic barons bereft of credible policy commitments.

Although almost all sub-Saharan African states have adopted some form of electoral democracy in which the highest political offices are filled through regular, multiparty elections, there should be a radical redefinition of democracy that goes beyond the mere regular conduct of free and fair elections. With a public outcry of 'stolen elections' in nearly all countries in Africa every election cycle, it can arguably be observed that elections have become mere ritual events aimed at meeting some of the minimal conditions of liberal democracy, as perceived on the global scene (Eggen 2012). This is likely to create apathy among the majority of voters on the value of these elections since the outcome seems to be always predetermined. To most ordinary citizens, elections then become just mere rituals that rubber-stamp those in power with democracy being just a mere "set of rules intended to legitimize bourgeois power" (McNair 2003: 24) with no checks and balances to ensure the will of the people is manifest.

Over the past three decades, violence has featured prominently either on a large or small scale during elections in most African countries such as Côte d'Ivoire, Kenya, Nigeria and Zimbabwe, Cameroon, Democratic Republic of Congo, Liberia, Equatorial Guinea, Gambia, Guinea, Madagascar, Sierra Leone, Senegal and Uganda just to mention but a few (Adolfo et al. 2012). In theory, elections ought to be the bedrock of democratic governance by facilitating representation, ensuring accountability and peacefully regulating access to political power. But in countries where the winner literally takes all, as is the case in most of Africa, the stakes of elections are high, and the costs of defeat devastating making political competitions fertile ground for violence (Soderberg Kovacs and Bjarnesen 2018). As Wiredu (1996) observes, this adversarial winner-takes-all nature of majoritarian liberal democracy is one of the major weaknesses of periodic elections as a yardstick of a functional democracy. Wiredu argues for a system of governance based on consensus rather that competitive party politics. For him, the process of deliberation on issues rather than resorting to a popular vote can promote mutual tolerance, thereby contributing to de-marginalization in the society (Wiredu 1996; 2001).

There is also the tendency of many African states to concentrate power and resources at the centre, even in countries where this has been addressed on paper through a devolved system of government as is the case in Kenya. This effectively turns politics into a zero-sum game which is a recipe for violence (Diamond 2008). Nearly all countries in Africa are also characterized by what is popularly known as 'Big man politics' which gives near-divine powers to the one who occupies the executive seat of the Presidency, despite the re-introduction of multiparty democracy in the early 1990s. With weak justice institutions which are more often than not disregarded and ignored with impunity by those in power, elections become a 'do or die' affair and aspirants, especially the incumbent use all means possible to stay in power. In the postcolonial state in most of Africa, "political power gives its holders disproportionate access to resources such as land, public jobs, and business opportunities, so that the lack of political power often results in the lack of these other social goods" (Oduor 2018: 54). This makes all elections in most of Africa high stake elections with a high likelihood of electoral violence.

Characterized by patron–client networks commonly organized along ethnic lines or regional constellations, elections in Africa are frequently marked by the direct or indirect mobilization of ethnic or regional votes (Mueller 2020; Arriola 2009; Posner 2007; Fjelde & Hoglund Kristine 2018). Most societies in Africa are deeply divided into highly politicized and ethnicized groups, with each group perceiving political behaviour solely in zero-sum terms. The democratic process of holding periodic elections therefore becomes a tool of conquest and domination of the ethnic minorities by the ethnic majority groups (Oduor 2018). Throughout Africa, like many other developing countries, voting is still largely determined by ethnicity, kinship and neighbourhood (Mbaku 2020). Politics is largely organized around the crucial variable of ethnicity, and that those in society who share the ethnicity of those in power are often privy to a range of benefits to which non-co-ethnics may not have access. Thus, ethnicity has been hypothesized to be key in shaping political institutions (Posner 2005) conflict (Horowitz 1985) and attitudes of legitimacy (Schatzberg 2001). The principles of representation, legitimacy and transfer of power are subverted when the dominant group: seizes control of the state machinery; allocates to its segment a disproportionate share of the state's resources and services and entrenches a political hegemony at the expense of less powerful groups (Cobb 1989: 4).

Any form of electoral violence, physical, psychological or structural (Ashindorbe 2018: 95), is a political vice that erodes public trust in governance institutions, compromises political legitimacy of the elected leaders, undermines the integrity of the democratic process and as has been witnessed in many countries in Africa, reduces voter turnout due to voter apathy. Further, election violence undermines the foundational elements of democracy such as choice and consent, civic participation, accountability and rule of law (Animashaun 2020: 20). The main aim of electoral violence is to manipulate the electoral process (Birch 2011) and this has a direct impact on the consolidation of democracy. The political, economic, social and humanitarian costs related to electoral violence are high whether it occurs in a transitional or developed democracy. Election violence causes loss of human life, and affects the outcome of elections and their perceived legitimacy. In extreme situations, it may increase the risk of armed conflict or civil war (Birch et al. 2020: 4).

Which Way Forward? Elections, Violence and Consociational Democracy in Africa

How can most African countries end the cycle of electoral violence that has characterized multiparty democracy over the decades? Is politics of accommodation/consociationalism through political coalitions the solution? Globally, political polarization is increasingly weakening democratic norms, compromising basic legislative processes, exacerbating intolerance and discrimination, diminishing societal trust and increasing violence throughout the society (McCoy et al. 2018). In the recent past, there have been attempts in several countries in Africa such as Kenya, Zimbabwe, South Africa and Rwanda to resolve election-related conflicts and violence to minimize polarization through the formation of consociational democracies/ political coalitions based on different power-sharing formulae. There seems to be a gradual shift from the traditional tenets of liberal democracy such as multipartyism and 'free and fair' periodic elections as the basis for political legitimation to power sharing between political elites where all segments of the population ought to be represented. Discussions and justification of consociational democracy stem from Arend Lijphart's study of the Netherlands in the *Politics of Accommodation* (1968 and 1977) in which he proposed a system of multi-ethnic power sharing as opposed to majority rule. As a theory, consociationalism, which is also known as non-majoritarian democracy/consensus democracy attempts to explain how societies that are deeply divided along ethnic, racial, religious or otherwise as is the case in most African countries can establish functional democracy. As a system, it is anchored on the concept of power-sharing between and among elites from the various divided social groups (Lijphart 1968; 1984; 2012).

Arend Lijphart (1968) outlined the political features of consociational democracy as follows: government by a grand coalition of segmental elites, a proportional electoral system and proportionality in the allocation of jobs and other resources, segmental autonomy both territorial and/or functional and a mutual veto-implicit or explicit. Western/European consociational democracies are or were the Netherlands, Belgium, Switzerland and Austria (Ertman and Steiner 2002). In Africa, we have had Kenya, Zimbabwe, South Africa and Rwanda. However, most of what we have had in Africa and Kenya in particular is what Horowitz (1985) calls multi-ethnic alliances and multi-ethnic parties respectively that do not last past an election period. Under the Alliance model, the consociational party is made up of separate organizational entities that function as a unity in the context of competitive multiparty elections.

Using Kenya as a case which has had multiple alliances in the last decade to illustrate Horowitz's point, in 2002 there was the National Rainbow Coalition (NARC) coalition bringing together the major opposition political parties with the main aim of ousting the long-serving former President Daniel Moi who had been at the helm for 24 years. When Mwai Kibaki took over power from Daniel Moi in 2002, his cabinet appointments had to uniquely reflect the diversity that led to his historic victory. His victory was spearheaded by a multi-ethnic coalition and thus the cabinet formed after the elections had to reflect pre-election agreements. The NARC, the party that put Kibaki to power in 2002 was an ethno-regional coalition comprising of the National Alliance Party of Kenya (made up of 13 different parties) and the Liberal Democratic Party (LDP) formed just before to the elections. Although the coalition achieved its objective in the 2002 elections; to oust Daniel Moi from power, it fell apart soon after due to an alleged pre-election memorandum of understanding between the coalition partners that was not honoured by the Kibaki administration. In the 2007 elections, there were two main coalitions: ODM as the lead opposition party and PNU, which comprised of political parties sympathetic to the Kibaki administration. Just like in the 2002 coalition, the two alliances brought together political leaders from the major ethnic communities and their sympathizers in different camps and just like in the 2007 case, the coalition did not last until the next elections in 2013. In the 2013 elections, two new major political alliances were formed yet again, the Coalition of Reform and Democracy (CORD) and the Jubilee Alliance.

The CORD coalition brought together the Luo and Kamba communities under their 'ethnic big men', Raila Odinga and Kalonzo Musyoka respectively while the Jubilee Alliance brought together the Kikuyu and Kalenjin communities under Uhuru Kenyatta and William Ruto respectively as 'ethnic Big men'. There was also the Amani coalition, which was largely associated with the Luhya community under Musalia Mudavadi. The presidential elections vote count points to a strong ethnic voting bias. For instance, the Jubilee Alliance received 93.92% and 72.22% in Central and Rift Valley provinces; the ethnic strongholds of the Kikuyu and Kalenjin respectively. The CORD coalition received 86.83 and 48.8% in Nyanza and Eastern provinces pointing to the strength of ethnic numbers of the Luos and Kambas respectively. In the spirit of politics of accommodation, Uhuru Kenyatta's cabinet under the Jubilee Alliance in 2013 has been deemed as the least balanced since independence. Kikuyus and Kalenjins, which are the president and deputy president's ethnic groups, were disproportionately overrepresented. It was evident that half of the cabinet slots were evenly distributed between his own ethnic group and that of his deputy (Kivuva 2018). This generated a lot of public outcry on the skewed public service appointments raising concerns as to whether consociational democracy through such ethnic/regional alliances remedies or worsens political tensions in deeply divided societies such as Kenya that are a sure recipe for election-related violence.

In the current era of multiparty politics in Africa generally and Kenya in particular, characterized by ethno-regional coalitions for convenience to win elections, it is difficult to find a party or coalition that is founded on ideology. For instance in the case of Kenya, although the ruling Jubilee Alliance survived till the last elections in 2017, it has since been a scene of ethnic battles between the deputy president's sympathizers and those of the president. The opposition alliance NASA under Raila Odinga which was formed in the run-up to the 2017 elections is also technically dead since the leader, Raila Odinga "shook hands" in the now famous March 2018 "Handshake" with President Kenyatta, unofficially crossing over to the government side. This is seen as a basis to form new coalitions ahead of the 2022 elections bringing together Uhuru and Raila on the one side and the deputy president William Ruto and his sympathizers on the other. In the just concluded August 9th, 2022 general elections, the two main political alliances were the Azimio la Umoja Kenya Alliance led by Raila Odinga and the Kenya Kwanza Alliance led by deputy president and now president-elect William Ruto. Just like in previous coalitions, these two alliances brought together leaders of different ethnic groups to consolidate the vote. Although there have been claims that these ethnic groups coalesce into a political party or seek alliances with other ethnic groups as part of a political struggle to correct what they perceive as historical injustices, the rate at which they disintegrate waters down this otherwise noble objective.

If what has been happening in Kenya as illustrated here is anything to go by, which is not very different from what has been happening in other countries that have embraced the politics of accommodation such as Zimbabwe, political coalitions/parties seem to draw the majority of their membership from and are founded to basically advance the interests of specific ethnic groups, and by extension, to counter the interests of perceived enemy ethnic groups (Biegon 2018). The only distinguishing feature in these coalitions seems to be "who" rather than "what" they represent. Most of the times, the only unifying ideology for alliances/coalitions for the opposition is to unseat the incumbent and for those in government they form ethno-regional alliances to consolidate their numbers to stay in power. Therefore the verdict on whether ethno-regional coalitions are the solution to political polarization cum conflict is still debatable.

The net effect for the politicization of ethnic identity and increasing political polarization in most of Africa has been the significant erosion of public trust in institutions of governance especially the presidency, the legislature, electoral management bodies and the judiciary. This has also weakened the formal structures of political parties, posing a serious challenge to the consolidation of democracy (Hsieh 2013). Ideally, the aim of consociational democracy is to 'manipulate a society's pluralism in order to create the conditions under which political power can be shared, a maximisation of interests aggregated, and compromises obtained between all significant segments in the system' (Cobb 1989: 9). It seeks to ensure that democratic processes prevail in systems hostile to traditional, majoritarian assumptions of democracy. If this will be the solution to the persistent election-related violence in Africa, the jury is still out there.

Conclusion

This chapter has analysed the issues of periodic elections as a yardstick of electoral democracy and political legitimation in Africa and the persistent electoral violence as a major challenge to the realization of majoritarian democracy. It has been argued that although free and fair elections are universal tenets of a functional electoral democracy, the recurrent violence and claims of fraudulent elections compromise the quality of democracy in Africa. Political violence still remains a pervasive trait of electoral processes in most of Africa's multiparty systems. Such violence threatens to undermine not only electoral integrity, but also democratic gains in these countries. It has been observed in this chapter that although democratic institutions and procedures, including elections, have been introduced and/or reinforced since the (re-)introduction of multiparty politics in sub-Saharan Africa in the early 1990s, the underlying structures of power in society and the norms governing the political system have often not yet been transformed. Therefore, from an African political philosophy perspective, any discussion about the status of electoral democracy in Africa must critically analyse the everyday experiences of citizens and the ways in which recurrent electoral violence undermines political legitimation.

References

Adolfo, Eldridge, Kovacs, Mimmi, Nyströ, Daniel and Utas, Mats. *Electoral Violence in Africa*. The Nordic African Institute. 2012. ISBN 978-91-7106-726-5.

Animashaun, Mojeed Adekunle. "Democratization Trapped in Electoral Violence". *Contemporary Journal of African Studies*, Vol. 7, No. 2, 2020, pp. 18–30.

Arriola, Leonardo. "Patronage and Political Stability in Africa". *Comparative Political Studies,* Vol. 42, No. 10, 2009, pp. 1339–1362.

Ashindorbe, Kelvin. "Electoral Violence and the Challenge of Democratic Consolidation in Nigeria". *India Quarterly,* Vol. 74, No. 1, 2018, pp. 92–105. DOI: 10.1177/0974928417749639 http://journals.sagepub.com/home/iqq

Biegon, Japheth. "Politicization of Ethnic Identity in Kenya: Historical Evolution, Major Manifestations and the Enduring Implications". *Ethnicity and Politicization in Kenya*, edited by Japheth Biegon, Joshua Kivuva, Patrick Asingo and Winluck Wahiu, Kenya Human Rights Commission, 2018, pp. 8–50.

Birch, Sarah. *Electoral Malpractice*. Oxford University Press, 2011.

Birch, Sarah, Daxecker, Ursula and Hoglund, Kristine. "Electoral Violence: An Introduction". *Journal of Peace Research*, Vol. 57, No.1, 2020, pp. 3–14.

Bratton, Micahel. "Vote Buying and Violence in Nigerian Election Campaigns". *Electoral Studies*, Vol. 27, No.4, 2008, pp. 621–632.

Burchard, Stephanie. *Electoral Violence in Sub-Saharan Africa: Causes and Consequences*. Lynne Rienner, 2015.

Carter, Danielle. *Sources of State Legitimacy in Contemporary South Africa: A Theory of Political Goods*. Working Paper No. 134. Afrobarometer, 2011 https://www.afrobarometer.org/wpcontent/uploads/migrated/files/publications/Working%20paper/AfropaperNo134.pdf

Cobb, Shane. Consociational democracy: the model and its relevance to conflict regulation in South Africa. University of Cape Town. Unpublished MA thesis, 1989.

Diamond, Larry. "The Rule of Law versus Big Man". *Journal of Democracy*, Vol. 19, No. 2, 2008, pp. 138–149.

Eggen Oyvind. "Performing Good Governance: The Aesthetics of Bureaucratic Practice in Malawi". *Ethnos*, Vol. 77, No. 1, 2012, 1–23. DOI: 10.1080/00141844.2011.580357.

Englebert, Pierre. *State Legitimacy and Development in Africa*. Lynne Rienner Pub, 2002.

Ertman, Thomas and Steiner, Jürg (eds.) *Consociationalism and Corporatism in Western Europe: Still the Politics of Accommodation?* Meppel: Boom, 2002.

Fayemi, Ademola. "Towards an African Theory of Democracy". *Thought and Practice: A Journal of the Philosophical Association of Kenya (PAK)* Premier Issue, New Series, Vol. 1, No. 1, 2009, pp. 101–126.

Fjelde, Hanne & Hoglund Kristine. "Ethnic politics and elite competition: The roots of electoral violence in Kenya". *Violence in African Elections: Between Democracy and Big Man Politics*, edited by Mimmi So''derberg Kovacs & Jesper Bjarnesen. London: Zed, 2018, pp. 27–46.

Fjelde, Hanne and Höglund, Kristine. "Electoral Institutions and Electoral Violence in Sub-Saharan Africa". *British Journal of Political Science*, Vol. 46, 2014, pp. 297–320.

Gaus, Gerald. 2014. "The Turn to a Political Liberalism". *A Companion to Rawls*, edited by Mandle, Jon. And Reidy, David. John Wiley & Sons, Vol. 2, 2014, pp. 233–250.

Gibson, James and Caldeira. Gregory. "Defenders of Democracy? Legitimacy, Popular Acceptance, and the South African Constitutional Court". *Journal of Politics,* Vol. 65, No.1, 2003, pp. 1–30.

Gilley, Bruce. *The Right to Rule: How States Win and Lose Legitimacy.* New York: Columbia University Press, 2009.

Gillies, David. *Elections in Dangerous Places: Democracy and the Paradoxes of Peacebuilding.* Montreal: McGill-Queen's University Press, 2011.

Grauvogel, Julia and von Soest Christian. Claims to legitimacy count: Why sanctions fail to instigate democratisation in authoritarian regimes. *European Journal of Political Research*, Vol. 53, No. 4, 2014, pp. 635–653.

Horowitz, Donald. *Ethnic Groups in Conflict*. University of California Press, 1985.

Hsieh, John. "Arend Lijphart and Consociationalism". *Taiwan Journal of Democracy*, Special Issue, Vol. 87, 2013, pp. 87–101.

Hurrelmann, Achim, Steffen, Schneider and Jens, Steffek. *Legitimacy in an Age of Global Politics*. Palgrave Macmillan, 2007.

International Peace Institute. *Elections in Africa: Challenges and Opportunities.* 2011. Available at www. ipinst.org, Accessed on 12/08/2021.

Kanyinga, Karuti, Okelo, Duncan and Akech, Akoko. 2010. "Contradictions of Transition to Democracy in Fragmented Societies: The Kenya 2007 General Elections in Perspective". *Tensions and Reversals in Democratic Transitions: The Kenya 2007 General Elections,* edited by Karuti Kanyinga and Duncan Okello. 2010, pp. 1–20.

Kasanda. Albert. *Contemporary African Social and Political Philosophy Trends, Debates and Challenges.* Routledge. 2018. ISBN 9780815381662

Kasanda, Albert. "Analyzing African Social and Political Philosophy: Trends and Challenges". *Journal of East-West Thought,* 2019, Vol. 5, pp. 29–50.

Kellner, Douglas. "Media Spectacle and Media Events: Some Critical Reflections". *Media Events in a Global Age,* edited by Nick Couldru, Andreas Hepp, and Friedrich Kotz. 2010, pp. 76–91, Routledge.

Kivuva, Joshua. "Negotiated Democracy and its Place in Kenya's Devolved System of Government: An Examination of the 2013 General Elections". *Ethnicity and Politicization in Kenya,* edited by Biegon J., Kivuva, J., Asingo P. and Wahiu W. Nairobi: Kenya Human Rights Commission, 2018, pp. 53–76.

Kovacs, Mimmi and Bjarnesen, Jesper. *Violence in African Elections: Between Democracy and Big Man Politics.* Zed Books Ltd, 2018.

Laakso, Lisa. "Insights into Electoral Violence in Africa". *Votes, Money and Violence: Political Parties in Sub-Saharan Africa,* edited by Basedau, Matthias, Erdmann, Gero and Mehler, Andreas. Nordic Africa Institute, 2007, pp. 224–253.

Lajul, Wilfred. "A Critical Analysis of Political Philosophy in African Political Discourses". *Art Human Open Access Journal,* Vol.4, No.5, 2020, pp. 176-185. DOI: 10.15406/ahoaj.2020.04.00168

Lijphart, Arend. *The Politics of Accommodation: Pluralism and Democracy in the Netherlands.* University of California Press, 1968.

Lijphart, Arend. *Democracy in Plural Societies: A Comparative Exploration.* Yale University Press, 1977.

Lijphart, Arend. *Democracies: Patterns of Majoritarian and Consensus Government in Twenty-One Countries.* Yale University Press, 1984.

Lijphart, Arend. *Patterns of Democracy: Government Forms and Performance in Thirty-Six Countries.* Yale University Press, 2012.

Lipset, Seymour. "Some Social Requisites of Democracy: Economic Development and Political Legitimacy". *The American Political Science Review,* 1959, Vol. 53, pp. 69–105.

Mbaku, John. *Threats to Democracy in AFRICA: The Rise of the Constitutional Coup,* 2020. Available at https://www.brookings.edu/blog/africa-in-focus/2020/10/30/threats-to-democracy-in-africa-the-rise-of-the-constitutional-coup/ Accessed on 29/08/2021.

McCoy, Jennifer, Rahman, Tahmina and Somer, Murat. "Polarization and the Global Crisis of Democracy: Common Patterns, Dynamics, and Pernicious Consequences for Democratic Politics". *American Behavioral Scientist,* Vol. 62, No.1, 2018, pp. 16–42.

McNair, Brian. *An Introduction to Political Communication.* Routledge, 2003.

Mueller, Sussane. "High Stakes- Ethnic Politics". *The Oxford Handbook of Kenyan Politics,* edited by Nic Cheeseman, Karuti Kanyinga and Gabrielle Lynch. Oxford University Press, 2020, pp. 343–355.

Oduor, Reginald. "Nationhood and Statehood: The Impact of a Conflated Discourse on African Polities and Their Non-Dominant Ethnic Groups". *Utafiti,* Vol. 13, No.2, 2018, pp. 45–67.

Omotola, Shola. "Explaining Electoral Violence in Africa's 'New' Democracies". *African Journal on Conflict Resolution,* Vol. 10, No.3, 2010, pp. 51–74.

Peter, Fabienne. "Political Legitimacy under Epistemic Constraints: Why Public Reasons Matter". *Political Legitimacy, Nomos,* edited by Jack Knight and Melissa Schwartzberg, Volume LXI, Nyu Press, 2019. pp. 1–19.

Posner, Daniel. "Regime Change and Ethnic Cleavages in Africa". *Comparative Political Studies,* Vol. 40, No.11, 2007, pp. 1302–1327.

Posner, Daniel. *Institutions and Ethnic Politics in Africa.* University Press, 2005.

Rawls, John. *Political Liberalism.* Columbia University Press, 1993.

Redie, Bereketeab. "State Legitimacy and Government Performance in the Horn of Africa". *African Studies,* Vol. 79, No.1, 2020, pp. 51–69. DOI: 10.1080/00020184.2020.1724767

Reyes, Giovanni. "Theoretical Basis of Crisis of Legitimacy and Implications for Less Developed Countries: Guatemala as a Case Study". *Tendencias,* Vol. 11, No.1, 2010, pp. 145–163.

Ripstein, Arthur. "Authority and Coercion". *Philosophy & Public Affairs,* Vol. 32, 2004, pp. 2–35.

Schatzberg, Michael. *Political Legitimacy in Middle Africa: Father, Family, Food.* Indiana University Press, 2001.

Sil, Rudra, and Chen. Cheng. "State Legitimacy and the (In) significance of Democracy in Post-Communist Russia". *Europe-Asia Studies,* Vol. 56, No. 3, 2004, pp. 347–368.

Steyn, Ibrahim. "The Shorthand of Electoral Democracy: Democracy for Some". *South African Civil Society Information Service (SACSIS),* 2008. Available at http://www.sacsis.org.za/site/news/detail.asp?idata. Accessed on 6/10/2019

Stremlau, Nicole and Price, Monroe. *Media, Elections and Political Violence in Eastern Africa: Towards a Comparative Framework,* 2009. Available at https://www.ifes.org/sites/default/files/electionviolenceineastafrica.pdf.Accessed on 27/7/2020.

Voltmer, Katrin and Kraetzschmar, Hendrick. *Investigating the Media and Democratisation Conflicts: Research Design and Methodology of Media, Conflict and Democratisation* (MeCoDEM), 2015. Available at http://www.mecodem.eu /wp-content/uploads/2015/06/Voltmer-Kraetzschmar -2015_Investi gating-the-Media-and-Democratisation-Conflicts.pdf. Accessed on 15/5/2020.

Weber, Max. "Legitimacy, Politics and the State". *Legitimacy and the State,* edited by Connolly, William, University Press, 1984, pp. 32–62.

Willems, Wendy. "The Ballot Vote as Embedded Ritual: A Radical Critique of Liberal-Democratic Approaches to Media and Elections in Africa". *African Studies,* Vol. 71, No. 1, 2012, pp. 91–107. ISSN 0002–0184.

Wiredu, Kwasi. *Cultural Universals and Particulars: An African Perspective.* Indiana University Press, 1996.

Wiredu, Kwasi. "Tradition, Democracy and Political Legitimacy in Contemporary Africa". *Rewriting Africa: Toward Renaissance or Collapse?,* edited by Kurimoto, Eisei, The Japan Center for Area Studies, 2001, pp. 161–172.

20

DEVELOPMENT AND HUMAN RIGHTS IN AFRICA

A Theoretical Proposal

Martin Odei Ajei

Introduction

I aim in this paper to defend the proposal that an ethic of communalism, derived from African concepts of personhood, is appropriate foundation for conceptualizing development and human rights for application in Africa. These two concepts have been the subject of intense academic and policy disputation since the end of the Second World War (WW2), and have undergone several iterations in the course of these debates. Their protracted consideration may underlie Paul Zeleza's suggestion that scholars of social processes in Africa should concentrate on understanding the nature and implications of the strategies of development, especially rights-based ones, and spend "less time offering more prescriptions" of theoretical and strategic directions, as Africa has received "an overabundance [of them] and is no better for it" (Zeleza, 2009). I disagree with Zeleza's advice, and maintain that the wealth of ideas of development and human rights that have made their mark in Africa are liable to review precisely because they have fallen short of the expectations of their intended beneficiaries. I consider as good cause for revisioning, the stranglehold that non-African paradigms have taken on theorizing these concepts. The scant visibility of African scholarship in these efforts is substantiated by Hyden's observation that such scholarship has tended to "echo, often in an opportunistic fashion, the voices of theorists elsewhere in the world (Hyden, 1994)". Zeleza point in saying that many African perspectives have emerged after Hyden's observation cannot be dismissed hastily. There is reason for concern that that in spite of these multiple perspectives, Africa hasn't yet succeeded to free itself from the theoretical sway of external theorizing of these notions.

Even though functionally different concepts, human rights and development share in common a status as normative tools in pursuit of a desirable end: the preservation and improvement of human life, dignity and welfare. They share the aspiration to guiding conduct towards "what conduces to living well" (Aristotle, 2000) in society. Mainstream ethical theories accept this practical conclusion[1]. Proceeding from a virtue-ethicist point of view, for the moment, suitable visions of this end would imply that their anticipated beneficiaries should possess the ability (virtues) to deliberate appropriately on their goals. Development and human rights are, thus, the "stuff" of Aristotle's "practical wisdom" as their object (beneficiaries) ought to possess the attributes of practically wise subjects: they should have

DOI: 10.4324/9781003143529-23

the capacity for "good deliberation". This means they should think correctly, in the sense that their thought processes should yield a beneficial end (Aristotle, 2000). Thus, their good deliberation must achieve three intents of good judgement – i.e. the understanding that development (or human rights) are worthy goals to pursue; the understanding of what this pursuit involves; and the ability to experience and act intelligently towards achieving those ends. If this is a good picture of what a vision of development and human rights involves, then the strategies for their application must be contextually derived. Accordingly, I maintain that the weak African theoretical grip on these notions is undesirable. Hence Zeleza's advice is disputable.

In pursuit of justifications for my proposal, I begin with an overview of conceptions of development since WW2, and argue their lack of appreciable African inputs. I then introduce Kwame Gyekye's account of development as a viable alternative to the dominant concepts. I embark on a similar historical analysis of human rights in the following section. Section three discusses Peter Ekeh's analysis of the problematic structure of the public sphere in post-colonial African states, as the starting point for the search for conceptual foundations. Ekeh identifies two distinct publics that operate with dissimilar norms in the African state, and argues that this dual normative structure subverts meaningful citizenship and the discharge of the state's duties to its citizens. I argue that the failures of the hegemonic conceptions in Africa are indicators of the problems identified by Ekeh. The final section elaborates and justifies my thesis: it argue that Gyekye's idea of development and the African Charter of Human and Peoples' Rights (ACHPR) are consistent with the ethical foundations that I propose, and should therefore be considered as viable starting points for constitutional reform to facilitate the formulation of visions of development, and of human rights, for practice in Africa.

A Whirl of Development at Cross-Purposes

So, what is it for an object to be developed? A good starting point to addressing this question would be Martinussen's distinction between concepts, theories and strategies of development (Martinussen, 1997). I understand him to mean that in the context of societies, a development concept professes an answer to the question: *what* "it is for that society to be developed"?. A concept of development thus specifies goals pertaining to improvements in the lives and welfare of members of a society and in their natural and social environment. It is thus value-laden, as it condenses visions of what a desirable life is. Development theories, on the other hand, seek to elaborate directions for achieving the goals conceived. They specify conditions that facilitate or impede processes towards development as conceived, and the causal relationships that obtain amongst those processes, and grounds for judging the effectiveness of those processes. Conversely, strategies refer essentially to the interventions that seek to transform the society towards their theorized goals. Thus, ideally, the normative content of concepts should be sieved into theories and strategies by virtue of the derivation of these from concepts (Pickering, 1992). I am concerned principally in this paper with development at the conceptual level.

Until WW2, development was envisaged as a goal to be attained by colonized territories through bilateral relations with their colonizing powers. After the war, this conceptualization changed to an emphasis on multilateralism, spearheaded predominantly by the emergent Bretton Woods institutions – the International Monetary Fund (IMF) and the International Bank for Reconstruction and Development (World Bank) (Cooper and Packard, 1997) – whose functions were predicated on the liberalization of trade (Preston, 1997). But the multiple visions of Africa's development obtained from both emphases have steadfastly promoted economic progress and idealized forms of the achievements of Western society. I have indicated elsewhere that it is not unreasonable to suppose that from their genesis to date, the Bretton Woods institutions have remained apathetic to a favourable imagination of the continent's development (Ajei, 2022). The IMF's mandate continues to absolve it from perpetuating the Debt Trap in which sub-Saharan Africa is currently enmeshed (Parfitt, Trevor, and Stephen, 1986); and an analysis of the World Bank reports that the voices of developing countries are inadequately represented in the Bank's operations (The World Bank, 2006). I maintain that this deficiency has conditioned development visions formulated by African institutions.

Theorizing Western achievements as development goals for Africa, after WW2, begins with the modernization school, whose assumptions still hold sway on development theory. Modernization construed countries in the "Third World" as "backward" and prescribed as a solution to this backwardness a phased and irreversible process of evolution modelled on the experience of "developed" North America and Western Europe (Himmelstrand, 1994). This prescription stemmed from modernization's heritage in evolutionary theory (Portes, 1980), and functionalism (So, 1990) and a blend of classical economic theory/Keynesianism (Preston, 1997). Rostow's theory of economic growth (Rostow, 1960), an apogee of modernization theory, seeks to demonstrate that modernization is a phased and linear process towards economic development. Given this, the process tends towards the kind of homogeneity assumed in Talcott Parsons' structural functionalist theory, particularly his claim that "the patterns of modernization are such that the more highly modernized societies become, the more they resemble one another (Levy, 1967)". The upshot of these assumptions is that the liberal economic and democratic course that typify current Western societies are models that Africa should emulate, even though this vision implies that cherished values of the continent's indigenous cultures are eliminable on the path to development (Tipps, 1976). The African development landscape is replete with policy goals that pay allegiance to these assumptions[2]. Among these are the Structural Adjustment Programs (SAPs) imposed in the 1980s as conditions for concessionary loans and debt repayment arrangements by the World Bank and IMF (Preston, 1997), even though they worsened "development" outcomes in implementing countries (Stiglitz, 2002); and Poverty Reduction Strategy (PRSs) introduced by the same institutions in sequel to the SAPs, even though they failed to free African countries that subscribed to them from the debt trap[3].

At the dawn of the 1990s, a "paradigmatic crisis" of development was declared by social scientists who proceeded to embark on a quest for "new paradigms"[3]. The hope was that these new pathways will centre on "homegrown" models. They did. But I maintain that the four foremost models of development that follow the call for revisioning – two formulated outside Africa (The Millennium Development Goals and Sustainable Development Goals) and two formulated by Africans (NEPAD and Agenda 2063) – are also aligned with modernization theory. Although the MDGs and SDGs have been driven by the UN rather than the Bretton Woods institutions, they exhibit no difference in *kind* from the SAPs and PRSs. The MDGs and SDGs, like the SAPs ad PRSs, adopt a "one size fits all" approach that displaces African cultural values[4]. The MDGs established "universally-agreed objectives" for tacking human needs[5]. The SDGs likewise adopt this structural-universalist approach. As with the formulation of the SAPs and PRSs, it is arguable that the representation of African thought in formulating the SDGs is negligible. African representation in the UN's Open Working Groups (OWG)[6] that drafted the SDGs, and in their adoption in 2015, is merely formal and cannot be taken to translate into the inclusion of substantive African content in the goals.

Likewise, the two pan-African models – NEPAD[7], and Agenda 2063[7] – do not fare better in representing African thought. Far from fulfilling its self-definition as an "African-owned and African-led development programme" (NEPAD Secretariat, 2001), NEPAD affirms modernization-theoretical assumptions by de-emphasizing the role that African cultural values should play in the continent's development (Ajei, 2011a). It acknowledges "Africa's rich cultural legacy", and assigns to this legacy merely the role of "consolidating the pride of Africans in their own humanity" (NEPAD, 2001). Clearly, "a rich cultural legacy" is capable of achieving more than this in a homegrown continental framework for development. Like NEPAD, AGENDA 2063 professes to be a pan-African "strategic framework [...] for inclusive and sustainable development" (African Union, 2020a). Yet, of its fifteen "flagship programs" (effortlessly aligned with the 17 SDGs), only one pronounces on how African cultural values can be harnessed to mobilize energies towards achieving its goals. Even so, this solitary recognition is geared towards establishing a museum "to create awareness about Africa's vast, dynamic and diverse cultural artefacts and the influence Africa has had and continues to have on the various cultures of the world" (African Union, 2020b). Again, it is difficult to fathom out how delicate reverence to museum artefacts can serve to highlight the merits of Africa's cultural heritage in a "home-grown" vision for transformation. Thus, neither NEPAD nor Agenda 2063 offer theoretical contributions that differ in kind from modernization-inspired paradigms that fostered and continue to perpetuate the "crisis of development" for which "new paradigms" were sought. (Ajei, 2011b). Although they may be "homegrown", one can hardly perceive them as products nourished by the intellectual soil of Africa.

Gyekye's Dismissal of Economism

Two features typify the span of development visions from modernization to Agenda 2063: their exaggerated emphasis on measurable economic progress along with the assumption that proceeds from such advancement will be harnessed for poverty reduction (Ake, 1996). The other feature is the scant attention paid by these visions to knowledge and values systems evolved in Africa[8]. Kwame Gyekye has coined the term "economism" (Gyekye, 1994) to describe the first of these two features. He dismisses the reduction of development to economic progress as "lopsided, inadequate and unrealistic (Gyekye, 1994)" because the narrowness of this approach renders the visions derived from it incapable of coming "to grips with the complex nature of human society and culture" (Gyekye, 1994). Economistic conceptions of development are particularly objectionable because of the fallacy of composition they exhibit, for "a species is never identical with its genus (Gyekye, 1994)". Hence economic growth cannot be identified with development. Gyekye then proposes a behavioural concept as an attractive alternative. For him, an object is developed that has acquired the "capacity to perform the functions appropriate to its welfare satisfactorily" (Gyekye, 1994). This functional capacity inheres in a society's ability to respond adequately to the entire existential conditions in which its citizens function (Gyekye, 1994). Gyekye's behavioural concept thus requires reasoned agency and inventiveness – behavioural characteristics – that define and refine an object's ability to function satisfactorily (Gyekye, 1994). As such, his object of development ought to be, simultaneously, an agent of development.

Gyekye's idea carries an inherent weakness, embedded in his claim that "the process of development cannot be endless" (Gyekye, 1994). He justifies this claim on the ground that were development an endless process "it will be impossible to justify a claim to the knowledge of a developed object, for an object in a continuous, infinite process of development cannot be fully known; it cannot therefore be characterised as developed" (Gyekye, 1994).

I am inclined to think that Gyekye's position is problematic because his application of "behaviour" to society ought to imply the possibility of perpetual changes to the challenges to which behavioural responses will be required. Accordingly, when such responses to existing problems evolve in a manner that exemplifies attainment of development (adequate responses to addressing those problems), it is reasonable to foresee – or even expect, – the emergence of new problems that necessitate a set of new responses. Such are to be expected because development processes are, by their nature, "crisis ridden" (Ekeh, 1986). Instability and dynamism are necessary attributes of social formation. Therefore, arguably, the only plausible limit to development challenges – challenges that require behavioural responses for a particular society, and the criteria for assessing the satisfactoriness of those responses - is the cessation of that society. Even when that society ceases to exist, such criteria may continue to influence thought and conduct in another (the future of the same society, or a geographically distinct) society. Accordingly, there can hardly be a time limit on a society's development goals, and the criteria for their assessment. Hence, Gyekye's satisfactory behavioural responses cannot have a terminal, but require continually imagining development-bearing criteria for present or future segments of a society.

Admittedly, this weakness in Gyekye's conception becomes less censurable when placed in the context of his article's aim and time of authorship. The work, which arguably counts as the first African philosophical analysis of development and challenge to economism[9], the Bretton Woods institutions and Western governments had powerful influence on the direction of Africa's development. The nomenclature applied to Africa then was interchangeably "the Third World" and "developing" world. Writing in the context of these labels and in a "crisis" precipitated by the uni-dimensional focus on economic growth and denigration of African knowledge and value systems, Gyekye's time-bound concept was hardly out of tune. His reliance on the intuitive appeal of the use of language against an endless (which topographically represents the idea of universal) character of development, and his affirmation of its bounded (both in time and historical context) character, assumes considerable merit when situated in the conventional vocabulary at the time of writing his paper. So in spite of my disagreement with part of Gyekye's conclusions, I find a useful resource in his teleological conception of development as a contextually grounded, self-conscious and deliberate behaviour that is functionally directed towards the welfare of its object-agent.

What Rights Are Whose?

Compared to the crisis of development proclaimed in the 1990s, a "crisis of citizenship" in Africa has been mooted recently (Hunter, 2016). A feature of this latter crisis involves difficulties in delineating an idea of human rights that effectively serves the ends of citizens. As normative tools for improving the processes of social formation and human welfare, human rights instruments have, paradigmatically, been promoted as standards of justice that merit observance[10] because they facilitate a life worth living and promoting. But as with development, African thought has hardly been prominent in the framing of human rights as desirable ideals. The International Bill of Human Rights (IBHR)[11] enjoys acclaim as the best source of human rights standards for universal application. But the universality of its aspirations remain in question, because of its undoubted liberal inspiration and orientation (Ajei,

2015). I believe that cumulatively, the IBHR standards tilt towards the idea of human rights as essentially "natural rights accruing to persons in virtue of their humanity" (Beitz, 2009). This destabilizes their proclaimed universality, for two reasons. First, it de-emphasizes the importance of duties which I argue is foundational to a notion of human rights that is consistent with African thinking; and second, it harbours ambiguities that make way for a liberal seizure of the rights agenda in Africa.

Given its genesis in liberal ideals, the IBHR is committed to an ontology of personhood that upholds the primacy of the human individual over community. As such its norms tend ultimately to prioritize civil and political rights over economic and social rights and the rights of community[12]. The philosophical relevance of such prioritization is that the IBHR fails to accord weight comprehensively to the rights of human beings; and to take seriously the idea of duties as responsibilities that societies must afford to human beings by virtue of their being human. Yet, such responsibilities are foundational to the ethics of personhood in African thought. Reasonable arguments may be advanced against my assessment of the IBHR's orientation by citing the intentions and content of its instruments and those of its correlate, the Vienna Declaration and Programme of Action[13]. Nevertheless, there is good reason to persist in the claim that the IBRH's intentions to affirm the equal weight of rights is defeated by the structure and content of various sections of its instruments, which contrive to depict a hierarchy of rights in favour of the civil and political rights of individuals, and a de-emphasis on duties[14]. As we will see shortly, the bias reflected in the IBHR's assumptions was inserted in the institutional arrangements for the transfer of political power from colonial administration for African self-rule, included the liberal tradition of rights, which conceives a nation as a bearer of the collective right to self-determination and its citizens as bearers of human (civil and political) rights. Such a polarity of rights flagrantly disregards the relationship between state and citizens in indigenous African political formations (Mamdani, 2000); particularly, the continuity of the space between state, community and citizen and their rights and obligations to each other (Wiredu, 2012). Arguably, this initial disconnect between context and theory underpins the problems attending to the fragmented nature of citizenship as well as of rights and duties, discussed in the next section. Such fragmentation, arguably, underlies the failure of IBHR norms on the continent. It is not far-fetched, therefore, to assign responsibility for the well-documented failures of these standards in practice in Africa to the theoretical bias in preferring some rights over others in an internally weighted set of standards.

A House Divided against Itself: Ekeh's Two Publics and the Problem of Citizenship

The observations on the eccentric relationship between state and citizen alluded to in the previous Section are theorized by Peter Ekeh in his "Colonialism and the Two Publics in Africa". This work analyses a unique phenomenon in post-colonial Africa: the existence of two publics – the civic public and the primordial public – which operate with dissimilar norms of behaviour. The primordial public represents elemental groupings, sentiments and activities that bear on the public interest; and subscribes to moral imperatives that align with those in the private domain of citizens (Ekeh, 2012). Conversely, the civic public is "amoral and lacks the generalized moral imperative in the private realm and in the primordial public" (Ekeh, 2012). Citizens and managers of this public measure their relationship with it in terms of what they can gain materially from it, such that their "duties are de-emphasized while rights are squeezed out of the civic public with the amorality of an artful dodger" (Ekeh,

2012). This dual structure of the public realm muddles the notion of citizenship, as citizens see their duties primarily as moral obligations for the benefit of their primordial communities, to which they willingly contribute resources and expect nothing back but only benefits of identity and psychological security (Ekeh, 2012).

Ekeh points out that this duality in the structure of the relationship between state and citizen defies the orthodox definition of a state as a social unit configured by a cohesive private realm and a corresponding public realm, both of which subscribe to a common moral foundation. A norm of reciprocity is pivotal for this definition in Western thought. Harold Laski invokes this norm when he says that the state should first fulfil its obligations to citizens (i.e., observe their rights) before it can legitimately demand duties from them.

For Laski, the purpose which legitimizes and justifies the coercive authority of a state is the acceptance of citizens of the measure of the state's effort to maximize the satisfaction of their demands. And, it is not the "intention merely to achieve this end that is its title to allegiance....it is not the purpose announced but the purpose realized" that is the criterion of the legitimation of the power of the state (Laski 1935). This is so, for "the obedience [i.e. legitimation] that counts is the obedience of an actively consenting mind; and such a mind is concerned less with the source of law than with what the law proposes to do", whether it does it or not, and how it does it when it does (Laski 1989). Thus, a state's sovereignty is subject to limitation by a principle of right conduct of authority, which should be written into the fabric of the state. This principle limits what authority can do by establishing a minimum threshold of conduct state as the basis upon which citizens lay claim to the rights and privileges provided by the state, in a state seeking to construct citizenship and belongingness in the state. It is a threshold beneath which a state seeking legitimation ought not to fall. The principle of right conduct is the norm of reciprocity in application, and the fulfilment of the state's obligations constitute an essential right conduct of its authority. Ekeh argues that the two publics constitute the anomalous outcome of the application of this principle to Africa without due regard to contextual norms that governed the idea of citizenship and the citizen's relationship to the state[13].

A strength of Ekeh's theory lies in its problematization of rights and duties in the two publics. Why is duty the focus in the primordial public, while rights are taken for granted there? And why are rights the focus in the civic public, and duties problematic there? The theory shows the flawed nature of the assumption that the norm of reciprocity will work in post-colonial Africa without leveraging on indigenous norms. But why is that? It is precisely because the frame of reciprocity in the African setting proceeds from communal belongingness, which takes rights and duties as integral parts of an individual's identity. The consequence of the African state's disinterest in promoting this kind of belongingness is that "bonds of mistrust between states and individuals in Africa are replaced with bonds of moral sentiments binding individuals who share a common ethnicity [or alma mater, or religious affiliation]" (Ekeh, 2004). Citizens feel this sense of belonging (and ownership) in their primordial publics and find in them protection from the state. The lesson here is that rights and duties, as organic elements of citizenship, become more meaningful once citizens' belongingness to the state are resolved. Where a misalignment obtains, "the national interest is not promoted and protected from exploitation" (Ekeh, 1986).

How, then, may we transcend this consequence of the two publics in an inherently pluralistic post-colonial African society whose basic regulatory norms are progressively being dominated by liberal thought? In my view, a short answer to this question is: by making rights and duties organic elements of citizenship. Such an approach would imply discarding the limited scope of the dominant imagination of rights (tilted towards liberal values), and of duties (de-emphasized by the processes of state formation and the IBHR) for a framework modelled on the norms of the primordial public. Such a model can accommodate an imaginative blend of the concepts of development and human rights, grounded on African social and ethical values. A homegrown moral and social normative base is needed to provide the stimulus for self-sustained conceptions of progress, and for the entitlements and obligations that accrue to citizens by virtue of their human beings to whose nature communal belongingness is integral. The idea of "home-growing" to which I allude here differs from the use of the term in NEPAD and Agenda 2063, as mine hinges on the requirement that the intended beneficiaries of development and human rights should make sense of the concepts at the time of their formulation and, as argued, such an understanding is hardly discernible in NEPAD and Agenda 2063. Access to the means to 'home-grow' one's conceptions on this view becomes a "fundamental human right of decisional representation" (Wiredu, 1996); and supplies a negotiated and shared normative perspective by rational agents – a social morality – from which the creativity for the transformation of social norms and structures can proceed. A judicious employment of this access can direct how subjects construct what they construct, and for what ends they exert their efforts. Historical and cultural contexts are important resources for this right of decisional representation. I maintain that weak representation by Africans in the formulation of development and human rights goals is a key cause of their failure in Africa. Had decisional representation been actively at work, the process of state formation would most likely been grounded on a supposition the relationship between public institutions and rational citizens who consider social belongingness to be an inherent feature of their personhood, and who take individual rights and duties as equally integral aspects of that identity[14]. In such a framework of state formation, a frame of reciprocity would have evolved that aligns citizen and state, and bring values into play that can end the exploitation of the state characterised by Ekeh's civic public.

Towards a Solution: A Bill of Duties from an Ethics of Mutual Responsibility

Several philosophers have defended the notion of personhood indicated in the preceding section, which entered philosophical debate with Mbiti's claim that an African perceives her being as dependent on the being of others (Mbiti, 1970). A human being is, on this view, born into a community of well-defined social affiliations (Wiredu, 1992), and remains dependent on these for her existence and sustenance of her aspirations. She comes to conceive of her identity as "part of an ordered whole whose principle of order is the ethic of the community" (Wiredu, 2009). This ethic of mutual interdependence is what makes persons naturally orientated towards others, for it emphasizes solidarity and cooperation as necessary requirements for a life lived well. The idea of mutual interdependence as a human mode of being in African thought, and the reciprocal responsibility it solicits from everyone, is expressed in Masolo's view that to be human is to differ and be different, but not to be indifferent in the social setting (Masolo, 2004). One ought to value such a life because human life is an enterprise of mutual aid[14], therefore human fellowship is the most important human need. The upshot of this ethic is that it solidarity, cooperation and reciprocal responsibility, are necessary conditions for the sustenance and flourishing of a life well lived.

In my view, a state's observance of duties to citizens would be less problematic were the relationship between citizen and state structured by such an ontology and ethic of personhood. For, the relationship between citizens would unfold in a harmoniously contiguous space between state, community, and citizen (Wiredu, 2012). Where this obtains, the problem identified by Ekeh, of ownership of, and belonginess to, the state will be resolved;

and the "bonds of mistrust between states and individuals" and the "bonds of moral sentiments binding individuals who share a common ethnicity [or alma mater, or religious affiliation]"(Ekeh, 2004) as occurs in the two publics, is likely to dissipate. But practically, this solution, grounded on an ethic of mutual responsibility, necessitates the reform of African constitutions. There is a need to insert into them a Bill of Duties[15] that matches their provisions on human rights. The Bill of Duties would elaborate the foundational obligations of the state in relation to its citizens in a manner that accords with the ontology of belongingness of indigenous African cultures. Such elaboration should proceed from a moral imagination that transcends the structure of the current binary construction of rights and duties, by integrating them in a manner that makes rights derivative from duties. The relationship between rights and duties in this framework can be characterized thus: if I (or the state) owe X a duty to do Y, X also owes another person the duty to do Z, and in this string of relations of duties, rights are derived because those duties are owed to individual citizens (or distinct groups of citizens), and by owing them to citizens and performing them, the recipients of the outcomes of those duties which are owed, assume a right to expect to be recipients of that which is owed to them. So, being a recipient of a duty renders one automatically a recipient of the rights that those duties imply. And because one's life unfolds in the context of mutual aid, one is likely to feel the need to reciprocate the entitlements that one has with performing one's duties to others.

The proposals on duties enshrined in the African Charter of Human and People's Rights (ACHPR)[16] serve as a good starting point for this strategy. A unique feature of the Charter is the clear footprints of the African cultural values it contains. The Committee of Experts that drafted the Charter was invited to produce a Charter that reflects "the African conception of human rights, [and] African philosophy of law"[17]. This invitation appears to have generated distinctive ideas that depart from the temperament of the IBHR conventions, in explicitly recognizing the validity of culture-specific values in conceiving human rights standards. These unique features of the ACHPR are as well relevant to the notion of development.

Two such relevant ideas deserve mention. One is the Charter's introduction of the notion of "peoples' rights" to human rights language[18]; and the other is the subject-matter of the duties it catalogues for the state and individuals. The Charter doesn't define "peoples", but the tone of its provisions suggests it can be interpreted in terms of John Rawls's notion of "Society of Peoples", i.e. as well-ordered societies that seek "proper self-respect of themselves as a people, resting on their common awareness of their trials during their history and of their culture with its accomplishments" (Rawls, 1999). Construed as such, it becomes obvious that this right is distinguishable from the UN's notion of the right to self-determination as "one of the pillars of the international human rights order"[19]. This is so, because in the Covenants of the IBRH, "self-determination" is restricted principally to a people's resolve on their political status within the international system of polities, and their right to choose their domestic constitutional arrangements (El-Obaid and Appeagyei, 1996). However, I think the African Charter's "self-determination" demands more than this. It is highly unlikely that the drafters of the Charter, stimulated by the entreaty to be sensitive to African normative frameworks, would construe the right to choose one's own constitutional arrangements in a manner that is premised on the Western norm of reciprocity discussed above. They are unlikely to simply draft peripheral variations on IBRH norms, or repeat them. In my view, therefore, the Charter's right to self-determination should be read as establishing a foundational right for African peoples to seize a "decisional representation" in determining what they take to constitute human rights. The Charter's introduction of "peoples' rights", as distinct from, and complementary to, "human rights", would seem to constitute this determination. It points to a new conceptual direction in the history of rights discourse. The constitutional reform I am advocating should interpret this right as the right to ground human rights and development goals on an African theory of persons – and by extension of citizenship – that prioritizes duties.

The Charter is unique also in the manner and content of the duties it outlines: specific ones for states, and others for citizens. A state duty that I find relevant for my proposed solution appears in Article 18, which prescribes a duty to recognize and assist the family as the natural and basic unit of the community. This identification of the family, rather than the individual citizen, as the basic unit of society is notable in the way it mimics traditional African ideas on the composite units of society. The family is indeed the basic unit of the network of relationships in the relational ontology discussed, and so this duty requirement seems to me to hit at the core of the ethics of mutual dependency. Furthermore, among duties of the individual relevant for my argument are her "duties towards the family, society, state, other legally recognized communities" (Article 27); her duty to "preserve the harmonious development of the family, to work for its cohesion, and to maintain one's parents at all times" (Article 29.1); her duty to serve one's national community (Article 29.2), her duty to "preserve and strengthen social and national solidarity" (Article 29.3), and her duty to "preserve and strengthen positive African cultural values" (Article 29.9). These duties of the individual accord with the ethic of life as mutual aid, and the ontology of personhood, in several indigenous African cultures, and can serve as the beginning point for an explicit bill of duties that orientates the individual towards the state in the manner she relates to others in Ekeh's primordial public.

The integration I am proposing is not one-sided. Emphasis on community and duties in the proposed constitutional reform should not be interpreted as counting for degrading individuality. Articles 2–22 of ACHPR outline rights that basically imitate the civil and political rights in the IBHR. The Charter, thus, affirms the hybridity of human nature by assigning in tandem the enjoyment of rights and performance of duties to persons and peoples. It merely suggests the necessity to expand the focus of the individual's communal relations "to bring to bear a sense of [her] liberation, initiative and creativeness" (Abraham, 1962). This should be done, as I have suggested above, in a manner that makes the status of rights derivative from duties.

The constitutional integration of rights and duties neither envisages an unrequited extension of the domain of duties owed by members of primordial publics to the state, nor the state's duties to its citizenry. The state owes a duty to harness prevailing positive norms in the primordial setting in constructing a homogeneous citizenry and in sorting its interest in the legitimation of its power. Thus, the solution to Ekeh's duality of citizenship becomes not so much of overcoming society-improving primordial loyalties in order for a meaningful citizenship model to evolve that can sustain successful practices of development and human rights. Rather, such loyalties should be harnessed by the state and incorporated into the processes of harmonizing the status of citizenship.

Conclusion

The President of the United States of America and the Chancellor of Germany, in the *Washington Declaration*, publicized on the 15ᵗʰ of July 2021, affirmed their commitment to promoting peace, security and prosperity around the world. Towards this goal, they affirmed their "responsibility to lead in the development of global solutions to shared challenges" and to work together "bilaterally, as well as in the G7 and G20", to ensure the multilateral system, including the UN system, can meet contemporary global demands (The White House, 2021)

Reference to global demands suggests that the two heads of state had in mind solutions to human problems – to problems that afflict or threaten the whole of humanity. Yet, they conceived solutions to these to reside in the domain of the G7 and G20, to which Africa has but a negligible voice[20]. This is one more evidence of the endurance of the historical inattention to African agency in finding solutions to its developmental problems, for the right to decisional representation dictates that solutions to threats to African aspirations should be, at least partly, African. This calls attention to Okeja's recent thesis that a desirable African future is contingent on, first, admitting, and then working through, the failure of politics on the continent (Okeja, 2022). One of the ways in which political philosophers can contribute to this task of clarifying the failure of politics and tackling its consequences is to assess the manner in which African conceptual resources can be brought to bear on conceptualizing and theorizing development and human rights.

I have proposed that the notion of duties enshrined in ACHPR should serve as the foundation for framing a Bill of Duties that have unequivocal relevance for accounting for the relationship between citizens and the state because the ACHPR notion is consonant with normative values and the ontology of personhood in several indigenous African cultures, and that these values and theories of personhood have the capacity to accustom the individual to bridging the gap between the state and her primordial public. The principle of order of such a Bill of Duties should be the ethic of mutual interdependence of citizens, and the reciprocal responsibility it elicits from the state. Such an instrument, grounded in such an ethics, is likely to address the powerlessness that citizens feel in the face of the state, and provide normative grounds to compel the institutions of state to act in ways that inspire confidence in citizens of their belonging in the state. Success with drafting such a Bill of Duties will serve, among others, to uncover flaws in the marginalization of African perspectives on development and human rights; and enrich global theorizing of these concepts through the inclusion of African inputs, and further balance the historical neglect of Africa in conceiving these normative tools for social formation.

Notes

1 Except that the reasons that they offer for this will differ: utilitarians will maintain that what makes this right is that it results in the greatest amount of well-being, overall; whereas Kantians will maintain action towards this is right if it accords with the law of reason. Virtue ethicists will assign the rightness of action towards this to its being virtuous.

2 An exemption to these is the challenge to modernization that was mounted by dependency theory in the 1970s and 1980s. Although the critique originated in South America, substantial theoretical inputs were made by Africans to it. However, this challenge faltered in the face of modernization because dependency "remained a theory of criticism [of Modernization and Western theoretical hegemony], not of substantive engagement with the issues of development" (Ekeh, 1986, p. 6).

3 One academic response is "In Search of New Paradigms for African Development (ISENPAD)", through which the publication *African Perspectives on Development* (Himmelstrand, U, Kinyanjui, K., and Mburugu E (eds), 1994) that professes a number of "homegrown" development strategies.

4 I mean by this that of the substance of five of the eight goals (a) are wrongfully assumed to be accessible to universal meaning and (b) are easily measured by some economic index or the other.

5 Endorsed by African Heads of State and Government in October 2001 as the main development agenda for the continent.

6 Adopted at the 50th Anniversary of the formation of the OAU/AU, in May 2013.

7 In addition to the classical theorists of modernization, Hyden affirms the view that relations that have economic and social value in indigenous African social organization are impediments to development (Hyden, 1983, 8–11).

8 This statement needs qualification. Odera Oruka's applied philosophy is undoubtedly on development, even though he didn't undertake a conceptual analysis of the term. Oruka advocated for "ethically appropriate actions" into development thinking and practice in Africa, and an "ethical minimum" driven by a humanistic morality that aims for "the quality and security of human life" (Oruka, 1997, 138). His developmental thinking is also implicit in his view that civil liberties (political freedom) can hardly be effective without economic freedom – access to a decent standard of living, and at worst to basic needs (1996, 66). As Masolo points out, the duty to fulfil Oruka's right to an ethical minimum is not incumbent only on national governments, but rises to the level of global justice (Masolo, 2012, 25). However, Oruka identifies "ethno-religious solutions" with "dogmatism and non-philosophy", and excludes these from any role in addressing the "current prevailing and dehumanizing ethics of political might" (Presby, 288). Although the term "ethno-religion" is not clarified by Oruka, it is reasonable to suppose that he meant by it aspects of what I consider to be salient tenets of indigenous African ontology, epistemology and values. If my interpretation of Oruka's claim holds, then there is cause to see Gyekye's paper as the first African philosophical paper on development that consciously advocates the relevance of traditional African knowledge and value systems.

9 Either by state action or by the action of some determinate entity

10 This consists of the Universal Declaration of Human Rights (UDHR), adopted in 1948; the International Covenant on Civil and Political Rights and the International Covenant on Economic, Social and Cultural Rights, both of which came into force in 1976.

11 This does not constitute a distinction between "negative" and "positive" rights, and identify negative rights with those that do not require State action (e.g. refraining from torture) and positive ones where civil and political liberties are "negative" and economic rights etc. are "positive". I accept the position that such a dichotomy is not helpful, as for example, refraining from torture requires committing resources to train the police (positive), and the right to food sometimes just means refraining from depriving small-scale farmers of their lands (negative). I accept therefore that these two supposed categories of rights are not diametrically opposed but dovetail into each other.

12 The World Conference on Human Rights adopted the Declaration and Programme of Action in Vienna on June 25, 1993.

13 Although the UDHR renders no explicit endorsement of liberalism, its liberal orientation can be intuited in the ubiquitous presence of paradigmatic terms of liberalism, like "freedom", "liberty", "equality", "reason"; and in the preponderance of the provisions affirming personal civil and political rights over those that espouse social and economic rights. Of the 30 Articles of the UDHR, only one – Article 29 – makes any statement on the individual's duties to the community. Further, although the International Covenant on Civil and Political Rights (ICCPR) and International Covenant on Economic, Social and Cultural Rights (ICESCR) advocate the right of all peoples to self-determination and to economic, social and cultural development. However, I have argued in "Ontology and Human rights" that various sections of these Covenants indicate a bias for civil and political liberties.

14 By "ontology" I mean a philosophical account of things as that are, i.e., of "being".

15 This conclusion is Wiredu's interpretation of two Akan maxims "*onipa na ohia*", which he interprets as yielding two simultaneous meanings: "human interest is the basis of all value" and "and "human fellowship is the most important of human needs". These meanings serve as the premise to another maxim "*obra ye nnoboa*", which means "life is an enterprise of mutual aid" (Wiredu, K., "An orap philosophy of personhood: Comments on Philosophy and Oralitry", in Research in African Literatures, 2009, Vol. 40, No. 1, pp. 8–18, p. 16

16 I owe this idea to Professor Edwin Etieyibo, but not the content I am endeavouring to give to it. I heard the phrase for the first time in Edwin's inaugural lecture, titled "An African Ethics of a duty and Cultural Justice and injustice". on 21st September 2020. I attended the lecture via webinar, but the connection was so unstable I could also hear fragments of the speech. Since then I have asked Edwin to share a copy of the lecture with me, but I have not received it yet. So I have not had occasion to see exactly how he conceived this Bill to be like.

17 Adopted by the Organization of African Unity (OAU), a precursor to the African Union, on June 27, 1981. But the Charter entered into force on October 26, 1986.

18 Quoted in Amnesty International, *The Organization of African Unity and Human Rights,* AI Index IOR 03/04/87, p. 8

19 This notion occurs in several provisions of the Charter, including (a) the promotion and protection of morals and traditional values recognized by the community (Article 17.3); the "unquestionable and inalienable right to self-determination" of peoples (Article 20.1); the right of peoples to their economic, social and cultural development (Article 22.1); and a peoples' right to an environment favourable to their [own] development (Article 24).

20 South Africa is the only African member of the G20. In the non-Western world, South America is represented by three countries (Argentina, Brazil and Mexico), whereas Asia is represented by four (China, India, Indonesia and South Korea) The scant African representation is significant, given that G20 Countries together represent around 90% of global GDP, and two-thirds of the world's population.

References

Abraham, W., E., 1962 [2015], *The Mind of Africa*, Oxford: Oxford university Press [Accra: Sub-Sahara Publishers].

African Union a: https://au.int/en/agenda2063/overview [21 May 2020].

African Union b: https://au.int/en/agenda2063/flagship-projects [21 May 2020].

Ajei, M.O., 2011a, *Africa's Development: The Imperatives of Indigenous Knowledge and Values*, Saarbrucken: Lambert Academic Publishing, pp. 79–80.

Ajei, M.O., 2011b, "Africa's Renaissance and the Challenge of Culture: The Failures of NEPAD", in *Identity Meets Nationality: Voices from the Humanities*. Lauer, H., et al. (eds), Accra: Sub-Saharan Publishers, pp. 242–264.

Ajei, M.O., 2022, An African philosophical perspective on barriers to the current discourse on sustainability, *The Philosophical Forum*, 53 (1):31–45 (2022), p. 34.

Ake, C., 1996, *Democracy and Development in Africa*, Ibadan: Spectrum Books, p. 127.

Aristotle, *Ethics*, Book VI, Chapter 9, 1142b.

Aristotle, *Nicomachean Ethics*, Edited by Roger Crisp, Cambridge: Cambridge University Press, 2000, Book VI, Chapter 5, 1140a. See also Aristotle, *Politics*. Translated by C. D. C. Reeve. Indianapolis, IN: Hackett, p. 3.

Beitz, C.R. 2009, *The Idea of Human Rights*, New York: Oxford University Press, p. 60.

Bradshaw, J., 2009, *Reclaiming Virtue: How We Can Develop the Moral Intelligence to Do the Right Thing at the Right Time for the Right Reason*, New York: Bantam, p. 55.

Cooper, F. and Packard, R., 1997, "Introduction", in *International Development and the Social Sciences: Essays on the History and Politics of Knowledge*. Cooper, F. and Packard, R. (eds), California: University of California Press, pp. 1–6.

Ekeh, P.P., 1986, "Development Theory and the African Predicament", *Africa Development*, Vol. 11, No. 4, pp. 1–40, p. 9.

Ekeh, P.P., 2004, "Individuals' Basic Security Needs and the Limits of Democracy in Africa", in *Ethnicity and Democracy in Africa*. Berman, B., Eyoh, D. and Kymlicka, W. (eds), Athens: Ohio University Press. p. 36.

Ekeh, P.P., 2012, "Colonialism and the Two Publics in Africa: A Theoretical Statement with an Afterword", in *Reclaiming the Huamn Sciences and Humanities through African Perspectives*. Lauer, H. and Anyidoho, K. (eds), Accra: Sub-saharan Publishers, pp. 200–232, p. 201.

El-Obaid, E. A & Appiagyei-Atua, K., 1996, "Human Rights in Africa – A New Perspective on linking the past to the present", *McGill Law Journal*, Vol. 41, pp. 819–859, p. 839.

Gyekye, K., 1994, "Taking Development Seriously" *Journal of Applied Philosophy*, Vol. 11, No. 1, pp. 44–56.

Gyekye, K., 1995, *An Essay on African Philosophical Thought: The Akan Conceptual Scheme*. Philadelphia: Temple University Press.

Gyekye, K., 1997, *Tradition and Modernity: Philosophical Reflections on the African Experience*. Oxford: Oxford University Press.

Laski, H. J., 1935, *The State in Theory and Practice*. London: Allen and Unwin, *pp. 19–20.*

Laski, H. J., 1989, "Law and the State", in *The Pluralist Theory of the State*. Paul Q. Hirst (ed.), London: Routledge, pp. 195–227, p. 105.

Himmelstrand, U., 1994, "Perspectives, Controversies and Dilemmas in the Study of African Development", in *African Perspectives on Development*. Himmelstrand, U., Kinyanjui, K. and Mburugu, E. (eds), London: James Currey Ltd., p. 37.

Hunter, E., 2016, *Citizenship, Belonging, and Political Community in Africa: Dialogues between Past and Present*, Cambridge: Centre of African Studies.

Hyden, G., 1983, *No Short Cuts to Progress: African Development Management Perspectives*, Berkeley: University of California Press, p. 8–11.

Hyden, G., 1994, "Changing Ideological and Theoretical Perspectives on Development", in *African Perspectives on Development*. Himmelstrand, U., Kinyanjui, K. and Mburugu, E. (eds), London: James Currey Ltd., p. 318.

Levy, M.J., 1967, "Social Patterns (Structures) and Problems of Modernization", op. cit., p.

Mamdani, M., 2000, "Democratic Theory and Democratic Struggles in Africa." in *Government and Politics in Africa*. Nnoli, O. (ed.), Harare: AAPS Books, pp. 220–239, p. 228.

Martinussen, J., 1997, *Society, State & Market*, London: Zed Books, pp. 14–15.

Masolo, D.A., 2004, "Western and African Communitarianism: A Comparison", in *A Companion to African Philosophy*. Wiredu, K. (ed.), Malden: Blackwell Publishing, pp. 483–498, p. 495.

Masolo, D.A., 2012, "Care Versus Justice: Odera Oruka and the Quest for Global Justice", *Thought and Practice*, Vol. 4, No. 2, pp. 23–49.

Mbiti, J. S., 1970, *African Religions and Philosophy*, London: Heinemann, p. 141.

NEPAD Secretariat, 2001, *The New Partnership for Africa's Development Development*, Midrand: NEPAD Secretariat, paragraph 60.

Okeja, U., 2022, *Deliberative Agency*. Bloomington: Indiana University Press, p. 4.

Oruka, H.O, 1996, *The Philosophy of Liberty: An Essay on Political Philosophy*, Revised ed. Nairobi: Standard Textbooks Graphics and Publishing.

Oruka, H.O., 1997, *Practical Philosophy: In Search for an Ethical Minimum*. Nairobi: East African Educational Publishers.

Parfitt, T.W., and Stephen, P.R., 1986, "Africa in the Debt Trap: Which Way Out?" *The Journal of Modern African Studies*, Vol. 24, No. 3, pp. 519–527.

Pickering, A. (ed.), 1992, *Science as Practice and Culture*, Chicago: Chicago University Press.

Portes, A., 1980, "Convergences between Conflicting Theoretical Perspectives in National Development", in *Sociological Theory and Research*. Blalock, H. (ed.), New York: Free Press, p. 223.

Presby, G.M., 2002, "African Philosophers on Global Wealth Redistribution", in *Thought and Practice in African Philosophy*. Presby, G.M., et al. (eds), Nairobi: Konrad Adenauer Stiftung, pp. 283–300, p. 284.

Preston, P.W., 1997a, *Development Theory*, op. cit., p. 168.

Preston, P.W., 1997b, *Development Theory*, op. cit., pp. 153–165.

Preston, P.W., 1997c, *Development Theory*: An Introduction, Oxford: Blackwell Publishing.

Rawls, J., 1999, *Law of Peoples*, p. 34.

Rostow, W.W., 1960, *The Stages of Economic Growth: A Non-Communist Manifesto*. Cambridge: Cambridge University Press. According to Rostow, his five stages of economic growth "constitute in the end both a theory about economic growth and a more general, if still highly partial, theory about modern history as a whole" (p. 1).

So, A.Y., 1990, *Social Change and Development*, op. cit., p. 18.

Stiglitz, J., *Globalization and Its Discontents*, New York: W. W. Norton and Co. 2002, p. 86.

Tipps, D.C., 1976., "Modernization Theory and the Comparative Study of Societies: A Critical Perspective" op. cit., p. 81.

The World Bank, 2006, *Evaluating the World Bank's Approach to Global Programs: Addressing the Challenges of Globalization*. http://www.worldbank.org/ieg/gppp/index.html

The White House, 2021, The Washington Declaration. https://www.whitehouse.gov/briefing-room/statements-releases/2021/07/15/washington-declaration/ [30 June 2021]

Wiredu, K., 1992, "The Moral Foundations of an African Culture", in *Person and Community, Ghanaian Philosophical Studies I.* Wiredu, K. and Gyekye, K. (eds), Washington, DC: Council for Research into Values and Philosophy, pp. 193–206.

Wiredu, K., 1996, *Cultural Universals and Particulars*, Bloomington and Indianapolis: Indiana University Press, p. 180.

Wiredu, K., 2012, "State, Civil Society and Democracy in Africa", in *Reclaiming the Human Sciences and Humanities through African Perspectives II*. Lauer, H. and Anyidoho, K. (eds), Accra: Sub-Saharan Publishers, pp. 1055–1066, p. 1055.

Zeleza, P.T., 2009, "What Happened to the African Renaissance? The Challenges of Development in the Twenty-First century", *Comparative Studies of South Asia, Africa and the Middle East*, Vol. 29, No. 2, pp. 155–170, p. 170.

http://www.undp.org/content/undp/en/home/sustainable-development-goals/background.html [21st May 2021].

https://sustainabledevelopment.un.org/owg.html [21 May 2020].

http://www.imf.org/external/np/prsp/prsp.asp [21 May 2020].

PART IV

Emerging Concepts and Topics

21

RELIGION AND POLITICS

Learning to Navigate a Slippery Slope

Jare Oladosu

Introduction

Many are the afflictions of democratic evolution in post-colonial Africa; it is not clear if and to what extent it can be delivered from any of them. Most of the problems retarding Africa's democratic progress are man-made; only a few can be classified as acts of nature. But even about the latter, humanity has been severely complicit as an active contributory agent. By their acts of omission (sheer negligence) or commission, human beings have facilitated, albeit in a negative way, nature's devastating rampage on the physical environment, which in turn has contributed in no small measure to the impoverishment of the populations of African nations, which in turn has contributed significantly to stymie the robust evolution of democracy and its attendant virtues on the continent.

While the exploration of the nexus between environmental crises and mass poverty is a fascinating subject,[1] the focus of this chapter will largely be on the man-made factors militating against the entrenchment of the democratic ethos in contemporary Africa. These man-made obstacles to Africa's democratic progress are very serious and they tend to be resistant to resolution. But some are more serious and more resistant to resolution than others. The commonly acknowledged obstacles include, in no particular order, chronic insecurity, ethnic chauvinism, restive and professionally undisciplined armed forces, and a rigged globalized economic order. In my view, these well-known factors are more amenable to scientific resolution in the final analysis because the issues that precipitate them are almost always based on a scientific ontology. Matters concerning religion and spirituality, on the other hand, underwritten as they often are by a transcendental ontology, tend to be inherently resistant to resolution.

In this essay, I will start by highlighting some of the more commonly acknowledged obstacles in the path of democratic progress in post-colonial African nation-states. I will then isolate, for a more detailed analytical engagement, the one factor which I consider most intractable, or at least seemingly so, namely the disruptive impact of religion on the politics of most contemporary African nation-states. My overall strategy is to set out a constitutional/legal framework that would enable us to avoid inquiring into the murky contents of religious doctrines and the underlying theologies altogether. The critical objective is the affirmation of the incontestable sovereignty of the "secular" state and the supremacy of its law-making authority and power. The essay will be in two main parts. The highlight of

DOI: 10.4324/9781003143529-25

some difficult, but as they will turn out, lesser obstacles in the path of democratic progress, will be presented in part one. I will take up the matter of religion in the politics of African states in part two.

The Lesser Hurdles

Among the perennially difficult hurdles in the path of political progress, which I would equate with democratic evolution, in post-colonial Africa, is the deep-seated ethnic suspicion, rivalry and contestation for political power, which in turn has routinely been used to garner socio-economic advantages and even dominance. It is a historical truism that various ethnic nationalities occupying contiguous, sometimes overlapping, geographical spaces were arbitrarily lumped together when the colonizing European powers drew the boundaries of their territorial holdings in Africa. Accounts of the Berlin Conference of 1884, at which the European overlords carved up for sharing, pieces of the African continent (like so many pieces of a giant cake) have been variously rendered.[2] In effect, what the departing colonial administrators left behind in the guise of modern nation-states all over Africa, perhaps with the rare exception of Somalia, were actually federations of ethnic nationalities, where the "federating units" had no hand in the composition of the resultant federations.

Whether the European colonizers reconfigured the African continent that way with the express aim of sowing the seeds of discord, as conspiracy theorists might insist, or they embarked on the arbitrary ethnic partitioning primarily for administrative convenience, as more optimistic souls might grant, could be a prime subject for scholarly debate. What is incontrovertible, however, are the pernicious effects of those involuntary ethnic realignments of African societies on the social and political experiences of the resultant nation-states.

The ethnic fault lines opened up with a vengeance immediately after the flag independence in each of the new nation-states, as the elites from the various ethnic nationalities jostled to fill the vacancies left by the departing European administrators. Since the overriding goal in this contest was not the entrenchment of democratic norms and ethos as such, but the almost single-minded pursuit of ethnic advantage, with the ultimate aim of furthering personal interests, all but little efforts were made to nurture democratic ideals. Indeed, democratic institutions and processes such as free and transparently fair elections, independent judiciaries, free press, robust civic involvement in political discourse and negotiation, were routinely compromised, sometimes blatantly perverted in the early post-colonial African states – the period commonly referred to as the first republic in many parts of the continent.

More pertinent for our concern here, is the fact that the ethnic factor still looms large in the politics of most contemporary African countries, several decades after independence from colonial rule and the subsequent era of self-government. For the most part, elections are still won/lost with votes cast along ethnic lines.[3] Even where the electorates would prefer to transcend ethnic barriers, say, to endorse demonstrable virtue and competence, desperate politicians would sooner goad them back into tribal line. African politicians still scurry back to their ancestral enclaves to rally support from their kith and kins, whenever they run into trouble "outside", i.e., at the national arena.

The most notorious recent instance of this phenomenon has to be what, for want of a better label, I would call the Zuma affair.[4] Certainly, South Africans and indeed the whole of Africa cannot soon forget the ugly spectacle of vandalism, looting and mindless arson that were committed in July 2021, by Mr. Zuma's supporters, mostly his fellow Zulus, when the former President of South Africa was to be arraigned in a court of law for trial for alleged corruption and abuse of his office as President between 2009 and 2018.

Whereas the Zuma affair may stand out as particularly odious, given the scale of destruction wrecked on the society and being so recent, thus fresh in our memories, it is by no means isolated or rare. African politicians resort to the elicitation of ethnic protection at the slightest provocation. From the first republic to-date, Nigerian politicians, for example, have availed themselves of the unfailing understanding and protection of their kinsmen. It is not uncommon to hear that communities in Nigeria form a human shield around the homestead of their "illustrious son", so as to prevent the arrest and prosecution of such ethnic heroes and benefactors. Such a human barricade was reportedly mounted to prevent the arrest of a former Governor of Delta State, in Nigeria, James Ibori.[5] Can anyone possibly be in doubt that were any attempt to be made to arrest and prosecute any of Nigeria's former Presidents or (especially) the incumbent President after he leaves office, presumably in 2023, Nigeria and Africa would witness a level of violent resistance that might surpass the Zuma affair?

Surely, the democratic credentials of a polity where some individuals are treated as sacred cows, immune from accountability for their deeds in office through the due process of the law, must at best, be suspect. Where public officials and their ethnic supporters are able to successfully negotiate "political solutions" to their otherwise clear legal infractions, thereby truncating the normal processes of the law, there we can be sure that the development of democratic norms is at best inchoate. The indispensable anchor for a democratic polity is the adherence to the due process of the law; the rule of law, in other words, is the engine that makes democracy run.

Until the tall weeds of ethnic interests and calculations are first eradicated, no seed of democracy that falls on the African political soil would flourish. But, and here is the rub, there is little indication that these weeds would be eradicated anytime soon. The hope of their eradication must remain nugatory as long as members of the political elites, who manipulate the primordial ethnic divisions for their own selfish interests, actively nurture them.

Another potent obstacle in the path of democratic progress in Africa is an unconscionable level of poverty. Majority of the populations of virtually all African countries live below the World Bank prescribed index of about two United States' dollars per day.[6] And the situation seems to be getting direr in many of these countries, where a concatenation of factors is conspiring to render entire populations desperately impoverished. These factors include what we might surmise as bad governance, i.e., lack of basic managerial and technical competences by those running the affairs of the African states, coupled with a crippling level of corruption, fueled by impunity. To compound the misery are natural disasters like inclement weather, problems such as desertification, coastal erosion, and other forms of environmental problems. Man-made calamities like full-blown wars and other forms of insecurity, from insurgency and banditry to inter- and intra-communal conflicts, in some cases, hangovers of ancient animosities, also contribute their ample quotas to the pauperization of Africans.

In a class all by themself, among factors making the average African the "wretched of the earth", are the deleterious effects of a globalized world economy. Unable to compete meaningfully, African nations are often left holding the proverbial bag. They are perennially at a disadvantage in a global economy whose terms are invariably written and enforced by the economically powerful nations of Western Europe, North America, and the economic powerhouses of Asia, namely, China and Japan.

The cumulative effects of these and other factors have plunged overwhelming majorities of the populations of African countries into a deeply entrenched poverty. For example, Nigeria was reported to hold the unenviable distinction of being the poverty capital of the world, having overtaken India, according to World Bank records, sometime in 2018.[7] This is statistically depressing; what it means is that nominally there are now many more poor persons in Nigeria than in India, even though at about 1.4 billion the population of India is roughly seven times that of Nigeria, which is estimated to be about 200 million. Other African countries may not have this dubious distinction of being the poverty capital of the world, but they are not fairing any better either. Everywhere one turns on the continent, one is confronted by a mind-numbing level of poverty.

It is trite to acknowledge that democracy and its concomitant ideals and processes would be the last thing on the mind of a person so destitute as to not know where his next meal would come from or if the meal would come at all. Right from the advent of participatory democracy in the ancient Greek city-states till today, a certain irreducible minimum level of material and emotional comfort is a prerequisite for an active participation in democratic discourse and practical engagement. As one might expect in this kind of political ecosystem, characteristic of contemporary African nations, voting in Nigeria, for example, as in many other African countries, are sometimes openly staged electoral bazars, where votes are delivered on a cash-and-carry basis. Clearly, the result of such exercises would hardly amount to the free expressions of democratic preferences. Such a display of crash opportunism by all the actors – office-seeking politicians and the electorate to varying degrees – can only be a cynical perversion of the democratic ideal.

Another major obstacle in the path of democratic progress in Africa is the phenomenon of military coup d'état. In most parts of the twenty-first century world, a military take-over of government would be regarded as the ultimate political horror, a mind-jarring throwback to the dark ages of socio-political underdevelopment, an atavistic abomination. That would be the case in many parts of today's world, but evidently not in Africa, where coup d'états still occur with embarrassing frequency. Africa's coup plotters have been especially busy in the last couple of years. The year 2021 was perhaps the most prolific in this regard, with successful coup d'états in Mali, Sudan, and Guinea Bissau, a failed one in Niger Republic, all in the course of the year. 2022 is shaping up to be as eventful in this regard too, with a successful coup already recorded in Burkina Fasso, and a failed one in Guinea Conakry.

Colonialism had bequeathed to the majority of African nation-states, restless armed forces, too weak to defend the territorial sovereignty of their countries any way but powerful enough and often lacking in professionalism and discipline to let democratic experiments flourish. It is difficult to think of any African country where the military would not have hijacked the civilian coup that was staged in the United States of America, on January 6, 2021, when supporters of former President Donald Trump invaded the U.S. Capitol in a bloody siege. Yet the armed forces of the United States were sufficiently disciplined to keep a clear professional distance from the entire chaotic scenario, allowing the politicians the opportunity to clean up their mess.

Yet another source of hinderance to the evolution of a democratic culture in Africa is the tenacious hold of the traditional kingship institution. This is particularly the case in the West African sub-region. Virtually all post-colonial nation-states in Africa proclaim themselves as republics. Indeed, many prefix their names with the title "republic", as for example, in the Democratic Republic of Congo (DRC), the Republic of South Africa (RSA), the Federal Republic of Nigeria, etc. This mode of self-identification would convey the impression that the old monarchical orders which held sway in these nations in pre-colonial times are now a thing of the past and that what currently subsist are bona fide republics. In reality however, the surviving vestiges of the ancient kingdoms and empires still wield considerable socio-cultural influence on the people, which often translates to real economic and political clout.

Africa's traditional kings and chiefs exercise informal, unofficial, but nonetheless wide-ranging powers on land use. This is truly remarkable because in many of these countries, there are extant formal legislations enacted to regulate land use and tenure. And in Africa, as it is too well known, it is all about land; land is the king among economic resources, and it is the ultimate factor of production. Therefore, he who controls the use of land controls quite a lot. The traditional kingship institutions are able to keep an effective control on land use by leveraging on the primordial loyalty and allegiance of their subjects. For the same considerations, Africa's traditional kings are able to exact real influence on the politics of their respective nation-states. In this regard, Eswathini, formerly Zwasiland, stands as the exemplar of backwardness, being the sole surviving absolute monarchy on the continent and one of the few remaining in the world.

It is rather curious, nay regrettable, that African political theorists and commentators have largely shied away from exposing the traditional kingship institution in Africa for what it represents in the context of modern democratic governance, namely a malignant anachronism. If, as I have argued elsewhere,[8] democracy can only survive and grow in a republic, then democracy cannot flourish in many contemporary African nation-states until the remaining vestiges of the ancient monarchies hanging on their necks like an albatross are totally cast off. Democracy and monarchy are not just different forms of government, they are mutually incompatible; the one excludes the other.

To make matters worse, the above-highlighted factors militating against democratic progress in post-colonial Africa tend to be mutually reinforcing. It is almost a given that insecurity aggravates the problem of poverty. When a community comprising of persons hitherto earning their livelihood by subsistence occupations (peasant farmers, local hunters, petty traders, village fishermen, basket weavers, etc.) are uprooted from their ancestral land, by life-threatening insecurity, and cramped into internally displaced person camps (IDPCs), sometimes far away from home, it is obvious that while in the IDPC such individuals would not have access to their regular means of subsistence. Often, they would have to depend on handouts from governments at different levels, supplemented by local and foreign private donors. This has been the situation in many parts of northern Nigeria for more than a decade. The increasing levels of poverty, as one might expect, has, in turn, resulted in the further deterioration of the security situation. Due to displacement and the inevitable destitution, hordes of young persons – out-of-school children and other frustrated youths – become readily available as cheap recruits into the armies of insurgents and bandits.

In the same vein, destitution and hopelessness render people vulnerable to ethnic manipulation by self-seeking politicians. It also bears noting that some traditional rulers have been fingered as sponsors, at least as aiders and abettors of banditry and insurgency. This has been the case, for quite some time, in North East and North West of Nigeria, and it has started manifesting in parts of the middle belt too.[9] No doubt, the problem of traditional rulers being complicit in the sponsorship of insurgency and other forms of peace-compromising criminalities is to be encountered in other parts of the continent.

Finally, pervasive insecurity could be exploited as a justification for a military incursion into government. Such was the professed excuse for the recent (and we may add, the latest) coup d'état in the West African nation of Burkina Fasso, where mutinous soldiers sacked the civilian government of President Roch Kabore, on January 24, 2022.[10]

Confronted by these obstacles, clearly, the survival and growth of democracy in the toxic socio-political environment of many post-colonial nation-states in Africa is a daunting task. But by far the most intractable obstacle in the path of democratic evolution in contemporary Africa is, in my view, not any of the factors enumerated above, nor, for that matter, their various combinations. The greatest hinderance to democratic progress in Africa is religion. Presently, I explain why I think this is so.

Poverty can be alleviated. China is perhaps the latest nation to provide the world with a viable model of how to lift masses of people out of poverty.[11] Singapore offered another model earlier. Equally impressive is the spate of wealth creation and the resultant socio-economic upwards mobility of millions of people in the United States. A cursory look at the comparative socio-economic indices in the U.S. in the one hundred years, from 1900 to 2000, reveals an unprecedent uptick in human development indices and well-being. Obviously, some models of poverty alleviation are more rights-friendly than others.

For example, the Chinese model of economic growth and the accompany prosperity and upwards social mobility of the people has come with serious challenges: the most noticeable drawback of the Chinese economic miracle is the cost denominated in lack of respect for human rights. Thus, while China may be an economically open society, in the sense of being a major player in the globalized economic order, it is a politically and socially closed society. The closeness is evident in the absence of democratic governance and in the nonobservance of standard principles and procedures in dealing with issues of human rights.

As they strive to expand their economies with the aim, *inter alia*, of lifting their populations out of poverty, African nations should take the best available clues from the Chinese experiment, they should learn how to unleash the latent forces of economic productivity in their populations, while avoiding the negative traits seemingly endemic to the Chinese model, as manifested in the extreme lack of pollical and social inclusiveness and openness. Being an economically buoyant and an open society should not be mutually exclusive. If anything, as the American and (arguably) the Singaporean models tend to show, democratic openness and inclusiveness could be a veritable catalyst to greater economic prosperity.

Insurgencies can be defeated or at least sufficiently degraded to the level where they would constitute no more than occasional sources of irritation. The definitive routing of the Tamil Tigers in Sri Lanka, after more than a quarter century of insurgency, offers a clear contemporary illustration of how this could be accomplished.[12]

On the tenacious hold of the traditional kingship institutions, perhaps the surest way to abolish them is by constitutional means. It is not enough for the constitutions of post-colonial African nation-states to not assign any role to traditional rulers; modern African constitutions should contain provisions expressly abolishing the institutions. Such constitutional provisions would be the logical requirement to perfect the national profession of republicanism. In other words, the formal constitutional step which I am suggesting, is an imperative for our democratic progress in Africa. For African nation-states to be true to their professed allegiance to republicanism, the traditional kingship institutions have to be totally abolished. Whatever relics and paraphernalia of the ancient institutions are left could be appropriated for scientific management under a ministry of culture and tourism. That, in my view, is about all that is left of the English monarchy. As democracy grows, and with a significant reduction in poverty, normally there should be a proportional reduction in the people's vulnerability to the sway of ethnic or tribal sentiments and manipulation.

To dissuade military interruption of democratic progress, two salient measures are necessary. The first is a universal rejection of coup d'état and any other form of undemocratic mode of changing a government. The rejection should be demonstrated in global condemnation, isolation and comprehensive boycott of the regimes of military power usurpers. The second necessary measure is that coup plotters and their collaborators – local and foreign – should be subjected to criminal prosecution and punished to the full extent of the law, whenever, as it is inevitable sooner or later, their illegal reigns are terminated. To facilitate the efficacy of these coup-dissuading measures, the doctrine of non-interference in the domestic affairs of sovereign nations,[13] an article of faith of public international law, would have to be circumscribed appropriately. The doctrine is rapidly being supplanted by humanitarian considerations anyway. In Africa, the doctrine has often served as a convenient shield for military power usurpers and other garden-variety dictators. Humanity must realize that the only way for the flower of democracy to bloom in peace anywhere is for it to be nurtured everywhere. It is not fortuitous that democracies rarely wage wars against each other. Next, I turn to the subject of religion, a factor which in my view, constitutes a more difficult problem to surmount in the politics of contemporary Africa.

Religion and Politics in Africa

The Primordial Need for Religion

A modern democratic state truly desirous of social harmony and its attendant benefits of economic development and political progress must learn to handle matters pertaining to religion with utmost care and sensitivity. To say this is merely to repeat the obvious. However, in the affairs of a multi-ethnic multi-religious polity as is the case in most post-colonial African nation-states, this seemingly platitudinous admonition, to deploy the proverbial Solomonic wisdom in managing issues relating to religion, assumes a more urgent imperative.

Religion is a formidable social institution whose impacts on human life ramify wide and deep. This is by no means a new phenomenon; the human need for some form of spiritual anchor or refuge is virtually instinctive. It is a primordial need that predates all but the most basic requirements for man's physical survival, namely, nutrition, clothing and shelter. For believers, the stakes could not be higher, it is the ultimate destiny of one's soul. Indeed, for many adherents of monotheistic faiths, the primary (perhaps the sole) purpose of man's earthily sojourn is to prepare him for eternal life in heaven or in hell, as the case may be. Even the atheists and the agnostics must contend with having to endure the inevitable disturbances to their ears and toes and other forms of irritations resulting from the acts of worship of practicing theists. Think of the holy noises bellowing out of worship centres on a daily basis, in some cases several times daily, and which not uncommonly spill out unto the public space.

Religion has always been a harbinger of good and evil, possibly in equal proportions. Legions of human lives have been saved, who otherwise would have perished, by having their basic needs for subsistence provided by religious organizations. Faith-based charities have fed and continue to feed the hungry; they have clothed the naked; they have comforted the distressed and the destitute in a myriad of other ways. Religious organizations have, in other words, ministered to men's bodily needs even as they have ministered to their spiritual needs.

On the other hand, religion has also served as an unrivaled dispenser of destruction and misery. Uncountable numbers of innocent souls have perished in religion-induced conflicts and pogroms. Populations have been rendered hungry, homeless and destitute, all for the sake of religion. So, it stands to reason that a social institution with such a checkered reputation for good and evil should be regarded with awe and handled with care.

Religion in African Culture

Modern African nation-states have additional and quite peculiar reasons to tread cautiously on matters of religion. It is true that neither religion nor ethnic/cultural pluralism is alien to the African civilization. Indeed, as J.S. Mbiti once famously observed, Africans have always been "notoriously religious".[14] However, what contemporary African nation-states have to contend with is a religious phenomenon totally alien to the traditional African attitude to religion and spirituality. Put simply, the challenge today is how to manage the contestations between two proselytizing religions, Islam and Christianity (both spiritual imports from the orients) on one hand, and how to manage the various points of intersection between these religions and others and the operations of the "secular" state on the other. Not only does each one of these two religions seek to dominate the other religions, but it is also patently in their character to contend with the state for power and authority to control people's lives and in general the affairs of the society. The inevitable conflicts are problems that Africans are not culturally equipped to handle.

As a matter of historical fact, and this is without prejudice to their spiritual authenticity, the two oriental religions, Islam and Christianity, were brought to Africa as elaborate sectarian facades to conceal the real intentions of those who brought them. Both were introduced to Africa as spiritual sweeteners to aid Africans in swallowing the bitter pills of colonialism. First to come was Arab colonialism and slavery, which came bearing the religion of Islam. Much later was the Christian faith which accompanied and greatly facilitated European colonialism slavery and the trans-Atlantic slave trade.

By their nature, proselytizing religions are harbingers of strife and conflict, both internally within their own respective folds, and externally with other religions and creeds. The reason may not be too far to seek. There is only a finite pool of humanity to win souls from; a finite number of potential recruits into the columns of the matching saints, who are as such veritable targets of evangelical campaigns. Thus, a soul won by one faith is to that extent lost to another. In this winner-takes-all scramble for the souls of men, it is not surprising that neither Christianity nor Islam has a benign disposition toward the apostate. Orthodox Islam punishes apostasy with death; the apostate was once treated as an anathema on the body of the Christian faith, an execrable incubus. The bottom line is to win as many souls as possible for God and to keep them in one's religious fold. By some happy coincidence too, each bearer of a soul is also a potential payer of tithes and offerings and other forms of religious taxes.

In contrast to these imported religions, African traditional religions do not proselytize, they do not win converts by evangelism. Perhaps, this is just as well. Imagine, for a scary moment, the level of sacred chaos society would be confronted with, if practitioners of African traditional religions were to engage in proselytizing and thereby to troop out in their glorious legions, bearing the various items of their worship, life chicken and all, for vigorous or even aggressive evangelism. In traditional (Yoruba) African society, a man may be a devotee of the God of thunder, Sango, while his wife worships the arch goddess of the river, Yemoja. Each of their adult children may choose to follow other deities. Not only would this not be considered a cause for domestic and or social disharmony, but it would actually be a cause for celebration. On the occasions of the periodic festivals as required by the different deities, the whole community would enthusiastically participate in the feasting and merry-making. More pertinently, practitioners of African traditional religions do not, as a matter of routine everyday engagement, seek to confront the state in open contestation for power and authority to control the affairs of the society.

It is not surprising, therefore, that apostasy does not bear the same negative connotations in African traditional religions as it does in Islam and Christianity. African traditional religions do not proselytize anyway; every adult person is at liberty to choose what deity to worship. Indeed, not only is the apostate not vilified, but in some cases swamping of deities to follow is actively encouraged. In some traditional settings, the relationship between deities and their devotees seems to be purely transactional. The Yoruba of southwestern Nigeria would say, for example, "orisa bi oole gbemi, semi bi o se bami": o ye deity if you are unable or unwilling to confer blessings on me, at least restore me to the original position you met me. Again, the Yoruba would often say, "bi orisa kan ko ba gbeni ki a wa omiran sin": if a deity is not conferring blessings on one, then one should select another deity to worship.

These doctrinal variations may actually be indicative of more fundamental theological differences between African traditional religions on one side and the judeo/Christian/Islamic faiths on the other. For example, Kola Abimbola has called into question the presumed supremacy of Olodumare, the Yoruba analogue of the Christian and the Muslim God. Abimbola has argued that "a close analysis of the roles and functions of Olodumare in Ifa literary Corpus (and in the practice of the religion) reveal that Olodumare cannot be a Supreme Being!"[15]

It is against this cultural background that I propose to carry out the remainder of this discussion. I will start with a brief explication of what I regard as the pernicious impacts of religion on the Nigerian society. Here, I take Nigeria as a typical contemporary African nation-state, from whose experience we can profitably extrapolate to the situation of most other African nations. I will then provide a concise analysis of why religious disagreements and the resultant conflicts are characteristically difficult to resolve. Finally, I will present the highlights of a proposal on how to manage our religious diversity, to minimize conflicts and maximize socio-political harmony. I will label this concluding section of the essay "learning to ride a bull in a China shop", in obvious allusion to the title of the chapter.

Religion and Social Disharmony in an Africa Nation, Nigeria as Point of Reference

Contemporary Nigerian society is a perpetually simmering hotbed of religious disharmony. To be sure, the destructive manifestations of religious intolerance vary from region to region. The spectrum ranges from severe intolerance in the "core" north, roughly the whole of the northwest and the northeast, on one extreme end, to the happy accomodationism in the southwest on the other extreme end, where Christians and Muslims not only live side-by-side in virtually unbroken peace but for the most part, have also, to a significant extent, learnt to demonstrate a progressive attitude of live-and-let-live towards the followers of other religious creeds, including African traditional religions. The middle belt of Nigeria, the north-central geopolitical zone, is where the two great religions, Islam and Christianity, meet. (Interestingly, this is the region where the two great rivers that define modern Nigeria, river Niger and river Benue also meet) With Islam striving to expand southwards and Christianity striving to expand northwards, it is hardly surprising that this spiritual confluence is the most volatile region in Nigeria. The region has been a theatre of endless religious disputes, not infrequently accompanied by the carnage.

The casus belli are never in short supply. They range from the relatively inconsequential matters such as the wearing of the hijab (the head Scarfe) by female students in public schools, to more important issues over political representation, conflict of laws, especially between the laws enacted by the "secular" legislatures and the Shariah legal system. Other causes of religious flare-ups include perceived blasphemy, apostasy, same-gender sexual orientation and open profession of atheism or agnosticism.

Overall, religion has done considerably more harm than good to Nigeria's democratic progress. Attempts to enact even the most progressive pieces of legislation have, for example, been opposed on religious grounds. Such, for example, is the otherwise inexplicable failure to domesticate the child rights Act in some northern states,[16] and the serial parliamentary rejection of a Bill to enforce gender equality in the country, sponsored by a female Senator from the southwest.[17]

The most damaging impact of religion occurs when it is weaponized into a fine instrument of ethnic suspicion, as it has been, not uncommonly, done in Africa. Karl Marx once described religion as a potentially addictive drug – the opium of the people.[18] In Nigeria, as in other parts of Africa, that spiritual opium is daily been force-fed into the masses of the regular citizens by politicians and other socio-cultural elites. The administration of the opium of religion starts, in most cases, very early in life. In the course of their socialization, children are taught in mosques and in churches, especially the Pentecostal denominations, to regard adherents of other faiths as the unredeemed, spiritually unclean, and morally suspect.

Explaining the Resistance of Religious Disagreements to Resolution

Overcoming these pernicious influences of religion in order to liberate our democracies for true evolutionary advances would require deliberate, sustained, well-thought-out measures. I will provide, albeit, in broad strokes, the highlights of a constitutional/legal proposal to address the problem, presently. But first, a word on why religious disagreements often seem intractable. According to William Clohesy, "religion is a deeply important way of being human: relating oneself to the universe, to God, and to a moral framework of life that transcends the secular toward the spiritual".[19] It is this transcendental dimension of religion that makes it a poor candidate for definitive scientific understanding and analysis. It is this other-worldly feature that renders the deployment of the scientific tools of conflict resolution often ineffectual in the resolution of religious disagreements and the resultant conflicts. The nurturing of religious beliefs and the commitment to the prescribed doctrines and observances, is not wholly a matter of reason; it is only partly a matter of reason and largely a matter of faith. It is, therefore, a matter of both the head and the heart. And, going by Blaise Pascal's insightful contention, "the heart has its own reason that reason knows nothing of … it is the heart which experiences God, and not the reason".[20] These ontological and epistemological peculiarities of religious discourse informed my decision to treat it as uniquely resistant to resolution.

As it is invariably the case in a philosophical engagement such as we are about here, the scholarly tools of critical analysis and ratiocinative argumentation, all within the framework of a purely scientific ontology, inconclusively effectual as they may be, are all we have got. With this methodological presupposition in mind, I turn to the next and final subsection of the chapter to highlight some constitutional and other measures which African nations should consider for adoption to tame the menace of religion in their politics.

Learning to Ride a Bull in a China Shop

In elucidating the problematic relationship between politics and religion there is the tendency to conceive the relationship as subsisting purely between two institutions, religion on one hand, and the state on the other. Though usually unstated, this presupposition informs the popular analogy of the wall of separation between the church and the state. Or, in multi-religious societies like a typical modern African nation-state, the wall of separation between the state and the church/mosque/synagogue/temple/shrine etc. Analytically useful as this analogy has been, I am of the view that the conception of politics implicit in it is rather too narrow. I propose that we work with a wider conception according to which politics would be implicated whenever and wherever a need arises for the intervention of the state in regulating conduct. A promising approach is through J.S. Mill's much-debated distinction between the private and the public spheres of human conduct; the Harm Principle would then provide the guide rail. Conduct falls within the purview of the public, is subject to regulation by the state, implicates politics, if and only if it bears harmful consequences for the well-being of someone else other than the acting rational agent.[21]

Presently, I provide a tentative list of five points of contact between politics and religion, where the intervention of the state could be warranted to prevent or manage discord and conflicts, that may ultimately result in harm to third parties. The first ones are the interactions between believers and "unbelievers". How is the state to regulate the unnecessary but common hostility between theists and atheists/agnostics? Second, are intra-faith disagreements leading to conflicts. Usually, these are matters of doctrinal disagreements traceable in most cases to conflicting or even contradictory interpretations of religious texts. The discordant reactions of some of Nigeria's leading Islamic clerics to the recent blasphemy killing of a young college student, Deborah Samuel, in Sokoto, is a case in point. While some prominent Islamic scholars and clerics condemned the killing in very strong terms, as ungodly (clearly un-Islamic), immoral and criminal, others, equally revered for their learning, hail it as deserved and justified.[22] Such intra-faith disagreements could precipitate harmful behaviors targeted at others. How is state intervention to be deployed to prevent or sanction such harmful conducts?

Third, there is the problem of inter-faith conflict: Islam against Christianity, Islam and or Christianity against African traditional religion. How is the state to mediate in these inter-religious disputes? The fourth point of contact and possible conflict is between individual believers and the state. For example, an individual theist might, on the grounds of conscientious objection informed by his or her faith, refuse to comply with a government-directed course of conduct, say in withholding a particular form of tax or refusal of military draft to participate in a particular kind of war, or for that matter, all kinds of war. Such individual acts or omissions must be distinguished from the acts of commission or omission done by religious bodies as corporate entities. A religious congregation for its part might, for example, refuse to remit taxes to the government, or refuse to make records of its activities available for audit by officials of the state, invoking the principle of the separation of politics and religion. Fifth, there is the relationship between religious organizations as corporate entities and the "secular" state. As I indicated above, this is the problematic relationship that has attracted much scholarly attention, perhaps appropriately so. The point here is not to produce an exhaustive list. In principle the list is open-ended. More points of contacts/conflicts between politics and religion would have to be added as they are indicated by practical experience. The list is offered to suggest the sort of measures, constitutional, legal (even extra-legal as desirable) to be designed in negotiating a harmonious, ideally mutually beneficial relationship between politics and religion in Africa's emerging democracies.

I start with constitutional provisions that must be put in place to secure our democracies and enthrone religious harmony. These measures, expectedly, would touch on the very existence of the commonwealth and fundamental considerations pertaining to the relationship between politics and religion. The purpose of putting these measures in the constitution is to safeguard them from the vagrancies of changing political sentiments. Presently I explicate two basic provisions the constitution of a multi-religious polity should contain.

1   There should be a provision in the constitution affirming the inviolability of the sovereignty of the state and, derivatively, the supremacy of the state's law-making powers. One salient characteristic of modern sovereign states is that they do not share the glory of their legislative powers with any other body or institution.

2   There is a need for a provision in the constitution establishing and protecting the mutual independence of the state and religion. John Locke has admonished that, in order to prevent anyone from

> imposing on himself or others by the claim that he is loyal and obedient to the monarch or that he is sincere in his worship of God, it is utterly necessary that we draw a precise boundary line between (1) the affairs of government and (2) the affairs of religion.[23]

Locke warned that failure to establish such a clear boundary between religion and politics would "[lead to endless] controversies between those who have (or at least pretend to have) a concern for men's souls and those who have (or at least pretend to have) a care for the commonwealth".[24] To firmly erect this wall of separation, religion should stay clear of the administration of the commonwealth, while for its part, "the civil power should not try to establish any articles of faith or doctrine, or any forms of worship by the force of its laws".[25]

Happily, we do not have to reinvent the wheel here, we only have to finetune it to local specification. For these insights by Locke, Jefferson[26], and others across the ages have since been encoded into some national constitutions. The most well known is the extensively debated Establishment Clause of the First Amendment to the Constitution of the United States (1791), which provides that "Congress shall make no law respecting an establishment of religion, or prohibiting the free exercise thereof". This provision in the 1st Amendment to the U.S. Constitution is a pertinent addendum to Section (3) of Article Vi of the U.S. Constitution (1787), which provides that "no religious Test shall ever be required as a Qualification to any Office or Public Trust under the United States".

Similarly, Section 10 of the Constitution of the Federal Republic of Nigeria (1999) provides that, "The Government of the Federation or of a State shall not adopt any religion as State Religion". The import of the second half of the Establishment Clause of the 1st Amendment to the U.S. Constitution (the non-prohibition of people's freedom of worship) is, in my view, likewise amply captured by Section 38(1) of the Nigerian Constitution. It provides that,

> Every person shall be entitled to freedom of thought, conscience and religion, including freedom to change his religion or belief, and freedom (either alone or in community with others, and in public or in private) to manifest and propagate his religion or belief in worship, teaching, practice and observance.

The freedoms enumerated in this section of the Nigerian Constitution are, of course, to be taken as fundamental rights, their existence must be understood to predate their incorporation in the Constitution.

Going Forward

Going forward, it is imperative for all the parties in this "negotiation" to acknowledge the inevitability of significant compromises to be made by everyone. What we are trying to constitute here is a federation of some sort – a federation of faiths. No federating unit can insist on having all its desires granted. Where a unit in a federation insists on having it all its own way, then perhaps what it actually wants is not a fair and just federation but a scheme of domination. To take one major illustration, it has been argued that the proclamation of the sovereignty of the state as inviolate and the supremacy of its law-making powers and author-ity as unassailable run contrary to the basic tenets of the Shariah legal system.[27] For there to be harmonious co-existence with non-Muslims, Muslims would have to concede that a substantial chunk of the Shariah legal system will be supplanted by, or at least, subjugated to, the constitution and other "secular" laws of their country. The burden of the sacrifice of important tenets of one's religion is, of course, not one-sided; adherents of other faiths too would likewise be required to make comparable forbearances, as necessary.

Let us now examine how our analyses thus far would bear on four phenomena that have often served as sources of religious crises: apostasy, heresy, blasphemy, and the legal status of atheists/agnostics in a democratic society. My selection is random, the list is not exhaustive and it may not yet include all the major sources of religious conflicts. Of the four, apostasy should be the easiest to deal with in a nation with constitutional provisions like Section 38(1) of the Constitution of the Federal Republic of Nigeria, and the Establishment Clause of the 1st Amendment to the U.S. Constitution. Among the freedoms guaranteed to the Nigerian citizen or resident therein, is the "freedom to change [one's] religion or belief…" I have suggested above, that the enumerated freedoms in this Section of the Nigerian Constitution be regarded as fundamental rights. This being the case, the notion of apostasy and the ven-omous reactions and sanctions it tends to evoke from Christians and Muslims is rendered meaningless, i.e., no longer applicable in Nigeria and any other nation with a similar consti-tutional provision, by constitutional fiat. It should be recalled that the notion of an apostate is alien to African traditional religions anyway, religions which are integral aspects of our indigenous cultures.

Heresy by its nature is an intra-faith problem. It typically arises out of a disputed under-standing of some core doctrines of a religion. Ordinarily, the state and others who are not followers of the religion in question should be content to stand aside, leaving members of the sect alone to resolve their differences. However, the state might be compelled to wield its regulatory powers, for two cardinal reasons. The first is to protect the larger society from the nuisance and other forms of harm that may be suffered by by-standing third parties, when such intra-faith squabbles spill unto the public arena. The second justification for state inter-vention in matters of heresy is equally paramount. It is to lay down the parameters defining clearly, the limits of the authority of religious sects to punish heresy. In the exercise of its freedom of association, nay, the freedom of association of its members, a religious sect could always expel a person it has adjudged to be a heretic, perhaps with all their prescribed rituals of excommunication. The freedom to associate implies the freedom to refuse to associate. But can an aggrieved religious sect subject a heretic to corporal punishment? No. Can it bombard his estate, as a form of fine? No. Can it incarcerate him at some private prison dug in the basement of their temple; or, worse, simply put him to the sword? No. In principle, only the state may impose these latter forms of punishment, which, for want of a better label, I would call kinetic forms of punishment. In a multi-religious polity, the presumption is that individuals are citizens or residents of the nation first before becoming members of their chosen religious associations. Meanwhile, an unassailable characteristic of a sovereign state is the insistence on the monopoly in the deployment of kinetic coercion and violence. Thus, any form of punishment that would involve the use of coercion or physical force can only be imposed by the state.

I should remark, in passing, that it is this feature (among others) of the Shariah legal system, as it has been adopted in several states in northern Nigeria, which I consider most objectionable. In a multi-religious, multi-ethnic polity, no religion or ethnic group should arrogate to itself the licence to set up agencies to enforce its own laws, parallel to the law enforcement machinery of the nation-state. Entities like the Hisbah in Shariah states in northern Nigeria are, in my view, a clear constitutional anomaly. In general, the adoption of the Shariah legal system in northern Nigeria, designed initially to operate in the area of family and other private laws and then especially its subsequent extension to criminal matters is a huge elephant in the sitting room. It deserves all the full-fledged scholarly treatments it has received and some more.

Blasphemy is another thing that has provoked much outrage both in its commission and the usually extreme reactions to it. In the afternoon of Thursday, May 12, 2022, Deborah Samuel Yakubu, a second-year, Christian student of Shehu Shagari College of Education, Sokoto (in Nigeria's northwest geopolitical zone), was murdered in cold blood by her fellow students. They had accused her of expressing allegedly disrespectful, i.e., blasphemous views against the person of Prophet Muhamed, Islam's most venerated icon. After first pelting Deborah with stones and sticks, the irate Muslim students then set her on fire, probably while she was still alive. Deborah's murder was not the first nor for that matter the last blasphemy killing in Nigeria. Nonetheless, her gruesome murder made headline news around the world. Nigeria was thrown into a palpable apprehension, especially against the nagging background of preexisting and pervasive insecurity in the country. While many commentators demanded the arrest and prosecution of the murderers, others, from the fundamentalist fringes of Islam, hailed the killers as exemplars of Islamic virtue, who did what they had to do in the fulfilment of their religious duty, as the occasion demanded. Leading Islamic clerics, divided roughly along northern and southern Muslim lines, provided conflicting interpretations of the Quran on the subject of blasphemy.

In the ensuing cacophony of opinions and suggestions, some Islamic clerics came up with the proposal for the nation-wide criminalization of blasphemy, presumably, by an Act of the National Assembly.[28] That way, they reasoned, a regime of sanctions would be statutorily laid down to punish the offence across religious divide. Though it may seem prima facie plausible, the proposal is unavailing. The criminal law is the inappropriate legal instrument to redress the wrong of blasphemy. The criminal law is a tool designed and entrusted in the hands of the state, to redress wrongs done to the society as a whole. We could label such wrongs against the commonwealth as *wrongs in rem,* to distinguish them from *wrongs in personam,* those committed against individual persons. For example, when murder is committed, the murderer kills an individual or in some cases, multiple individuals with distinct identities. But the killer does more than that, so the theory goes: the killer inflicts serious harm on the society in general. On the organic conception of society, the killer's wrong against the society is akin to attempted murder, or at least the infliction of grievous physical or emotional harm on the society. Therefore, on this view, punishing a criminal conduct is an act of self-defense: society avenging and defending itself against an act that threatens its existence or at least its health.

Now, having no religion of its own, the state (the agent of the commonwealth) cannot be harmed by blasphemy. Having no injury of its own to avenge or defend against when blasphemy is committed, the state cannot criminalize it. Were the state to deploy the exclusive instruments of its criminal law to punish blasphemy on an occasion, the state would thereby have constructively, or put less euphemistically, through the back door, adopted the religion whose object of worship is deemed to have been maligned by the blasphemous act. But that is precisely what the constitution says the state is prohibited from doing.[29] Our resourceful clerics could retort by pointing out that their proposal is to criminalize blasphemy across board, irrespective of whose religious symbol is disrespected. By this regime, which could be described as equal opportunity criminalization of blasphemy, the state would not have adopted any particular religion, it would instead have demonstrated its even handedness (neutrality) in matters of religion. But now the state would have merely further compounded the problem, for it would thereby have adopted not one but all the religions and other belief systems represented in the polity.[30] This, in turn, would be the height of constitutional absurdity: a constitution that prohibits the state from adopting any state religion could not reasonably be construed to permit it to adopt many.

Apart from this constitutional incongruity, there is another impediment, one of a practical sort that would stand in the way of a universal criminalization of blasphemy. There will be no objective standard for determining when the offence has been committed. Because criminal conducts harm society as a corporate entity, there are well-articulated indices and procedures for ascertaining the presence of the elements of a crime. For example, one who takes the life of another without justification and, as lawyers would add, with malice aforethought, would have committed the crime of murder. Such a standardized procedure for establishing the elements of the wrong would be unavailable for blasphemy. To begin with, there are religious sects, such as followers of African traditional religions, who do not even recognize the offence of blasphemy. Or, perhaps to state it more accurately, there are those whose religions do not impose on them the duty to avenge conducts that could otherwise be regarded as blasphemous. Practitioners of African traditional religions normally do not feel obligated to intercede on behalf of their deities; the belief is that the gods are quite capable of looking after themselves. The relativism runs deep. The selection of what objects and symbols to venerate is relative to each religion. Thus, one religious sect's venerated prophet could be regarded from the point of view of another religion as a shameless pedophile or a thief. As John Locke claims in regards to doctrinal differences among Christian sub-sects, when it comes to the matter of orthodoxy, "every church is orthodox to itself and erroneous or heretical to the others".[31] We move much further away from a consensus of opinions on religions and their symbols, if we extrapolate from the contestations within a single body of faith to the differences among many religions.

What I have demonstrated thus far, I should hope with some persuasion, is the non-applicability of criminal sanctions to cure the offence of blasphemy. I have, by no means, denied the reality of the offence. It would be extremely uncharitable, indeed profoundly insensitive to dismiss, say, with a bemused wave of the hand, the complaints of those who claim that they have been harmed by blasphemy, as some form of fanatical self-indulgence or that such complainants are otherwise delusional. But if blasphemy cannot be criminally punished, how is it to be redressed? What alternative remedy might be available to those who may indeed feel genuinely harmed by the offence? My proposal would be to seek remedy in a civil court. An injured party could litigate a course of action under some suitable theory in tort. Suppose, for example, that upon witnessing, hearing, seeing, smelling, etc., a blasphemous act done to a revered symbol of his or her religion, a person instantaneously experiences a severe shock or emotional breakdown sufficiently intense to require some period of hospitalization or a course of costly counselling. Such a person, in my view, should be able to bring a civil suit under the tort theory of Intentional Infliction of Emotional Distress (I.I.E.D). To be sure, while I.I.E.D is a universally recognized course of action in tort, it could be especially difficult to prove, given that the complainant (plaintiff) must bear the burden of proof, and the difficulty of marshalling relevant and compelling evidence to prove it. But to say that it is difficult is not to say that it cannot be done. I should note also that the lower standard of proof, namely, proof with a preponderance of the evidence, which is much lower than proof beyond a reasonable doubt required in criminal matters, could be helpful to the complainant/plaintiff in a civil litigation.

The last item on our list is atheism/agnosticism. What should be the constitutional/legal status of the atheist and the agnostic? In my view, one of the most unconscionable practices in this matter of religion is the persecution of agnostics and atheists. It is an egregious scandal, that even John Locke, a foremost ancestor of liberal thought in western civilization, the author of the hugely influential "Letter Concerning Toleration", does not consider the atheist as worthy of toleration. "None should be tolerated", Locke had warned, "who denies the existence of God. Promises, covenants, and oaths, which are the bonds of human society, can have no hold on an atheist: this all dissolves in the presence of the thought that there is no God".[32] This piece of defamatory nonsense, based on a hasty generalization, is all the more outrageous coming from an icon of enlightenment liberalism and tolerance. In many African countries too, an open profession of atheism could put one in grave jeopardy or at least serious social disadvantage. Just like John Locke in the seventeenth century, many in today's religion-crazy Africa find it uncomfortable to have any kind of dealing or enter into any form of association with someone they consider Godless. It is bad enough to ostracize the atheist and the agnostic, for such attitudes of rejection are invariably based on prejudice and pointless suspicion. However, the real harm is done, when atheists and agnostics are lined up for persecution. Now we ask, what, precisely, is the crime or offence of the atheist/agnostic? In what specific ways does atheism/agnosticism harm any other person's interest or the interest of the society as a corporate entity? Under what theory of tort might an individual bring a civil action in a court of law against his fellow man who only professes atheism? In each case, I can think of none. We must always bear in mind that the race to salvation is not a team sport. Each individual soul must face judgement alone. So, as John Locke himself points out,

> if someone strays from the right path, that is his misfortune, not yours; and your belief that he will be miserable in the after-life is not a reason for you to give him a bad time in his present life.[33]

Luckly for mankind, Locke's admonition of intolerance toward the atheist/agnostic seems to have been roundly rejected by drafters of national laws and constitutions of subsequent ages. Surely, the drafters of the Constitution of the United States (1787) expressly rejected Locke on this point, by the provision of Art. Vi (3), which removes any form of religious test as part of qualification for holding public office. Similarly, in guaranteeing, in Sec. 38, the enumerated freedoms, which include the freedom of thought, conscience and religion, and crucially, the freedom to change one's religion or belief and to propagate such religions or beliefs as one chooses, the Constitution of the Federal Republic of Nigeria (1999) has conferred equal recognition and protection on the atheist and the agnostic. Atheism and agnosticism are bona fide forms of beliefs in their own right. Atheism is the belief that there is conclusive reason to believe that God does not exist. Agnosticism, on the other hand, is the more nuanced belief that there is no conclusive reason either way, i.e., either to believe that God exists or that God does not exist. Once this acknowledgment is made, it becomes clear why atheism and agnosticism must enjoy the same degree of constitutional protection as any manifestation of theism or other forms of beliefs. The only caveat in regards to atheism/agnosticism, as it is for theism, is compliance with the Harm Principle: that the belief be not harmful to the interest of nonconsenting others.

Atheists and agnostics can bask in their constitutionally protected right not just to hold their respective beliefs but actually to freely propagate those beliefs. There can be no lawful impediment to atheists/agnostics, either as individuals or as groups, to embark on their own evangelical crusades, to win souls lost to theism back to the belief in the nonexistence of

God.[34] The theist who wishes to dissuade the atheist from embarking on this soul-winning campaign and redirect him to the way of the Lord has his work cut out for him. There is but one only appropriate and efficient way to convert the atheist, John Locke got it right this time: it cannot be by fire and sword, it can only be by the deployment of persuasive reason. "The only way to propagate truth", says Locke, "is through reasoning and argument, combined with gentleness and benevolence".[35] For emphasis, he adds later in the "Letter", that, "nobody ought to be compelled in matters of religion either by law or force".[36] Two hundred years later, J.S. Mill expressed similar insights, with characteristic trenchancy. Mill had vowed not to obey any God who would not provide him a reason why His commandment should be obeyed:

> Whatever power such a being may have over me, there is one thing which he shall not do: he shall not compel me to worship him. I will call no being good, who is not what I mean when I apply that epithet to my fellow creatures; and if such a being can sentence me to hell for not so calling him, to hell I will go.[37]

Conclusion

The primary subject of this essay is the problematic nature of religion in the democratic evolution of modern, that is, post-colonial African nation-states. While it is true that the path to democratic progress in contemporary Africa is strewn with obstacles large and small, in my view the most difficult one to deal with is religion. This is because of the recondite nature of religious discourse, which is to a significant extent shrouded in dogmas and mystery and only partly an affair of reason and logic.

I have presented the essay in two main parts. In part one, I explored what I consider the lesser obstacles in the way of Africa's democratic progress. These "lesser evils" are, inter alia, the problem of endemic poverty, ethnic chauvinism, official corruption and gross abuse of public office, chronic insecurity, lack of basic managerial competencies by those in charge of our nations, the hangover of traditional kingship institutions, restive and professionally undisciplined, coup-plotting militaries and the pernicious effects of a globalized economic order.

I took up the examination of the more intractable problem of religion, in part two. My submission here is that with the establishment of an appropriate constitutional foundation, and with all the major parties and stakeholders primed to make sacrifices and concessions as are required for the success of our federation of faiths, all should be well with African democracy. Put in more specific terms, if each of these entities, i.e., the "secular" state, the various religious organizations, subscribers to other belief systems, would keep to the constitutionally negotiated terms of co-existence, then we can conveniently side-step the more dogmatic and subjective contents of religious creeds. Provided the parties and stakeholders are willing to stay in their respective lanes, today's generation of Africans could afford to be as notoriously religious, as their ancestors were reputed to have been, without compromising social harmony and real democratic progress.

Notes

1 A classic instance are the myriad of socio-economic crises created by the environmental degradation of the Lake Chad basin. On this, see, for example, Leon Usigbe, "Drying Lake Chad Basin Gives Rise to Crisis", *Africa Renewal*, Dec. 24, 2019; for a more scholarly rigorous discussion of

the problem, see, Freedom C. Onuoha, "Environmental Degradation, Livelihood and Conflicts: A Focus on the Implications of the Diminishing Water Resources of the Lake Chad for North-Eastern Nigeria", *African Journal of Conflict Resolution*, Vol.8, No.2, Jan. 2009, pp. 35–61.

2   This cake-slicing imagery is the conventional rendition of the "raison d'etre" of the proceedings at, and the end result, of the 1884 Berlin Conference. There are, however, credible alternative accounts, according to which the impetus for the convocation of the conference was primarily to further the nationalistic agenda of a wily German prince, Otto Von Bismarck. On this, see, for example, Daniel De Leon, "The Conference at Berlin on the West-African Question", *Political Science Quarterly*, Vol. 1, No.1, (Mar. 1886), pp. 103–139.

3   On this, see, Aluko, M.A.O. and Ajani, A.O. "Ethnic Nationalism and the Nigerian Democratic Experience in the Fourth Republic", *African Research Review*, Vol. 3, No.1, (2009), pp. 483–499. For a pan-Africanist coverage, see, Ake, Claude. *The Feasibility of Democracy in Africa*, Dakar, Senegal: Codesria, (2000).

4   For a fairly detailed chronology and helpful analysis of the causes and consequences of the Zuma affair, see, Clayton Hazvinei Vhumbunu, "The July Protests and Socio-Political Unrest in South Africa: Reflecting on the Causes, Consequences and Future Lessons", *Accord*, Dec. 10, 2021.

5   On the James Ibori saga, see the news report by Monjola Sotubo, "How Ibori Was Arrested in Dubai after Failed Attempt in Delta", *PULSE.ng.*, Dec. 22, 2016.

6   See, "March 2021 Global Poverty Update from the World bank", compiled by R. Andres Castaneda, et al., *Data Blog*, Mar. 16, 2021.

7   On this, see, "World Poverty Capital: Nigeria's Weighty Burden", *The Sun* newspaper, Oct. 8, 2018.

8   Jare Oladosu, "Designing Viable Republican Constitutions for Modern African States: Why the Institution of Traditional Kingship Must Be Abolished", *African Journal of International Affairs*, Vol. 8, No. 1&2, (2005), pp. 45–63.

9   On this, see, Great Ozozoyin's report, "Insecurity: Ishaku Warns Traditional Rulers as Terrorists Move to Take-Over Taraba", *Daily Post*, Dec. 16, 2021.

10   Some commentators seem to agree with this narrative by the coup plotters. For example, see, Ornella Moderan and Fahiraman Rodrigue Kone, "What Caused the Coup in Burkina Fasso?", *Institute of Security Studies[News Lette]r*, Feb. 03, 2022.

11   Some analysts are skeptical about the sustainability of the so called Chinese economic miracle. For a critical commentary on the Chinese model, see, Burton G. Malkiel, "The Chinese Economic Miracle: Can It Last?", *Proceedings of the American Philosophical Society*, Vol. 153, No.2, (June, 2009), pp. 193–199.

12   Neil A. Smith, "Understanding Sri Lanka's Defeat of the Tamil Tigers", *Joint Forces Quarterly*, Issue. 59, 4th Quarter (2010).

13   Article 8 of the Montevideo Convention (Convention on the Rights and Duties of States) of December 26, 1933, provides that: "No State has the right to intervene in the internal or external affairs of another". The eight articles of the Montevideo Convention are reproduced in Mark W. Janis and John E. Noyes (eds.), *International Law – Cases and Commentaries*. St. Paul, MNN: West Publishing C., 2001, pp. 403–404.

14   Mbiti, J. S. *African Religions and Philosophy*, London: Heinemann, 1969, p. 1

15   Abimbola, K. *Yoruba Culture (A Philosophical Account)*, Birmingham: Iroko Academic Publishers, 2006, p. 51.

16   Currently, 11 out of the 36 states in Nigeria are yet to domesticate the Child Rights Act of 2003. All the defaulting states are in the northern region of the country. See *This Day* news paper of July 27, 2022, for an earlier reportage, see *Premium Times* of May 11, 2019.

17   A Bill for an Act to provide for the equal rights in marriage between men and women was first submitted to the Nigerian Senate, during the 8th Assembly, by Senator Abiodun Olujimi (representing Ekiti South). The Bill was rejected on March 15, 2016, at the 2nd reading (see, *tori.ng* of March 15, 2016). The Bill was represented to the Senate in the 9th Assembly, where it was again rejected. Not even the sponsor's concession to substitute the word "equity" for "equality" could safe the Bill. See the reportage in *The Guardian* Newspaper of Nov. 26, 2019, and *Vanguard News Nigeria* of Dec. 16, 2021.

18   Karl Marx, *Critique of Hegel's Philosophy of Right*, (1843), translated by Joseph O'Malley, Oxford: Oxford University press, 1970, p. 3.

19 Clohesy, William W. "The Separation of Church and State: Truth, Opinion, and Democracy", *Public Affairs Quarterly*, Vol. 23, No. 1, Jan. 2009, pp. 49–66, at 54.

20 Pascal, Blaise. *Pensees* (1660), Translated by W.F. Trotter, Grand Rapids, MI: Christian Classic Ethereal Library, 2002, parag. 277 and 278.

21 Mill, J. S. (1859), *On Liberty: Annotated Text Sources and Background Criticism*, edited by David Spitz, New York: W.W. Norton and Company, 1975, p. 11.

22 Conflicting reactions by Islamic clerics to the blasphemy killing of Deborah Samuel.

23 Locke, John. *A Letter Concerning Toleration* (1689). I am quoting from the version prepared by Jonathan Bennet, first launched in May 2010, p. 3.

24 Ibid.

25 Ibid. p. 4.

26 Thomas Jefferson's Letter to the Danbury Baptist Church, Connecticut, of January 01, 1802. A copy is available at billofrightsinstitute.org/primary sources/danburybaptists.

27 On this, see, Abikan, AbdulQadir Ibrahim, "Constitutional Impediments to the Enthronement of Shariah in Nigeria", *The University of Ilorin Law Journal*, Vol.1., No. 2, (2006), pp. 185–215, at 187. Abikan discussed a number of other points of disagreement between the Constitution of the Federal Republic of Nigeria (1999) and the Shariah legal system. They include the constitutional separation/dichotomy between the state (politics) and religion, the exercise of the power of *nolle prosequi,* the exercise of the prerogative of mercy, executive immunity. The inevitable conclusion from Abikan's analyses is that a full-blown Shariah legal system cannot be realized in a multi-religious federation like Nigeria, that would be attainable only in an undiluted Islamic theocracy. In such a theocracy, the Shariah would not only be the sole legal system in operation, it would also regulate every aspect of a citizen's life. Under the authentic Shariah, there can be no wall of separation between religion and politics; the state would serve as an agency of the mosque.

28 On this advocacy, see, "MURIC and Other Muslim Groups Ask FG to Criminalize Blasphemy", in *The Paradise* news paper of May 23, 2022. MURIC: Muslim Rights Concern, is an Islamic NGO under the leadership of Professor Ishaq Akintola.

29 See the 1st Amendment to the Constitution of the United States (1791), and Section 10 of the Constitution of the Federal Republic of Nigeria (1999). The suggestion here is that multi-religious African nation states should enact similar prohibition of state religion.

30 The Islamic clerics who are promoting this idea of a universal criminalization of blasphemy would do well to consider carefully what they are praying for, just in case their prayer is answered. Among the religions that the state would be adopting as state religions are the motley varieties of African traditional religions. It could even get worse. Followers of A.T.R., for their part, would not have any problem with the proliferation of religions, or with the idea of the state serving as the patron to them all. Their mantra is to live and let live, to let a thousand flowers of faith flourish together. The grumblings of intolerance often emanate from the other side; serious opposition to accommodation often come from the covens of worshippers of jealous gods.

31 Locke, John. *Letter Concerning Toleration*, p. 8.

32 ibid. p. 21.

33 ibid. p. 8.

34 Here is another reason for our resourceful clerics to be wary in their advocacy for the criminalization of blasphemy. Atheism and agnosticism, being bona fide bodies of beliefs in their own respective rights, they would also have to be adopted by the state along with other beliefs and religions represented in the society for the criminalization project to be feasible even in principle.

35 Locke*, Letter Concerning Toleration*, p. 22.

36 Ibid.

37 Mill, J. S. *An Examination of Sir William Hamilton's Philosophy*, Boston: Spencer, 1865, p. 131, quoted in Sellers, Wilfrid and Hospers, John (eds.), *Readings in Ethical Theory*, Englewood Cliffs, NJ: Prentice-Hall Inc., 1970, p. 740.

22
AUTONOMOUS WEAPONS AND THE FUTURE OF WARFARE IN AFRICA

Karabo Maiyane

Introduction

For as long as humanity has existed, there has been warfare. These wars have been engaged differently, from world wars to inter- and intrastate wars. In Africa alone, there have been over 100 wars recorded since the first independence (Ugwuanyi, 2020). Over this time, there has been an academic interest in evaluating whether these wars were just or unjust. These evaluations are conducted from different perspectives, such as the traditionalist perspective (Walzer, 2015), revisionist (Orend, 2013; Lazar, 2017), and African perspective (see Badru, 2019; Okeja, 2019; Ugwuanyi, 2020; Cordeiro-Rodrigues, 2021). Although there are some differences in these approaches, the framework of the evaluations remains similar, focusing on the three parts of evaluating the morality of war: justified reason(s) to go to war *(jus ad bellum),* the justified conduct of war *(jus bello),* and the justified conclusion of the war *(jus post bellum).* These three principles constitute what we regard as just war theory.

There is a vast amount of literature that covers this topic. This chapter will pay particular attention to the ethics of war in light of the African experience, particularly the means used to fight a just war. This chapter investigates the ethical implications of the development and possible deployment of autonomous weapons systems (AWS) in warfare in Africa. AWS are weapons systems that, once activated, can select and engage targets without human intervention (Sparrow, 2007; ICRC, 2018; Sharkey, 2019). As far as we know, no such weapon has been used in warfare, but there has been a keen interest in developing them. The chapter specifically investigates whether the application of such weapons would undermine the ethics of war in African social and political thought. Looking at two African conceptions of the ethics of war: limited realism and just war theory, it argues that autonomous weapons would not undermine the ethics of war in Africa, particularly regarding the conduct of war and the means applied because limited realism does not restrict how war should be conducted and what means are permissible. Also, autonomous weapons would not undermine provided they are deployed only when they can distinguish between legitimate and non-legitimate targets. To ensure this condition, the chapter proposes the introduction of a *weapons prohibition principle* as one of the main principles governing the conduct and means of warfare. This is important because the rules governing which weapons are permissible

DOI: 10.4324/9781003143529-26

are as important as the discrimination and proportionality principles. Thus, they should be prioritised as such.

To make this point, the chapter will outline the contentious debate surrounding AWS. It will highlight and respond to the arguments made against them. In this regard, the it aims to show that many arguments against AWS are based on misunderstanding these weapons' role in warfare. If AWS are considered instruments and not agents of war, many arguments against them do not hold. It will then briefly explain the principles of a just war in African thought to evaluate autonomous weapons. Lastly, the chapter will make some recommendations considering the African articulation of a just war.

Autonomous Weapons and Warfare

This section offers a background of autonomous weapon systems as weapons technologies likely to feature significantly in future conflicts. It will start by explaining what AWS are. Following this, it will outline the ethical debates and responses surrounding them. It argues that most arguments against AWS are based on a misunderstanding of the role of AWS in warfare. The arguments assume that AWS could have the capacity to become political actors or have human autonomy. Taken as instruments and not agents, most of the arguments fall short.

One of the issues associated with autonomous weapons is that they are, as far as we know, conceptual, which means that there have not been any weapons deployed that can be rightly articulated as AWS. They are essentially imagined as the next step in weapons technologies based on the currently used weapons. AWS are weapons systems that, once activated, can select and engage targets without human intervention (Sparrow, 2007; Asaro, 2012; Sharkey, 2014; Heyns, 2017; ICRC, 2018; Sharkey, 2019). This implies that once programmed, AWS can determine when and how a target is executed without any human intervention. Such functionality falls out of the parameters of our current understanding of the role and capability of weapons. Weapons are usually operated by combatants who are responsible for making the critical decisions of targeting and pulling the trigger.

Given that AWS would be making such decisions, it makes some uncomfortable that they have banded together to form a campaign calling for their outright ban. The Campaign to Stop Killer Robots was launched in 2013 as a coalition of experts and government organisations to raise awareness about the dangers of developing and deploying autonomous weapons. In addition to this campaign, some authors have also argued against using AWS. I outline the arguments below.

One of the arguments against AWS is that these weapons' development and possible use would encourage political leaders to go to war, given the minimal cost of human casualties, thus encouraging other political actors to develop them as well. The potential diminished human cost would make states less hesitant to launch war campaigns. Such actions would cause another arms race (Sparrow, 2007; Asaro, 2012; Sharkey, 2014). In response to this point, Keith Abney (2015) argues that these arguments are not based on the weapons themselves but on the actions of political actors who would possess them. Political actors are the ones who declare wars; weapons are just means by which a war can be fought. Thus, no matter how sophisticated the weapon might be, they remain the means, never the actors that can declare war.

Regarding the argument that AWS has the probability of causing another arms race, one could argue that developing such capabilities could serve as a deterrence, discouraging political actors from attacking each other. When the prospect of success is less, it is less likely for one to launch an attack. Such is the case in terms of countries possessing nuclear weapons. Following the bombing of Hiroshima and Nagasaki, there was a consensus that such weapons should never be used in warfare. This consensus, based on the principle of "Mutually Assured Distraction", is why there has not been such an attack since. Thus, if one considers the development of autonomous weapons in this regard, one might argue that such a development would lessen the prospect of going to war in the long run, as no state or political actor would want to attack a country with such military prowess.

Another argument against AWS is that they would not comply with laws of armed conflict. Noel Sharkey (2014, p. 116) argues that "allowing robots to make decisions about who to kill could fall foul of the fundamental ethical precepts of a just war under *jus in bello*", specifically principles of discrimination and proportionality. Essentially, in a situation where the war is conducted in a place where people live, these weapons would be unable to distinguish between legitimate targets and non-legitimate ones. In a situation where combatants are targeted, Antonio Gutteres (2018) argues that "the prospect of machines with the discretion and power to take human life is morally repugnant". Similarly, Christof Heyns (2013, p. 10) argues that autonomous weapons lack "human judgment, common sense, appreciation of the larger picture, understanding of the intentions behind people's actions, and understanding of values and anticipation of the direction in which events are unfolding". For him, these qualities are important for making decisions about human lives. Peter Asaro (2012, p. 700) also argues that "the very nature of IHL [International Humanitarian Law], which was designed to govern the conduct of humans and human organisations in armed conflict, presupposes that combatants will be human agents".

The challenge with the arguments above is that they assume the status of AWS in warfare as that of agents. That is why they liken their conduct to that of combatants. However, there is insufficient evidence to suggest that AWS would assume the status of agents. The claim that they could is based on a misunderstood notion of what an autonomous agent is from a functional perspective and what it is from a human perspective. Functional autonomy is related to robots having the capacity to perform certain functions without direct supervision, whereas human autonomy is much more complicated, involving not only how one acts but how one wills to act. Will, in this regard, means the conscious capacity that enables human beings to act in certain ways or change their minds. Since AWS are like any other weapons, they would be considered instruments, not agents. As instruments, they would only need to comply with weapons treaties. There are already existing weapons treaties[1] that specify what is required and what is prohibited. They would also need better target precision to ensure that they comply with the principles of discrimination and proportionality.

Another argument against the use of AWS is one based on responsibility. The argument is that it is unclear who, if anyone, could be held responsible for unlawful acts caused by a fully autonomous weapon: the programmer, manufacturer, commander, or the machine itself. The accountability gap proposed here would make it difficult to ensure justice, especially for victims (Heyns, 2013; Roff, 2013; Sharkey, 2014; Gerdes, 2018). Accordingly, the issue of accountability is significant because IHL "emphasise [s] a clear chain of accountability as a prerequisite" (Gerdes, 2018, p. 238). Heyns (2013, p. 14) also argues that "robots have no moral agency and as a result, cannot be held responsible in any recognisable way if they cause deprivation of life that would normally require accountability if humans have made the decision. Who, then, is to bear the responsibility?" given that "you cannot punish an inanimate object" (Sharkey, 2014, p. 117).

The response to the responsibility issues is that if the status of AWS is that of an instrument, then the responsibility would lie with the agent using it. Since AWS would be programmed based on the instructions of the commander in charge, the responsibility would lie with the commander using a principle known as command responsibility. It states that

> commanders and other superiors are criminally responsible for war crimes committed by their subordinates if they knew or had reason to know that the subordinates were about to commit or were committing such crimes and did not take all necessary and reasonable measures in their power to prevent their commission, or if such crimes had been committed, to punish the persons responsible
>
> *(Walzer, 2015, p. 317)*

Therefore, the commanding officer is the first locus of responsibility regarding the conduct of war. As such, they can be held responsible for the conduct of their combatants and the arsenal at their disposal. In every declared conflict, a commander is appointed and made responsible for carrying out the interests of their representative state. The commander takes charge of the entire infantry, from the combatants to medical staff and weapons. Thus, Michael Walzer argues that:

> The moral responsibility is clear, and it cannot be located anywhere else than in the office of the commander. The campaign belongs to the commander as it does not belong to ordinary combatants; he has access to all available information and also the means of generating more information; he has [or ought to have] an overview of the sum of actions and effects that he is ordering or hoping for.
>
> *(ibid.)*

Nothing happens or should happen in war without the commander's knowledge. It is because of this that she bears the primary responsibility. Also, as an accounting officer, she could hold programmers responsible if they misunderstood the instructions or decommission the AWS if she realises it is faulty. Essentially the commander is responsible for all actions in the field. They even have the power to hold others responsible. It is for this reason that they are the locus of responsibility.

This section highlighted the arguments favouring and against the development and use of AWS. It argues that many of the arguments provided tend to misunderstand the role AWS would play in warfare in three ways. Firstly, autonomous weapons are not political actors. As such, they cannot encourage or discourage anyone's prospect of going to war. Secondly, although they might have some autonomy only in terms of their functions, they are not autonomous in a human sense. Thus, their role will be as instruments, perhaps with extended capabilities, but not combatants. Lastly, as instruments used in war, all responsibility related to their actions would befall their user. Although there could be a need to evaluate the existing weapons treaties to ensure that AWS does not contravene the principles of a just war, none of the arguments proposed against them is sufficient to justify a claim for an outright ban. If the weapons treaties are insufficient, we can rely on existing just war theory principles. The following section outlines these principles of just war theory with a particular interest in the African conception of a just war

Ethics of War in African Thought

A just war is a war that is fought to maintain some form of justice. Justice in that the hostilities in question do not regress to all-out war. To engage in such a war, actors must adhere to certain principles. There are three main categorisations of the principles of war: (1) *Jus ad bellum* – the principles related to the reasons for engaging in war; (2) *Jus en bello* – the principles related to how war is conducted; (3) *Jus Post Bellum* – the principles related to the manner which war should be concluded. This section outlines these principles, paying particular attention to African conceptions of a just war in light of how and with what means a war should be conducted. Specifically, it investigates whether the application of autonomous weapons in war would undermine the African conception(s) of a just conduct of war. Looking at two African conceptions related to the conduct of war, limited realism (Okeja, 2019) and proportionality and participatory pain (Ugwuanyi, 2020), it argues that the application of autonomous weapons in warfare does not undermine African principles of acceptable conduct of war. It will first briefly outline just war theory and the principles involved in positioning the African conception in line with the existing literature on the subject. It will pay particular attention to the conduct of war specifically the means applied in conducting war to position autonomous weapons as the means to conduct these hostilities.

Most literature on just war theory is centred on the Western normative frameworks. Within this framework, just war is framed under three categories: *jus ad bellum, jus en bello* and (recently) *jus post bellum. jus ad bellum* principles are concerned with a set of conditions that political actors must consider before engaging in war to determine whether entering the war is morally and legally permissible. There are six necessary conditions under *jus ad bellum* that a state (or other political actors) needs to fulfil before going to war. These are Just Cause; Legitimate Authority; Right Intention; Reasonable Prospects of Success; Proportionality: Last Resort (Necessity) (Lin, Bekey and Abney, 2008; Orend, 2013; Abney, 2015; Lazar, 2017).

Jus in bello refers to the principles and laws concerning the acceptable conduct of agents during a war. Unlike *jus ad bellum*, where responsibility rests on the state (or the political actor instituting the conflict), with responsibility "rests with those commanders, officers and soldiers who command and control the lethal force set in motion by the political hierarchy" (Walzer, 2015, p. 39). Some principles serve as necessary conditions which combatants must abide by, such as Discrimination, Proportionality and Necessity (Lazar, 2017)

Jus post bellum principles involve the law concerning acceptable conduct following the official or declared war's end. It is a relatively new field, and as such, there is not much literature regarding the principles categorised under it. Orend (2013) proposes the following moral principles: Proportionality and publicity; Rights vindication; Discrimination; Punishment; Compensation and rehabilitation. He suggests these principles would benefit the countries who engaged in war after the war. As such, they must be considered as part of just war theory. These principles – *jus ad bellum, jus en bello & jus post bellum* – collectively cover the institution of war from when it starts until it officially ends and must be followed for a war to be considered a just war.

Recently there has been a development in the philosophical literature on just war theory from an African point of view (see Metz, 2019; Okeja, 2019; Ugwuanyi, 2020; Cordeiro-Rodrigues, 2021). I briefly outline some key arguments. Luis Cordiero-Rodrigues (2021) provides an overview of contemporary African perspectives on a just war. He outlines the main arguments concerning the moral justifications to initiate or abstain from war (*jus ad bellum*) by looking at works from twentieth- and twenty-first-century African philosophers. He argues that within African thought, there are four kinds of arguments for going to war:

> Firstly, there are consequentialist rationales for starting a war, which in fact constitute the dominant perspective in African thought. Secondly, there are African thinkers who uphold that for initiating or abstaining from entering war one needs to look at the

therapeutic impact that war or peace may have and, from this impact then deliberate on whether it is justified or not to enter war. A third category of arguments defend that entering war is justified if it is a response to a wrong committed. Finally, some African philosophers uphold that wars are justified only if they have been agreed upon, under certain conditions.

(Cordeiro-Rodrigues, 2021, p. 9)

He argues that it is for these reasons that the bulk of theorisation in the African context emanated. In this text, he only focuses on *jus ad bellum* principles, arguing that that is where a large amount of literature emanates. Given that he does not pay much attention to the principles of the conduct of war, his conception then does not assist in evaluating whether the use of autonomous weapons would undermine *jus en bello* principles. I now turn to Uchenna Okeja.

Looking at wars fought pre-colonisation, Okeja 2019 outlines both the motivation to go to war (*jus ad bellum*) and the conduct of war (*jus in bello*) to address the question: what makes a war morally justified? In terms of *jus ad bellum*, he (ibid., p. 195) argues that "consensus is the basis for the determination of the morality of the recourse to war in traditional African contexts". Essentially, he argues that even in the different types of conflicts that occurred in different military organisations, common to these conflicts was that chiefs and council members had to consent to any decision to go to war. The motivation for this was the just cause claims that required deliberation and agreement by the parties affected or their representatives before such a war could ensue.

Okeja (2019) argues that the conduct and means of war at this time had flexible moral requirements. Essentially there was no legislation regarding how the conflict could be conducted or what means were permissible. All means accessible to the warring parties to subdue the enemy could be used, ranging from "charms, talismans, amulets, chief priests" (ibid., p. 194), to name a few. He thus summarises the conduct of war as an endorsement of limited realism, meaning that "considerations of what is permissible or impermissible in war is confined to the domain of expediency, taboos and customs" (ibid., p. 195).

Given the chapter's interest in *jus en bello*, it will not focus on the justification for the recourse for war. It will only address questions of the conduct of war. Regarding Okeja's (2019) conception of limited realism, I argue that using AWS would be permissible because limited realism does not restrict how war is conducted and what means would be permissible. Realism goes as far as to argue that there is no such thing as the morality of war. Once a conflict starts, then it is everything goes. It would not matter what weapons would or should be in use. That decision would depend on the military capacity of the warring parties based on what would give them a more strategic advantage. Thus, in this context, using autonomous weapons would not contravene any principle, especially in Okejas's case, where there are no principles governing the conduct of war. Lawrence Ugwuanyi (2020) holds a different view in terms of the principles governing the conduct of war

Looking at wars fought in Africa post-1957, Ugwuanyi (2020) articulates an African theory of just war. In his paper titled "Towards an African Theory of Just War", He (ibid., p. 51) argues that

a just war in African thought is a war fought to protect the corporate harmony of a people who are bound and bonded together through the land, resources, and other symbols and traditions that make them distinct.

Essentially, the primary interest of African communities is peace and harmony, not war. So even in cases where they must resort to war, they would have to abide by certain principles. He lists four fundamental principles of a just war in Africa: (1) last means of addressing conflict; (2) proportional means and ends; (3) participatory pain; (4) Harmony. He argues that these principles are informed by the norms, values and principles that drive philosophical inquiry in Africa and thus constitute a just war. Some of these principles are similar to those expressed in the Western normative conception of just war theory. Others, such as harmony and participatory pain, are unique to the African conception.

He proceeds to explain each of these principles in detail. This section will only address principles 2 and 3 concerned with the conduct of fighting a war. The principle of proportional means and end suggests that war is not meant to annihilate the other party. Instead, it must be "executed in a manner that would provide for and make up for the harm that caused the dispute in question and lead to what can be called a measured restoration" (Ugwuanyi, 2020, p. 62). This principle is closely linked with participatory pain, which emphasises that "war in Africa observed such ethics that forbade the total annihilation of an opponent" (ibid.). These two principles emphasise that the conduct and means by which hostilities are conducted must always ensure the least damage in acquiring whatever goals the hostilities envisage. So whatever weapon is used cannot, for example, be indiscriminate or annihilate the other party. It must be targeted with the aim of minimal harm and suffering.

These requirements are like the current conventions regarding the conduct of conflict[2] and the means. Thus, based on the requirements of Ugwuanyi's conception, using autonomous weapons would be permissible if the weapons can discriminate between legitimate and legitimate targets and, in targeting legitimate targets, use only the amount of force needed to achieve the political goal. So, if autonomous weapons can comply with existing weapons treatise, they would not contravene this conception of a just war. I argue that they would even be better suited to execute tasks with minimal casualties. For example, a drone a size of a hornet with just enough explosives and facial recognition camera can aim at and only cause damage to the intended target and no one else. This success would come at a lesser human cost than sending in a small unit that would need to target other people to reach the intended target. Thus considered this way, using autonomous weapons would not contravene the African principles of a just war.

This section outlined African conceptions of just war theory with a particular interest in evaluating whether using autonomous weapons would undermine African principles of just conduct of war. It found that Looking at two approaches related to the conduct of the war in Africa: limited realism (Okeja, 2019) and just war principles of proportionality and participatory pain (Ugwuanyi, 2020) shows that the application of autonomous weapons in warfare does not undermine African principles of acceptable conduct of war. In terms of limited realism, it argued that given that conduct and means of war are not regulated within this paradigm, any means would be permissible. In terms of the principles of proportionality and participatory pain, it argued that autonomous weapons would not contravene these principles if, in use, these weapons are not indiscriminate and do not seek complete annihilation of other actors. Now that we have established that the development and use of autonomous weapons would not undermine just war theory, what follows is to outline how these weapons can be applied in future conflicts.

Imagining the Future Warfare in Africa

What does the future of warfare look like in Africa? This section outlines how we should think about the future of warfare. It begins by making some recommendations regarding *jus ad bellum* and then proceeds to *jus en bello*. It argues that the current African conception of just war theory does not pay much attention to *jus en bello*, specifically on the means of fighting a just war. Most literature focuses on the justifications of war, and not much is said about the conduct or the means. In terms of resolving the issue of war means, it proposes that a principle of weapons prohibition should be one of the key principles of *jus en bello*. This principle would greatly assist in evaluating current and future weapons such as AWS to ensure they align with jus en bello principles.

Regarding *jus ad bellum*, there is work done to address the legitimate causes for engaging in war (Metz, 2019; Cordeiro-Rodrigues, 2021) and to show that war occurs after lengthy deliberations and only as a last resort (Okeja, 2019; Ugwuanyi, 2020). Much work needs to be done in considering the principle of legitimate authority. Who has the authority to enter these negotiations, and how is this determined? These questions are critical in African conceptions of just war theory because most contemporary African wars involve states versus non-state actors. For example, the current civil war in Ethiopia is a civil war between the state and a political actor called the Tigray People's Liberation Front (TPLF). This development is not conventional in just war theory and thus requires its articulation.

Traditional just war theory considers war as a conflict between states (Walzer 2015). Even the rules outlined in International Humanitarian Law (IHL) are primarily meant for inter-state conflicts. There are minimal provisions for non-state and intrastate conflict (ICRC, 2004). Revisionists have done some work to try and resolve this (Lazar, 2017). Some of the changes instituted in this school include the definition of war which has now changed from being a conflict between states to being a conflict between *political actors* (Orend, 2013; Lazar, 2017), meaning that war is not only a conflict between states but can include parties who intend to become states. This slight change in the definition of war enables a greater appreciation of other political actors in warfare, such as insurgents (Umkhonto we Sizwe), transnational organisations (Al Qaeda), and terrorist groups (Boko Haram). Considering war this way empowers the *jus ad bellum* to have a broader scope in determining which actors would have the legitimate authority to declare war.

This is already something that happens. It is evident in recent conflicts where peace negotiation involves both state and non-state actors. Considering the Ethiopian conflict, for example, the actors involved in this conflict are varied. On the side of the state is a coalition of "Ethiopian military, ethnic militias and troops from neighbouring Eritrea" (Walsh and Dahir, 2022). From this example, one can conclude that even non-state armed groups are considered legitimate political actors. As something that already happens, it would be beneficial for the African conception of just war theory to document as a principle to consider.

Regarding the conduct of war, Ugwuanyi (2020) does well to highlight the principles necessary to ensure a just war. He argues that the conduct of war must not aim to annihilate the opponents, which means that in fighting, there must be discrimination in terms of who can be targeted and who cannot. Also, the means used must ensure that the damages are not indiscriminate. To make this point, he invokes the principles of proportionality, discrimination and participatory pain. These principles ensure that in a conflict, only those that have consented to hostilities can be legitimate targets, and the means must be proportional. What is missing in the literature is an articulation of what acceptable *means* can be applied in conflict. Should certain weapons be prohibited, and how would we evaluate such?

Ugwuayi (2020) tries to respond to these questions by arguing that whatever means applied must not discriminate or seek to annihilate the other. However, he does not articulate how such means would be evaluated to ensure they do not cause unnecessary harm or destruction. This issue is not unique to the African conception of just war theory. Even Walzer (2015, p. 42) argues that "rules specifying how and when soldiers can be killed are by no means unimportant, and yet the morality of war would not be radically transformed were they to be abolished altogether". What he means here is that although it might be noteworthy to address the questions of when and how legitimate targets are targeted, not doing it would not fall foul of *jus en bello* principles, which are primarily concerned with distinguishing legitimate and non-legitimate targets.

Walzer is correct in arguing that the foundation of just war theory is the principle of discrimination. However, He is incorrect that it makes no difference what weapons must be used. Evaluating weapons plays a significant role in ensuring the discrimination principle is upheld by ensuring that the means used can distinguish between legitimate and non-legitimate targets. This is also why international law has clear weapons prohibition treaties. Thus, I agree with Orend (2013) that rules governing which weapons are permissible should take as much priority as the principles of discrimination and proportionality. I thus propose that as part of the principles governing the conduct of war and the means used, there must be a weapons prohibition principle. The principle would read as follows:

Weapons Prohibition: weapons used in war must comply with international weapons treaties and just war principles

Such a principle would ensure evaluation of the weapons used by the warring parties and ensure that in their use, they do not contravene just war principles, thus minimising potential damage. It would also ensure accountability even for non-state actors who are not signatories to the existing treaties. This principle would also be prudent because it can evaluate even weapons not covered by international treaties, using just war principles. Having such a principle in place ensures that the development and use of conventional weapons, such as autonomous weapons, do not undermine *jus en bello* principles. Because before they can be used, any party involved must fulfil the necessary conditions as stated in the just war principles.

So, to answer the question of what the future of warfare would look like in Africa. The ideal response is that Africa would be relatively peaceful without acquiring or using weapons. However, history has shown us that this has never occurred anywhere. So, it is likely that we would have to deal with the advent of war for decades. The best we can do is to use war as a last resort and ensure that we adhere to the principles of just conduct and means of fighting when engaging in hostilities. Autonomous weapons can help us achieve this. Better target precision comes with better technology, meaning most non-legitimate targets will be spared. Better technology also ensures that conflicts do not take as long as they do now. However, for this future to be possible, we must abandon our fears and embrace new technologies such as autonomous weapons. In embracing them, however, we must ensure that we are aware of the risks and do our best to mitigate them.

Conclusion

This chapter has endeavoured to show that the development and possible deployment of AWS in warfare would not undermine African conceptions of just war theory. This point was made based on two African conceptions of the ethical conduct of war: limited realism and just war theory. Limited realism does not impose any rules regarding the conduct of war. Taken this way, the use of AWS or any other weapon, for that matter, would be permissible. Regarding the just war perspective provided by Ugwuanyi (2020), it argued that using AWS would be permissible if they complied with participatory pain and proportionality principles. The paper went on to show that the African literature on just war theory pays very little attention to the conduct and means of warfare. In this regard, the paper proposed that we should consider weapons prohibition as a necessary condition in the conduct of war. This would ensure that weapons are evaluated as critically as their users, thus ensuring fewer casualties than necessary.

Although we would like to imagine the future of Africa without any war, the current reality is that there is a lot of it. Part of mitigating this is ensuring that people's socioeconomic conditions are improved. In tandem with this, we must invest in the necessary technology, such as AWS, to ensure the effective defence of our people. Such an investment would assist in two ways; firstly, it would ensure a swift response to threats and secondly, by acting as a deterrent. Imagined this way, the future could be free of conflict sooner rather than later.

Notes

1 The varied weapons treaties that are current in place. For a list, please refer to https://www.icrc.org/en/document/weapons
2 The first additional protocol of the Geneva conventions

References

Abney, K. (2015) 'Autonomous robots and the future of just war theory', in Alhoff, F. (ed.) *Routledge Handbook of Ethics and War: Just War Theory in the 21st Century*. London: Tailor & Francis, pp. 338–351. doi: 10.4324/9780203107164.ch25.

Asaro, P. (2012) 'On banning autonomous weapon systems: Human rights, automation, and the dehumanisation of lethal decision-making', *International Review of the Red Cross*, 94(886), pp. 687–709. doi: 10.1017/S1816383112000768.

Badru, R. O. (2019) 'An African philosophical account of just war theory', *Ethical Perspectives*, 26(2), pp. 153–181. doi: 10.2143/EP.26.2.3286746.

Cordeiro-Rodrigues, L. (2021) 'African perspectives on just war', *Philosophy Compass*, 17(3). doi: 10.1111/phc3.12808.

Gerdes, A. (2018) 'Lethal autonomous weapon systems and responsibility gaps', *Philosophy Study*, 8(5). doi: 10.17265/2159–5313/2018.05.004.

Gutteres, A. (2018) *Address to the General Assembly, United Nations*. Available at: https://www.un.org/sg/en/content/sg/speeches/2018-09-25/address-73rd-general-assembly (Accessed: 15 March 2022).

Heyns, C. (2013) *United Nations Report of the Special Rapporteur on Extrajudicial, Summary or Arbitrary Executions*.(Issue A/HRC/23/47). https://www.ohchr.org/sites/default/files/Documents/HRBodies/HRCouncil/RegularSession/Session23/A-HRC-23-47_en.pdf

Heyns, C. (2017) 'Autonomous weapons in armed conflict and the right to a dignified life: An African perspective', *South African Journal on Human Rights*, 33(1), pp. 46–71. doi: 10.1080/02587203.2017.1303903.

ICRC (2004) 'What is international humanitarian law?', *Icrc.Org*. Available at: https://www.icrc.org/en/document/what-international-humanitarian-law

ICRC (2018) *Ethics and Autonomous Weapon Systems: An Ethical Basis for Human Control?* (Issue August). Available at: https://www.icrc.org/en/document/ethics-and-autonomous-weapon-systems-ethical-basis-human-control

Lazar, S. (2017). 'War', in E. N. Zalta, (ed.). *Stanford Encyclopaedia of Philosophy.* Available at: https://plato.stanford.edu/archives/spr2017/entries/war/

Lin, P., Bekey, G. and Abney, K., (2008). *Autonomous Military Robotics: Risk, Ethics, and Design.* San Luis Obispo: California Polytechnic State University. Available at: http://ethics.calpoly.edu/ONR_report.pdf

Metz, T. (2019) 'An African theory of just causes for war', in Cordiero-Rodrigues, L. and Singh, D. (eds) *Comparative Just War Theory. An Introduction to International Perspectives.* London: Rowman and Littlefield, pp. 131–155.

Okeja, U. (2019) 'War by agreement: A reflection on the nature of just war', *Journal of Military Ethics,* 18(3), pp. 189–203. doi: 10.1080/15027570.2019.1690115.

Orend, B. (2013) *The Morality of War.* Second Edition. Toronto: Broadview Press.

Roff, H. M. (2013) 'Killing in War: Responsibility, liability, and lethal autonomous robots', in Allhof, F. Evans, N.G. & Henschke, A. (eds.) *Routledge Handbook of Ethics and War: Just War Theory in the 21st Century.* New York: Routledge, pp. 352–364.

Sharkey, N. (2014) 'Killing made easy: From joysticks to politics', in Lin, P., Abney, K., and Bekey, G. (eds) *Robot Ethics: The Ethical and Social Implications of Robotics.* Massachusetts: MIT Press, pp. 111–128.

Sharkey, A. (2019) 'Autonomous weapons systems, killer robots and human dignity', *Ethics and Information Technology,* 21(2), pp. 75–87. doi: 10.1007/s10676-018-9494-0.

Sparrow, R. (2007) 'Killer Robtos', *Journal of Applied Philosophy,* 24(1), pp. 62–77.

Ugwuanyi, L. (2020) 'Towards an African theory of just war', *Revista de Estudios Africanos,* (1), pp. 51–65. doi: 10.15366/rea2020.1.003.

Walsh, D. and Dahir, A. L. (2022) *Why Is Ethiopia at War with Itself, The New York Times.* Available at: https://www.nytimes.com/article/ethiopia-tigray-conflict-explained.html (Accessed: 10 March 2022).

Walzer, M. (2015) *Just and Unjust Wars: A Moral Argument with Historical Illustrations.* Fifth. New York: Basic Books.

23

AFRICA'S DIGITAL PUBLIC SPHERE

Nanjala Nyabola

Defining the Public Sphere

In 1975, Jurgen Habermas defined the public sphere as "a realm of social life within which some kind of public opinion could be formed" (1964). Habermas asserted that wherever individuals come together to form a public body, they needed to create opportunities for deliberation in order to make sure that the body they were building aligned with their individual aspirations and values. For Habermas, a public body is constituted, not just by the presence of individuals and institutions within it, but also by a context that creates space for unrestricted deliberation: "with a guarantee of freedom of assembly and association, as well as freedom to express and publish…opinions" (1974). The public sphere is not characterised merely by its existence, but by the nature of relation it makes possible between those who have power and those who do not. In this vein, the public sphere is the space of relation between the society and the state, shaped by the rules of engagement that coordinate this relation. In the pre-industrial period, this space might have been physical, but today the media – both digital and analogue – are the space through which the deliberation occurs.

Crucially, within this approach, the health of a society is characterised, not by the ability of the government to communicate to the people but by the ability of the people to communicate to government. Habermas argued that a functional democracy is one in which "political control is effectively subordinated to the democratic demand that information be accessible to the public" (1964). This approach recognises that there is a power differential between those who are governed and those who governed, and that the ability to influence the avenues for communication vests significant power to alter the public sphere within the state. A state in which debate is unilateral is akin to a feudal monarchy rather than the democratic public sphere that Habermas envisions.

Once individuals came together to constitute a public sphere in this way, then they created a narrative about what their particular political entity represents and to some extent what are the roles of the various entities – individuals, governments, corporations, etc. – within that public sphere. The process through which this narrative is delineated is known as the rational-critical debate. The rational-critical debate within the Habermasian public sphere is both an ideal and a means of action, which of course raises practical challenges. The idea of a rational-critical debate presumes certain structures, not least of which perfect rationality and

DOI: 10.4324/9781003143529-27

the capacity to criticise. Habermas not only argued that the rational-critical debate was integral to the idea of a public sphere, but he also prescribed that without meaningful political participation, there was no meaningful self-determination. As such the public sphere makes both a national narrative and a national identity possible. The national narrative is the outcome of the rational-critical debate and therefore, information and the platforms that carry information between states and their governments are crucial to determining the bounds and content of the rational-critical debate.

Similarly, ideas are crucial to the functioning of the public sphere. A public sphere is also one where ideas can come together in a meaningful way, and this means that language has particular significance in determining what voices are amplified and what voices are diminished within the national narrative. When powerful interests disproportionately curtail the participation of specific groups then they also undermine the integrity of the public sphere. The Habermasian public sphere is about convergence and exchange. Habermas' concept of a public sphere unwittingly rests on notions of literacy, and the ability to speak the language of power (Nyabola, 42). The stories we choose to tell and the ways we choose to tell them are central to how we see our place in our state.

One key characteristic of Habermas' definition of the public sphere is that it is both descriptive and normative, and this gives it tremendous rhetorical and analytical value even if it creates contradictions of use. The Habermasian public sphere was produced through an analysis of Western European political history charting the development of representative democracy within these societies. But Habermas was also defining an ideal type of society within which democracy could flourish. Fraser (2017) notes that within his own analysis of the public sphere, Habermas routinely oscillates between these two functions, for example shifting the meaning of concepts like "public opinion". In the historical register, Fraser notes, Habermas describes the history of the public sphere as "a history of decay" but in the normative register emphasises its emancipatory and critical power (245).

For Habermas, the public sphere is distinct from both the state and the market. His approach presumes free, rational and unrestricted communication which is practically unsustainable within most societies. Frictions of identity and belonging necessarily slow down the process of communication, as do basic limitations of comprehension.

Habermas grounds his concept of the public sphere in the development of a post-feudal polity in Europe, but arguably its roots go further back to the idealised narrative of Athenian democracy. Athenian democracy, in turn fuelled political structures in much of Western Europe at the time Habermas developed his idea. Within the Athenian social practice, public life and private life were strictly demarcated, and public interactions were often characterised by an element of performance, that is that individuals did not generally have authentic and unguarded interactions with each other but instead with versions of each other calibrated to suit the demands of the specific contexts they were in. Goldhill and Osborne (1999) write that connections in this period "depended on a set of barely concealed, if rarely articulated, assumptions about the subject and the subject's relation to social norms and agendas ... each activity forms an integral part in the exercise of citizenship" (1). To be a citizen in this context necessarily meant a separation between the informality of private life and that of public life, where in the public domain unspoken rules and codes were integral to fulfilling or upholding those duties.

Speech acts are a central part of this performance of public life and the Habermasian public sphere saw deliberation or discourse as the core process through which relation is established within the polity. Habermas stated that public opinion – the narrative about the polity's self that emerges from these interactions – was created primarily through the process of conversation or debate. Again, in the Athenian model these conversations would occur in physical sites like the gymnasium or symposium and the output of these conversations would feed directly into how the city-state was governed. These conversations, characterised by specific and previously agreed upon rules and mores, produced a specific type of outcome. Overall therefore, the public sphere from Habermas' perspective is the space in which all conversations with power and between various groups collide to produce a national narrative.

One of the earliest critiques of Habermas' concept of the public sphere came from Negt and Kluge (2016) who argued that Habermas was essentially describing the development of the European bourgeoisie rather than a distinct mode of political action. They argued that Habermas did not see the proletarian public sphere, and particularly did not ascribe rationality to modes of political participation that distinctly act against the interests of the bourgeoisie. Rationality is presupposed as a value and a normative good but it is not universally ascribed to all people in a society. In this analysis, protest for example which is a rational political action for an exploited underclass would likely be described as irrational because it may result in the destruction of property or disruption of work. But for those who exist at the margins of power even destructive protest is perfectly rational action. The discursive practices of those who are removed from power might seem irrational to those who are accustomed to interacting with responsive and representative systems, but they are a form of rationality and a contribution to the rational-critical debate of the entire nation, albeit not in the language of power.

Michael Warner (2002) put forward the idea of "counterpublics" as sites where different types of rationality take shape and define alternative public spheres (76). Counterpublics refers to modes of social organisation within the society that reject many of the fundamental norms that would define the public sphere. Counterpublics in his definition are not created by strategic actors motivated power and subordination (76). They may be motivated purely by the rejection of the principles of the public sphere; the rejection of the principles of the public sphere becomes its own rationale. Counterpublics may include music scenes like punk and reggae that evolve into distinct political ethos, or gender and sexual cultures like drag. These counterpublics have different rules for both public and private performance, and have distinct orientations towards power and how to distribute it. Discourse within these counterpublic is governed by separate rules of style and but they share identical political and social space with the mainstream public sphere. For Warner, counterpublics are not merely reactionary but they also "describe the world it attempts to circulate, projecting for that world a concrete and liveable shape, and attempting to realise that world through address" (81).

Other critics have also taken issue with the idea that debate within the public sphere must be rational. Wahl-Jorgensen (2019) argued that Habermas' conception of the public sphere necessarily excludes discourse that is emotive and subjective as being peripheral to the rational-critical debate (2). They find that in fact, even within the mainstream public sphere people are more responsive to emotive or subjective presentations of information than they are to information that is presented otherwise. In fact, they argue that there must be a role for emotion as an alternative way of knowing and experiencing the world, rather than as something that is fundamentally at odds with the idea of debate in the public sphere.

Feminist critiques of Habermas elaborate this critique on the absence of alternative approaches to rationality or reasoning. Landes (2012) points out that for Habermas the exclusion of women from the physical sites of practice for the public sphere – the coffee houses and the salons – was not an inherently bad thing because their discourses might have been "inconsequential" (96). She suggests that had women been involved in the earliest forms of the literary and cultural debates that occurred in these salons, they may never have naturally deviated towards political and economic discussions precisely because the mores of gender relations prevented them from doing so and were less likely to be violated in mixed-gender groups. The exception to this was the women patron of the arts and landowners of various backgrounds who were permitted by virtue of their economic standing to at least involve themselves in conversations about literature and the arts (97).

Landes notes that this conception of the role that women played in bourgeois society is inaccurate and perpetuates an untenable distinction between the private and the public. She points out that intimate relations have a direct impact on how the individual was able to perform their roles and duties in the public sphere (97). Indeed, the fundamental feminist maxim that "the personal is political" speaks against this distinction. Intimate relations include the management of domestic affairs like household finances and labour, but also sexual relations between individuals that include gender performance and sexuality. Intimate relations are shaped by discourses that may not be easily articulated in the mainstream public sphere where conversations about sex for example might be viewed as lewd or offensive. And yet sex has been a key method for political organisation and participation for African women. Luise White (1990) for example documents the ways through which prostitution allowed black women in racist and colonial Nairobi to claim political space in a city in which they were legally forbidden to live, to demand protection from the colonial state, and to accumulate wealth beyond that which was thought possible for African women. Sexual relations can replicate or undermine prevailing networks of power and allow women and sexual minorities access to spaces that may otherwise be denied them in patriarchal systems, but the Habermasian public sphere might see these actions as irrational and extraneous to the rational-critical debate. Beyond failing to explain or understand it properly Habermasian public sphere simply does not see the politics of the intimate sphere even though it does influence the public domain.

Similarly, feminists argue that the Habermasian concept of the public sphere does not see the methods of the private sphere, and particularly the methods employed by women to navigate exclusion from the mainstream political arena. Research on women's political action around the world reveals that this inability persists today and women's political organisation is often characterised as peripheral. For example, women's marches for peace and calls for sex strikes betray a specific understanding of intimate politics but they are often reported as irrational and unbecoming actions rather than fundamental resistance to the politics of the day.

Habermas himself later conceded that his concept of the public sphere did not sufficiently take into account the experiences of women and other marginalised groups within European bourgeois society. Landes questions his latent idea of the masculine as "objective" and "universal" and the feminine as "particular" (98). This tendency to ascribe rationality to the work and public functions of men is embedded in several patriarchal contexts and is an easy way through which women's political behaviour is ignored. In reviewing colonial records on women's revolts in Kenya, Cameroon and Nigeria for example, Shanklin (1990) finds that the colonial officers routinely diminished the impact of women's political spaces and action, characterising them as "disturbances" or "riots", seeking the action of men in influencing their activity where such organising was successful, betraying their belief that women – and African women especially – were incapable of organising independently.

African Critiques of the Habermasian Approach

The idea of deliberation and exchange as being central to constituting a national discourse is in itself broadly accepted. But scholars from various backgrounds have criticised the Habermasian approach for its limited understanding both of how power shapes different individual's ability to participate, as well as the idea that the public and the private can be seen as fundamentally separate. With its deep roots in Western political philosophy, the Habermasian approach inherits the tendency to ignore the disparities of power and access that characterised the Athenian public sphere and Europe's pre-war societies. Post-colonial scholars especially, looking at societies whose experiences are framed by power disparities within the societies as well as the imposition of colonial authority, have criticised the tendency to overlook social forces like racism, misogyny and ableism, as well as the class disparities that undermine the full presence and participation of certain groups within the public sphere. Much like the idealised narrative of Athenian democracy, the Habermasian model does not seem to see that participation was the province of white, landowning, able-bodied men and that this approach overlooks the political action that their wives, slaves and others undertook within the private domain. The failure to account for the political stratification of a society in deploying theories about how society functions only deepens the marginalisation of these groups.

Peter Ekeh's (1975) foundational essay on Africa and the two publics explores the impact of imperialism on the idea of an African public sphere. Ekeh argued that the Western concept of a public versus a public realm rests on the assumption that the two realms are united by a common moral foundation and that what distinguishes the private and the public is the subject matter of the opinion rather than the framework on which opinion is based (96). In contrast, Ekeh argues that Western imperialism introduced two parallel moral frameworks within African societies and that the distinction was not between private and public but between these two contesting publics. The primordial public is shaped by the ties, sentiments and groupings that characterised pre-colonial society, while the Western-facing realm is characterised by the moral codes imposed through force. Imperialism creates this bifurcation within invaded societies by using force to compel indigenous communities to embrace and exist within these parallel frameworks, and because they are fundamentally irreconcilable, the existence of the indigenous individual is characterised by negotiation and navigation between the two.

Ekeh argues that many of the political developments in Africa including clientelism, ethnonationalism and more are products of the navigation between the primordial and the civic realm. Colonisation was not merely a political project but also a cultural one, and western imperialism was the exportation of European bourgeoisie values and politics onto other parts of the world and imperial ideologies, not only imposing authority on Africans but also providing racial superiority as an organising principle to keep a separation between the white and black bourgeoisie. For the African subject therefore the ability to navigate the imperial society without allowing it to change you was a crucial tactic for survival. For the Europeans, generating even the illusion of mass compliance was a victory for imperial politics. Within this framework, both the coloniser and the colonised had a significant incentive to accept the African performance of compliance and to ignore the slow and steady bifurcation of the public sphere. As in the Athenian case, both publics require an element of performance, but the actors read from two different scripts with irreconcilable premises and more importantly, in different languages. For Ekeh, the African bourgeois accepts the principles implicit in colonialism but rejects the foreign class imposing them. It claims to be competent enough to rule but with no traditional legitimacy.

Raufu Mustapha (2012) expands Ekeh's thesis to argue that there could not be a single public sphere because political action is bounded by various factors that sever relation. Habermas' approach rested on a distinction between public opinion and ordinary opinion that Mustapha argues was inaccurate (29). All opinions could ultimately be a form of public opinion under the right circumstances, and the emergence of the digital age has made this even more apparent. Mustapha is especially concerned with the continued influence of Western bourgeois politics on the African public sphere, lately through the projection of supposedly neutral expertise through international organisations (37). Mustapha argues that elite capture of political life in Africa is a facet of cohabitation between African elites and Western elites who share a bureaucratic language, economic aspirations characterised by a hunger for accumulation, and the inability to completely understand the interests of the majority. As for Ekeh, language is one way through which Mustapha identifies the contradictory priorities and desires for these two public spheres, with the indigenous bourgeois sharing English as a language for political action with the European elites, while the indigenous proletariat public sphere is dominated by the use of local languages (37).

Mustapha similarly insists that there is still a power differential between the putatively "neutral" foreign expertise that insinuates itself into the African public and African people, and that this power differential further undermines the rational-critical debate within African societies. He highlights the model of the foreign expert who reorganises key public sectors in Africa without due consideration for its social and historical context and does not rely on deliberation or participation of African people (37). Nor does it make efforts to include through processes of translation. Much like the colonised African, the African in the neoliberal era is the subject of deliberation between the local bourgeois and the foreign bourgeois but never an agent taking action and participating in the domestic public sphere.

Boaventure de Sousa Santos (2021) is even more explicit in his criticism of the Habermasian public sphere. He argues that the idea of a public sphere is a stylised account of public life in Europe that does not reflect the structures of other societies. In a special volume edited by Mustapha, he wonders explicitly if the concept of a public sphere is applicable in African contexts given that it proves inadequate to capturing the complexities of race, gender, class, age, ethnicity, foreignness etc. that characterise African societies, particularly after Ekeh's observation on the bifurcation of the African post-colonial society (45). He argues that what gives Habermas' conception of the public sphere such utility is actually the ability of Western countries to project their ideas and their practices to post-colonial nations, such that the ontology of the public sphere as a concept is never questioned because it is so easily embedded into how these societies see themselves (45). Essentially, Habermas was writing from within a very specific theoretical tradition, and while his genealogy of Western European modernity is accurate and useful for that context, it only seems useful outside Europe because of the connections between the colonised societies and the metropole. Habermas himself acknowledged that his was a decidedly Eurocentric view whose utility in post-colonial contexts may be marginal (1984). Santos therefore urges the African scholar to "keep distance" from Eurocentric epistemologies – use them, but in a transgressive way that reads them always in opposition to epistemologies of the South, always with an ear to the limits they inherently contain to how African societies might define themselves.

There are other key sociological phenomena that undercut the idea of a unitary public sphere in African societies. For example, religion is also a key distinguishing feature of the African publics that challenges the notion of a unitary public sphere. The case of Islam highlights the limits of a Eurocentric epistemology to understanding the African public sphere. More than Christianity, Islamic practices of different traditions prescribe not just religious practices but also codes for private and public action. Tayob (2012) writes that public Islam was always discursively formed but through the actions of intellectuals and spiritual leaders rather than through the work of the bourgeois (144). Moreover, the influence and practices of Muslim publics in Africa have always been transnational including on the Internet. Despite many frictions, the Umma is a superseding idea that unites Muslims beyond national, racial and ethnic boundaries, and provides a template for relation and engagement to those who practice the faith that is portable and easily translated into many contexts. Tayob emphasises that because Islamic religious and social practice was so extensively codified and transmitted throughout the continent, the arrival of colonisation created unique opportunities for Muslims to participate in and shape the public sphere (144). Even so, it is important to note that Islam in Africa is not a monolith, and the different expressions or traditions of Islam on the continent have varied experiences with the public sphere even within one country. Liberal Sufi traditions in Sudan have clashed with a more conservative Sunni practice that traces its origins to the Gulf, and the arrival of Ahmadi and Shia Muslims from the Indian sub-continent has added further complexity to the place for Muslims in Africa's publics.

Even so, Islam in Africa reminds the observer that in the Western approach concept of the public sphere, religion is classified as belonging to the private domain and yet in many African publics it is integral to the norms and codes – the rules of performance – that shape an individual's ability to participate in the public. The Internet has only accelerated the blurring of these distinctions. Anderson (2003) writes that the Internet is democratising information channels within Islamic societies, wresting control from traditional sites of authority towards "younger and subaltern elites" (891). The media allows for the development of "found communities" or spaces where people can find others with more particular practices of Islam perhaps bounded by multiple ideas of identity. Standard religious texts like the Qu'ran exist within the Islamic public sphere, but so do digital communities supporting women Imams and extensive debates over what it means to be a Muslim. Both narrow extremism and unprecedented broad interpretations of Islam have found a natural home on the Internet echoing the discursive practices of the religion back onto the analogue spaces.

Today, Africa's digital publics are intimately connected to analogue public life even while their contours do not always perfectly overlap. Online identities are bifurcated and made even more complex through deep connections to other parts of the world, e.g. in the emergence of cryptocurrency communities in countries like Nigeria that do not even have stable electricity supply. Factors like language, colonial histories, transnational identities that supersede colonial boundaries and more complicate the politics of African digital public spheres.

Mapping Africa's Digital Publics

The form and scope of digital publics in African societies vary considerably, given the aforementioned influence of imperialism and culture. Individuals necessarily curate the versions they present of themselves online narrating versions of their own histories, including images and stories that they share. Nyabola (2018) argues that some of the socio-cultural characteristics that exist offline are replicated offline, where the digital necessarily builds on and then intensifies the offline nature of the society that is building it online. Ethnonationalism, religious practices, gender identity and expression are all factors that can be hidden behind anonymity or expressed vocally depending on the preference of the individuals, shaping how other individuals from within their chosen communities interact with the person in question. As such, Africa's digital publics are a complex medley of offline characteristics of the various societies that constitute them, as well as the heightened aspects of identity that individuals curate in order to project themselves into various narrow audiences. As Banda et al., the terrain in which technology is deployed shapes how that specific technology will be experienced (1).

One key question that underscores any analysis of the form of Africa's digital publics is the question of access. Understanding who has access illuminates who is able to participate in discourse online and therefore whether or not any concept of an African digital sphere mimics the contours of exclusion that leads critics to discount the Habermasian ideal of a public sphere. Mobile infrastructure has brought the Internet closer to more users in Africa, with most internet users on the continent connecting through their mobile phones. Significant research has been conducted into the structural barriers to the inclusion of women, persons with disabilities and rural communities into Africa's digital cultures. The African Development Bank (2022) estimates that the time of writing only 6% of Africa's rural communities was connected to the Internet. The cost of Internet remains prohibitively high in many African countries, and layered with these concerns about gender and ability, it is clear that while Internet use is growing dramatically, it does not yet map perfectly onto the size of the population more generally.

However, access is not a perfect metric of the impact that digital cultures have on the public sphere. For one, the amplification of online discourse onto other media platforms like television and radio increases the reach and the impact of these conversations in these spaces. Nyabola shows that budgets for traditional media decrease and the cost of creating new content increases, traditional media in many African countries turn to online conversations as a ready source of information and content (79). Many countries like Kenya build entire programming strands around amplifying digital content to their audiences, and this keeps their audiences current while also creating a link between the digital public sphere and the analogue. Similarly, efforts to make their content "go viral", i.e. become extraordinarily visible in the digital space, leads the content producers on this platform to adapt their content and attune it to these platforms, increasing their popularity and visibility overall in a mutually symbiotic relationship. Going viral also has negative outcomes outlined subsequently.

Language is a key element within Africa's digital public sphere. Ngugi (1981) wrote that language is "central to a people's definition of themselves in relation to their natural and social environment" (9). For him, language is a tool through which power is distributed in a society including through pedagogical and administrative methods. Making people speak European languages was a crucial part of the colonial project and remains one of the main ways through which the post-colonial state defines itself. Ekeh's conception of two publics in African societies roughly corresponds to language, where a formal European language was forced on African populations as part of the cultural project of colonisation while an African mother language is spoken at home or in informal contexts as a way of preserving the connection to what Ekeh calls the primordial. Githiora (2018) points out that in countries an informal patois develops as a linguistic manifestation of the negotiation that young Africans especially developed to navigate the tensions between the imperial legacy and the severed connection to the indigenous past (2). Language is crucial in Africa's public spheres therefore for establishing a relation between the past and the present, as well as articulating new forms of connection across geographies and locations.

The use of language in Africa's digital spheres roughly corresponds to the analogue in that colonial languages dominate at the expense of mother languages. Western languages and specifically English dominate the discourse online. And while Africa is home to at least one-third of the world's linguistic diversity, only an estimated 0.1% of the content on the Internet today is produced in African languages[1]. This means that the Africa's digital publics roughly correspond to the European imperial public established in the colonial era, a somewhat formal space characterised largely by bourgeois concerns and discourse. The ability of proletariat public spheres to enter these spaces is dependent in large part on the willingness of Africa's bourgeois to make space for these concerns.

One major exception to this situation is Kiswahili, the most widely spoken African language in the world and an official language in Kenya, Tanzania and the DRC, yet spoken in at least 11 countries in East and Southern Africa. Kiswahili occupies an unusual space in the analogue publics of these countries because of its unusual encounters with imperialism. Mazrui and Mazrui (1993) call Kiswahili "preponderant" because it has numerous speakers even though the ethnic group that developed it is not dominant in the African country where it is spoken, affirming that the language has major value (276). The Swahili people of the East African coast are small in number but were leaders in the region's long-distance trade including the East African slave trade, and this means that its associations with non-Swahili communities are not necessarily positive. It provides a bureaucratic alternative to European languages in the region, allowing speakers to cultivate a sense of national identity independent of imperialism, but the uptake of Kiswahili itself was a mixture of organic use because of the long-distance trade and the impact of the imperial desire to homogenise the African population by forcing them to speak a single language.

Although English still dominates by a great margin, a significant amount of the digital content produced in East Africa is produced in Kiswahili. Some of this is the consequence of bureaucratic action where governments are compelled by law to translate their key documents and platforms into the second official language. But some of it is also the consequence of the utility of the language in articulating a distinctly African post-colonial identity.

Another key outlier in this situation is the use of patois or slang like sheng' or pidgin which reflects the dominance of youth culture in Africa's digital publics. These patois are not merely languages but are also indicators of counterpublics that exist within African societies. These counterpublics are in turn marked as youth cultures by generational markers such as choice of dress and address or speech. Because these patois are malleable and able to use the tools of English, French or Portuguese to create new forms of speech and narration, they are much easier adapted to the digital space unlike mother languages that may not have specialised technical support like diacritics and intonation marks, or even a written language to begin with. The Internet is optimised for European languages with the ability of other languages to catch up dependent on national investments in developing first the language to describe the Internet and second the tools to help citizens participate in it. Mandarin, Cantonese, Korean and other Asian languages have significant support for specialised language characters albeit not as much as the Western languages around which the Internet was built.

The use of patois languages online is a reflection of how digital cultures in many African countries are also youth cultures. This is in part a product of demographics given that Africa is the youngest continent in the world with an average age of 19.7 years old.[2] But it is also a reflection of the broader situation in which young people are more likely to take up online spaces as they interact with them organically through the process of maturing rather than having to learn them retroactively. These patois also lend themselves to political action because they are inherently rebellious, breaking the rules of grammar and creating an informal register that is loaded with its own rules of performance and organisation. Githiora (2018) argues that patois like sheng' – a combination of English, Kiswahili and Kenya's various mother languages – are a linguistic manifestation of the negotiation that young urban Africans pursue every day between age, and class, rural and urban divides (2). These patois are also at the cutting edge of linguistic innovation on the continent, sometimes changing vocabulary multiple times within a single generation, echoing the sentiment that the digital should be a space for innovation and experimentation. Popular culture like music videos and television shows only enhance the popularity of these registers of languages. Still, while the use of patois is increasingly popular European languages continue to provide the baseline for Africa's digital publics, particularly given the resistance of bourgeois society in Africa to the ascendance and dominance of these languages.

Africa's digital publics are also characterised by distinctions of gender. Gender is a key driver of disparities on the Internet. For instance in many families access to mobile phones is determined within family units on the basis of gender and age. Sanya (2013) points out that African women therefore are the least likely to have consistent access to the Internet in part because of restrictions to the mobile phone as an object but also because of the vagaries of the distribution of labour within rural families especially (69–75). Similarly, African women are uniquely subjected to novel forms of harm and abuse online because they are women including practices like doxing in which the private addresses of individuals are shared in order to invite abuse or even violence against them; revenge pornography in which intimate videos of women with high profiles are leaked in order to intimidate them; or systemic harassment through coordinated inauthentic action as outlined above. The same patterns of abuse that characterise women's presence in the patriarchal public spheres are often replicated and intensified online, with women resorting to tactics like anonymity and using masculine pseudonyms in order to evade them.

However, the Internet has also made new forms of mobilisation possible within African communities, evidenced by the rise of radical feminist discourse online. Social movements like #MyDressMyChoice in Kenya and #RhodesMustFall in South Africa and Zimbabwe are driven to a large extent by the organising activities of radical feminists online. Tiernan and O'Connor (2020) argue that in analogue societies women may be reluctant to self-identify as feminists, viewing the word as a distinctly Western construct. But online, given the preponderance of avatars and the measure of safety they provide, many radical feminists are not only self-identifying as such but building communities to engage with the key women's rights concerns within their communities. Rukondo (2018) emphasises that figures like Stella Nyanzi successfully use the Internet to mobilise their followers, embracing transgressive practices like vulgarity or publicly discussing sex to draw attention to their causes and find followers across national boundaries in unprecedented ways.

Protest remains a key function of African digital publics, particularly in societies where the freedom of expression remains precarious. Some key social movements like #RhodesMustFall, #FeesMustFall and #MyDressMyChoice on the continent owe their proliferation if not expressly their creation to the emergence of digital technologies. For women especially, digital spaces have created room for a voice that allows for organising around radical demands that do not otherwise find articulation in the public sphere. Nyabola (2018b) charts the emergence of #MyDressMyChoice in Kenya through the emergence of social media. Langmia (2013) points out that social media was crucial to monitoring and organising resistance to state excess during the 2011 presidential election in Cameroon, particularly in bringing women's voices into the mainstream.

Other groups have benefited indirectly from the space created by radical feminist organising online. LGBTQ+ communities in Africa are core allies to the radical feminist movements in African countries, and this alliance routinely places concerns that would otherwise be censored or muted in the analogue public sphere at the centre of political discourse in many African countries. LGBTQI+ Africans are able to be visible, vocal and political online in ways that were hitherto prohibited, rallying support for causes like the repeal of colonial-era criminalisation of homosexual acts or promoting events like Pride that are technically banned across much of the continent. In 2019 for example, LGBTQI+ activists in Kenya and Botswana rallied to demand the repeal of the colonial-era section of the penal code in both countries that criminalises homosexual acts. Members of the community not only turned up in court but did so flamboyantly, claiming a right to visibility that was hitherto denied. Within one month of each other, the high court of Botswana decriminalised homosexual acts but the Kenya High Court declined to do so, although it remained a victory as the first time the law was challenged in the courts.[3]

One last key characteristic of Africa's digital public spheres is the renewal of Pan Africanism or the embrace of working transnationally and across cultures as a political strategy. Perhaps because of the usually low personal cost of participating in online civic spaces during mass mobilisations, Africans online routinely contribute to narratives of dissent across international boundaries, expressing support for movements outside their own countries. For instance, when Ugandan opposition candidate Bobi Wine (Robert Kyalanguni) was arrested by incumbent Yoweri Museveni, 67% of the #FreeBobiWine tweets demanding his release came from Kenya.[4] Similar patterns have emerged during Internet shutdowns in Sudan and Cameroon, with mobilisation across borders evolving as a key tactic to sustain these movements. Contemporary Pan Africanism as articulated online is a youth discourse that usually turns away from ethnonationalist discourse in favour of solidarity narratives. It is also largely critical of institutional power, particularly long-serving African presidents and the inability of institutions like the African Union to hold them accountable.

However, Africa's digital publics are not only characterised by positive developments. Given the speed at which power is adapting to the potency of the spaces, there have also been a significant number of negative developments. For one, there has been a marked increase in the presence of inorganic or computer-generated individuals in Africa's online discourse. As the timber and tenor of political discourse online in Africa has risen, so too has attention from governments and power. Online discourse and coordinated protests have led to significant social change because they allow youth activists to find each other and amplify messages that would be difficult to amplify in analogues spaces characterised by state capture. Online mobilisation is a key part of youth political movements like Y'en a marre, Lucha RDC, and Balai Citoyen all of which have played a key role in political transitions in Senegal, the Democratic Republic and Burkina Faso respectively. The acceleration of these movements soon after the experience of the Arab spring fuelled anxiety in many African countries that there would be similar protests across the continent. In 2015, Glez and Andleman (2015) analysed the experience of Burkina Faso as the possible advent of an African spring particularly across French-speaking Africa.

No African spring materialised, in part because vulnerable African governments have adapted their tactics of repression and manipulation to quell dissent online. Internet shutdowns where the entire country is taken offline are an extreme yet increasingly common example of the kind of actions that governments are taking in reprisal. Also increasingly common are social media shutdowns where only access to social networking platforms like Facebook and Twitter are implemented. Throttling, where the speed of the Internet is deliberately slowed down at source is also a marked behaviour of authoritarian regimes trying to frustrate communication during politically sensitive moments like elections. 12 African countries shut down the Internet 19 times in 2021, an increase from previous years[5].

Dangerous groups also make use of the Internet in order to amplify their message. Al Shabaab, a terrorist group operating primarily in Somalia but that has conducted serious attacks across the border in Kenya, relies on the Internet to distribute much of its recruitment materials. Moreover, Menkhouse (2022) suggests that Al Shabaab takes specific advantage of the "echo chambers" that exist on social media, as well as the amplification effect between social and traditional media, to project greater influence than it actually has. Similar dynamics have occurred with groups like Boko Haram operating in the Sahel and with the Islamic State in Africa.

Subtler but no less noxious forms of interference have also emerged. On social media, given the sheer volume of information that is shared at any moment, the ability to parse through the signal and the noise is a critical way of building online networks and discourse. The social networking site Facebook developed the term "coordinated inauthentic behaviour" to refer to individuals who are paid by other groups or parties to influence political discourse online by either drowning dissent in noise – hijacking hashtags with offensive or irrelevant information – or by targeting individuals with abuse in order to discourage them from participating in online conversations. In May 2020, for example, Facebook removed 446 pages and 96 groups in Tunisia that were creating and disseminating political misinformation into various countries in Africa south of the Sahara[6]. And African governments are increasingly likely to use these automated inorganic users or bots to either influence opinion online or silence critics[7]. In 2020, Twitter also removed over 220,000 automated accounts run by individuals from various backgrounds most of which were designed to influence political discourse, but also by extension reducing the size and scale of accounts that would purchase access to these accounts in order to boost their appearance of popularity.[8]

Surveillance is another tactic increasingly deployed by African governments to control political discourse. In July 2021, an international coalition of media outlets revealed a cache of documents that confirmed that African governments were amongst the key customers for surveillance technology from Israel's NSO group.[9] Much of this surveillance was levelled against critics of the state, where for example the government of Morocco sought access to at least 10,000 phone numbers through the software, while the government of Rwanda went as far as attempting to hack a mobile phone belonging to the president of South Africa amongst others[10]. This surveillance targets critics of the state, some of whom were later killed or arrested, as well as chilling dissent within the public sphere. Surveillance therefore curbs the freedom of expression of individuals in the various public sphere.

Conclusion

In conclusion, the African digital public sphere builds on histories of pluralism, imperialism and sub-national diversity to challenge the Eurocentric notion that there can be such a thing as a single public sphere. These publics are ecumenical in interests and approaches, but increasingly subject to draconian and unilateral interference both by governments and corporate commercial interests. They are multifaceted and split along several lines that reflect the various cartographies of power that are overlain on the continent. Imperial and resistance histories create one line of fracture but so too do the rise and dominance of youth culture and the Internet as a youth-driven space, gender and sexual identities, and the complexities of language on the continent. These complexities further challenge the notion that there can be such a thing as a unitary Habermasian public sphere given how many counterpublics are sustained within African digital publics. However, there are emerging discourses that suggest that these publics and counterpublics are connected in an intricate balance, and in a constant tension with the desire of power to extend its analogue influence onto the digital space.

Notes

1 'What If the Internet Were an Ally of Linguistic Diversity?' *CCCB LAB*, 29 Oct. 2019, https://lab.cccb.org/en/what-if-the-internet-were-an-ally-of-linguistic-diversity/

2 Statista. 'Median Age in Africa 2000-2030'. https://www.statista.com/statistics/1226158/median-age-of-the-population-of-africa/. Accessed 17 April 2023.

3 'Kenya: Court Upholds Archaic Anti-Homosexuality Laws'. *Human Rights Watch*, 24 May 2019, https://www.hrw.org/news/2019/05/24/kenya-court-upholds-archaic-anti-homosexuality-laws.

4 Nyabola, Nanjala, et al. "#Freebobiwine and Today's Pan-Africanism for the Digital Age." *African Arguments*, 23 Aug. 2018, https://africanarguments.org/2018/08/freebobiwine-today-pan-africanism-digital-age/.

5 Anthonio, Felicia. 'Report: Who Shut down the Internet in Africa in 2021?' *Access Now*, 28 Apr. 2022, https://www.accessnow.org/internet-shutdowns-africa-keepiton-2021/.

6 'Facebook statement on UReputation - May 2020 Coordinated Inauthentic Behavior Report'. *Business & Human Rights Resource Centre*, https://www.business-humanrights.org/fr/derni%C3%A8res-actualit%C3%A9s/facebook-statement-on-ureputation-may-2020-coordinated-inauthentic-behavior-report/. Accessed 19 Sept. 2022.

7 'How Social Media Bots Became an Influential Force in Africa's Elections'. *Quartz*, 18 July 2018, https://qz.com/africa/1330494/twitter-bots-in-kenya-lesotho-senegal-equatorial-guinea-elections/.

8 Russell, Jon. 'Twitter Is (Finally) Cracking Down on Bots'. *TechCrunch*, 22 Feb. 2018, https://techcrunch.com/2018/02/22/twitter-is-finally-cracking-down-on-bots/.

9 Kirchgaessner, Stephanie, and Diane Taylor. 'Nephew of Jailed Hotel Rwanda Dissident Hacked by NSO Spyware'. *The Guardian*, 18 July 2022, https://www.theguardian.com/world/2022/jul/18/nephew-of-jailed-hotel-rwanda-dissident-hacked-by-nso-spyware.

10 Kirchgaessner, Stephanie, et al. 'Revealed: Leak Uncovers Global Abuse of Cyber-Surveillance Weapon'. *The Guardian*, 18 July 2021, https://www.theguardian.com/world/2021/jul/18/revealed-leak-uncovers-global-abuse-of-cyber-surveillance-weapon-nso-group-pegasus.

Works Cited

"Al-Shabaab and Social Media: A Double-Edged Sword – The Brown Journal of World Affairs." https://bjwa.brown.edu/20-2/al-shabaab-and-social-media-a-double-edged-sword/. Accessed 19 Sep. 2022.

Anderson, Jon W. "New Media, New Publics: Reconfiguring the Public Sphere of Islam." *Social Research*, vol. 70, no. 3, 2003, pp. 887–906. *JSTOR*, http://www.jstor.org/stable/40971646. Accessed 19 Sep. 2022. 40971646

Anthonio, Felicia. "Report: Who Shut Down the Internet in Africa in 2021?" *Access Now*, 28 Apr. 2022, https://www.accessnow.org/internet-shutdowns-africa-keepiton-2021/.

Bank, African Development. "Digital Connectivity and Infrastructure." *African Development Bank - Building Today, a Better Africa Tomorrow*, 2 Feb. 2022, https://www.afdb.org/en/topics-and-sectors/sectors/information-communication-technology/digital-connectivity-and-infrastructure.

Brunkhorst, Hauke, et al., editors. *The Habermas Handbook*. Columbia University Press, 2018.

Ekeh, Peter P. "Colonialism and the Two Publics in Africa: A Theoretical Statement." *Comparative Studies in Society and History*, vol. 17, no. 1, 1975, pp. 91–112. *JSTOR*, http://www.jstor.org/stable/178372. Accessed 19 Sep. 2022.

"Facebook Statement on UReputation - May 2020 Coordinated Inauthentic Behavior Report." *Business & Human Rights Resource Centre*, https://www.business-humanrights.org/fr/derni%C3%A8res-actualit%C3%A9s/facebook-statement-on-ureputation-may-2020-coordinated-inauthentic-behavior-report/. Accessed 19 Sep. 2022.

Fackson Banda, Okoth Fred Mudhai and Wisdom J. Tettey. "Introduction: New Media and Democracy in Africa - A Critical Interjection" in *African Media and the Digital Public Sphere*, Okoth Fred Mudhai, Wisdom Tetey and Fackson Banda (Ed.). New York: Palgrave Macmillan, 2009.

Frances, Nancy. "The Theory of the Public Sphere" in *The Habermas Handbook*. Brunkhorst, Hauke, et al. (Ed.). New York: Columbia University Press, 2018.

Githiora, Chege. *Sheng: Rise of a Kenyan Swahili Vernacular*. NED-New edition, Boydell & Brewer, 2018, https://doi.org/10.2307/j.ctv1ntfvm.

Glez, Damian, and Andelman, David A. "An African Spring." *World Policy Journal*, vol. 32, no. 1, 2015, pp. 77–85. *JSTOR*, http://www.jstor.org/stable/44214211. Accessed 19 Sep. 2022.

Goldhill, Simon, and Robin Osborne, editors. *Performance Culture and Athenian Democracy*. Cambridge: Cambridge University Press, 1999.

Habermas, Jurgen et al. "The Public Sphere: An Encyclopedia Article (1964)." *New German Critique*, no. 3, 1974, p. 49, https://doi.org/10.2307/487737.

Habermas, Jurgen, *The Theory of Communicative Action* (2 vols), Boston: Beacon Press, 1984/1987.

"How Social Media Bots Became an Influential Force in Africa's Elections." *Quartz*, 18 July 2018, https://qz.com/africa/1330494/twitter-bots-in-kenya-lesotho-senegal-equatorial-guinea-elections/.

"Kenya: Court Upholds Archaic Anti-Homosexuality Laws." *Human Rights Watch*, 24 May 2019, https://www.hrw.org/news/2019/05/24/kenya-court-upholds-archaic-anti-homosexuality-laws.

Kirchgaessner, Stephanie, and Diane Taylor. "Nephew of Jailed Hotel Rwanda Dissident Hacked by NSO Spyware." *The Guardian*, 18 July 2022, https://www.theguardian.com/world/2022/jul/18/nephew-of-jailed-hotel-rwanda-dissident-hacked-by-nso-spyware.

Kirchgaessner, Stephanie, et al. "Revealed: Leak Uncovers Global Abuse of Cyber-Surveillance Weapon." *The Guardian*, 18 July 2021, https://www.theguardian.com/world/2021/jul/18/revealed-leak-uncovers-global-abuse-of-cyber-surveillance-weapon-nso-group-pegasus.

Langmia, K. (2013). "Social Media Technology and the 2011 Presidential Elections in Cameroon" in *Media Role in African Changing Electoral Process: A Political Communicative Perspective*. C. U. Nwokeafor & K. Langmia (Eds.). pp. 111–123. Lanham, MD: University Press of America.

Mazrui, Alamin M., and Ali A. Mazrui. "Dominant Languages in a Plural Society: English and Kiswahili in Post-Colonial East Africa." *International Political Science Review / Revue Internationale de Science Politique*, vol. 14, no. 3, 1993, pp. 275–292, https://www.jstor.org/stable/1601194.

Meehan, Johanna, editor. *Feminists Read Habermas: Gendering the Subject of Discourse*. 1. iss. in paperback, Routledge, 2014.

Mustapha, A. R. "The Public Sphere in 21st Century Africa: Broadening the Horizons of Democratisation." *Africa Development*, vol. 37, no. 1, 2012, pp. 27–41, https://doi.org/10.4314/ad.v37i1.

Negt, Oskar, and Alexander Kluge. *Public Sphere and Experience: Toward an Analysis of the Bourgeois and Proletarian Public Sphere*. Verso, London, 2016.

Ngugi wa Thiong'o. *Decolonising the Mind: The Politics of Language in African Literature*. Reprint, Transferred to digital print, Currey [u.a.], 2005.

Nyabola, Nanjala. *Digital Democracy, Analogue Politics: How the Internet Era Is Transforming Kenya*. ZED, London, 2018a.

Nyabola, Nanjala. "Kenyan Feminisms in the Digital Age." *Women's Studies Quarterly*, vol. 46, no. 3 & 4, 2018b, pp. 261–272. JSTOR, www.jstor.org/stable/26511346. Accessed 30 July 2021.

Nyabola, Nanjala, et al. "#Freebobiwine and Today's Pan-Africanism for the Digital Age." *African Arguments*, 23 Aug. 2018, https://africanarguments.org/2018/08/freebobiwine-today-pan-africanism-digital-age/.

Rukundo, "Solomon, My President Is a Pair of Buttocks': The Limits of Online Freedom of Expression in Uganda." *International Journal of Law and Information Technology*, vol. 26, no. 3, Autumn 2018, pp. 252–271, https://doi.org/10.1093/ijlit/eay009.

Russell, Jon. "Twitter Is (Finally) Cracking Down on Bots." *TechCrunch*, 22 Feb. 2018, https://techcrunch.com/2018/02/22/twitter-is-finally-cracking-down-on-bots/.

Santos, B. de Sousa. "Public Sphere and Epistemologies of the South." *Africa Development*, vol. 37, no. 1, 2012, pp. 43–67, https://doi.org/10.4314/ad.v37i1.

Sanya, Brenda Nyandiko. "Disrupting Patriarchy: An Examination of the Role of e-Technologies in Rural Kenya." *Feminist Africa*, vol. 14, 2013, pp. 69–75.

Shanklin, Eugenia. "Anlu Remembered: The Kom Women's Rebellion OF 1958–61." *Dialectical Anthropology*, vol. 15, no. 2/3, 1990, pp. 159–181. *JSTOR*, http://www.jstor.org/stable/29790346. Accessed 19 Sep. 2022.

Tayob, Abdulkader. "Politics and Islamization in African Public Spheres." *Islamic Africa*, vol. 3, no. 2, Oct. 2012, pp. 139–168, https://doi.org/10.5192/215409930302139.

Tiernan, Alix, and Pat O'Connor. "Perspectives on Power over and Power to: How Women Experience Power in a Mining Community in Zimbabwe." *Journal of Political Power*, vol. 13, no. 1, Jan. 2020, pp. 86–105, https://doi.org/10.1080/2158379X.2020.1720089.

Wahl-Jorgensen, Karin. "Questioning the Ideal of the Public Sphere: The Emotional Turn." *Social Media + Society*, vol. 5, no. 3, 2019, p. 205630511985217, https://doi.org/10.1177/2056305119852175.

Warner, Michael. "Publics and Counterpublics." *Public Culture*, vol. 14, no. 1, 2002, pp. 49–90, https://muse.jhu.edu/article/26277.

White, Luise. *The Comforts of Home: Prostitution in Colonial Nairobi*. Chicago: University of Chicago Press, 1990.

24

HIJACKED NARRATIVES AND THE MARGINALISATION OF WOMEN IN AFRICA

Fatima Doumbia

Introduction

A disturbing event took place in Abidjan on August 30, 2021 on the set of a prime-time television programme in Côte d'Ivoire. On this occasion, a famous TV host whose programme was supposedly aimed at denouncing rape, welcomed on his set a convicted sex offender, and then pointing to a mannequin on set, beckoned on his guest to re-enact how he committed the act of rape that sent him to prison. Relaxed, the host questions his guest about his methods, his tastes in the choice of his victims, "thin or with buttocks", wanting to know "if women still take pleasure when they are raped", before asking to the "ex-rapist" some advice to give to women on how to avoid being raped. Facing the host who was laughing through vile and violent details of the host's depraved actions was an equally laughing and applauding audience. Curiously, there was as well as a famous female influencer, seemingly cheerful in the face of this calamitous programme. Outraged by the show, feminist associations denounced the trivialisation of rape and called for the host, known for his sexist comments and who was set to host the Miss Côte d'Ivoire election evening, to be replaced. The legitimacy of the facilitator to present this competition was questioned, without the sexist nature of the competition being questioned, as if women had themselves made peace with what tends to reduce them. At conferences, pretty, well-dressed and silent hostesses picket, flanking learned men while they speak.

In the shadow of the sexual violence that makes the headlines, exists sexist violence, which can be symbolic, insidious, silent and deaf to the women themselves, and which ought to be interrogated given how it fosters a certain representation of women, which confines them to the private sphere and erases them from the public sphere and decision-making positions. A key assumption of this work, therefore, is that representations stemming from a specific historical narrative can determine reality. This idealist principle would therefore make it possible to say that it is rather towards representations that we must first turn so that changes in society are effective and values can be transformed. Before proceeding, one would need to ask how these representations are formed, or where they come from. For a thing to be able to be represented at the level of consciousness, it must be seen to have manifested. Thus, let us change assumptions and start from reality. By committing ourselves this time to the materialist path, we note that the realities have indeed changed since the conditions of women have

DOI: 10.4324/9781003143529-28

clearly improved. However, the representations of "the woman" do not change. The pitfalls into which we fall from these two assumptions lead us to formulate the problem of how to change the realities of women in Africa when changes in their social conditions do not lead to a change in the way they are imagined or otherised. The objective of this study is to show that the question of the status of women in Africa is poorly apprehended, stifling the ability of society to respond effectively to the challenge of marginalisation. In interrogating how the politics of narratives accounts for the flawed representation of women, we gain some clarity on a better vision of emancipation for women in Africa.

Tell me the Untold of the History You Are Talking about: The Event and Its Story

Some Erased Facts from the Great History of Africa (understood as seen by men).

"In the past, our country was called Gaul and its inhabitants, the Gauls". This was the first sentence of Ernest Lavisse's French history manual, written after the defeat of Sedan in 1870, taught in France until the 1960s, and even in certain French colonies. According to Mamadou Dia, "Our ancestors the Gauls" would have been taught only in Senegal where the students were being prepared to be future French citizens, hence the need for French education. In his memoirs (1985, p. 29), he writes:

> Until upper primary school, we knew nothing of the History of France, of the Geography of France. We taught, above all, the geography and history of Senegal and the AOF. We knew the Samorys, the Mamadou Lamines, etc. I think it was excellent. It was only from William Ponty that we began to study the History and geography of France and Europe.

On the other hand, Boubou Hama has different memories and remembers that, as students, they recited like parrots "Our ancestors the Gauls had blue eyes and blond hair", without asking questions about these Gallic ancestors. If Mamadou Dia finds it excellent to have been able to study "the Samorys, the Mamadou Lamines", Boubou Hama, for his part, explains that when he entered the upper primary school of Ouagadougou in 1924, he knew Charlemagne, Louis XIV, Napoleon, etc. However, he writes, "we ignored Moro-Naba, Sundiata, Kankou Moussa, Mohammed Bello, El hadj Omar, Samory [...]. All the glories of our past". (Hama, quoted by Labrune-Badiane & Smith, 2018, p. 125).

A noteworthy observation from these examples is that stories or history about a people are often created, amongst other reasons, to serve an ideological objective. Whether we choose to focus on the works of Mamadou Dia or Boubou Hama, we still arrive at the realisation that the great figures of African history; the glories of the continent's past are men. The questions arising from this observation then are to ask: where are glorious women in the history of Africa? Why are women absent from this great African history or lack any considerable prominence from the narrative of this history?

Several examples come to mind regarding this lack of representation of women in the political history of Africa. Can we talk about those who fought against the Portuguese colonists and ignore the story of Anne Nzinga (1581–1663), Queen of Ndongo and Matamba in Angola who challenged the Europeans for almost 40 years? Can recall those who fought against the British colonists and ignore the story of a 50-year-old Yaa Asantewaa (1840–1921)?

After ruing the men's lack of temerity against the British, she led an army of 4,000 insurgents in attacking the fort where the British representatives, including the governor, lived. Can we talk about those who fought against the Italian colonists and ignore the story of Taitu Betul (1851–1918)? We know the singular history of Ethiopia and of Menelik II, the king of kings, but not that of his wife Taitu Betul, great empress and strategist who is said to have a remarkable intelligence and to whom the country owes the victory of the Battle of Adwa in 1896, which was the finest victory of an African country against a colonial army.

Can we recall also, those who fought against the French colonists and ignore the story of the young Aline Sitoé Diatta (between 1910 and 1920–1944)? Heroine of civil disobedience in Casamance, nicknamed "the woman who was more than a man", she called on the Senegalese to fight against the colonists. Can we discuss the resistance put by the native African population against colonial and male domination without mentioning the one who was nicknamed "the mother of women's rights", "the lioness of Lisabi", Funmilayo Ransome-Kuti (1900–1978)? Arrested, imprisoned, exiled, defenestrated, is the story of many other women who gave their lives for their country as Sylvia Serbin recounts in *Reines d'Afrique et héroïnes de la diaspora noire* [Queens of Africa and heroines of the black diaspora]. How then can we explain the absence of these valorous women and important political figures from Africa's political history? One way of explaining this is to understand history as a site of contestation and power play, in which male dominance has been reinforced through the (mis)representation.

Construction of the Historical Narrative

When we speak of history, we must distinguish between the event and its rendition; in other words, what difference exists between the official account of the history and what really transpired. Ricœur, in his book *Temps et récit* [Time and Narrative], clearly shows the distinction between what happened, which belongs to the past, and the story or narrative, which is the rendition of the event. The question of the narrative is related to what is said, and therefore to the speech. Thinking about history requires thinking about the very form of the narrative, and Ricœur is surprised that the narrative is not questioned:

> The most surprising thing, for those of us who question the narrative status of history, is that the notion of narrative is never questioned for itself [...] Nor did it ever occur to Lucien Febvre [...] that his vehement criticism of the notion of historical fact, conceived as an atom of history all given by the sources, and his plea for a historical reality constructed by the historian, fundamentally brought historical reality, thus created by history, closer to the fictional narrative, also created by the narrator.
>
> *(Ricœur, 1983, p. 146–147)*

The historical fact is not given by itself. We can only know it by the account given by the historian. The question of narration is therefore just as important as that of events since it is through narration that what happened is transmitted. In other words, the story is a connection between the event and the producer of the discourse on the event. This leads us to question ourselves as cautioned by Mamadou Diouf (2002, p. 59) on "[...] the status and identity of producers, the regime of truth that founds adherence to the narrative and, above all, the relations between institutionalised national academic history and the disparate memories of communities and individuals".

This questioning of institutional history makes it possible to understand that it can be written with a political or ideological objective, which can easily be understood by taking up the example of the myth "Our ancestors the Gauls" that historians of the time like Ernest Renan in *Qu'est-ce qu'une nation?* [What is a nation?] set out to deconstruct it by qualifying it as a geographical and historical fiction with an ideological aim because Gaul did not exist, nowhere was this unified territory found. It was about building the nation through a common narrative, that of a common history in order to create a patriotic feeling.

One then wonders, is this patriotic feeling so far from the historical consciousness that Cheikh Anta Diop wanted to arouse in his project of narrating this common history aimed at founding a common unity? It is because there is a construction that there can also be deconstruction. In addition, it is indeed through this process of deconstruction of the history written by ethnographers and other missionaries and settlers that African historians come to reflect on the African condition, appraising the narrative of colonial and imperial powers as falsified narratives that erases the glorious past of Africa. Moreover, it is necessary to understand not only who narrates, but also why they narrate. These first African historians write because the history of Blacks has been denied because it has been falsified, and set themselves the task of rewriting and reconstructing it, by inscribing the names of the glories of our past. The objective of Cheikh Anta Diop, for example, is clear: to restore historical truth in the face of falsification. To transform alienated African historical consciousness, Diop studies and restores some modicum of greatness to the narrative of Africa's past. However, for Mamadou Diouf, Diop's very goal is first and foremost political:

> Cheikh Anta Diop's inevitably polemical work is not primarily concerned with retracing the history of Egypt (...) nor with doing the work of a historian, but with solidly rooting the political project of intellectual and scientific liberation, on the one hand, and economic development, on the other hand, of the African continent. This strong determination organises and directs the Egyptian-Pharaonic narration of Cheikh Anta Diop.
>
> *(Diouf, 2002, p. 60)*

The story we tell of history is therefore strongly linked to the person and the motivation of the narrator. To the questions of who speaks, why and when do they speak, we must add the question of the method used by the person who constructs the historical narrative. We see then that unlike the Indian historiography of Subaltern Studies, Diop remains a prisoner of a linear, progressive conception of history inherited from the *Lumières* [Enlightenment]. In other words, it is from a universalising conception of history similar to the European conception that he imagines this African history. However, says Diouf (2002, p. 62), "this conception erases the plurality of modes of expression, encoding, ordering of historical narratives and exhibition of regimes of truth which present themselves as competing histories, refusing the embrace of linear history as the dominant figure of modernity".

The rewriting of history through postcolonial studies thus makes it possible to think about all forms of domination; it integrates the plurality of modes of expression, particularly those that are not expressed. Consequently, it is a question of thinking about the violence that is the erasure of part of the population, both by colonial historiography and by the first African academics. Among these subjects are the women who we are accustomed to hearing that they occupied fundamental roles in the tradition, which would have been erased by colonisation. The question that arises therefore aims to understand what led to their marginalisation, which requires returning to colonisation, but also pre-colonial Africa.

Historical Reasons for the Marginalisation of Women in Africa

The Exclusion of Women from Knowledge and Possessions: Male Domination during Colonisation

Erasing means causing disappearance without a trace of what was. To imagine that these African women of historical importance were subjects of attempted historical erasure is to appreciate the political nature of historical narratives. Thus, the question that arises becomes: who made these attempts and why? Such an attempt can precisely be made by only someone with the resources to do so; to be understood in the sense of possibility (conditional) but also in the sense of power (effective). Ideological power and economic power are to be related and involve the questions of knowledge and having, says Marx in *L'idéologie allemande* [The German Ideology] (1982, p. 338–339):

> In every era, the ideas of the dominant class are the dominant ideas; in other words, the class that is the dominant material power in society is at the same time the dominant spiritual power. The class which disposes of the means of material production thereby also disposes of the means of intellectual production, so that in general it exercises its power over the ideas of those who lack these means [...].

In the ideology of the civilising mission of colonisation in Africa, Blacks or the native population so to speak, had to be educated. For the Fathers of the Holy Spirit who settled on the banks of the Niger in the nineteenth century, there existed a goal to socially re-engineer the society through the instrumentality of religion. Doing so therefore meant the need to "change the African woman", to distance her from her "dissolute mores", to fight against local cults, nudity, the Mpobo-Nkukho, polygamy, the wearing of ornaments and rings, it was better to bring her up and take care of her from an early age (Pagnon, 1997, p. 37).

The exclusion of women from knowledge can be partly traced to the sexism of these early missionaries. They considered the education of girls and women as "a useless work" and explained the poor results of the girls by "the lightness of spirit of the weaker sex" (quoted by E. Pagnon, p. 39). It is also necessary to take into account the lack of qualification of the Sisters to whom the education of the girls was subsequently entrusted. A factor that is not always mentioned in this exclusion of girls from knowledge, and to which we will pay particular attention, is the parents themselves, whose responsibility is often overlooked.

Various reasons are invoked to explain the reluctance of parents to send their daughters to school, including marriage (made difficult by the confrontation with customs and the increase in the dowry entailed by educated daughters, their difficulty in accepting polygamy after going to school, etc.). In addition, notes Estelle Pagnon, Igbo men accepted that their boys be educated but questioned the teachings given to their daughters, finding it unnecessary for girls to receive a thorough education. This explains why the education of girls was more accentuated on home economics, considered much more useful than book learning. This also accounts for why Housekeeping Training Centres were opened in the Onitsha region, which were more successful than schools for girls. However, according to Estelle Pagnon, the mothers, Igbo women, Ibibio and Effik, did not see the point of this Western female education because it did not allow the girls to integrate into their traditional living environment or the society which colonialism had reconditioned. Moreover, with the opening of these schools, the role of the women in the transmission of knowledge was also denied. In addition, because of their instruction in new commercial techniques, men, unlike women, were able to integrate easily into the modalities of the new commerce with foreign firms, which women were denied the aptitude to participate in nor benefit from. As Pagnon (1997, p. 53) notes

> The fate of peasant women therefore worsened during the colonial period. The "market queens" saw pricing completely slip away from them with the entry of the country's economy into the market and international speculation. This role of traders, which gave them political and social independence, diminished. [...] With the new British laws, they could no longer practice the boycott (the love, cooking and childcare strike), an effective means of pressure to win their case. Victorianism confined them totally to their homes, politics being entirely a man's business.

Among the elements of the decline in women's rights, was also the ban on boycotts, as Estelle Pagnon further reckoned. However, we must dwell on the content of the boycott which consists of the love, cooking and childcare strike. If it was through this practice that women could win their case, then it would seem that Victorian ideology only reinforced a certain representation of women.

Sex, cooking, and children belong to the domestic sphere. This is where women are confined or rather the space which the colonial power desired them to occupy. Would it not then be more accurate to qualify the remarks and to see in colonisation, not what is responsible for the exclusion of women from the public sphere, but rather something which reinforced this domination. This would suggest that male domination existed in pre-colonial societies in Africa.

The Subalternity of Women or Male and Elders Hegemony in Pre-colonial Africa

[...] "it is possible to affirm that what led to the loss of the privileges of women, to the strengthening of male hegemony and to the aggravation of female subjugation, is to be largely sought, in the upheaval of economic structures, under the effect of the shock caused by exogenous factors. (Djibo, 2001)". It was the colonial power with a patriarchal social project, reinforced by foreign religions, which excluded women from the public space by refusing them any possibility of participating in the political sector. From a position where they were kingmakers and where they led their people, women suddenly found themselves excluded from everything.

(Sarr, 2009, p. 86)

Although Hadiza Djibo, quoted by Fatou Sarr, uses the terms "reinforcement of male hegemony" and "worsening of female subjugation"; Fatou Sarr seems to affirm that male hegemony was a feature of pre-colonial society in Africa, which then came to be reinforced by the colonial experience. Sarr highlights the role of women as kingmakers, but not as political actors who led their people. She conceives the role of women here based on their positions as the wives of chiefs and queen mothers. This also advances a notion of their marginality when historical records prove otherwise.

We can cite the example of Madame Yoko, chief of the Kpaa-Mende who used both her position as a wife and as a local authority recognised by colonial powers to achieve a political status that enabled her to sign pacts with the British. It was this alliance that protected British traders even before the annexation of the Protectorate. It was Madame Yoko who collaborated with the British during the suppression in 1898 of the Hut Tax War following a tax revolt. Odile Goerg in "Femmes africaines et politique : les colonisées au féminin en Afrique occidentale" [African Women and Politics: Colonised Women in West Africa] explains that after this insurrection, other women were chosen as leaders to replace the men who participated in the insurrection, specifying that this "invention" of colonial administrators and the strategies of certain women was then presented as a matter of tradition.

Interestingly, the point has also been made that regardless of the importance of their role, these wives remained wives of the chief. In other words, it was the hierarchical position of their husbands that conferred on them the status that they instrumentalised. Thus, Catherine Coquery-Vidrovitch (2004, p. 20) writes:

> Women were tools, not political actors. They were not married for sentiment; their function was to ensure descent and to provide the labour force for subsistence, mainly hoe agriculture, especially in non-slavery societies. The intellectual, even political, complicity between the chief and his wife or wives was not expected. Even if the matrimonial alliance obeyed a political imperative, it was a matter of clans and not of individuals.

It was the husband who accepted in certain cases to delegate part of his power, which places this power, from the outset, under the dependence of the men and relegates these women to a subordinate status. To adopt a Gramscian ideation of this concept, subordination proceeds from the condition of subalternity. Gayatri C. Spivak advances the term subaltern taken up by Guha, one of the founders of Subaltern Studies, by including Third World women, without distinction of class. Spivak considers the subalternity of women as stemming from both colonial and traditional male domination and domination by elders.

The role of elders in traditional societies has been studied by Claude Meillassoux who observes that within a pyramid-type community, there is the elder who has authority over the group. It is up to him to redistribute products within the community. At the bottom of the hierarchy are the cadets. "In such a system women work for their husbands who give the product to the elders who redistribute it to the whole community directly or through married men" (Meillassoux, 1960, pp. 43–44). It is the possession of knowledge that would justify the power of the elders over the younger ones. They have control over the products insofar as they are the ones who hold the knowledge learned over time. Age and power are linked and combined in the masculine. "Above all, it is logical in an economy where one can only control the product of labour by controlling the producer directly to control also and perhaps more the producer of the producer, that is to say, the procreative woman" (Meillassoux, 1960, p. 50). We talk about the control of women, which allows this male hegemony to be expressed.

This status of the procreative woman, of the mother, also allows us to dwell on the second example often given as an illustration of the fundamental status of women in traditional Africa, that of queen mothers. Note that these were not necessarily the mother of the chief, but could be an aunt, a sister, like Yaa Asantewaa who was named by her brother. They had an important place, especially in Akan matrilineal societies. However, their major role was to advise the chief, which always places them, except in exceptional cases like Yaa Asantewaa, at the second level:

> On the other hand, in Benin, the social representation of women requires them to be discreet and conciliatory. Like the queen mothers or the favourite wives of the monarchs of the ancient Beninese kingdoms, she can be very influential, to the point of

contradicting the royal will in the privacy of the night, but she must remain very discreet in public.

(Tozzo, 2004, p. 78)

Women could therefore speak in domestic, intimate, non-public spaces. This social representation of women, according to Catherine Coquery-Vidrovitch, would not be applicable only to Benin, but to all of Africa.

From the foregoing, it would appear that the ideation of women as people who could wield political power in pre-colonial times but are only able to do so discreetly subtly reinforces their marginality. Does it not also explain today the difficulty of entrusting positions of responsibility to women, and the need to keep them in subordinate positions in relation to men? In essence, does this narrative regarding the role of women in pre-colonial Africa provide a persuasive critique against the subjugation of women during colonialism? Ultimately, there is a need to dredge up a counter-narrative that challenges these representations.

The Difficult Question of the Emancipation of Women in Africa Today

Changing Representations?

Whether it concerns the domination of women in colonial societies or their subalternity in traditional societies, in both cases, it is on the representation of "the" woman that the discourses that depict them are constructed. Representation here refers to presence and replacement because, in representation, something takes the place of something else. This means that representing a person leads to speaking in their name; that is, representation by proxy. Nevertheless, the representation in another sense can also be by portrait. Here the meaning of the image looks appropriate. Edward Saïd brought greater clarity to the role of the image as a qualification in the process of representation. These qualifications contain something peremptory which, by the force of repetition and the use of the "eternal timeless", take on the appearance of truth, of what the thing truly is. As he asserts,

> For all these functions, it is often sufficient to use the simple verb "is". Thus, Muhammad is an impostor [...]. No justification is necessary; the proof needed to convict Muhammad is contained in the word "is". [...] It is repeated, he is an impostor; each time it is said, it becomes a bit more of an impostor, and the assertor gains a bit more authority for having said it. [...] Finally, it is obvious that a category like impostor (or Oriental for that matter) implies, even requires, an opposite which is neither something else fraudulently nor endlessly seeking identification explicit. In addition, this opposite is "Western", or, for Muhammad, Jesus. From a philosophical point of view, therefore, the type of language, thought and vision, which I have very generally called Orientalism, is an extreme form of realism. It consists of a habitual way of dealing with supposedly oriental matters, objects, qualities and regions; those who use it will designate, name, indicate, and fix what they are talking about with a term or an expression. We then consider that this term or this expression has acquired a certain reality, or, quite simply, is the reality.
>
> (Said, 2005, p. 89–90)

Generally, Saïd's arguments on Orientalism illuminate the concept of representation as a political act that goes through a process of framing until what is being framed becomes real. In the case of the historical representation of "the African woman", one finds in the narrative

337

the reproductions of prejudices that tend to substantialise "her" identity. These prejudices come from tradition and Western cultures that lead to a representation of what "woman is". This determination is always made in relation to the other that is man, who does not need to be represented. This attention to the verb to "be" is decisive for understanding the structure of these representations. In the introduction to the *Deuxième sexe* [Second Sex], Simone de Beauvoir already pointed out that it is necessary to take an interest in the verb "to be," which loses its dynamic meaning in favour of a "substantialism" on which inequality is based. In the work, she maintained the following:

> We know the quip of Bernard Shaw: "The white American, he says, in essence, relegates the black to the rank of shoe shiner: and he concludes that he is only good at shining shoes. "We find this vicious circle in all analogous circumstances: when an individual or a group of individuals is maintained in a situation of inferiority, the fact is that he is inferior; but it is on the scope of the word being that we must agree; bad faith consists in giving it a substantial value when it has the dynamic Hegelian meaning: to be is to have become, it is to have been made such that one manifests oneself; yes, women as a whole are today inferior to men, that is to say that their situation opens up fewer possibilities for them: the problem is to know whether this state of affairs should continue.
>
> *(de Beauvoir, 1976, p. 25)*

We thus understand that the woman is not, but has become because of the position that has been conferred on her. It is after the fact that she "is" by force of circumstance, like the shoe shiner who is only good at shining shoes. Any representation is taken in a given context and is not the reproduction of an object after observation, but rather a construction before observation by the scholars in pursuit of an end, hence the ideological role of the representation which sustains the stories. It has been said that she is only good for the domestic space after having confined her to this space, making it her "natural" space because she is the one who gives birth. This association with maternal capacity leads to the construction of these women as passive and to their exclusion from political activities or decision-making roles.

Moreover, this construction goes hand in hand with a hierarchy: the one who represents has power over the one who is represented insofar as it is what he says about her that will be. In other words, the way in which the represented will be seen depends on the way in which the person who says it presents it, hence the power of the latter over the other. Moreover, it is for this reason that for Saïd, no representation can be faithful. These are discourses that construct these representations of women. In the preface to the first French edition of *Orientalism*, Tzvetan Todorov writes:

> Saying to someone: "I have the truth about you" not only informs about the nature of my knowledge, but also establishes between us a relationship where "I" dominates and the other is dominated. Understanding means both, and for good reason, "interpreting" and "including": whether it is passive (understanding) or active (representation), knowledge always allows those who hold it manipulation of the other; the master of the discourse will be the master full stop.
>
> *(Todorov, in Saïd, 2005, p. 8)*

The solution to transforming society does not therefore consist of a change of representations, which would leave the question of domination untouched. If it is a question of fighting against domination, then it means that what is at stake is fighting against the structures that entrench this domination. However, how to bring about a change when we fail to identify the alienating elements, like the fight for the replacement of the animator instead of a fight for the abandonment of these competitions?

Fighting, Yes, But Against What?

"The master of speech will be the master full stop," says Todorov. What can the master do to remain the master? Stay in control. In addition, for that, all means are good to prevent the other from becoming a master of the discourse, including humiliation and contempt. Thus, in the professional and political public sphere, we see men cut women off, we hear them call them by their first names and call each other by their names when they call each other. Calling by first name is one of the signs of this non-acceptance of their presence in the public space. As Marlène Coulomb-Gully points out (2016, p. 42), "the use of the first name is the rule in private life and in the intimate space, its use in the public space contributes to discrediting the action of women". This non-acceptance of women in the public space amounts to a lack of social recognition.

> Insofar as the experience of social recognition is a condition on which the development of personal identity as a whole depends, the absence of this recognition, in other words contempt, is necessarily accompanied by the feeling of being threatened of losing one's personality [...] There is therefore a close link here between the damage suffered by the normative conditions of social interaction and the moral experiences that subjects have in their daily communications. When these conditions are violated and a person is denied the recognition they deserve, they usually reacts with moral feelings that accompany the experience of contempt, and therefore with shame, anger or indignation.
>
> *(Honneth, 2008, p. 193)*

Shame, anger, and outrage are feelings that lead women to give up politics or resign from leadership positions.

In professional and public spaces, women still have to contend with or endure sexist and paternalistic remarks that serve as enactments of male hegemony in socio-political life. Top-level managers or leaders of political parties would typically refer to a junior colleague (but a colleague nonetheless) as "my daughter," a subtle reminder of the gendered power dynamics between them. This situation also serves to collapse the public sphere into the family sphere, effectively eliminating the space for contestation or talking back from the one who cannot act outside of her status as a "daughter" in the African cultural imagination. When you know that contradicting your father is inadmissible in society, you understand that these remarks which pass for affectionate only hinder by preventing any possibility of speaking out or raising a voice against your oppressed condition, which then deepens, your alienation in society. What to do? How to overcome this spectre of invisibility? How to make the action of women credible? Certainly not by instituting gender-parity through quota appointments or related forms of affirmative actions.

Gender-parity, which is often proposed as an effective means of improving the material condition of women vis-à-vis men, is the surest way to reinforce male domination. Recognition, to be effective, must not only be a recognition of rights. The problem of parity means that competence is no longer what is visible, but ethical decency. This "promotion" of gender at all costs can become a misfortune for women because a woman appointed, not for her skills, but for the sake of respect for numbers, will show her shortcomings which will only reinforce the representations that people have of all women as incompetent. In addition, this promotion of gender-parity at all cost, which leads to a certain complacency in mediocrity, are sometimes set in motion to advance the ideological objectives of women or women groups with self-serving goals. Furthermore, it must be understood that the person who appoints is de facto in a superior hierarchical position.

We thus see that women construct themselves through the gaze of those who represent them, thus perpetuating or reinforcing the very conditions they purport to address. Just as we have shown how the first African academics, although in a critical stance vis-à-vis colonisation, extended colonial thought structures, following the example of Cheik Anta Diop, it is a question of saying that the women who have also become these "others" have integrated androcentric structures of thought and thus come to reproduce their own inferiority. However, how to understand this determination of the superior element? Because, according to Simone de Beauvoir (1976, p. 17),

> [...] no subject arises immediately and spontaneously as the inessential; it is not the Other who defining himself as Other defines the One: he is posited as Other by the One positing himself as One. However, so that the reversal of the Other to the One does not take place, he must submit to this foreign point of view.

However, it is precisely because women have submitted to these male gazes and representations that they manage to integrate them and not consider as alienating what nevertheless demeans them, such as for example these beauty contests which speak of symbolic violence. Symbolic violence is open but masked violence, based on the recognition of the dominant and the ignorance of the two groups, unaware that their relations are unequal. This directs the question of domination towards that of knowledge, in other words of education. However, this solution may only be half effective. Because we must see both in the educational system and traditional "values" instances of reproduction of relations of domination. It is to this invisible, symbolic violence that we owe eternal vigilance given the domination it perpetuates. As Bourdieu surmises,

> Symbolic violence is this coercion which is instituted only through the admission that the dominated cannot fail to grant to the dominant (therefore to domination) when he / she has at hand only the instruments he / she has in common with the dominant [...] to think him and to think himself or, even better, to think his / her relationship with the dominant [...].
>
> *(Bourdieu, 1997, p. 204)*

It should however be specified that this membership is in no way a voluntary servitude insofar as this subjugation is not a conscious or voluntary act. This comes from this repetition which ends up becoming this "eternal timelessness" and remains inscribed in the bodies themselves. This is undoubtedly the reason why those who become aware of this violence experience a wound in their flesh. It is this wound that can lead to orienting the struggles towards what remains invisible, yet decisive. All practices must be questioned. And this should take us back to the indifference of a female influencer being a cheerful spectator to the re-enactment of a rape scene. We see women's indifference to practices that deserve to be challenged. It is necessary to know how to identify the overt and subtle ways in which the politics of history and narrative condition women to naturalise or eternalise their inferiority as opposed to challenging it.

Conclusion

The chapter interrogated the attempted erasure of women in the historical discourse of politics in Africa, which serves to render invisible the contribution of women as political actors in the pre-colonial and colonial period. The argument advanced is that in dealing with the marginalisation of women in contemporary Africa, there is a need to imagine the role of women as represented in the historical narrative of the continent, and how their near erasure from history reproduces forms of oppression they contend with in reality. At any rate, responding to the problem of marginalisation of women with quota appointments in public or political positions is also fraught with several challenges. While they are intended as a means of establishing gender-parity, they also possess a tendency to infantilise women and entrench the very domination they are meant to eliminate. For the emancipation of the African women to go beyond rhetoric and cosmetic remedies, there is a need to examine how they are represented in the historical materials and narratives that the larger society relies on to make sense of the world. Acknowledging the active role and contributions of women in colonial resistance would represent an important starting point in altering historical narratives that (mis)represent women and which provide the building blocks for their marginalisation in the here and now.

References

Bourdieu, Pierre, 1997, *Méditations pascaliennes*, Paris, Seuil.

Coquery-Vidrovitch, Catherine, 2004, "Des reines mères aux épouses de président" in *Premières dames en Afrique*, Paris, Karthala, "Politique africaine", 2004/3, N° 95, p. 19–31.

Coulomb-Gully, Marlène, 2016, *Femmes en politique, en finir avec les seconds rôles*, Paris, Belin, coll. Égale à égal.

de Beauvoir, Simone, 1976, *Le deuxième sexe*, tome I, Paris, Gallimard.

Dia, Mamadou, 1985, *Mémoires d'un militant du Tiers-Monde*, Paris, Publisud.

Diouf, Mamadou, 2002, "Sortir de la parenthèse coloniale. Un défi fondateur pour les historiens africains" in *Le Débat*, 2002/1 (N° 118), p. 59–65.

Djibo, Hadiza, 2001. *La participation des femmes africaines à la vie politique: les exemples du Sénégal et du Niger*, Paris, L'Harmattan.

Honneth, Axel, 2008, *La société du mépris*, translated by Olivier Voirol, Pierre Rusch and Alexandre Dupeyrix, Paris, La Découverte.

Labrune-Badiane, Céline and Smith, Etienne, 2018, *Les Hussards noirs de la colonie. Instituteurs et petites patries en AOF*, Paris, Karthala.

Marx, Karl and Engels, Friedrich, 1982, *L'idéologie allemande*, translated by Maximilien Rubel, Louis Evrard and Louis Janover, in Œuvres III Philosophie, Paris, Gallimard, Bibliothèque de la Pléiade.

Meillassoux, Claude, 1960, "Essai d'interprétation du phénomène économique dans les sociétés traditionnelles d'auto-subsistance", in *Cahiers d'études africaines*, 1960/1 (N°4), p. 38–67.

Pagnon, Estelle, 1997, "'Une œuvre inutile?' La scolarisation des filles par les missionnaires catholiques dans le Sud-Est du Nigéria (1885–1930)" in C. Coquery-Vidrovitch (ed.), *Femmes d'Afrique*, Clio. Histoire, femmes et sociétés 6/1997, Toulouse, Presses Universitaires du Mirail, p. 35–59.

Ricœur, Paul, 1983, *Temps et récit*, Tome I, Paris, Seuil.

Said, Edward W., 2005, *L'orientalisme. L'Orient créé par l'Occident*, traduit par Catherine Malamud, Préface à l'édition française de Tzvetan Todorov, Paris, Seuil.

Sarr, Fatou, 2009, "Féminismes en Afrique occidentale? Prise de conscience et luttes politiques et sociales" in C. Verschuur (ed.), *Mouvements de femmes et féminismes anticoloniaux*, Vents d'Est, vents d'Ouest, Genève, Berne, p. 79–100.

Tozzo, Émile A., 2004, "Rosine Soglo, Famille et entreprise politique" in *Premières dames en Afrique*, Paris, Karthala "Politique africaine" 2004/3 (N° 95), p. 71–90.

25

VIOLENT DEMOCRACY AND THE PROMISE OF PEACE

Anthony C. Ajah and Mfonobong David Udoudom

Introduction

How can we reimagine the conception and practice of democracy to reduce democratic violence in contemporary African societies? This is one of the most urgent issues in African political philosophy, considering the spate of violence in many democracies in Africa. We make this claim for two reasons. First, from the 2015 'Rhodes must fall' campaign in South Africa, to the 2020 '#EndSARS' campaigns and heightened violent secessionist agitations in many parts of Africa, there is reason to believe that as long as majorities determine the direction and content of social policies, violence will remain an undetachable cloak from democracy, despite the promises of its ardent proponents. Second, several scholars that study Africa have continued to argue how democracy is unfit for a social organization of societies in this context. For many, the mere practice of the democratic form of governance is itself violence in Africa. For others, democracy is impracticable in Africa because it is alien to the continent. The claim is that because democracy is imported, it is a source of violence. Addressing the questions we have raised will contribute insights into how we can tackle some of the practical and theoretical concerns about the practice of democracy in Africa.

Our focus is not on what it means to talk about violent democracy generally. Daniel Ross (2004) discussed the implications of the idea of violence in democracies. Our focus is also not on the new forms of violence that result in reorganization of institutions of democracy, state–system–control, and terror (Ross, 2004). These points have been highlighted by critics of democracy (see Nichols, 2021; Fukuyama, 2015; Diamond, 2015; Krastev, 2011; Collier, 2009). We are instead interested in examining violence as a central yet reducible element of current predominant conceptions of democracy. Particularly, we explore how the 'people' in the definition of democracy as 'government of the people' has been subtly replaced by the 'majority'. The result is that democracy is reductively conceptualized and operationalized as 'government of or by the majority'. We demonstrate that the default distinction between majority and minority groups along various identity and interest lines constitutes a fundamental root of democratic violence. These problems make democracy to be basically prone to violence. To solve these problems, we consider three ways out of violence-prone democracy. Among other things, we assess the possibilities of putting 'the people' back into the concept and practice of democracy. We analyse the possibilities of weakening the practice of

DOI: 10.4324/9781003143529-29

having permanent majorities and minorities. The practice technically and practically usually warrants that as long as a certain democratic regime obtains in a society, specific persons and groups are steadily advantaged by default, and others continue to be disadvantaged no matter what they do.

To achieve our goal, this contribution is divided into two sections. In the first section, we explore the ideas behind the lure and spread of democracy as well as the reasons behind its rejection and rollback in more recent decades. In doing this, we debunk the claim that democracy ensures peace by default. We also highlight how the predominant conceptualization and practice of democracy is based on an almost strict dichotomization of groups into permanent minorities and majorities. We then show how this is a formalization of violence even by those who do not consciously mean to exert violence against others. The second section is titled 'Three ways beyond violence-prone democracy'. There, we explore possibilities of reducing the problems that we highlighted in the previous section. Specifically, we offer three ways to improve the conceptualization and practice of democracy.

Democracy's Promise of Peace

Democracy was attractive as a political ideal to the post–Cold War nations, especially countries in the global south and the former Soviet bloc. In principle, this was largely a function of the liberal interpretation of the democratic peace theory which holds that modern democracies have rarely, if ever, fought each other, though they might wage wars on non-democracies (Simpson, 2018; Hobson, 2011, 147; Richmond, 2014; Elman, 2001, 758; Doyle, 1983, 226). To effectively drive home their point, proponents of the democratic peace theory advance the monadic and dyadic democratic peace theories to further explain the sweeping generalization of liberal democracy. According to the dyadic democratic peace proposition, democratic states seldom go to war against each other, though intolerant and sometimes bellicose towards non-democracies. The proponents explain that two factors proscribe the use of violence between democracies. The first are institutional constraints on decision-making choices of democratic leaders. The second are shared democratic norms of compromise and cooperation (Chernoff, 2014; Doyle, 2012; Múller & Wolff, 2006; Daase, 2006; Pugh, 2005; Henderson, 2002; Owen, 1994). Dyadic democratic peace proposition is a theory of peace that supports its kind. It works in conformity with Kant's peace plan, seeking 'democratic enlargement' in order to validate the perception that joint democracy is a 'sufficient condition for peace' (Henderson, 2002, 3). On the other hand, monadic democratic peace proposition, in its normative version, suggests that democratically socialized citizens, leaders, and rational citizens in liberal capitalist societies are generally peace prone. Since violence would endanger their lives and economy, they would prefer and agree to resolve their conflicts in peaceful and consensual manners (Múller & Wolff, 2006, 43–44). Ish-Shalom (2011, 178) suggests that these rational and normative explanatory frameworks reveal that democratic peace theory is a theory of democracy, by democracy, for democracy.

The generalization of democratic peace theory is yet to be contradicted by any major historical case. However, since the wake of the twenty-first century, many scholars of democracy have argued that democracy is backsliding and rolling back into authoritarianism. The acclaimed 'zone of democratic peace' is losing its attraction. Some of the indices claimed to be responsible for the decline in global democracy include national and international racial prejudices and discrimination, corruption, underdevelopment, and poor health care. Others are ethnic chauvinism, religious conflicts, and election-related violent conflicts. This last set of indices more easily poses as regular features of dichotomized majority–minority relations in democracies. In a nutshell, the attractiveness of the promise of democratic peace proposition has waned. According to this view, the failure in practice is leading to a situation where a culture of violence manifests periodically in democracies. Violence is the result of the failures of democratic governments to establish peace and prosperity at home (Nichols, 2021; Fukuyama, 2015; Diamond, 2015; Krastev, 2011; Collier, 2009; Diamond, 2008). This implies that democracy is not inherently an antithesis of authoritarian governments. To argue otherwise would be to 'obscure the true nature of democracies, and in the process mask democracy's true grounding and continual fragility' (Ross, 2004, 183).

Realists were among the first to criticize the world's pacification project as proposed and projected in the democratic peace theory by liberal thinkers. The realists continue to conceive the world as eternally bounded to power struggle and war. They seem unable to imagine the possibility of a pacified world order. The liberalism that subsequently emerged challenged the idea that violence and war were part of the natural order of things (Richmond, 2014). It is easy to see why realists closely examine the claims of liberal democracy by identifying salient flaws that expose the fragility of liberal democracy. Coetzee and Hudson (2012, 259–264), for instance, summed up realists' objections to the democratic peace theory in two parts: the institutional and the normative. The institutional reductive provision of democratic peace theory holds that liberal states would be peaceful. The realists consider this proposition as weak. It lacks a causal mechanism to establish peace. Granted the failure to establish a causally valid link between democratic peace and liberal peace, realists correctly observe that liberal democracies are equally war-prone as authoritarian states. Hence, the source of waning enthusiasm and growing discontent about democracy.

Negative events in both advanced and recent democracies give impetus to this discontent. Various engagements by citizens with their home governments over their dissatisfaction have resulted in domestic violent conflicts that unsettle democratic peace. The normative interpretation of democratic peace theory holds that liberal democracy externalizes their norms of compromise and non-violent conflict resolution. Realists challenge this on two counts. First, there is little effect of this norm on the pacifistic nature of inter-liberal relations. They stress the absence of valid historical records to prove the claim of non-violent conflict resolution among liberal states. Second, democratic states undermine the trust and respect underpinning normative theories of democratic peace whenever they intervene against fellow democracies. Thus, the realists insist that it is the issue of relative capabilities of states, rather than liberal forces, that explains the foreign policy behaviour of states. In an anarchical international system, it is expedient that states continue to build capabilities to shield themselves from eminent tendencies of attack by others.

Assessing the positions of both realist and liberal theories of the democratic peace, Coetzee and Hudson (2012, 274) argue that 'their attendant manifestation within level-exclusive explanatory frameworks do not provide a credible avenue for the theorization of the democratic peace.' Aligning with neoclassical realists, they conclude that the social world holds more things in stock than the realist and liberal theories of democratic peace acknowledge. They argue that neoclassical realism is a credible alternative to the shortcomings inherent in liberal and (neo) realist conceptions of democratic peace. This is premised on the promise of neoclassical realism to provide a comprehensive explanatory framework that considers the complex nature of the interaction between the agent-structure problem and the level-of-analysis problem (Coetzee and Hudson, 2012, 268). This means that neoclassical realists give adequate attention to the importance of both human agents and social structures in the attainment of democratic stability and peace.

Within the framework of neoclassical realism, there is more to the social system and the democratic peace than reductive structuralism, individualistic ontologism, liberalism, and neorealist conceptions of democratic peace could admit. The democratic peace debate in its final analysis is a case of *reducio ad absurdum*. What seems to unite the structuralist, individualist, normative and ontological positions in this debate is their reductive understanding of peace as the absence of physical violence. This would be a negative interpretation of peace. Peace scholars understand peace beyond its negative imagination upon which the debate on democratic peace hinges. They consider the idea of positive peace as implying the absence of violence in all its manifestations, be it direct, cultural or structural (Ramsbotham, Woodhouse & Maill, 2011; Jeong, 2000; Galtung, 1996; Burton, 1990). Negative peace, on the other hand, focuses on the cessation of direct violent behaviours by conflict stakeholders against either friends or foes. The implication of the positive conception of peace is that it is wrong to judge democracy as successful in its promises simply because there is a reduction in international wars. Rather, all forms of international interactions that involve cultural humiliation as well as structures in democracies that sustain violence against individuals and groups, imply that democracy does not essentially nor sufficiently conduce to ending violence. Thus, Tony Smith (2011, 154) argues that as an explanation of the logic of international relations, democratic peace theory could only posit the emergence of a world of peace and freedom, should democracy and markets expand worldwide.

The consensus in scholarly research on the democratic peace hypothesis, at least among realists, is that democracies are not more peaceful than non-democracies (Kaarbo & Ray, 2011, 151). By taking this stand, scholars involved are debunking the idea that democracy necessarily ensures peace and reduces violence. The supposition in this regard is that the mutual nonaggression pact of liberal democracies is a limited and exclusive pacification. It is insufficient to guarantee a stable international system in the long run. It is also not enough basis to describe democracy as non-violent by default.

The fear which has manifested in various democracies is about democratic dictatorship and the negative effects of free trade on liberal democracy. Capitalism opens doors for incessant crave for materialism and related consumption of raw material. Considering the system-level economic and biospheric stress, liberal democracy could ultimately lead to a hollow victory or environmental collapse (Richmond, 2014). Resource conflicts in states of the global south are largely the effects of unheeded warnings about possible consequences of environmental collapse. The representative structure of liberal democracy pits people of the same ancestral origin against each other. In doing this, it divides the citizens of states into a majority group which dominates a minority group. This core feature of democracy is a source of violence. It is a formalization of violence because, among other things, it creates a situation where there is an ever-widening pacification of the liberal pacific union. A dichotomous local politics in states in the global south seems to be erasing the zone of peace from national politics. In concrete terms, therefore, it is reasonable to hold that the great limitations of democracy have foisted cruelty upon the social life in many cases.

We argue that the establishment of permanent dichotomies by the current conceptualization and practice of democracy is responsible for the creation and sustenance of permanent groups of minority and majority. In our view, the various forms of formal acceptance of groups in democracies as if they are natural and immutable, imply the formalization of violence. We operationalize the word violence as including any action or word that intentionally or unintentionally hurts or dehumanizes others. This understanding of violence balances both direct and indirect forms of violence. Direct violence involves physical harm or hurt done to the body – the human body. Here, the performer of the act of violence is known. In the case of indirect violence – otherwise known as structural violence – there may not be obviously identifiable persons as perpetrators of the violence. This kind does not immediately manifest as violence. It arises from particular forms of social organisation and process, and is expressed in conditions such as domination, exclusion, deprivation and poverty (Ramsbotham, Woodhouse & Mall 2011; Jeong 2000). To say, then, that the predominant practice of democracy necessarily sustains/formalizes violence implies that it consistently hurts those in the minority, and in some cases, dehumanizes them. On this note, we recall Plato's critique of democracy for being full of varieties and disorder. So how can we improve the conceptualization and practice of democracy?

Three Ways beyond Violence-Prone Democracy

In the last section, we showed how the currently predominant conceptualization and practice of democracy structures, formalizes and sustains violence. We emphasized that the core issue is that in the current conceptualization and practice of democracy in Africa, groups are divided into permanent majorities and minorities. In this section, we explore three related ways to reimagine democracy, weaken the permanence of dichotomies in current imagination, and reduce the violence the dichotomies breed.

The first way is to deemphasize the unrealizable promise that democracy ensures non-violence as well as transcend the assumption that democracy is a sufficient condition for peace. The premise of this assumption is unrealizable. We think realists are correct to argue that no system of social and political organization can guarantee non-violence by just being adopted. We also deemphasize the idealistic promises that are implied in the definition of democracy. This implies that concrete persons in concrete democratic contexts need to consistently pay attention to possible sources of violence as well as regularly aim at not being violent. The realist disposition in relation to the promise of democracy to offer nations a path to peace seems more apt than the assumption by most democratic peace theorists that by merely adopting democracy a society has severed ties with violence.

The second possibility to resolve the problem of violent democracy is to reconsider the argument that democracy is desirable because it depends on the direct and representative choice of the majority of the people – a government 'by the people'. By this definition, it is assumed that social organization is under the direct control of the people rather than a group of political elite. This picture of democracy is not accurate. The reality about democracy is that it is mediated by representations. As such, it is not the people that govern, but the most populous group, or sometimes groups with the highest lobbying capacity and skills. In most cases, only what suits this group will be approved for implementation. Minorities are therefore left to live as if they are trapped. Majority of decisions hurt them rather than improve their wellbeing. Their interests do not seem to matter. Usually pushed to their limits in the long run, they react violently in response to the disregard and violence they experience regularly.

This leads to the entrenchment of majority–minority antagonistic divides that breed more violence at various levels. To curb this violence, democracy maybe reimagined, first as a government by the people, and second as a government aimed at the reduction of human suffering. This is different from merely operationalizing democracy as a government of the people defined by majority and their group interests. The form of operationalization we suggest requires that the adoption of policies is not decided based on the interests of the majority that could have as well been lobbied. Policy decisions would rather be driven by a fundamental question: How may the implementation of a particular policy better the condition of those who are most dehumanized by suffering? This question is also suitable to guide decision-makings on whether to engage in war with others; whether to continuously take loans on behalf of citizens, and whether to continue production patterns that have negative impacts on the climate. These questions rarely come into consideration when democracy is driven by the idea of how many persons support the adoption of a policy. Yet, they are important questions that will ensure mutual recognition of groups of human beings of varied sizes and interests.

Finding the right answers to these questions promises three gains. First, it will ensure that minority groups are not pushed to their limits. Second, it ensures such groups are not ignored to the point that where they inhabit become ungoverned spaces, denied of government presence, and easily subdued by non-state and anti-government groups. Third, it recognizes the needs of groups, to reduce their sufferings even when their number places them in the minority. The outcome will be a reduction of various forms of violence. Replacing 'the most populous people' with 'the most needy group' in the conception of democracy on the one hand, and focusing attention on reducing human suffering on the other hand, can dismantle structures that sustain various forms of violence in democracies.

The idea that underlies this suggestion is that the basis of group identification is fluid. It fades away when human beings are confronted with despair and suffering. The forms of identification that define social groupings into majority or minority, fade away when we carefully notice that human beings share the same set of problems and suffering. In suffering, more than in any other existential situation, human beings are united. If 'the people' are reinstated in the conceptualization and operationalization of democracy, the practice of democracy will improve and the rollback of democracy will be slowed. We take this position because whereas democracy is anchored on 'the people', the practice rather focuses on 'the most populous group'. This makes democracy to be predominantly practiced as a government of the most populous group. A possible response to our suggestion here is that theoretically there are many safeguards put in place to ensure that democracy does not degenerate into a government of the most populous group. A critic of this position may add that in Nigeria, for instance, one does not just have to get the highest votes to become president. They must get a specific percentage from every region in the country. We respond to this position from two angles. First is that many of the safeguards are mainly in principle, not in practice. Second is that even in the example of Nigeria, efforts are still made to ensure that specification about percentage amounts to numerical support for the candidate. In many cases, this support is organized by members of the opposition (see Ngwu and Ajah, 2022, 198–206).

The third way to resolve the problem of violent democracy follows from the second. We propose that citizens need to rally around the common human need to reduce suffering rather than their micro and macro identities. Minority identities disable and disadvantage groups more than they enable them. Majority of social identities, on the other hand, make those who belong to such groups to directly or indirectly, consciously or unconsciously, participate in inflicting pains, violence, and suffering on others. Thus, it is in making and maintaining permanent minorities (Mamdani, 2020) that citizens contribute to sustain democratic violence. Our guiding assumption is that all forms of social organization are the outcome of social construction. Such constructions depend on the dynamics in society for sustenance. To overcome conceptions and practices that sustain violence in democracies, citizens and representatives of groups should be willing to switch party affiliation based on the consideration of what best serves the wider interests of the people at the time. This is a more promising alternative compared to ideological loyalty to political parties and party leadership, regardless of their performance. We take this position because there is nothing to suggest that ideologies are immutable. The measure of all ideologies should be how best they enable the realization of human wellbeing.

Let us consider the example of gender pay gap to buttress our point on how the majority always have their way in democracies, and how this makes democracy prone to violence. Let us imagine that a few women involved in policy-making belong to party X which is 'the ruling party' in a particular context. Let us also imagine that the leadership of this party drafts a document about the payment of wages to citizens. This document specifies that men should be paid higher wages than women for doing similar works. Now, imagine that the party presents this document to the parliament for assessment and adoption. Evidence from various contexts where democracy is practiced reveals that women who are members of party X will vote in favour of adopting the policy items suggested in the document. They do that even though items in the document imply formalization of inequality against them, and therefore a form of democratic violence against all women in their society. Most of the women in party X will support the document because they are expected to not vote against their party. Should they vote otherwise or support members of another party in rejecting their party's position, they will be accused of engaging in anti-party activities. Members of the opposition party will also see them in this light even though they are joining voices with them to correct potential source of violence in a policy draft.

This fact that members of the opposition will see these supporters from the ruling party as engaging in anti-party activities, buttresses the point about the wrong conceptualization of democracy. In this conception, the practice is not based on humane issues of interest at the time, but on party affiliation. To therefore stick to the decision of the party, rather than resist policies that are inimical to the welfare of all the women in the society, the women in our example undermine their agency, self-respect, and responsibility to guarantee the welfare of others in society. Our point, therefore, is that citizens and representatives in democracies should be free to make political choices, even when it demands far-reaching ideological changes and practical choices that differ from the collective position of their party. Our arguments about gender pay gap in this paragraph apply in cases where men and women perform comparably the same work of comparably equal results in the society. Our position will be the same in situations of an electoral contest for political power. People should vote not because particular persons are affiliated with their party. Political responsibility demands that they choose the best candidate or support the most humane policy suggestion, regardless of party affiliation.

These last points imply that reducing violence in the predominant conceptualization of democracy requires transcending partisan politics. It requires that individuals need not be so strongly committed to policy suggestions from members of their political party to the extent that they are reluctant to compromise and do what is best for everyone in the society. Overcoming partisan politics in this way is necessary for a new face of democracy to emerge. This new democracy will engage citizens as agents in theory and practice. It will be a democracy in which citizens deliberate consciously to decide the result of social actions and inactions (Okeja, 2022). Specifically, we think the end of rigid party politics is a prerequisite for a more successful consolidation of deliberative agency in democratic contexts in Africa, as Okeja (2022) suggests. The picture and practice of democracy that we suggest will be a more humane democracy. It can create a reliable structure for fewer cases of violence since citizens have good reasons to adopt a political approach built on the imperative to ameliorate suffering. Partisan politics made it possible for several authoritarian rulers to perpetuate themselves in power in many countries in Africa. If some of the members of the parties in power were to publicize their honest sentiments about the leaders who represent their parties, they would acknowledge the inadequacy of perpetuating one-party rule.

Notwithstanding, people support policies that will make their party remain in power for as long as possible, because 'it is in the interest of their party'.

Our idea that citizens should be motivated by the common human need to reduce suffering can be further explained from two angles. The first is that by means of this process, the power to determine how the society is governed still resides with the people. But in this case, the people are not defined by a majority but by a central idea capable of pulling people together to tackle entrenched forces that structure and sustain human suffering. Thus, it is not the will of the majority that matters but political action that reduces suffering.

The second angle is that the need to reduce human suffering trumps the need to unite around exclusive identities and interests. In view of this, we recall our argument that all forms of identities become irrelevant when human beings are confronted with suffering. This implies that to reduce violence in democracies, the first action to undertake is to limit the influence of seemingly exclusive identities on political imagination and action. Political imaginations as well as the prism they create and sustain, could lead people to believe that the humanity, interests, and aspirations of specific groups are less important or unworthy of recognition. This might make them not care that members of such groups suffer within the conventional majority–minority struggles in democracies. The question therefore is not 'which group among the citizens of democratic states should be allocated what', but 'which group is in greatest need of available resources, at a given time'.

Conclusion

We set out in this contribution to reimagine the conceptualization and practice of democracy in contemporary Africa. We showed that democracy has succeeded in enhancing peace among democratic nations by drastically reducing the number of international wars. However, its predominant mode of practice divides populations into national antagonistic groups of seemingly permanent majority and minority. In each case, the permanent majority is advantaged, while permanent minorities are continuously marginalized, ignored, hurt, and dehumanized. This is a major challenge wherever democracy is being practiced. The result is intractable contestation and violence of various scales.

We showed how to overcome this challenge. Specifically, we explored three ways democracy can be reconceptualized and practiced in Africa to reduce the violence that results from majority–minority dichotomy among citizens. The first way is to deemphasize the unrealizable promise that democracy ensures non-violence. The second is to see democracy as a government for greater reduction of human suffering rather than the government of groups who are majority. The third way is to encourage citizens to unite around the common human need to reduce suffering. This approach to democracy promises to be better than their disabling micro-social identities that make them minorities by default, or their majority identities that make them exert violence on others who are different from them only by accidents of history.

References

Burton, J. (1990). *Conflict resolution and prevention*. London: Macmillan.
Chernoff, F. (2014). *Explanation and progress in security studies: Bridging theoretical divides in international relations*. Stanford: Stanford University Press.
Coetzee, E., & Hudson, H. (2012). Democratic peace theory and the realist-liberal dichotomy: The promise of neoclassical realism? *Politikon*, 39(2), 257–277.
Collier, P. (2009). *Guns and votes: Democracy in dangerous places*. New York: Harper Collins Publishers.

Daase, C. (2006). Democratic peace – Democratic war: Three reasons why democracies are war-prone. In A. Geis, L. Brock & H. Múller (Eds.), *Democratic wars looking at the dark side of democratic peace* (pp. 74–89). New York: Palgrave Macmillan.

Diamond, L., & Plattner, M. F. (Eds.), *Democracy in decline?* Baltimore: Johns Hopkins University Press.

Diamond, L. (2008). The democratic rollback: The resurgence of the predatory State. *Foreign Affairs*, 87(2), 36–48.

Doyle, M. (1983). Kant, liberal legacies, and foreign affairs. *Philosophy & Public Affairs*, 12(3), 205–235.

Doyle, M. W. (2012). *Liberal peace: Selected essays*. London: Routledge.

Elman, C. (2001). Introduction: History, theory, and the democratic peace. *The International History Review*, 23(4), 757–766.

Fukuyama, F. (2015). Why is democracy performing so poorly? In L. Diamond & M. F. Plattner (Eds.), *Democracy in decline?* (pp. 11–24). Baltimore: Johns Hopkins University Press.

Galtung, J. (1996). *Peace by peaceful means: Peace and conflict, development and civilization*. London: Sage Publications Ltd.

Henderson, E. A. (2002). *Democracy and war: The end of an illusion?* London: Lynne Reinner Publishers, Inc.

Hobson, C. (2011). Roundtable: Between the theory and practice of democratic peace. *International Relations*, 25(2), 147–150.

Ish-Shalom, P. (2011). Don't look back in anger. *International Relations*, 25(2), 178–184.

Jeong, H. (2000). *Peace and conflict studies: An introduction*. Aldershot: Ashgate Publishing Ltd.

Kaarbo, J., & Ray, J. L. (2011). *Global politics* (11th ed.). Boston: Wadsworth Cengage Learning.

Krastev, I. (2011). Democracy and dissatisfaction. *Journal of Globalization Studies*, 2(1), 22–32.

Mamdani, M. (2020). *Neither settler nor native: The making and unmaking of permanent minorities*. Cambridge, MA and London: Harvard University Press.

Múller, H. & Wolff, J. (2006). Democratic peace: Many data, little explanation? In A. Geis, L. Brock, & H. Múller (Eds.), *Democratic wars: Looking at the dark side of democratic peace* (pp.41–73). New York: Palgrave Macmillan.

Ngwu, E. C., & Ajah, A. C. (2022). Intra-party chicanery and electoral outcomes in Nigeria's presidential elections. In O. Ibeanu, I. K. Okoye, I. M. Alumona, & E. T. Aniche (Eds.), *Anonymous power: Parties, interest groups and politics of decision making in Nigeria's fourth republic (Essays in honour of Elochukwu Amucheazi)* (pp. 191–210). Singapore: Springer Nature.

Nichols, T. (2021). *Our own worst enemy: The assault from within on modern democracy*. New York: Oxford University Press.

Okeja, U. (2022). *Deliberative agency: A study in modern African Political Philosophy*. Bloomington: Indiana University Press.

Owen, J. (1994). How liberalism produces democratic peace. *International Security*, 19(2), 87–125.

Pugh, J. (2005). Democratic peace theory: A review and evaluation. CEMPROC Occasional Paper Series.

Ramsbotham, O., Woodhouse, T., & Maill, H. (2011). *Contemporary conflict resolution: The prevention, management and transformation of deadly conflicts* (3rd ed.). Cambridge: Polity Press.

Richmond, O. P. (2014). *Peace: A very short introduction*. Oxford: Oxford University Press.

Ross, D. J. (2004). *Violent democracy*. Cambridge: Cambridge University Press.

Simpson, S. (2018). Making liberal use of Kant? Democratic peace theory and perpetual peace. *International Relations*, 0(0), 1–20.

Smith, T. (2011). Democratic peace theory: From promising theory to dangerous practice. *International Relations*, 25(2), 151–157.

PART V

Global Perspectives

26

PAN-AFRICANISM AS COSMOPOLITANISM

Pius Mosima

Introduction: African Philosophy as a Political Issue

The discipline and practice of academic African philosophy, in the course of the twentieth-century, have been greatly influenced by colonial rule, decolonization and the post-colonial experience. Kenyan philosopher Dismas Masolo depicts the origins of the debate on the history of African philosophy with two related happenings: the Western discourses on Africa and the African response to these discourses (Masolo, 1994, p. 1). Western discourses were steeped in racism and Eurocentrism which opened the floodgates to colonialism and slavery. These discourses did not only reject the identity but considered the African as one who was incapable of rigorous and dialectical inquiry. The black man's culture and even mind were devalued and claimed to be extremely strange to reason, logic and various habits of scientific scrutiny. The dominance of this colonial mentality and the subsequent ideological devaluation of the Africans were couched in Eurocentric discourses by philosophers like Hegel, Kant, Hume and anthropologists like Lévy-Bruhl (1910) and Brelsford (1935, 1938) who considered the Africans as the impenetrable other. This self-declared European ethnocentrism sustained the colonial ideology and paved the way for the so-called "mission to civilize" Africans through colonization, and Christian evangelization (Mudimbe, 1988, p.136). Consequently, Africa became an idea (Mudimbe 1994) and had to be invented (Mudimbe 1988) based on the body of texts and epistemological order which construct Africa as a symbol of otherness and inferiority, which Mudimbe refers to as the Colonial Library (Mudimbe, 1994, p.38). Conversely, the African reaction to the Western self-proclaimed hegemony was radical criticism that challenged this dominance with a renewed understanding of their human possibilities. This could be seen with the emergence of ideologies of otherness and resistance such as Pan-Africanism, Negritude, Black Consciousness Movement (BCM), etc., which were not just literary activities but also universalist movements, aimed at rehabilitating and expressing the black personality. In fact, Pan-Africanism remains one of the most outstanding philosophical doctrines that have dominated and influenced discourses among scholars, philosophers and politicians. Even though Pan-Africanist ideas began to circulate in the mid-nineteenth century, starting in West Africa by a few educated black elites as a revolt against European contempt about everything African, this concept continues to be more prevalent and discussed among educated Africans of the upper-middle class. Pan-Africanism is a socio-cultural precedent to Negritude, and both

DOI: 10.4324/9781003143529-31

movements exerted immense influences on the other in challenging European prejudices and racist mindsets about Africa. Négritude as a literary, ideological movement, for example, was developed by Francophone black intellectuals, writers and politicians in France in the 1930s. This group included Leopold Sedar Senghor from Senegal, Martinican poet Aimé Césaire and the Guianian Léon Damas. Defenders of Négritude share solidarity in a common black identity as a better tool against French colonial racism. The violent colonial encounter between France and her African colonies, which led to the ideological devaluation of the Africans and the entire black race, triggered these intellectuals to come up with Négritude as a tool for assertive cultural nationalism. They believed that the shared black heritage of members of the African Diaspora would help in fighting against French political and intellectual hegemony and domination. They formed a realistic literary style and adapted Marxist ideas as part of the ideological base of this movement. Senghor's conception of Négritude influenced black African intellectuals in retrieving the epistemological basis of their identity and worldview in a bid to articulate their distinctive mode of relating to the world. Negritude exerted immense influence on Pan-Africanism, the idea of one Africa, as a form of literary protest by African Americans against the racism of the white community. It is very common to see how, when travelling in different African countries, many young people relate to the concepts of African identity and unity. Nevertheless, there is a tendency to limit Pan-Africanism to the actual physical African continent over the last several decades. This is perhaps due to the conception of an invented Africa, a homogenous socio-cultural group ...a unanimous ethno-political Sovereign (Eze, 2013), the postcolonial other who is confined to live in such logic of otherness. It is precisely such unanimous conceptualization of Pan-Africanism that gave a certain view of African philosophy in the wake of independence, as radically different from Western philosophy.

An example is the debate about the nature and existence of African philosophy, a debate which was largely sustained by the first generation of university-trained African philosophers. The first inspiration for the debate was provided by Placide Tempels' *La philosophie bantoue*, first published in Dutch (*Bantoe-filosofie*) in 1945. Academic African philosophy in the 1970s and 1980s was dominated by the heated ideological debate between defenders and critics of ethnophilosophy. The two main groups were the "traditionalists", with a particularizing perspective, and the *universalists* or *modernists*, with a universalizing point of view (Oruka 1975, 1990; Mudimbe 1988).

African philosophy is a way to do philosophy, and to understand the reality that roots in cultural practices and patterns that are pervasive in (sub-Saharan) African cultures. Hence, African philosophy encompasses those works and thinkers and reflective practices that arise out of and dig into specific questions that come from specific shared histories of sub-Saharan African countries and their peoples. It is a specific way to understand community and the dynamics between individuals and society; a way to understand matter and non-matter as inseparable aspects of one reality; a strong sense of the divine/sacred character of being; interconnectedness of the natural world and human societies.

African philosophy has been too limited to differences with the West, and as I have argued elsewhere (Mosima, 2016, p.11), a new perspective is required "...we can also broaden the adjective 'African' to designate cultural, historical, political, ideological, and social realities". To this, we may include the concept Africana Philosophy, all "Black" philosophy, and African Diaspora philosophy. Africana philosophy refers to the works of philosophers of African descent and others whose work deals with the subject matter of the African Diaspora. The notion *African Diaspora*, modelled after the concept of *Jewish Diaspora,* was coined in the 1990s and entered common usage in the 2000s. It pertains to the various communities all over the world that come from the historic movement of peoples from Africa, primarily to Europe, the Americas and other areas around the globe. Historically, this notion was used to refer to the descendants of West and Central Africans who were sold as slaves and taken to Brazil and the United States of America, or those who voluntarily migrated to other continents. The connections between African and diaspora black thinkers have always been there, though sparse during the time of Trans-Atlantic slavery, but when American blacks returned to the continent, mainly as pastors after abolition, it is the case. After 1956 when the famous Pan-African conference took place in Paris, we see a systematic exchange, resulting in thinkers connected to or doing mental work for real-life political struggle, around the fight for independence and nowadays the fight against neocolonial extraction (Césaire, Fanon, Nkrumah, Mbembe). Prominent Africana philosophers include Lewis Gordon, Frantz Fanon, W.E.B. Du Bois and Robert Bernasconi.

This explains the rationale of this chapter: to broaden the concept of Pan-Africanism to include the realities of Africans in the continent and Africans in the diaspora; inviting us to perceive Africa as both continental and transcontinental. In our time characterized by globalization and multicultural society, my aim is to (re)construct, re(create) a new and complex conception of Pan-Africanism which takes into account many contemporary currents of thought in different philosophical traditions. I focus on how a new idea of one Africa could have been imagined and historically realized in light of the contemporary challenges it faces and must answer. I argue for a creative imagination of a Pan-African identity that is rooted in Africa but transcendent of it. This is where I suggest and situate a new Pan-Africanism which is to be connected to knowable African communities, nations and traditions, but also to live a life divided across cultures, languages and states, with new challenges. Can a locally rooted political ideology and practice like Pan-Africanism be adequately articulated onto cosmopolitan political scenes? Is it of any global significance today? I begin with a brief discussion of African philosophy as a political issue, in which I situate and articulate the conditions of the emergence of Pan-Africanism. As a next step, I explain the concept, ideology and phenomenon of Pan-Africanism by sketching its history, trends and development that led to the idea of one Africa. This permits us to discuss Pan-Africanism as an invention of the postcolonial other. But, as a next step, I argue for a new conception of Pan-Africanism by broadening its scope, from a cosmopolitan perspective. This gives us a way forward to deconstruct and reconstruct Pan-Africanism beyond colonialism and othering ideologies, and also think of a new African identity beyond fundamental differences. Finally, I conclude with some implications on this cosmopolitan orientation for the future of political theorizing in Africa and beyond.

What Is Pan-Africanism?

It is not easy to define Pan-Africanism because it has taken on various meanings and manifestations. In spite of the long-standing definitional difficulties that have plagued Pan-Africanism since its inception, W.E.B Dubois defines Pan-Africanism as a socio-cultural phenomenon that emerged for the industrial and spiritual emancipation and an integral promotion of African cultural values (Esedebe, 1994). It is a simultaneously intellectual, cultural, social, political, economic and artistic project that calls for the unification and liberation of all people of African ancestry, both on the African continent and in the African Diaspora (Rabaka, 2020, p. 8). Keisha Blain revealingly wrote:

> In the broadest sense, Pan-Africanism refers to a movement and ideology centered on the belief that peoples of African descent throughout the continent and in the diaspora share a common past and destiny. This shared understanding of the past and future

informs how people of African descent mobilize against racial discrimination, colonialism, and economic, political, social, and cultural oppression. Throughout history, Pan- Africanism has taken on various meanings and manifestations. This includes, but is certainly not limited to, Ethiopianism (race redemption ideas derived from a biblical conception of Ethiopia) and Garveyism (the political teachings of the charismatic Jamaican Black Nationalist Marcus Garvey).Perhaps the most well-known manifestation of Pan-Africanism is the series of Pan-African congresses of the twentieth century (1900–1945), led primarily—but not exclusively—by W. E. B. Du Bois.

(Blain quoted in Vaggalis, "Women, Gender Politics, and Pan-Africanism.")

In spite of the definitional difficulties, Pan-Africanism centres on liberation and integration. Pan-Africanism of liberation is one concerned with the revolt and rupture of colonial historicity and its consequent dehumanization of black people. Pan-Africanism of integration is concerned with the alliance in terms of free trade, economic union, or a homogenous socio-political unit (Mazrui, 1995; Campbell, 1996). Pan-Africanism is therefore a representative discourse of Black experiences; harmonizing these experiences into an ideological unity in order to undermine the imposed colonial condition and generate a new era of socio-political and economic independence (Eze, 2010). Hence, it is neither located on the African continent, nor is it an "elitist-centred" movement (Shepperson, 1953), but one that is a metaphysical sense of unity for all peoples of African origins as inspired by a shared historical memory. The most important early Pan-Africanists were Martín Delaney and Alexander Crummel, both African Americans, and Edward Blyden, a West Indian. They emphasized the commonalities between Africans and Black people in the United States. Delany, who believed that Black people could not prosper alongside whites, advocated the idea that African Americans should separate from the United States and establish their own nation.

Crummel and Blyden, both contemporaries of Delany, thought that Africa was the best place for that new nation. Motivated by Christian missionary zeal, the two believed that Africans in the New World should return to their homelands and convert and civilize the inhabitants there. Although the ideas of Delany, Crummel and Blyden are important, the true father of modern Pan-Africanism was the influential thinker W.E.B. Du Bois who articulated on the Negro problem in America and the effects of European colonial hegemony in Africa. Among the more-important Pan-Africanist thinkers of the first decades of the twentieth century were Jamaican-born Black Nationalist, Marcus Garvey, George Padmore, C.L.R. James, Léopold Sedar Senghor, Aime Cesaire and Jomo Kenyatta. From the 1940s through the 1980s there were prominent thinkers too like Kwame Nkrumah, Julius Nyerere, Sekou Toure etc. Since then, perhaps the most-prominent current of ideas that can be called Pan-Africanist has been the Afrocentrist Movement as espoused by such Black intellectuals as Molefi Asante and Cheikh Anta Diop of Senegal. Michael Eze (2013) summarizes the outcomes of the idea of Pan-Africanism in the following:

(i) an idea of a shared Africana historical consciousness, (ii) intellectual revolt to colonialism and its exploitative ideology, (iii) a sense of socio-political identity different from given impressions of colonialism but grounded in Africa's historical past, (iv) a sense of subjective autonomy culminating in socio-political independence, (v) a vision of history that is typically African in premise, content, context, and conclusion, (vi) a metaphysical sense of unity for all peoples of African origins as inspired by a shared historical memory.

Pan-Africanism as Inventing the Postcolonial Other

In order to better understand a particular concept, ideology or phenomenon such as Pan-Africanism, one must attend to its history, i.e. the developments which led to its formulation. And so, while we can of course engage in dialogues with authors from the past, it is also essential to take into consideration the questions and theoretical or practical needs they were a response to. This would consist in tracing its different steps of historical development across time, focusing both on what changes at each step and on what stays the same.

Pan-Africanism, as a search for Africa's shared historical and cultural identity, is linked to the idea of nationalism, a national imaginary it has inherited (Eze, 2010). Nationalism is the abstract feeling of togetherness, of a shared homogenous empty in time which we identify with the lives, goals and aspirations of countless millions we shall never know, of a "territory which we shall never visit in entirety" (Kohn, 2005, p. 9). The idea of nationalism is essentially based on the relationship between the nation-subject, on the one hand, and the external "other", on the other hand. Hence, nationalism is enhanced by a call to recognize otherness to the point of difference from an "other", from whence the "national" begins to assume an identity, an identity by sameness which is modulated by shared imaginaries (Eze, 2010, p. 5).

As stated above, colonialism thrived through a denial of historical culture to Africans with a false promise of a "civilizing" the barbarian – a strategy that evacuates all possibility of human enterprise. This logic of colonialism, based on the regime of power through colonialist representations (Said, 1978), did not only invent knowledge about "other" people but aimed at justifying the "truth" of their assumptions that became accepted as scientific truths and psychological legitimation for colonialism. This explains why at political independence, colonial discourses were premised on a new discourse of "fictitious fabrication" of the other (Said, 1978; Bhabha, 1994), an invention of an "exotic" other, which resembles a form of narrative whereby the productivity and circulation of subjects and signs are bound in a reformed and recognizable totality... a regime of truth structurally similar to realism (Bhabha, 1994, p. 71), an imposed hegemonic truth without historical veracity or actual verification (Eze, 2010, p. 5). This is what Edward Said meant by Orientalism, an illusory binary construct created by the West to assume a power/knowledge position (Foucault), as the norm and other knowledge systems as inferior. He argues that "the West" created the cultural concept of "the East", which according to Said allowed the Europeans to suppress the peoples of the Middle East, the Indian Subcontinent and Asia in general, from expressing and representing themselves as discrete peoples and cultures. Orientalism thus conflated and reduced the non-Western world into the homogeneous cultural entity known as "the East". Therefore, in service to the colonial type of imperialism, the us-and-them Orientalist paradigm allowed European scholars to represent the Oriental World as inferior and backward, irrational and wild, as opposed to a Western Europe that was superior and progressive, rational and civil—the opposite of the Oriental Other. This acquisition of an empire of overseas colonies influenced the Europeanization of the globe (Ashcroft, Griffiths, &Tiffin 2000), from a metropolitan centre and created distortions negative labelling and deficit binaries of the West and the Colonized Other (Bhabha 1994).

Said's orientation has been endorsed by Valentin Yves Mudimbe whose writings have transformed the intellectual history of Africa by challenging the dominant historic reconstruction of Greek philosophy, which according to him, was racialized. For him, the Western power/knowledge system has had far-reaching implications for the constitution of knowledge about African realities. Mudimbe shows that without critiquing the epistemologies which were the basis of the discourses about Africa critical approaches can become fruitless. He deconstructs the very notion of Africa as a colonial invention aimed at othering the colonized subject, in which the colonial subject becomes implicated in the very process of invention.

He presents colonialism, through the lens of anthropologists, missionaries and colonial adventurists, as a hegemonic project aimed at organizing and transforming non-Europeans areas into fundamentally European constructs. The colonial structure was designed to ensure the domination and marginalization of the colonies. In this way, these structures controlled the spiritual, human and physical aspects of the entire colonizing experience. They denied any attributes of humanity to the colonized peoples, and this dehumanization was achieved by physical and mental violence. This hegemonic relationship is also identifiable in knowledge production in which Europe would pose as a superior location of knowledge, seeking to impose European *cogito* on what they invented as the radical "other". The Colonial Library (*bibliotheque coloniale*) then becomes an instrumental body of knowledge in which the "other" becomes an object to be studied and understood, on the one hand, and a medium in which the other reveals its wholeness to the alluring gaze of a master who guarantees his "civilization; through colonialism, slavery, apartheid, etc. (Eze, 2010, p. 20). It follows, therefore, that knowledge production about Africa is never unbiased but hegemonic or counter-hegemonic—that is, it strengthens a particular hegemonic structure or seeks to destroy that structure. This means that knowledge production is always characterized by the vested interests of those producing it. It is knowledge produced by the "captive mind" (Alatas, 2004), "colonized the minds" (Fanon, 1967; Ngũgĩ wa Thiongo, 1986; Appiah, 1992; Wiredu, 1995), which produce knowledge by uncritically imitating Western research methods and paradigms. Against this conceptual framework, Mudimbe largely leans on the works of French philosophers such as Derrida and Foucault and the French sociologist Bourdieu for his archaeological constructions. For example, he uses Foucault's paradigm of power/knowledge to deconstruct the Eurocentric invention of Africa. Said (1978) argues that power and knowledge are central in the way Occidentals claim to have knowledge of the Orient. It is this knowledge that allowed Occidentals to change the Orient into imperial colonies. This power/knowledge binary relation is vital for our understanding of colonialism, and it shows us that the thought patterns in Africa, Europe and Asia can hardly be neutral relative to the hegemonic or counter-hegemonic representations of power. The former colonized and marginalized people are stripped off their knowledge and belief systems and replaced them with that of the colonizers. Following this power imbalance, Mudimbe argues that:

> The history of knowledge in Africa and about Africa appears deformed and disjointed, and the explanation lies in its own origin and development.
>
> *(Mudimbe, 1988, p.175)*

Consequently, Western colonialism and its hegemonic influence on knowledge production of Africa provoked Negro activism as we see in Pan-Africanism and Negritude. The term "Negro" means "black" in both Spanish and Portuguese, where English took it from. It was a derogatory, racialized term used to classify persons of black African heritage during the colonial era.

Michael Eze (2010, p. 23) notes that Pan-Africanism, Negritude, Black Consciousness Movement, etc. will all become categorized as African discourses of and ideology of otherness. Contrary to such models of otherness that are closed, and based on the confines of a culture, in the sections that follow, I propose an open and globalized Pan-Africanism based on intercultural exchanges.

Rethinking Pan-Africanism in Contemporary Intellectual History of Africa

Michael Eze (2010) makes an interesting critique of Pan-African historicism. His main argument is that it rests upon the assumption of a pristine, homogenous memory of a historical unanimity and as such misconceives the reality of Africa. It projects African's social imaginary as one which can only be validated through a paradigm of difference to the Western "other". It argues, not for an African philosophy and history by analogy, but for a creative historicism that is intellectually elastic and politically plural (Rabaka, 2020). According to Eze (2010, p. 13), the analytical model of historicity exhibits the following character: *Inversion:* challenging colonialist discourses and representations through a differentiating order of "otherness" or negation of the colonial "other" and "order". *Redemptive teleology:* Africa's intellectual history would conjecture a redemption of Africa's subjectivity through historical enactment, an instantaneous narrative in which Africa is promoted as a superior location of knowledge, an authentic bastion of subjectivity through discourse reversal and historical analogy. *Paradigm of difference:* a discourse reversal that mutates into a dualistic disjunctive: (1) the admiration for an idealized past and a lethargic feeling or longing for such a past, and (2) fashioned as a displacement narrative to colonial discourse that destroyed life patterns. *Historical analogy:* an invention of Africa through an alien epistemological paradigm that de-historicizes the subject insofar as it is a "given" historicism and by extension insensitive to context.

Hence, according to Eze, if we proceed from the Pan-African historiography by analogy, we realize that it not only suffocates the different cultural memories of Africa, but also produces a false consciousness and conceptual blunders which becomes an identity reservoir to preserve the illusion of continuity with an idealized past and becomes a tool for political domination. This is a very similar critique Paulin Hountondji makes against ethnophilosophy. He thinks that ethnophilosophy is an ideological myth because it has to account for an imaginary unanimity…that nowhere exists and has to be constantly reinvented. He reveals that Tempels' *Bantu Philosophy* was meant for a foreign audience in a bid to satisfy ideological aspirations (Hountondji, 1996, pp. 50–62).

In this way, knowledge is formulated in an alien format, where identity and difference remain given to the African "other", who assimilates these narratives within a given paradigm of Western episteme. Africa is conceived and treated in isolation from the West with a fantasized alterity that provokes an emotional unity in the name of Pan-Africanism. This emotional unity creates a community and extols the common good, public interest, collective attachment and respect for tradition. This community attaches much worth to group loyalty, patriotism and seeks to establish a close-knit, self-contained, family-like, social units based in a particular locality, culture, politics and philosophy is prevalent and somewhat natural. This explains why national boundaries are morally relevant and take priority as moral commitments. This is because the cultures, traditions and social conditions a person is born in and grows up with make us who we are. They deeply shape us and give us the framework through which we see the world, ourselves, others, morality, politics, and our duties and obligations. Since the community provides us with our values, and it is the source of values, it is to be protected, sustained and valued highly and it is where our responsibilities squarely lie.

We may cite the impact of the anthropological discourse on African ethnicity largely influenced by colonialism. This discourse was based on closed entities, cultural pluralism and separateness of cultures with no room for finding a common ground. In this way, the population of Africa is arranged into different "tribes", each tribe having its own fixed "culture", art, language, somatic features, political organization (including "tribal chief") and "tribal territory". If we rely on this anthropological discourse on African ethnicity, which hinges on differences all we can have is more ethnic divisiveness, conflicts and violence than is already there in Africa. Moreover such difference also offers an illusive character of a homogenous racial enemy and closes the possibilities for creative dialogue (Appiah, 1992, p. 285).

Pan-Africanism from a Cosmopolitan Perspective

Cosmopolitanism today is widely growing and possibly rivals globalization and transnationalism as a focus for research in fields of research in the social and human sciences. In its broadest sense cosmopolitanism pertains to the extension of the moral and political horizons of people, societies, organizations and institutions. It implies an attitude of openness instead of closure. It is the belief that human beings belong to the same community and that they have a responsibility towards each other. Cosmopolitanism does not go against prevailing conditions, but thrives on our interconnected globalizing conditions and recommends that within this condition we need to look for solutions to our global problems while taking into consideration the perspectives of others beyond our own context. These solutions to global problems are not found in a predetermined, an absolute category, but should be seen as potentials within the present; a dimension of social life that must be actively constructed through practices of meaning-making in social situations. Cosmopolitanism is grounded on the premise that human beings belong to the same community and that they have a responsibility towards each other. The heart of cosmopolitanism is the concern for another person's pain and suffering. It argues that the desire to act in order to relieve another person's misery and distress is a common human response and not abstract.

The word "cosmopolitan" is a combination of "cosmos" which means "world" and "polites" which means "citizen" and comes from "polis" the Greek word for city. It means a citizen of the world. It suggests identifying with the whole of humanity rather than with a particular place, nation, or people. A cosmopolitan thinker is one who is free from local, provincial, or national ideas, biases, prejudices, or attachments and being familiar with and interested in many cultures.

The first philosopher to use this expression was Diogenes the Cynic, a Greek philosopher, who was born in the Black Sea Greek colony of Sinope (modern-day Sinop in Turkey) and was a contemporary of Plato. According to Diogenes Laertius (early Third Century A.D.), "When the question was put to him what country he was from, he replied, I am a citizen of the world" (The Lives VI 6).13 Martha C. Nussbaum argues that by this answer "Diogenes meant that he refused to be defined simply by his local origins and group memberships, associations central to the image of a conventional male [citizen]; he insisted on defining himself in terms of more universal aspirations and concerns" (Nussbaum, 1997, p. 52). Consequently, cosmopolitanism focuses in the idea on the idea of citizen of the world and its development. The Stoics expanded the Hellenic cosmopolitanism of Diogenes and gave it content and a firm basis with their concepts of rationality and virtue. For the Stoics, identifying oneself as a cosmopolitan suggested a kind of uniting oneself with the whole of humankind and brought about a greater sense of comradeship. So for them, its use promoted peaceful and harmonious co-existence with other human beings. During the Enlightenment, the authority of reason came to prominence along with the idea that every person has some measure of reason. The new weight and influence of reason and science ushered in values such as free inquiry, openness and tolerance. The Enlightenment was also an age of democracy and freedom, both of which underline human equality. And the idea of allegiance to humanity came to prominence in these circumstances. The idea of oneness and interconnectedness of humanity is central to Kantian ethical and political thinking. In his *Groundwork of the Metaphysics of Morals* (1785), Kant defends universality as a test for determining the rightness of actions. He puts the ultimate moral value on humanity as an end in itself and demands that we never treat others as a means to an end. Universality is also a prominent feature of Kant's conception of justice, which he thinks must be cosmopolitan. In *Perpetual Peace: A Philosophical Sketch* (1795), he advocates for what is needed for achieving a peaceful world, and exhorts all states to protect the basic rights and their citizens and must have a republican constitution. Kant's cosmopolitan right stems from an understanding of all human beings as equal members of a universal community.

Cosmopolitan right thus works in conjunction with international political rights, and the shared, universal right of humanity. This is because, given our increasing interconnectedness, violation of human rights in one state is felt throughout the globe. The respect for these shared political rights across humanity, according to Kant, would serve as guiding principles to help global society achieve permanent, enduring peaceful and harmonious co-existence with other human beings. This shows the practical relevance of a cosmopolitan idea of international law and world citizenship. Following Diogenes, the Stoics and Kant, the political philosophy of cosmopolitanism has always upheld the spirit of openness and a perspective of the world that emphasizes uniting oneself with the whole of humankind, the extension of the bonds of inclusivity. It focuses on shared values and ideas that can bring together our common humanity, how we should relate to each other as human beings and how to perceive our connections with each other. It brings forth the idea that every human being is an equal member of the human community and generates certain universal moral obligations. It entails obligations, duties that have a universal scope; that we must treat each other well and to look out for each other. This is where Levinas and Derrida, for example, ground their foundation of moral universal obligations: to respond to the Other. In Being for the Other, Levinas writes that there is no *a priori* "universal moral law", only the sense of duty for goodness, mercy and charity that the Other, in a state of vulnerability, requires. The proximity of the Other is an important part of Levinas's concept: the face of the Other is what compels the response (1999/1974). For Derrida, the foundation of ethics is hospitality, the readiness and the inclination to welcome the Other into one's home. Ethics, he claims, is hospitality. Pure, unconditional hospitality is a desire that underscores the conditional hospitality necessary in our relationships with others (Derrida 1999, 2000). And these cosmopolitan virtues are what Kwame Appiah (2006) proposes if we have to live together in peace in today's multicultural societies. He urges us to consider these virtues which recognize the worth of each human being no matter where they live and that everybody is entitled to have their basic needs met. For Appiah, there are a plurality of values and perspectives, and that moral and cultural issues are subject to disputation within every society as well as across societies. Living together peacefully requires that we engage in the practice of "conversation across boundaries of identity – whether national, religious, or something else" (Appiah, 2006, p. 85). These conversations, according to Appiah, "begin with the sort of engagement you get when you read a novel or watch a movie or attend to a work of art that speaks from some place other than your own" (Appiah, 2006, p. 85). He adds: "conversation doesn't have to lead to consensus about anything, especially not values; it's enough that it helps people get used to one another" (Appiah, 2006, p. 85). Hence, through many cross-cultural conversations and debates, what he calls cosmopolitan curiosity (Appiah, 2006, p. 97), we get to understand the position of each other. He asserts that

> The points of entry to cross-cultural conversations are things that are shared by those who are in the conversation…. Once we have found enough we share, there is the further possibility that we will be able to enjoy discovering things we do not yet share. That is one of the payoffs of cosmopolitan curiosity. We can learn from on another; or we can simply be intrigued by alternative ways of thinking, feeling, and acting.
>
> *(Appiah, 2006, p. 97)*

The revival of cosmopolitanism thought today has to do with the tremendous changes that occurred in the 1990s in the aftermath of the end of communism in the USSR and Central and Eastern Europe. In this period we also saw the end of Apartheid in South Africa, The Tiananmen Square Movement, movements towards the democratization of the Arab world, the internet, all brought cosmopolitan appeal as framework of interpretation. In this light, Pan-Africanism ought to take into consideration an understanding of major social and political changes across the world, shifts in the social imaginaries of societies and the emergence of ethical and political responses to global changes. Hence it is an expansion of the space for Pan-Africanism, a new way of imagining the dynamics of Pan-Africanism as cosmopolitanism embodies universal norms and values and it is often criticized on the same grounds. And this is precisely where critical questions pertaining to the definitional difficulties, intellectual elasticity and political plurality of Pan-Africanism emerge (Rabaka, 2020).

Nevertheless, there have been criticisms or anti-cosmopolitan movements too. Many critics think that cosmopolitanism rejects real communities, is politically abstract, lacks contents (Walzer, 1996) and de-contextualized to have relevance (Caney, 2006; Calhoun, 2007) and is more likely to rob us of our concreteness and immediacy as it offers little or nothing for the psyche to fasten on (Barber, 1996). Gertrude Himmelfarb is also sceptical about whether there are any substantive, universal, common values, "specifically, concretely, and existentially". She argues that cosmopolitan values of justice, reason, rights and love of humanity are not universal values, but "they are in fact predominately, perhaps even uniquely, Western". She stresses that cosmopolitanism is utopian… "an illusion, and, like all illusions, perilous" (Himmelfarb, 1996, pp. 72–77).

Another critique could be that it is another theory from the West, originating from the Stoics through Kant to Levinas, hence a Western approach to history and modernity. Nevertheless, is cosmopolitanism un-cosmopolitan because it originates from the West? Should we ignore the historical experiences of non-western parts of the world? In spite of these criticisms, cosmopolitanism looks plausible as an open-ended approach that is not based on a fixed set of values but which upholds universal values for humanity. Moreover, it is also endorsed by the rights of groups that were previously excluded from political communities, minorities, marginal groups and it is very much bounded with dissent and protest. It is produced by de-colonialism in the Global South (Mignolo) Appiah talks of rooted cosmopolitanism (2010) meaning to be embedded in a specific history, nation or people; to be a cosmopolitan is to declare oneself a citizen of the world. For Appiah, however, these two are inseparable. Local histories, he reminds us, have themselves been shaped by the movements of peoples and their communal practices (let's not call them cultures) as old as human history itself. The implication is that one can pledge allegiance to one's country and still conceive of oneself in terms of global identities or universal values. Hence for Appiah, without a deeply felt commitment to the local, there can be no genuine sense of obligation to the universal and vice versa. This can be facilitated by conversations that are to take place in a world, as we struggle to negotiate the "global village" of the contemporary world, where multiple affiliations are increasingly becoming the norm.

Hence what cosmopolitanism enriches Pan-Africanism with are not hybridity or homogeneity (Bhabha, 1994; Spivak, 1999) but an overlap, a creative interaction of cultural orientations (van Binsbergen, 2003; Mosima, 2016) and an exploration of shared worlds. In this era of globalization characterized by migration, integration, trade, ICT, the boundaries and borders between countries and cultural orientations are becoming blurred. For people to cooperate and live together it is crucial that we understand each other. It is vital for the inevitably interconnected future of all human beings that cross-cultural dialogue and mutual understanding be given a rethought. This gives us the opportunity to rethink or reconsider a bigger picture of Pan-Africanism.

More and more, another generation of African migrant writers is beginning to question those ideologies and to recover alternative narratives of African identity in search of a "hermeneutics of redemption" (Webb, 2001). In their writings, the idea of Afropolitanism, as a new form of African cosmopolitanism, constitutes a significant attempt to rethink African identity outside the trope of difference and isolation (Selasi, 2009; Mbembe, 2020; Eze, 2014; 2016, 2021).

Deconstructing and Reconstructing Pan-Africanism beyond Colonialism and Othering Ideologies

Pan-Africanism needs to continuously reinvent itself and that self-reinvention is not to be separated from the question of Africa's self-reinvention in this context in a bid to create new meaning. This implies a new version of Pan-Africanism, which could be considered as a philosophical foundation of black solidarity in all spheres of life, beyond the physical continent and beyond binaries like black /white, Africa /Europe, Afrocentrism/Eurocentrism. It calls for Black solidarity between Africans and the African Diaspora in their common response to the situation of submission to colonialism and racism (an oppressive colonial order) on the one hand, and the emotional cultural unity (Community and Identity). First of all, it entails a counter-hegemonic, decolonizing, inclusive and interdisciplinary approach in which the impact of colonialism and othering ideologies are radically interrogated in a constant power struggle between the interests and ways of knowing of the West and that of the "colonized Other" (Chilisa, 2020, pp. 9–16). The notion of colonized Other emphasizes the fact that the communities described still suffer scientific colonization as well as colonization of the mind (Ngũgĩ wa Thiong'o, 1986; Wiredu, 1995). Rediscovery and Recovery refers to the process where the colonized Other rediscover and recover their own history, culture, language and identity. It is a process of interrogating the captive mind so that the colonized Other and the historically oppressed such as women, the deaf, children, the disabled and the elderly are able to define in their own terms what is real to them. They can also define their own rules on what can be known, spoken, written about them, how when and where.

Rethinking Pan-African Identity Beyond Fundamental Differences

We also need to liberate ourselves from the incarcerating conception of identity. The idea of a Pan-African consciousness as conceived by Africans and Diaspora blacks for much of the nineteenth and twentieth centuries was based on the experiences of racism, exclusion, marginalization due to the corrosive effects of slavery, colonialism and neo-colonialism. This consciousness was a survival strategy with the vision of an eventual triumph and regaining an African identity with the view that such an identity was fundamentally, different and distinctive from that of the colonial masters. The vision was that the answers to ethical and political problems and to some extent the question of identity can be found in this community and community values and commitments. Yet, this vision downplayed the massive cultural continuities through space and time, on a transcontinental scale, and profoundly involving Africa. Under postmodern conditions typical of globalization, North Atlantic societies, too, have experienced large-scale erosion of meaning and consensus, the blurring of binarism between Africa and the North Atlantic region, fragmentation of identity and erosion of the nation-state by elusive intercontinental corporate powers in the economic domain. In Africa ICT, has brought the forms of African socio-cultural life closer to those in other continents today. Increasingly the neat compartmentalization of the world into continents has become an idea of the past, and the concerns of North Atlantic political, ideological and economic hegemony and of Islamic counter-hegemony have found their way to what used to be distinct and distant local settings in Africa. Moreover, the religious, ethnic and cultural expressions which used to be restricted to local settings in Africa, in the course of recent globalization have spilled over to African communities across the globe. Recent technologies make it possible for local African religious and artistic expressions to assume a new global and commodified format. This offers them a new lease of life albeit that in the process they have become greatly transformed, shedding much of their original local symbolic frame of reference. For the first time in post-Neolithic history, distinctive local and regional African religious expressions (music, dance, divination, specific cults and spirituality) have gained a substantial presence and impact in the North Atlantic also among people not of recent conscious African descent. The latter effect is caused both by the increasingly diasporic demographic presence of Africans, and by their appropriation of recent communication technologies also for the expression of local (and not just global) religious ideas and practices and points to a new collective shared meaning not just in Africa but the rest of the world (van Binsbergen, 2004)

With globalization, cosmopolitanism and the growth of hybridization such an approach of conceiving identity, which is largely an ideological construct, has become problematic and obsolete. Identity is a complex process of becoming; a very fluid process and evolutive spaces that replicate experiences of the in-between. It is therefore difficult to argue for a monolithic, glorified African experience as one where there was no conflict, resistance and struggle. I think that this kind of veneration of community is to a large extent just a yearning for simplicity, purity, certainty and absolutes. However, this is an attempt to give a simple answer to complex questions and issues by locating them in a familiar and ordinary place, a place where there is no conflict of values, commitments and obligations. But in reality, there is no such place or refuge.

Moreover, problems of multiple overlapping identities and loyalties come up and it is very important to pay enough attention to African identities. There are a lot of diverse kinds of demands and pressures on the contemporary self. There are many diverse ways of living, values and commitments, and many competing voices vying for our attention. Many people now live with and amongst peoples of a variety of different backgrounds and nationalities. All of this can be too much for the individual to cope with and may bring on a lot of anxiety and worries. This in turn can lead the individual to long for a safe space that is untouched by these competing voices that are making claims on us. Similarly, we may posit an emotional unity and identity as a solution to the supposed problems of fragmentation of culture and the self by recourse to a Pan-African community, tradition, culture, place and roots. But it is important to recognize that there is no site, which is free from conflict and disagreement. There is no site of absolute belonging. There are no forms of solidarity that could make one feel completely whole, take all our insecurities away, and overcome the disunity of the contemporary self. Moreover, nostalgia for home leaves us unprepared to deal with the complexities of life, different and critical points of view, and social and political conflicts. Hence it becomes problematic to continue framing Pan-African nationalism even as globalization shrinks and erodes the boundaries of race and ethnicity on which such nationalism had thrived in the past.

So, is it not time to look at new meanings of and for Africa? Meanings that could be newly constructed and imbued with more progressive images for action and transformation which transcend earlier meanings of Africa? Emmanuel Eze (2001) exhorts us to create meaning beyond the African particularity as a viable strategy towards achieving our humanity. Even though the idea of an African unity and identity is an emotional, seductive imagination (the earlier meanings were to transform and transcend the corrosive effects of colonialism, slavery and racism on the Africans), it is time to reconstruct our cultural, social identities by integrating global challenges and opportunities. It is one that reimagines the African in a broader, richer field beyond mere geographic reference to include Africans in the diaspora. This is because the new African identity is hybrid, creole and ever-changing which needs to encompass this promising universal perspective. The key to, as cosmopolitanism evokes, is in transcending particularistic traditions, cultivating broad and international perspectives in African thinking. It is crucial in counterbalancing the nativistic and nationalistic tendencies that prevent one from realizing the full scale of our contemporary experiences in a bid to recreate and reinvent our identities.

Pan-Africanism may be a cultural and political phenomenon that regards Africa, Africans and African descendants abroad as a unit, but one must also recognize the different local historical contexts of its emergence. This means we need to broaden the scope of Pan-Africanism to include even the diaspora. Yet this idea of one Africa should be rooted from below couched in an African renaissance that seeks to redefine the African self by invoking a cultural tradition as a challenge to the logic of coloniality and seek a revival of the African spirit and image through a reenactment of an assumed era of a pristine paradise and its celebration thereof. The longing of an African renaissance, in this sense, becomes a prophetic symbol for a future generation of Africa. It is not a call for a homogenous retrieval of every detail of our cultural history and its associated discontinuities but a rehabilitation of the goods internal to the past historical narratives and practices of our community in a bid to complement the task of nation building, restoring civic virtues, promoting civic right and responsibilities and enhancing democratic humanism. Furthermore, Eze proposes an anti-essentialist, dynamic inclusive and accommodating idea of an African renaissance and identity. The "African" is an individual, a member of an "ethnic" group whose identity interfaces with that of others as a global citizen (Eze, 2010, pp. 181–182). Consequently, the new Pan-African identity entails venturing beyond one's own chosen boundaries, regardless of whether such boundaries are defined in a geographical, an identitary, a disciplinary, or a logico-conceptual one. The new home is nowhere, the new boundary is situational and constructed, and the new identity is performative (Mosima, 2016, 14).

Conclusion

Throughout this chapter, I have argued that Pan-Africanism, as an ideology, a concept and a phenomenon has been instrumental in decolonization of the continent and the improved position of Africans in the diaspora. Nevertheless, there is an urgent need for a critical appraisal of twenty-first-century Pan-Africanism. I have asserted that if Pan-Africanism has to be relevant in the twenty-first century and beyond, it needs to cross the boundaries of colonialist discourses, be willing to question its methodology, and articulate it from the contemporary global realities and within a broader intellectual tradition of renewal. This, I think is really, hard work: But it can and should be done. Doing so will help Westerners liberate themselves from oppressive, hegemonic frames of thought they have inherited—even though they might not have been aware of- and also encourage Africans to adopt a non-essentialist conception of being African. I have also argued for a non-essentialist, intersubjective and creative approach that different "traditions" meet and create something new instead of withdrawing into demarcation and involution. The national-cultural qualifiers inherent in our vision of Africa can be important and practically helpful in decolonization but should not be the end goal of cultural and intellectual pursuits. In this sense, I regret that decolonization movements around the world often led to nationalist movements instead of the fundamental emancipation of human beings from the notions of "nationality" and "identity". These notions should always be seen as work in progress to be constantly enriched with new encounters and new relationships, and never to be confined by geography, political or disciplinary boundaries. Moreover, the broader conception and expression of Pan-Africanism and the consciousness that is fundamental to it should not merely be expressed by radicals, social leaders, politicians and intellectuals, but also by, folk artists, filmmakers, novelists, playwrights, poets, painters, dancers, musicians and highlighting Pan-African women and their struggles against sexism and for gender justice. The new idea of Pan-Africanism must give continental and the global African family the tools they need to practice self-reliance and solve their own (and global) problems. We must remind ourselves that many of the most pressing challenges of our time (climate change, refugee crises, financial and economic crises, the rise of nationalist movements, terrorism etc.) are global. This approach, hopefully, will keep with the overarching international, intersectional and interdisciplinary/transdisciplinary approach to Pan-Africanism that Rabaka (2020) suggests. Moreover, the implications of a cosmopolitan imagination of Pan-Africanism for future political thought in Africa could bring in new perspectives on debates about remaking today's international order. This would mean remaking not only African nations but the world as a whole (Getachew 2019). Adom Getachew makes the interesting claims that those anticolonial visions of self-determination, as seen in the political thoughts of Nnamdi Azikiwe, W.E. B. Du Bois, George Padmore, Kwame Nkrumah, Eric Williams, Michael Manley and Julius Nyerere, exceeded the national frame and were, first and foremost, projects of remaking the international order. These thinkers, according to Getachew, had world-making aspirations and projects that they viewed as necessary to securing independence after empire. Consequently, African political theorizing, leaning on the works of Pan-Africanist thinkers cited above, should be a reconsideration of decolonization and Pan-Africanism from a world of nations to a post-imperial world order. This would require revising the rapport between sovereignty and empire, critiquing the racialized international hierarchy created by empire, and celebrating the cosmopolitan emphasis on the moral dignity of persons with attention to collective claims of independence and non-domination.

References

Alatas, Syed H. 'The Captive Mind and Creative Development', in: *Indigeneity and Universality in Social Science: A South Asian Response*, Partha N. Mukherji and Chandan Sengupta (eds.). New Delhi: Sage Publication, 2004, pp. 83–98.

Appiah, Kwame A. *In My Father's House: Africa in the Philosophy of Culture*. Oxford: Oxford University Press, 1992.

Appiah, Kwame A. *Cosmopolitanism: Ethics in a World of Strangers*. New York: W.W. Norton & Co., 2006.

Appiah, Kwame A. *The Ethics of Identity*. Princeton, NJ: Princeton University Press, 2010.

Barber, Benjamin R. 'Constitutional Faith', in: *For Love of Country? Debating the Limits of Patriotism*, Martha Craven Nussbaum and Joshua Cohen (eds.). Boston, MA: Beacon, 1996, pp. 30–37.

Bhabha, Homi K. *The Location of Culture*. New York: Routledge, 1994.

Brelsford, William V. *Primitive Philosophy*. London: John Bale, Sons and Danielson, 1935.

Brelsford, William V. *The Philosophy of the Savage*. London: John Bale, Sons and Danielson, 1938.

Calhoun, Craig J. *Nations Matter: Culture, History, and the Cosmopolitan Dream*. New York: Routledge, 2007.

Campbell, Horace. 'Pan Africanism in the Twenty-First Century', in: *Pan Africanism: Politics, Economy and Social Change in the Twenty-First Century*, Tajudeen Abdul-Raheem (ed.). New York: New York University Press, 1996.

Caney, Simon, *Justice Beyond Borders: A Global Political Theory*. Oxford: Oxford University Press, 2006.

Chilisa, Bagele. *Indigenous Research Methodologies*. Second Edition. Los Angeles, CA: Sage Publications, 2020.

Derrida, Jacques. *Adieu to Emmanuel Levinas*. P.-A. Brault & M. Naas (trans.). Stanford, CA: Stanford University Press, 1999.

Derrida, Jacques. *Of Hospitality*. R. Bowlby (trans.). Stanford, CA: Stanford University Press, 2000.

Diogenes Laertius. *The Lives and Opinions of Eminent Philosophers*. C.D. Yonge (trans). http://www.classicpersuasion.org/pw/diogenes.

Esedebe, Peter. O. *Pan-Africanism: The Idea and Movement, 1776–1991*. Washington, DC: Howard University Press, 1994.

Eze, Chukwudi E. *Achieving Our Humanity: The Idea of the Postracial Future*. New York: Routledge, 2001.

Eze, Chielozona. 'Rethinking African Culture and Identity: The Afropolitan Model'. *Journal of African Cultural Studies*, Vol.26, No.2. (2014), pp. 234–247.

Eze, Chielozona. 'We, Afropolitans'. *Journal of African Cultural Studies*, Vol.28, No.1 (March, 2016), pp. 114–119.

Eze, Chielozona. *Justice and Human Rights in the African Imagination: We, Too, Are Humans* (1st ed.). London: Routledge, 2021.

Eze, Michael, O. *Intellectual History in Contemporary South Africa*. New York: Palgrave Macmillan, 2010.

Eze, Michael, O. 'Pan-Africanism and the Politics of History'. *History Compass* Vol.11, No.9, (September 2013), pp. 675–686.

Eze, Michael, O. *The Politics of History in Contemporary Africa*. New York: Palgrave Macmillan, 2018.

Fanon, Frantz. *Black Skin, White Masks*. New York, NY: Grove, 1967.

Getachew, Adom. *Worldmaking after Empire: The Rise and Fall of Self-Determination*. Princeton, NJ: Princeton University Press, 2019.

Himmelfarb, Gertrude. 'The Illusions of Cosmopolitanism', in: *For Love of Country? Debating the Limits of Patriotism*. Martha Craven Nussbaum and Joshua Cohen (eds.). Boston, MA: Beacon, 1996, pp. 72–77.

Hountondji, Paulin J. *African Philosophy: Myth and Reality*. Second Edition. Bloomington/Indianapolis: Indiana University Press; this English translation first published in 1983; first French edition published in 1976, 1996.

Kant, Immanuel. *Grounding for the Metaphysics of Morals*. James W. Ellington (trans.) [1785], Third Edition. Indianapolis, IN: Hackett, 1993.

Kant, Immanuel. *Perpetual Peace: a Philosophical Sketch*. Ted Humphrey (trans.). Indianapolis: Hackett Publishing, 2003[1795].

Kohn, Hans. *The Idea of Nationalism: A Study in its Origins and Background*. New Brunswick: Transaction Publishers, 2005.

Lévinas, Emmanuel. *Otherwise Than Being, or, Beyond Essence*. Alphonso Lingis (trans.). Pittsburg, Pennsylvania: Duquesne University Press, 1999 [1974].

Lévy-Brühl, Lucien. *Les fonctions mentales dans les sociétés inférieures*. Paris: Alcan; translated into English in 1926, *How Natives Think*. London: Allen & Unwin, 1910.

Masolo, Dismas A. *African Philosophy in Search of Identity.* Bloomington/Indianapolis: Indiana University Press/ Edinburgh: Edinburgh University Press, 1994.

Mazrui, Ali. 'Pan-Africanism: From Poetry to Power'. *African Studies Association: A Journal of Opinion,* Vol.23, No.1 (1995), pp. 35–38.

Mbembe, Achille. 'Afropolitanism', in *Africa Remix: Contemporary Art of a Continent,* Simon Njami and Lucy Duran (eds.) Johannesburg: Johannesburg Art Gallery, pp. 22–30.

Mosima, Pius M. *Philosophic Sagacity and Intercultural Philosophy: Beyond Henry Odera Oruka.* Leiden: African Studies Center, 2016.

Mudimbe, Valentin Y. *The Invention of Africa: Gnosis, Philosophy, and the Order of Knowledge.* Bloomington/Indianapolis/London: Indiana University Press/Currey, 1988.

Mudimbe, Valentin Y. *The Idea of Africa.* Bloomington/London: Indiana University Press/Currey, 1994.

Ngũgĩ wa Thiong'o. *Decolonizing the Mind: The Politics of Language in African Literature.* London: Portsmouth, N.H.: James Currey: Heinemann, 1986.

Nussbaum, Martha C. 'Kant and Cosmopolitanism', in *Perpetual Peace: Essays on Kant's Cosmopolitan Ideal,* James Bohman and Matthias Lutz-Bachmann (eds.). Cambridge: MIT Press, 1997, pp. 25–57.

Oruka, Henry O. 'The Fundamental Principles in the Question of 'African philosophy'. *Second Order: An African Journal of Philosophy,* Vol.4, No.1 (1975), pp. 44–55.

Oruka, Henry O. *Trends in Contemporary African Philosophy.* Nairobi: Shirikon, 1990.

Rabaka, Railand. *Introduction from: Routledge Handbook of Pan-Africanism,* 2020. Accessed on: 16 June 2021. https://doi.org/10.4324/9780429020193

Said, Edward. *Orientalism.* New York: Pantheon Books, 1978.

Selasi, Taiye. 'Bye-bye, Babar (Or: What Is an Afropolitan?),' in: *The International Review of African American Art,* Vol.22, No.3 (2009), pp. 36–38.

Shepperson, George. 'Ethiopianism and African Nationalism'. *Phylon,* Vol.14, No.1 (1953), pp. 346–358.

Spivak, Gayatri C. *A Critique of Postcolonial Reason: Toward a History of the Vanishing Present.* Cambridge, MA: Harvard University Press, 1999.

Tempels, Placide. *Bantu Philosophy.* Paris: Présence Africaine. First published as Tempels, P., 1955, *Bantoe-filosofie.* Antwerpen: De Sikkel, 1959.

Van Binsbergen, W.M.J. *Intercultural Encounters: African and Anthropological Lessons Towards a Philosophy of Interculturality.* Berlin/Boston/Muenster: LIT, 2003.

Van Binsbergen, W.M.J. 'Challenges for the Sociology of Religion in the African Context: Prospects for the Next 50 Years'. *Social Compass,* Vol.51, No.1 (2004), pp. 85–98.

Walzer, Michael. 'Spheres of Affection', in *For Love of Country?* Martha C. Nussbaum and Joshua Cohen (eds.). Boston, MA: Beacon, 1996, pp. 125–127.

Webb, William J. *Slaves, Women & Homosexuals: Exploring the Hermeneutics of Cultural Analysis.* Downers Grove: Inter Varsity Press, 2001.

Wiredu, Kwasi. *Conceptual Decolonization in African Philosophy: Four Essays.* Ibadan: Hope Publications, 1995.

27

POLITICAL PHILOSOPHY IN THE GLOBAL SOUTH

Harmony in Africa, East Asia, and South America

Thaddeus Metz

Comparing Political Philosophies Beyond the West

It is fairly common these days for a given political perspective from the Global South to be put into comparison with one from the 'modern' West. In particular, now it is not hard to find, say, an *ubuntu*-based account of distributive justice or Confucian theory of political power compared with Kantian democratic liberalism.

What is more rare is a direct comparison between accounts from the Global South, without the large mediation of a modern Western variable. This state of affairs is in some ways ironic, given how 'WEIRD' Kantian rights, utilitarian cost-benefit analysis, and social contract theory are. This acronym is often used to signify, not only the traits of being Western, Educated, Industrialized, Rich, and Democratic but also ones that are amongst the least representative of the world's population (eg, Henrich et al). It is unfortunate that global thought about political philosophy is dominated by perspectives that grow out of Euro-American-Australasian cultures, which are in the numerical minority and do not cohere well with the views of many long-standing intellectual traditions, which presumably have some insight into the human condition. What might we learn from South–South dialogues about the proper role of political organization?

If one considers worldviews beyond the modern West, at least as expressed in English-speaking literature (to which this essay is restricted), one encounters philosophies of politics that differ dramatically from salient Western ones. For many indigenous peoples, neither autonomy, utility, nor contract should be deemed foundational to politics, and, instead, 'harmony is mother of all values' (Bell and Mo). It is typical for philosophies from the Global South to hold that a political organization at the domestic level should harmonize with its citizens, foster harmonious relationships between them, and also promote such relationships between citizens and certain aspects of nature.

However, harmony is neglected in internationally influential philosophical discussions about rights, power, and other facets of public policy; it is not prominent in articles that appear in widely read journals or books published by presses with a global reach (although there are of course sprinkles, on which I draw here). Of particular interest, political philosophers and policy-makers remain ignorant of the similarities and differences between various harmony-oriented approaches to institutional choice from around the world.

DOI: 10.4324/9781003143529-32

In this chapter, I begin to rectify these deficiencies by critically discussing the way harmony has figured into political philosophies from three major traditions in the Global South, namely, African *ubuntu* (humanness in the Nguni languages there), East Asian Confucianism, and South American *buen vivir* (good living in Spanish). I point out that, although harmony is at the core of all three political philosophies, it is conceived in different ways, entailing incompatible prescriptions about things such as who should make laws and which sorts of beings have rights against the state. Such contrasting views call for rigorous cross-cultural dialogue amongst theorists of harmony, beyond mounting challenges to more individualist approaches that have been salient in modern Western political thought. While there have been comparisons of *ubuntu* and Confucianism (Bell and Metz; Anedo; Metz 2014, 2020) and *ubuntu* and *buen vivir* (Graness; van Norren), there have not been any of all three, let alone in terms of their conceptions of harmony and their bearing on political philosophy.

Note that, when expounding the conceptions of harmony that have been prominent in the three Global Southern bodies of thought, I downplay appeals to imperceptible agency or a spiritual realm. For instance, I spell out *ubuntu* harmony without reference to ancestors and Confucian harmony without mentioning Heaven. I do this in part because contemporary philosophical exponents writing in English are generally not placing such considerations at the heart of their analyses, and in part because setting aside contested metaphysical claims would make it easier to facilitate cross-cultural debate about moral-political ones.

In the next section 'Harmony as an Ethical Orientation', I briefly provide a broad analysis of what a harmony-based moral-political orientation is, contrasting it with those that have been prominent in the West for the past few hundred years. Then I spell out three different conceptions of harmony and their implications for politics from the Global South (Sections 'African *Ubuntu*', 'East Asian Confucianism', and 'South American *Buen Vivir*'). Finally, I suggest some ways forward for scholarship in regards to non-Western political philosophies that appeal to harmony, particularly in the light of their differences, after which I briefly summarize (Section 'Comparing Three Political Philosophies from the Global South').

Harmony as an Ethical Orientation

Although I focus on respects in which conceptions of harmony in the Global South differ and have competing implications for politics, it is worth pausing to consider how they are similar. What makes a value system harmony-based? How does such an ethic differ from others that have been prominent in English-speaking political philosophy?

Although the focus of this chapter is on philosophies from the Global South, in this section, I do address salient Western approaches, to illustrate what the former have in common in contrast with the latter. There is a large kernel of truth in the claim that modern Euro-American-Australasian moral-political philosophies are individualist. Too often that has been construed in terms of egoism, self-ownership theory, or some other orientation that does not prescribe weighty duties on a moral agent to help her society. It is true that these ethics are respectable parts of the modern Western philosophical tradition, but are largely anathema to African philosophy. However, even more commonly held than they by philosophers in the West for the past 250 years or so have been utilitarian and Kantian principles, both of which not only ascribe moral status to those besides the agent but also demand much of her in terms of helping others.

I think the relevant respect in which the modern Western tradition counts as individualist is not the presence of egoism and similarly undemanding ethical views, but rather a feature that these views share with utilitarianism, Kantianism, and still other influential theories such as respect for human life and biocentrism (a point I first made in Metz 2012). What all these theories have in common is a certain understanding of what it is that makes something merit moral treatment. Specifically, they all include the view that there are certain features intrinsic to an individual in virtue of which it is owed duties for its own sake or 'directly'. The following are all individualist features grounding moral status, in the sense that none of them makes essential reference to anyone but the individual with the feature: being an agent, owning oneself, having the ability to feel pleasure/pain or to have preferences dis/satisfied, having the capacity for autonomy or rationality, being a member of *Homo sapiens*, possessing a soul, and being a living organism.

Individualism is what has been salient in the modern Western tradition. Such an account of moral status has grounded conceptions of institutional obligations in which notions of cost-benefit analysis, ownership, contract, self-governance, individual rights, and desert have been prominent. Again, there have obviously been some exceptions, such as Aldo Leopold's land ethic, but my claim is that individualist analyses of how a political organization such as a state ought to be oriented have been the rule for Euro-American-Australasian philosophy for many decades.

Many readers will know that the African tradition has been substantially different, with relationality being salient in accounts of human dignity and moral status. One scholar remarks, 'The dignity of human beings emanates from the network of relationships, from being in community; in an African view, it cannot be reduced to a unique, competitive and free personal ego' (Botman), while another says, '(T)he human person in Africa is from the very beginning in a network of relationships that constitutes his alienable dignity' (Bujo 88), and still another notes, '(T)he dignity and importance of the individual human being can best be understood in terms of relations with other human beings as well as relations with physical nature' (Ramose 312). There have been apparent exceptions, with the appeal to life-force as grounding moral status potentially viewed as a form of individualism (on which see, eg, Magesa). However, many in the African tradition would argue that the nature of a given instance of life-force cannot be comprehended except by its relationships with other life-forces, ie, that it is ultimately a relational feature.

There are different views on precisely which relations matter, but one common view is that a being has in fact engaged in harmonious interactions with a clan or a specific community (eg, Cobbah; Ikuenobe). Another view, which this author has championed, is that it is the capacity to relate to others in harmonious ways, not actual relations with them, that confers moral status (Metz 2012, 2022).

None of these views is individualist, for they all entail that what it is that gives one a moral standing cannot be understood without reference to a positive interaction with someone else. Relational views maintain that some kind of desirable interactive property between oneself and others is what entitles one to moral treatment or to being the object of direct duties. Insofar as the relevant interaction involves harmony, the straightforward view to hold is that a being merits moral consideration insofar as it either is or can be a party to harmonious relationships. That could mean one harmonizing with others or others harmonizing with one (or both).

Since, for many traditions in the Global South, what makes human beings and other parts of nature special is their having related harmoniously or the capacity to do so, the kinds of institutional obligations that follow tend to differ from the Western ones mentioned above. In contrast to those, prominent have been prescriptions for a political organization to balance, integrate, align, and smooth (Anedo 16). Additional salient obligations, discussed below, involve advancing the common good, caring for people, fostering inclusion and togetherness, acknowledging interdependence, cooperating to realize shared ends, and interacting in ways that create something new and useful. Consider how different this batch of ethical concepts is from, say, a person's happiness counting for one when maximizing outcomes, rights to own oneself and property, and respect for another's ability to govern her own life.

In the following, I bring out some of what the relational concepts entail for politics in the contexts of three different worldviews from the Global South. While all broadly share the harmony-centric value system sketched in this section, they interestingly have different understandings of how to understand harmony. I first spell them out on their own terms in the next three sections, after which I highlight areas of difference between them that warrant sustained philosophical enquiry.

African *Ubuntu*

In this section, my aim is to expound a widely held interpretation of *ubuntu*, particularly as it bears on issues in political philosophy. The word '*ubuntu*' literally means humanness in the Nguni languages of southern Africa, but is these days often used to refer to a sub-Saharan ethic (or even broader philosophy) that includes the prescription to develop one's humanness by relating to others in more or less harmonious ways. Despite the linguistic origin of the word, the approach to morality associated with it resonates with many philosophies from other indigenous parts of the continent.

Probably most southern African thinkers hold that certain harmonious or communal ways of relating merit pursuit as ends or for their own sake, a view that is shared by philosophers from other countries, too. However, also common, particularly elsewhere on the continent, is the view that harmonious relationships are essential means by which to promote other, logically distinct ends, such as meeting everyone's needs (eg, Gyekye 35–76) or promoting life-force (eg, Magesa). Regardless, it is standard amongst African philosophers to hold that morality must be informed by relational considerations, and, in the following, I spell out a prominent way to understand them and their implications for political choice.

To begin to say more about what an *ubuntu* approach to moral-political philosophy involves, consider two representative quotations about it. The first is from Desmond Tutu, renowned Chair of South Africa's Truth and Reconciliation Commission (TRC) who appealed to *ubuntu* when considering the TRC's ethical foundations. He remarks about African peoples,

> When we want to give high praise to someone we say, '*Yu, u nobuntu*'; 'Hey, he or she has *ubuntu*.' This means they are generous, hospitable, friendly, caring and compassionate....We say, 'a person is a person through other people....I am human because I belong.' I participate, I share....Harmony, friendliness, community are great goods. Social harmony is for us the *summum bonum*––the greatest good. Anything that subverts or undermines this sought-after good is to be avoided like the plague.
>
> *(Tutu 34–35)*

Consider, too, the following characterization of an *ubuntu* morality from Yvonne Mokgoro, a former Justice of South Africa's Constitutional Court who had invoked in her judicial reasoning:

> (H)armony is achieved through close and sympathetic social relations within the group - thus the notion *umuntu ngumuntu ngabantu* (a person is a person through other

persons—ed.)....which also implies that during one's life-time, one is constantly challenged by others, practically, to achieve self-fulfilment through a set of collective social ideals....a morality of co-operation, compassion, communalism.

(Mokgoro 17)

Notice that, for both thinkers, one is to become a genuine human being or realize oneself and to do that by prizing harmonious relationships with other persons. Those who fail to do so are routinely called 'non-persons' or even 'animals' in extreme cases (see, eg, Nkulu-N'Sengha 143–144).

These views are in the first instance accounts of how to become a good person, and not so much about which public policy would be just. However, it is not a stretch to interpret them in ways that are relevant, say, as holding that just institutions are those that promote harmony or that treat people as special because of their capacity to be a party to harmonious relationships.

As Tutu and Mokgoro implicitly suggest, harmonious relationships are not merely those of any stable, peaceful group. For instance, a dictator whose subjects do not rebel because they are afraid does not have a harmonious relationship with them in the relevant, morally attractive sense. The harmony to prize is instead a way of relating in which people 'participate' and are 'close', on the one hand, and 'share' and are 'sympathetic', on the other, a characterization echoed by other African thinkers (on which see the quotations in Metz 2022: 92–93). The former is a matter of cooperative engagements or joint projects, while the latter consists of aiding others for their own sake, which in the African tradition is centrally to meet their needs, including the need to exhibit humanness. These ways of interacting are often thought required to respect the dignity of human persons, and note how they are characteristic of an (extended) family, with a common thought being that politics and society ought to be modelled on appealing familial relationships (eg, Nyerere 12; Oruka 148–150). A dictator hardly cooperates with his subjects, and nor does he reliably do what is expected to be good for each of them.

Instead, the default position amongst African philosophers is that political power must be allocated democratically and, more specifically, according to a consensual agreement. While details naturally vary thinkers, a prominent view is that, although there should be elected representatives (say, because they are likely to be more experienced or because direct democracy is impractical in a mass society), Parliamentarians should have to come to a unanimous agreement in order for a statute to be valid (eg, Wiredu). It is thought that requiring consensus amongst legislative representatives would make it most likely that the good of all citizens would be sufficiently advanced and would constitute the most intense form of cooperation possible at the political level. Settling for majority rule is thought to degrade those in the minority, as a failure to harmonize adequately.

Turn from the question of how power should be allocated to how it should be used. That is, let us consider which laws a state should enforce, given a prescription to respect people's dignity by relating to them harmoniously, roughly with cooperation and aid.

On the one hand, many African philosophers believe that such an orientation requires enforcing human rights, with violations of them consisting of degrading treatment in the forms of killing, subordination, or harm. Unlike the philosophical liberalism of John Rawls, Robert Nozick, and Ronald Dworkin, for the African tradition, the state should not be neutral with regards to conceptions of the good life. For it, human rights violations are commonly conceived at least partially in terms of actions that severely reduce the quality of people's lives (and not merely remove primary goods or freedoms), and, furthermore, the state is routinely thought to have an obligation to meet people's needs, including their social or moral need to relate harmoniously.

On the other hand, it is also a salient feature of the African tradition to deny that human rights are the be-and and end-all of the function of a political organization. Some suggest that duties are prior to rights in some way, say, in that it would be preferable for people's needs to be voluntarily met by others, without them having to invoke rights-claims against anyone (eg, Molefe). Others maintain that in addition to individual rights, there are group rights, where *relationships* of cooperation and aid amongst a clan or nation must be protected beyond the interests of the individuals who are party to them. Something like that approach is enshrined in the African ('Banjul') Charter on Human and Peoples' Rights adopted by the member states of the Organization of African Unity. Some rights of a people include the entitlements not to be dominated and to resist domination (Article 20), while others involve claims to natural resources, socio-economic development, and an environment necessary for the latter (Articles 21, 22, 24).

East Asian Confucianism

Confucianism is another long-standing and influential philosophy in which harmony plays a central role. It goes back more than 2500 years to the time of Confucius (551–479 BC), and it has been not merely the dominant philosophical orientation of the large population of China, but also quite influential in neighbouring countries that include Korea, Taiwan, and Japan. There have naturally been a variety of interpretations of Confucianism over the millennia. To obtain focus, I concentrate on the ethical ideas of its two most influential exponents, namely, Confucius as his ideas were compiled in *The Analects* and Mencius (372–289 BC) as per the book titled *The Mencius*, particularly as interpreted by contemporary East Asian philosophers. Upon doing so, one sees that talk of 'harmony' is salient, but understood differently from the way it is construed in the African tradition.

It is literally just in the past decade or so that philosophers have become aware of some striking similarities between *ubuntu* and Confucian thought (with early texts being Bell and Metz; and Anedo). Like the *ubuntu* tradition, the Confucian one tends to distinguish between a lower, animal nature that we have and a higher, human one that we should instead strive to develop. For instance, one scholar remarks in a text introducing Confucianism that

> the potentiality within individuals that enables them to be finally differentiated from birds and beasts is yet to be developed and cultivated as actual qualities of their character.... (The goal of self-cultivation) is to fully develop original moral senses, is to become fully human, while to abandon or neglect it is to have a deficient character which is not far from that of an animal.
>
> *(Yao 154; see also Li 2008: 428)*

Another similarity between indigenous African and Chinese thought is the centrality of harmony as the key way to develop humanness or develop a moral character. Harmony (*he*) has been variously labelled as 'the highest virtue' for Confucians (Yao 172), 'the most cherished ideal in Chinese culture' (Li 2006: 583), and the Confucian 'grand ideal' (Chan 2). As the influential scholar Wei-Ming Tu remarks, 'If someone is able to uphold the harmony in family relations, neighborly relations and in the relations between the upper and the lower ranks....then we can call him a Confucian' (254).

Confucian thinkers are often at pains to make it clear that harmony for them is neither mere peace, sameness, nor agreement. Although Confucian harmony often includes peace, it is not reducible to it and includes more integration than mere détente. It is also by definition, not sameness, as it necessarily (or at the very least ideally) includes differential elements; indeed, one of the most commonly quoted sayings of Confucius is: 'The gentleman seeks harmony not sameness, the petty person seeks sameness not harmony' (translation from Chan 91). Harmony is also not simply agreement, for those who have contrary opinions and perspectives can harmonize in the relevant way.

Instead, Confucian harmony is characteristically (perhaps essentially) a matter of different elements coming together, where differences are not merely respected, but also integrated in such a way that the best of them is brought out or something new is created. According to Chenyang Li, the scholar who has studied it the most in recent Confucian scholarship:

> (H)armony is sustained by energy generated through the interaction of different elements in creative tension....Through mutual adjustment and mutual accommodation we reshape the situation into a harmonious one.
>
> *(Li 2006: 589, 600)*

> Harmony is an active process in which heterogeneous elements are brought into a mutually balancing, cooperatively enhancing, and often commonly benefiting relationship.
>
> *(Li 2014: 1)*

Aesthetic analogies are often used to illustrate this concept of creative tension or mutual benefit between disparate properties; think of instruments that make music together or ingredients that constitute a tasty soup. Human beings are meant to integrate into analogous ways, where differences amongst them come together to complement each other and form a productive unity.

One key kind of difference amongst people for the Confucian tradition is the position in a hierarchy, to which Tu alludes in the quotation above. That is, a desirable kind of harmony comes in the form of there being superiors who are educated and virtuous and who guide the lives of inferiors who are not to the same degree. Here, harmony is to be realized within, and by means of, such hierarchical roles between rulers (the 'upper ranks') and citizens (the 'lower ranks'), parents and children, older people and younger people. Harmony arises when those in the lower position are respectful and deferential towards those in the higher one *and* when those in the higher position work for the benefit of those in the lower one. Then, differences are brought together such that a productive relationship is realized.

This conception of harmony has probably been largely responsible for the absence of a tradition of democratic governance in China. It is well known that prior to Communism in the twentieth century, a characteristically Confucian approach to politics, of seeking rulers qualified by their literate education and moral character, had supported a highly skilled public service for literally thousands of years. Confucian philosophers in the twenty-first century continue to be sceptical of sharing power equally, and instead, tend to favour an arrangement in which those with the most qualifications hold the most power (Bell and Li; Chan; Bai). Benevolent dictatorship or autocratic meritocracy are the watchwords in regards to the question of who should rule the state; popular voting is unwelcome or at least should be of secondary influence on the allocation of power, given Confucian harmony as an ideal.

Notice, though, that appeal to benevolence or meritocracy means that the elites who have secured political power are not meant to use it for selfish purposes; instead, the point of decision-making being done by the most qualified is so that they will exercise it in a way that is expected to promote the well-being, and especially virtue, of citizens. Conceiving of harmony in terms of participation in a productive hierarchical role further entails that paternalism is often viewed as an acceptable means by which to realize the end of fostering the good of citizens, particularly their relational excellence. Although it would be sensible for those in charge to consult with those they are seeking to help, ultimately it is their decision to make, with coercion and deception being deemed acceptable tools to use. 'Confucian values have nothing to do with personal and economic freedoms, per se....The moral goal according to Confucianism is to develop our humanity, and that entails our learning to fulfill the responsibilities that we have to others' (Bockover 160), where this goal might be advanced by, say, restricting people's access to the internet (see also Wong).

South American *Buen Vivir*

Let us now turn away from what is East of Africa to what is in the opposite direction, albeit in the Global South. South America includes yet another long-standing tradition in which harmony features prominently and foundationally. Common English descriptors of this strain of moral-political thought are 'good living' or 'plentiful life', variously called '*buen vivir*' in Spanish or '*sumak kawsay*' in Quechua, an indigenous language spoken mainly in Peru but also in some neighbouring countries such as Ecuador and Bolivia.

There is debate about how talk of *buen vivir* and *sumak kawsay* relate to each other (Waldmüller), and both phrases have been used in various ways, including as picking out indigenous values, contemporary 'post-development' or leftist philosophies, as well as laws and policies that have been adopted by certain states (Waldmüller and Rodriguez 236). In the following, I focus on works in English, which happen to have been composed mainly by those who speak Spanish (and other European languages) as opposed to Quechua, and hence I consider mainly what has been put under the heading of '*buen vivir*'. Furthermore, I consider English works addressing *buen vivir* in the light of what they might offer to political philosophical reflection, and not so much intellectual history or some other empirical enquiry. With this approach, therefore, I am not trying to represent beliefs that have been widely held amongst indigenous peoples in South America or track the ways the phrase '*buen vivir*' has been used; instead, my goal is to expound some prima facie attractive ideas inspired by beliefs associated with the phrase that are relevant to contemporary political philosophy.

Consider the following summarizing statements of *buen vivir* that have been advanced in academic forums:

> As an alternative to the neoliberal growth model, *Buen Vivir* seeks to establish a harmonious relationship between mankind and nature and a social equilibrium within societies....It requires acting in concert with others in a community with reciprocity as key element and the aim of living well, but not necessarily living better than others. Hence, it demands that human well-being should not be grounded in the exploitation of others nor should it destroy our natural environment.
>
> *(Agostino and Dübgen 6)*

> (*Buen vivir* is) a way of living the present in harmony, that is, assuming and respecting differences and complementarities (among humans and between humans and non-humans)

from an ecological perspective that could be described as holistic and mutualistic. Hence *Buen vivir* breaks away from the reductionist Cartesian worldview to adopt a systemic perspective encompassing the entire ecosphere (including abiotic components). It also breaks away from the idea of cultural and social homogeneity....and posits instead a path of harmony and 'unity in diversity'.

(Vanhulst and Beling 56)

Like many other characterizations of the core of *buen vivir*, one finds explicit mention of harmony in the above.

What is notable about the articulations of *buen vivir* is that two distinct forms of harmony are mentioned and given what appear to be comparable standing. On the one hand, there is the idea of relating to other people in mutually supportive ways to achieve an objectively decent quality of life. Instead of encouraging gross inequalities of wealth, self-interested trading, consumerist goods, and a focus on subjective well-being, *buen vivir* prescribes sharing resources, cooperating, meeting needs, and a focus on culture and relationality. 'In opposition to Western concepts of exclusivity, categorization, competition, subjectification, etc., *Buen Vivir* puts emphasis on key values such as solidarity, generosity, reciprocity and complementarity' (Waldmüller 21).

On the other hand, there is the idea of people relating to nature in ways that 'enable the natural environment to regenerate itself' (Agostino and Dübgen 6) and that treat it 'as having inherent, and thus never merely instrumental, value for humans' (Waldmüller and Rodríguez 240). Notice that we are to harmonize not merely with certain parts of nature, such as animals, but rather with nature as a whole, including 'abiotic components', ie, non-living parts that nonetheless might be understood to be part of a grand process.

The principal way that scholars have invoked *buen vivir* when thinking prescriptively about politics has been to cast doubt on dominant ways of conceiving economic progress. As mentioned above, the 'neoliberal growth model', whereby governments aim to expand gross domestic product (GDP) indefinitely, is invariably rejected as incompatible with both sorts of harmony. That approach not merely separates people from each other and from nature, but also involves relations of domination and destruction that are anathema to *buen vivir*.

However, many scholars have also invoked *buen vivir* as an alternative to a development model of economic progress. Although most interpretations of sustainable development these days focus on a metric that, unlike GDP, is plausibly understood to focus on human well-being and to require some consideration of nature, many friends of *buen vivir* criticize it for being technocratic, individualist, and anthropocentric. Instead, for one striking contrast, *buen vivir* is often taken to require seeking out 'harmony with Mother Earth', where 'Mother Earth is a sacred, living being' (Plurinational State of Bolivia 22, 12) towards which we have direct duties. *Buen vivir* grounded a Bolivian law prescribing the right of the Earth 'to support the restoration and regeneration capabilities of all its components that enables the continuity of life cycles' (Plurinational State of Bolivia 29), a non-anthropocentric approach to economic production and consumption that far transcends sustainability for long-term human use.

When it comes to political power, *buen vivir* clearly favours democracy, but one of a sort that is more participatory than what one typically finds in Parliamentary states. For example, key *buen vivir* concepts include decentralization, ie, giving power to local communities, and inclusiveness, engaging with civil society and citizens and not leaving governance up to (national) elites (Friant and Langmore 65; Meyberg 5–6, 8; van Norren 443–446). Another salient theme is appeal to 'radical pluralism', 'pluriculturality', or 'plurinationality', the thought being that, taking advantage of 'indigenous self-government' (van Norren 444), we should welcome a variety of forms of life in a certain territory that co-exist without conflict and, indeed, instead with mutual support (Walsh; Friant and Langmore 64; and van Norren 444, 446, 452).

Comparing Three Political Philosophies from the Global South

Having spelled out key elements of the political philosophies of *ubuntu*, Confucianism, and *buen vivir* individually, it is time to consider them in relation to each other. I begin by pointing out some salient differences between them, noting debates that should take place internal to the Global South amongst theorists of harmony there (Section 'Differences'). I then step back and conclude by noting some respects in which the three political philosophies are similar and should collectively ground challenges to views salient in the modern West or Global North (Section 'Similarities'), after which I briefly sum up the project undertaken here (Section 'Summarizing Conclusion').

Differences

Despite *ubuntu*, Confucianism, and *buen vivir* all appealing to harmony as a basic (or at least central) value, the conceptions of harmony fascinatingly differ amongst all three. Here I consider some of the more prominent divergences and their implications for political philosophy. One difference that is more purely ethical, with less obvious ramifications for governance, concerns the role of self-realization in regards to harmony. The ideal of moving away from an animal self towards a human self, and doing so by relating harmoniously and particularly within the family, is prominent in both *ubuntu* and Confucianism (on which see, eg, Metz 2020: 183–184), whereas it does not appear that the good life is essentially a more human one for *buen vivir*.

One major difference in respect to politics concerns environmental matters, with *buen vivir* on one side and Confucianism and *ubuntu* on the other. Although all three approaches prescribe harmony with aspects of nature, *buen vivir* stands out for deeming that sort of harmony to be of comparable moral importance to interpersonal harmony. For it, the latter must never be undertaken in a way that would undermine the former, and instead is circumscribed by and even informed by it. In contrast, contemporary expositions of an *ubuntu* ethic usually invoke the maxim, 'A person is a person through other persons', meaning that one can become a genuine person by prizing harmonious relations with other persons. Harmonious relations with nature are either ultimately anthropocentric, such that destroying nature is understood to be stealing what the clan owns or disrupting places where ancestors reside, or, if not anthropocentric, then of secondary importance. Similarly, although Confucian harmony does allow for integration between persons and non-persons, it is almost never given as much prominence. Instead, for Confucian thought, 'The family was not seen as a necessary condition for the good life, it was the good life' (Bell 145; see also Li 2008: 429–430; Fan).

The three approaches differ in terms of not only the importance of harmony between humans and nature relative to that between humans alone, but also the aspects of nature with which we should harmonize. As indicated above, for adherents to *buen vivir*, the Earth or nature as a whole has moral rights, a perspective enshrined in the Bolivian Constitution and also the Ecuadoran (Republic of Ecuador Articles 71–73). In contrast, normally for contemporary exponents of *ubuntu* and Confucianism, there are only certain parts of the natural world with which we ought to harmonize, at least for their own sake. For instance, some Confucian scholars have pointed out that we are to develop our human nature by being humane and empathizing with others, orientations that are naturally extended to animals (Nuyen), but not, say, to plants or ecosystems. Similarly, according to some interpretations of *ubuntu*, we should positively orient ourselves towards values such as 'life, vitality, sentience, and well-being' (Chemhuru 43) and recognize that 'community comprises of both the human and biotic community' with the aim to prize 'wellness and the wellbeing of all' (Lenkabula 385, 386); these prescriptions naturally suggest relating harmoniously with animals and plants. For neither view is it normal to suggest that the Earth *qua* Earth merits a harmonious relationship (though there are exceptions, including other passages in Lenkabula). Insofar as we should treat the Earth well, the standard approach of Confucianism and *ubuntu* is more instrumental, prescribing protection of ecological systems in order to sustain individuals (whether human, animals, or plants) or to respect people's property (whether of ancestors, the clan, or God) (eg, Li 2008: 434; Ramose 308–309, 312–313). In contrast, it appears much more common for proponents of *buen vivir* to hold that the Earth or natural world has value in itself, apart from its bearing on persons or even individuals more broadly.

Hence, philosophers in the Global South need to find ways to debate with each other about what it means to harmonize with nature in morally relevant ways and how weighty a consideration that is compared to interpersonal harmony. Upon reflection, is there reason to view the Earth as a whole as having merely instrumental value for the sustenance of the individuals residing on it? Should we want an account of harmony with nature that fits neatly with interpersonal harmony, where ways of relating such as supporting individuals' goals, welfare, and excellence could apply to both? Or, in contrast, should we find, say, the complexity of the Earth's ecosystem to ground moral status and invite a type of harmonization different from what would be apt for individuals? And, then, however harmony with nature is best understood, is it so important as to warrant legal enforcement, which presumably would take some resources away from the protection and flourishing of human persons?

Focusing strictly on interpersonal harmony in the rest of this section, consider some contrasts between the three conceptions of it spelled out above. One has to do with the role of differences and whether they are expected for harmonization. Confucian harmony is normally understood as requiring different elements that are brought together into a unity; as Confucius suggests above, where there is sameness there is no harmony. In addition, *buen vivir* is often interpreted as, if not requiring differences, then at least working with a conception of harmony that is enhanced when they are present and brought into a mutually supportive relationship.

In contrast, adherents to *ubuntu* harmony are more welcoming of a culture of sameness. Cooperative engagements that are expected to meet people's needs could (even if they need not) involve people having adopted the same ends and more generally living in the same ways. Salient forms of cooperation in the African philosophical tradition are residing with a family and engaging in the rituals and customs of one's society, which hardly seem essentially to include people adopting divergent lifestyles. As Kwame Gyekye says of the African tradition,

> Communitarian moral and political theory, which considers the community as a fundamental human good, advocates a life lived in harmony and cooperation with others, a life of mutual consideration and aid and of interdependence, a life in which one shares in the fate of the other.
>
> *(75–76)*

From this perspective, it could be appropriate for a state to protect a culture in which people live in quite similar ways.

Furthermore, amongst Confucianism and *buen vivir*, there is disagreement about how best to understand what counts as a relevant kind of difference that is to be integrated. For Confucianism, an essential difference concerns place in a hierarchical role, with the central sort of harmony consisting of the more qualified influencing the lives of the less qualified in productive and beneficial ways. That conception is quite out of place in *buen vivir*, which is much more egalitarian in regards to the allocation of power. *Buen vivir* instead finds the relevant sort of difference to be between ways of life, particularly amongst various communities that need to engage with one another in a common territory. Relatedly, recall that most political philosophers who adhere to *ubuntu* favour consensual democracy and hence an equal distribution of political power; the suggestion that a single person, party, or other group ought to have all the power is not salient in contemporary African philosophy.

So, here is another cluster of issues that merit debate amongst philosophers in the Global South. Is there something undesirable about a kind of interpersonal harmony in which people's ways of life are similar, or could that rather be a welcome, and even intense, sort where people have chosen to come together in that way meriting support from the state? In Confucian terms, should the field perhaps not be more acknowledging of the potential desirability of *tong* (often rendered as 'sameness') as opposed to *he* (harmony)? Another key issue that needs to be addressed is the role of hierarchy and how to organize politics and society when there are some who have markedly greater education and virtue than others.

Perhaps both issues would be best considered in the context of an extended family or small-scale community, as all three traditions can be viewed as providing accounts of what makes them attractive. Harmony-based ethics characteristically take familial relationship as an ideal to extend to the rest of society, and so it is worth considering what precisely makes it valuable and the implications of that for our best understanding of harmony and politics.

Similarities

If I am correct about the state of the literature, this discussion has been the first to consider contrasts between conceptions of harmony prominent in three major intellectual traditions in the Global South and to recommend some ways forward for debate amongst them. The time is ripe for cross-cultural argumentation amongst African, East Asian, and South American philosophers without the mediation of a modern Western (or Global Northern) variable. However, another project that these thinkers should consider undertaking is looking for common ground and giving their individualist interlocutors in the West (Global North) pause about how to do political philosophy. In support of that project, I note that mainstream adherents to *ubuntu*, Confucianism, and *buen vivir* would all readily accept the following prescriptions for institutional choice.

Political leaders ought to seek out win/win solutions to conflict, in which all parties come away with enough to be satisfied. Such an approach contrasts with resting content with helping the majority or doing the most that one can for one's side (let alone dominating others for the sake of one's own profit or power).

Neither government nor business should pursue economic growth as an end or use it as a marker of progress. GDP, roughly the amount of goods and services that have been sold, does not reliably track harmony in whichever way harmony is plausibly construed by the three Global South perspectives.

The state should enforce fairly radical redistributions of wealth. It is unjust both within a country and between countries for some to have enormous amounts of wealth on the order of billions of US dollars when others cannot meet their needs. All the views of harmony here would count this state of affairs as its discordant opposite.

A given Constitution should feature socio-economic rights, and they should be deemed of comparable importance to rights to civil liberty. For example, the state and other agents in society should be considered to have a duty to ensure that each citizen has access to food, water, education, housing, healthcare, and the like.

Beyond meeting the biological and psychological needs of citizens, a state has good reason to foster various ways of relating in society, whether that is engaging in community service, volunteering at a charity, developing a sense of national unity, improving relationships between romantic partners and between them and their children, or reintegrating offenders into society. Note how these ends differ from satisfying people's various preferences or self-chosen ends, particularly in a market.

It is imperative for the state to fight global warming and more generally environmental degradation such as acidified oceans, depletion of the ozone layer, reduction of species diversity, and destruction of natural beauty. Regardless of whether one conceives of harmony strictly in terms of relations with individuals or also with the Earth as a whole, it requires confronting the environmental crisis and furthermore doing so in ways that involve the participation of all countries, particularly those most responsible for it.

If I am correct that the above prescriptions constitute overlap amongst the three harmony-based approaches to political philosophy explored here, then Global South adherents ought to strive together to see such approaches taken seriously. They must harmonize in their efforts to contest alternative approaches, which is true when it comes to not merely globally influential theoretical analyses of values, policy, and law, but also international practice.

Summarizing Conclusion

The main aim of this chapter has been to advance cross-cultural reflection amongst those working within political philosophical traditions in the Global South. I have contended that large swathes of indigenous moral-political thought in Africa, East Asia, and South America are plausibly understood as relational in nature and specifically as grounded on an ideal of harmony. This shared value of harmony is usefully invoked to structure debate amongst adherents to *ubuntu*, Confucianism, and *buen vivir*. On the one hand, there are important differences between the ways these thinkers tend to interpret the nature of harmony. I identified some of the differences in this chapter and drew out implications for various aspects of politics, ranging from how power should be distributed to which sorts of things have rights against the state to which kind of culture the state should support. On the other hand, despite the differences in the ways adherents to *ubuntu*, Confucianism, and *buen vivir* understand what counts as harmony, there is substantial common ground amongst them that should be identified. I noted that a harmony framework in general is quite distinct from more individualist values such as autonomy or preference satisfaction, and also identified several respects in which the three different interpretations of harmony nonetheless prescribe similar approaches to politics, ones that provide reason to question a number of dominant practices and influential Western principles.

References

Agostino, Ana and Franziska Dübgen. "*Buen Vivir* and Beyond: Searching for a New Paradigm of Action." Degrowth Conference Venice, 2012, http://www.socioeco.org/bdf_fiche-document-3878_en.html.

Anedo, Onukwube. "A Cultural Analysis of Harmony and Conflict." *Unizik Journal of Arts and Humanities*, vol. 13, 2012, pp. 16–52.

Bai, Tongdong. *Against Political Equality: The Confucian Case*. Princeton University Press, 2019.

Bell, Daniel A. *Beyond Liberal Democracy*. Princeton University Press, 2006.

Bell, Daniel A. and Chenyang Li, eds. *The East Asian Challenge for Democracy*. Cambridge University Press, 2013.

Bell, Daniel A. and Thaddeus Metz. "Confucianism and *Ubuntu*: Reflections on a Dialogue between Chinese and African Traditions." *Journal of Chinese Philosophy*, vol. 38, supp., 2011, pp. 78–95.

Bell, Daniel A. and Yingchuan Mo. "Harmony in the World 2013: The Ideal and the Reality." *Social Indicators Research*, vol. 118, 2014, pp. 797–818.

Bockover, Mary. "Confucian Values and the Internet: A Potential Conflict." *Journal of Chinese Philosophy*, vol. 30, 2003, pp. 159–175.

Botman, H. Russel. "The OIKOS in a Global Economic Era: A South African Comment." *Sameness and Difference: Problems and Potentials in South African Civil Society*, edited by James Cochrane and Bastienne Klein. The Council for Research in Values and Philosophy, 2000, pp. 269–280.

Bujo, Bénézet. *Foundations of an African Ethic: Beyond the Universal Claims of Western Morality*, translated by Brian McNeil. Crossroad Publishers, 2001.

Chan, Joseph. *Confucian Perfectionism: A Political Philosophy for Modern Times*. Princeton University Press, 2014.

Chemhuru, Munamato. "Using the African Teleological View of Existence to Interpret Environmental Ethics." *Philosophia Africana*, vol. 18, 2016, pp. 41–51.

Cobbah, Joseph. "African Values and the Human Rights Debate." *Human Rights Quarterly*, vol. 9, 1987, pp. 309–331.

Friant, Martin Caliso and John Langmore. "The *Buen Vivir*: A Policy to Survive the Anthropocene?" *Global Policy*, vol. 6, 2015, pp. 64–71.

Graness, Anke. "*Ubuntu* and *Buen Vivir*: A Comparative Approach." *Ubuntu and the Reconstitution of Community*, edited by James Ogude. Indiana University Press, 2019, pp. 150–175.

Gyekye, Kwame. *Tradition and Modernity: Philosophical Reflections on the African Experience*. Oxford University Press, 1997.

Henrich, Joseph, Heine, Steven, and Ara Norenzayan. "The Weirdest People in the World?" *Behavioral and Brain Sciences*, vol. 33, 2010, pp. 61–135.

Ikuenobe, Polycarp. "The Communal Basis for Moral Dignity: An African Perspective." *Philosophical Papers*, vol. 45, 2016, pp. 437–469.

LenkaBula, Puleng. "Beyond Anthropocentricity – Botho/Ubuntu and the Quest for Economic and Ecological Justice in Africa." *Religion and Theology*, vol. 15, 2008, pp. 375–394.

Leopold, Aldo. *A Sand County Almanac*, 2nd edn. Oxford University Press, 1968.

Li, Chenyang. "The Confucian Ideal of Harmony." *Philosophy East and West*, vol. 56, 2006, pp. 583–603.

Li, Chenyang. "The Philosophy of Harmony in Classical Confucianism." *Philosophy Compass*, vol. 3, 2008, pp. 423–435.

Li, Chenyang. *The Confucian Philosophy of Harmony*. Routledge, 2014.

Magesa, Laurenti. *African Religion: The Moral Traditions of Abundant Life*. Orbis Books, 1997.

Metz, Thaddeus. "An African Theory of Moral Status." *Ethical Theory and Moral Practice*, vol. 15, 2012, pp. 387–402.

Metz, Thaddeus. "Harmonizing Global Ethics in the Future: A Proposal to Add South and East to West." *Journal of Global Ethics* vol. 10, 2014, pp. 146–155.

Metz, Thaddeus. "Communication Strategies in the Light of Indigenous African and Chinese Values: How to Harmonize." *Philosophia Africana*, vol. 19, 2020, pp. 176–194.

Metz, Thaddeus. *A Relational Moral Theory: African Ethics in and Beyond the Continent*. Oxford University Press, 2022.

Meyberg, Adriana Yee. "Buen Vivir: A Revolutionary Version of Governance?" 2017, https://www.academia.edu/35154395/BUEN_VIVIR_A_revolutionary_Version_of_Governance.

Mokgoro, Yvonne. "*Ubuntu* and the Law in South Africa." *Potchefstroom Electronic Law Journal*, vol. 1, 1998, pp. 15–26, https://www.ajol.info/index.php/pelj/article/view/43567.

Molefe, Motsamai. *An African Philosophy of Personhood, Morality, and Politics*. Palgrave Macmillan, 2019.

Nkulu-N'Sengha, Mutombo. *Encyclopedia of African Religion*, edited by Molefi Keti Asante and Ama Mazama. Sage, 2009, pp. 142–147.

Nuyen, Anh Tuan. "Confucian Role-based Ethics and Strong Environmental Ethics." *Environmental Values*, vol. 20, 2011, pp. 549–566.

Nyerere, Julius. *Ujamaa: Essays on Socialism*. Oxford University Press, 1968.

Organization of African Unity. "African Charter on Human and Peoples' Rights." 1981, https://au.int/en/treaties/african-charter-human-and-peoples-rights.

Oruka, Henry Odera. *Practical Philosophy: In Search of an Ethical Minimum*. East African Educational Publishers, 1997.

Plurinational State of Bolivia. "Living-Well in Balance and Harmony with Mother Earth." 2014, https://www.genevaenvironmentnetwork.org/wp-content/uploads/2020/05/living-well_pdf.pdf.

Ramose, Mogobe. "Ecology Through Ubuntu." *African Ethics: An Anthology of Comparative and Applied Ethics*, edited by Munyaradzi Felix Murove. University of KwaZulu-Natal Press, 2009, pp. 308–314.

Republic of Ecuador. Constitution of the Republic of Ecuador. 2008, https://pdba.georgetown.edu/Constitutions/Ecuador/english08.html.

Tu, Wei-Ming. "Confucian Encounter with the Enlightenment Mentality of the Modern West." *Oriens Extremus*, vol. 49, 2010, pp. 249–308.

Tutu, Desmond. *No Future without Forgiveness*. Random House, 1999.

van Norren, Dorine. "The Sustainable Development Goals Viewed Through Gross National Happiness, Ubuntu, and Buen Vivir." *International Environmental Agreements*, vol. 20, 2020, pp. 431–458.

Vanhulst, Julien and Adrian Beling. "*Buen Vivir*: Emergent Discourse Within or Beyond Sustainable Development?" *Ecological Economics*, vol. 101, 2014, pp. 54–63.

Waldmüller, Johannes. "Buen Vivir, Sumak Kawsay, 'Good Living': An Introduction and Overview." *Alternautas*, vol. 1, 2014, pp. 17–28.

Waldmüller, Johannes and Laura Rodríguez. "*Buen Vivir* and the Rights of Nature." *Routledge Handbook of Development Ethics*, edited by Jay Drydyk and Lori Keleher. Routledge, 2019, pp. 234–247.

Walsh, Catherine. "The Plurinational and Intercultural State: Decolonization and State Refounding in Ecuador." *Kult*, vol. 6, 2009, pp. 65–84.

Wiredu, Kwasi. "Democracy and Consensus in African Traditional Politics." *Polylog: Forum for Intercultural Philosophy*, vol. 2, 2000, http://them.polylog.org/2/fwk-en.htm.

Wong, Pak-hang. "Confucian Social Media: An Oxymoron?" *Dao*, vol. 12, 2013, pp. 283–296.

Yao, Xinzhong. *An Introduction to Confucianism*. Cambridge University Press, 2000.

28

NON-STATE ACTORS, FREEDOM AND JUSTICE

Should Multinational Firms Be Primary Agents of Justice in African Societies?

Thierry Ngosso[1]

Introduction

Freedom and justice are two major political ideas that continue to generate enormous philosophical interest and debate. The diversity of conceptions of freedom and justice makes it even more difficult to grasp their respective definitions or concepts. African political philosophers are therefore no exception on this point. For a continent that has lived through the turpitudes of slavery, the throes of colonization, the mischiefs of neo-colonialism and post-colonialism, the disruptions of globalization, the notions of justice and freedom are more than academic or intellectual concepts. Their quest is embodied in the daily life of many African citizens.[2] Instead of delving into a definition or a concept of justice or freedom that will remain disputed, perhaps a better way of grasping these political ideas would be to present those situations Africans are facing that can be unjust or where people can feel or are unfree. We can then ask ourselves if non-state actors and particularly firms should count among the agents who have the responsibility as *primary agents of justice* to address them. The concern here is not merely to know if non-state actors have any duties at all when it comes to addressing situations of injustice or to contributing to the promotion of freedoms in African societies as *secondary agents of justice*. Rather, the issue is to examine if, given their contribution to justice and freedom, especially in contexts of failed African States, they can be considered as *primary* agents of justice.

That concern is morally relevant. States have traditionally been regarded in the field of international relations and even of political philosophy as the privileged habitat of power and authority, and as such, as the guarantor of justice and the protection of fundamental rights.[3] These are the features that historically differentiate the Westphalian State as an institution from other so-called 'non-state' actors whose contribution to justice and the protection of fundamental rights only require compliance with the standards, rules and public policies established by the state actor.

That said, the role of private and non-state actors in shaping the contours of globalization, and their involvement in the fabric of the global public discourse has also been a subject of academic interest. Whether it is non-governmental organizations working for the global protection of human rights, civil society organizations such as trade unions working to improve the conditions of workers[4] or even companies/firms called upon to contribute more

DOI: 10.4324/9781003143529-33

proactively to the economic development of peoples[5] and to the promotion or protection of human rights,[6] the boundary that separated state and non-state actors stemming from the Westphalian conception of the state seems to be increasingly blurred. If there is a particular non-state actor that has been the focus of scholarly work in this area it is the business corporation or firm, and especially the multinational corporation.

The acknowledgement of that evolution or questioning of the traditional 'state/non-state actors' distinction, especially when it comes to some powerful transnational or multinational corporations, has led the British philosopher Onora O'Neill to provide an interesting reformulation of that state/non-state actors' distinction. The key difference in that evolution is that all social actors – not the state only – are agents of justice, although in different capacities or roles. Instead of a 'state/non-state actors' distinction, she suggests we should distinguish between *primary agents of justice* which have the authority and capacity to determine the way principles of justice will be institutionalized and operationalized in a certain domain and *secondary agents of justice* whose main task is to comply with the state requirements.[7] But even that new approach and normative reconceptualization of the 'state/non-state actors' distinction is literally and theoretically challenged not only by the phenomenon of globalization,[8] but also by the failure of the state to advance justice and secure fundamental rights in most parts of the world and especially in most African societies. O'Neill writes:

> any firm distinction between primary and secondary agents has a place only where there are powerful and relatively just states, which successfully discipline and regulate other agents and agencies within their boundaries. But once we look at the realities of life where states are weak, any simple division between primary and secondary agents of justice blurs. Justice has to be built by a diversity of agents and agencies that possess and lack varying ranges of capabilities, and that can contribute to justice - or to injustice - in more diverse ways than is generally acknowledged in those approaches that have built on supposedly realist, but in fact highly ideologised, views of the supposed motivation of potential agents of justice.[9]

In other words, if the normative distinction between primary agents of justice or formerly so-called state actors and secondary agents of justice or formerly so-called non-state actors solely can still hold in what Rawls calls 'well-ordered societies',[10] it is irrelevant in 'non-well-ordered societies',[11] which certainly includes most of the African societies. The normative implication is that in those settings where the ordinary primary agent of justice is unwilling or unable to perform its duties, a door is open for ordinary secondary agents of justice like firms to become exceptionally and provisionally primary agents of justice.[12]

This chapter questions and cautions about that normative implication *even* in the African context where States or governments are 'weak' and relatively 'unjust' while disputing the moral relevance of the characterization of the primary/secondary agents of justice or State/non-state actors' distinctions more broadly. It argues that if addressing the situations of injustice and unfreedom can take forms in African societies that are different from those in 'well-ordered societies' because the state actor or the primary agent of justice can actually be considered unable or and most of the time unwilling to perform its duties, there remains a stronger moral case to maintain some sort of moral division of labour between several social institutions. My argument is that we should reject the binary distinction either between state actors and non-state actors or between primary agents of justice and secondary agents of justice and adopt a trinary distinction between state actors, hybrid actors and non-state actors. That trinary distinction acknowledges that some social institutions like multinational corporations are hybrid institutions[13] and do not completely fit in either of the formerly conceptual camps. Based upon that new recalibration of the entire 'agents of justice' debate, we can properly contextualize the contribution of firms, especially multinational corporations, in addressing situations of injustice and unfreedom in Africa.

The chapter is divided as follows. Section I briefly presents several situations of injustice and unfreedom as the default reality in most African societies. Section II considers the primary/secondary agents of justice and discusses two claims in favour of considering some firms as primary agents of justice in African societies. Section III suggests why considering some firms as primary agents of justice in African societies can be operationally ineffective and morally problematic. Section IV presents a trinary approach that includes some firms with a hybrid status and suggests the proper contribution to the justice of those firms in African societies. Section V concludes.

The Face of Injustices and Unfreedom in Africa

Africa as a continent is home to varying forms of injustices, a place where many freedoms are under threat and where human rights are violated on a daily basis.[14] Despite six decades of gaining sovereignty and embarking on self-rule, the quest for justice remains elusive while injustices remain widespread. Unjust situations manifest in numerous ways that it would simply be impossible to make an exhaustive inventory of them here. Their face is both domestic (social justice, intergenerational justice, criminal justice, ethnic justice), intra-African (transitional justice) or international (global justice, restitutive justice) and covers many aspects such as health, education, income, the environment, gender, the workplace, amongst others.

Consider for example health disparities and inequalities in many African societies. While some in the Global North enjoy a longer and healthy life in part because of a better access to health care from childhood, others in the Global South contend with a higher mortality rate, given the poor access to effective healthcare and lack of preparedness for health emergencies. The situation is particularly concerning in sub-Saharan African countries where the medical gaps relative to most countries in the West in terms of health expenditures, physicians and other health workers' availability, medicine accessibility[15] faces a host of social and structural challenges (poverty, education, gender discrimination, employment, environment, unrest, etc.). The absence of access to basic health care for most African citizens seriously affects the life expectancy in countries like Sierra Leone or Central African Republic where it is about 51.4 years so far behind countries like Japan where it is around 83.6 years.[16] Those circumstances of global health inequalities very often shadow huge domestic health inequalities between urban and non-urban areas in most of these metrics.

Consider also environmental injustices[17] which deny many African citizens access to clean water, clean air and other relevant elements. These environmental injustices can take several forms such as the overexploitation of Africa's natural resources that has led to many armed conflicts in several parts of the continent, the most notorious being in the great Lake area of the Democratic Republic of Congo. It has also led to the displacement of many populations from their ancestral land in order to set up the national park to signal environmental solidarity with countries of the Global North. An additional form of this environmental injustice is the dumping of very toxic waste by Western governments and companies in African countries that lack serious environmental policies and law with the 2006 Probo Koala scandal[18] in Ivory Coast being one of the most recent and prominent examples.

Consider also gender inequalities and how much such injustices affect young girls in the area of education[19] or women in general when it comes to income and social representation at the workplace[20] or the poor labour conditions of most workers both in the public and private workplace or even issues pertaining to criminal justice with many inmates whose sole crime is often to be from the opposition political party or because they have lifestyles that are counter to the dominant local values.

Consider finally, matters of international justice where the unfair economic and political arrangements and judicial order by the most powerful and rich countries and their business corporations make it harder for many African countries to achieve economic development by fighting poverty or human development by instating the rule of law.

At any rate, the quest for justice is not the only Herculean challenge facing many African citizens. There is a constant attempt or at least desire by citizens to escape or overcome the unjust structures that impose various forms of suffering upon them. People's fundamental freedoms are violated on a daily basis whether it is the human right to security, to food, to health, to education, etc. They are mostly violated by the very institutions, the state, which is supposed to protect them. At the heart of this lack of emancipation is an ever-escalating cycle of poverty that undermines the basic capabilities or freedoms that every individual should enjoy.

These violations of fundamental rights are not only experienced in times of latent armed conflicts, as can be seen today in Mali, the DRC or even Rwanda. Many African citizens experience them on a daily basis. And one can see on the ever-growing phenomenon of emigration of many African citizens to the Global North does not suggest merely the quest for a better economic fortune, but above all, an essential step towards personal emancipation and access to fundamental freedoms that the African States are unable or unwilling to guarantee.

The above-mentioned examples represent a fraction of the dreadful ways life unfolds for most African citizens and how the absence of justice and freedom serves to cement this reality. The quest for justice, therefore, is to see to the dismantling of unjust structures and to herald the possibility of each African citizen to see their fundamental liberties protected. I consider the realization of justice in African societies as intrinsically linked to the protection of fundamental freedoms or human rights.[21] There is no protection of fundamental rights when the basic structure of society is unfair. Likewise, a just and fair society functions to protect the fundamental or human rights of its own people. In this respect, the contribution of non-state actors in advancing/promoting justice, to which I turn now in the next section, will necessary advance also the protection of fundamental freedoms. My focus here will therefore be only on the ways firms should or should not contribute to justice as primary agents of justice.

Reasons to Consider Firms as Primary Agents of Justice in African Societies

African societies still face several issues related to domestic and international justice and many African citizens are still deprived of fundamental freedoms. Curiously, while the ideological basis of colonial resistance and demand for self-rule by African states was anchored on the quest for freedom, these independent states have continued to restrict the freedoms of their own people. Given this context, would it not be reasonable to stop relying on those failed States (alone) to advance justice in African societies and instead call upon so-called non-state actors, particularly firms, to do so?

There is a growing call and an emerging public sentiment to take that path. Public opinions in many states around the world, especially in developed countries, seem to be increasingly in favour of greater involvement of non-state actors, especially multinational corporations in the public domain.[22] Given the difficulties of state and government actors in effectively tackling situations of injustice that arise at the domestic and international levels, citizens have turned more and more to firms and especially to the most powerful and influential among them which are multinationals to tackle the injustices linked to global poverty, global inequalities, climate change or violation of human rights. This way of rethinking the role of firms beyond the private sphere and to consider firms as political actors[23] is increasingly echoed in academic literature. Far from the warnings of economists like Milton Friedman who reduced corporate social responsibility to profit maximization and favour the strict division of moral labour between private and public actors, scholars like the British philosopher Onora O'Neill or the Swiss business ethicist Florian Wettstein either see firms as potential primary agents of justice[24] or as quasi-governmental institutions.[25]

To understand their position, it is important first to recall how they characterize the distinction between primary and secondary agents of justice. As I mentioned already above, O'Neill considers as agents of justice all actors with the ability to avoid, inflict or maintain any situation of injustice. But among the different social actors or social institutions that exist, they don't contribute to justice in the same way. Some will be considered as primary agents of justice, in this case, state actors, since they contribute to justice by defining and setting up the principle of justice that will apply in a certain domain or in what Rawls will call the basic structure of society. Others will be considered as secondary agents of justice, non-state actors and other individuals because they will contribute to justice only by abiding or complying with whatever demand the primary agents of justice will require of them. According to O'Neill, in some circumstances, some secondary agents of justice are in a position to change an unjust situation into a just one, especially when the State is unable or unwilling to do so, and should do so.

Florian Wettstein reformulates the distinction between primary agents of justice and secondary agents of justice into a distinction between agents of justice in *a wide sense* and agents of justice in *a narrow sense*.[26] In a wide sense, agents of justice show their commitment to justice beyond mere compliance to the demands of state actors. They actively contribute to maintaining just structures and upholding them where they already exist. In a narrow sense, beyond compliance with the demands of state actors, agents of justice proactively work to transform existing structural injustice into a just one. They act as political agents or actors. Where O'Neil sees firms as mere agents of change which avoid maintenance of situations of injustice when they are able to change them, Wettstein considers firms as state-like agents with the duty to promote justice where the need arises.

Beyond these characterizations and nuances, both O'Neill and Wettstein affirm that some firms meet the criteria to be considered primary agents of justice or as agents of justice in the narrow sense. There are broadly two claims they make to support that position. Let us call the first claim 'the competence claim'. The claim suggests that firms have the moral and the political competence to contribute to justice as primary agents of justice. The competence claim imagines multinational firms to embody the state capacity to be a vehicle for justice because it is able to act in two crucial ways. First, in their internal structure, some firms have developed some sort of capacities or authority that make them look like States.[27] Second, in their interaction with society, the social position of many firms has made them significant agents of change shaping substantially social phenomena like globalization, but more importantly transforming the daily lives of many people around the world with significant impacts. As agents of impactful change which happen to share several attributes with States, firms have the competence to be considered *de facto* primary agents of justice in certain circumstances. As such, they should also take on some responsibilities to advance justice that are consistent with their new status, beyond their compliance with the regulatory frameworks handed down by the state.

Aside from the competence claim, there is also the second claim, which is an 'effectiveness claim'. The effectiveness claim also comprises at least two components. First, there is the idea that the State is no more effective in acting as a primary agent of justice and in such circumstances, there is no clear distinction on who constitutes a primary and secondary agent of justice. While O'Neill thinks that the blurring of that distinction is circumstantial and provisory (only in non-well-ordered societies) Wettstein considers that the blurring of that distinction should be more permanent given the structural injustices inherent in the process of globalization in the post-Westphalia era. The second component of the effectiveness claim is that the ineffectiveness of the State coincides with the effectiveness of many global firms. The idea here is that while many African States are either unable (because they are too poor) or unwilling (because they are undemocratic) to play their governmental role adequately, some firms are financially more powerful than those states and demonstrate a stronger capacity to address situations of injustice. They are better disposed to address injustice because they are mostly bound by the democratic values of their countries of origin where they can be held accountable by public opinions and regulatory structures that emanate from strong ethical principles. Thus, in the absence of governments that have abdicated their responsibility to ensure that justice prevails in the society, these firms should take a greater role in advancing justice and protecting freedoms in African societies.

Can Firms Better Advance Justice Than 'Failed African Societies'?

The notion that some firms are increasingly more powerful than certain states is factual. This reflects in their ability to influence policies both in their home countries or in their foreign abode of operation. Given the enormous influence some of these firms wield and given the desperate conditions of injustice and unfreedom that the majority of those living in Africa have come to find themselves today, is there an opportunity here to reimagine how we advance and promote justice? Why should we continue to rely on African States to advance and promote justice when those same States have consistently proven to be primary agents of injustice? Moreover, how do we justify the need to stick to a normative state/non-state actors or primary/secondary agents of justice distinction if we acknowledge that the majority of African States have been unable to enforce the very laws and regulations they created?[28] One may agree with these sets of assertions and observations, but disagrees with the normative implications O'Neill and Wettstein put forward. I argue that, even if one acknowledges these observations, there are still reasons to doubt that some firms may do a better job than failed African States in advancing justice in African societies.

Consider the effectiveness claim first. This claim hides an implicit claim that some firms are more ethically disposed to advance the course of justice for citizens in Africa where their governments have failed. But there is much more than circumstantial evidence to consider many firms operating in Africa as 'failed' social institutions themselves. When they are not directly responsible for grave violation of human rights or agents of exploitation of vulnerable people in poor settings of many African societies, they collude with self-serving political elites in perpetuating and worsening the conditions of the social injustice. In this respect they are neither 'morally' nor 'politically' disposed to succeed on the score of justice where the state in Africa has failed.

Consider also the competence claim. It is in part based on the misleading argument that some firms are significantly more powerful than most African States. Some firms may be richer or wealthier than some African States, but financial power does not necessarily translate into political power.[29] Wettstein could object that he is not basing his own claim exclusively on the financial power, but on a form of political authority that some firms have recently developed. If we focus solely on the financial power which is often the currency of their political influence (as they deploy this to lobby politicians and dictate policy directions), we miss the point of how justice should be pursued and how it should function in society. We also fail to ask the question of whether economic entities that exist primarily to make a profit can become an institutional vehicle for justice in the state. Each society that has the ideal of justice as its overall goal needs a multitude of social institutions playing each a key role to achieve that overall goal. The existence of such diverse institutions and roles calls for a division of moral labour that should be aligned with the necessary division of social labour.[30] If that is the case, we should acknowledge that there are critical state responsibilities that even the most powerful firms with the best of intentions should not usurp in the interest of maintaining a fair judicial system. Furthermore, for the sake of justice in African societies and interest of protecting the fundamental freedoms of African citizens, there may be strong moral reasons not to rely on big corporations because doing, as Nien-hê Hsieh rightly pointed out, may significantly undermine the way we see individual and citizens as morally equal persons[31] or as Chiara Cordelli has shown, may undermine several aspects of the democratic fabric.[32]

If turning some firms into state-like institutions is not the best way to contribute to justice, what should be the way forward?

Rethinking the Contribution of Firms in Advancing Justice in African Societies

Perhaps, the best way to reimagine the contribution of firms in advancing justice is not to transform some firms into state-like institutions hoping that they succeed where actual state actors are failing, but to completely reset our models of the moral division of labour between state actors and non-state actors, particularly here between the state and the firm and the entire public/private divide.[33] In this respect, we need to rethink and reconsider the role of business corporations in given societies while acknowledging their internal transformations as social institutions in the last decades alongside many other social institutions. Looking at them more as social institutions rather than economic institutions only could be a better path in grasping their contribution to just societies, including in African societies.

Such as reset of the state/firm moral division of labour starts by recognizing that there are two metrics to assess our moral expectations regarding different kinds of social institutions: one is their power or capacity, and the other is their role or function in society. If one looks at the power or the capacity metric, it is reasonable to infer that States are increasingly structurally weak while firms are increasingly structurally powerful in the context of globalized economies. But it is also reasonable to consider that moral responsibility or obligations are not exclusively drawn upon from the power or the capacity of a specific institution. It may depend more importantly on the specific role they play or function they have in society. The role some institutions play may afford them the capacity other institutions lack in order to perform a specific duty. Because of their specific function in society, States will always have a 'power-wise' advantage over firms even in poor countries.

Still, the fact the power of States has shrunk while the power of firm has expanded should also have an impact on the way we reassess their respective functions and role as contributors among other to the overall objective of fair and just societies. A reassessment of the function of the firm that will determine its responsibilities and part of moral labour alongside the State should lead to a special status of the firm[34] as a hybrid institution, where the firm occupies a slightly elevated position compared to other non-state actors and a little bit less than a State. This is particularly applicable to big or multinational corporations.

There exist also the belief that there is a difference in functionality between firms and States. States are public institutions whereas firms are private institutions, and both types of institutions are not governed by the same rules and do not abide by the same principles. Charles Larmore suggests one key aspect of that difference in kind when he writes regarding the principle of neutrality that

> for the liberal, neutrality is a political ideal. The state's policies and decisions must be neutrally justifiable, but the liberal does not require that other institutions in society operate in the same spirit. Churches and firms, for example, may pursue goals (salvation, profits) that they assume to be ideals intrinsically superior to others. In other words, neutrality as a political ideal governs the public relations between persons and the state, and not the private relations between persons and other institutions[35]

The main reasons behind that difference in kind are first the *involuntary* nature of state that its members do not choose whereas the firms are a voluntary association where workers come and go and second, its political/public feature which includes the fact that the State should essentially treat its members on egalitarian terms whereas the firm predominantly treats members on meritocratic terms.

For others however, there is a difference in degree between States and firms.[36] Jeffrey Moriarty rejects the 'voluntary argument' when he writes that it "is obvious that leaving one's country is difficult. It is not appreciated how difficult leaving one's job can be. For many workers, leaving a job means losing seniority, retirement funds, health benefits, job-specific skills, community ties, and friends".[37] Likewise, the growing literature on firms as political actors or agents attests to the fact that firms are no more considered strictly as private actors, but as public institutions of a different dimension.

This debate can be a complex one, and part of the complexity comes from the fact that firms or states are considered as monolithic categories. There is a distinction that can be made between small firms, middle-size firms and transnational or multinational corporations. If the former two categories could be considered 'strict' non-state actors, the status of the latter seems more ambiguous and can fall into both the non-state or the state actors' category. Multinationals share with state and non-state actors some relevant features. Like non-state actors, they still have private interests stemming from their roles as economics institutions. Like state actors, they have influential and financial power that put them in some areas in a position to do good and advance justice better than some states. A testament to their overlapping characteristics. This is a hybrid status that needs to be acknowledged and probably sharpened in a normative sense. Relying on that hybrid status of the firm, the state/firm division of moral should lead to complementary instead of separate responsibilities.

If we consider firms as social institutions and some of those firms, multinationals, as hybrid actors, they have a moral obligation as all social institutions to contribute to promotion and advancement of justice. Given their hybrid status and those subsequent moral obligations, I see three ways some firms can discharge their duties to contribute to justice in African societies. First, firms should help promote just institutions where they are unavailable. To assist in the promotion of just institutions means (a) that firms should collaborate with other social institutions to meet their own duties, (b) that the collaboration between firms and other institutions aims at the one hand at upholding and maintaining fair social structures that already exist, and (c) on the other hand at transforming unjust structures where they exist. Firms do not need to become quasi-governmental institutions to do so.

Second, firms should not be accomplices to governments that violate the human rights of their own people. This is of course a difficult ask, especially where profits are threatened. Moreover, if firms seek to protest injustice of a human rights-violating state by leaving, such a decision would also come at the cost of job losses for the locals and impact adversely on the livelihood of more citizens. Firms can also choose to stay in order to help improve the situation from within, but with the risk of being accused of indifference in the face of injustice. The moral challenge or dilemma is real, and it is one faced by multinationals on a daily basis in most African countries. Whatever path that each firm can take depending on its mission and values, there is a need to recognize the influence that they wield and to leverage this in their interaction with state actors to bring about a just society. In this respect, the moral leadership many key firms played in contributing to the end of the Apartheid regime in South Africa[38] is a model other firms can emulate.

As hybrid actors, firms should change their own internal private governance in a way that can set an example for 'failed' state actors to emulate. Being a kind of social institution, firms can become a small laboratory of fair and just societies. If firms cannot set up internal constitutions, rules or model of governance that improve the social conditions of their workers, protect their fundamental freedoms wherever this is compatible with their core functions or give them a voice in the way the workplace is governed and considered as equal partners with shareholders and other stakeholders in the wealth creation process, they will simply lack the moral and political authority to address the flaws and unjust situations that take place in the general population. Setting that example will not only have the benefit of improving the daily conditions of many African citizens who happen to work in those firms, but it will also provide some sort of guidance for African states to reflect on. Here also, those firms may substantially contribute to advancing justice in African societies in a way that is both beyond their 'current' status as non-state actors and below their 'call-for' status as quasi-governmental institutions.

Conclusion

The consequences of globalization and the incapacity of many failed states in Africa to secure fundamental freedoms for their people and establish more just societies have triggered a robust debate on the contribution of non-state actors to advance these causes. In this chapter, I tried to consider that paradigm shift while cautioning about relying on business corporations to address the most pressing issues (injustices and unfreedoms) African citizens are facing daily. I suggested that we should redefine the role of the firm, especially multinational corporations, as a hybrid social institution and that its collaborative responsibility in advancing justice and helping to protect fundamental freedoms in Africa should focus on helping to promote justice institutions where they are lacking. These big firms must, as a matter of ethical responsibility, avoid complicity in state violation of human rights and (re)calibrate their internal governance culture and apparatus in ways that advance justice and protect the fundamental rights of the working community. By so doing, they are able and set an example for African societies where they operate and advance the course of justice through this relational interaction.

Notes

1   University of Maroua, Catholic University of Central Africa & University of St. Gallen.
2   Chabal, Patrick, *Africa: The Politics of Suffering and Smiling*. Zed Books, 2009.
3   Bieler, Andreas, Higgott, Richard & Underhill, Geoffrey (Eds.), *Non-State Actors and Authority in the Global System*, 1st ed. Routledge, 2000. https://doi.org/10.4324/9780203165041.
4   Vosko, Leaf F., "'Decent Work': The Shifting Role of the ILO and the Struggle for Global Social Justice", *Global Social Policy* 2, no. 1 (2002): 19–46. https://doi.org/10.1177/1468018102002001093
5   Madeley, John, *Big Business, Poor Peoples: The Impact of Transnational Corporations on the World's Poor*. Zed Books, 1999, xvii, 206p.
6   Wettstein, Florian, *Multinational Corporations and Global Justice: Human Rights Obligations of a Quasi-Governmental Institution*, 1st ed. Stanford University Press, 2009. Ruggie, John Gerard, *Just Business: Multinational Corporations and Human Rights*. W.W. Norton & Company, 2013.
7   O'Neill, Onora, "Agents of Justice" *Metaphilosophy* 32, no. 1/2 (2001): 180–195, p. 181.
8   Bieler, Higgott & Underhill, op. cit.
9   O'Neill, "Agents of Justice", p. 194.
10 John, Rawls, *The Law of Peoples*. Harvard University Press, 1999.
11 Idem.
12 O'Neill, "Agents of Justice", pp. 193–194.
13 Actors which cannot fall completely in one or the other category completely, like multinational corporations.
14 Many reports of either international governmental organizations like the UN or international non-governmental organizations like Amnesty International or Human Rights Watch, and domestic organizations in several African countries show how in a wide-range of issues social inequalities grow while the size of freedom and liberties shrink.
15 Kruk, Margaret E. et al., "Mortality Due to Low-Quality Health Systems in the Universal Health Coverage Era: A Systematic Analysis of Amenable Deaths in 137 Countries", *The Lancet* 392, no. 10160 (2018): 2203–2212.
16 United Nations, World Mortality Report 2017.
17 Kelbessa, Workineh, "Environmental Injustice in Africa", *Contemporary Pragmatism* 9, no. 1 (2012): 99–132. https://doi.org/10.1163/18758185–90000219
18 Denoiseux, Delphine, « L'exportation de déchets dangereux vers l'Afrique : le cas du Probo Koala », *Courrier hebdomadaire du CRISP* 2071, no. 26 (2010): 5–47.
19 Ombati, Victor & Mokua, Ombati, "Gender Inequality", *Journal of Women's Entrepreneurship and Education* 3–4 (2012): 114–136.
20 Nicoleta, Isac, "Gender Inequalities in the Workplace: Case Study of South Africa", *Management and Economic Review* 6, no. 1 (2021). https://doi.org/10.24818/MER/2021.06-06.
21 Mbonda, Ernest, *John Rawls. Droits de l'homme et justice politique*. Presses Universitaires de Laval, 2008.
22 See for example Wettstein and Bauer who argue that business corporations should care about issues like marriage equality and other topic discussed in the public domain. See Wettstein, Florian & Baur, Dorothea, "Why Should We Care about Marriage Equality?": Political Advocacy as a Part of Corporate Responsibility", *Journal of Business Ethics* 138 (2016): 199–213. https://doi.org/10.1007/s10551-015-2631-3.
23 Néron, Piene-Yves, "Business and the Polis: What Does It Mean to See Corporations as Political Actors?", *Journal of Business Ethics* 94, no. 3 (2010): 333–352. http://www.jstor.org/stable/40784698.
24 O'Neill, "Agents of Justice", 2001.
25 Wettstein, *Multinational Corporations and Global Justice: Human Rights Obligations of a Quasi-Governmental Institution*, 2013.
26 Wettstein, Florian, "From Agents of Change to Agents of Justice. The Role of Multinational Corporations in a Globalizing World", *Theories de la justice. Justice globale, Agents de la justice et Justice de genre*, T. Ngosso & E. Mbonda (eds.), Presses Universitaires de Louvain, 2016, pp. 109–119.
27 Wettstein, *Multinational Corporations and Global Justice: Human Rights Obligations of a Quasi-Governmental Institution*, 2013.
28 Ihonvbere, Julius O., "The 'Irrelevant' State, Ethnicity, and the Quest for Nationhood in Africa", *Ethnic and Racial Studies* 17, no. 1 (1994): 42–60. https://doi.org/10.1080/01419870.1994.9993812

29 Brian Barry provides a very interesting exegesis of power when it comes to the comparison between firms and states and questions the notion that firms are taking over States in ruling the world today. See Brian, Barry B., "Capitalists Rule Ok? Some Puzzles About Power", *Politics, Philosophy & Economics* 1, no. 2 (2002): 155–184. https://doi.org/10.1177/1470594X02001002001

30 Ngosso, Thierry, «Quatre approches de l'entreprise responsable», *Philosophiques* 47, no. 1 (2020): 117–137. https://doi.org/10.7202/1070253ar.

31 Hsieh, Nien-hê, "Should Business Have Human Rights Obligations?", *Journal of Human Rights* 14, no. 2 (2015): 218–236. https://doi.org/10.1080/14754835.2015.1007223

32 Cordelli, Chiara, "How Privatization Threatens the Private", *Critical Review of International Social and Political Philosophy* 16, no. 1 (2013): 65–87. https://doi.org/10.1080/13698230.2011.640482

33 I will not address directly the issue of the public/private divide more broadly here, even if it is at the root also of the state/non-state actors' distinction.

34 Probably some particular firms.

35 Larmore, Charles, *Patterns of Moral Complexity.* Cambridge University Press, 1987, p. 45.

36 Moriarty, Jeffrey, "On The relevance of Political Philosophy to Business Ethics", *Business Ethics Quarterly* 15, no. 3 (2005): 455–473.

37 Moriarty, Jeffrey, "On the Relevance of Political Philosophy to Business Ethics", p. 460.

38 Mangaliso, Mzamo P, "South Africa: Corporate Social Responsibility and the Sullivan Principles", *Journal of Black Studies* 28, no. 2 (1997): 219–238. http://www.jstor.org/stable/2784852.

29

AFRICA IN THE POLITICAL IMAGINATION OF THE AFRICAN DIASPORA

Omedi Ochieng

Introduction: Contours of the Diasporic Imagination

The word diaspora is drawn from the Greek prefix *dia-* (meaning "across" or "through") and the verb *sperein* (meaning "to scatter" or "to sow"). Though initially the word mainly referred to Jewish communities that were dispersed across the Mediterranean during the Hellenic period, the term now is broadly used to designate a wide variety of populations that claim historical and imaginary affiliative ties to a separate geographical locale. In the case of the African diaspora, the term has mainly come to designate the dispersion of African-descended people across the continents, beginning with the slave trade from the fifteenth century through to the end of the nineteenth century.

In what follows, I will limn the constructions of "Africa" in the political imagination of its diaspora. Both the terms "political" and "imagination" are contested terms and therefore worth explicating. By political imagination, I mean primarily the sensory and affective forms in and through which a population constructs boundaries of belonging, the institutional structures constitutive of what they take to be their identity and sustenance, and the myths, ideologies, and stories through which they narrate their histories and chart their futures (Ochieng, *Intellectual Imagination*). The imagination, then, is neither defined in what follows as a faculty opposed to reason nor a romantic emanation distinct from "reality." Rather, it is constitutive of reality. Moreover, the imagination is constituted by a full range of sensory and affective forms—the visual, auditory, olfactory, tactile, and gustatory senses. Thus, unlike North Atlantic accounts of the imagination that privilege the visual, this essay seeks to be attentive to other modalities of the imagination. To be clear, the sensory and the affective ought to be seen as mediated by the institutions and formations of politics and culture. It therefore follows that this essay will pay particular attention to signs and language—especially the metaphors through which the political is constructed and given salience.

The "political" is no less contested than the imagination. By the political, I mean principally the range of institutions, ideas, and practices in and through which humans imagine, contest, and transform power. Considered as such, the political ought not to be seen as encompassing only the institutions of state or officially designated governmental institutions. The relationship between the political and the "economic," or the "cultural," is not seen in the order of distinct spaces, or artifacts, or objects of interest. Just as the economic and the cultural are political if we

DOI: 10.4324/9781003143529-34

conceive of power as saturating and interanimating all practices, so the political is itself structured by the economic ("the formations, systems, and practices in and through which humans adjudicate matters of subsistence, exchange, and distribution") and the cultural ("the *how tos* of any practice, institutionalized or heterodox") (Ochieng, *Groundwork*).

Below, I will chart some of the main articulations of Afro-diasporic political imaginations. Though I endeavor to engage with some prominent thinkers and texts that shaped Afro-diasporic imaginations about Africa, this essay does not claim to be exhaustive. Its goal is oriented, rather, to sketching out some significant landmarks in the historical and geographic map of Afro-diasporic thought.

Abolitionist Africa: Between "Barbarism" and "Refuge"

'Twas mercy brought me from my *Pagan* land,
Taught my benighted soul to understand
That there's a God, that there's a *Saviour* too:
Once I redemption neither sought nor knew.
Some view our sable race with scornful eye,
"Their colour is a diabolic die."
Remember, *Christians, Negros,* black as *Cain,*
May be refin'd, and join th' angelic train.

This poem, entitled "On Being Brought from Africa to America," by Phillis Wheatley was first published in 1773. Wheatley is reputed to be the first African American woman to publish a book of poetry. Born c. 1753, it is likely she was in her early twenties when the poem was first published. Her poem echoes some of the major tropes that Europeans fashioned from the very beginnings of the trans-Atlantic slave trade about Africa. Her account of Africa as a land of heathens plays to a European notion of the continent as the antithesis of Christian civilization. Black skin is made a metonymy for the "darkness" of Africa, which Wheatley alludes to by describing her soul as "benighted" before conversion.

Many scholars have argued, however, that Wheatley should not be read unimaginatively. Against the idea that she is simply parroting the racist ideas of her white captors, they point to how the poem subtly pushes back against the idea that blackness is a "diabolical die" (Loving). This was significant at a time when one of the justifications for slavery held that Africans were cursed by God. Others have argued that Wheatley's lines, "Remember, *Christians, Negros,* black as *Cain/* May be refin'd, and join th' angelic train" introduces the idea that even Christians—here a reference to white people—were themselves also sinners (Scheick).

Wheatley's poems presaged heated clashes among Afro-diasporic people about the meaning of Africa and the relationship they ought to take toward it. The context was in part poisoned by bitter recriminations over whether free African Americans should colonize or emigrate to Africa. A great deal of what made the issue combustible was the American Colonization Society, a white-led movement that sought to remove free black people from the United States for resettlement in Africa. Frederick Douglass, the most electrifying abolitionist in the United States, took a principled stand against colonization. Though, undoubtedly, correct in exposing the racist motives of white advocates for colonization, Douglass was prone to conflate the stance of white-led colonization with that of African Americans who were championing emigration. Among the latter were the likes of Martin Delany. "We are a nation within a nation, as the Poles in Russia, the Hungarians in Austria, the Welsh, Irish and Scotch in the British dominions," Delany argued in his book *The Condition, Elevation, Emigration, and Destiny of the Colored People of the United States, Politically Considered.* He argued that African Americans should therefore find a new nation on the eastern coast of Africa.

Douglass's unstinting opposition to the white-led colonization movement was in no small part made ironically distinctive by how deeply he himself had absorbed their racist assumptions. "There is nothing in reason why anyone should leave this land of progress and enlightenment and seek a home amid the death-dealing malaria of a barbarous continent," he wrote in an editorial (Martin, jr. 208). His descriptions of Africa drew on the hoary binaries that white elites had long circulated about Africa. He juxtaposes the "splendors of Europe" with the "wilds of Africa"; portrays Africa as backward in comparison to Europe; and is prone to compare the abject state of the slave to the life of Africans on the continents. Douglass's contemptuous legacy has redounded across history, as seen in the writings of the likes of Richard Wright and Henry Louis Gates, Jr.

Anti-emigration abolitionists like Douglass and pro-emigration proponents like Delany, however, agreed that ancient Egyptian civilization represented the best of historic African capabilities. They spoke at a time when sentiment prevailed in elite Euro-American circles that ancient Egypt was primarily a white civilization. Douglass cannily turned their very assumptions against themselves. For example, prominent white archaeologists like Samuel G. Morton argued that even though the ancient Egyptians were a mixed race, the "Caucasian" ingredient of the mixture was predominant over the "Negroid" element. Douglass countered that by the logic of the "one drop of blood" rule—which held that the slightest African ancestry made one black—that would immediately mean that the ancient Egyptians would be classed as "Negroes" in nineteenth-century America. Whatever the color and features of the ancient Egyptians, Douglass wrote after his visit to Egypt in 1887, there was no doubt that they would have been classed as Negroes according to the criteria of white supremacists (Martin, jr. 206).

The writings of the likes of Wheatley, Douglass, and Delany by no means offer an exhaustive account of Afro-diasporic political imaginations in the nineteenth century. And yet, they stand as landmarks that have continued to deeply shape the contours of the Afro-diasporic imagination even today. One of its legacies has been the affects incited by Africa in the Afro-diasporic imagination: repudiation, ambivalence, and perhaps even shame (as seen in the writings of Wheatley and Douglass), on the one hand, and pride, desire, and identification (as seen in the writings of Delany, William Wells Brown, Edward W. Blyden, and Garnet) on the other.

And yet, for all their differences, it is striking how little prominent U.S.-based Afro-diasporic intellectuals cared to listen to Africans on the continent speak on their own terms. Alexander Crummell, for example, in celebrating the enduring connection between U.S. blacks and Africans on the continent, articulated a position in direct opposition to the views of Frederick Douglass. Still, he spoke about Africans with an unabashed paternalism and condescension that scarcely differed from Douglass's ideas. Writing in defense of the colonization of Liberia by emancipated black Americans, he characterized it as a mission to bring civilization to "this seat [Africa] of ancient despotism and bloody superstitions" (Wilson 242). In response to those who would object to such an endeavor, Crummell insisted that "both our positions and our circumstances make us the guardians, the protectors, and the teachers of our heathen tribes." (Wilson 246).

Pan-Africanism: The Limits of African Utopianism

In 1900, Henry Sylvester Williams, a Trinidadian lawyer, convened the first Pan-African Conference under the auspices of the African Association, an organization dedicated to fighting for the rights of Africans on the continent and in the Caribbean. The conference drew in luminaries from across the world, including WEB Du Bois, Anna J. Cooper, Anna H. Jones, and Benito Sylvain, a Haitian diplomat and writer, and representative of Emperor Menelik of Ethiopia. Plans for subsequent conferences did not materialize, in part due to the collapse of the African Association. The impact of the conference, however, cannot be gainsaid. Perhaps one of its most distinctive contributions consisted in making thinkable an institutional Pan-African network.

It is precisely these threads that Marcus Garvey, the Jamaican writer and activist, would pick up on and extend. Garvey founded the Universal Negro Improvement Association and African Communities League (UNIA) in Jamaica in 1914. In its manifesto, UNIA declared that would seek to establish "a universal confederacy amongst the race." The manifesto asserts that UNIA would seek to bring about "racial pride and love," contribute to "the civilizing of backward tribes in Africa," and promote "conscientious Christian worship." UNIA adopted the motto: "One God! One Aim! One Destiny!" (Adi 28).

To achieve these ends, Garvey thought that black people needed to establish a state and a government of their own. Writing about the process by which he came to found UNIA, Garvey writes: 'I asked "Where is the black man's government? Where is his king and his kingdom? Where is his president, his country, and his ambassador, his army, his navy, his men of big affairs?" (Garvey 5). In his book, *Philosophy and Opinions*, Garvey makes a case for the establishment of a continent-wide independent African republic that would safeguard the interests of black people worldwide. Garvey believed that he ought to be the leader of that future republic.

Garvey moved to the United States in 1916 and oversaw the rapid growth of UNIA. Scholars estimate that the organization's membership may have numbered over 2 million people, with up to a thousand branches across North America, Africa, the Caribbean, and Europe. UNIA also established several commercial ventures, including a shipping line, grocery stores, restaurants and a newspaper, *Negro World*.

UNIA's spectacular ascendance was in the end followed by just as spectacular a fall. UNIA's shipping line, the Black Star, went bankrupt, rendering Garvey vulnerable to his powerful enemies. The U.S. government charged Garvey with fraud and sent him to prison. His overtures to the government of Liberia, which he thought of as a foothold for his plans toward an independent African republic, also failed after the U.S. government forced Liberia to cut ties with him. After his release from jail, he was expelled from the United States leading to a split between the U.S. branches of UNIA and other chapters in the rest of the world.

Like the life of contrasts that he led, Garvey bequeathed a contradictory inheritance. The positive dimensions of his legacy ought not to be dismissed. Perhaps the most important was that Garvey understood correctly that any serious effort to confront white supremacist power had to take the form of a mass movement. The very composition of the mass movement that Garvey mobilized speaks to why it was so formidable. Of striking significance is that UNIA drew its support from working and lower middle classes in both rural and urban areas. In the United States, for example, UNIA chapters organized and established chapters in the South (Hahn).

But even from the start, it was clear that Garveyism was a flawed movement. A substantial reason for this emerges from the very form of mass movement that Garvey envisioned. UNIA articulated a largely racially essentialist mass movement. More specifically, he sought to gather members to the cause on the basis of their black identity. An ideological foundation of racial essentialism, however, had little chance of posing a sustained and radical threat to a global social formation constituted by capitalism, white supremacy, and patriarchy. In order to make such a sustained struggle possible, Garvey would have had to have a more sophisticated social ontology, one that, for example, recognized the differing, cross-cutting interests among black people. That Garvey's movement was impressive given the resources he started with and the powers ranged against him is undoubtedly true. But closer scrutiny also reveals that he was as much an obstacle to its growth as he was its engine for expansion. Rather than arrogate to himself leadership, he could have imagined a much more participatory, democratic movement. His arrogance was matched by his parochialism, as seen in the UNIA manifesto's Christian assumptions and his paternalism toward the people of Africa.

Few Afro-diasporic leaders have been able to match Garvey's organizational ambition and energy. But even fewer have matched the renown and influence of Garvey's most formidable critic—W.E.B. Du Bois. No serious engagement with Du Bois should pass without a deep acknowledgment that his life was characterized by remarkable transformations. From the liberal universalism of his early thought, he turned to a cultural nationalism in his middle years to a robust form of Pan-African Communism in the later decades of his life.

Du Bois was sharply critical of Marcus Garvey whom he once described as "the most dangerous enemy of the Negro race in America and the world" (Levering 340). The weaknesses of Garveyism, Du Bois argued in his book *The World and Africa*, "lay in its demagogic leadership, poor finance, intemperate propaganda, and the natural apprehension it aroused among the colonial powers" (Du Bois *The World* 149). Even so, the early Du Bois had much in common with Garvey, for all that he was keen to disavow their similarities. He, much like Garvey, took a largely paternalistic stance toward Africa, believing that enlightened, talented black people like him would lead Africa into civilization. For Du Bois, of course, that enlightened, talented group were mainly African Americans, whom he thought ought to be accorded the "natural" leadership role among the black peoples of the world. In *The Conservation of Races*, he cast African Americans as the "advance guard of the Negro people" (56). This was in keeping with Du Bois's elitist view of leadership. He called for the exercise of black leadership by a "talented tenth"—intellectually gifted, college-educated black people who would serve as leaders and exemplars of the black race.

Du Bois played a central role in organizing four Pan-African conferences after the First World War. He pointedly excluded Marcus Garvey from these conferences not only because he was intent on being seen as the lead representative for Afro-diasporic people, but also because he was at this time opposed to Garvey's populism. To that end, the conferences that he organized sought to bring about change by addressing and petitioning the leaders of the victorious world powers. One of the main successes of these conferences was that they facilitated deep and lasting forms of coordination and comity among Afro-diasporic leaders around the world. Nonetheless, they failed in realizing some of their immediate demands. Moreover, Du Bois's theory of change to the effect that political transformation could come about through elite negotiation at conferences also bequeathed a pernicious legacy that would ripple out for generations across Afro-diasporic history.

But by the fourth congress, held in New York in 1927, Du Bois was already showing signs that his political commitments were undergoing profound transformations. His visit to the Soviet Union in 1926 signaled his growing turn against moderate liberalism to a far more radical posture. Indeed, Du Bois's radical turn offers a remarkable portal both to the utopian possibilities unleashed by Pan-African internationalism and solidarity and its crushing failures, betrayals, and contradictions. The utopian potentialities were encapsulated in two directions: the emergence of communism as a revolutionary force in global affairs and the movements for self-determination across the world that fought back against colonialism and imperialism.

When, in his autobiography, Du Bois defiantly declares, "I now state my conclusion frankly and clearly: I believe in communism," (35) he was doing more than announcing a longstanding political practice. He also signaled his solidarity with the world that communism had made possible. From the time the Bolsheviks formed the Communist International in 1919, a countervailing force to global capitalist imperialism was transformed from an idea into material institutional forces—movements, parties, and state apparatuses. World revolution became more than simply an aspiration—it was an organized social formation.

In theory, at least, the Communist International unfolded a vision of the world beyond the global color line. But other ascendant global movements had been for a long time the driving engine of freedom from the domination of North Atlantic imperialists, sometimes but not always drawing their theoretical and affective inspiration from communism. Those global movements were disparate—some emergent from slave revolts such as the Haitian revolution; others formed in the wake of colonialism in places as diverse as South Asia, the Middle East, and Africa. But by the twentieth century, many had crystallized into struggles for national self-determination. Du Bois's stunning network of correspondents, confidantes, and comrades is a veritable who's who of the twentieth-century's most influential figures of the global south: Kwame Nkrumah, George Padmore, C.L.R. James, Jawaharlal Nehru, Mohandas Gandhi, Mao Zedong, and many more.

The undeniable banners of freedom borne aloft by communists and movements for self-determination in the global south were shot through with authoritarian and parochial interests. These contradictions were theoretical as well as historical. Even as the Bolshevik cadres advanced a vision of global class struggle, factions from within fought against democratic, participatory Soviets, culminating in Stalin's ascendance to power. Stalin would go on to dictate that Socialism in the USSR took precedence over the world revolution. In many ways, Du Bois embodied these contradictions as much as he lived them. His praise of Stalin jarringly contradicted not only his own continued aspirations for a global revolution but also, given his influence, contributed to legitimizing the authoritarianism germinating among the elite ranks of anticolonial movements.

To be sure, the political theorist Adom Getachew has argued for a conception of anticolonial nationalism as worldmaking. In her reading of political figures such as Nnamdi Azikiwe, W.E.B. Du Bois, Michael Manley, Kwame Nkrumah, Julius Nyerere, George Padmore, and Eric Williams, Getachew avers that "anticolonial nationalism envisioned a world where democratic, modernizing, and redistributive national states were situated in thick international institutions designed to realize the principle of nondomination" (28). Getachew charts the movement of decolonization through a number of phases. There was, first, the articulation of Pan-African internationalism as a revolutionary alternative to imperial universalism. This was followed by the negotiations that led to the adoption of the language of self-determination by the United Nations. The next phase focused on the institutionalization of regional federations such as the Union of African States and the West Indian Federation. The final phase then involved attempts to bolster economic self-determination by instituting a New International Economic Order (NIEO) in the 1970s.

Getachew's book offers a richly researched illumination of the intellectual history of decolonial self-determination. Nonetheless, her book also advances normative conclusions that call for a critical response. Getachew argues, correctly, that for too long anticolonial nationalism has been seen as a failed imitation of Western ideals of self-government. Seen as such, she continues, many scholars have argued that nationalism was doomed to failure. For its liberal critics, nationalism flouts the principle that the individual takes primacy over the collective. For traditionalists, nationalism was an artificial imposition on African polities that failed to accord with precolonial African forms of social organization. Getachew rejects both arguments. Far from being a failed imitation of Western nationalism, anticolonial nationalism articulated a compelling alternative to the racism and imperialism of the former. Moreover, there was nothing inevitable about the trajectory that anticolonial nationalism took. Its failures lay in contingent historical forces and decisions.

These arguments, primarily directed at liberal scholarship that has sought to enfold anti-colonialism within a hegemonic Western scholarly frame, are broadly right. And yet, precisely because Getachew's argument is mainly directed at a critique of liberal political theory, she fails to grapple with radical critiques of anticolonial nationalisms. The problems begin, perhaps, with her historiography. Her title and narrative frame the story of anticolonialism nationalism as a "rise and fall." For all that she insists on the contingency and contradictions of history, she is here still beholden to a largely linear historiography. Getachew, of course, would argue that her account of the rise and fall of self-determination is purely descriptive, indexing the ascendance and eventual etiolation in intellectual influence and institutional power of decolonial nationalism. And yet her narrative belies that characterization. Her book frames the limitations of anticolonial self-determination as subsequent to the grand visions unfurled by decolonial protagonists, emerging largely as an effect of their encounter with intractable historical forces. She argues in her epilogue, for example, that

> the preoccupation with the precarious nature of post-colonial independence had inspired demanding projects of worldmaking to secure international nondomination. But as these projects faltered and nationalists faced domestic opposition and international criticism, they increasingly embraced a more defensive posture toward the state.
>
> *(179)*

Getachew's book, then, fails to take as a *sine qua non* of her investigation, a thoroughgoing critique of what it would mean to limn the political imagination of a movement or tradition—the epistemic, affective, and aesthetic contours and limits of not just what thinkers and writers make claims on behalf of, but also what they cannot or will not imagine. Part of that task would have demanded a much more elaborate immanent critique of the visions articulated by anticolonial nationalists. As Nyerere himself would later concede when interviewed:

> I was not seeing Ujamaa outside of the nation-state. I've questioned many, many, many things from Europe, but I've not questioned the nation-state. I cannot think, how do I think in terms of not the nation-state? … My questioning did not reach the nation-state. My questioning focused upon the borders.
>
> *(Sutherland and Meyer 76)*

Such an immanent critique would have had to contend with the radical social collectives—many of these emergent from Indigenous people—that from the very start fiercely fought against the anticolonial nationalists that Getachew's book valorizes (Gnamo). Moreover, it calls for a more careful parsing out of the tensions and outright conflicting horizons between and among anticolonial nationalists. Here one calls to mind, for instance, the disagreements between Nkrumah and Nyerere over the primacy of the political over the economic; or the deep tensions between W.E.B. Du Bois and C.L.R. James over slave agency.

At stake in an immanent critique is the question of the radical imagination. And it is precisely here that Getachew's analysis proves particularly feeble. It is a glaring characteristic of the form of worldmaking advanced by the leading intellectuals she examines that they conceive of nationalism instrumentally. What's more, their *internationalist* strategy in response to imperialism evinced a remarkable faith in "high" contractarian politics, ultimately grounded in a doomed effort to preserve the nominal accoutrements of state autonomy rather than transform global politics. As Getachew argues:

> Anticolonial worldmaking offered a number of strategies to mitigate, circumvent, and undo the hierarchies that facilitated domination. First, through the right to self-determination, anticolonial nationalists strengthened the legal barriers against foreign intervention and encroachment. Through an expansive account of sovereign equality as equal legislative power and a redefinition of nonintervention that went beyond prohibiting military interventions, anticolonial nationalists sought to contain and limit domination through legal instruments. Second, in the constitution of regional federations in the West Indies and Africa, anti-colonial nationalists sought to evade the economic dependence inherent in the global economy by organizing regional institutions that were egalitarian and redistributive. Rather than a direct challenge to international hierarchy, federation was an attempt at a partial exit and insulation from the dependencies that facilitated domination. Finally, through the New International Economic Order, anticolonial nationalists directly challenged the economic hierarchies of the international realm. Laying claim to the expansive account of sovereign equality articulated in the right to self- determination, they envisioned an egalitarian welfare world that would be democratic and redistributive. In this final project, nondomination was refigured as a radical form of international equality.
>
> *(23–24)*

It is immediately striking that the global strategy articulated here is grounded in a juridical foundation, one that proved both a cause and consequence of the enmeshment of the anticolonial nationalist imagination in an ultimately abstract "rights" discourse. This juridical frame conducts international politics in a largely defensive posture, one that re-naturalizes the state as the proper guarantor of political self-determination. Even when this is leavened with regional federations aimed at securing economic benefits, the language of "partial exit," "insulation," and even "dependency" was at best naïve about what it would take to seriously take the fight to imperial capitalism. No wonder then that the economic imagination of the anticolonial nationalists turned out to be welfarist and redistributive, a telling concession to the capitalist world order.

The travails of Pan-Africanism cannot then be wholly attributed to exogenous factors: the authoritarianism of many of the anticolonial nationalists, their often narrow and cramped political imaginations, and their refusal to absorb the lessons of defeat played its part.

Post-Pan-Africanism: The Afterlife of Political Defeat

Saidiya Hartman's *Lose Your Mother* offers an entry into the post-Pan-African world. The goal of her monograph is to chronicle her journey to Ghana to retrace the routes of the Atlantic slave trade. But hers is not, as she is quick to warn the reader, yet another tale of an African American looking to find her roots in Africa. Rather, for her,

> the rupture was the story. Whatever bridges I might build were as much the reminder of my separation as my connection. The holding cell had supplanted the ancestral village. The slave trade loomed larger for me than any memory of a glorious African past or sense of belonging in the present.
>
> *(41–42)*

Toward that end, Hartman's monograph narrates a story in which Africans on the continent and African Americans encounter one another as strangers. Upon her arrival in Ghana, she quickly learns she is *Obruni*, a stranger, not kin. It is a label Hartman then embraces. Those sold into slavery by Africans, she points out, were strangers, not kin. In accepting that she is a stranger, she is also embracing the slave. Hartman chronicles an Africa in which slavery is simultaneously disavowed and monetized to attract tourist dollars.

The Ghana that Hartman visits is a decidedly postcolonial country, with frequent power cuts, the looming threat of a military coup, and widespread poverty. It is part of Hartman's intent to remind readers that, perhaps more consequentially than even colonialism, Ghana is a post-slave society. As such, Hartman wants to puncture what she sees as the romanticism of "Afrotopia," the idea of Africa as a hoped-for homeland for its scattered diaspora. Hartman's narrative is significantly informed by the perspective of an African American couple, Mary Ellen and John Ray, who at that time had been living in Ghana for over a decade. The couple is embittered by the way they have been treated in Ghana. "We have to stop bullshitting about Africa. The naïveté that allows folks to believe they are returning home or entering paradise when they come here has to be destroyed," John tells Hartman (33). Mary Ellen, for her part, rejects the appellation African American, deeming the *African* part of the name false. Instead, she confides to Hartman that the only identity she could claim was as a *black* American.

Perhaps what emerges most powerfully in Hartman's narrative is that Afro-diasporic solidarity can no longer rest on a metaphysics of kinship—and more specifically, kinship conceived of as biological relationships of descent. Instead, she gestures toward an invention of new identities fashioned out of dreams for freedom—on both sides of the Atlantic.

But for all of its undeniable power and insight, Hartman's narrative cannot entirely work through its contradictions and limitations. The trouble begins with form. In an interview, Hartman revealed that she "never thought [she] would write anything that anyone could attach the label memoir to" (Saunders 4). Following Foucault, she is wary of confessional genres. Nonetheless, *Lose Your Mother* does draw heavily on the conventions of memoir as a genre, even as it strives hard to explode the form's solipsism. To that end, Hartman moves fluidly from autobiography, to field observation, to historical research, to normative political critique. And yet as she moves across these differing registers, she does not foreground the tensions and outright contradictions that may emerge as she sutures these distinct genres. Her account comes across as seamless and thereby raises questions about how these forms of narration may not only enrich one another, but quite often contradict and upend the insights yielded by each. Hartman does not, however, pursue what it would mean to write an account that is as attentive to the internal tensions and contradictions of narration as to its content, the travails of Pan-Africanism, which she expertly skewers.

For example, at its very best, autobiography can yield "thick insights" about the texture and particularities of a place. Normative political critique, on the other hand, aspires to a certain level of abstraction insofar as it seeks to connect disparate peoples, places, and histories. And yet, by far the most dominant comparative frame in Hartman's narrative is that between Africans on the continent and Afro-Americans. She thereby sidles too easily between different spatial and historical scales—for instance, her encounters with the specific people she met are synecdochal for Ghana writ large, while Ghana is also in her narrative a sign of Africa as a whole. She fails to grapple with the complexities striating these differing scales.

One upshot of this critique is what her narrative ends up obscuring. Such is her focus on the trans-Atlantic slave trade, for example, that her narrative offers little to no insight into how this history intersects with Indigenous, Indian Ocean and trans-Saharan slave institutions and trafficking. Consequently, while she critiques the Africans she encounters for their disavowals and bad faith in regard to the devastation of the trans-Atlantic slavery, she is not altogether free from recapitulating the tropes and patterns of the U.S. imperial gaze. She misses several opportunities to stringently examine what it means to be a relatively wealthy person from the world's most powerful imperial power studying and critiquing (mostly) poor people on the African continent.

Perhaps the greatest weakness in Hartman's narrative, however, emerges as she reflects on what ought to follow from the ruins of Pan-Africanism. Her book ends with a soaring affirmation of freedom dreams as the basis of new global solidarities. But whatever the failures of twentieth-century Pan-Africanisms, their most gripping characteristic ought to be a commitment to material struggle—social movements, insurgencies, and, where possible, institutions of care and solidarity. Hartman demonstrates that she has a remarkable grasp of the limitations of twentieth-century Pan-Africanism. But in the upshot, hers is ultimately an idealistic, often even psychologistic indictment of Pan-Africanism. Pan-Africanisms, however, did not simply fail. They were also defeated. Hartman's inability to distinguish between failure and defeat is a compelling demonstration that the Pan-African political imagination is itself part of what demands an urgent reanimation.

Conclusion

This essay explores the meaning of "Africa" in the political imagination of the African diaspora. As pointed out, of course, the spectacular diversity of the African diaspora allows for no univocal statement about the meaning of Africa. Indeed, the very terms "Africa" and "diaspora" are furiously contested in these accounts.

The very earliest accounts—especially those that emerged from the North American context—clashed over whether Africa ought to be considered an ancestral land of refuge to which its stigmatized black descendants ought to return, or else whether it fit with its depiction as a savage heart of darkness from which its diaspora ought to be glad to have been "delivered." These early debates were followed, in the twentieth century, with the ascendancy of Pan-Africanism as not only a cultural but also a political force in the world. The fruits of Pan-Africanism were monumental, as seen in the wave of decolonization that swept the African continent and the equally powerful freedom rights movements across the diaspora. However, Pan-Africanism itself would founder as the century wore on from a variety of exogenous and endogenous factors.

We now live in the shadow of the defeat of Pan-Africanism. As dramatized poignantly in Saidiya Hartman's *Lose Your Mother*, past stories of a shared ancestry, experience, or even political aspirations no longer suffice to hold together Afro-diasporic groups. If there is value in Pan-Africanism or African and Afro-diasporic political and cultural constellations, it is precisely a material, planetary, and radical political imagination that is most urgently in need of articulation.

Such a task can begin by stringently raising anew what precisely is at stake when we endeavor to limn the Afro-diasporic political imagination. Here I can suggest at least one significant reason for the importance of an Afro-diasporic political imagination. It enables us to think and act across planetary scales. It stands in opposition to the fiction of the "nation" as the "natural" unit of political organization. Such a task is made even more urgent in light of both the reactionary power of the global order—the hegemony of capitalism, white supremacy, and patriarchy—and the defeats of erstwhile radical forms of planetary forms of political organizing such as the Communist International and Pan-Africanism. Ecological destruction, what we have come to know by the name the Capitalocene, only underscores the scale of what needs to be done.

The best of the Afro-diasporic imagination has insisted that this task must be a material and organizational one, not simply an idealistic and aspirational one. That will mean a renewed commitment to social movement organizing and insurgency. But militancy, as essential as it is, will only be one part of it. Another part will demand attempts to create durable institutional social constellations that can attend to questions of social reproduction, work and labor, and art, play, and socialization, precisely against and beyond the imperial-state-capitalist complex. For if the African and Afro-diasporic imaginations are to realize "the political"—in its most robust form as the art and practice of social flourishing— then its most urgent task will go toward the radical transformation of planetary life.

Works Cited

Adi, Hakim. *Pan-Africanism: A History.* Bloomsbury Academic, 2018.

Du Bois, W.E.B. *The Autobiography of W.E.B. Du Bois: A Soliloquy on Viewing My Life from the Last Decade of its First Century,* edited by W. Sollors. Oxford UP, 2007.

———. *The World and Africa.* Oxford University Press, 2007.

———. "The Conservation of Races." *The Problem of the Color Line At the Turn of the Twentieth Century: The Essential Early Essays,* edited by Nahum Dimitri Chandler. Fordham UP, 2015, pp. 51–65.

Garvey, Marcus. "The Negro's Greatest Enemy." *The Marcus Garvey and UNIA Papers,* vol. 1, edited by R. A. Hill. University of California Press, 1983, pp. 3–11.

Getachew, Adom Getachew. *Worldmaking after Empire: The Rise and Fall of Self-Determination.* Princeton UP, 2019.

Gnamo, Abbas H. *Conquest and Resistance in the Ethiopian Empire, 1880–1974: The Case of the Arsi Oromo.* Brill, 2014.

Hahn, Steven. *The Political Worlds of Slavery and Freedom.* Harvard UP, 2009.

Hartman, Saidiya. *Lose Your Mother: A Journey Along the Atlantic Slave Route.* Farrah, Strauss, and Giroux, 2007.

Lewis, David Levering (ed.). *W.E.B. Du Bois: A Reader.* Henry Holt and Company, LLC, 1995.

Loving, MaryCatherine. "Uncovering Subversion in Phillis Wheatley's Signature Poem: 'On Being Brought from AFRICA to AMERICA.'" *Journal of African American Studies,* vol. 20, no. 1, March 2016, pp. 67–74.

Martin, jr., Waldo E. *The Mind of Frederick Douglass.* University of North Carolina Press.

Ochieng, Omedi. *Groundwork for the Practice of the Good Life: Politics and Ethics at the Intersection of African and North Atlantic Philosophy.* Routledge, 2017.

———. *The Intellectual Imagination: Knowledge and Aesthetics in North Atlantic and African Philosophy.* University of Notre Dame Press, 2018.

Saunders, Patricia J. "Fugitive Dreams of Diaspora: Conversations with Saidiya Hartman." *Anthurium: A Caribbean Studies Journal,* vol. 6, no. 1, 2008, pp. 1–16.

Scheick, William J. "Phillis Wheatley's Appropriation of Isaiah." *Early American Literature,* vol. 27, no. 2, 1992, pp. 135–140.

Sutherland, Bill and Matt Meyer, *Guns and Gandhi in Africa: Pan-African Insights on Nonviolence, Armed Struggle and Liberation.* Africa World Press, Inc., 2000.

Wilson, Henry S. *Origins of West African Nationalism.* Macmillan, 1969.

30

UBUNTU

A Critique of Superiorization[1]

Mpho Tshivhase

Introduction

For centuries black people (and other non-white groups) have suffered the indignity of being dehumanized and have thus been treated in ways that devalue their selfhood among other prized human values. The reason that is peddled to defend the inhumane treatment of non-white individuals is their skin color. Mabogo More states that anti-black racism is built on the idea that blackness is a sin (2017). The black individual's sin is being born black where blackness connotes all that is negative (Mills, 1998). Herein lies an indicator of race as the problem of anti-black racism. One way of problematizing it is to illustrate race as an organizing tool used to oppress the other. That is to say that one's skin color is made a reason for a form of dehumanizing discrimination. Another way to problematize race involves turning the problem of race into a matter relating to what it reflects about those who use race to cushion their sense of self based on ideas of superiority. In other words, what do racism and the related superiorization of whiteness tell us about the moral fabric of racists?

The way the debate about racism and personhood has been framed has created the impression that black people need to prove that they too are persons. This has placed the burden of proof, so to speak, on black people to prove their humanity and the irrevocable and irreducible value of said humanity (Yancy, 2005; Sithole, 2021). This has been an unjustifiable challenge placed on black people by the purported (uncontested) superiority of whiteness. Society, as it were, has accepted whiteness as the yardstick for value and moral consideration. Even day-to-day standards of beauty, capability, and intelligence among many others, have been and continue to be measured against whiteness. Whiteness is consistently reproduced as the norm (Yancy, 2005, 217–220). The whiteness standards of beauty are evident in the way that people invest in whitening creams or in the way that they go through skin-bleaching therapies. Even complexion politics are based on the underlying assumption that lighter-skinned black beings enjoy forms of privilege within black societies. The trust deficit in black-owned or black-led institutions is an open secret. In any case, the point is that whiteness has enjoyed the place of superiority which has been unfairly justified through ideas of ancestry that enabled the colonial logic of elimination such as the 'one drop rule' to exclude and inferiorize non-whites (Wolfe, 2006).

In this chapter, I will explore two frames of racism namely, race as an organizing tool and what racism reveals about racists, with a larger interest in the second framing regarding

DOI: 10.4324/9781003143529-35

what racism tells us about racists. I will engage this second framing by applying Felix Murove's conception of ubuntu. Much like Murove, I do not apply ubuntu here with the aim to celebrate it as the solution to all of society's problem. Herein, I take Bernard Matolino and Wenceslaus Kwindingwi's caution against the overextension and bastardization of ubuntu quite seriously (2013, 204). I, therefore, follow Felix Murove's critical application of ubuntu to the issue of colonization with the aim to overturn the tone of depersonalization that has its stronghold in race, and rather question the humanness of those who think it is acceptable to own, use, and abuse other humans simply because of their non-white skin color.

My overarching aim in this chapter is to critically analyze racism in a way that will desuperiorize whiteness. I will use Kant's view of personhood as an instance of a racist philosophical theory. I choose to showcase Kant's conception of personhood because it forms part of his moral theory, which he purports to be a universal moral theory. I will employ Murove's lens on ubuntu and personhood to illustrate that when re-reading philosophical texts such as those produced by Kant, we should not limit ourselves to maintain the superficially race-neutral structural view of inferiorizing black people. Murove's view of ubuntu, and by extension personhood, invite black people to consider the absence of personhood in those who have found it essential to structure the world in ways that necessitate the devaluation of black people in order to legitimize their imagined existence as superior beings. In other words, given that all humans are equal, with none more equal than others, how do we, black people come to make sense of the moral values of those who think their whiteness makes them more equal than black people? In short, what is wrong with white people who consider themselves to be more valuable than black people? I will apply Murove's critical conception of ubuntu in an attempt to answer this question.

I will start by discussing the general view of ubuntu with the aim to explain what it entails and how it relates to the Afro-communitarian conceptions of personhood. Thereafter, I will show the dehumanizing narrative of personhood by focusing on Immanuel Kant's limited view of personhood. Following a brief overview of Kant's racism, I will analyze such racism with the aim to show that the view of personhood offered by Kant and his Enlightenment buddies – Hume and Voltaire among others – is racist (see Freter, 2018). I will construct this argument in order to show that desuperiorization of whiteness requires us to turn the mirror on those who place whiteness on a pedestal and ask them to tell us what their personhood consists of – test their personhood using a multifaceted moral theory such as ubuntu, which is constituted by aspects of virtue, duty, and utility – none of which anti-black racism displays. The colonization project has been extremely successful at dominating and oppressing all that is non-white. This domination was made successful by the myth of white purity which worked to erase the value of blackness. When we turn the mirror on whiteness, we expose its inhumanity to itself and the black society in order to inspire a black gaze on whiteness with the aim to show that to put whiteness on a pedestal is to revere cruelty. Perhaps this perspective is what the black society needs to reevaluate its value, autonomy, and general place in the world. The white imaginary is quite oppressively visible. It is time we pay attention to the black imaginary – an unencumbered, un-inferiorized black imaginary – and perhaps ubuntu can offer a useful framework for such an undertaking.

The Concept of Ubuntu

Ubuntu is generally understood to be an African ethic, which encompasses the right kind of principles that engender the good life, where the good life is a matter of pursuing moral perfection for the benefit of oneself, others, and the community as a whole. Herein the

407

common dictum used to capture the meaning or essence of ubuntu is '*muthu ndi muthu nga vhathu*'.[2] The direct English translation is 'a person is a person through other persons' – "the maxim underlines the vital importance of mutual recognition and respect complemented by mutual care and sharing in the construction of human relations" (Ramose, 2002, 329). One is expected to live well with other people in order to develop one's full humanness, where one is unable to develop into a full human in the absence of positive relationships with others (Munyaka & Matlhabi, 2009, 67). In other words, a person is understood to be a good human being when that person recognizes the need to belong to a community of persons where such belonging is preceded by an interest in the pursuit of solidarity within a community.

The theory of ubuntu offers the principles upon which moral behavior should be built and it also tells us what personhood entails. Part of what stands out about ubuntu, in relation to other moral theories, is its emphasis on relationality. Essentially, ubuntu captures what it means to be a person by indicating the importance of creating and maintaining positive relations with others in the community wherein such relations with others are guided by other-regarding moral principles that are aimed at contributing positively to the welfare of others (Metz, 2007, 330–323). Ubuntu emphasizes a communal way of living that enables one to develop a sense of personhood that is enjoined with the welfare of others (Murove, 2014, 42–44). Herein, what it means to be a person living among other persons is not characterized in terms of what constitutes one's personhood, but rather, in terms of how one should conduct oneself in relation to others. The expected way in which one should conduct oneself in relation to others ought to reflect a commitment toward pursuing goodness as a guiding principle of interaction (Masolo, 2018, 24–25). In keeping with goodness, ubuntu engenders respect, compassion, generosity, and kindness – in short, ubuntu is a pro-social moral theory geared toward creating a community of good persons.

Ubuntu can also be viewed as a theory that reflects different moral aspects. For instance, Fainos Mangena understands ubuntu to be a multifunctional theory involving aspects of virtue ethics, deontology, and utilitarianism (2012). That is to say, it aims to prescribe how humans ought to behave in interactions with each other based on domains that consider the consequences of one's actions (utilitarianism), the duty one has toward another's welfare by virtue of respecting their personhood (deontology), as well as a focus on the ethical construction of one's character (virtue ethics). This multifunctional structure of ubuntu, according to Mangena, is part of what makes ubuntu such a unique moral theory.

Apart from the moral principles that define ubuntu, one also finds that ubuntu offers a definition of a person. Herein, one's personhood depends on those moral relations with other people. John Mbiti's (1969) famous "*I am because we are, and since we are, therefore I am*" is used by thinkers such as Ifeanyi Menkiti and Dismas Masolo to capture the view that one's personhood is defined by the community (Menkiti, 1984, 171–174; Masolo, 2010; 2018). A person is inextricably connected to one's community so that one's personhood is immediately a feature that is grounded on one's interdependent values and goals, which form a picture of what it means to do well with others. Not only does the theory of ubuntu offer us the principles upon which moral behavior should be built, but it also describes what personhood entails. It is this virtuous sense of personhood that seems lacking in the devalued view of black persons. Ubuntu expresses virtuous personhood. In this way, personhood is a morally loaded sense of being that is informed by a concern for others which is expressed through relationality. The virtuous sense of personhood is withheld in instances where one is found lacking in moral regard for others (Metz, 2011; Banda, 2019).

Devaluation of Black Persons

The discourse that relates to blackness aims to portray blackness as a kind of ill that justifies the dehumanization of black people. For too long black beings have and continue to be viewed as less than human. The inferiorization of black humans is captured in George Yancy's assertion about the "...white social imaginary [apprehending] the Black body, *my* body, as pre-given in its constitution as inferior" (2005, 220). The existence of black people is also devalued through racism as a speech act. Claudia Brodsky Lacour explains dehumanization of non-whites as an act instigated by racism. According to Lacour, racism is a form of perlocution "...whose pervasive existence depends on its tenacious non-admission and complicitous nonrecognition" (1992, 139). It is the refusal to recognize the normative value of black humans that intends to diminish their value thereby enabling their subjection and exploitation.

Achille Mbembe characterizes blackness as a matter of subjection to whiteness, wherein such subjection is founded on the 'old myth of racial superiority (2017, 11). It is this myth that gave whiteness its power and priority – a kind of priority that thrives through a kind of predatory power that is only concretized in the subjugation of black bodies (Ekpo, 1996, 3–7).

> To produce Blackness is to produce a social link of subjection and a *body of extraction,* that is, a body from which great effort is made to extract maximum profit. An exploitable object, the Black Man is also the name of a wound, the symbol of a person at the mercy of a whip and suffering in the field of struggle that opposes socioracially segmented groups and factions.
>
> *(Mbembe, 2017, 18)*

The relation that Mbembe identifies between the black body and capitalism is articulated by Teresa Guess in her discussion of the social construction of whiteness as an activity that structures society in the process of race formation, where such race formation is an institutionalized feature of a system of social interactions that are informed by politics, economics, and power. In other words, racialization is a central organizing principle in the structuration of race relations which create patterns of social interaction that develop and protect white-skin privilege (2006, 657–662). Ekpo rightly explains that it is the power that characterizes the domination and legitimation of the social order of colonial structures designed by the west to oppress Africans wherein such power does not care for justice or moral rightness (1996, 9–11).

Racism and its dehumanizing machinations are most obvious in its physical violence, but there is also an epistemic violence that forms part of the racialized performative acts that aim to limit black people's normative value. Some performative racial acts appear in the form of theories. Theories written about humanity often, overtly or covertly, dehumanize black humans thereby devaluing them as lesser beings in comparison to their white counterparts. One of the covert ways in which racial theories are delivered to us involves racism that is hidden in theories that are purported to be race-neutral. Race-neutral theories are often theories that contain no racial discrimination, and so, they become relevantly applicable to all persons irrespective of color or creed. In Philosophy in particular, we have many theories that are celebrated as central to the foundations of Philosophy proper, but upon a re-reading of those theories, one finds that they are, indeed, racist. One such theory is Immanuel Kant's theory of personhood. On the face of it, Kant's moral theory, which includes his conception of personhood, is race-neutral. It is universal and applies to all persons.

Björn Freter (2018, 238–243) exposes the lack of race neutrality in the epistemology we inherited from the Enlightenment period. He argues that the epistemology of the human being is plagued with ideas about white superiority. He critically analyses the work of three Enlightenment thinkers namely, Voltaire, Hume and Kant to illustrate that the underlying anthropologies about the human being, which inform philosophical moral thinking, are not race-neutral – instead, they are about the white human being. The exclusion of non-whites in philosophical reflections about the nature of a human being indicate, for Freter, a contempt for non-whites, which makes him question the humanity of white scholars who produce work that maintains and champions white supremacy (2018, 243–246). Freter's broader view is that Eurocentric scholarship, especially philosophical scholarship has been careless with knowledge about humanity and this is a problem we inherit from eurocentrism that does not critically analyze Euro-Western traditions.

In my analysis of the arbitrary positioning of white superiority, I focus on Kant's personhood view. According to Kant, it is those people who are characterized as persons who are afforded moral worth (2002, 45; 52–53). Persons are beings of a rational nature. What it means to be a person is to display a capacity for rationality. Kant's concept of rationality is the grounding for dignity so that all individuals who are considered persons are understood to possess dignity, the correct response to which is respect. Put simply, all persons, by virtue of having dignity, are worthy of respect. Furthermore, Kant uses rationality to distinguish between persons and things. For Kant, the value of things is price, which makes them replaceable, and the value of persons is dignity, which makes them irreplaceable and incomparable. In this way, Kant offers us a theory of persons that does not discriminate across gender or race.

Emmanuel Eze revealed Kant's racism to the scholarship by analyzing Kant's racialized view on morality throughout several of his writings (1997). According to Eze, Kant's moral theory is not race-neutral. Eze's view is that if we interpret Kant's moral theory without ignoring his racial taxonomy then we will be able to see that Kant's moral theory is racist. Those who aim to challenge Eze's charge against Kant with the aim to defend Kant tend to want to argue that Kant's work could not have been racist – and that Kant himself was not a racist – because his transcendental theory is not the kind of theory that can be relativized in terms of race. The idea that his racial taxonomy is racist should be taken to be a consequence of his time which should not necessarily overshadow his work (Hill & Boxill, 2000).

It is important to note that Eze's analysis of Kant's racial taxonomy enables us to see that Kant regarded black individuals to be irrational and thus uneducable. According to Eze, Kant's advice to those who want to teach black individuals anything at all is that they should whip the black individuals till they bleed.

> The meaning of the distinction that Kant makes between the ability to be "educated" or to educate oneself on the one hand, and to "train" somebody on the other, can be surmised from the following. "Training" for Kant seems to consist of physical coercion and corporal punishment, for in his writings about how to flog the African servant into submission, Kant advises us to use a split bamboo cane instead of a whip, so that the 'negro' will suffer a great deal of pains (because of the 'negro's' thick skin, he would not be racked with sufficient agonies through a whip) but without dying.
>
> *(Eze, 1997, 116)*

This is considered morally acceptable treatment of black people because they lack true rational and moral character. Kant makes this judgment about black people based on their skin color. Eze asserts that Kant's (primitive) taxonomy of race, in part, classifies black people as inferior to white people (1997, 115–118). The fact of recommending corporal punishment is a practical repercussion of his morally exclusionary theory of personhood. Eze's main aim in his analysis of Kant's work was to illustrate that according to Kant black people do not possess rationality; black people lack dignity, and so, they are replaceable and comparable; and black people are not moral (1997, 112–119).

Following Emmanuel Eze's critique of Kant, Charles Mills problematizes Kant's distinction of the category of persons and things paying specific attention to the implications that his categories of persons and non-persons hold for black people (1998, 87–92; 2005). Simply put in Kant's view of personhood, *persons* are beings with rational capacity wherein such rational capacity grounds their dignity. In contrast, non-persons lack the capacity for rationality and for this reason their value is captured in terms of price. It is animals and objects that belong to the category of non-persons and humans who belong to the category of persons. Charles Mills is skeptical of the racial neutrality of Kant's conception of personhood, and so, he, in keeping with the logic of Kant's racial taxonomy, asserts that when Kant wrote on personhood what he was referring to was white people. In other words, personhood is a category reserved for white human beings. What seems obvious to Mills is that, if we take Kant's racial taxonomy seriously – and we should–then Kant's theory of personhood does not account for the moral value of black individuals. By virtue of lacking the capacity for rationality, black people are not persons (Mills, 1998, 106–110).

Nonetheless, black people are not animals in the narrow sense of the term, nor are they objects, and so, cannot be considered persons or non-persons in the Kantian sense of it. In an effort to find a way to make Kant's moral theory consistent with his racism, Mills introduces the concept of the *Untermensch* – sub-person. The idea of sub-person seems, to Mills, to be a fitting compromise given that black people were not considered to meet the threshold of personhood and they were not objects either – it made sense to create a middle category that would account for their moral status (or lack thereof). Mills is convinced that the category of subpersonhood was necessary for the maintenance of white superiorism.

> Subpersonhood has to be enforced and racial deference from subpersons maintained. Because of its self-sustaining symmetry, ideal Kantianism is inherently stable, since it rests on reciprocal relations between persons of acknowledged equal worth, involving a respect voluntarily given. *Herrenvolk* Kantianism, in contrast, required that a subset of the human population learn to regard themselves as subpersons and, as such, not of equal worth…Subpersons are not born but are made, and the making is not a once-and-for-all event, like slave-breaking or even the extended process of indoctrination known as education in colonial societies, but an ongoing political operation involving routine daily transactions of various kinds.
>
> *(Mills, 1998, 111)*

Subpersonhood forms part of the social order that is necessitated by the desire to dominate where such domination requires the creation of a hierarchy. Kant's personhood, understood as a category reserved for white people maintains the political practices of racial subordination upon which anti-black racism is founded. The point Mills aims to make is that there is a dynamic relation between personhood and subpersonhood in the superiorization of whiteness, which thrives only in the subjugation of blackness (or all that is non-white).

Lucy Allais (2016, 8; 18) argues that the introduction of the idea of the sub-person is unsuccessful given that it requires viewing Kant's notion of personhood as a threshold concept which implies a level of cognitive ability that some humans lack. Allais does not interpret Kant's use of rationality as a cognitive ability but rather as a motivating condition for our actions. Following Allais' interpretation, reason is to be understood as a capacity to act for ends – the capacity to pursue ends, not the capacity for intelligence or education. In her understanding of Kant, it is children who do not meet the threshold for personhood (Allais, 2016, 18–19). Allais' advise is that scholars should abandon the aim to make Kant's racism consistent with his universal moral theory and rather take the gaps that Mills has illustrated in his analysis of Kant's work to learn about the pervasiveness of racism (2016, 20). Overall, on Allais' understanding of Kant's moral theory, there is no room for the idea of the *Untermenschen* since his philosophy forbids the instrumentalization of all humans.

Other defenders of Kant such as Thomas Hill and Bernard Boxill do not concern themselves with making Kant's universal theory consistent with his moral philosophy. They simply argue that Kant's racist assertions, while they appear inconsistent with his moral theory, do not weaken his central philosophy, and so, critics of Kant should not take an isolated contradiction in his work to tarnish his central philosophy (2000, 458–469). In almost the same vein as Allais, Hill and Boxill recommend that we should use Kant's moral framework to challenge racism (2000, 470).

The arguments in defense of Kant against the charge of racism seem to downplay the levels of racism in Kant's universalism which makes one wonder what it is that philosophers are truly protecting in the face of the practical impact that theories have on human lives. Theories are not innocent tools; hence Mills argues in favor of re-reading classical texts to illustrate the role that philosophical texts have had on society, which necessitates serious consideration of the lack of race neutrality. (2005, 33–34). The advice to learn from Kant's mistakes without disrupting his central canon seems to perpetuate the devaluing of black people, which makes one wonder whether the defenders of Kant are not themselves overestimating rationality and underestimating the pervasive nature of racism to a point of underestimating the intimate relationship between the theories we write and their impact on real-life social concerns about autonomy, equality, identity and the other forms of discrimination that threaten these values. If we follow the logic of learning from rather than paying attention to the racist inconsistencies in his work, then we, as African philosophers, are complicit actors in the prolongation of the view that some philosophers' works, regardless of their devastating moral and political effects on some groups of humans, are untouchable.

While I remain curious about the prioritization of theory over desuperiorization of whiteness, what I want to focus on next is the racist structure of philosophical personhood theories. I want to apply Murove's view of ubuntu and personhood to analyze what could have gone wrong in the moral structure of those who have placed themselves at the top of the moral hierarchy at the cost of other humans' welfare. I want to claim that if we maintain the moral principles of ubuntu, it follows that it is the racists who lack personhood.

Racists Lack Personhood

Thus far I have discussed the theory of ubuntu with the aim to show its structure and principles as a moral theory. To this end, I have shown the relevance of ubuntu to personhood, wherein personhood is a matter of living well with others and maintaining interconnectedness through relational ways of being. Murove's account of ubuntu as he applies it to the colonizers and their mentality is unique in the sense that it turns an African gaze on white supremacy. Murove's approach is aimed at showing that there is something wrong with the white colonial slave masters and white supremacists who think themselves superior to black people and other non-white individuals. On his view, there is something morally suspect about humans who single out a trait and use it to simultaneously elevate their moral worth and oppress those that do not possess that trait. A thinker such as Kant is guilty of using one trait, that is rationality, to construct a hierarchy of moral status. Mills views Kant's threshold view of personhood as a racist theory that should be interrogated with the aim to uncover its divisive and dehumanizing structure (2005, 32–34).

On Murove's account of ubuntu, admittance into the category of personhood is over-turned and considered not in terms of rational capacity, but in terms of relationality that is based on virtues and moral duty (or obligation) to others. What Murove aims to show is, in part, that racism is not a black person's problem in the sense that being a victim of racism is not a reflection of the personhood of black people, but rather a reflection of the lack of personhood of white supremacists and those who think there is something about their ontological status that makes them better qualified to be persons. Part of what is wrong with this picture involves the idea that moral value is a privilege that is due to some humans but not all. One gets this tone of moral privilege in Kant's threshold conception of personhood wherein he seems to show that not all humans are persons even though the members of all races are considered human (Mills, 1998, 86–86; 2005, 14–16; Freter, 2018, 240–242).

What one should take issue with here, following thinkers such as Charles Mills and Emmanuel Eze, is that the exclusion of black people from the category of personhood is a racist attack on black people for the mere reason of their blackness. This dehumanization of black people is captured succinctly by Mabogo More who states that the black person's sin is being born black (2017, 43). The point is that it takes deep moral failure to be at ease with using the possession of one distinguishing aspect about humans to claim superiority over other humans and devalue them. This moral failure illustrates the lack of ubuntu, which Afro-communitarian thinkers such as Menkiti and Masolo would judge as a failure at acquiring personhood.

Apart from the obvious fact of racism, what is wrong with the picture wherein black people are devalued and dehumanized because of their skin color? Part of the problem is that this is packaged as a black people's problem. In other words, the onus is placed on black people to prove that they are persons; to prove that they deserve moral regard; to prove that they meet the requirement for personhood. This perspective is the problem that often goes unchallenged, which inadvertently contributes to the continued oppression of black persons. Murove writes that "[t]he behavior of slave masters and colonial settlers toward their African victims was devoid of humanness or ubuntu because ubuntu implies seeing another human being as yourself and treating them with respect" (2014, 38). Murove's view, which I agree with, seems to be that the racism inherent in colonialism is not a black people's problem. Racism is a white people's problem because it is the white colonialists who failed at being persons. It is the colonialists who failed to display humanness and take accountability for their moral failure toward others in community:

> A responsible person is thus characterized as *Unobuntu* (Zulu) or *Unohunhu* (Shona) – terms that imply that s/he/[they] has humanness or that s/he/[they] is a true embodi-ment of what it truly means to be human.
>
> *(Murove, 2014, 39)*

This idea of accountability makes sense when one understands one's relationship with others, as primarily based on relational rationality rather than individual autonomy (Murove, 2014, 37; 39). Furthermore, Murove asserts that

> [o]ne who has Ubuntu or Unhu takes into consideration the concerns of others in relationship to his personal concerns. This claim could not make sense in colonial social evolutionism because of the predominance that was given to individualism and the pursuit of self-interest in human socio-economic relations.
>
> *(2014, 39)*

Murove argues that greed and self-interest are inconsistent with ubuntu, and therefore, the colonial societies that aimed to universalize greed, would not understand ubuntu, let alone endeavor to espouse the principles of ubuntu due to their denigration of ubuntu theory (2014, 38; 42).

It is not black people who have to prove that they are morally valuable. It is not black people who have to provide evidence of their rationality. Instead, using the structure of Murove's criticism of the dehumanization of Africans by colonialists through ubuntu, it appears that it is the personhood of white racists that is questionable, or more directly, it is white supremacists who failed to become persons and are thus the ones who need to develop pro-social values that will enable them to live well with others. The notion of personhood involves the moral value of those who are considered persons wherein personhood is derived from the positive relationships that one forms with others. Personhood is a concept that is foundational to our understanding of how to construct moral regard for ourselves and others.

> The concept of persons—entities who, by virtue of their characteristics, are protected by a certain normative armor of rights and freedoms, entitled to be treated in a certain way—has become the central pillar of contemporary moral discourse. Thus debates about abortion are often fought over the actual or potential personhood of the fetus; animal rights theorists charge that restricting full moral concern to human persons is speciesist; and issues of metaphysical and political autonomy, of freedom of the will and citizenship rights, are discussed in terms of what personhood demands.
>
> *(Mills, 2005)*

Personhood permeates most if not all spheres of human and, sometimes, non-human interaction. We look to personhood as a category that enables us to determine the right treatment or morally acceptable behavior in a given situation. There are certain values that apply to persons because of the implied value that persons hold. If we hold white supremacists and racists to the standards of personhood, where we take personhood to be a matter of virtues, relationality, and an interest in securing the welfare of others, we should not be asking whether victims of racism are persons but rather, we should be asking whether white supremacists meet the requirements for personhood as set out by ubuntu theory, among other moral theories grounded on personhood. This move to turn the critical lens on racists is one way of desuperiorizing whiteness. How so? Here the standard of measure is not based on isolated phenotypical traits but rather, and rightly so, on behavior and the way in which one interacts with others.

Ubuntu theory asserts that those who fail to live well with others have failed to become persons. We say of such individuals that they lack ubuntu. That is to say, they lack the tools to recognize the moral value of another, their moral duty toward another and its connection to their own welfare, and sense of self, as well as the need to contribute to the overall welfare of the community. Those lacking in ubuntu have no sense of humanness and/or humaneness. Put differently, those who lack ubuntu are not persons. Racists lack ubuntu, therefore, racists are not persons.

Further Considerations

To put it succinctly, the myth of racial superiority is a product of the social construction of a racialized society. Power and domination solidified the structure of raced interactions and capitalism entrenched the racialized institutional structures that organize society (Guess, 2006). Racial formation is also responsible for the prioritization of whiteness. In a raced society, whiteness enjoys its self-given privilege at the intersections of power, race and privilege. A related element of whiteness is the white gaze, which dominates blackness in a way that negatively affects the black self-image and limits the social, political, and economic possibilities for the black body (Yancy, 2005; 229–231). In other words, the white gaze, in its mythical rightness, exerts ontological and epistemic violence on the black individuals. Such violence breeds black self-hatred. This black-self-hatred comes as a matter of the internalized white gaze. The internalization of the white gaze enables patterns of self-regulation that enable a self-surveillance and in-group policing, which is then captured in politics of respectability (Cohen, 1999, 71–774–76; Yancy, 2005, 233; Mbembe, 2017, 44).

In response to this epistemic and ontological violence, I suggest that we use the principles of ubuntu to turn the proverbial mirror toward whiteness. While Ekpo argues that there is nothing that can be done about Eurocentric superiority since it is, by its nature, evil and predatory, my view is that it is not enough to simply note its evil predatory nature and then ignore it (1996, 6–9). Colonialism has peddled whiteness as pure and right. In the same breath, it has positioned whiteness as the measure of all humanity with blackness as an inferior. This is bewildering given that oppressive whiteness had demonstrated that it is inhumane. To persistently measure blackness against whiteness is to aspire to an inhumane state of being. Reflecting on the content of oppressive whiteness should be viewed as an effort to illustrate to black people that they have been duped to aspire and bow down to an immoral form of existence.

The mirror that I champion is not just a mirror that displays oppressive whiteness on itself. The mirror serves black thought too, perhaps primarily so. What the mirror does for black people bears more value as it unveils the arbitrariness of oppressive whiteness. Sure enough, it may not be the task of oppressive whiteness to recognize and respect blackness. However, oppressive whiteness, in racializing society and inferiorizing blackness, has instilled a deep level of black self-hatred and the work of undoing this self-hatred to inspire black self-love, esteem, confidence, and autonomy, among other values, requires repetitive demonstration of the myth of whiteness – the shallow and inhumane character of oppressive whiteness. The display of the myth of whiteness, unpacked through the principles of ubuntu, offers a plausible framework through which the black body can escape seeing itself through the oppressive white gaze – that the dehumanization of blackness by oppressive whiteness, is a projection of the inhumanity of that oppressive whiteness. Nothing of estimable value can come from the inhumanity of oppressive whiteness, and blackness ought to then articulate itself in ways that resist amplifying whiteness.

Thus far I have been thinking about anti-black racism, dehumanization of blackness and white superiorism. I think there is a complex relation between all three categories which seem to coalesce in racism, which is an organizing tool in a racialized society. The dominant theme in racism seemingly involves the logic of domination and elimination, which are central to the structure of colonialism. Colonialism, for Wolfe, should be understood not as an event but as structure. It is in dissolving native societies and replacing them with colonial ones, that colonialism concretizes its totalizing presence and slips into unseen futures (Wolfe, 2006, 388). That is to say, the structures of colonialism persist into the postcolonial state in ways that perpetuate the dehumanization of black people. Herein, it matters to keep in mind that structures can be dissolved over time but that this kind of dissolution does not happen organically. Black people should commit to desuperiorizing oppressive whiteness and view it as a way to shift the framing of blackness from inferiority toward positive recognition. Part of the work includes picking at oppressive whiteness piece by piece and enabling the black gaze to eliminate the legitimacy of oppressive whiteness. What gets reflected by the mirror on whiteness is a necessary visual for the esteem and empowerment needed to desuperiorize whiteness.

Conclusion

In light of the reinterpretation of theories in philosophy that unveils their discriminatory assumptions, I think is it equally worthy to reframe other theories and apply them appropriately to certain behaviors in society. Some approaches in African philosophy appear to be reactionary to the western views in philosophy. In one sense this is troubling as it could unjustifiably imply that nothing original could be created by Africans. This sounds much like a racist claim against African scholarship. A more acceptable perspective could simply be that African scholarship was delayed and marginalized by racist systems that enforced gatekeeping. No matter the approach what is at issue is, in part, the intelligence, moral value, and capability of black scholars. The aim of this piece was to challenge the negative connotations of blackness that have been created to uphold the superiorized position of oppressive whiteness.

The white gaze on blackness has made it so that people believe that being black is unnatural, primitive, and not morally valuable. In this chapter, I showed that the picture looks differently if we turn a black gaze on oppressive whiteness. It is not that the black gaze on the superiorization of oppressive whiteness reciprocates the injustice by devaluing whiteness. No, the black moral gaze, in the way that I have discussed it using Murove's view on ubuntu, simply evaluates the behavior of those who think themselves superior by virtue of being white while using that superiority as a justification for abusing those who are non-white. In other words, ubuntu theory illustrates, like most moral theories, what counts as morally acceptable and what would count as morally blameworthy.

Given ubuntu's further tenets on what it means to be a person, where personhood is a matter of humanness that is characterized by kindness, altruism, respect, recognition of interconnectivity within community, and many other positive values, it would appear that white superiorists would be considered to have failed to act humanely, thereby showcasing their lack of ubuntu. Given that ubuntu principles are central to the communitarian view of personhood, it would follow that racists are not persons because of their failure to live well with others – their failure to see their humanity as inextricably connected with the humanity of others.

Notes

1 This paper has benefitted from comments and questions from fellow scholars who have an interest in the critical reflection on racism and other patterns of oppressive whiteness. I am grateful to John Sanni, Sepetla Molapo, and Uchenna Okeja for engaging my views to help me sharpen my thoughts and arguments.
2 I use the TshiVenda version of the Nguni expression *umuntu ngu muntu nga batnu* because TshiVenda is my mother tongue.

References

Allais, L., 2016. Kant's Racism. *Philosophical Papers*, 45 (1–2), pp. 1–36.

Banda, C., 2019. Ubuntu as Human Flourishing? An African Traditional Religious Analysis of Ubuntu and Its Challenge to Christian Anthropology. *Stellenbosch Theological Journal*, 5 (3), pp. 203–228.

Cohen, C., 1999. *The Boundaries of Blackness: AIDS and the Breakdown of Black Politics*. Chicago, IL: University of Chicago Press.

Ekpo, D., 1996. How Africa Misunderstood the West: The Failure of Anti-West Radicalism and Post-modernity. *Third Text*, 10 (35), pp. 3–13.

Eze E. C. 1997. The Color of Reason: The Idea of 'Race' in Kant's Anthropology. In *Postcolonial African Philosophy: A Critical Reader*, E.C. Eze (ed.). Malden, MA: Blackwell Publishers, pp. 103–140.

Freter, B., 2018. White Supremacy in Eurocentric Epistemologies: On the West's Responsibility for its Philosophical Heritage. *Synthesis Philosophica*, 65 (1), pp. 237–249.

Guess, T. J., 2006. The Social Construction of Whiteness: Racism by Intent, Racism by Consequence. *Critical Sociology*, 32 (4), pp. 649–673.

Hill, T.R., Boxill, B., 2000. Kant and Race in *Race and Racism*, B. Boxill (ed.). Oxford: Oxford University Press, pp.448–471.

Kant, I. 2002. *Groundwork for the Metaphysics of Morals*, A.W. Wood (Transl.). New Haven, CT: Yale University Press.

Lacour, C.B. Doing Things with Words: "Racism" as Speech Act and the Undoing of Justice. In *Race-ing Justice, En-gendering Power: Essays on Anita Hill, Thomas Clarence, and the Construction of Social Reality*, T. Morrison (ed.). New York: Pantheon Books, 1992, pp. 127–158.

Mangena, F. 2012. Towards a *Hunhu/Ubuntu* Dialogical Moral Theory. *Phronimon: Journal of the South African Society for Greek Philosophy and the Humanities*, 13 (2), pp. 1–17.

Masolo, D. A., 2010. *Self and Community in a Changing World*. Indiana: Indiana University Press.

Masolo, D. A., 2018. Self-constitution and Agency. In *Ubuntu and Personhood*, J. Ogude (ed.). Cape Town: Africa World Press, pp. 11–37.

Matolino, B., and Kwindigwi, W., 2013. The End of Ubuntu. *South African Journal of Philosophy*, 32, pp. 197–205.

Mbembe, A., 2017. *Critique of Black Reason*. L. Dubois (Transl.) London: Duke University Press.

Mbiti, J., 1969. *African Religions and Philosophy*. London: Heinemann Educational Books Ltd.

Menkiti, I. A., 1984. Person and Community in African Traditional Thought. In *African Philosophy: An Introduction*, R.A. Wright (ed.). New York: University Press of America, pp. 171–181.

Metz, T., 2007. Toward and African Moral Theory. *Journal of Political Philosophy*, 15, pp. 321–341.

Metz, T., 2011. Ubuntu as a Moral Theory and Human Rights in South Africa. *African Human Rights Law Journal*, 11 (2), pp. 532–559.

Mills, C., 1998. *Blackness Visible: Essays on Philosophy and Race*. Ithaca, NY: Cornell University Press.

Mills, C., 2005. Kant's Untermenschen, pp. 1–34. Available on https://pdfs.semanticscholar.org/7865/c7f24fa9bd68035e1db09b016d6732188a37.pdf, accessed August 2021.

More, M.P. 2017. *Biko: Philosophy, Identity, and Liberation*. Cape Town: HSRC Press.

Munyaka, M., and Mothlabi, M., 2009. Ubuntu and its Socio-moral Significance. In *African Ethics: An Anthology of Comparative and Applied Ethics*, F.M. Murove (ed.). Pietermaritzburg: University of KwaZulu Natal, pp. 62–84.

Murove, M.F., 2014. Ubuntu. *Diogenes*, 59, pp. 36–47.

Ramose, M.B., 2002. The Ethics of Ubuntu. In *Philosophy from Africa: A Text with Readings*, 2nd Edition, P.H. Coetzee and A.P.J. Roux (eds.). Cape Town: Oxford University Press, pp. 324–330.

Sithole, T., 2021. The Meditations on the Dehumanization of the Slave. In *Decolonising the Human: Reflections from Africa on Difference and Oppression*, M. Steyn and W. Mpofu (eds.). Johannesburg: Wits University Press, pp. 130–142.

Yancy, G., 2005. Whiteness and the Return of the Black Body. *Journal of Speculative Philosophy, New Series*, 19 (4), pp. 215–241.

Wolfe, P, 2006. Settler Colonialism and the Elimination of the Native. *Journal of Genocide Research*, 8 (4), pp. 387–409.

INDEX

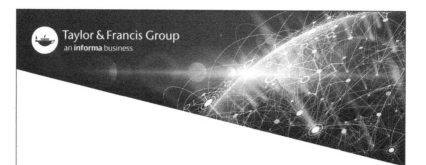